THE TRAVELLER'S CHOICE
MILLENIUM EDITION

Hotels, Inns, Restaurants, Places to Visit

ENGLAND
2nd e(

Potted History County by County
Exciting Attractions and Places to Visit
Great Venues, Great Food and Comfort, Great Value

THE PERFECT COMPANION FOR LOCALS & VISITORS
WHICH
YOU CANNOT AFFORD TO BE WITHOUT

Acknowledgements

Joy David would like to thank Andy and Marie Needham and Mick Devereux for their assistance in compiling this book. Their help and dedication has been invaluable. Sharon Bradley, Lisa Mitchell, Ian Pethers and Mick Devereux for their beautiful line drawings, Alison Fildew and Jayne Jackson for their unstinting assistance, and to Karen Vosper and Hilary Kent whose work in compiling the artwork has been beyond the call of duty.
Front & Back Cover: Gidleigh Park, Chagford, Devon.

© Joy David

First published 1998
ISBN 1 899311 505
All rights reserved

British Library Cataloguing-in-Publication Data
Catalogue data is available from the British Library

Typeset by :Traveller's Choice Publications Ltd. Plymouth, Devon. '(01752) 607141
Printed and bound in Great Britain by: Nuffield press, Abingdon, Oxon

INTRODUCTION

CONTENTS INCLUDES

INTRODUCTION

Over a decade I have written many books about the regions of England and stayed and eaten in a myriad of hotels, guesthouses, inns and restaurants. Some have given me greater pleasure than others but everywhere there has always been a wonderful welcome. In addition I have seen glorious countryside, fabulous stately homes, exotic and beautiful gardens, castles, churches and cathedrals which have left me breathless with their beauty and architecture, all of which has made me realise just what Britain has to offer - a fact that seems to escape a lot of people who feel they have not had a holiday or a short break unless they leave these shores. I hope that what has given me so much pleasure may change their minds. For visitors from overseas I hope Joy David's Choice will encourage them to leave the familiar tourist beaten track and explore some of the lesser known places.

In this second book I have endeavoured to put together a selection of some favourite establishments, beloved vistas, exciting places to explore and the odd watering hole or two in which to refresh ones body rather than ones mind. In my choice I have covered a wide spectrum in order to ensure that financially there is a sensible choice - not everyone can, or wishes, to. stay in a five star hotel, some prefer eating in pubs to restaurants. For myself I have frequently found as much, if not more, pleasure in staying in one of the Wolsey Lodges, than a more impersonal hotel. Here you are invited to stay with people in their own, very beautiful, homes and enjoy their conversation over a fabulous dinner. This choice will certainly not suit everyone but it gives me the opportunity of opening up new avenues for those who want to stay away. I have written the book county by county to make it user friendly and at the back you will find additional information which may prove of use to you, the reader.

Joy David

Chapter 1

BEDS. BERKS. CAMBS. BUCKS. & HERTS

INCLUDES

Chapter 1

BEDFORDSHIRE, BERKSHIRE, BUCKINGHAMSHIRE, CAMBRIDGESHIRE & HERTFORDSHIRE

The whole of the Royal County of Berkshire is really overshadowed by the majesty of Windsor Castle and its surroundings. This enormous fortress which dominates Windsor is the largest inhabited castle in the world. It has been one of the principal residences of the sovereigns of England since the days of William the Conqueror, who built it. When you come to examine it closely you will see that almost every monarch since William's time has taken a hand in rebuilding. For our present Sovereign Lady, Queen Elizabeth II, the rebuilding has been forced upon her by the devastating fire just five years ago which destroyed much of value, although the works of art, furniture and books were saved by a human chain passing these priceless masterpieces gently down the line hand to hand - hands that included the Queen, the Duke of York and many local people. The damage has now been restored and the castle is as magnificent and awe inspiring as ever. Three wards, or enclosures, make up Windsor Castle. The Round Tower in the Middle Ward was built by Henry II to replace the wooden Norman fortress; George IV added its upper half in 1828-32. The Lower Ward contains St Georges Chapel and the Upper Ward has the State Apartments.

Within the Castle, parts of which are open to the public, you must not miss the 15th and 16th century St Georges Chapel. It boasts some of the finest fan vaulting in the world, the helms and banners of knights, the tombs of Henry VII and Charles I and a memorial to Prince Albert. The State Apartments also must not be missed. These magnificently furnished rooms on the precipitous north flank of the castle are still used on official occasions. On a quite different scale is the world's most famous Doll's House designed by Sir Edwin Lutyens in the 1920's for Queen Mary.

Everywhere in Windsor there are Royal connections. Indeed the town grew up because of the presence of the castle. In St Albans Street, The Royal Mews has the elegant Scottish State Coach of 1830 in pride of place. Next door Burford House built in the 1670's for Nell Gwynn is used to display gifts presented to the royal family. Colourful uniforms of the Blues and Royals are on view at the Household Cavalry Museum in Combemere Barracks. Exhibits cover the history of the Regiments of Household Cavalry - bodyguards and escorts of the sovereign - from their beginnings in Charles II's reign through to the age of armoured and motorised transport. Then there is the Royalty and Empire Exhibition, mounted by Madame Tussaud's of London in the restored Eton and Windsor Central Station; a stunning recreation of Jubilee year in 1897.

Windsor itself is delightful with a good theatre, attractive shops and a beautiful parish church built in 1820 on the site of an earlier church. The building was supervised by Jeffrey Wyatt who later, as Sir Jeffrey Wyatville, designed the Castle's Waterloo Chamber for George IV.

Windsor Great Park off the A332 south of Windsor is the remnant of a much vaster royal hunting forest. It is marvellous for walking and has some superb views which include the vista up the famous Long Walk - a 3 mile avenue leading from the statue of George III on horseback, known as the Copper Horse, to the walls of the Castle. The park at its south-east corner, stretches into Surrey where two beautiful gardens - Savill Garden and Valley Gardens - spill to the shores of Virginia Water.

Eton is always inextricably mixed with Windsor but it is a little town in its own right. It has always had a fascination for people especially because of the world famous school, Eton College. It is an excellent place in which to stay because it is so convenient for London, and central for anyone who wants to explore the beautiful countryside surrounding the River Thames.

There are some wonderful drives along the River Thames to small towns and villages, **Maidenhead, Taplow**, amongst many. I always enjoy visiting **Cookham** the home of the artist Sir Stanley Spencer (1891-1959). He loved his birthplace with an intensity that shows in his paintings. Whatever the theme, Cookham, almost always provided the settings for his paintings. Cookham High Street, the parish church, the River Thames, the meadows are all recognisable in his works. It is fitting that Cookham should be the home of the **Stanley Spencer Gallery**. It stands in the centre of Cookham in the former Wesleyan chapel to which he was taken as a child by his mother. Pride of place is held by the immense, unfinished Christ Preaching at Cookham Regatta. There are also some touching reminders of this talented man; his spectacles, easel, palettes, sunshade and folding chair, and even a baby's push chair that he used to carry his equipment when he was off on a painting expedition.

Newbury is a busy, prosperous town which drew me because of its **Newbury District Museum** in the Wharf, off Newbury Market Place. It is situated in the town's beautiful **Jacobean Cloth Hall** and extends into a picturesque 18th century Granary. Its purpose is to tell of the history of Berkshire where, in centuries past, the Berkshire Downs were great sheep hills and Newbury was a thriving cloth town. There are all sorts of things to see connected with the history of local weaving. You can learn about the Kennet and Avon Canal which runs close-by. You can admire the old town stocks and there is an audio-visual show dramatising events of the Civil War at Newbury.

Two good hostelries were recommended to me in villages outside Newbury. The first at **Stockcross** just three miles from Newbury with easy access to the M4 motorway. Here The Lord Lyon has strong connections with the racing fraternity. In fact the pub was named after the racehorse which was the first horse to win the Triple Crown in 1866. For those not in the know the races included the 2000 Guineas at Newmarket, the Derby at Epsom and the St Ledger at Doncaster quite an achievement. The Lord Lyon is a traditional village pub offering tasty meals and bar snacks at sensible prices.

The second is at **Chaddleworth** which you can reach by going north from Hungerford up the A338, crossing the motorway at Junction 14. This is no more than a sleepy hamlet in the heart of the Berkshire Downs with wonderful uninterrupted views. The Ibex is a welcoming hostelry which is in the centre of the racing world and you will find that many interesting racing personnel frequent the bars.

One might not choose the busy commercial and industrial town of **Slough** as an ideal place to stay but **The Copthorne Hotel** in **Cippenham Lane** is outstanding and offers every conceivable service to the traveller, business man or woman. I recommend it heartily.

Over the Thames from Windsor and beyond the town of Slough, Berkshire joins the tall narrow county of **Buckinghamshire** on its short southern boundary. At this point Buckinghamshire is low and leafy, rising sharply further north to the Chilterns with its thick beechwoods, then further north still becoming a land of streams and marshes.

A prehistoric boundary known as **Grim's Ditch** runs across the Chilterns to **Great Hampden** and nearby are two crosses cut through the turf into the chalk. Not as exciting as the White Horse of Uffingham but nonetheless intriguing.

The Chilterns are renowned for the many footpaths and there are walks both short and long, but rarely strenuous, that can take advantage of the scenery, giving just occasional glimpses through the trees of distant views. The **North Bucks Way** starting near **Wendover** on the Chilterns escarpment takes walkers down to **Wolverton** in the vale of Aylesbury. On the North Bucks Way can be found the **Quainton Railway Centre** with trains in steam on the last Sunday of each month. The ancient trees of **Burnham Beeches** east of **Maidenhead** form a beautiful area which was bought for the people by the City of London in 1879. At one time this area was also home to Romany gypsies, now long gone.

Along the Thames, Buckinghamshire has some attractive towns such as **Marlow** which is particularly beautiful. This was the home of the poet Percy B. Shelley and Mary Shelley of 'Frankenstein' fame. The poet William Cowper spent the second half of his life in **Olney** where the **Cowper Museum** celebrates his works, including 'Amazing Grace' which was written here.

Stoke Poges church is where Thomas Grey wrote his 'Elegy written in a country Churchyard' and at **Beaconsfield** lived G.K.Chesterton and Enid Blyton who it is believed was inspired by the **Bekonscot Model Village** with tiny houses spread over a large garden. Milton lived in **Chalfont St Giles** when he fled from London to escape the plague and in addition to a small museum, his cottage is now open to visitors.

Near Beaconsfield the small town of **Jordans** was home to William Penn, the founder of Pennsylvania and he is buried at the small 17th century **Quaker Meeting House. The Mayflower Barn,** also open to the public, incorporates beams taken from the Mayflower after the Pilgrim Fathers sailed to America in 1620.

Hughenden Manor near **High Wycombe** was the home of Benjamin Disraeli and the house still contains much of his furniture and other belongings. Today's Prime Minister has a country residence southwest of **Wendover,** a Tudor house known as **Chequers,**presented to the nation for just this purpose during World War 1.

From pretty, small villages such as **Hambleden** to modern towns like **Milton Keynes,** Buckinghamshire has absorbed a large increase in population in the latter part of this century, yet outside these conurbation's retains its character as a rural area. **Bedfordshire** is a green and peaceful county where water meadows flank the River Great Ouse and the rolling downs climb towards the mighty Chilterns. John Bunyan was born in the village of **Elstow** in 1628. Later he was imprisoned for his religious views in the county town of

Bedford. Both places have much to remind us of this great man. **Elstow Moot Hall** is a beautiful timber and brick building built about 1500. Its purpose, to house the goods for the famous May Fair at Elstow. It was also used as a court house and it has been suggested that Bunyan might have had Elstow Fair in mind when he described the worldly 'Vanity Fair' in the Pilgrim's Progress. The Hall belonged to the nuns of Elstow Abbey and after the abbey was dissolved at the Reformation, the Moot Hall continued as a court house. For centuries it was neglected until in 1951 it was restored. The upper floor has been opened up to display the superb medieval roof, with massive beams and graceful uprights.

Two miles south west of **Dunstable**, the rolling hills of Dunstable Downs form the northern end of the Chilterns chalk escarpment and from them there are wide views over the Vale of Aylesbury and beyond. Thousands of years ago they were a highway for prehistoric man, who trudged along the Icknield Way (now the B489) at their foot. In a 300 acre area the ground has been left untreated by chemical weed-killers or fertilisers and the result is stunning. Rare plant species flourish, including fairy flax and chalk milkwort. Little muntjac deer browse among the scrub, and whinchats and grasshopper warblers dart over the hillside.

At Whipsnade Heath there is a reminder of the First World War. Here is the Tree cathedral, in a sun dappled grove, laid out to a plan of nave, transepts and chapels. It was planted in the 1930's by Edmund Kell Blyth in memory of his fallen friends. Quite moving and very beautiful.

Nearby on top of the downs, more than 2000 animals roam over 500 acres of **Whipsnade Park Zoo**, in conditions as nearly wild as climate and safety will permit.

If you are a narrow gauge railway enthusiast you will want to visit **Leighton Buzzard Narrow Gauge Railway**. An average speed of five and a half miles an hour might not seem much by today's standards but it is quite enough to the locomotives of the Leighton Buzzard Railway which was built to carry sand from the quarries north of the town to the main London and North Western Railway. Due to be scrapped at the end of the 1960's, it was saved by a band of enthusiasts who have acquired steam and diesel engines from as far away as India and the Cameroons, constructed rolling stock, and built an engine shed for maintenance.

This is a county full of wonderful stately homes including Woburn Abbey, the showplace home of the Dukes of Bedford and Luton Hoo standing in 1200 acres of a park laid out by Capability Brown. The plain exterior hides a glittering treasure house.

I listened to Jeffrey Archer once talking about **Cambridge,** a city he loves, and one in which he almost lives at **Granchester**, made famous by Rupert Brooke, only two miles away. He gave some very good advice to people wanting to visit the city. 'Do not allow the academics and students make you feel you have no right to be there. Cambridge is as much your city as theirs.' Good advice, for this famous seat of learning can be a bit intimidating.

There are all sorts of things you need to know about Cambridge. For example during the year there is constant activity and one thing is for certain one visit will not suffice. No matter when you come it is lovely and very special but if you remember that accommodation is difficult during major events such as May Week, Degree Days and the Festival, that may influence your decision.

If you have thoughts of going to Evensong in King's College Chapel, for example, the services only take place during University terms. Lastly during the University examination period, May to mid June, many of the Colleges are closed to the public.

So when are you going to visit Cambridge? Will it be to tour the Colleges? A wonderful experience. Strangers frequently ask 'Where is the University?'. Once an easy question to answer but today far more complex. The oldest buildings, which now accommodate the administration, form the complex called Old School's opposite Great St Mary's Church. This really is the heart of the University but its lecture halls, laboratories and libraries are spread through central Cambridge and west of the river as far as **Madingley.** You will see undergraduates darting about from one college to another in pursuit of their studies and of their social lives.

The only way to discover the joys of this magical city is on foot and the way I was shown, many years ago, is probably the best way. Over a period of days I was taken on various walks which took in the central area of Cambridge, including the oldest Colleges and University buildings.

There are many brilliant museums and perhaps I should mention that the beautiful green areas in front of the Colleges are known as 'Courts' whereas at Oxford they are called 'Quads'. You are welcome to visit these grounds and wander about at will but please remember that they are private establishments, and that their members live and work in them all year round. Many visitors takes this opportunity and because of this there are occasional restrictions especially during examination time. At most other times you can walk through the courts to visit the chapels, and in a few cases, the Halls and Libraries. Picnicking is not permitted nor may you bring prams, pushchairs or dogs.

I have to admit that most people come to Cambridge to take a look at the University which is fair enough, but a spin off from this is the excellence of the shops. The big stores are represented but the specialist shops are the really interesting ones and usually housed in old buildings. It is good to see the church like windows of **Heffers Children's Bookshop**, the elegance of Ryder and Amies Hosiers and Shirtmakers. There are fine antique shops, fine woollens, silver, shops specialising in herbs, and good bookshops naturally.

From Monday to Saturday you can wander around the bustling market which hides the unusual in the centre and keeps the outer stalls for fruit, flowers and vegetables. Keep looking and around the area you will find Flea markets and in the summer All Saint's Gardens provides the setting for displays of art and craft as well as artists selling their own paintings.

I went just a little way west on the A45 to **Stow-cum-Quy** and **Anglesey Abbey**, a place of great beauty bequeathed to the National Trust in 1966 by Lord Fairhaven whose nephew the third Lord Fairhaven now lives there.

Its history has been chequered, with several owners since the l6th century one of whom was a Carter from Cambridge, by the name of Hobson and from whom we have derived the expression 'Hobson's Choice'. Of the original Augustinian priory only the chapter house and the vaulted monks' parlour survive. It is a wondrous place to visit and the gardens are nothing short of superb. In spring cowslips cover the meadows and the sweet scent of some 4,000 white and blue hyacinths pervades the air. Next come the daffodils and their golden glory is replaced by dahlias and brilliantly coloured herbaceous borders. The autumn reminds us that winter is coming but throws out a warmth of its own with the varied array of trees and shrubs in every shade of bronze and red.

Then taking the A45 again out of Cambridge going west I made for **Caxton**. The village is on the A1198 11 miles north of Royston and 10 miles south of Huntingdon. My purpose was to discover why people who use Wolsey Lodges frequently, spoke so highly of Church Farm, a member of the Wolsey Lodge Consortium. Not hard to discover why because here is a house set in 3 acres of beautiful grounds that is elegant and spacious and a listed farmhouse. It retains original 16th and 17th century features with 19th century additions. A wealth of oak beams, antiques and English water-colours greet you, open log fires and very comfortable beds add the finishing touches. You will be wonderfully fed and truly cosseted but there is more besides. From here Peter and Maggie Scott run Heritage Leisure Courses. Two day Courses are designed to enhance the enjoyment of our heritage, whilst being informative. There is a strong element of participation and an exchange of ideas, knowledge and observations is encouraged. Most of the time is spent visiting historic locations - Cambridge University, Fitzwilliam Museum, Audley End House, Ely Cathedral, and sites of particular significance to the periods studied.

A little further north from here is **Waterbeach,** a pleasant village with the River Cam flowing nearby. The church is 550 years old and you can find out much more about it from the landlord of The White Horse where you will be well cared for.

If you went further west and then drove northwards up the A1 the Great North road, you would come to the historic village of **Buckden**. In 1533 King Henry VIII imprisoned his wife, Catherine of Aragon in Buckden Towers following the annulment of their marriage, allowing him to marry Anne Boleyn. Buckden also has the splendid and imposing 17th century George Coaching Inn. It must have looked like paradise to the 17th and 18th century stagecoach travellers on the road between London and York, with the ostlers scurrying to arrange a change of horse, as the weary travellers descended from their carriage, to enter the warmth of this welcoming hostelry. That tradition is still there today, fostered by the owners of this family run business, where quality and value for money go hand in hand.

Eight miles south west of Cambridge on the A603 is **Wimpole Hall**, the largest country house in Cambridgeshire with a landscape of rare historical worth. Not to be missed.

Sawston lies to the south of Cambridge. This small town has a bustling High Street in the midst of which is The Greyhound, a meeting place for locals and visitors. Sunday lunch is popular here. Booking is advisable for each of the two sittings, the first at noon and the other at 1.30pm. A good place to stoke up sufficient energy to visit the mighty **Imperial War Museum** at **Duxford,** two miles away.

This is much more than a museum. It is a different and fascinating outing for the whole family. It's fun, full of surprises and educational as well. There is the finest collection of military and civil aircraft in the country together with an incredible variety of tanks, vehicles, guns - even a lifeboat and midget submarines. Whatever the weather is like you can come here because thousands of square feet of undercover displays will keep you interested. The collection dates from the First World War right up to the Falklands conflict and the Gulf War. Restoration of historic aircraft is carried out here and you can watch this vital work in progress.

Melbourn was an important place in the Middle Ages. It still has moated houses and a medieval church as well as many attractive cottages. In its midst is Sheen Mill, a restaurant with rooms, in an idyllic setting overlooking the Mill pond and the River Mel, which actually runs beneath the restaurant. The 17th century mill has been fully restored and is a treasure. The original mill was listed in the Domesday Book. I only wish I had the time to stay in one of the 8 bedrooms overlooking the river.

Another delightful village within 2 miles of the Duxford Museum and also only 4 miles from the historic house **Audley Hall**, is **Hinxton**. It sits just one mile inside the Cambridgeshire border, 6 miles from Saffron Walden. It has no shops, just one street and its biggest disturbance is the River Cam flowing nearby.

The tiny spire of the old church rises from a dome set in the battlements of a 650 year old tower. The story of the church is older than that. It begins in 1080 and from that time comes the font and a doorway blocked up in the nave. The rest of the church is mainly 14th and 15th century. The chancel has old benches and there are old beams in the roof. A wonderful, inspiring house of God.

Another village gem is the 16th century pub, The Red Lion which boasts an old bread oven and was once a picturesque coaching inn. The pub is busy and justifiably so for it produces delicious food both in the restaurant and bar. It has a garden which is large and lovely, stables with horses, ponies and goats and a parrot called George who will be happy to talk to you!

Wisbech is situated in an area renowned for bulb growing and fruit cultivation, and fruit canning is an important local industry. The town stands on the River Nene, 12 miles from the sea - though at one time before changes in river patterns altered its relation to the Wash, it was only 4 miles away. From the North and South Brinks an impressive array of Georgian houses, several with Dutch characteristics, looks across the quays and the river; the most notable is **Peckover House** belonging to the National Trust and built in the 1720s, displaying some fine rococo plasterwork. The church of St Peter and St Paul is mainly Norman and Perpendicular with a fine 16th century tower. The Wisbech and Fenland Museum splendidly illustrates fenland life.

The small village of **Welney** on the edge of Norfolk, is a quiet, tranquil place which is known for its fishing of the rivers 'the Delph' and 'the Bedford'. In addition the well known Pisces fishing lakes are also very popular with bird watchers, largely because of the Wildfowl and Wetlands centre which has its headquarters in Pintail House, Hundred Foot Bank, Welney. It is one of eight national centres encouraging visitors to develop close, personal contact with a total of 7000 wetland birds of 200 different types; some species owing their very existence to the Trust. At Welney you can get close to nature along a carefully planned walk, with 21 camouflaged observation hides and a visitor building that provides, warm, comfortable shelter from even the harshest elements.

Ely will be somewhere you will not want to leave out. Charming in its own right it is enhanced by the glory of its beautiful Cathedral which can be seen for miles around. A few miles out of Ely going west on the A142 you will see the ancient village of **Witcham** signposted. At the end of the High Street is the beautiful Georgian **Witcham House** set amongst its own horse paddocks with views across the Isle of Ely to the Cathedral 5 miles away.

Now for **Huntingdon**, a county within the county of Cambridgeshire and famous as the home and constituency of the previous Prime Minister John Major. Here I want to bring two establishments to your attention. The first in the village of **Hilton**, a picturesque village tucked away on the B1040. It is The Prince of Wales, the only pub left remaining in the village and as such has become the centre of village life. It is a shining example of a traditional pub with hearty traditional food. Four en suite rooms make it a good place to stay for anyone wanting to see Cambridge, Huntingdon or St Ives.

There is a nice story about the next pub, Bennetts Restaurant and The White Hart at **Bythorne**. The bar of this 1771, timber-framed building was where two highwaymen stopped to spend some of their ill-gotten gains after robbing a coach in Kettering. They were arrested whilst in the bar but by then they had hidden their catch somewhere on the premises. To this day it has not been found. The landlord will be delighted to hear if anyone has any ideas on the subject The pub is charming and has almost the feel of a country house. The traditional food is first class and very good value.

Enjoy Huntingdonshire which is rich in history and has attractive countryside. It is a land of wide skies and church spires, pretty riverside villages, historic market towns and tranquil waterways.

Hertfordshire, along with the extinct county of Middlesex, made up the Northern Home Counties and it is here that the mix of grand country houses and new towns is in greatest contrast - or greatest harmony depending on your viewpoint. **Letchworth** was the first of the new 'Garden Cities', created as early as 1903 in a bid to bring better housing to ordinary people. Its **First Garden City Museum** tells the story of the somewhat radical social ideas which were held by those who originally created this town as well as those who lived here. **Welwyn Garden City** followed in 1920 and several other new towns, often around old town or village centres, sprung up in the post-war period of the 1950s.

I have to admit that for me, Hertfordshire is principally **St Albans** with its fine cathedral in which thousands of years of worship have continued on the site of St Alban's martyrdom. Many centuries ago Alban was the first Christian martyr in this county and his shrine has always attracted pilgrims in search of physical and spiritual healing. It is a beautiful place which emanates strength.

You feel as if the Almighty is reaching out for you and endeavouring to pour into your soul the fortitude shown by St Alban, and at the same time give you hope for the present and peace eternal. The history of the cathedral is well documented and you will do no better than to purchase the beautifully presented, Pitkin Guide to St Albans Cathedral which will cost you about two pounds and be a constant reminder of your visit.

Almost surrounded by motorways, St Albans is easy to reach and having done so you drive into quieter realms and begin to realise that you are going to discover in this one place, which offers the unusual combination of the dignity of a Cathedral City and the intimacy of a rural market town, the full span of British history. For a moment or two the sense of history is overwhelming. St Albans is full of museums, beautifully laid out and providing easily digested information.

A totally different atmosphere you will find at **The Mosquito Aircraft Museum** in Salisbury Hall, **London Colney**. The historic site of the moated Salisbury hall, mentioned in the Domesday Book, was chosen by the d'Havilland Aircraft Company in 1939 to develop in secret the wooden, high speed, unarmed bomber, the Mosquito; with 41 variants of the type of the most versatile aircraft of the war. This began the museum's long association with Salisbury Hall making it the oldest Aircraft Museum in the country. Visitors to the museum soon discover that it can offer more than a collection of static aircraft. Close inspection of the exhibits provide a unique hands-on experience. Members are always on hand to assist the visitor and demonstrate the working displays. With a varied programme of regular events that include flying displays, vintage car and motor cycle rallies and model exhibitions, there is always something to appeal to all ages.

From the air to the ground. **The Royal National Rose Society** at Chiswell Green, St Albans on the outskirts of the town, invites you to enjoy the world famous 'Gardens of the Rose' at the Society's showground where there is a collection of some 30,000 roses of all types.

The 12 acres of gardens are a marvellous spectacle for the casual visitor and fascinating to the rose enthusiast. The gardens are being continuously developed - in particular by associating roses with a great many other plants - to create greater interest for visitors and to stimulate ideas leading to more adventurous gardening.

The British Rose Festival is a spectacular national event held every year in July. It includes a magnificent display of roses organised by the Society and the British Rose Growers Association on an excitingly new and different theme each year. The competition is for the leading national amateur rose exhibitors and floral artists. All the best of British roses can be seen at this unique show.

Of particular interest in this county for vegetarians will be **Shaw's Corner** at **Ayot St Lawrence**. **Sir George Bernard Shaw,** playwright and critic, vegetarian and humanist, lived here for the second half of his long and active life. His vegetarian ideals were based on both moral and health grounds, proclaiming that 'Animals are our fellow creatures. I feel a strong kinship with them.' The house has been kept exactly as it was at the time of his death in 1950.

The many houses on a truly grand scale include **Hatfield House** originally home to the Bishops of Ely and later to Henry VIII's children and other members of the Royal family. **Brocket Hall** which was the home of Lord Melbourne and Lady Caroline Lamb, **Moor Park**, the historic home of Cardinal Wolsey later transformed into a Palladian mansion and now a golf club, and **Basing House,** home of William Penn founder of Pennsylvania.

Sadly others have fared less well, such as the Castle at **Bishop's Stortford** now just a mound, and another earthworks with just a little masonry which was the Castle at Berkhamsted, presented by William the Conqueror to his brother, later visited by Thomas a Becket, Chaucer and three of Henry VIII's wives and involuntarily visited for a long term, by King John of France. Another was Ware Park which originally housed the 'Great Bed of Ware' mentioned by Shakespeare in his plays, now in the Victoria and Albert Museum.

Near **Ware** at **Amwell** is one of the most unexpected museums in Britain, a Lamp-Post Museum!

GATEHANGERS INN

Lower End. Ashendon
Nr Aylesbury Buckinghamshire HPl8 OHE

Tel: 01296 651296 Fax: 01296 651340

Ashendon is an area of Buckinghamshire that is steeped in history and rewards anyone who takes the time and trouble to discover all its secrets. That makes it an essential stopping point for anyone visiting the county and this is reinforced by the excellence of the village's local, the Gatehangers Inn, which for the last four hundred years has been dispensing hospitality to travellers and never better than today in the capable and friendly hands of Susan and Michael Rand. As one would expect in a hostelry of this age, it is full of character with a wealth of old beams, nooks and crannies and uneven floors all adding to a great atmosphere of well being. The Rand's have the knack of making their customers feel relaxed and at ease as soon as they enter the pub's portals. The attractive furnishings in a cottage style are in keeping with the inn. Michael has a great knowledge of beer and you will not find better kept ale in the county. He also jealously guards his wine list which is chosen with great care and gives people the opportunity to sample wines from around the world at sensible prices.

The food, for which the Gatehangers is well known. provides an ever changing menu of delectable dishes. You might well start with fresh Mussels in a real home-made white wine sauce with a hot crusty baguette, freshly made soup of the day or home-made fish-cakes with a light cheese sauce and follow the starter of your choice with Chicken and Sage Pie with a Puff pastry top, Smoked Haddock rarebit made with gruyere cheese or a mouth-watering - and very filling - 120oz Rump steak with a grilled garnish. All the main courses are served with either fresh, seasonal vegetables, chips or a side salad. The emphasis is on quality with as much local produce used as possible.

For anyone wanting to stay in the area either for business or pleasure, the Gatehangers has five en suite bedrooms, all with extremely comfortable beds, pretty furnishings. colour television, direct-dial telephones and a generously supplied hospitality tray. Aylesbury is close-by and Oxford not far away. There is a wealth of places to visit within easy distance including a number of National Trust properties. Aylesbury is an interesting town in its own right and Oxford with its 'dreaming spires' will give you hours of pleasure. For the energetic there is fishing. golf, horseriding. cycling and good walks.

USEFUL INFORMATION

OPEN*; All year*
CHILDREN*; Yes, if well behaved*
CREDIT CARDS*; All major cards*
LICENSED*; Full On*
ACCOMMODATION*;: 5 en suite rooms*
PETS*; No*

RESTAURANT*; Good food, sensible prices*
BAR FOOD*; A good range, home-cooked*
VEGETARIAN*; Always a choice*
DISABLED ACCESS*; Not suitable*
GARDEN*; Yes*

HUNT HOTEL

Church Road,
Linslade, Leighton Buzzard,
Bedfordshire LU7 7LR

Tel/Fax: 01525 374692

Frequently one reads in this sort of write up the words 'warm welcome' and no doubt that is true but in the family run Hunt Hotel there is something very special about the welcome. You walk in through the doors and you are encompassed in an atmosphere of warmth and hospitality which seems as natural as daybreak. The hotel is owned by the Naylor family. It is an interesting 1850's building in its own right. In the 1930's it enjoyed tremendous popularity capped by such illustrious visitors as Edward VIII and Mrs Simpson who stayed whilst hunting with the Whaddon Chase. They would have found, as one does today, a very professionally run hotel.

You will find the hotel on a quiet road off Wing Road A418, overlooking parkland and adjacent to a fine example of an early Victorian Church, It has a large Car Park at the rear and the main London-Birmingham railway line is within easy walking distance. London is only 45 minutes away. Milton Keynes, renowned for its shops, is 20 minutes drive and Luton Airport 30 minutes. From the Hunt Hotel you are well situated to explore such places as Woburn Abbey, Knebworth House, Hatfield House, Luton Hoo, Silverstone Race Track, Towcester Race Course and Whipsnade as well as many other attractions. Within the hotel there are fifteen attractively and comfortably furnished en suite bedrooms, all of which have Telephones, TV, Radio and Video facilities as well as hairdryers and a well supplied Hostess Tray. The friendly bar is a popular meeting place where one can enjoy tasty bar snacks or simply relax with an aperitif before dining in the pretty restaurant which is open to non-residents. Here there is a comprehensive A La Carte menu with the emphasis on good traditional English fare. An extensive, well chosen wine list complements the meal perfectly. In addition there is a Function Room which is widely used for meetings, seminars, wedding receptions and private parties. Here as throughout the hotel, the service is immaculate.

USEFUL INFORMATION

OPEN: *All year*　　　　　　**RESTAURANT:** *Good English fare*
Lunch: 7 days a week A la Carte or Bar Meals 12-2pm
Dinner: Mon-Sat from 6.30pm (Sunday Residents only)
CHILDREN: *Welcome*　　　　**BAR FOOD:** *Good choice*
CREDIT CARDS: *All major cards*　**VEGETARIAN:** *On request*
LICENSED: *Full On*　　　　　**GARDEN:** *Large. Car Parking*
ACCOMMODATION: *15 en suite rooms*　**PETS:** *By arrangement*

THE HIGH FLYER

69 Newnham Street,
Ely, Cambridgeshire CB7 4PQ

Tel: 01353 669200

This friendly establishment is a hotel, a public house and a restaurant, and a pleasure to visit, largely for its friendly, genuine welcome. It is near the magnificent and sometimes awe-inspiring Ely Cathedral. From here you can take a short walk and find yourself at the river where you can hire a boat and idle away a delightful afternoon looking at this charming small town from the water - it gives one a totally different perspective. Oliver Cromwell had a house here which is open to visitors, there is a Nature Reserve at Welney with 900 acres of wetland. Windmills abound in this part of Cambridgeshire. Ely has a swimming pool and a cinema so there is plenty to see and do if you decide to stay at The High Flyer.

Oddly enough The High Flyer is not an ancient hostelry as one might expect but an attractively built and designed modern pub, just three years old. What it lacks in history it gains from all the modern amenities and you will find that the landlords, Neill and Annette Gwinnett have created a very pleasant, cheerful place in which one can enjoy a drink, have a good meal and stay a night or two. The busy bars are light and spacious, the Restaurant with its 86 covers is just the place for a meal and you will find the menu is wide ranging. Bar Food is very popular and there are always Daily Specials as well as a very good selection for Vegetarians. Every Thursday evening there is live music to which regulars and visitors look forward. There is a free Car Park.

The six en suite bedrooms are comfortably furnished and all have television with Skye channels. A generously supplied hostess tray is there for your use - what a boon at the end of a busy day or first thing in the morning. A direct dial telephone is also in every room. Breakfast each morning is a delicious meal and substantial enough to set anyone up for the day.

USEFUL INFORMATION

OPEN; *All day*
CHILDREN; *Welcome*
CREDIT CARDS; *Yes. Not Amex*
LICENSED; *Full On*
ACCOMMODATION; *6 en suite rooms*

RESTAURANT; *Extensive menu*
BAR FOOD; *Wide choice. Daily Specials*
VEGETARIAN; *Very good selection*
DISABLED ACCESS; *Yes*
PETS; *No*

PEKING RENDEZVOUS,
23 High Street,
Haddenham,
Aylesbury,
Buckinghamshire HP17 8ES

Tel: 01844 291468

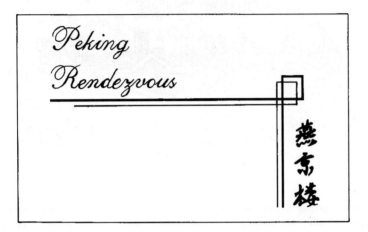

The Peking Rendezvous is well known far beyond the environments of Haddenham. You will find it in the High Street and probably be amazed to discover the ultimate Peking Experience in a big sleepy village in the heart of Buckinghamshire but this is exactly what the Peking Rendezvous is. Once a pub called the Wagon and Horses it was transformed into an Oriental paradise in 1986. Stephen Wong, one of the owners, has worked hard with his staff to produce a delightful and restful atmosphere in which to enjoy the excellent food. You sit at pleasantly furnished tables waited on by a staff who are determined to ensure you enjoy the ambience as well as the many delicious dishes.

The emphasis is on quality ingredients and special preparatory techniques, the end result of which produces a unique menu based on the traditional recipes from various regions of China including Peking, Szechuan and Cantonese. The Peking offers special things for special occasions such as Birthdays. The price ranges from twelve pounds to twenty pounds per head.
You will have a memorable meal at the Peking at any time of the year. The only time The Peking Rendezvous closes is Christmas Day and Boxing Day.

USEFUL INFORMATION

OPEN; *Mon-Sun 12-1.30pm & 6-10.30pm* ***VEGETARIAN;*** *Catered for*
(Last orders)
RESTAURANT; *Exciting Oriental Dishes* ***LICENSED;*** *Yes*
CHILDREN; *Welcome. Children's meals* ***CREDIT CARDS;*** *All major cards*
DISABLED ACCESS; *Yes*

LITTLE OFFLEY
Hitchin,
Hertfordshire SG5 3BU

Tel/Fax: 01462 768243

This wonderful l7th century house built about 1685, is set in 800 acres of farmland in the Chiltern Hills. The views over the garden and surrounding countryside from the windows of the house, are stunning. The home of Martin and Lady Rosemary French, it is a gracious, well-loved establishment in which guests are warmly welcomed and encouraged to enjoy all it has to offer. Everywhere you look there is something to please the eye from the Barley Twist Bannisters and the Panelling to the lawns at the front complete with a Ha-Ha. To reach Little Offley take the Luton-Hitchin road. At Great Offley, turn off for Little Offley.

Throughout the house there are some fine pieces of antique furniture and the spacious guest bedrooms - three in number - are beautifully appointed, each with en suite bathrooms and hostess trays. In fact one wing of the house has been set aside for guests and in addition to the bedrooms there is a large, elegant drawing room with a listed carved fireplace, and a dining room in which a delicious breakfast is served every morning. Accommodation is offered on a bed and breakfast basis but lunch and dinner can be provided for larger groups. There is also room for small conferences. An outdoor swimming pool and croquet lawn are available for guests' use in summer. Guests may leave their car at the house when flying from Luton Airport.

Little Offley is an ideal touring base from which to visit Hatfield House, Luton Hoo and Whipsnade Zoo, Woburn Abbey and Cambridge. The nearest town is Hitchin, which has large open markets on Tuesdays and Saturdays. London is 30 minutes by train.

USEFUL INFORMATION

OPEN; *All year*
CHILDREN; *Over 12 years*
CREDIT CARDS; *Visa/Master*
LICENSED; *No*
ACCOMMODATION; *3 rooms en suite*
PETS; *No*

DINING ROOM; *Excellent breakfast*
No evening meal except for large groups
VEGETARIAN; *Upon request*
DISABLED ACCESS; *Not suitable*
GARDEN; *Beautiful with swimming pool*
And croquet lawn

THE HARROW INN

Little Bedwyn, Nr Hungerford,
Wiltshire SN8 3JP
Tel:01672 870871 Fax: 01672 811231
email :josher@globalnet. co. uk

The small hamlet of Little Bedwyn is tucked away on the Eastern edge of the Vale of Pewsey, on the Wiltshire/Berkshire border. Little Bedwyn is ideally situated to explore the local area's attractions. Wiltshire is an extremely old part of the country, and Stonehenge, Avebury and Silbury Hill are close by. The Kennet and Avon Canal is a couple of hundred yards away from the Inn, and offers boating, fishing and good walking. Within easy reach are the antique shops in Hungerford and Marlborough, with Bath a little further away.

Dating from the 19th Century, the Harrow Inn is full of character and has the authentic atmosphere of a village Pub, something that is appreciated by the many people who treat it as their local - even if they live some distance away. Michael Chinner, the Chef and Landlord, is ably assisted by his staff, who go out of their way to give a warm and courteous welcome. The decor in the Inn is warm and country style, which emphasises the attraction of the Inn itself. Upstairs there are two Bed and Breakfast rooms with full en suite facilities. The rooms also have televisions and tea and coffee making facilities. Breakfast the next morning is sumptuous!

The Restaurant seats 25 in comfort and style, and the food is delicious. The menu is comprehensive in style and price offering something for everyone and every budget. Typically dishes range from Spicy Thai Prawns to a Traditional Roast Beef lunch on Sunday. All the food is freshly cooked and is presented in a relaxed, informal 'bistro' style. The Restaurant Wine List features wines from 6 different countries. Additionally, their Premier Wine List offers a select range of fine wines which are very competitively priced.

If you have ever wanted to sample a bit of the 'real' England, this is a perfect opportunity.

USEFUL INFORMATION

OPEN; 11-3pm & 6-11pm
CHILDREN; Welcome
CREDIT CARDS; Visa/Master/Switch
LICENSED; Full On & Off
ACCOMMODATION; 2 en suite rooms
GARDEN; Yes
PETS; Yes, by arrangement.

RESTAURANT; Modern English. Wide choice of dishes at varying prices
VEGETARIAN; Yes, also special diets by arrangement
DISABLED ACCESS; Ramp access to Inn but not to toilets

ABBEY HOUSE AND COACH HOUSE
West End Road,
Maxey, Peterborough
Cambridgeshire PE6 9EJ

Tel: 01778 344642

This must be one of the most fascinating houses in Cambridgeshire. An earlier building was adapted for use as a Rectory in 1454. In 1540, at the time of the Dissolution of the Monasteries, ownership passed from the Abbey to the Dean and Chapter of the cathedral and subsequent renovations took place in 1817 and 1881. It is full of nooks and crannies and oozing with character. Throughout the house the walls are colour washed in pretty pastel shades which help to make every room feel light and airy. The furnishings are traditional and well suited to the age of Abbey House. The Dining Room, where you will be served a delicious breakfast, has French windows opening on to a large mature rear garden containing the oldest Yew tree in the county. The house is beautifully run, warm and welcoming and the ideal place in which to stay to explore this part of England which abounds with stately homes, castles, former monasteries and delightful stone built villages. Peterborough has its Cathedral and Museums, Stamford its wonderful architecture and the scene of much film making. There are private lakes for walking and fishing at the end of the road, several golf courses within a short distance and many small villages, quaint hostelries and other places to see.

Abbey House has 10 en suite bedrooms most of which are in the Coach House, each attractively and individually furnished and with television, direct dial telephone and a hospitality tray. You order your breakfast the night before from a menu which offers a Farmhouse Grill with bacon, sausage, mushrooms, fried egg, tomatoes and fried bread, or Scrambled or Poached Eggs. There are fruit juices, grapefruit segments or cereal to start with and plenty of freshly made toast with marmalade or jam. No evening meals are served but local pubs serve good food at sensible prices. This is a house which is as good for the businessman as it is for the visitor; somewhere in which to relax, unwind and enjoy the friendly hospitality.

USEFUL INFORMATION

OPEN; *All year*
CREDIT CARDS; *Not at the moment*
LICENSED; *No*
ACCOMMODATION; *10 en suite rooms*
PETS; *No*

DINING ROOM; *Excellent breakfast*
VEGETARIAN; *By arrangement*
DISABLED ACCESS; *Yes*
GARDEN; *Yes*

THE GEORGE AND DRAGON
Watling Street,
Little Brickhill,
Milton Keynes, Buckinghamshire MK17 9NB

Tel: 01525 261298

One would not be incorrect if one were to refer to The George and Dragon as a Restaurant with a pub attached rather than the other way round. The reason is simple; the Chef/Patron, Ronnie Noble has a passion for food and has created a clientele who find their way to the inn especially to try some of the exciting and innovative dishes on offer. Imagine starting a meal with a salad of smoked chicken and crispy bacon or a Lobster Bisque followed by Cajun spiced Pink Snapper with a sweet red pepper sauce. There is a wide choice from the simple to the exotic with fresh fish a speciality but whatever you have will have been freshly prepared; Ronnie is a stickler when it comes to demanding the freshest local produce and the very highest quality meat and poultry. The full A la Carte menu is available in the pretty, intimate Garden Room Restaurant every evening except Monday and on Sundays a delicious, traditional Sunday Lunch is served. A very popular institution for which it is wise to book in advance.

In addition to the stunning food, the whole atmosphere of The George and Dragon is one of warmth, cheerfulness and a joie de vivre which is so often missing today. You will find regulars enjoying International fayre in the newly refurbished lounge bar with a wide selection of traditional ales. There is a large, beautifully kept garden at the rear of the building in which it is relaxing and therapeutic to sit with a drink in peaceful surroundings. Summer Sundays from July to September, weather permitting, provide an opportunity to have a barbecue in the garden. A fun occasion when the food is very special. If you are feeling really decadent after Sunday lunch in the summer then you can laze about surrounded by the scents and sounds of the garden and wait for a delicious afternoon tea to be served, complete with scones, jam, cream and cake.

You will find that The George and Dragon is the closest restaurant to Woburn Championship Golf Course and you will find it 100 yards off the new A5 By Pass.

USEFUL INFORMATION

OPEN; *All day Sat & Sun. Mon-Fri 11.45am-3pm & 5-11.30pm*
CREDIT CARDS; *Visa/Master/Switch*
CHILDREN; Welcome
LICENSED; *Full On*
PARKING; *Large car park*

RESTAURANT; *Modern Anglo/French Rest: 12-2.30 & 6.30-10pm*
BAR FOOD; *Wide range*
VEGETARIAN; *Catered for*
DISABLED ACCESS; *Yes*
GARDEN; *Large & beautiful. Barbecues Afternoon Teas*

THE TUDOR TAVERN,

28 George Street,
St Albans, Hertfordshire AL1 4ES

Tel: 01727 853233 Fax: 01727 854737

Steeped in history, The Tudor Tavern dates back to the 14th century and when one walks in through its sturdy doors one can almost imagine that one is stepping back in time. The atmosphere has been built up over the centuries and is nurtured today by the landlord Colin Dixon, who, with his staff, welcomes everyone who comes here whether for a meal or just for a drink in the cosy bar. Surprisingly, the upstairs restaurant, which is full of character, has high ceilings and the original beams - one tends to look for low ceilings in the 14th century. The restaurant has an attractive small and very comfortable bar area where you may sit and enjoy a drink whilst taking a look at the extensive menu. The food is traditional English, beautifully presented and value for money. Well behaved children are very welcome and there is a Vegetarian selection; special diets are available by arrangement. At lunchtime there is an attractive bar menu which offers daily specials. The Tudor Tavern is close to St Albans magnificent Cathedral and just the place to visit having sated oneself with the beauty of the Cathedral.

USEFUL INFORMATION

OPEN; *All year*
CHILDREN; *Well behaved welcome*
CREDIT CARDS; *Most major cards*
LICENSED; *Full On*
PETS; *No*

RESTAURANT; *Good, traditional English*
BAR FOOD; *Lunchtime only*
VEGETARIAN; *Yes*
DISABLED ACCESS; *Not suitable*

THE ALEXANDRA HOTEL
Queen Alexandra Road,
High Wycombe, Bucks HP11 2JX

Tel: 01494 463494 Fax: 01494 463560

This very modern building has 28 en suite rooms and 4 flats and is also well equipped for conferences, seminars etc. The emphasis throughout the hotel is on quality, service and cuisine and this is achieved. It is run with great efficiency by a staff who not only know their jobs but perform them with pleasure. Guests feel important and very welcome; something that is frequently missing in today's world and something that is very much appreciated by the travelling public. Whether you come to stay at the Alexandra Hotel for pleasure or business you will enjoy your stay and appreciate the comfort and excellent food that is on offer. Every bedroom has remote control Sky television, direct-dial telephone, pre-set alarm calls, trouser press, hair dryer, teas and coffee courtesy tray and a mini bar. A great boon for the business traveller is the speedy check in/check out system in which no time is wasted at reception.

The Carrington Restaurant is a delightfully relaxed place in which to eat. It provides full English or Continental breakfast, together with a range of light meals and is suitable for small private lunches or dinner parties. The four flats are situated next door at Kingfisher Court. All four, luxuriously appointed, have a twin or double-bedded room, bathroom, kitchen and lounge area. Restaurant, Bar, Laundry and Housekeeping facilities are readily available for guests staying in the flats as well as the hotel itself.

USEFUL INFORMATION

OPEN: *All year*
CHILDREN: *Welcome*
CAR PARKING: *Yes*
CREDIT CARDS: *All major cards except Diners*
CAR PARKING: *Yes*
PETS: *No*

RESTAURANT: *Excellent high quality cuisine*
BAR FOOD: *Light snacks, sandwiches*
VEGETARIAN: *Catered for*
DISABLED ACCESS: *Yes*
LICENSED: *Full On. Good wine list*
ACCOMMODATION: *28 en suite rooms 4 flats*

Chapter 2

CHESHIRE, LIVERPOOL & MANCHESTER INCLUDES

Chapter 2

CHESHIRE, LIVERPOOL AND MANCHESTER

One tends, as a stranger, to think of Cheshire as a county almost swallowed up by Merseyside and Greater Manchester in some parts a fair assumption but in the main this is a county which is particularly interesting to study.

Chester, for example, was one of the great Roman legionary fortresses, and has considerable Roman remains. This beautiful city, and then as the Dee became less navigable, the towns of the Wirral, were the major ports for crossing to Ireland. We would not recognise the picture that would have confronted travellers of the Middle Ages, when the great forests of Mara and Modrem, Wirral and Macclesfield dominated the uplands. Now we see moors and valleys, historic churches and oil refineries, rich farmland and the creeping suburbs of the big towns and cities. There are country villages and mill towns, salt flashes and the coastline. The famed Mersey estuary has great mudbanks and the power stations of the Wirral stand unabashed. Mine is only a fleeting visit to this county of marked contrasts.

Chester appears to have been founded by the Romans, using its strategic position at the mouth of the Dee. It may well have seen its first fort in AD59 built by Suetonius during his campaign against the Deceangli and Ordovices of Northern Wales, but medieval legend has it that Chester was built by 'Leon Gawer, a mighty strong giant; which builded caves and dungeons, many a one, no goodly buildings, ne proper, ne pleasant' The Romans called it Deva, their camp, and no one can come here without their minds turning back to far off days. There is no walled city in these islands to surpass it in completeness. From its famous walls one looks down on a spectacle that would be hard to match anywhere. Chester stands on a rocky sandstone spur at the head of the River Dee, set in the midst of rural countryside about which still hangs the air of medievalism that I have never felt anywhere else in England.

It was the Middle Ages that brought fortune to Chester when it became the most important port in North West England. The city's merchants exported candles, salt and cheese, and trade flourished. This peaceful prosperity was shattered in the 17th century by the English Civil War as the armies of Charles I and Cromwell battled for control. Chester supported the Crown and was besieged by Parliamentarian forces for two years after the Battle of Rowton Moor in 1645. Many buildings were destroyed and the city had to melt the civic plate to make coins for the soldiers' pay. At last starvation and plague forced the King's loyal citizens to surrender. Revolution of the industrial kind has left its mark on the city too, a network of canals, railway bridges and roads heralded a new age and leadworks, foundries and shipyards transformed the landscape. You will see this prosperity mirrored in the wealth of Georgian and Victorian houses. Chester is vitally important today as the county town of Cheshire and 'Gateway to North Wales'. It stands at the heart of the national communications network and is easy to reach from anywhere in the world.

Chester is a city of steps. There are flights of them everywhere, to the houses, to theRows, to the gates in the walls. These famous walls of red sandstone are nearly two miles round, making a raised walk from which many of Chester's interesting things can be seen. Wandering around the city is rewarding at every turn especially when you come to the unique and world famous 'Rows'. Among the interesting buildings are the 17th century **Bishop Lloyd's House**. Nearby is **God's Providence House,** the only building untouched by Black Death during the city's 17th century plague years. Two fine museums in Bridge Street are both worthy of a visit; **The Chester Heritage Centre** and **The Toy Museum**.

In Eastgate Street, The Chester Grosvenor is surely one of the finest hotels in the whole of Britain. I heard it described as one of life's memorable experiences, something with which I wholeheartedly agree. From here one can set out to explore and revel in this superb old, unique city. There is so much to see and do. Racegoers will love the beautiful racecourse. Wanting to know about the past is dealt with in a plethora of Museums. **Chester Zoo** is in a wonderful setting and has all kinds of animals from over the world. It has 110 acres of natural enclosures and parts can be toured by waterbus.

If you want to stay in one of the grandest Bed and Breakfast establishments imaginable then go to The Redland at 64 Hough Green, just a mile from the city centre. Here in a Victorian mansion you will find wonderful antique furniture, suits of armour, antique teddy bears with dolls making an appearance everywhere. Every room is delightful and the grander rooms have out-of the-ordinary bathrooms with maybe a shell-or-oval-shaped bath. In the handsome beamed dining room where you will be served a first class breakfast at tables covered in delicate white lace cloths, you will be overlooked by stern Victorian portraits reminding you of your table manners! A fascinating place.

The magnificent Cathedral is superb and should not be missed. It has both a sense of majesty and humility and is totally beautiful.

Just south east of Chester off the A41 is the rural village of **Rowton** and within it the elegant Rowton Hall Hotel standing in 8 acres of award winning gardens and pastureland, enjoying far reaching views across the Cheshire Plains to the hills of Wales. It is hard to imagine that this peaceful setting was once the battle ground of Rowton Moor in the Civil War. This is an hotel for all ages and all seasons.

Nantwich is always a delight to visit. This was once the most important town in the shire after Chester, and certainly the most famous of the three wiches.

The Domesday Book tells us that in the time of King Edward the Confessor there were eight salt-pits here. The Welsh were always trying to get their hands on the town. The brine-pits attracted them and at one time Henry III closed them down to try and curb the Welsh attacks. The local people were not having their livelihood destroyed and they were soon in production again. Richard II stayed here before he abdicated. In 1604 the plague hit Cheshire and the Chester Assizes were moved to Nantwich. This was to no avail, the plague struck the town and killed nearly 500 people before it abated in March 1605. The town recovered and thrived and has done so virtually ever since.

One of the most famous of Nantwich's houses is **Churche's Mansion**, which being outside the town, was not touched by the 1583 fire. This wonderful house is a restaurant today which has been decorated in a style fitting to the period, with traditional tapestries and fabrics complementing the interior. Meals are served in both the 'Buttery' and the impressive 'Long withdrawing Room'. Here you can enjoy superb food and perhaps meet with the ghostly figure of William Churche whose portrait hangs in the panelled lounge.

There is a good pub here as well. The Red Cow in Beam Street is the oldest building in Nantwich to have survived the devastating fire of 1583. It is a High Street pub standing opposite the Library and the Bus station with the Market two minutes walk away. It became a pub in the 17th century and it was here the Roundheads had their meeting place and it is still used as such on Holy Holy Day which is re-enacted every January to celebrate the Battle of Nantwich in 1644. The pub is heavily beamed with lots of nooks and crannies and beautifully cared for.

Nantwich has several attractive places to visit including **Stapley Water Gardens** where the magic of water is everywhere. As the world's largest water garden centre, there are acres of covered and outdoor areas devoted to water gardening, from modestly priced pool construction kits to colourful fountains with constantly changing spray patterns and lighting in time with the music!

Bridgmere Wildlife Park set in 35 acres of pleasant rolling countryside is ideal for a varied day out in the country.

On the B5074 out of Nantwich and going marginally north, is the village of **Worleston** which has the most beautiful hotel and conference centre, Rookery Hall. A delightful place to stay either for a break, a holiday or on business. Run with a degree of professionalism that many establishments will envy, you will be cared for the moment you step through its elegant portals.

Another of the wiches is **Middlewich** which goes back, according to the records, to the 13th century. Here we have a pleasant litde salt town with timber and brick houses. The church is mainly 14th century Perpendicular with a square 15th century tower. The gravestones amused me. One said:

> *Here lies Anne Barker*
> *Some have children some have none*
> *But here lies the mother of twenty-one*

There is an old font in the graveyard and stocks as well. You will see the tower is marked by cannon shot which is said to have been acquired in the Civil War during the battles of Middlewich when the town stood for the church and king.

At Middlewich one is right on the banks of the Trent and Mersey Canal and it is here you will find **The Big Lock** in Webbs Lane. It took vision, courage and dedication for Tony Hatton to restore an almost derelict building into the delightful free house it s today. The Big Lock provides overnight canal mooring and you can enter it both from the road and canalside. Middlewich is on the River Croco, which flows down from **Brereton** to join the Dane just outside the town.

Up the A51 from Nantwich is **Tarporley**, a village of brick buildings and with a famous pub The Swan, noted as a meeting place of the Tarporley hunt. It is an attractive area made even more so by Willington Hall, a delightful hotel, superbly appointed and serving delicious food. Ideal for anyone who wants a pampered break or visiting Cheshire on business.

From here a visit to **Beeston Castle** is simple. This 12th century fortress towers above the Cheshire Plain and is worth seeing if only for the breathtaking views. Nor should one forget **Peckforton Castle** of which Sir Gilbert Scott said 'the largest and most carefully and learnedly executed Gothic mansion of the present day, is not only a Castle in name but it is a real and carefully constructed medieval fortress, capable of standing siege from an Edwardian army... the very height of masquerading.' Here time stands still and dreamers may dream of recapturing and preserving forever the spirit and atmosphere of a medieval fortress. A wonderful place to be.

Winsford to the east can only be called an 'expanding town'. In 1878 it was the centre of the Cheshire salt industry, although now it is far outstripped by the brine pumps of the third of the wiches, Northwich.

I drove a little south along country roads to **Wettenhall** where I found The Boot and Slipper, an old coaching inn with an excellent restaurant and five very comfortable en suite bedrooms. It is only a short drive from Tatton Park, Stapeley Water Gardens, Beeston Castle and the Candle factory, with two golf courses and the canal thrown in for good measure.

From **Middlewich** to **Congleton** is no distance along the A54. For a long time its prosperity was linked with gloves, lace and ribbons. It has fine houses and from the streets, hill climbers can recognise in the distance their favourite Mow Cop. That was not my purpose. I had been told of an interesting hostelry, a canal pub, The Wharf Inn on the Macclesfield Canal. It stands side by side Tudor and Georgian buildings and harmonious modern developments. A short walk along the canal will introduce you to 'The Macc' which is renowned for the beautifully designed stone bridges crossing the canal. Within easy reach of the Wharf Inn are places such as **Gawsworth Hall, Biddulph Grange Garden, Little Morton Hall** and the fascinating **Congleton Antique Market and Fayre.**

Canals are very much a part of life in Cheshire and close to the M6 Crewe and Middlewich road is **Wheelock** a pretty village through which runs the Trent and Mersey Canal. Here is The Cheshire Cheese, an attractive pub offering excellent hospitality. It is a sheer pleasure to sit outside in the waterside gardens and frequently enjoy a barbecue. Canal moorings are available and clay pigeon shooting is organised every Sunday. It is a good place to be.

Allgreave sits alongside the A54 as it goes east from Congleton. Here is yet another attractive place with a delightful pub, The Rose and Crown where the friendly mine hosts, have a great ability to turn strangers quickly into friends. Just off the A523 from Macclesfield is the cotton town of **Bollington**, which always seems to be quietly bustling, if that is not a misnomer, with a railway viaduct of 20 arches over the River Dean. Climb up the hill to **White Nancy**, a round stone tower, 920ft above sea level and you will see wide views all around which allow you to look over Cheshire into industrial Lancashire, and as far as the hills of the Derbyshire Peak.

The old silk town of **Macclesfield** should be included in your itinerary. It is full of quaint cobbled streets which remain inspite of this being a bustling town today. In **Backwallgate** which used to form part of the old castle walls, is an interesting restaurant, Yorkes, in a building which dates back to the 18th century and has an interior that retains much of the old charm and character with its stone flagged floors and old oak beams. The Mexican, Cajun and Creole cuisine is reflected in the antique jazz instruments and artefacts which adorn the walls.

This part of my journey comes to an end at **Alderley Edge** where I was to stay with friends who were kind enough to take me for a meal at The Brookfield, a pleasing pub which was once the club house for the well known 9 hole, **Alderley Edge Golf Course**. The terrace is somewhere that regulars make a beeline for in summer in order to enjoy an alfresco meal or a quiet drink. I was happy to follow their example.

For me Merseyside is inextricably a mixture of **Liverpool, Anfield, Goodison Park** and **The Grand National at Aintree**. There is something very exciting about this great city which has seen so many swings of fortune. The roar from the Kop End at Anfield when Liverpool Football Club are playing at home is my strongest memory of this unwieldy city. It is the spirit of the club that highlights all that is good about Liverpool; the sporting spirit, the ability to climb back after disaster, the solidarity in time of the greatest need. It is not only at Anfield that this shows but also at adjacent Goodison Park where Everton have their base, and in the other spirited Merseyside team, Tranmere Rovers. It is the strength of the rivalry between Liverpool and Everton that, on local Derby weeks, can split streets and families in two; people who normally live in total harmony. This rivalry lives on throughout Liverpool and has helped it through the years to rise above depression, war and poverty.

I have been a Liverpool supporter for over twenty years and the club to me has been an example of greatness in true sporting fashion. It has produced great players and great Managers. Today the success of the club is legendary and its sons are managing equally successful clubs. Liverpool Football Club Visitors Centre Museum at Anfield captures the history and success of the club from the beginning right up to the present Tours operate Monday to Friday except on mid-week match days, at 2pm and 3pm. Advance booking is essential.

Liverpool also boasts the most spectacular and thrilling horse race in the world, The Grand National run on the Aintree Course and attended annually by thousands of excited spectators waiting for the thrills and spills - although 1993 gave them thrills they did not expect and is best forgotten. More recently the threat of terrorism almost spoiled a unique day, but showed the true grit of the Brits in friendliness and generosity, when thousands of people were stranded without transport or a place to stay. Locals rallied round to provide hospitality for one and all, and the spirit of kindness won over what could have been a horrific experience.

This is a city that has produced a plethora of talent from John, Paul, George and Ringo - The Beatles - to the inimitable Ken Dodd, the fun loving comedian Jimmy Tarbuck, the Nazi hater, funny man Stan Boardman, and the much loved Cilla Black, she of 'Blind Date' fame and known for her funny teapot wedding hat - forgive me Cilla, but as one of your fans, I cannot write about Liverpool without a mention of THAT HAT! Liverpool has been the seat of successful politicians - Harold Wilson, our Prime Minister for so many years, to name but one. It is also the home of the **Liverpool Royal Philharmonic Orchestra**. The Royal Liverpool Philharmonic Society was founded in 1840 as a concert-giving body, making it one of the oldest such organisations in the world. The Society celebrated its 150th anniversary in 1990. During its long and distinguished history, the Society's principal conductors have included such famous names as Max Bruch, Sir Henry Wood, Sir Thomas Beecham, Sir Malcolm Sargent and Sir Charles Groves, Walter Weller and Marek Janowski. Each year the orchestra gives almost 100 concerts in Liverpool in the Philharmonic Hall. The current hall, a classic example of 1930's acoustics and its distinctive art deco murals and glass decorations.

But what of Liverpool's past? The north bank of the famous River Mersey was first settled in the 1st century AD and by 1207 was a sizeable village with a Charter granted

34

by King John. It was Liverpool's coastal location which influenced its great development, first as one point in the triangular slave trade with Africa and the West Indies; then with the American Colonies and the young Republic whose cotton fuelled the textile industry of north west England. By the mid 19th century Liverpool was bustling as a principal port. It was the point of massive emigration to the New World by the starving Irish escaping the famine of the 1840's, and the centre of trade. Parts of Liverpool's docks have become redundant today but have found a new and splendid use whilst others remain to keep its importance as a port to the forefront. Its crowning glory is the famous Royal Liver Building where you may join in on one of the special organised tours which take place daily by appointment from April to September. The old Cunard building, now the Customs house, reminds us of the famous family who built up such enormous shipping interests operating first on the North American coast and then Transatlantic from the United States and Canada to Britain.

No one would call Liverpool architecturally beautiful, at least I would not I have none the less found it a city of such wide interests and tastes that one could never be bored. It has the remarkable and probably unique achievement of having built two cathedrals in this century. The Roman Catholic Metropolitan consecrated in 1967 is unusual. Designed in contemporary style by Sir Frederick Gibberd, it is capped with a stained glass lantern tower, and is sometimes referred to as a 'wigwam wearing a lantern crown.

The Anglican Cathedral was commenced as an act of faith in 1904 and continued to be built even throughout the traumatic days of World War II when the Germans were doing so much to destroy Liverpool because of its strategic importance. The aftermath of the bombing and its industrial decline has left Liverpool with many problems but the act of building a cathedral, eventually to be completed at a time in 1978 when many dreams remained unfulfilled, is the essence of the spirit of a city which has had sufficient faith in itself to see this, and so much more achieved against a background of adversity. The site chosen could not have been better. It commands on one side the whole city and riverside, and on the other, a deep ravine enclosing an old churchyard. All around it were Georgian houses and attractive terraces.

The sheer scale of the building is stunning, the Gothic arches the largest ever built. You stand there in awe of this vast expanse and yet wrapt around by the great love of God - His presence is real here unlike many cathedrals I have visited. John Betjeman summed up the Cathedral in a nutshell;

'This is one of the great buildings of the world.... the impression of vastness, strength and height no words can describe...suddenly, one sees that the greatest art of architecture that lift one up and turns one into a king, yet compels reverence, is the art of enclosing space.'

Liverpool has so much to see as you will discover in The Albert Dock. There are Museums galore, wonderful Art Galleries, The Beatles Story in the Britannia Vaults. You can have a day out on the famous Mersey Ferries and much more.

Manchester is somewhere that I lived in for a short time in 1961 when I thought it rather a dirty city - anyone who lives, as I do by the sea in Plymouth, does not react kindly to vast cities anyway. Since those days Manchester has improved out of all recognition. Here is a bustling city busy with commercial life, its Universities, its theatres and concert halls. Life is rich, the shops are good, there are eateries of every nationality and superb hotels. I can wholeheartedly recommend The Normandie Hotel, in Manchester itself. The height of comfort and elegance. Within walking distance of the Airport is another of my favourite places, Ethrop Grange, standing in its own grounds, and giving everyone who stays there a feeling of tranquillity hard to find in this busy world. Without doubt somewhere that is unique both for its standards and its ambience.

I look forward to returning to this part of the world and spending more time in order to write a book devoted to Cheshire, Manchester, Merseyside and The Wirral.

ROWTON HALL HOTEL

Whitchurch Road,
Chester CH3 6AD

Tel: 01244 335262 Fax: 01244 335464

This elegant hotel situated in the rural village of Rowton, was built in 1779 as a private residence and still retains many original features including a Robert Adam fireplace and a superbly carved staircase. It stands in 8 acres of award winning gardens and pasture land, enjoying far reaching views across the Cheshire Plains to the hills of Wales. It is hard to imagine that this peaceful setting was once the battle ground of Rowton Moor in the Civil War. The battle was centred on the city of Chester which was held by the Royalists but had been under siege for sometime. 1995 was a memorable year in the history of both Rowton Hall Hotel and the village. Events marking the 350th anniversary took place and included a re-enactment of the battle in costume.

Today Rowton Hall has 42 bedrooms all with en suite bathrooms. The Langdale Restaurant opens for luncheon and dinner with a full a la carte and table d'hote menus. Non residents are welcome. The Cavalier Bar is a place to meet friends for a social drink or enjoy a lunchtime snack. For the business fraternity there is a choice of 5 Conference/Meeting rooms with facilities for up to 200 delegates. The Adam Lounge or Inglenook are ideal rooms for hosting private luncheons and dinner parties, whilst the Ballroom provides a grand venue for banquets and dances. For an informal gathering, to enjoy morning coffee, afternoon tea or cocktail reception, The Hamilton Lounge has the added bonus of overlooking the garden. You are invited to relax in Hamiltons Leisure Club which is available to club members and hotel guests, the facilities include swimming pool, multi gym, sauna and solarium. This is a hotel for all ages and all seasons.

USEFUL INFORMATION

OPEN; *24 hour*
DISABLED ACCESS; *Yes*
CHILDREN; *Welcome. Baby listening*
CREDIT CARDS; *Amex/Visa/Master/ Diners/Switch*
GARDEN; *8 acres. Patio area*

RESTAURANT; *High standard. International*
BAR FOOD; *Wide range, freshly cooked*
ACCOMMODATION; *42 en suite Leisure & Conference facilities*
LICENSED; *Full*

THE CHESTER GROSVENOR

Eastgate Street,
Chester CH1 1LT

Tel: 01244 324024
Fax: 01244 313246

Chester is England's best preserved walled city, a living part of recorded history since AD79 when the Romans arrived on the banks of the River Dee and built their fortress which they named Deva. Its importance as a port, trading and social centre continued through the middle ages and since the 16th century at least, a hostelry has stood on the present site of The Chester Grosvenor within the city walls next to the old East Gate. By 1800 the Grosvenor family had acquired the Royal Hotel which by then, had replace the medieval 'Golden Talbot, and this quickly became the premier hotel of the county town, a stopping place for visiting royalty and other important dignitaries. On January 11th 1866, Richard, second Marquis of Westminster officially opened the Grosvenor which had been erected on the same site re-using many of the materials, including the fine entrance pillars, from the old Royal Hotel. Listed as a Grade II building of historic and architectural interest, the Grosvenor has long been acknowledged as the centre of the county's social scene. In the winter of 1987-88 the Grosvenor underwent its most impressive transformation yet. No expense was spared to make it the most luxurious hotel in Britain and at the same time never neglecting its unique heritage.

Everywhere within the hotel is beautifully appointed. The reception is spacious and comfortable, setting the style and standards for which the hotel is renowned. The Library and Drawing Room provide two delightful rooms where coffee and afternoon tea is served or simply to meet friends over a pleasant drink. The Arkle Restaurant, named in honour of the famous steeplechaser, provides wonderful food in the most opulent and sophisticated surroundings whilst La Brasserie, open every day from 6.30am-11.30pm is delightfully informal, whether you want a croissant and coffee or a complete meal. Every one of the Grosvenor's 8 sumptuous suites and 78 luxury bedrooms is individually designed and furnished to the very highest international standards with hand-made furniture from Italy, the finest fabrics and silks from France and America and the best of true British craftsmanship. The Grosvenor caters for a full range of business and social events including conferences, meetings, banquets and private dining.

USEFUL INFORMATION

OPEN; *All year*
CHILDREN; *Welcome*
LICENSED; *Full.*
CREDIT CARDS; *All major cards*
ACCOMMODATION; *8 suites,*
78 luxury bedrooms

RESTAURANT; *Superb cuisine in the Arkle Restaurant*
LA BRASSERIE; *Anything from a croissant & coffee*
VEGETARIAN; *A wide choice of dishes*
DISABLED ACCESS; *Yes*

YORKE'S RESTAURANT
5 Backwall Gate,
Macclesfield,
Cheshire SK11 6LQ

Tel/Fax: 01625 431990

The original occupants of 5 Backwall Gate in the 18th-century would have been delighted with the charm and character, the stone flagged floors, oak beams and nooks and crannies but they would have been astounded by the food provided by the present occupants, Yorke's Restaurant. Here, in this unique atmosphere you can sample dishes from all over the world especially Mexican, Cajun and Creole. Try Fajitas for example, served sizzling at your table and beef or chicken Chimichanges. The character of the 18th-century remains but is heightened by the use of antique jazz instruments and artefacts which adorn the walls. Live Jazz entertainment stirs up the digestive juices on Wednesday, Friday and Saturday evenings. At other times unobtrusive background music helps to portray the ambience of Yorke's.

This is a family business, the latest incumbents are Steve and Debbie Black who continue the family tradition of good food and good service but have brought in new and innovative ideas of their own. Yorke's is one of those places that will always be remembered by anyone who visits the old silk town of Macclesfield. The restaurant opens for lunches starting at 11.30am providing an intriguing range of inexpensive dishes including fresh and well filled sandwiches, pizzas and pasta. It is a busy establishment and it would be wise to reserve a table for Friday and Saturday evenings.

USEFUL INFORMATION

OPEN; *Mon-Sat 11.30-2.30pm*
CHILDREN; *Welcome*
CREDIT CARDS; *Master/Visa/Switch*
LICENSED; *Full License*
DISABLED ACCESS; *Limited*
ACCOMMODATION; *Not applicable*

RESTAURANT; *International 6.30-10.30pm*
Specialising in Cajun, Mexican and Creole
BAR FOOD; *Not applicable*
VEGETARIAN;: *10 dishes*
GARDEN;: *No*

LAUREL FARM (A NON-SMOKING HOUSE)

Chorlton Lane,
Malpas,
Cheshire SY14 7ES
Tel/Fax: 01948 860291

In an outstanding, peaceful situation, surrounded by acres of glorious countryside, yet only minutes from the attractive market village of Malpas, Laurel Farm is set off by a large landscaped duck pond to one side of the drive, (a bevy of cheeky ducks may greet you!). You stand momentarily before entering the front door and take the pure air into your lungs and looking about you see some truly lovely views. A good start but when you enter the house the ambience just jumps out at you. It is warm and welcoming and a perfect place to stay. Anthea Few is your hostess and this lady has a great eye for colour and detail, something she has given to the furnishings of Laurel Farm. Her taste is exquisite, not only is the furniture a mixture of antique and traditional, it gleams with the patina of age. Warmth, welcome and comfort are the hallmarks of this elegant house which dates from the 17th-century. The atmosphere is very relaxed - something guests always remark on at Laurel Farm. Sympathetically restored, it retains all its original character and charm enhanced by exposed beams, old doors, mellow Welsh quarry tiled floors and much more besides.
There are stunning views from each individually furnished bedroom - here again comfort is the key - a well stocked hot drinks tray, remote colour TV, hairdryer and the many personal touches finish the rooms off beautifully. Never over the top however! To one side of the house there is a private suite of two bedrooms plus a sitting room - excellent for parties of four to We people. Here guests have their own keys and are most welcome to come and go at their own leisure. A lovely, very English dining room awaits you in the morning. An excellent variety of food and splendid cooked breakfasts - always freshly cooked when you arrive - a friendly affair which will be a highlight of your visit
Situated on the North Wales/Shropshire borders, the area offers a wealth of interesting places to visit - Chester, Shrewsbury, some glorious countryside, a bit of 'hidden' England and the dramatic and spectacular scenery of North Wales together with castles, fine houses, some magnificent gardens and wonderful walks on the Sandstone Trail. Close by are numerous golf courses and the excellent sporting and leisure facilities at Carden Park. Locally there is an excellent range of good pubs and restaurants. In all Laurel Farm makes an ideal base for a break, or for those on business who prefer a more restful stay in quality surroundings. To reach Laurel Farm from the attractive village of Malpas, go down the High Street and in the centre of the village take the 85069 towards Bangor-on-Dee. One mile take the first right to Chorlton. After one mile turn right opposite the red telephone kiosk. The farmhouse is less than a 1/4 mile on the right hand side

USEFUL INFORMATION

OPEN; *All year*
CHIILDREN; *Over 12 years*
CREDIT CARDS; *None taken*
VEGETARIAN; *Upon request*
LICENSED; *No*
ACCOMMODATION; *4 en suite rooms*
PETS; *No*

DINING ROOM; *Traditional breakfast*
Dinner by arrangement Light suppers
(Minimum 4 guests-48hours notice)
DISABLED ACCESS; *Ground floor*
bedroom.Not suitable for wheelchairs
GARDEN; *Lovely with ducks & pond*

ROOKERY HALL

Worleston,
Nantwich,
Nr Chester,
Cheshire CW5 6DQ

Tel: 0l270 610016   Fax: 01270 626027

Rookery Hall, near the historic town of Nantwich, was built in 1815 by a wealthy English landowner, William Hilton Cooke. The house is set in 200 acres of gardens and pastures fringing the banks of the River Weaver which ensures complete tranquillity. Later that century in 1860 Baron Von Schroder of the banking world purchased the Hall and changed the traditional Georgian Mansion into a fine Victorian House with a hint of his ancestry coming to the fore in the form of a magnificent German Schloss like tower. Rookery as a hotel opened under private ownership with eleven bedrooms in the 1970's when it gained much acclaim, especially for its' food. The hotel is now owned by Select Hotels, and in 1990 a new wing was harmoniously added, providing more bedrooms and a state of the art Conference Centre. Rookery now has 45 luxury bedrooms.

That in a nutshell is the history of Rookery but however well appointed the building might be it is nothing without the backing and enthusiasm of a General Manager and a first class staff who pull together as a team. Rookery has just that in the shape of Jeremy Rata, as General Manager, a man with a wealth of experience and someone who actively encourages his staff to lend their own style to the hotel. For example, Rachel in Reservations supplied the ducks who now roam the 200 acres (surely the most pampered ducks in England) and it was Eileen in house-keeping who suggested it may be a good idea to keep a supply of Wellingtons at the front door for those guests wishing to walk the estate, as this way her carpets would stay cleaner for longer! I doubt if you will find a better trained, more contented staff anywhere and of course this reflects in the whole atmosphere of this stunning hotel.

Great emphasis is placed on really welcoming guests at Rookery. All the guests are greeted at their cars and escorted to Reception the personally taken to their rooms. However the core of Rookery has always been and still is the restaurant. Head Chef David Alton, formerly of The Chester Grosvenor, leads his team with skill and innovation. Food is bought locally from first class suppliers, with all bread, sorbets, ices, indeed everything served in the Restaurant being produced by the Kitchen. A fixed price lunch and dinner menu with at least six choices on each course is changed regularly to reflect the best produce available. The wine list now incorporates a cellar listing, whereby guests are offered the opportunity of actually venturing into the cellar to select their bottle. The Cellar can also be offered for private dining parties up to 16 complete with candlelight. Rookery Hall is superb.

USEFUL INFORMATION

OPEN; *All year, 24 hours*
CHILDREN; *Welcomed if well behaved*
CREDTT CARDS; *All major cards*
LICENSED; *Full On*
ACCOMMODATION; *45 luxury bedrooms*
GARDENS; *200 acres*

RESTAURANT; *Superb, innovative dishes from a Master Chef*
BAR FOOD; *Available*
VEGETARIAN; *Always available*
DISABLED ACCESS; *Not easy*

Chapter 3

CORNWALL INCLUDES

Chapter 3

CORNWALL

I have an unashamed love for Cornwall with its incredible mixture of glorious coastline running up either side of the peninsula until it joins Devon across the River Tamar, the Atlantic and the English Channel, and in the middle of the sandwich the extraordinary mining villages, some of which would not be out of place in a Science Fiction film! Mineral wealth below ground, shaped the destiny of Cornwall and the Cornish for hundreds of years, changing the landscape and creating these unique villages, harbours and quays. The National Trust now owns a third of the coastline of Cornwall, more than 100 miles of magnificent walking country including many spectacular stretches and popular holiday resorts.

The coastal villages have always been among the most picturesque and sought after for film makers and artists, some liking the softer south side and others the incredible, harsh beauty of North Cornwall. Whichever way you go you are never far from the sea and for the purpose of this chapter I intend to start across the Tamar and work my way down to Penzance and then up the northern coastline to Bude. It is a county that will give you something new to see every time you cross its borders. It is magical, full of legend, tales of the sea and endless fishing yarns.

Crossing the Tamar is simple today with the Tamar Bridge linking **Plymouth** and **Saltash.** Three decades ago the river could only be crossed by car ferries which traversed the river from **Devonport** to **Torpoint** and **St Budeaux** to Saltash. The town of Saltash has now been bypassed making it once more a pleasant place to stop a while either in the busy little town or down the steep hill to the river where a variety of pubs wait for you at the water's edge. Just outside for those who want to stay in complete peace and quiet in a delightful home, **Erth Barton** is well worth seeking out. It has been inhabited since the days of Edward III and is stunning. A member of Wolsey Lodges, please do not arrive without booking.

The car and foot passenger, **Torpoint Ferry** still operates twenty-four hours of every day and takes those who live and work either side of the river to their destinations as well as carrying thousands of visitors every year who enjoy the pretty countryside around Torpoint and the magic of the golden beaches in **Whitsand Bay**. Two small villages, **Kingsand** and **Cawsand** are tucked away to the left of Torpoint; villages almost untouched by the modern day because of their inaccessibility. They both have beaches, good pubs and a friendly welcome for visitors. Both villages are part of the **Mount Edgcumbe** estate which starts at **Cremyll** and carries far on right out to the glorious isolation of **Rame Head**. Wonderful coastal walks from **Mount Edgcumbe Park** and within the park itself make this a popular area for visitors and local people. **Mount Edgcumbe House and Gardens**, the seat of the Earls of Mount Edgcumbe for centuries is open to the public.

The traffic from the ferry and from the Tamar Bridge meet at **Trerulefoot**, where maybe you will decide to carry on deeper into Cornwall or cut off to the east and through the pretty **Hessenford Valley** until you reach the quaint fishing villages of **East** and **West Looe**. Here river meets the sea, picturesque houses climb the steep hills, fishermen set sail every day in their colourful boats and visitors set out with some of them to go shark fishing. For the less adventurous Looe itself is fascinating, full of good pubs, sandy beaches and a plethora of hotels from which to choose should you decide to stay.

Turning right over the bridge which divides East and West Looe, you would be on the road for **Talland Bay,** surely the most beautiful stretch of smuggling coast in Cornwall!! The colour of the sea, the green of the lush grass and the lack of houses make this very special but even more special is the award winning Allhays Country House which offers its guests a wonderful holiday in a house full of warmth and charm.

From Looe to **Liskeard**, a small market town which you could easily bypass on the dual carriageway, but which is worth a stop and a wander round. It still retains it's steep and narrow streets, it has views of Dartmoor, two ancient crosses and a fine, mainly 15th century church in which there is a little low window, with two mullions a few inches apart, which is probably Norman, and the bowl of the Norman font is built into the north porch. One curious feature is that the windows of the north wall are three recesses with stone roofs; one was a porch, the other two were chapels.

Fowey with its spectacular harbour is the obvious next step after first stopping at the ancient town of **Lostwithiel** which you might be tempted to pass through because of its comparatively uninteresting main street. Please don't, this is somewhere that needs exploring on foot from the majesty of the ruins of **Restormel Castle** which watch over the town to the river which flows gently through. The Castle is a delightful place to be, the ruins enhanced by magnificent rhododendrons, trees and shrubs. Built in the 13th century it was a ruin by the 16th. In Duke Street, The Royal Oak you will find is a very welcoming hostelry which will provide you with both food and accommodation if you should so wish. Lostwithiel was strongly Royalist in the Civil War and legend has it that Charles II was hidden in an oak at Boconnoc, hence the name of the pub. Lostwithiel was once the capital of Cornwall. It is an ancient borough with a working community who will tell you that they do not put on a special face for holiday makers for a few weeks in the year but aim to give the same friendly welcome all year round. It is an excellent centre for fishing, walking or just relaxing and enjoying the Cornish countryside. The 13th century church of St Bartholomew is worth a visit.

Fowey is a place of discovery; narrow winding streets where flower decked houses and cottages jostle side by side with quaint little shops and pubs on the hillside that slopes down to the glory of the Fowey river and its fine, colourful harbour. From the days of pirates and smugglers with their barges and brigantines brazenly at moorings, to the hundreds of colourful craft that now fill what is undoubtedly one of the most enchanting harbours in this country, time has changed very little. Fowey has a splendid old medieval church and a wonderful house simply named **Place.** The house is undoubtedly Tudor, it has two exquisite bays of the time of Henry VII, the hall and porch, and many traces of the Elizabethan building. It is the family home of the Treffrys and of Sir John who won fame at the Battle of Crecy. Queen Elizabeth I was a frequent visitor and her high-backed chair is still a proud possession. Some of the panelling is said to have come from the ship that took Napoleon to St Helena. Fowey has some superb restaurants. The Restaurant Cordon Bleu on the Esplanade is known world-wide and every meal is a gastronomic delight. More simply Crumbs Tea Rooms offers good wholesome food and their speciality is the traditional cream tea with home-baked scones.

Rising in Bodmin Moor, the River Fowey has always been the life-blood of those towns and villages through which it flows on its way to the open sea at St Austell Bay. From Lostwithiel it continues meandering past the lovely little church of St Winnow on the east bank, which dates mainly from the 15th century, although there are some remains of Norman and 13th century architecture. A little further on is the creek that leads up to the pretty waterside village of **Lerryn,** where once sailing ships came to discharge their cargoes of road-stone from the quarries at St Germans. Now it is so silted up that you must keep a watchful on the tide if you are water-borne.

On the west bank is an even smaller village, **Golant,** much beloved by small boat owners. They come to enjoy the sailing but also to visit The Fishermans Arms which you will find at the end of a road marked 'Road liable to flooding at high tide'. The pub overlooks the water but it is out of harm's way - even the pavement is 2 ft high!

Directly opposite Fowey and reached by a ferry is **Bodinnick** and its heart is The Old Ferry Inn which has one of the world's most picturesque views from its lounge right over the estuary, past Fowey and Polruan to the sea. It is a great place to stay and full of the atmosphere built up over the four hundred years of its existence. Had I not taken you down off the main road to Fowey you would have continued on towards **St Austell Bay** and its many attractive offshoots. I am always drawn to the small and so far unspoilt, harbour village of **Charlestown** where the small entrance to the harbour defies belief that any vessel of size, let alone the big clay carrying ships can enter its sheltering arms, but they do and demonstrate this every day. It is the home of **The Shipwreck Museum** which is Britain's biggest exhibition of shipwreck artefacts. **The Heritage Centre** in the village shows vividly how people used to live and it is built right on top of one of the old tunnels, through which dried clay was formerly transported underground from drying kilns to waiting ships, and you will walk through some of these on your way round the centre.

St Austell is one of the busiest towns in Cornwall. It does not have a great deal to offer the visitor other than its fine church which stands among palm trees, rising from a beautifully manicured lawn, right in the heart of the town opposite its premier hostelry The White Hart. It has a tower well over five centuries old but the church's rarest possession is its massive Norman font with a bowl carved with extraordinary creatures and resting on columns ending in human faces. One of the main attractions of St Austell Bay is **Mevagissey,** the largest fishing port in the bay and probably one of the most photographed harbours in Cornwall. Colourful fishing boats still sail out from here and nothing can take away the charm of the whitewashed cottages as they cling to the steep sides of the roads to Fore Street, where attractive shops flank the inner harbour. **Gorran Churchtown** should not be missed. Just one and a half miles from Mevagissey, it has a pub, The Barleysheaf, built in 1837 by a Mr Kendall who, hearsay states, had it erected for his own use because he was barred from every other hostelry in the area! You are close here to the wild headland that sailors call **The Dodman** with its 550-year-old tower, a massive structure rising 110 feet; a famous landmark from the sea.

Going marginally inland and only 3 miles from Mevagissey The Kilbol Country House Hotel at **Polmassick** has to be the epitome of Cornish peace! This 16th century hotel is totally remote and yet has abandoned none of the modern conveniences. Certainly a place to recommend. It caters for non-residents as well as those lucky enough to be staying there.

From St Austell the road to Bodmin takes you through English China Clay country. If you go via **Nanpean** and **Carthew** you will come to the **Wheal Martyn Museum**. This will give you an unforgettable insight into Cornwall's single largest industry. Great white, eerie mountains appear on all side, evidence of the industry that has provided so much of Cornwall's employment. In **Bodmin**, the handsome church of St Petrock delights all who see it. It is the biggest in the county, 151 ft long and 65 ft wide. Mainly 15th century, it has been much restored. On Beacon Hill, looking down on the town, is a great column of granite rising 144 ft high. It is in memory of Sir Walter Raleigh Gilbert, a brave soldier, and belonging to the family of Sir Humphrey Gilbert who was the stepbrother of Sir Walter Raleigh.

Just outside Bodmin is **Washaway** where you will find Pencarrow House, the home of the Molesworth family and has been so since it was completed by Sir John Molesworth, the 5th baronet about 1770. Essentially a family home, it is a delight to explore. For Gilbert and Sullivan fans it is interesting to know that Sir Arthur Sullivan composed the music for Iolanthe here. **The Pencarrow Gardens** cover some 50 acres. Huge rhododendrons and camellias provide a wonderful display every spring. There are several gardens within striking distance from here which should not be missed. At **Prideaux Place, Padstow**, there is a deer park and a newly restored garden overlooking the Camel estuary. **Lanhydrock** has rare trees and shrubs, the unique circular herbaceous garden and exceptional magnolias. **Lancarffe** at Bodmin has four and a half acres of sheer beauty and then there is the fabulous **Longcross Victorian Gardens** at **Trelights**, near **Port Isaac**, which is open all the year round from 10.30 am until dusk. It has fascinating maze-type walkways and one of the best cream teas anywhere!

Bodmin has a lot to offer including **The Bodmin and Wenford Railway** which allows you to explore some of Cornwall's finest countryside from a steam-hauled branch line train. **The Light Infantry Museum** is opposite the station and **Bodmin Town Museum** is a short walk away from the town centre. **The Camel Trail** paths to Wadebridge and Padstow starts near the historic Bodmin Goal.

Wadebridge is a splendid little town where the magnificent bridge with its 13 arches carrying it 320 ft across the River Camel is wonderful to see. Strangely, Wadebridge has no church so in the 15th century, Thomas Lovibond, built the beautiful church at **Egloshayle** on the Bodmin side of the town. Its chief possession is a lovely old pulpit with richly carved panels dating before the Reformation. Wadebridge is a busy market town which at the time of the Royal Cornwall Show in June feels as though it could not take one more person. Local people have their own favourite pubs but perhaps mine is the 16th-century coaching inn, The Molesworth Arms. It is said that at midnight on New Year's Eve, a ghostly coach-and-four clatters through the courtyard and the headless coachman steers his eerie charges across the yard and out the double doors of the hallway.

Down the road from St Austell and just a few miles north of **Truro** one can visit one of the loveliest houses in Cornwall, **Trewithen.** This Georgian beauty, houses fine paintings and furniture and is surrounded by gardens designed by that truly great gardener, George H. Johnstone. The magnolias and rhododendrons are superb and only matched by the camellias and azaleas in the spring, plus the special varieties of Trewithen daffodils. The house is just outside **Probus** where the church has a tower that is the tallest in Cornwall. The road that leads from here into Truro is by far the prettiest entrance to Cornwall's county town. It winds upwards through the woods leaving the Tresillian river behind.

CHAPTER THREE

Here is a city that seems to grow lovelier with age. Its heart lies around the cathedral, a majestic building which has only in the last decade celebrated its centenary. It gives the appearance of having been there forever and certainly holds this fine city together. If you can take a short while to sit within its walls, taking stock of life, you will find it rewarding. You may be lucky to have chosen a time when evensong is being sung by the splendid choir. The music soars into the rafters and the whole church is uplifted.

Understanding that Truro is the acknowledged county town and also Cornwall's centre of administration, the planners ensured that as the city grew it would have reasonable parking space. You will find there are five council car parks with a capacity for accommodating 14,000 cars. Strangely this planning has not been so thoughtfully dealt with when it comes to accommodation. It always seems to me to lack sufficient hotels. I like The Royal Hotel in Lemon Street. It has character and feels as though it is in the heart of the city, which it is. In Tregolls Road, the main thoroughfare leading from St Austell into the city, there is the efficiently run Brookdale Hotel and opposite it The Alverton Manor which has been converted from a nunnery in recent years and is beautifully done.

Truro which dates from Norman times lies at the head of the Truro river where the Kenwyn and Allen rivers become one. The water tumbles out into the Tresillian river at **Malpas** where it becomes the River Fal flowing on to **Falmouth** and then into the English Channel. Strategically its navigable position did much to influence the growth of the town as a centre for merchants and I suspect a smuggler or two, not to say that the odd pirate did not make his way up the river as well.

Falmouth and Truro have not always been friendly neighbours. In 1663 Truro was punished for its role in the Civil War and the whole river from **Tregothan Boathouse** was given to the new Co-operative of Falmouth. It was hard on Truro and it took from then until 1709 to assert its rights over Falmouth harbour, a claim strongly contested by Falmouth, which was by then a port of some consequence and saw no reason for Truro to have any say in the matter. It took the courts to settle the matter.

From Truro, the rivers leading to the great **Carrick Roads** wander through some of the most beautiful scenery in the world. There are pleasure boats that will take you on a voyage of discovery that is a never ending delight, right the way down to Falmouth at **St Mawes**. Inland the road from Truro to St Mawes is almost like trying to find the pot of gold at the end of a rainbow. You seem to drive forever, sometimes through delightful scenery, and at others indifferent, in the way that Cornwall has of teasing those who seek to know all about her. Finally, less than twelve miles from Truro you are rewarded by the sought for treasure, St Mawes. Everything is beautiful here, the glory of the sea, the majesty of **St Mawes Castle**, and it is surrounded by the villages of **The Roseland**. No nothing to do with roses. In this instance, Roseland means promontory or commonland.

St Just in Roseland is a famous beauty spot with its pretty church nestling against the banks of the river. It has curious stones inscribed with slightly mawkish sentiments lining the steep path through the churchyard down to the church. I heard it described once as 'the sort of churchyard one would be happy to be buried in.' The church is open daily and I would list it as a must for visitors.

On the other side of the Fal, **Pendennis Castle** guards the entrance to Carrick Roads as it has done, together with St Mawes Castle, for hundreds of years. Both castles can be visited. The easy way to get across the river to Falmouth is to take the little passenger ferry, or go further up the river and take your car across on the **King Harry Ferry**. The road from there will take you via **Perranarworthal.** There are few better stopping places en route in which to get a drink or a good meal than The Norway. From here you are in easy reach of the enchanting inlets of **Feock, Mylor** and **Restronguet.** Wonderful places in which to wander and spend the most contented of days.

Before you reach Falmouth you will come to **Penryn**. It always seems to me that it is a resentful place, the pavements and walls are built of forbidding granite and it has a sombre air. Its problem is that Falmouth became the chosen port and successful, leaving Penryn behind as the poor relation. Penryn would probably call Falmouth, a modern upstart and they would not be far wrong; a fact only denied by the seafarers who have used the haven of the Carrick Roads for centuries. Tourism in Falmouth is obviously important but for all that the town is a very busy port with ship repairing facilities and a dry dock which is capable of taking vessels up to 90,000 tons.

It is a pleasant town in which to wander and some of it will excite those who seek out fine architecture. Particularly the charming Georgian houses of the Post-Captains in the Service, such as **Marlborough House** which stands above Swanpool in all its glory, built for Captain Bull, a famous and gallant seaman in his day. **The Falmouth Maritime Museum** is a good place to visit. In there you will find evidence of Falmouth's long maritime history. **Jacob's Ladder** is another feature of Falmouth. Not to be tackled by the faint hearted for there are 111 steps which take you from **The Moor** to **Vernon Place**. The good news is that you can stop for a glass of medicinal brandy at the top and bottom; pubs have situated themselves very sensibly at both ends. With the mild air of Falmouth, gardens flourish including palm trees and the town must have some of the most beautiful public gardens in the county. **Gyllyndune** is particularly well endowed.

If you love gardens there is none more enchanting than **Glendurgan Garden** at **Mawnan Smith**. It lies in a valley and it is a marriage of man and nature. There are fine trees and shrubs, walled and water gardens, and a wooded valley runs down to the tiny village of Durgan on the river. You can lose yourself in the Maze if you wish, or just stand and stare at the wondrous beauty around you. Wander up the river and you will come to **Gweek** where there is a Seal Sanctuary. There is something appealing about these animals, possibly because of their sad eyes. Anyway it is a super place to visit and the dedicated people who run it should receive our grateful thanks for their caring attitude.

It would be sad, once you have got this far down into Cornwall, not to stretch out a little further to the east and visit the remote and wildly beautiful villages of **Manaccan, St Keverne**, and **Coverack**. Manaccan hides itself in its hilly slopes. No matter which way you approach it you have to come down or climb up hills. Indeed the whole coastline of this region is on the descent. One incline goes to St Keverne, another down the pretty valley to **Gillian Creek** and yet another to the Helford River.

The sea has never been kind to St Keverne and if you wander in the churchyard you will see the graves of 400 people who have drowned off this shore in ships brought to their doom on the dreaded **Manacles**. On a calm summer's day when the sea is a brilliant blue and the little church surrounded by palms and hydrangeas it is hard to conjure up the harshness of this piece of coast in the height of a storm. But be there when a storm is raging and you will never ever again doubt the power of the ocean. Man has conquered most things but the sea will always be the master.

Coverack is more sheltered and is charming. From there you need to go inland a bit to pick up the lanes that will lead you down to **Ruan Minor** and **Cadgwith**, two delightful spots. Ruan Minor is not quite a mile away from the sea. Its houses cluster round the tiny church which must be well over five hundred years old. You round **The Lizard** and on the downs above **Mullion Cove** are the graves of some Ancient Britons. The cove is lovely and has an impressive cavern and the striking **Lion Rock.**

If you have never heard of **Flambards**, I can recommend it to you as an excellent day out for all the family no matter what the weather. It is close to **Helston,** famous for the annual Floral Dance which is performed through the town rather like the Hobby Horse in Padstow on the north coast. The Royal Navy have a presence at Helston. The air station at **Culdrose** is home to several squadrons of helicopters, and it is a rare day when you do not see these ungainly creatures of the air, landing and taking off. The skill of the pilots and the crews is unmatched. Many a sailor and a visitor has been saved from certain death by the efficiency of their rescue skills and their bravery.

Another great place to visit is at **Wendron. The Poldark Mine Heritage Complex** has won many awards. The Poldark Village is based on Winston Graham's famous novels which became such a successful television series. It depicts the true living conditions of the mining community in the early 19th century. Like every mine it has to be kept free of water and more than 30,000 gallons are pumped out every day, just to keep the parts that the public visit dry. The gardens are lovely and the amusements for the children well thought out.

Three miles south of Helston, just off the A308 in a combe, stands the church of **St Winwalloe,** in solitary state with only the call of the seabirds for company. The isolation merely adds to the romanticism. Sheltered by a cliff it is the site of the 'Church of the Storms' founded in the 6th century by Winwalloe, close to the manor of one Roger de Carminowe, who was described as a descendant of King Arthur. There are sandbanks here where treasure chests were buried by pirates, and a ship sunk just offshore carrying her treasure with it. The church is lovely with a beautiful wagon roof, a granite altar and parts of a wonderful 16th century rood screen. You should see this church and soon; constant erosion of the cliff threatens it.

Before you look at Camborne and Redruth, may I suggest that you take the A30 a little to the north of Redruth and seek the turning for **Chacewater**. It lies in the heart of the Cornish mines - most no longer working - and had the richest vein of copper in the world. It can boast the first steam pumping engine in a Cornish mine made by James Watt. Today Chacewater is a pleasant rural village with some nice houses, and a fine pub The Rambling Miner in Fore Street. From the village it is simple to visit the famous **Wheal Jane** mine and the entrancing **Blissoe Valley.**

Camborne is famous worldwide for its School of Mines but apart from that it is a busy market town. The fine medieval church is well worth visiting with a churchyard crammed full of interesting gravestones many with entertaining epitaphs. Near Camborne is **Magor Farm** where, in this century, ruins of a Roman Villa were found.

Redruth is almost joined to Camborne these days but it still has its separate existence. William Murdoch lived in one of the plain little houses here. It was he who gave us gas light and invented the locomotive. A Scot by birth he married a Redruth girl and it was their house which had the very first gaslit home in the whole of the country. If you find the tin-mining industry interesting, you will not want to miss **Cornish Engines** at **East Pool**. Here there are impressive relics of these great beam engines which were used for pumping water from over 2,000 ft deep, and for winding men and ore. The engines exemplify the use of high pressure steam patented by the Cornish engineer, Richard Trevithick of Camborne in 1802. It is open Good Friday to the end of October, daily from 11-6 pm or sunset if it is earlier.

High above Redruth stands **Carn Brea Castle**, silhouetted against the sky, and near it is a great column in memory of Francis Basset who did so much for Cornish miners. It is worthwhile making the effort to climb up the inside stairway of this monument which stands 90 ft high. From the top you get the most amazing view of the whole of this mining area and the sight of more coastline than anywhere else in the county.

Where did miners go if they had free time? **Gwennap Pit**. This was the place where they would listen to the stirring oratory of John Wesley preaching in this naturally tiered open-air amphitheatre. In my imagination I can hear the great sound of the Wesley hymns resounding around the place from the glorious Cornish voices. John Wesley converted the Cornish to Methodism in their thousands.

Penzance brings us ever nearer to the tip of Cornwall. It is a nice old town with a busy port and wide promenade. The Queens Hotel on the promenade has always been a favourite of mine. It is within sight of the hotel that The Scillonian sails daily for the **Scilly Isles**, twenty eight miles south west of **Lands End**. These islands are addictive but more of that later. On the Penzance to **Morvah** road is **Trengwainton Garden** overlooking Mounts Bay. Here in the shelter of the walled garden you will find many tender plants which cannot be grown in the open anywhere else in England.

You can see the majesty and mysticism of **St Michael's Mount** rising out of the sea in Mounts Bay. Originally the site of a Benedictine Chapel established by Edward the Confessor, this spectacular castle dates from the 14th century. To get there you can walk across from **Marazion** when the tide is out, or during the summer months take the ferry at high tide. It is a wonderful experience and the gardens which seem to grow out of the rock, are unique. Because of the narrow passages within the castle, it is necessary to limit the numbers of visitors at any one time.

Winding roads lead from Penzance to the fishing village of **Newlyn**, beloved by artists and then to **Paul**, the last village in Cornwall to speak the Cornish language back in the early 1700's. **Lamorna** next, right by the sea and so beautiful. Then **Porthcurno** and **St Levan** before we reach Lands End. Once I used to be filled with an enormous excitement at standing here at the very end of Britain but those days have gone. It now has a smart hotel, endless attractions and restaurants - not the same at all.

Now for our journey up the Atlantic Coast. First of all **Sennen** - America's nearest neighbour! It stands high above the sea with a deep cove into which the sun hardly ever shines in winter. There is an odd story about the little medieval church. A great stone stands outside and round it seven Saxon Kings dined and wined, so the story goes, and then continues to say that when another seven kings dine here the end of the world will come!

The church may have its story. The village hostelry, The Old Success Inn, which has a beachside location, has many more. Built in the 17th century, it has always been the haunt of fishermen and smugglers; in recent years it has also become a watering hole for the brave lifeboat crew. Open all year, it is as good to stay here at Christmas, when there is a special break, as it is at any time of the year.

St Just, not to be confused with St Just in Roseland, although Spring comes early here with the beauty of the hedgerows ablaze with wild flowers - autumn lingers and in winter frost and snow are rare visitors. But the exhilaration of facing up to the wild Atlantic gales is an experience you are unlikely to forget! Wonderful place to stay and Boscean Country Hotel cannot be bettered whenever you come. One visitor from the States wrote that 'It is as if we had stepped back in time. The Edwardian house with its beautiful panelling, fireplaces, a grand staircase with a view of the sea from the landing, a grandfather clock, and lovely paintings, has an air of gracious living about it all.

St Ives is the home of so many artists that it does not need me to paint in words how attractive it is. It was much frequented by Whistler and Sickert who delighted in the light which has a high ultra violet content. The whole reach of St Ives Bay from Navax Point to St Ives itself is glorious. The sea always seems to be bluer here than anywhere else in Cornwall. The streets are narrow and it is hellish for drivers. You are well advised to leave your car at **Lelant** and use the excellent park-and-ride service which operates with stops all along the bay. As you wander round the centre of this town you will find pretty aspects at every turn. Little houses jut out at funny angles and lead to other houses, until you have climbed steadily to St Ives Head under which the town snuggles, safely sheltered. There are pubs and restaurants galore with a wide choice of hotels and guest houses.

Perranporth with its sand dunes and vast beach is always popular in the summer for family holidays and for day visitors especially at weekends. The bustling holiday resort of **Newquay** with its spectacular beaches has for so long been a holiday Mecca for people from the North of England. It is so busy in the season and there are so many places to stay and eat that it becomes impossible to select a variety of establishments. Conversely in the winter, when I find it the most appealing with its great empty stretches of beach washed by the mighty Atlantic rollers, so many places are closed. It has been referred to as the 'Blackpool of Cornwall'.

Cornwall has few Elizabethan manor houses which have escaped extensive alterations. One of the few is **Trerice** only three miles from Newquay and approached by high hedged lanes. For 400 hundred years the home of the Cornish Royalist Arundell family, this glorious house still retains most of its 16th century glass in the great hall window of twenty-four lights, comprising 576 panes. It was acquired by the National Trust in 1953.

To the north of Newquay there will be few people who do not know of the existence of **Bedruthan Steps**, a famous beauty spot owned by the National Trust. The question is how many have braved the descent and ascent from the beach! It is definitely demanding but the rewards far and away outweigh the puffing and panting of those of us who are more used to driving in our cars than taking such strenuous exertion.

There are some delightful seaside villages just north of Newquay like **Port Gaverne**. Here you will find the well established and totally delightful Port Gaverne Hotel, known by thousands throughout the world. For over 350 years it has been dispensing hospitality and never better than today.

Port Isaac has charming, irregular steep streets with cottages that lead down to the harbour. It is a village that is the essence of a Cornish fishing port. It has been a Conservation Area since 1969. For those looking for somewhere to stay that has good food and is slightly different, then The Old School Hotel or The Slipway Hotel will fill the bill. I do not know which I like best. If you would like to stay in a pub that is only a little way from Port Isaac but inland, then The White Hart at **St Teath** has for many years been one of my favourite watering holes.

The estuary of the River Camel divides **Rock** from Padstow. Each side of the estuary has its aficionados. One of the strange things about Rock is that it lost its church in the sand! Perfectly true. Sand dunes on the banks of Padstow Harbour engulfed an ancient chapel and it was out of use for ages until the middle of the l9th century when it was restored. You can see it now as it stands on the sand with a fine view across to Padstow. The famous **St Enodoc Golf Club** is within easy reach.

It is the stunning views over the Camel estuary and away to **Bodmin Moor** as you come from Wadebridge to this coast that will first strike you about Padstow. This little town has clung on to its ways and traditions for centuries. Its narrow streets wind down to the quay and the fishing boats. For most people Padstow will be synonymous with its curious May Day custom of welcoming summer with songs and dancing in the streets while a man in a mask dances in front of a Hobby Horse. It is a day when the town is filled to overflowing.

Before the Reformation there were many chapels and shrines in Padstow which was a privileged sanctuary for criminals for some reason. Now there is only the stately church of St Petrock's standing high in the town, framed by trees. There are remains of ancient crosses in the churchyard, and the 8-holed stocks are housed in the porch. It is a church that gives everyone who enters it pleasure.

There are so many beautiful places around Padstow that you are truly spoilt for choice but you would be foolish to miss the delights of **Trevone Bay** or **Harlyn Bay**. The latter boasts everything that a true Cornish beach should have. A wide golden expanse of firm, clean sand with rock pools either side just waiting for the intrepid explorer. There is safe bathing, fantastic surf for the novice and the champion wave rider. The coastal path winds around the Bay with breath-taking views. It is a favourite spot for birdwatchers and the area is steeped in ancient history. There is an excellent hotel here, The Polmark Hotel, built in Cornish stone, with an old-fashioned elegance which will provide you with a truly relaxed holiday in a friendly, casual atmosphere.

Continuing up the coast you will come to **Tintagel.** I wonder what you will make of it? To enjoy it you must be prepared to believe in legends. Tintagel is said to be the birthplace of King Arthur and he is supposed to have lived here with his Queen Guinevere and the Knights of the Round Table. Every year tourists come here from all over the world to see **King Arthur's Exhibition Hall** and **Halls of Chivalry** which were built in 1933 and between them have 72 stained glass windows and many murals depicting symbolic scenes and the virtues of this legendary king and his beautiful queen.

I lived in this village for a while in 1950 and every Sunday I used to walk up the long hill to the l4th century church which is the oldest in Cornwall. It is set high on the Clebe Cliff exposed to the ravages of the Atlantic storms. The wind here can be of such force that it has been necessary for some of the gravestones to have tiny buttresses. Few would argue that the most popular and famous attraction is the medieval castle. One wonders how it ever got built because it stands on the wildest and most windswept part of the North Cornwall coast. I have no idea whether King Arthur ever set foot here but I am willing to believe it. It is romantic, identifiable as a settlement from AD400 in the time of the Celts. In the 12th century it became a royal castle but by the 1500's the central portion had been washed away by the erosion of the sea. Edward, The Black Prince is supposed to have stayed here, and if you climb down the path that leads to the shingle beach you will find Merlin's cave where it is alleged that King Arthur spent his childhood.

Close to Tintagel there are a number of small beaches and coves that are not well known. Soft golden sand is to be found at **Bosinney Cove** and it is here that you will find Willapark Manor Hotel surrounded by stunning views. It is very comfortable, with a warm, friendly and informal atmosphere. The lawns at the back of the house sweep down to meet the cliffs, and on balmy summer evenings, you can sit with your after-dinner drinks and watch the sun set over the sea. A path leads from here to a side gate opening onto **Bosinney Lands** and **Benoath Cove** - a haven for the bather and sun-worshipper. Close by are the islands known as **The Sisters**, the precipice of a great headland overgrown with lichen and the cliff in the cove which is remarkably like an elephant. **Trebarwith Strand** with its sandy beach is another popular place for surfing; the tide roars in here and it is not always safe.

Boscastle must have been known to sailors since men first sailed the English seas. If you have a choice of roads then to see Boscastle at its most spectacular, approach from **Camelford** on the B3266 where the road rises until you suddenly see the most glorious prospect over the **Valency Valley** and the Atlantic Ocean, before you drive down the twisting road into the village. This is somewhere you will want to stay and there is no better place than the very old, historic Wellington Hotel. It is totally comfortable and full of interest.

There is no doubt that the little harbour is one of the oddest in the country. It has a medieval breakwater, a long greasy slipwater and a huge dog-leg opening into the ocean. For those who pass the stone jetty and clamber over the slippery rocks, the sea opens out in front of them to a sight that is unforgettable. If the tide is right you will not be able to miss the famous blow-hole working and rumbling. It is a natural curiosity throwing out a cloud of spray with a deep rumble like a tiny volcano. I have heard it called the **Devil's Bellows**. In Fore Street there is a non-conformist chapel which, in a perfectly true story, is linked with this odd harbour and the very best of wines and spirits. The story begins with a French Privateer attempting to ambush a vessel belonging to Boscastle wine merchants, Messrs Sloggett and Rosevear: the Cornish captain applied full sail and headed for the port. The Frenchman chased him hard until they were both just off the entrance to Boscastle harbour. The Frenchman was not privy to the secrets of the hidden harbour and thought the Cornishman was sailing for certain destruction on the rocks, so he sailed away disgruntled, but pretty sure he had left nothing to chance. It was with great relief that Messrs Sloggett and Rosevear saw their cargo landed. In gratitude they contributed a large sum of money for the improvement of the teetotal chapel!

Thomas Hardy came here as a young architect to help in the restoration of the church where he met his wife, Emma Gifford. This was not a marriage made in heaven although it lasted over 30 years. Oddly enough after her death in 1912, Hardy returned to Cornwall and the memory of their early romance at Boscastle inspired him to write some of the greatest love poems ever. Wherever you go around Boscastle it is magical. You can walk inland or take the coastal path from the harbour to **Penally** and on to **Pentargen** or climb the lane linking Boscastle with **Lesnewth** and nearby **Minster** with its church in an almost theatrical setting with not a house in sight and tall trees forming a backdrop. In spring the whole of the floor of this imaginary stage is covered with a carpet of bluebells and daffodils. Today the walls and pews are in need of repair and you are asked to give generously towards the restoration fund. The walk along the coastal path from Boscastle to Tintagel is nothing short of stunning. When the sun is shining, the sea is an unbelievable blue and laps the rocks below with a caress. When the wind blows it lashes the ocean into a ferment. It makes it difficult to stand upright but what a sight; the fury of the anguished sea is awesome.

In North Cornwall, we come to **Bude** which Sir John Betjeman described as the 'least rowdy resort in the county'. Certainly it is a well behaved sort of place and one in which families will delight. The sea and sand are superb, the Atlantic rollers rise to heights which please surfers. Strangely enough at the beginning of the last century Bude was not even on the map. Next door **Stratton** was the established market town where the famous Battle of Stamford Hill took place in 1643 when Sir Bevil Grenville defeated the Parliamentary forces led by the Earl of Stamford. Every year in May this battle is re-enacted by members of the Sealed Knot Society.

Last but by no means least is **Launceston**, which until 1838 was both the capital and Assize town of Cornwall, just over the border from Devon. You may wonder why the county court was so close to the Devon border - the reason is simple, judges were too scared to go further! These days Launceston is mainly an agricultural town and sleepy to boot, but it has a great charm and is crammed with history and beauty.

The stately castle with pile upon pile of round towers gives pleasure to those who climb to its summit and are rewarded by the beauty of the view across Cornwall into Devon. The ruins of the ancient priory keeps safe the monks who lie at their rest beneath it, and as you enter the town from the Tavistock side you come through the gateway of the old town wall.

The church of St Mary Magdalene is superb. The exterior walls are uniquely carved with intricate designs and the roof inside was allegedly carved by one man. He carved more than half a mile of oak, covered with ferns, foliage and heads. Sir John Betjeman described it as a medieval triumph of Cornwall.

The Launceston Steam Railway gives a great deal of pleasure to many people. With a train every 40 minutes or so, many passengers choose to enjoy a picnic or walk in the valley and return on a later service. It runs for two miles through the valley of the River Kensey, a tributary of the Tamar.

THE SCILLY ISLES

Warmed by the Gulf Stream, buffeted by the Atlantic, dependant on sea and air links with the mainland, the unique Isles of Scilly and the islanders willingly let you share a quality of life that is totally different. Whenever I think about taking a break which will give me rest, peace and a complete recharging of my batteries, it is always to these magical islands that I am drawn. Whether you decide to go by sea or air it is immaterial; it is all beautiful.

CHAPTER THREE

The Scillonian carries everything the islanders need and whilst you wait to sail you can watch the cargo being loaded. It is a two and a half hour voyage and part of its charm is watching the sights of the Cornish coast slip past. St Michael's Mount, Newlyn, Mousehole, Lamorna Cove, the Minack Theatre and finally Land's End. You will catch sight of the Wolf Rock Lighthouse, see a variety of shipping ploughing its way, seabirds in profusion and sometimes dolphins and sharks.

After two hours you will see the group of granite islets, the Atlantic outpost of England. Hopefully you will have come to stay on one of the islands but if not it still makes a wonderful day out, and you are pretty sure to acquire the taste for more next time.

The islands have their own history inextricably linked with the mainland. They are on the route taken by intrepid sailors who first came from the coasts of Portugal, Spain and Brittany and who, in the course of centuries, left traces of their religion behind them. Some never went back and there are more prehistoric chambered graves of these seamen and stone builders than in the whole of mainland Cornwall.

The soft, mild airs which breathe over the islands when no wind blows, and a warm current possibly from the Gulf Stream, gives them a semi-tropical climate where the myrtle and palm trees flourish. Even bananas and eucalyptus will grow in the open. The chief industry of the islands is the cultivation of flowers and early vegetables. In early spring the fields, sheltered by thick hedges of tamarisk and laurel are covered with daffodils, narcissus, wallflowers and lilies. Everyone joins in the picking. Picked, packed and despatched the same day, these flowers delight us all with their intoxicating perfumes and their freshness. You may find someone who will tell you that in the past this was not the chief industry of the islands. Wrecking took precedence, a slander for which the enormous number of ships lost on the rocks appear to give it some credence.

St Marys is the largest of the islands, yet still only two and a half miles by one mile. It is the hub of commercial and social life with **Hugh Town** as its capital. There are two excellent places to stay. The Harbourside Hotel and The Wheelhouse at Porthcressa. Both are welcoming and generous in their hospitality.

From St Mary's you will probably set off every day by boat to explore the other islands, the largest of which is **Tresco.** This is an island of amazing scenery as well as the wonderful **Abbey Garden** with its sub-tropical and exotic plants growing with a luxuriance unknown elsewhere in the United Kingdom. **St Martins** is the most north-easterly with cliff scenery along the north side and many magnificent beaches of fine, white sand along the southward coastline. Wonderful to explore, there are two landing quays, at Higher Town and Lower Town, at either end of the two-mile-long island, each used at different states of the tide.

The charm of **St Agnes** lies in its remoteness and rugged nature, where a friendly looking disused coal-burning lighthouse, overlooks an island of cottages, bulbfields and tamarisk hedges. To the westward the island consists of heath and downs with some striking granite outcrops. From here the views towards the Bishop Rock Lighthouse and the Western Rocks mark the resting place of countless wrecks from the days when great sailing ships plied the Western Approaches.

A sandbank links St Agnes to **Gugh** at low water. Gugh has many megalithic remains and outstanding views from the summit but for heavens sake check the tide before exploring, otherwise you may have to paddle across the bar! The unmistakable twin hills of **Samson** will make photographers eager to test their skills at sunset. No one lives here any longer. Poor shelter and a lack of water make it impossible.

I have left **Bryher** until last because here, in an island of low hills, wonderful beaches, rugged, wild and untamed even by Scillonian standards, is The Hell Bay Hotel, which belies its name. It is a wonderful place to stay in the greatest comfort. Away from the world, pampered, surrounded by scenery of unsurpassed beauty, it has to be my idea of heaven. In fact every time I come to the Isles of Scilly, I firmly believe I am in a corner of heaven.

THE CLIFF HOTEL
Crooklets, Bude,
Cornwall EX23 8NG

Tel/Fax: 01288 353110

The Cliff Hotel has been awarded the prestigious '4Q Selected' and RAC 'Highly Acclaimed' classifications in addition to the English Tourist Boards 3 Crown Highly Commended which gives you some idea of how good this small, immaculately run hotel is. The location is perfect - only 200 yards from the famous Crooklets Beach and just five minutes from the town centre. The views down the coast from the hotel are quite spectacular stretching some thirty miles down to Trevose Head.

Wonderful as the setting is, that is only a part of the pleasure that guests derive from staying at 'The Cliff'. The bedrooms, some with balconies and sea views, are large, purpose-built and each is decorated charmingly. All the rooms are fully en-suite and have Colour and Sky televisions with a Video and Radio. Direct Dial telephones make communication simple and the fully stocked beverage tray is an added bonus. Meal times are eagerly looked forward to. The pretty cream and green dining room has beautifully appointed tables, soft lighting and a very relaxed atmosphere. On the menu you will find dishes that have given The Cliff an enviable reputation throughout the area for its cuisine. Breakfast consists of a buffet style arrangement for fruit juices, grapefruit and cereals (including the hotels home-made muesli). Then there is waitress service for the cooked breakfast of your choice. At lunchtime there are freshly prepared bar meals which are served either in the friendly bar or on the sun terrace. Dinner is a feast of three courses with excellent choices - something to suit everyone. The Cliff is particularly famed for the Greek dish Klef Tico where they use up to 10 legs of prime English lamb on the bone and herbs from the garden. Delicious and very tender. Local seafood specialities include whole Crab platters. For those with a sweet tooth the sweet trolley will prove irresistible.

Leisure facilities are well catered for with a superb indoor heated swimming pool, spa bath, tennis court, both a pitch-and-put and a separate putting green; an archery range and a large lawn for your own games. For young children there is a sandpit and swings. There is a fine 18-hole golf course within five minutes walk, riding stables and an Adventure Centre. Walkers love the coastal footpaths especially along the old Bude Canal, the only remaining canal in Cornwall.

USEFUL INFORMATION

OPEN; *April-October*
CHILDREN; *Welcome*
CREDIT CARDS; *All major cards*
LICENSED; *Yes*
ACCOMMODATION; *Fully en suite*

DINING ROOM; *First class food with fresh produce, local seafood & other specialities*
BAR FOOD; *At lunchtime. Wide variety*
VEGETARIAN; *Catered for*
GARDEN; *Yes +indoor heated swimming pool Beach 200 yards*

HURDON FARM,
Launceston,
Cornwall, PL15 9LS.

Tel : 01566 772955

Just south of the old Cornish capital town of Launceston you will find this charming 18th century stone and granite farmhouse. It is RAC listed, 2 crowns Highly Commended, and AA 'QQQQQ' Premier Select! These are just the official accolades, but there are many warm personal ones by guests. Situated in the peace and harmony of the surrounding countryside, this beautiful house is at the end of a tree lined drive in expansive cultured gardens. Margaret Smith is your hostess and provides a welcoming warmth in a congenial atmosphere for all her guests. The bedrooms are delightfully decorated in co-ordinating fabrics and colours, and all have facilities of full central heating, hair dryers, hospitality tray, colour TV, and thoughtful extras such as books, games, sewing kits, writing paper and even a hot water bottle! The lounge features a wonderful log stove, colour TV, and big comfy chairs for guests to relax in. Food is traditional English cooking ...but with 'flare'. Dishes such as 'Prawn Rouladen' are on the starter list, followed by delicacies of perhaps 'Chicken with Dijon mustard and mushrooms' and to finish 'Pineapple & Cream filled brandy baskets' or 'Steamed sticky toffee pudding'. All are very imaginative (and delicious), and the farms own produce is used where possible. The meal is always followed by various cheeses and 'pots of coffee'. Vegetarian dishes are not a problem and you are welcome to bring your own wine. This is a beautiful house with much character retained from times gone by. The large kitchen with it's open granite fireplace, original Dutch oven, and collection of old jacks and trivets is just one of the features. Hurdon Farm is a working farm of 400 acres, with dairy cows, sheep, pigs, and it is an ideal place for children to experience farm animals.

Although rurally situated to give you the tranquillity and relaxation of a country setting, Hurdon Farm is perfect for visiting many of the local attractions. The north and south coasts are within driving distance, and both Bodmin and Dartmoor, with their rugged haunting scenery, are also within easy access. There are two impressive National Trust properties close by; one being the charming Cotehele with its house and wonderful gardens, and the other being Landhydrock House, a magnificently preserved example of Victorian and Edwardian country house living. For the steam engine enthusiast Launceston has its own, and there are many more attractions, within easy distance, to suit all. This is the perfect location for relaxation, but at the same time gives you an opportunity to visit the wide variety of amenities there for your enjoyment.

USEFUL INFORMATION

OPEN; *April - Nov*
CHILDREN; *Welcome*
PETS; *No*
CREDIT CARDS; *None taken*
ACCOMMODATION; *6 rooms*
4 en suite 1 private bathroom.

DINING ROOM; *Wonderful cuisine*
VEGETARIANS; *Catered for*
DISABLED ACCESS; *Partial (by arrangement)*
GARDEN; *extensive*

THE OLD RECTORY COUNTRY HOUSE HOTEL
St Keyne, Liskeard
Cornwall PL 14 4 RL

Tel: 01579 342617

If one were to quote from the Bible 'The peace that passeth all understanding' it would be as applicable to the Old Rectory as it is in the biblical sense. The house is encompassed in an aura of peace and tranquillity, standing in a secluded setting in its own three acres of grounds and surrounded by farmland. The view from the grounds and the windows merely enhances the image. Built in the early 1800's this is a family run hotel with Pat and John Minifie at the helm. It combines the gracious charm of bygone days with cheery log fires on cooler evenings and modern central heating to ensure your creature comforts. The furnishings and decor are in total harmony with the original architecture. Panelled doors, a black marble fireplace, a handsome staircase with barley-twist balusters, and velvet sofas add to the elegance.

There are eight en suite bedrooms, tastefully decorated and all with tea/coffee making facilities and colour television. Two rooms have four-posters and there is a ground floor en suite room to accommodate the disabled. A sumptuous breakfast and an a la carte dinner including traditional fine English cooking and the adventure of Continental cuisine complete the picture. St Keyne is delightfully 'off the beaten track' on the little used B3254 but it is only 5 miles from the picturesque fishing village of Looe and 3 miles from the market town of Liskeard. Safe beaches, wonderful walks, sailing, tennis, fishing, riding and golf are just some of the activities readily available.

USEFUL INFORMATION

OPEN: *Closed at Christmas*
CHILDREN: *Over 12 years A La Carte dinner*
BAR FOOD: *Not applicable*
VEGETARIAN: *Catered for on request*
DISABLED ACCESS: *One ground floor room suitable*
PETS: *Well behaved with prior arrangement*

DINING ROOM: *Full English Breakfast*
CREDIT CARDS: *All except AMEX*
LICENSED: *Yes*
ACCOMMODATION: *8 en suite rooms*
GARDEN: *3 acres*

TRELASKE COUNTRY HOTEL,

Polperro Road, Looe,
Cornwall, PL13 2JS.

Tel : 01503 262159

Set in one of Cornwall's most charming holiday locations is the exquisite Trelaske Country Hotel and Restaurant. Luxury combined with the best service is standard here, and the peace and tranquillity of a break at this superb hotel will ensure complete relaxation and revitalisation. The hotel is set in four beautifully groomed acres and is just 3/4 mile from the beach. Wander the grounds or relax in a deck chair, and enjoy the quiet and solitude of this country paradise.

Silvia Rawlings is your hostess and exudes a friendly personal welcome to all her guests, ensuring you feel at home immediately and enjoy the particular attention which all staff exercise. The bedrooms are delightful with individuality in each, and are enhanced by the soft furnishings and quality bed linen and towels provided. All are equipped with colour TV, phone, hair dryer, complimentary bathroom accessories, and that ever essential tea/coffee tray. The bedrooms are en suite, and three have Jacuzzi baths. The views from the bedrooms are of open countryside and farmland, and it is a pleasure to awaken in one of these rooms. Breakfast is a traditional English affair, and home grown and local produce is used where possible. A continental breakfast is available in your room, and for that special occasion a champagne breakfast may be ordered. An evening meal is also available and the excellent menu offers many choices for the discerning palate. The roast duck is renowned here, but there are also many delightful seafood dishes (Looe being close by) and a variety of fresh home grown vegetables to complement. Vegetarian meals are available by prior arrangement. The wine list adds to the high standards, and all is served by unobtrusive, friendly, attentive staff.

The lounges offer relaxation with their open fires and welcoming warmth, and it is a pleasure to relax and unwind here after a days activities. Enjoy a drink from the bar while you plan the next outing or share some moment with friends or acquaintances.

This is a delightful part of the country, and the character of the local Cornish people will have you captivated very quickly. The vistas are stunning, the beaches glorious, and the towns and villages charming. You will not be disappointed whatever your age, as there is a wealth of activities here from water sports, to just walking and enjoying the scenery. Keep your camera close by as you will want to capture the memory of this holiday and you will find yourself returning time and time again to enjoy this haven of Cornish hospitality.

USEFUL INFORMATION

OPEN; *All year*
CHILDREN; *Welcome*
PETS; *By arrangement*
LICENSED; *Full*
CREDIT CARDS; *All major*
ACCOMMODATION : *7 luxury rooms en suite:*
4 dbl, 2 twin, 1 sgl, 2 fml. suites.

RESTAURANT; *Exquisite cuisine*
VEGETARIAN; *By arrangement*
DISABLED ACCESS; *Yes*
GARDEN; *4 acres including 3 hole Golf course*

PEREGRINE HALL
Lostwithiel,
Cornwall PL22 OHT

Tel/Fax: 01208 873461

Built in 1864 in Gothic style by George Edmund Street, architect of the Law Courts in London, its purpose was a nunnery and a home for wayward women - history does not relate what success rate the nuns had! Today Peregrine Hall has a vastly different role. You will be warmly welcomed into the house by the owners, Jo and Barry Nicolle, where four bedrooms are dedicated to bed and breakfast. All are en-suite and highly individual. One room has a 5ft canopied bed and a sitting area as well as a sleigh dressing room; two have four-poster beds and the other is twin bedded. All are equipped with television and generously supplied beverage trays. A delicious full English breakfast is served every morning either in the dining room or in the conservatory. All the rooms face south over the long broad terrace and the gardens, which together with the solar heated swimming pool, you are most welcome to use.

If for no other reason you should come to Peregrine Hall for the stunning views from many of the rooms and the terrace. From April to October given that the soft Cornish rain holds off, the hills and valleys are an arresting sight. The cool bright light of early morning sparks and flashes through the trees; because the house is south facing, the sun warms the old flags throughout the day and in the evening it is time to sit out and watch the scene before you gradually soften in golden light - the sheep and lambs turn almost a pinkish colour reflecting the peachy pink clouds; the sense of peace is timeless and disturbed only by rooks and smaller birds hurrying late to their nests, and occasionally an early owl. As the sun finally goes down over the western aspect and the majesty of Restormel Castle, the lights of the small town of Lostwithiel far below are a friendly reminder that 'civilisation' is not far away. Turn away from looking west and look across the valley in front of you, lift up your eyes to the glorious beauty of the night sky - it is breathtaking.

Lostwithiel is an excellent centre for anyone wanting to explore the magic of this part of Cornwall. Within six miles is Lanhydrock House and Gardens, Bodmin Steam Railway, Restormel Castle, Fowey, the Eden project, and the South Coast. Many other National Trust properties, Padstow and Newquay and family attractions are within easy reach.

USEFUL INFORMATION

OPEN; *2nd Jan-22 December*
CHILDREN; *Welcome*
CREDIT CARDS; *None taken*
ACCOMMODATION; *4 rooms en suite*
GARDEN; *10 acres gardens & grounds*

DINING ROOM; *Delicious English breakfast*
VEGETARIANS; *Catered for*
DISABLED ACCESS; *No facilities*
PETS; *Guide dogs only*

TREWITHEN RESTAURANT

Fore Street,
Lostwithiel,
Cornwall
PL22 0BP

Tel: 01208 872373

If you like to eat in a relaxed unhurried cottagey atmosphere, then the Trewithen Restaurant is the place for you. This friendly place is owned and run by Brian and Lorraine Rolls; Brian has a Diploma in wine and chooses all his own. It was established in 1980 and this cosy converted 300-year-old dwelling has already gained favour with locals and visitors alike. Nestled in the Fowey River Valley The Trewithen is situated in the charming town of Lostwithiel. During the summer south coast Lobsters are available, then in the winter, there is local Venison and Game.

Also for your delight are Steak, Scallops, local Fish and wonderful Crispy Duck. The menu is supplemented by a Specials blackboard. There is an appealing vegetarian selection. All dishes use local produce including the delicious home-made ice-cream. A truly special restaurant.

USEFUL INFORMATION

OPEN; *All year, closed Sun & Mon-Winter Sun-Summer*
CHILDREN; *Yes*
CREDTT CARDS; *Visa/Master/ Diners/Switch/Delta*
LICENSED; *Yes*
ACCOMMODATION; *Not applicable*

RESTAURANT; *Excellent food, specialises In Steak, Duckling, Lobster, Local fish*
BAR FOOD; *Not applicable*
VEGETARIAN; *At least 2 dishes*
DISABLED ACCESS; *Not really*
GARDEN; *No*
PETS; *No*

BALMORAL HOTEL
1, Mount Wise,
Newquay, Cornwall TR7 2BE

Tel: 01637 851736

There is a growing number of people who have discovered that Newquay with its wonderful beaches and stunning sea views, is even nicer off-season than it is in the summer. This has meant the need for good hotels open all year who have warmth, comfort, drying facilities for those who enjoy walking when the weather is perhaps not so kind, and the wind whips up the spray sending the rollers crashing down on the beach - something that is quite awe inspiring. The Balmoral Hotel is just that sort of place. Furnished with excellent taste and in the capable hands of Karen, Ann and Mark Webster and their friendly, competent staff, the hotel is just right for breaks at any time of the year. From here in addition to spending time strolling around the harbour, walking or sunbathing on the beach, surfing or swimming, one can go river or sea fishing all year round, ride, walk, play golf on more than one course within easy reach, and amuse oneself with a host of activities. Where coarse fishing is concerned, Mark is an able tutor and fishing tackle is available with storage facilities and fridges. The coarse fishing in and around Newquay is the best in the South West with Gwinear Pool, Whiteacres and Porth Reservoir only a short journey from the hotel.

Within the hotel you will find that the 21, mainly en suite, bedrooms made up of a good choice of single, double and family suites, are newly decorated, have very comfortable beds, television, a beverage tray, radio intercom and a baby listening service. It is a peaceful and happy establishment with a degree of informality which is delightful. Freshly prepared meals with seasonal vegetables are served in the spacious dining room, which hosts varied menus of English and Continental cuisine for evening meals and a full English breakfast. The Balmoral will willingly pay special attention to anyone requiring a vegetarian or special diet.

Most people gather in the bar lounge in the evenings which is a convivial place and ideal for relaxing, chatting over the days happenings and planning for tomorrow. Throughout the season entertainment is provided, including quiz nights, etc. There is also a games area where you can take on someone at pool or throw a mean dart. In fact at the Balmoral there is every ingredient to make a splendid holiday.

USEFUL INFORMATION

OPEN; *All year*
CHILDREN; *Welcome*
CREDIT CARDS; *All major cards*
LICENSED; *Yes*
ACCOMMODATION; *21 rooms*
mainly en suite

RESTAURANT; *Freshly prepared meals*
VEGETARIAN; *Upon request*
DISABLED ACCESS; *No facilities*
PETS; *Yes*
PARKING; *Ample*

FAR HORIZONS
Pentire Avenue, Pentire,
Newquay, Cornwall TR7 1PF

Tel: 01637 873378

With one of the finest positions on the picturesque Pentire Headland commanding panoramic views across the River Gannel Estuary and the magnificent Fistral Bay Beach, it would be hard to find a better place to stay in this part of Cornwall. Just below it are the seven stretching miles of scenic coast enticing you to stroll or to follow one of the National Trust walks from nearby Pentire Point. Far Horizons has recently been refurbished and prides itself not only on the comfort, the tasteful decor and comfortable beds but also on hygiene matters, where from the scrupulously clean kitchen the talented chef prepares delicious and varied meals always using the highest quality ingredients. The resulting dishes make meals an eagerly waited occasion. Special diets can be catered for.

The thirteen bedrooms, eleven of which are en suite are all attractively decorated and have stunning views. Each bedroom is equipped with television, direct-dial telephone, hospitality tray and hairdryers. The hotel is licensed and has a well-stocked bar which is a meeting point for guests whether they are here on holiday or business - the latter come especially because of the relaxed atmosphere and the sense of it being a 'home-from-home'. The comfortable television lounge opens onto a south facing terrace and lawn. Ideal for enjoying a coffee and newspaper or just relaxing in the sun and enjoying the view.

Warm in winter and in the colder months, Far Horizons is an ideal place for a break. Many people prefer the quiet of the off season months and enjoy the bracing air knowing that they can scurry back to the welcoming warmth of the hotel if the weather is inclement.

USEFUL INFORMATION

OPEN; *All year*
CHILDREN; *Welcome*
CREDIT CARDS; *All major cards*
LICENSED; *Yes*
ACCOMMODATION; *13 rooms 11 en suite*

DINING ROOM; *Good, traditional fare*
VEGETARIAN; *Catered for*
DISABLED ACCESS; *No. Ground floor bedrooms but not suitable for wheelchairs*

THE TOLVERNE HOTEL

45 Edgcumbe Avenue,
Newquay, Cornwall TR7 2NL

Tel: 01637 874359

The Tolverne Hotel is quite unusual inasmuch as it is a Cornish chalet-style bungalow which has been converted into a prestigious small hotel owned and run by Pat and Mike Blake who have that inborn quality that makes some people natural hoteliers. The hotel is relaxed and informal in many ways but that feeling is achieved by total efficiency behind the scenes. The 8 en suite bedrooms are either double or twin beds. Each room has colour TV and a generously supplied tea and coffee tray. The meals are always looked forward to with a full English breakfast and an excellent evening meal with lots of delicious sweets prepared in house which are served with lashings of Cornish Clotted Cream. The hotel is licensed and has a small bar serving a limited selection of drinks as well as a comfortable lounge with colour television. Centrally heated the hotel is as good to stay in during the off-season times as it is in the summer. In fact many people prefer the quieter months. One of the services offered by the Blakes is a mini coach service which collects people from Birmingham and Reading and having brought them to the happy atmosphere of The Tolverne, they are then taken for three or four outings during their weeks stay.

The hotel is situated close to the Trenance Leisure Park which incorporates Animal World, Swimming Pools, various activities and beautiful gardens in which to stroll. The glorious sandy beaches of Newquay are only a few minutes walk away and the town centre too. You may care to explore the Cornish countryside with its enchanting villages or perhaps fish, go horse riding or pursue other country activities. It is all there for you.

USEFUL INFORMATION

OPEN; *April-October*
CHILDREN; *Over 5 years*
CREDIT CARDS; *None taken*
LICENSED; *Yes*
PETS; *Yes*

DINING ROOM; *Good traditional meals*
VEGETARIAN; *Upon request*
DISABLED ACCESS; *Please ring*
ACCOMMODATION; *8 en suite rooms*
GARDEN; *Yes*

PORT GAVERNE HOTEL,
Nr Port Isaac,
North Cornwall PL29 3SQ

Tel: 01208 880244 Freephone 0500 657867

Twenty-nine years ago you would not have given this hotel a second glance. Then it only had nine habitable rooms, none of which were en suite, and a staff of seven which included the owners. Now there are 17 en suite rooms, a staff of 30 and a hotel of such a standard that the guests want for nothing. The determination not to spoil the charm, character and general ambience of this exceptional old inn was always paramount in the planning; the successful outcome speaks for itself.

Over more than a quarter of a century thousands of people have stayed in the Port Gaverne Hotel, coming from all parts of the globe and closer to home. It is universally acclaimed for its genuine atmosphere and for the welcoming presence of Midge Ross, the owner. That the hotel has achieved Four Crowns status from the Tourist Board is not surprising. The chef produces delicious food using fresh and wherever possible local produce. The staff are caring, efficient and obviously take pleasure and pride in their jobs. One great boon is that the attractive restaurant is strictly non-smoking.

The hotel is close to the beach and surrounded by spectacular and beautiful coastal scenery. In addition to the rooms in the hotel there are also 6 self-catering cottages which all sleep four people and like the 2 large flats which sleep 8, are beautifully appointed and equipped, situated almost on the beach.

USEFUL INFORMATION

OPEN; *All year except early Jan to mid Fe*
CHILDREN; *Welcome*
CREDIT CARDS; *Visa/Master/ Diners/Switch/Amex*
ACCOMMODATION; *17 en suite rooms 6 self-catering cottages sleeping 4 2 large flats sleeping 8*

RESTAURANT; *High standard. Delicious*
BAR FOOD; *Lunches & Suppers*
VEGETARIAN; *Upon request*
LICENSED; *Full Licence*
DISABLED ACCESS; *Not level. Possible*
GARDEN; *Yes, tables & chairs*

LLAWNROC INN,
Gorran Haven, St. Austell,
Cornwall, PL21 6NU.

Tel : 01726 843461

Gorran Haven is one of those postcard Cornish villages, with a sheltered sandy bay and beautiful views out to sea. The Llawnroc Inn overlooks the village and is ideally situated for enjoying the wonderful Cornish coasts and sea views. John and Jan Gregory are the owners of this friendly, family run hotel, and contribute to the ambience and well-being of their guests with their good natured, courteous manners. A home from home is the best way to describe this establishment, and home cooking is one of the specialities. Meals are served in the public lounge bars, both at lunch time and in the evenings. Additional, in the summer, are the picnic tables on the terraced lawns, where you can dine al fresco on those balmy evenings watching the sunset over the water. Sounds wonderful , doesn't it! Fish is a great speciality, as are various home-made pies such as steak and stilton, and the chicken breast stuffed with brie and mushroom sauce sounds delicious. Breakfast is a traditional English meal, and is served in the sunny breakfast room which has stunning views over the water - there are very few rooms which do not have wonderful views - all bedrooms have seaviews and a more pleasant sight upon awakening is hard to imagine. Vegetarian dishes are available and all meals are of excellent quality. There is in addition a games room , a family eating area, a lounge and the locals bar, which gives you plenty of choice and a range of activities for all the family. The eight bedrooms are very well appointed with quality furnishings and the essentials such as colour TV and a hospitality tray. They are all en suite apart from the single room, and non-smoking rooms are available on request. This is the perfect choice for that summer holiday with the children, or for that quiet weekend away in late season. John and Jan offer special breaks at certain times of the year, and a short phone call will give you the information.

This is a wonderful part of the country, and walking can be enjoyed along the coastal paths to the quaint fishing village of Mevagissey in one direction, or to the secluded Vault Beach in the other, with miles of National Trust property including Dodman Point, and its breathtaking views down to the mouth of the River Fal. There are plenty of water sports - St.Austell is only 20 minutes away by car - and there are excellent roads to nearly all parts of Cornwall from here. Castles, druids, gardens and moors are all accessible, and the wonderful hospitality of the Cornish people is a memory you will cherish along with the special quality of a memorable holiday.

USEFUL INFORMATION

OPEN; *All year*   **DINING AREA;** *Excellent choices*
CHILDREN; *Welcome*   **VEGETARIANS;** *Catered for*
PETS; *By arrangement*   **DISABLED ACCESS;** *Yes*
LICENSED; *Full*   **GARDEN :** *Terraced lawns*
CREDIT CARDS; *All major* **AMPLE PARKING**
ACCOMMODATION; *8 rooms: 7 en suite,*
6 dbl or twin, 1 fml & 1 sgl.

THE GARRACK HOTEL & RESTAURANT

Burthallan Lane,
St Ives,
Cornwall TR26 3AA
Tel: 01736 796199 Fax: 01736 798955

The Garrack is justifiably proud of its widespread reputation for freshly prepared and, whenever available, locally produced food, with vegetables from its own garden in season. Open to non-residents, every visitor to St Ives should have a meal here. The fishing port of Newlyn lands the second largest quantity of fish in the country and is the hotel's source of supply for seafood of exceptional quality and freshness - an opportunity not to be missed. The Garrack has its own storage tank for live lobsters. The extensive wine list is notable for its variety of choice, including Cornish wines. The unique pricing policy offers exceptional value for the more expensive wines.

Secluded and away from the noise of traffic, The Garrack stands in two acres of gardens overlooking Porthmeor Beach, The Island and the St Ives Tate Gallery. Beyond this can be seen the breathtaking sweep of St Ives Bay and thirty miles of coastal scenery stretching away to Trevose Head. Owned and run by the Kilby family, this stylish hotel has public rooms which invite you to relax. For example the comfortable lounges have both magazines and board games for all and open fires for colder days. When it comes to bedtime there are rooms in the original house which are in character with the traditional granite house and in the wing built by the owners the rooms are more modern in style. Most of the rooms have superb sea views.

There are three rooms on the ground floor with level access to all public rooms and therefore suitable for the partially disabled. All the rooms have private bath or shower, some have four-poster beds and some have personal spa baths. Direct dial telephone with baby listening facility, and remote controlled television are common to all rooms. There is also a cottage which has two en suite rooms.

There is a small leisure centre, a most attractive place in which to relax whatever the weather. It contains a heated swimming pool, an integral spa and a swim jet. There is also a sauna, a sunbed and cardiovascular exercise equipment. A licensed coffee shop serves light meals and refreshments throughout the day. A conference or small meeting room is well equipped to meet in comfort for groups of up to sixteen in boardroom plan or twenty-five to thirty people in theatre style.

USEFUL INFORMATION

OPEN; *All year*
CHILDREN; *Welcome*
VEGETARIAN; *Several dishes daily*
CREDIT CARDS; *All major cards*
LICENSED; *Restaurant & Residential*
COMMODATION; *16 en suite rooms*
Cottage has 2 en suite rooms

RESTAURANT; *Freshly prepared to a very high standard English with Continental influence Open to non-residents*
DISABLED ACCESS; *Yes. Ground floor rooms*
OFFEE SHOP; *Light meals & refreshments* **AC-**

THE WHITE HART,
The Square, St Teath,
Cornwall, PL30 3JX.

Tel : 01208 850281

Situated in the delightful Cornish village of St Teath, this traditional inn has been in the Burton family for 45 years. Barry and Rob, the owners, offer great hospitality to their guests, local and visitor alike, and you are sure to enjoy the warm atmosphere of this great establishment. Whether it is a quiet drink you want or a superb meal, then The White Hart can cater to your needs. The attentive, unobtrusive staff help you enjoy your visit, and ensure your requirements are met. Food is very much to the forefront here, and a steak at The White Hart is well known. The menu is good English fayre at very reasonable prices, and is served in the charming dining room just off the 'snug' and saloon bar. Home-made pies and puddings are on offer and there is a special children's menu, as well as vegetarian food. In addition to the house wine, there is a good wine list for you to choose from.

This is what we imagine a good country pub to be, with its 'olde worlde' surroundings of settles, oak beams, brass, and delabole slate floor. It is comfortable and caters to both the young and the 'not so young', and has a wealth of ales and spirits to tantalise your tastebuds! The company is both varied and interesting, with many of the locals being regulars. Woodbine is the well known resident barman, and takes his name from a certain brand of cigarette that he smokes. (A lot, I would think!) There is a games room, and a pool and darts room for those who wish to play, and this is very popular with the younger generation. Upstairs are two luxurious en suite bedrooms which have full facilities for overnight guests. This is a great pub with plenty of character, and one which shows the hospitality and friendship the Cornish people have to offer.

The village of St Teath is well situated for visiting much of Cornwall. This is a wonderful county with scenic beauty around every corner, and many historic houses and castles to visit. Other attractions include a great many water sports (Newquay with its surfing is within a car journey), and walking is always a favourite here. Shopping in Truro or historic Plymouth is a great day out, and you can round off the day with a visit to the theatre or one of the many night spots.

USEFUL INFORMATION

OPEN; *All year*   **RESTAURANT;** *Excellent food*
CHILDREN; *Welcome*   **VEGETARIAN;** *Catered for*
PETS; *Welcome*   **DISABLED ACCESS;** *No*
LICENSED; *Full*   **BEER GARDEN;** *Yes*
CREDIT CARDS; *All major*
ACCOMMODATION; *2 en suite bedrooms.*

ROYAL HOTEL,
Lemon Street, Truro,
Cornwall, TR1 2QB.

Tel : 01872 270345
Fax : 01872 242453

The Royal Hotel in Truro is one of Cornwall's finest, and being in the administrative capital of the county, it plays host to many of the business people and visitors to this fine area. This 17th century hotel is of a very high standard, and Lynn Manning, the owner, ensures a warm welcome and a quality of service difficult to compare. The staff are all very professional and wholly committed to the comfort and ease of the guests, and amid the many accolades are those of the visitors who return again and again to stay in the warm atmosphere of this efficient hotel. One of the hotels admirers included Prince Albert who stayed here in 1846 and experienced 'a much enjoyed visit'. The standards still encourage much praise today. All the bedrooms are of a very high criteria and are decorated beautifully. Each is en suite with many facilities including satellite TV, direct dial, hair dryers and a hospitality tray of tea and coffee. For the business guest there are 'Executive Rooms' which thoughtfully provide in addition, a workdesk, fax machine, CD player and those little extras necessary for the business day. The hotel also boasts a fitness room, or for those who require a rather sedate method of exercise, a good snooker room! Food is high on the list of priorities and you can enjoy a wonderful meal at 'Meanings Brasserie'. Here are wines, beers and cuisine from around the world, and in an atmosphere of soft lighting, congeniality and warmth. The attentive, unobtrusive service only adds to this special experience of fine foods and refreshments. Vegetarians are well catered for and the restaurant can cater for up to 80 persons.

Truro is a fine city with its beautiful 19th century cathedral, museums, charming shops and many eating and drinking establishments. There are good connections to the rest of the world with its rail link, and Newquay airport a short drive away. This is a sophisticated city in a wonderful county that has stunning scenery and something for everyone, whether you are taking time out from a business meeting or just here to enjoy the hospitality and friendliness of the Cornish people, the Royal Hotel is definitely the place to experience the wealth of Cornish outgoing cordiality.

USEFUL INFORMATION

OPEN; *All year (Except Xmas)* **RESTAURANT;** *Excellent cuisine*
CHILDREN; *Welcome*   **VEGETARIAN;** *Catered for*
PETS; *No*   **DISABLED ACCESS;** *No*
LICENSED; *Yes*   **CREDIT CARDS;** *All major cards*
ACCOMMODATION; *37 rooms en suite*
4 Exec/ 3 twin/ 12 dbl/ 11 sgls..

THE LUGGER HOTEL,
Lugger Hotels Ltd.,
Portloe, Near Truro,
Cornwall, TR2 5RD.

Tel : 01872 501322
Fax : 01872 501691

The Lugger Hotel is a family-run business in one of Cornwall's picturesque fishing villages, and is a haven of relaxation and tranquillity. Stephen Powell and his family have been here for over three generations, and are the epitome of Cornish hospitality. The hotel is to very high standards, and there is a lovely mixture of cottage style pine furniture and modern. All the bedrooms are colour co-ordinated, and the personal touches of prints and other small details add to the warmth and homeliness all guests feel. Each bedroom has en suite facilities, colour TV, direct-dial telephone, individually controlled central heating, hair dryers and a hospitality tray of tea and coffee.

The hotel has a comfortable lounge adjoining the bar and restaurant, and with its oak beamed ceiling and open stone fireplace, it is the perfect place to relax after a days exploring. There are facilities for cards, chess and backgammon, and a entertaining evening is usually to be had! The cocktail bar opens on to the terrace which has stunning views, and here you can enjoy a drink or something from the bar lunch menu which includes local seafood and the traditional Cornish pasty. Morning coffees and afternoon teas are also served here, and the Cornish clotted cream tea is high on the list of favourites! The intimate restaurant seats 40, and offers a varied menu of English and Continental dishes. Good local produce is used where possible, and vegetarians are well catered for. There is an excellent wine list from all over the world, including a local Cornish wine which is produced just 2 miles away.

This is a wonderful part of the world, and you will feel as if time has passed you by as you enjoy the hospitality of this charming family. There is over 300 miles of coastal scenery in Cornwall, and some of the finest beaches in Europe are here. It is rugged, wild and just stunning, and you will be amazed at the variation and diversity of the scenery. There is plenty for the whole family with National Trust houses and gardens to visit, a wealth of water sports, walking, and for the artists, the most glorious vistas to be put on canvas. For us lesser mortals (I cannot draw to save myself) a camera is one way of forever keeping the memory of this perfect part of Britain alive. The Lugger Hotel is in the most unique position for visiting Cornwall, and you will surely be entranced by the warmth and hospitality you are offered by the gracious Powell family.

USEFUL INFORMATION

OPEN; *March - Nov*
CHILDREN; *Over 12 years welcome*
PETS; *No*
LICENSED; *Restaurant/Residential*
CREDIT CARDS; *All major*
ACCOMMODATION; *19 rooms en suite:*
9 dbl, 7 twin, 3 sgl.

RESTAURANT; *Excellent choice*
VEGETARIANS; *Catered for*
BAR SNACKS *Available*
DISABLED ACCESS; *No*
GARDEN; *Patio & terrace*

Chapter 4

DEVON INCLUDES

Chapter 4

DEVON

D evon is a county of extremes. It has more roads than any other county in England, which will lead you through highways and byways, sometimes amid leafy hedge rows teeming with plant and wildlife, sometimes along a coastline that is breathtaking or on the busy A38 which traverses the county to the borders of Cornwall and beyond. The roads will take you to the romantic and stark beauty of Dartmoor and Exmoor, the lush glory of the South Hams, the attractive resorts in Torbay, the spectacular coastline of North Devon, countless pretty villages tucked away and to the two cities of Exeter and Plymouth whose history goes back hundreds of years. It is a county that begs to be explored and will reward anyone who takes the time. It offers an abundance of stately homes, wildlife parks, museums, glorious sandy beaches, safe bathing, water sports and enough golf courses to satisfy even the most ardent golfer. Fishing has always been part of Devonian life whether it be along the banks of flowing rivers or from a boat that will take you out from a sheltered harbour to spend hours of pleasure surrounded by the sparkling blue sea with the backdrop of the coast - it almost makes the catch unimportant!

Plymouth tucked away and separated from Cornwall by the River Tamar is a super centre for anyone wanting to tour the county and maybe pop over the border into Cornwall. This is a city which rose from the ashes after the German bombing in World War II. The bombing, horrific as it was, made way for a new city centre to grow, dispensing with the colourful, old narrow streets that would have crucified modern commerce. There is no finer vantage point than Plymouth Hoe to take in the brilliance of Plymouth Sound on a sunlit day, its waters dotted with the white and often brightly coloured sails of the innumerable boating enthusiasts who flock to the Marinas and Yacht Clubs here. Plymouth has been host to many people over the centuries. Catherine of Aragon first stepped ashore in Plymouth when she came to marry the unfortunate Prince Arthur and later Henry VIII. She would have seen a very different city from the one we know today. The narrow winding streets of the Barbican would have been unpaved. I doubt if any of the buildings now exist. Southside Street now the main thoroughfare of the busy Barbican is first recorded in 1591. What an exciting place this city must have been in the time of Drake and Hawkins. It was from Plymouth that Drake sailed on the 19th July 1588 to defeat the Spanish Armada, and it was on Plymouth Hoe that he played his famous game of bowls. The construction of the Breakwater by Rennie (1812-1840) gave Plymouth one of the largest and safest harbours in Britain.

Good hotel accommodation is available close to Plymouth Hoe and the City Centre. It is not all expensive and you can choose from a simple, comfortable bed and breakfast hotel like The Bowling Green at 9 Osborne Place, The Hoe or the splendid Grand Hotel right on the Hoe with spectacular views. It is from a balcony in this hotel that Prime Minister Gladstone addressed a crowd of some 100,000 on a cold winter's night in 1889. He might have been very surprised to know that less than 200 yards along the Hoe, and just a quarter of a century later, Parliament's first woman member, Nancy Astor, would take up residence with her husband in Elliott Terrace. An elegant house with wonderful views which the Astors gave to the city, and when not in use for official entertainment, is open to the public. Then there is what Sir John Betjeman described as 'the finest building in Plymouth', the Duke of Cornwall Hotel in Millbay Road which is dignified and gracious.

I have always had an affection for the Forte Post House which is not a pretty building but stands high on Plymouth Hoe and probably has the best views in Plymouth. If you do not want to stay here do at least make the effort to have tea or a cup of coffee in the lounge; the view over the sea is totally therapeutic! Plymouth's premier hotel has to be The Moat House, Plymouth Hoe. Wonderful views, delightful bedrooms, good food and so much more makes it an ideal place to stay. If you want somewhere to stay that is not too far away from the city then you will not do better than to visit two of my favourite places; The Moorland Links Hotel at Yelverton which is just on Dartmoor and Alston Hall at Holbeton, a quiet country retreat. Both are within fifteen minutes drive.

Plymouth has a vast number of restaurants and eateries but for me the most exciting has to be Chez Nous in Frankfort Gate, where Le Patron, Jacques Marchal cooks 'Cuisine Spontanee' with wonderful results. Then hidden away just off Durnford Street, Stonehouse, is the stylish Trattoria Pescatore, owned by Piero and Rita Caligari. They are a couple committed to their profession and it shows not only in the food which is a delight, but in their insistence on high standards from their suppliers. Their clientele comes from discerning local people who have discovered them and told their friends. Plenty of parking space and in summer you can sit outside in what is no more than a flower filled passageway. I love it and I am not alone - it won a Plymouth in Bloom award. If you want something a little cheaper and simpler, then a fun place to be is Pissarios Wine Bar in St Andrews Street in the heart of the city centre. Good food, excellent wine and invariably a lively, friendly crowd frequent the bar both at lunchtime and in the evening.

With the **Theatre Royal**, one of the finest in the country, **The Pavilions**, a complex which offers ice skating, a swimming pool and a venue for concerts of all kind from Shirley Bassey to the Bournemouth Symphony Orchestra, **Plymouth Dome** on The Hoe and many more attractions including the National Trust's **Saltram House**, Plymouth should always be high on a visitors list.

If you would rather not stay in the city, then you could do no better than to stay at Ermewood House at **Ermington** near **Ivybridge**. This beautiful hotel overlooking the River Erme offers complete relaxation and charming hosts.

There are many counties envious of Devon's good fortune in having **Exeter** as its capital. It has everything. The River Exe wends its gracious way through the heart of the city, stopping every now and again to prepare itself for the opening of the swing bridge which lets small coasters upstream for unloading. The jewel in the crown is the magnificent cathedral which dominates the city centre and dictates much of the life-style immediately around it. Exeter is Roman, Saxon and Norman; it has walls and a tower built by Athelstan, the first King of England, but most of all it is medieval. There are still miles of quaint streets and passageways, rambling walls, a plethora of churches and of course the cathedral bequeathed to us by many generations of the finest builders, apart from its Norman walls and towers. Of course the 20th century has crept in and much has had to be changed, but on the whole it has been done with the greatest care and dedication to the preservation of all that is good. Shopping is a pleasure, with the big stores living comfortably alongside medieval buildings. As in most county towns there are innumerable small shops which entice - most of them hidden away in enchanting alleyways. All the time you are wandering in and out of these alleyways you will probably be getting ever nearer to the cathedral. Such is the dimension of its beauty that I find it hard to do it justice on paper. Gazing at the outside will give you hours of pleasure and probably an aching neck!

I love walking along the little Cathedral Close and Southernhay with its beautiful buildings, almost entirely occupied by professional people rather than residents. Perhaps I will walk in the garden of the 14th century Bishop's Palace, with its fine trees taking shade from the great walls of the cathedral. Certainly I will look at the Deanery where Catherine of Aragon stayed a night on her way to meet her fate - Henry VIII - I wonder how she felt. Once inside the Cathedral I am always mesmerised by the beauty around me. It is almost like being in a heaven in which modern man is allowed to go about an ordered, peaceful existence which in no way lacks purpose. There is no strife, no threat of war, no anger, just a great sense of the presence of God in the most wonderful surroundings. If there is any cry for help at all it comes from the need to keep this treasure safe. The years are telling on it and constant war is waged against decay. It takes an immense amount of money which is mainly raised by the public. It is not only money that is needed, craftsmen are continually at work and some of them are getting very old. Finding replacements becomes quite a battle in itself.

Exeter is blessed with many fine churches, some of which are never used but most have stories attached to them. One entrance into the close is by the tiny church of St Martin with its porch looking across to the Cathedral. It is quite easy to disregard this little gem because of the stunning beauty of the Elizabethan structure alongside, which was known once as Moll's Coffee House. The tiers of windows lean out and are crowned by a little gallery. Its front reminds one of an old ship - not surprising because it was here that Drake used to meet his captains. Nothing much has changed since his time. The oak panelling is almost black with age, and there is an intriguing gallery painted with 46 different coats of arms. The most fascinating sight though is the whole front of the low room, which is glass. I am told that there are no less than 230 panes and no two the same size.

Apart from the Cathedral, nothing can compare to the **Guildhall**, whose walls have stood for 650 years. It makes sure you will not miss it for it thrusts itself out into the busy main street, in amongst all the 20th century buildings. I can almost hear it saying 'I bet I will be here still when you are long gone.' Quite right too. Can you imagine C & A or Marks and Spencers still being there in 600 odd years? Inside it is quite lovely. The hall has a superb roof with gilded beams, from which hang dazzling candelabra. The city arms were carved and painted for Elizabeth I to give to Exeter in Armada year. Displayed elsewhere are royal and other gifts that have been collected over the years, including a sword used by Nelson and some of the rarest seals in the land. One dates back to 1175 and is believed to be the oldest in the country.

Next door there is something quite different but equally ancient. **The Turk's Head** which has been a hostelry since 1330, is now an eating house. The pub has been retained downstairs and eating areas have been created at other levels so that you can choose your venue. If you just want to eat and be away from the hustle and bustle of the bar, then a rear entrance takes you to the attractive first floor where food is foremost in everyone's Exeter is an ideal base for people wanting to explore East Devon and perhaps somewhere like **Ottery St Mary** which has a fabulous church of cathedral proportions modelled on Exeter Cathedral. There is a strange story about this church, that is if you believe in fairy-folk, particularly pixies. The church is supposedly home to a marauding band of them! Their life's work is to try and abduct the church's bellringers in order to prevent them ringing out their joyous peals. To banish this threat someone has to say 'Bless my Soul' after which the pixies disappear until their next opportunity. The secret password has worked so far and never once have the bells failed to be rung, except during the 1939-45 war of course, when all bells were silenced, only to sound if invasion was imminent.

Ottery like so many places, has an annual carnival which takes place on November 5th. Nothing strange in that but here young men rush through the main street carrying barrels of flaming tar, a sight worth beholding. Although two horrific fires in 1767 and 1866 destroyed most of the thatched cottages in Yonder Street and beyond, Ottery still has many Georgian buildings. One fine example, in Silver Street, houses one of the best restaurants in the county, Oswalds. Here you will sample French food in intimate and charming surroundings.

Exmouth, the oldest seaside town in Devon, is a cheerful, peaceful resort with a good beach. Not the most attractive place architecturally, apart from the rather distinguished houses on the Beacon, where Lady Nelson lived at No.6. and Lady Byron at No.19. Even these are strange houses. From the front they are beautiful but at the back nothing short of a mess. It was the practice at that time for developers to build outstanding facades, and let the owners decide on the rest. What a sad lady Nelson's widow must have been. Upon her death she was buried in the sublime cemetery attached to the church at Littleham just two miles away. In this overcrowded burial ground, her tomb, a copy of Nelson's in St Pauls Cathedral, albeit less ornate, rests under a great yew tree.

Pleasant hotels, a nice shopping area and still almost living in the past describes Exmouth. I like the solidity and sense of permanence at the Balcombe House Hotel standing in a delightful half acre of its own level lawns and gardens. It is a privately owned and run hotel where the simple policy is - the guests come first. **A la Ronde**, an 18th century Octagonal House belonging to the National Trust is one of the gems of the area along with the beautiful Bicton Gardens, a wonderful place for a day out for all ages.

The typically Devon village of **Otterton** is another place to visit and in its midst is the **Domesday Mill**. What a fantastic place and how nearly it was ruined by its former owners without a sense of history. Fortunately a teacher of Medieval Archaeology, Desna Greenhow, lived directly opposite this extraordinary place. She acquired the lease and set about restoring and running Otterton Mill. Today it is not only a great tourist attraction but, as originally intended, a mill working as it has been, grinding grain, since before the Norman Conquest. Several of the barns have been converted as well and turned into craft workshops for local crafts people. The restaurant serves excellent home-made fare using flour from the mill and in the shop you can buy home-baked bread and cakes. It is quite enthralling watching the two water-wheels and the mill machinery, part of which is wooden and part cast iron. The wheels vary from the 18th to the 19th centuries, and the great spur and crown wheels have applewood cogs. Milling on average, occurs only three days a week, but the machinery and restored wheel turns every day. Guided tours for groups must be booked in advance, although the miller often takes groups round informally on summer afternoons.

On my way to Otterton I stopped for a short while in **East Budleigh**. What a pretty place it is with some delightful cob-and-thatch buildings. Sir Walter Raleigh was born just a mile west of the village at Hayes Barton, which is a fine example of a Tudor house. I have always been attracted by bench ends in churches and the parish church of All Saints has more than sixty, most of them 16th century, if not older. They had been splendidly carved, probably by local craftsmen. The church is mainly 15th century although it was sympathetically restored in 1884. Decorating its walls are several memorials to the Rev. Ambrose Stapleton and his family. He was a beloved vicar who cared deeply for his parishioners, but like his counterpart at Thurlestone he is better known for his involvement in the smuggling industry, rampant in the early 1800's. Many a barrel of brandy was stored in his vicarage which was perhaps marginally less reprehensible than the vicar of Thurlestone who used the church roof.

No distance at all from East Budleigh is **Budleigh Salterton**, one of Devon's most charming and unspoilt places. There is a gentle brook running right through the street that houses the friendly shops. The brook starts its run at Squabmoor, a drab name for such a beautiful spot adjoining Woodbury Common. Like most beaches along this part of the coast with its red cliffs, the pebbles do not entice you to walk barefooted - but it is of no importance, the scenery makes up for any minor inconvenience.

Further along the coast you will come to one of my favourite parts of the Devon coast. Seemingly not quite of the 20th century, **Seaton, Sidmouth** and **Beer**, have altered little since coming to prominence in Victorian times. Sheltered in Lyme Bay, all sharing shingle and pebble beaches and the dignity of yesteryears, these are not places to visit if you want a sophisticated life.

Sidmouth springs into frenetic activity for the annual Folk Festival which has become the Mecca for entrants world wide. The first time I saw it I could not believe there were so many variations of Morris Dancing and Folk Singing, let alone the clacking Clog Dancers. Once over, Sidmouth returns to its demure, elegant self. You can stroll along the Regency Esplanade where, as a child, Queen Victoria was pushed in a little carriage by her father, the Duke of Kent. He would stop people and tell them to look carefully at the little girl for one day she would be their Queen. The house they lived in is now The Royal Glen Hotel. This charming place in which to stay, still has a sensitive understanding of the house's historical value and is kept very much in the style that was prevalent in the young princess's time. There is even a bullet hole in the window of Victoria's bedroom which happened when a small boy shooting sparrows, missed his target and the bullet smashed one of the nursery windows. It missed the future monarch by inches.

One of the most gentle and loving places in Sidmouth is **The Donkey Sanctuary**. For the last twenty four years Elizabeth Svendson MBE has devoted her life to the care and welfare of donkeys. This remarkable woman, furthermore, in 1975 increased her work to include handicapped children. Utilising the donkey's gentle nature, they were taken to special local schools where the children could ride and pet these loving animals. Her work since then has been unceasing and more and more children have been able to enjoy the donkeys.

Between Sidmouth and Seaton is **Branscombe** sprawling over two miles through a valley that is a delight. I love the thatched cottages and the narrow streets which have not widened since medieval times. **Beer;** the place and not the drink, is a particular personal favourite; little more than a fishing village which attracts an influx of visitors in the summer, but unlike many similar seaside haunts, it does not die in winter. The inhabitants have all sorts of activities, from amateur dramatics to coffee mornings. They are such friendly folk, too - quite willing to talk, especially the fishermen. Some of the older ones will tell of the days of smuggling which was rampant here. The notorious activities of one Jack Rattenbury are especially popular. He, it would seem, had in some way been in league with Lord Rolle, lord of the manor. It is difficult to pinpoint the relationship but Rolle history discloses that the infamous Jack was given a pension by his lordship. Lord Rolle lived at Bovey House just off the Beer to Sidmouth road. Turning into the drive of the house (one I would not care to walk alone at night) you can well believe in the spirits which reputedly haunt the trees to either side. One wonders, though, if these spectres were not the smugglers' inventions conjured up to deter unwanted visitors, whilst they stored their ill-gotten gains in the house. Certainly no one within living memory has seen a ghost.

Today Bovey House is an entrancing hotel. Built in the 16th century, it once belonged to Catherine Parr, to whom it was given by Henry VIII as part of her dowry. The opportunity to stay in an historic house is rare, so seize this chance if you can.

Seaton has that rare item today, a tramway. It is even more a rarity to find a tramway working on an old railway line. Once run along the promenade at Eastbourne, and doomed when the promenade's extension was planned, the tram was rescued by the enthusiast who cares for it today - a considerable benefit for Devon. The hour's journey travelling the three miles aboard the double-decked tram, through the Axe and Coly valleys along the route of the old railway, will take you to **Colyton** one of the prettiest small towns in Devon.

Colyton was settled as early as Saxon times and has a number of very attractive buildings. It stands at the mouth of a beautiful combe running into the Blackdown Hills. There is something very satisfying in walking along the many combes in this parish with their network of lanes linking farm to farm. Most of them have been there since medieval times and I wondered what the hedgerows housed then. They are beautiful now and alive with wildlife.

The village's 13th century parish church of St Andrew has been altered over the years with the aisles being rebuilt in 1765 and 1816 giving the arcades a curious style. If you look closely at the stone parclose screen, erected by the incumbent, Thomas Brerewood, who held the living from 1524-44, you will see the initials TB and a briar bush, obviously a pun on his name and evidence of a sense of humour which appeals to me.

In recent years **Honiton** in the east of the county has been bypassed and at last one is able to enjoy its wide main street and its street markets without the constant rush of impatient traffic. Elizabethan times accounted for the towns initial prosperity; lace makers were much sought after and business flourished. It was also reputedly the first town in Devon in which serges were made.

Two miles from Honiton off the main A30 London to Exeter road there is a turning to the left that will bring you into the delightful hamlet of **Gittisham** with its wide street, pale stone houses, lovely old cob-and-thatch cottages, and its church enshrining 500 years of the community's history. Ideally placed for easy access to the fine golf courses at Honiton, Sidmouth and Budleigh Salterton. However it is not just the hamlet that one wants to see. Turn into a winding drive through magnificent parkland and you will come to **Combe House Hotel**, a stately Elizabethan mansion, originally founded in the 1400's. Some of the attractions of Combe are the perfect serenity, beautiful walks and fine views; all of this I could appreciate as I sat in my car, in awe of the grandeur about me, almost hesitant to open the heavy main door in case I would be disappointed. How foolish! John Boswell, a direct descendant of James Boswell, the biographer first came to Combe, with his wife Therese, in 1970 with the intention of creating a hotel that they themselves would like to stay in. They have achieved a house of total grace and comfort combined with excellent service, facilities and the glory of the past. The house is totally welcoming and you will be pampered in the nicest way.

If I were using Honiton as a base for sightseeing, I think I would take a look at the little hamlet of **Yarcombe**. Still owned by descendants of Sir Francis Drake, now named Meyrick, there are tenant farmers round here who still pay rent to the family. Yarcombe is situated between Honiton and **Chard** on the A358, almost at the gateway to Devon. Dorset and Somerset are on the doorstep, yet it is only a tiny hamlet with a few houses, scattered farms and an ancient church, St John the Baptist. Probably little changed since Saxon times, then named Erticombe, it was owned by Earl Harold, of Battle of Hastings fame. It was renamed Herticombe in Elizabeth 1's reign, when the Queen granted part of the manor to Robert Dudley, Earl of Leicester. Subsequently sold to Sir Richard Drake, the third son of John Drake of Ashe, it was in turn conveyed to Sir Francis Drake, to whom Elizabeth granted the remainder of the estate. Quite a history for such a little place.

Driving from Yarcombe through the Blackdown Hills, in and out of the small lanes, is pleasurable and in due course you will come to **Chardstock**, not a spectacular place but it does have a very good hotel, The Tytherleigh Cot, built round a courtyard with super bedrooms, and a charmingly light and pretty Conservatory restaurant which is open to non-residents.

Three miles down the road from Chardstock, **Axminster** comes into view, currently a horror in which to drive. The curious shape of the town centre, dominated by the parish church of St Mary's does nothing to alleviate the traffic. However when you consider its town planning evolved through the last 2,000 years, perhaps it is no wonder. Upon entering St Mary's, I was flabbergasted to see a church so wonderfully carpeted, with its pews set back far beyond the norm so that one can take in its magnificence. The shock should be expected perhaps as Axminster is the home of carpeting. One of the earliest Axminsters made in 1775, can be seen in the Guildhall in which is also housed the original market charter dated 1210. Thomas Witty pioneered the carpet industry in Axminster, having discovered the techniques from the Turks. His first carpets were produced in a little building alongside the church, and so important was the completion of each carpet that the church bells were rung in celebration.

Musbury on the A358 between Axminster and Seaton is fascinating because of the Drake connections. His kinsmen lived here for generations, some rising to even greater heights than Sir Francis, and their memorials in the church make very interesting reading. John Drake, depicted together with his wife kneeling at a prayer desk was the father of Sir Bernard, who was knighted upon becoming an Admiral by Elizabeth I. A lasting memory of him and his wife is present as well, also one of his sons, John, and spouse. Another Sir John Drake is remembered by a stone in the aisle. It was his daughter Elizabeth, who married a Sir Winston Churchill, known for having lost all his estates and wealth trying to prop up the toppling Stuart throne. Their children are the stars of this story. Arabella was a royal favourite and John became the first Duke of Marlborough.

Ever onwards, completing the round trip to and from Honiton you find yourself passing a turning for **Dalwood**. Not a particularly remarkable place except for **Burrow Farm Garden**, a large bog garden in a Roman clay pit creating such fertile soil to produce a profuse display of azaleas, rhododendrons and roses. A wondrous sight at the right time of the year. Also, the National Trust own **Loughwood Meeting House** at Dalwood. Nearby **Kilmington** was a stronghold of Baptists about 1653 and this simple, unadorned building was for their regular use until 1833. Surviving intact, it can now be seen throughout the year by one and all.

Wandering about Devon is one of the great pleasures of my life and I find myself equally enchanted with every corner. For those who like a resort atmosphere **Torbay** has to be the answer. It always gives one the feel of being on the French Riviera. The sea is a brilliant Mediterranean blue coming ashore to sandy beaches and row upon row of sparkling white buildings which range from high class hotels like the world famous Imperial Hotel set in 5 acres of lush gardens, in a sheltered position commanding a view across the English 'Bay of Naples'. From the day it opened its doors in 1866 The Imperial has been the haunt of royalty and film stars, famous people and those who just want to be pampered and indulged in what must be England's foremost resort hotel. At the other end of the scale there are many welcoming small guest houses whilst in between there is every variation on accommodation including holiday apartments. Torbay is made up not just of **Torquay** but of **Paignton** and the old fishing port of **Brixham** as well. It is as welcoming out of season with comparatively mild weather. In recent years it has become very popular for those who like to take short breaks in addition to their longer holidays. You will find a whole range of themed breaks including those devoted to Ballroom Dancing.

Brixham has always been the home of fishermen, whose houses perch on the side of the hills, leading to Higher Brixham. Some are close to the harbour or open onto little streets or steps bringing their occupants to the seafront. Whilst tourism is not ignored here, it has always had to take second place to the fishing industry, and so the character of the town has changed little over the centuries. More homes have been built on the outskirts but no one can change its narrow streets and its charm. For me Brixham will always stay in my mind whenever I hear that wonderful hymn 'Abide with me'. It was written by Henry Francis Lyte, vicar for quarter of a century, of the 19th-century All Saints Church. It is a hymn that has been sung throughout the Christian world by people in times of great emotion. My father told me that in World War I it was sung by men in the trenches and when they had finished the Germans would take it up from their dug-outs. It has brought peace to thousands. Henry Lyte wrote it in the dusk after evening service. He did not know that he had taken his last service in the church. He died not long afterwards. If you listen you will hear the bells of All Saints ring out his hymn every night.

Paignton is renowned for having one of the best Zoos in the country. The town and seafront are gentle places generally. Flowers and rockeries along the promenade and a wonderful park, man-made out of marsh this century, are the outstanding features. Paignton is the sort of place that people of my age enjoy in the spring, autumn and even the winter but who will probably avoid it like the plague in the height of the season.

No one comes to Torquay without seeing **Cockington**. If you want to see it at its best go early in the morning, soon after sunrise when it is still. Later it will be swamped with visitors and all you will remember will be the crowds and perhaps the thatched cottages. Seen early it is as if you were back in the 16th-17th century when Cockington Court was first built.

A cut through the lanes from here brought me back to the **Newton Abbot** bypass, a busy road but one that cuts down the endless traffic jams of not so many years ago. Just off the road and surrounded by narrow lanes and bridleways meant for pack horses and pedestrians rather than the mechanised 1990's. Take a look at **Ipplepen**, a village as old as time. Conan Doyle spent many a happy visit here with his friend Bertie Robinson who lived at Parkhill House. Exploring Dartmoor was one of his great pleasures and he used to be driven in a horse and carriage by the Robinson groom, one Harry Baskerville. Did you ever wonder where the title 'Hound of the Baskervilles' originated? Now you know.

Ipplepen is surrounded by attractive places. **Torbryan-through-Ipplepen** is one of the most picturesque districts of Devon, far removed from the bustle and turmoil of the modern world. It has a superb church and another showpiece of tremendous interest, The Old Church House Inn, which stands almost in the shadow of the church. It is a hostelry that must be visited.

No one ever denies the beauty of **Broadhempston** reached through a network of small lanes. Its church is 15th century with graceful arcades, old carved beams and bosses in its porch and roofs. The hostelry, The Coppa Dolla Inn, is mentioned in the Domesday Book. It is a memorable experience to take a meal here. For longer than one cares to remember it has been the meeting place for many local farmers and has a welcoming buzz of conversation as you walk through the doors.

If you take the coastal road out of Torquay you will come to **Teignmouth** and **Dawlish** two unashamedly Victorian resorts of great charm. On the approach to Teignmouth a turning off at **Shaldon** just before the bridge will take you to **Stoke-in-Teignhead**. It lies in one of Devon's combes by the mouth of the Teign. Full of pretty cottages and an old church which must have been here in Norman times. When you look at the mosaics in the sanctuary, you will wonder how so many years ago, such work was done by Italian craftsmen. Where did they stay, how did they cope with the language barrier and how long did their journey take?

Dawlish is close to **Powderham Castle**, one of the quiet glories of Devon, built between 1390 and 1420. It has been the home of the Courtenay family ever since. Sir Philip Courtenay was the first occupant, the sixth son of the second Earl of Devon, from whom the present Earl is directly descended. If you look at the castle you will see that every generation has made some form of alteration in order to keep up with the changes of their time. None of this has detracted from its beauty. A visit to Powderham will always remain in your mind as a red letter day.

Taking the road out of Teignmouth towards the busy market town of **Newton Abbot** do not miss the little village of Bishopsteignton and especially the 16th century Cockhaven Manor Inn, one of the most romantic inns in Devon.

Going further south west one comes to **The South Hams**, one of the prettiest areas in the whole of Devon. It is far quieter than its next door neighbour, Torbay, and for the most part less commercial. I started this journey by having coffee in Modbury, built on the slopes of a valley with four main streets intersecting at right angles. The main street is full of nice buildings and innumerable little shops. Always busy it has the bonus of a free car park. After climbing up hill and down dale you might enjoy The Exeter Inn where you will find evidence of the Civil War. It was used as the headquarters for the Royalist forces under the command of General John Trevanion, prior to the battle of Modbury. It is full of character, low ceilings, rich dark beams, wooden settles and tables. The menu is ever changing and there are six very differently decorated bedrooms with very comfortable four-poster beds.

DEVON

The road from Modbury towards the sea, winds its way towards **Kingsbridge** but every so often there is a turning right which will take you down a narrow lane to a beach. The first one is **Kingston** which boasts The Dolphin Inn, a popular place serving good food. A short walk from there will take you to **Wonwell** beach which I think is at its best in the winter or early spring, when you can walk along its deserted sandy stretch almost to **Bigbury-on-Sea**. Here the beach gives immense pleasure to thousands of people every summer. It is quite heavily commercialised.

What is exciting though is **Burgh Island**, which lies off the coast and is accessible by foot across the sand at low tide and by sea tractor from the car park at high tide. Small and magical, the island was first inhabited in AD 900 by a Monastic order who built a chapel on the summit. Slowly a fishing community came into being and by the 14th century it was thriving. There is only one cottage left today and that is now The Pilchard Inn, a delightful port of call after a walk across the sands. Burgh Island also has a famous hotel of the same name, owned by Tony Porter and his wife. Built in the 1920's it was almost derelict when they bought it in 1985. Now they have restored it superbly and once again it has the 1920's look beloved of the rich and famous who used to stay here in the 1930s including the then Prince of Wales and Wallis Simpson. Noel Coward stayed here and so did the Mountbattens. By the mid-1930's it had become the 'in' place to be and known as the smartest hotel west of the Ritz. The Porters love affair with the island and the hotel became almost a cult story with magazines and newspapers, so when they re-opened in March 1988, the word had spread across the world. People came from London, New York, Los Angeles and Europe and loved every moment of their stay. You will find Saturday nights are particularly good fun. Everyone dresses in 1920's style and the live music rapidly gets people in the mood for dancing to tunes of the era. The food is excellent, the friendly informality superb and the Porters are wonderful hosts.

From here back on the main A379 going towards Kingsbridge there is a turn on the right which will take you to the village of **Thurlestone.** It stands on the craggy South Hams coastline with marvellous views of Thurlestone Rock, an extraordinary natural arch on the seashore, and Bigbury Bay, with its vast expanse of sands. On a summer's day it is a still, calm haven, but the winter winds rise and the seas thunder in, roaring through the rock and pounding the shore, creating a noise that is peculiarly its own. Once the village was the hideout for many smugglers who foiled the excisemen by hiding their contraband in the roof of the church, with the full permission of the vicar who expected a keg or two of wine or brandy for his trouble! Baiting the excisemen was the sport of the day all the way along this coast. Sport today is mainly golf.

Although Thurlestone's course is not championship quality, it is one of the most sought after in the county and one of the most difficult to play. The village is a gentle place and in its midst is The Thurlestone Hotel. There is something about privately owned hotels that cannot be beaten. David Grose and his brother Graham are the inspiration behind this family business today emulating the standards that their great-grandmother Margaret Amelia started in 1896. The hotel is top notch, run beautifully and has a staff who change rarely. Ideal for anyone wanting a quiet, pampered holiday.

Another narrow lane off the A379 will take you down to **Hope Cove**. So many people miss Thurlestone and Hope Cove because they are tucked away. A sad omission. There is nothing much to do at Hope Cove except enjoy the sea and sand, water ski or just take off in a boat. Fishing was once the main source of income for the village, especially for mackerel and pilchards. Huge shoals used to be caught not far offshore. In fact the first little bay below **Bolt Tail** is still known as Pilchards Cove. The few remaining fishermen take their boats out to catch lobsters and crabs, which are eagerly awaited by locals and visitors.

And so to **Salcombe**, a place that never fails to stir my soul with its beauty. Its harbour is always full of all sorts and sizes of marine craft. Yachtsmen throughout the world make for the shelter of this wonderful estuary. Its narrow streets and charm attract thousands of visitors every year. I like it best out of season when one can enjoy its beauty without the congestion. Salcombe is full of memories. Tennyson adored it. The harbour entrance has the ruined wall of a medieval castle which guarded shipping 450 years ago and stood for King Charles against Cromwell. The little town is delightful to walk through and almost all the time you can catch glimpses of the ever changing scenery and colours of the estuary. It is a place to stand and stare and certainly to stay if you can. There are many hotels, pubs and guesthouses which offer excellent accommodation.

Just across the estuary from Salcombe is **East Portlemouth**. The easiest way to get to it is by the little ferry from Salcombe, which runs during the summer months. To get there by road you have to go right round the top of the estuary and then face the nightmare of traffic in narrow lanes. The beaches are the real attraction but everywhere there is something to see. The National Trust own the cliffs and you can walk as far as **Prawle Point**, Devon's southernmost tip. Had you come by car, more narrow lanes would have taken you to **East Prawle** and then to the ghost village of **Hallsands,** which hangs over the sea, disappearing more every year. This once prosperous little fishing village died in a storm in 1917 when it was washed away. It is something that should never have happened. Shingle was needed for the Dockyard in Plymouth and at Hallsands it was easy to dredge. The loss of the shingle left the village unprotected from the savage sea. Wandering the lanes going northwards for a few miles you will come to **Beesands** where the fishermen's cottages are right on the shore. It is a nice way to while away a lazy hour watching the fishing boats being launched from the foreshore.

Torcross is a place, tranquil in summer, which turns to the seething fury of a witches, cauldron when the ferocious gale force winds and thundering seas shake the exposed coastline. It is the beginning of an area which was totally taken over by the Americans in World War II. At the end of the village there is a Sherman tank which was raised from the sea just offshore in 1984, forty years after it was sunk in rehearsals for the D-Day Normandy landings. 749 Americans lost their lives off this beach when preying German E-Boats pounced on them unawares. Looking at it today it is hard to believe that Slapton Sands and Torcross were the hub of American activity in 1943-4. The beach was in constant use for practising the amphibious landings. Whole villages were evacuated and the villagers found homes elsewhere. In recent years an obelisk has been erected to commemorate this piece of history. Behind is the **Slapton Ley Nature** reserve which is both beautiful and full of wildlife. There is a Field Studies Centre too.

Continue along this route through the village of **Strete,** perhaps stopping at the little cove below **Stoke Fleming** where Warwick the Kingmaker is said to have landed. It is a small world of its own and strangely named **Blackpool.**

Kingsbridge is charming. It rises steeply from the Salcombe estuary. The tower of the church stands on massive 13th century arches; much of the rest is anything from the 15th century to the nave and aisles of the 20th century. There is a wonderful inscription on the wall outside the priest's doorway which must have been there for hundreds of years. It says:

Here lies I at the chancel door,
Here lies I because I am poor,
The farther in the more you'll pay,
Here lies I as warm as they.

For such a small town it has produced some remarkable people. George Montague, whose collection of animals and birds is in the British Museum; John Hicks, the Protestant minister who was persuaded to march under Monmouth to Sedgemoor and, after defeat, found a hiding place with Lady Alice Lisle at Ellingham in Hampshire. She, poor soul, had no idea he was escaping and when he was discovered she was hauled off to Wincheser for trial by the brutal Judge Jeffreys, who sentenced her to death. Then there is William Cookworthy who found a way of using Cornish China Clay to make English porcelain. He is remembered in The Cookworthy Museum of Rural Life, in Fore Street. Housed in a wonderful 17th century school building, it has period costumes, porcelain, old local photographs, a complete Victorian pharmacy and a magical world of dolls houses and toys which delight children of all ages.

The A381 takes you from Kingsbridge to **Dartmouth** the undoubted 'show stopper' of the South Hams but just before you reach it take a look at **Stoke Fleming**, two miles outside Dartmouth. It stands three hundred feet above Start Bay. Its streets are narrow and a walk along the cliff will leave you spellbound. You can almost imagine that you are in Atlantis when you see traces of a submerged forest along the shore, and the great rocks called, for some unknown reason, the Dancing Beggars. It is a village of little activity; not the place to stay if you need entertaining but the sheer beauty of the surroundings is reason enough. The place to stay is Stoke Lodge Hotel where comfort and good food are the order of the day.

You approach Dartmouth from the top of a steep hill. If the traffic permits stop for a moment or two to catch the stunning panoramic view of the town and the river. The town's dramatic scenery is heightened by the tiers of houses which cling for dear life to the hillside overlooking the River Dart. I have never thought of it as being a very comfortable place to live because of the endless hills, but nonetheless it is a town I love visiting.

The waterfront is always busy no matter what the time of the year. In the summer the pleasure traffic on the river is accompanied by the thousands of boats of the yachting fraternity. There are constant passenger and car ferries crossing the busy river to **Kingswear** on the other side, from whence it is an easy run into Torbay. A lot of people come down to Kingswear and leave their cars there, then take the ferry across to explore the delights of this very old town which has seen more history than most. There is a method in their madness. Dartmouth is one of the most difficult places in which to park during the season.

Dartmouth was important as early as 1147 when it was used as a point of assembly for the Second Crusade. Much of the waterfront land has since been reclaimed making the New Quay. As late as 1567 ships were still tied up to the churchyard wall of St Saviours. This is quite the most interesting church in the town. It was dedicated in 1372 but much altered in the late 15th century and again in the 1630's. If you take a look at the magnificent west gallery and take a guess at the astronomical sum it would take to build today, you will be astonished to know that at that time it cost just fifteen pounds.

Because of the sheltered deepwater, the harbour has always been sought after and in the 12th century Dartmouth rose to being the fourth most important town in Devon after Plymouth, Exeter and Barnstaple. All the cloth trade from Totnes came down to the Dart; wine from France was the main import and wealthy merchants and shipmasters made it their home. John Hawley was the greatest of them all and his driving force took the town forward. Chaucer visited in 1373 and his meeting with Hawley probably inspired him to uses the man as the Shipman in the Canterbury Tales. After Hawley's death Dartmouth lost its way until around 1580 when trade again flourished. Many of the wonderful buildings which fill the eye with pleasure, were built between this time and 1643. Much of the old town has either been preserved or restored. I wandered along the Butterwalk, revelling in the black-and-white houses and shops and then along the frontage of the quay. Up the steps by the side of the Harbour Bookshop, once owned by A.A. Milne's son Christopher Robin, is The Cherub Inn, the oldest building in Dartmouth.

Britannia Royal Naval College, a splendid red brick building, stands high above Dartmouth and contributes largely to the prosperity of the town. It is the home for all basic naval officer training, both male and female. Gone are the days when boys used to come here at the age of thirteen to finish their schooling and be trained as young naval officers at the same time. Today's young men and women are never less than eighteen and frequently graduates. The decision to build the college was made by the Admiralty in 1896 and the foundation stone laid by Edward VII on 7th March 1902. Since then it has produced some famous naval officers, amongst them Prince Philip. It was here that he first met our Queen when, as Princess Elizabeth, she came with her parents, King George VI and Queen Elizabeth, to the college for the spectacular passing out parade. This takes place on the quarterdeck of the college every year but not always in the presence of the monarch.

Along the quayside you will see notices advertising river trips up to **Totnes** and elsewhere. If you have time, take to the water, for the trip covers some of the most beautiful scenery in the county. On a sunny day the brilliant blue of the water finds it hard to compete with the endless variation of greens to be seen in the trees and fields. You will see **Dittisham**, a village of thatched stone cottages winding through plum orchards and daffodil fields down to the river. From the quay by an old inn, a passenger ferry plies its trade, signalling its approach by ringing a large brass bell. It is the epitome of a peaceful English scene, but remember this river, arguably the most beautiful in England, has been the means of bringing wealth to many places throughout our history. From choice I would always approach Totnes by river, but more practically, the pretty A3122 leads through the village of **Harbertonford**, an awkward place with an even more awkward bend as you approach it but for me it has two special places. The Maltsters Arms, a hostelry of great repute and the Maryland Health Hydro and Country Hotel, a place in which to stay, relax, be pampered and be well fed on a wonderfully varied menu of healthy well presented food.

Totnes, first mentioned in the reign of Edgar about AD 959, was probably a small settlement. Since then many tales have been told about this busy, attractive town which is not much more than one long beautiful street climbing up a hill by the River Dart. It has a superb, old guildhall which houses the museum.

Every Tuesday morning in the summer **Totnes Elizabethan Society** members and local traders dress in Tudor costume to raise thousands of pounds for charity. It has become a world famous spectacle and celebrates the town's 16th century heritage. During the English Civil War, a major turning point in British history, Oliver Cromwell, Charles I and General Fairfax were all to be seen in the streets of Totnes during their campaigns.

Totnes mathematician, Charles Babage built the first prototype computer here as long ago as the 1820's. You can see and hear more about this in the museum. Daniel Defoe wrote about Totnes and the world famous artist, Turner, painted its valley and castle. The town has a proud monument to the famous Australian explorer William Wills, who died opening up the outback in 1861; a Totnes man, he is a national hero the other side of the world. The great Victorian engineer Isambard Kingdom Brunel built the pumping station for his ill-fated 'Atmospheric Railway' which can be seen alongside the railway line. Sixty years ago, pioneering American millionairess Dorothy Elmhirst and her husband set up the Dartington Hall Trust to promote rural regeneration. Today the Dartington complex is a world leader in the fields of education, arts promotion, research, farming and business innovation.

Agatha Christie thriller writer, Desmond Bagley, and modern novelist Mary Wesley are just three famous writers who have made the Dart Valley their home. While you are in Totnes there are many things to see and do. Looking for somewhere to stay then I suggest The Old Forge in Seymour Place, a fine building converted from a 600-year-old stone built smithy, complete with a wheelwright's workshop, coach house and stables which served Berry Pomeroy Castle and its estate in the old days. Now it provides bed and breakfast accommodation in great comfort for travellers, business people and the holiday visitors. A coach arch through the building gives access to a delightful walled garden where cream teas are available on summer afternoons.

Talking of **Berry Pomeroy**, I recommend a visit to reputedly Devon's most romantic and mysterious **Berry Pomeroy Castle**.For me exploring the South Hams is a never ending treasure hunt with constantly different and unexpected clues to its beauty.

Wherever you are in Devon **Dartmoor** is not far away. There are do's and don'ts for exploring the moor. Make sure before you start any excursion on Dartmoor that you have with you stout walking shoes and a good map. Dartmoor is without peer in its beauty but it is treacherous. Sudden changes of weather are frequent leaving the unwary caught in swirling mists which descend fast.

What is unchanging about Dartmoor is the love affair that people have with it. It is almost like a good marriage; it is sometimes turbulent, sometimes inexplicable, mysterious exciting, infuriating, but always beloved. Within its encompassing arms you wake in the morning never knowing what the day will bring. People who live on the moor are a breed of their own, generous enough to want to share their love affair with outsiders and astonished if your reaction is not the same as theirs. No intrusion of man since prehistoric times has managed to conquer the wildness of the granite mass, some 130,000 acres in all.

There are fundamental lessons to learn about Dartmoor before you start exploring. It is a National Park, but that does not mean you have unlimited access. For example, it is an offence to drive a car more than 15 yards off the road. You are asked not to feed the ponies because it encourages them to stray on to the roads, putting themselves and road users into danger. There is a severe fine for those who do not heed this request. One other important point is to take note if red flags are flying on the north side of the moor. This means that the army is at work. Disobey the warning and you could get shot!

On this flying visit to Dartmoor we will assume I have started from Plymouth. Just outside the city the National Park starts and as I drive on to the moor I am immediately enthralled by the vast panoramic view as the road crosses the distance from **Roborough** to **Yelverton**. I stop at Yelverton to take a look at the fabulous **Paperweight Centre** at **Leg**

O'Mutton Corner, with its overwhelming beauty of colour. To the left is the little village of **Buckland Monachorum** with The Drake Manor Inn next to the church. You might come here before visiting **Buckland Abbey.** Whether you come from the pub or Yelverton, the little time it takes to get there is insufficient to prepare you for its beauty. it lies tucked away in a valley, surrounded by trees, and no one would imagine today, how much a part it has played as home to the masters of some of the most thrilling episodes in English history. Cistercian monks from Quarr on the Isle of Wight, first came here in 1278, and then after the Dissolution it was bought by Sir Richard Grenville for his son, Roger. His son, Richard, the most famous of all the Grenvilles, lived here whilst he planned a voyage to seek a southern route around America to the Pacific. He never got the opportunity because he was beaten to it by his rival, Drake. His chagrin was so great that he sold the Abbey and went to a retreat in Cornwall. Buckland was purchased by John Hele but he was only acting as a nominee. Drake was the true purchaser which was like rubbing a salt in a wound to Grenville. Even being knighted by the Queen did not make it any better. Had he known that Drake was going to live at Buckland he would never have sold it.

On now to the Stannary town of **Tavistock**, a favourite haunt of mine. I love its sense of pride and stability. It has so much history which started a hundred years before the Conqueror, and was originally controlled by its Abbey. You can seek out a great deal of the past in the fine medieval parish church, with its pinnacled tower, its wide nave, and countless gables that dominate the streets. It may well have been here that Francis Drake was taken to worship as a child for Tavistock is his hometown, something one is never allowed to forget. The Bedford Hotel is probably the best hotel here. It has great charm and character and is one of Forte's more individual establishments. It stands opposite the church and next door, is the vicarage. Between them they hold precious pieces of the past. The hotel has a fragment of the old abbey within its walls, and in the Vicarage gardens is the Great Gate with the abbot's prison in the ruined tower above it. Betsy Grimbal's Tower stands here as well. Betsy was a nun murdered by a lovelorn monk.

From here one ought to take a look at Morwellham Quay, a restored Victorian copper port. Here you can take a train ride into a copper mine, board an old ketch in the harbour, go on a carriage ride, watch the splendid shire-horses or take a look at the various exhibitions.

Many small villages surround Tavistock, all of which are worth seeing. On the Okehampton road there are two Tavys, Mary and Peter, the twins who grew out of the settlement on either side of the River Tavy. Each has a church linked together by a bridle path and a little bridge over the river, known as 'The Clam', an old name for a bridge. The Peter Tavy Inn is very old and world famous. It has recently been beautifully refurbished, losing none of its old character. Great food, good company and comfortable rooms make this a good stopping place.

Mining was the main industry in the two villages until the 1920s and you can see many remains of the old workings. The engine house of Wheal Betsy for one, which was part of the extensive workings of an old silver and lead mine. Women worked on the surface of this mine breaking up ore. They were known as Bal Maidens. Bal is an old word for mine which is more often used in Cornwall than Devon. There is still a Bal Lane in **Mary Tavy.** The village pub is The Royal Standard run by Rob Fairy, his daughter Lynne and his son-in-law Tony. A good pub which got its name from royalty at some time staying there.

No one should miss seeing **Lydford Gorge**, an unsurpassed beauty spot now in the care of the National Trust. Water pours off the moor onto the boulders of Lydford Gorge with a ferocity that would overshadow a witches cauldron. You can stand on the little footbridge looking 300ft down the gorge and see nature at its most beautiful and mysterious. Close by is **Lydford Castle** - not a happy place. The horror of the past still lingers and it is said that you will never see a bird perching on its walls; they have an inborn alarm system that steers them away from evil. All that remains of the castle now is the keep, but for a long time it was used as a prison for Stannary Law offenders. These Tinners had the so-called privilege of being tried by their fellow tradesmen under the unique Lydford Law. Quite horrendous was the outcome. More often than not the offender was hung, drawn and quartered in the morning and the trial held in the afternoon! What if the man were innocent? You can still feel the sense of evil today.

Lydford has a wonderful church that stems from the 7th century but is mainly 15th century. Look around the churchyard and you will spot the fascinating epitaph to George Routleigh, watchmaker:

He had the art of disposing of his time so well that his hours
glided away in one continual round of pleasure and delight
till an unlucky minute put a period to his existence.

A mile or so away is **Lewtrenchard** where the famous Sabine Baring-Gould was the rector for 43 years. He gave so much to the world apart from the restoration of this lovely old church and his wonderful hymns. Who could ever forget 'Onward Christian Soldiers' or 'Now the Day is Over'? Close by his old home Lewtrenchard Manor is now a stunning country house hotel. It was Sabine who embellished Lewtrenchard and made it quite out of the ordinary. He was an intrepid traveller and a compulsive collector which resulted in his bringing home interesting architectural features, so much part of the house today. It is wonderful and after a day of enjoying the fabulous countryside coming home to this glorious house, dining supremely well and then sleeping in the greatest comfort in a room named after one of Sabine's hymns -'Now the Day is Over' perhaps - confirms the reason to make a visit here a must.

Another place worth a mention here is **Liftondown**. This is a great place from which to visit the surrounding area as it is situated between the two moors Bodmin and Dartmoor, and at the same time is only 18 miles from the North Cornish coast. Next door at **Milford, Lifton** is **Dingles Steam Village** which offers a unique opportunity to view our industrial heritage in a beautiful location. Dingles features a wealth of working traction engines, steam rollers, vintage machinery and exhibits that will evoke fond memories of an earlier era. Much of the collection was used by the original Dingle family, one of the largest firms of road makers in the area.

Housed in 20,000 sq.ft. of undercover exhibition space the working machinery combines with heritage material and displays. The village also offers walks and picnic spots along the banks of the rivers Thrushel and Wolf, as well as Mrs. Dingles Kitchen for the best in home baking, a gift shop and children's play area.

Facilities are first class and geared to cope with any visitor's needs and include large coach and car parks, smooth pathways and disabled access ramps and toilets. Special groups are always welcome and guided tours, seated talks and party meals can be arranged by request.

The Steam Village- situated 1 / 2 mile from the A30 dual carriageway (exit for Roadford Lake) at Stowford Cross is open 6 days a week 10 a.m. - 6.00 p.m. from Easter until the end of October (closed Fridays). For more details and party rates please contact Dingles information line 01566 783425.

Also nearby is **Ashwater** where you will find the wonderful Blagdon Manor which as well as being a delightful place to stay, has history oozing out of every pore.

To the north of the moor is **Okehampton**, a town which does not really get the attention it deserves. It is a market town selling the agricultural produce of the surrounding area, but for the visitor it is an excellent centre for touring and exploring this part of the moor. If you want to walk the moor and would like to stay with someone who is an experienced wildlife and walking expert then I wholeheartedly recommend Heathfield House on the outskirts of the town. Owned and run by Jane Seigal, the house literally backs onto the edge of the moor. Jane has converted quite an ordinary house into a comfortable hotel in which every bedroom is en-suite. She is a superb cook and housekeeper which, one would think, would take all her time but, not a bit of it, she is so well organised that part of staying at Heathfield is walking with her on the moor to all her favourite places. She will take you to little known spots, and point out to you, on the way, the bird life, which is her great love. Jane is not a bossy walker! You can take the walks at your own pace and enjoy them. If she is not with you, she will map a route out for you, or perhaps direct you to somewhere other than the moors. Heathfield is a non-smoking house. Perhaps one of the greatest pleasures whilst staying at Heathfield, is that at night everyone tends to sit around after dinner, sipping a glass of wine and chatting over the day's activities.

Two places should be included in a visit to Okehampton. The first is the romantic **Okehampton Castle**, and the second **The Museum of Dartmoor Life** set around a pretty courtyard, in an old mill, off the High Street. Full of interest, with ever changing exhibitions.

One walk Jane Seigal might take you on is to **Throwleigh** (pronounced 'Ow' as in cow). What a pretty place, unbothered by time. It has a village cross, a church with a thatched lychgate and an ancient thatched church house surrounded by other attractive cottages. Once at Throwleigh you are almost at one of my favourite hotels in the whole of Britain. A tortuous one and a half miles from Chagford is Gidleigh Park. It is a road that goes nowhere apart from one or two houses and finally ends up at the hotel. In front of you, you will see a pretty, 1920's black and white house sitting gracefully above a tiered garden that runs down to the River Teign. Once inside it is quietly sumptuous, furnished with comfortable restraint and exuding an air of well being and welcome. Expensive but worth every penny.

Chagford is the nearest small town to Gidleigh and should not be missed. It is a sleepy place that has grown over the centuries round the village square. Do visit James Bowden & Sons. It is an experience. Founded in 1862 it can only be called an emporium. It calls itself an ironmongers but that only just touches on all that it sells. This is a Stannary Town where tinners would come from miles around to have their precious metal weighed and given the King's Stamp before it was sold. Farmers too would come to sell their cattle and sheep and, in particular, their fleeces, for wool was an important industry. All this activity was watched over by the most distinctive of the town's many historic buildings; the old market house in the middle of the square.

Just across the way is **Drewsteignton**, home to the amazing **Castle Drogo**, the last castle to be built in this country. Julius Drewe was responsible for it and got Sir Edwin Lutyens to design it. Lutyens plans were a bit too ambitious and expensive. Julius Drewe had allowed ,60,000 for the building and the gardens in 1910. It does not sound much today but remember at that time you could buy a four bedroomed house for ,200! What was built was a third of the size intended but it is still huge and Lutyens has managed to capture a sense of medieval times, even without the great hall and other rooms that his original plans demanded. The windows with their small panes are distinctly in the manner of Tudor times. There are many grand and stately chambers and the gardens are lovely. Now owned by the National Trust.

From Castle Drogo, which got its name from the Drogo who owned the manor in the days of Richard the Lionheart, it is only a stone's throw into the village of Drewsteignton, standing high above the wooded valley of the River Teign. It is a village of total charm with its thatched cottages and a hilltop church from medieval days.

The enchanted world of **Fingle Bridge** is just below Drewsteignton. You do not simply arrive there, you have to look for it. It is hidden away at the end of a long, winding leafy lane that seems to descend for ever, until suddenly there it is; a low pack horse bridge which dates back to Elizabethan times, if not earlier, straddling a river dancing and cavorting as it plays with the boulders strewn in its path. Once across the bridge you will find that the road comes to a grinding halt. The paths leading away from the bridge were probably the way that merchants came with their laden pack-horses and the terrain was too difficult to develop further. We can count ourselves lucky that this was so, otherwise Fingle Bridge might not have survived the wear and tear of men and vehicles over the years. For refreshment at Fingle Bridge, The Anglers Rest is excellent. Run by the Price family for several generations, it has high standards and caters for everyone.

There are three Iron Age hill forts around Fingle Gorge. **Prestonbury** you can see clearly from the bridge. **Wooston** is down river and if you see it on a spring morning with the sun behind you, it is breathtaking. The third **Cranbrook,** is higher up.

At **Shilstone** to the west is the best known of the cromlech or dolmens in Devon with the odd name of **Spinster's Rock**. Legend has it that three spinsters put it in place, but fact says it is the remains of a Bronze Age megalithic tomb.

Moretonhampstead holds the key to so much that is beautiful. Within my lifetime it has changed considerably. Forty years ago it was a shopping centre for farmers and people living in outlying hamlets. It had everything a community needed. Today the butcher is still there and the chemist, but the general store is no more and it is only recently that a baker returned. It gets its livelihood mainly from tourists. The hampstead part has been added in the last century or so and most local people ignore it, calling the little town Moreton, derived from the Saxon Mor Tun. The 15th century church of St Andrew, standing on high ground, has tombstones in the porch in memory of two French officers who lived at Moreton during the Napoleonic Wars, when they were on parole from their prison at Princetown.

What an extraordinary race we are! Given half a chance the French would have invaded and made Britain hell had they succeeded and yet we let prisoners wander at large. I wondered who paid for them and where their spending money came from. Were they persona grata at social occasions or were society matrons warned to lock up their daughters?

Four major fires occurred between 1845 and 1892 and many of the old buildings were destroyed. Apart from the almshouses, which were built in 1637 and narrowly missed demolition in the 1930's because they were not considered hygienic, the most stunning building, and the oldest is **Mearsden Manor**, a reminder of medieval times. Inside Mearsden Manor is an Aladdins Cave of treasure from all round the world which you are encouraged to take a look at and make your purchases. It is fascinating and totally unexpected in Moreton. Having wandered round it is well worth being tempted into the oak-panelled tea rooms, where you can get a light lunch or enjoy a piece of home-made cake with a piping hot cup of fresh coffee or tea.

If you have time do take a look at the villages of **Doccombe, Dunsford, Bridford**, and **Christow**, each has its own merits and all are part of the Dartmoor scene.Close to Moreton is one of my favourite places **Becky Falls**. High up in the solitude of Dartmoor you approach it through glorious woods. On one side of the road there is a car park, where, if you have any sense, you will don stout shoes or wellies, before making the descent alongside Becka brook, where the water cascades over and between massive boulders until with a roar it reaches its peak, and falls in sparkling torrents, on its way to the sea. This enchanted world is at its best after the mid-winter rains. I saw it on a sunlit morning in November when the autumn colours of the leaves and the bushes added lustre to the silver-grey of the tumbling water.

Moments up the road is the isolated village of **Manaton**, with its green nestling beside the church. It is mentioned in the Domesday book and seems to have been there forever. Overlooked by the lofty **Manaton Tor**, which if seen in autumn, aglow with the berries of holly and mountain ash, will remind you that there are not many more shopping days to Christmas. Away to the south the great rocks known as **Bowerman's Nose** look like a petrified sentinel guarding the rugged hills, or a man with a sense of humour wearing a cardinal's hat playing God.

Whilst Manaton remains essentially Dartmoor, **Lustleigh** to the east, like Moreton, has changed completely in the last two decades. There was a time when this rural community lived simply in the beautiful valley of the Wrey. They gained their livelihood from small holdings and cultivating productive vegetable gardens, seldom venturing away. A journey to Exeter was a once in a lifetime experience. Nowadays the 13th century church still stands. Look out for the mischievous carving of the small heads on top of the screen which was erected in Tudor times. The craftsman obviously had likes and dislikes; all the heads facing the chancel have a secret grin on their faces and those towards the nave, a scowl. The village is still beautiful, with thatched cottages surrounding the village green. Village cricket still flourishes and at weekends you can sit and watch on a field, fringed with alders, and make believe that the noise and trauma of the 20th century does not exist.

Bovey Tracey is one of the Gateways to Dartmoor, and an attractive place in its own right. It has been important since the days of the Normans, when the manor was held by Edric, a Saxon thane. In the last few years it has lost much of its peacefulness with the arrival of new businesses, which have taken the opportunity of entrenching themselves close to the A38. It still has delightful narrow streets and sits sedately overlooking the River Bovey. Newcomers may not know some of the wonderful legends that exist about the town and if they did I am not sure they would believe them. Would you believe that Sir William Tracy built the 12th century church of St Thomas a Becket as a penance for being one of his murderers? Not satisfied with one church, he built three. Sir William's church went up in flames 150 years later, but what has been left for us to enjoy is a 15th century building with a 14th century tower, which contains some of the finest treasures that Devon has to offer. The fine brass lectern for example which tells us another story. In the 17th century, James Forbes was chaplain to Charles Stuart and also to the forces in the Netherlands and

Germany. Having had enough of the hardships and discomfort of this sort of life, he settled down to become vicar of Bovey church, only to find himself ousted by the Puritans. He was able to save the Elizabethan chalice and the registers. Not only that, he preserved the fine brass lectern, - an eagle with silver claws and three lions at its feet - by throwing it into a nearby pond, praying that a drought would not occur!

With the Restoration and the return of the king, James Forbes set to work to undo all the damage the Puritans had done to his church. The chalice was put back in place, together with a pewter alms dish and flagon which he presented to the church in thanksgiving. Finally the lectern was rescued, and all traces of pond life removed from it. How proud he would be to know that his action saved one of only 50 left in England today.

Bovey Bridge was built during the Civil War and herein lies another tale. Royalists occupied Front House when it was attacked by Cromwell. They were playing cards and had not a hope of beating the number of men set against them. With great presence of mind they scattered all the stake money out of the window and whilst the poverty stricken Parliament men scrambled to retrieve it, the crafty Royalists escaped poorer, but unharmed.

There is no doubt that battles were fought at Bovey and Chudleigh Knighton Heath and it is said that ghosts of soldiers in Royalists and Cromwellian clothes still haunt the area. Unfinished business do you suppose?

The road from Moretonhampstead to Yelverton virtually cuts Dartmoor in half. The scenery is nothing short of stupendous and en route are some superb walks and climbs. Bowerman's Nose stands high on a hill, looking as though it is a man petrified by the sight of the Hound of the Baskervilles and left there for evermore to gaze across the moor. Within easy distance is the Bronze Age enclosure of **Grimspound**, the remains of the homes of some of Dartmoor's earliest settlers. **Blackingstone Rock** just outside Moretonhampstead has a legend woven around it. For once, King Arthur ventured into Devon. That is unusual in itself and here at the rock, Arthur came face to face with the Devil and won. There seems to be no justification for the story but I do like believing in weird tales.

Postbridge is a delightful spot on this road and just before you get there you will come across The Warren House Inn, one of the loneliest but most welcoming pubs in England. Finding somewhere to stay will pose no difficulty but for people who want assistance in understanding Dartmoor and its history, then I wholeheartedly recommend The Cherrybrook Hotel at **Two Bridges.**

To describe routes that one can take on the moor to get the greatest pleasure out of walking, takes more space than I am permitted. **The Dartmoor Visitors Centre** at **Princetown** will provide you with a comprehensive choice of books and pamphlets on the subject. The sort of things I look out for are the old guide posts which are no more than pieces of granite standing on end. Each is marked with a letter. From Two Bridges one would be marked P showing the direction of Princetown, or M for Moretonhampstead. It is primitive but effective. Sometimes they may be used as boundary stones between parishes. Frequently, you will come across the remains of Bronze Age dwellings, just circles of stones which once were a hut. Sometimes you will see the remains of beehive huts. Not that they ever housed bees; they were used by medieval tinners for hiding their unsold tin, tools and other bits and pieces.

The clapper bridges are to be seen quite regularly over the streams that run through Dartmoor. Postbridge has one of the best examples. It is a tribute to the skill of 14th century builders. You will see that all the bridges are made of huge slabs of granite balanced one upon the other. Built so well that they have withstood, the onslaught of human feet, the insistent hammering of the river and the Dartmoor climate for centuries.

It is the immensity of this wonderful tapestry that catches my breath and at the same time I marvel at the variety of flora and fauna. Pale green lichens cling to the blackthorn along the roadside. Polytrichum piliferum grows on the walls near brooks.

Then there are the Dartmoor 'Letter Boxes'. If you know nothing about them; it is purely a fun thing that has developed over the years into quite a serious hobby. You seek out the positions of these boxes, usually tucked away in a crag somewhere, quite well hidden. You then post your own cards and take out any that are already there, which then become your duty to post on. Inside the hiding place you will find a visitors book for you to sign, a rubber stamp and an indelible pad, and you have to stamp your cards with the Dartmoor Letter Boxes' own crest. One for instance, is to be found at **Cranmere Pool**, south west of Okehampton, another at **Crow Tor**.

At Two Bridges you have a choice of road either to Tavistock or to Yelverton.

To reach Princetown, always an attraction because of the infamous **Dartmoor Prison**, built by French Prisoners of War, you take the Yelverton road. The prison is a threatening place and dominates this small village. Even on the sunniest of days it still looks formidable and extremely depressing. One happy place at Princetown is **The Plume of Feathers** where mine hosts are James and Linda Langton. This lively pub is a favourite watering hole for people from miles around and is equally popular with visitors who find the informality and fun infectious. Accommodation of varying kinds is available here.

I am addicted to the road that runs from Two Bridges to **Ashburton** which has endless places of enchantment that run off it. Past **Dartmeet** and onto **Poundsgate, Widecombe-in-the-Moor** can be seen from miles away with its tall church tower, built 400 years ago, by tin miners in thanksgiving for the thriving industry. It is dedicated to St Pancras and known as 'The cathedral on the moor'. For centuries the village remained almost unknown and it was not until 1850, when the vicar decided to hold an annual fair and Sabine Baring-Gould popularised an old folk tune that Widecombe became world famous. There will be few who do not know the old song 'As I was going to Widecombe Fair wi' Bill Brewer, Jan Stewer, Peter Cobleigh an all.' If you are one of the few you may rest assured that someone in Widecombe will tell you the story of Uncle Tom Cobleigh and his grey mare. Whether he was fact or fiction is tenuously argued. What is a fact is that a Thomas Cobleigh was born nearby in the village of **Spreyton** in 1762 and died there in 1844. It could well be that he brought his grey mare and his motley crew to Widecombe for the fair.

Buckland-in-the-Moor is a different kettle of fish. Standing high on Buckland Beacon with the Ten Commandments carved in stone beneath your feet, you are 1,280ft above the sea, looking out as far as the Devon coast at Teignmouth and Torquay and below is **Holne** where Charles Kingsley was borne.

What a beautiful hamlet Buckland is, with some of the loveliest thatched cottages I have ever seen. On a hill stands the 15th century church with carved bosses in the porch and old tiles under the tower. When you look up at the clock you will note that it does not have numerals. In their places are the words 'My Dear Mother' and its bells chime out 'All things bright and beautiful'. There is no official explanation for this curiosity but legend has it that it was placed there by a man in memory of his mother. This remarkable lady, when told the news that her son had been lost at sea, refused to believe it. Every night she lit a candle and placed it in the window to guide him home. Her faith was rewarded, he did return. When she died this is how he repaid her faith.

It is not often that one finds a village of less than 300 inhabitants but this is so at Holne. A charming place made memorable by the nearby Holne Chase Hotel just up the Princetown road from Ashburton, a drive that takes you along winding roads, through a canopy of trees and then across a narrow bridge over the Dart. It is so pretty and so peaceful. The hotel is the sort of place that wraps its welcoming arms around you. Informal enough to bring your wellies with you but beautifully appointed. I cannot imagine anyone would find it difficult to occupy their time whilst staying at Holne Chase. For keen fishermen the hotel has a mile of water, single bank, fly only. If you want to ride, Holne Chase has some of the best stables on Dartmoor within less than half an hour's drive. Fox hunting can usually be arranged in season.

Ashburton is a town of contrasts and beauty. In 1305 it was designated a Stannary Town. Tin mining and the wool industry brought great wealth and with it the building of some fine houses. One in North Street remains. It was a 17th century gambling house, known as the Card House. You will see the reason why because of the clubs, diamonds, spades and hearts that form the pattern of its slate-hung facade. What is now the ironmongers on the corner of North Street was once the Mermaid Inn where the Roundhead, General Fairfax, had his headquarters after defeating the Royalists nearby. That many people were Royalists and prepared to risk their lives hiding soldiers is evidenced by the little carving of a man on horseback on one of the houses - a sign that Royalists were safe there.

Buckfast Abbey must be one of your ports of call. Not during the day although it is beautiful then, but at night. Buckfast Abbey during Compline is magical. The monks come silently down the aisle, the only sound the swish of their long robes as they pass by, the only light the bidding one high over the altar. As they reach their stalls, they push back the cowls from their heads and the service starts. Its simple message is chanted and reaches out to every corner of this great building. One cannot doubt that God is present. Going up the M5 northwards from Exeter towards the exit for Tiverton and the road to North Devon, you will come first to **Cullompton** and just outside on the B3181 the little hamlet of **Westcott** between Cullompton and **Broadclyst.** Here there is a small, unpretentious hostelry, The Merry Harriers, where you will be very welcome and find a generous meal at reasonable prices - better than stopping at a service station. At Broadclyst you will find the glorious **Killerton House.** It is from here that the National Trust carry out all the administrative work for their properties in Devon. The home of the Acland family, it is a delight to explore and the 15 acres of hillside gardens are beautiful. A wonderful day out.

Tiverton is a place that grows on you. The prettiest way to approach this very old town is by the Exe valley road. It goes back to Saxon days when it had fords across the Exe and Loman, and it is where these two meet that the town looks down from its high ground between the rivers. Right by the medieval gateway of **Tiverton Castle** is the 15th century St Peter's Church. Its spacious windows glisten in the afternoon sunlight highlighting its pinnacles and battlemented parapets. The centuries have not destroyed the wonder of the carving on the outside walls. Look for a bear that creeps along a hollowed wall, a monkey holding fast to its baby and the proud lions which crouch on the buttresses. On the north side there are two vast gargoyle heads and more carved animals interspersed with odd human faces. Tiverton Castle built by the Normans is still important to the town but it was the wool merchants who provided Tiverton with many of its finest buildings.

The rivers are not the only waterways in Tiverton. The reach of the **Grand Western Canal** has been lovingly and carefully restored and is now open to the public who can enjoy the gentle trip, by horse drawn boat along this beautiful canal as far as **East Manley**, where you can disembark and take a short walk to the aqueduct, which crosses the disused Tiverton railway line.

The road that takes you from the very old town of **Crediton**, with its ancient and very beautiful cathedral like church, to Tiverton takes you close to **Cadbury**, a small village amongst the hills, with wonderful views over the Exe valley. The tall church tower which has stood for over 500 years dominates all around it at first sight, until you realise that it, in turn, is overshadowed by the mighty **Cadbury Castle**. Standing 700ft up, it is a fort of the ancient Britons. Nothing much left there now other than two ramparts enclosing a great space. It was here that General Fairfax pitched his camp in the Civil War.

Fursdon House stands just a mile away. The Fursdon family have lived in this beautiful house or its forerunner, since the signing of Magna Carta. The yard, which surrounds the 15th century church, is the last resting place of many members of this family. They must have worshipped here regularly. Perhaps they were responsible for the installation of the complete panel of ancient glass which has an extraordinary representation of the Crucifixion. Jesus is dressed in purple, white and gold and coming from five wounds are long lines of red. Underneath this haunting depiction are the words, in old English, 'Is it nothing to you, all ye that pass by?'

So much beauty and history is crammed into the scenic village of **Bickleigh**. It has everything; a castle, a river flowing under a superb bridge, thatched cottages, an award-winning mill and two very good hostelries.

Before I leave this part of mid-Devon I would like to tell you about two splendid villages. **Bampton** first, about 8 miles north of Tiverton. Somewhere that should be visited if only to discover the ducks and the tablet on the west wall of the 15th century church which says:

In memory of the Clerk's son
Bless my little iiiii's
Here he lies
In a sad pickle
Kill'd by an icicle
In the year 1776.

The Swan Inn close to the parish church is the place to stay or eat. Originally built to house the craftsmen who were building the church in the early 1400's.

The second village is **Holcombe Rogus**. It is south of Bampton and slightly north-east of Tiverton. Mentioned in the Domesday Book, the Bluett family were lords of the manor from Tudor times and they have their own chapel in the small Perpendicular church. The Bluetts built Holcombe Court, a fine Tudor mansion which lies in its walled grounds sheltered by a wooded hill overlooking the village.

Nothing curious about any of this but when you learn that much of the carving in the Court was done by Spanish prisoners from the Armada, that Dutch refugees carved the large Court pew in the church, and that tough American servicemen billeted there during the Second World War, were frightened out of their wits by the persistence of an unknown ghost, then, if you are as nosy as I am, you do want to take a look.

There are so many places that need your attention in North Devon that it makes it difficult to decide where to go. **Holsworthy** for example, is a quiet market town with two striking viaducts and a good pub, The White Hart. One must never forget **Black Torrington**, almost on the banks of the Torridge, with its long street that leads up a hill to the fine tower of the Tudor church. The local hostelry, The Torridge Inn, in Broad Street has cheerful landlords who will tell you that 'The Welcome's Warm - the Beer's Cold.! It was from them that I discovered the 'Black' in the village's name refers to the stones in the nearby river which turn black with iron oxide in the water.

I wondered why friends of mine were so keen on **Sheepwash**. It seemed an isolated place without much going on but how wrong I was. For those who want a base for a holiday it could not be better and the hospitality and comfort of The Half Moon Inn make it special. There are many beautiful and interesting walks along the Torridge valley and the local countryside. The game fishing attracts keen anglers with salmon, sea trout and brown trout all providing excellent sport at different times of the season. Pony trekking and riding are available nearby. There are good golf course and it is heaven for eager ornithologists. If I were in this area I would probably add a visit to **Rosemoor Garden** as well. It is only a short journey from Sheepwash and one mile south east of Great Torrington.

Hatherleigh is another place where fishermen come for a quiet holiday. It is a charming village with the river flowing through it and two others close by. It is surrounded by acres of moorland and a church which is crowned by a shingle spire. Most of the church is well over 550 years old but I am not sure that 15th century builders would have approved of what has been done to the interior. In **Great Torrington** roughly 13 miles north of Hatherleigh I am always reminded of its past. It was literally blown into history by the great explosion of eighty barrels of gunpowder. It happened in the Civil War, when General Fairfax, marching from the east, took the Royalists by surprise, and captured the town. The prisoners were shut off for safety in the tower of the church. They were held in complete darkness and had no idea that they were scrambling about in what had been the arsenal of the Royalists. Somehow the powder was set alight and the ensuing explosion shattered the church, killed 200 men and nearly killed the General as well. **Dartington Glass** has made Torrington its home and in less than 30 years its crystal has become world famous. It stemmed from Dartington Hall, of course, when the founders of the Dartington Trust, Dorothy and Leonard Elmhirst, turned their attention from that estate to the needs of North Devon, which was suffering badly, economically. The Trust hoped that a glass factory making English lead crystal by hand in the traditional way, would not only provide work for local people, but also opportunities for them to develop specialised skills and improve their quality of life.

CHAPTER FOUR

North-west of Torrington is **South Molton**. This ancient sheep and cattle market town is on the edge of Exmoor. It dates back to the 12th century and until the middle of the 19th century thrived as a centre of the wool trade. **The South Molton Museum** housed in a 17th century building has a number of fascinating exhibits. There are fine Georgian houses and a nice early 15th century parish church, St Mary Magdalene, which you approach along an avenue of limes.

For anyone staying around South Molton **The Exmoor National Park** will beckon. Wild and wonderful and probably at its best when seen from the back of a horse, there are few more splendid and awesome places in the country. It is romantic and made more so by anyone who has read Lorna Doone. The villages hide in the valleys and combes and one of them, **Simonsbath**, is an ideal stepping stone on your way to discover this stark beauty. I cannot say the village excites me for it does not but it is a wonderful foil to the exquisite scenery which surrounds it on every side. However within the welcoming walls of The Exmoor Forest Hotel you can plan expeditions to the many wonderful places nearby like **Tarr Steps** perhaps. This is one of the finest examples of a clapper bridge. It is a very popular spot and although there is plenty of parking, the approach road tends to get a bit congested. Tarr Steps Farm will provide you with excellent morning coffee, lunch and cream teas.

From Simonsbath the winding B3223 will take you to the fabulously beautiful **Lynmouth** and its twin village **Lynton**. The Napoleonic wars were responsible for the rising popularity of the two villages. Restrictions on travelling abroad made people look for alternatives and here they found comfort and beauty. Shelley and Coleridge were regular visitors. Indeed Shelley spent his honeymoon with his 16-year-old bride in Lynmouth in 1812, in a cottage now known by his name which is part of one of the county's most beautiful and respected hostelries, The Rising Sun. Shelley wrote of this hotel 'The climate is so mild that myrtles of immense size twine up our cottage and roses bloom in the open air in winter'. It would have been romantic then and still is today with its double bedroom and four-poster bed, sitting room and private garden. The views are spectacular and it really is something special. But that goes for everything about The Rising Sun. A place to stay and revel in the atmosphere or just drop in for a drink and a meal. R.D. Blackmore is said to have written Lorna Doone whilst staying in the inn.

The River Lyn runs through Lynton and tumbles over moss strewn rocks and boulders, through thickly wooded hills as it falls to the sea at Lynmouth. It is an ideal base in which to stay if you want to explore this glorious stretch of North Devon often called 'Little Switzerland' Lynton and Lynmouth are linked together by a remarkable **Cliff Railway** which opened in 1890. It climbs 500ft above sea level along a 900ft track. Worked by water and gravity it must have seemed terrifying to the intrepid users when it first started, they never having seen anything like it before. Sir George Newnes was the driving force behind its construction because he saw the need for easier access between the two villages.

The main road from Lynton will take you to **Combe Martin** but there are some spectacular walks in between which should not be missed, nor should you leave out the little village of **Parracombe** which lies between steep hills and must have been one of the first places in Devon to have a Christian church, for 1450 years ago, St Petrock came here and built a little chapel of cob and wattle, with a roof of straw.

Close to Parracombe is the stunning **Heddons Mouth** and it is here that an inn and a hotel must be mentioned. Heddons Gate Hotel is the epitome of a country house, which

100

guests for the length of their stay can call 'home'. Hunters Inn is a completely detached chalet style building of immense character and charm with about 4 acres of landscaped gardens. The National Park footpaths lead from the inn and take you along the Coastal Footpath to Lynton. Both are fabulous places for different reasons.

Combe Martin has one of the longest village streets in the country and a strange 18th century inn, The Pack of Cards. It was built by a man who was said to have been a great gambler and from his winnings he built the inn to resemble a child's house of cards, with each storey smaller than the one below and chimneys arising from every possible corner. The village became part of history over 750 years ago when its silver mines produced the wherewithal to pay for the Hundred Years War. So rich were these mines that 300 men were brought from Derbyshire and Wales to help work them. I have no idea whose money went into building the church but it is a splendid place full of interesting things. Its striking tower stands 100ft high and is well over 550 years old. Inside you will find a memorial to George Ley who built the Pack of Cards.

Ilfracombe is the next stop and as you drive from Combe Martin you will be bewitched by the panoramic and stunning views glimpsed only occasionally over the cliffs to the sea. The town tends to die in the winter which is an enormous pity but it wakes up in the spring ready for a lively and vibrant summer. Wonderful scenery, a good beach, friendly pubs and the unpretentious Sunnymeade Country House Hotel at Dean Cross, West Down close by are good reasons for coming here.

A winding coast road will take you to the seaside villages of **Mortehoe, Woolacombe** and **Croyde** with their magnificent beaches beloved by surfers and families. They are all just big enough to have a life style of their own but small enough to remain intimate. From Woolacombe you can just see, far out to sea, **Lundy Island**, the granite haunt of pirates long ago and now chiefly the haunt of sea birds; the island stands out 400 ft above the sea.

Baggy Point offers some outstanding walks and this may attract you to Croyde which is tucked away on the southern flank of the peninsula. If you want to stay within sight and sound of the sea where it is informal and carefree, The Croyde Bay House Hotel in Moor Lane is the answer. **Saunton** three miles away is renowned for its **Championship Golf Course.**

A busy main road will lead you from here through **Braunton** and into **Barnstaple** which claims to be the oldest borough in England. Much of the old has had to give way to the new to allow the town to become the business centre of North Devon. It has an excellent theatre. From Barnstaple to **Bideford** you have the choice of two roads. The main A339 or the small B3233. The latter allows you to take a look at the villages of **Fremlingham** and **Instow** on the banks of the River Taw as it comes out to the sea at Bideford Bay.

From Instow a ferry trip across the river to **Appledore** is rewarding. It is here the two great estuaries of the Taw and the Torridge meet. Appledore is charming and picturesque. The little street running up from the quay is nothing short of beautiful. Anyone with the slightest talent for painting will itch to get their easel out, and for those of us unable to do so....well, we can just stand and stare. Next door is **Westward Ho,** another beautiful village with panoramic views out to sea.

Bideford is an excellent base for anyone who wants to explore the coast and villages between itself and **Hartland Point**.

Nothing ever changes in **Clovelly.** It is an artist's paradise. Forget your car you will have to leave it in a park at the top of the village. You descend down the cobbled street which tumbles for half a mile to the sea. On either side are old cottages with flowers and creepers climbing up their walls. Unless you are of Olympic fitness standard you will be forced to stop every now and again to catch your breath. You will be grateful for it because the scenery is unforgettable. High above you trees reach for the heavens whilst below the sea sparkles in the sunshine.

Hartland is a place that goes to no other town, which is part of its charm and a good place to end this potted insight into Devon. **Hartland Abbey** stirs the romantic soul of everyone who goes there. It is the sort of place that would inspire Barbara Cartland to write one of her famous books. It dates from the 12th century, is situated near the wild, desolate coastline, has monastic origins and has been lived in by the same family, although frequently inherited through the female line, since the Dissolution, when Henry VIII gave it to William Abbot, the Sergeant of his royal wine cellars. There are many lovely rooms and the grounds are outstanding. The valley is still as beautiful as it must have always been to the Abbots, Luttrells,Orchards and Stucleys who have been lucky enough to live amongst this majesty for centuries. The present owner is Sir Hugh Stucley who opens the house from May-September on Wednesdays, Bank Holiday Sundays and Mondays from 2-5.30pm. Dogs on leads are allowed in the grounds.

BLAGDON MANOR COUNTRY HOTEL,
Ashwater,
Devon EX21 5DF

Tel:01409 211224 Fax: 01409 211634

This wonderful, old, Grade 2 listed, typically Devonian manor house is one that will remain in your memory for ever once you have stayed beneath its friendly roof. From the outside it lives comfortably with the stunning scenery and the lawned garden which surrounds the house but it is within that it becomes remarkable. One can only suppose that it was always a happy house and this sense of well-being is still there today enhanced by the present owners, Tim and Gill Casey, two exciting people who are gregarious and genuinely enjoy the ever increasing number of people who beat a path to their welcoming door. It is Gill whose artistic flair has transformed the rooms. Every room has been recreated with floor coverings, drapes and beds all harmonising with the colour scheme appointed for that room. When you retire to bed you will appreciate the individual and attractive furnishings.

The house varies in age with anything from the 12th century to the mid-1600's and the sense of the past is everywhere with heavy oak beams and worn flagstones. As evening falls, the bar beckons with its enormous log fire with the hint of wood smoke tantalising your nostrils, or maybe you would prefer the peace of the library, a game of snooker or just the quiet of the drawing room. Dinner will be the highlight of your stay. It is as though you are invited to a dinner party with some old and some new friends. You sit at a long table, beautifully appointed with gleaming silver and sparkling glass. Candles throw a gentle light over the old beams and as each course is served you will discover what a superb cook Gill is. An array of fine wines complements the food.

Within the eight acres of Blagdon Manor grounds one can stroll, use the golfers practice ground or show how aggressive you can be when you take on someone at croquet. Fly fishing, rough shooting or horse riding are all available close by. Dartmoor, Exmoor and the Heritage coastlines of the south-west are accessible, as are many stately homes.

USEFUL INFORMATION

OPEN; *All year*
CHILDREN; *Not suitable*
CREDIT CARDS; *All major cards*
LICENSED; *Yes. Fine wines*
ACCOMMODATION; *7 en suite rooms*
Facilities for small conferences
Self catering cottage available (2 bedrooms)

DINING ROOM; *Superb, home-cooked food*
VEGETARIAN; *Upon request*
DISABLED ACCESS; *Not really*
GARDEN; *Beautiful 8 acres. Practice Golf*
Croquet

HEDDONS GATE HOTEL,
Heddon Mouth,
Parracombe,
North Devon EX31 4PZ

Tel: 01598 763313 Fax: 01598 763363

Heddons Gate may call itself an hotel but what the owner, Robert de Ville has achieved in the thirty years since he bought the almost derelict house, has made it the epitome of a country house which guests, for the length of their stay, can call 'home'. Robert married Heather who has been at the hotel for ten years, in January 1997 and so you now have a double welcome to this happy establishment. Run on friendly, informal but totally professional lines the house is luxurious but nonetheless you need never fear that your 'wellies' will not be welcome in the porch! No two bedrooms are alike and vary enormously in size and aspect. Bedrooms are named either according to their original use - the house built in 1890 was a hideaway for a famous Jam Manufacturer and his mistress - the Dressing Room, the Servants Quarters, the Indian Room and so on. Bedrooms for romantics include a magnificent half-tester bed and a four-poster complete with interior lighting and wrap around-drapes. The room with the least view is Nannies Room. Years ago this would have been spartan, but now has five lovely old stained glass windows, comfortable furnishings and a splendid Victorian bathroom. Two American guests who enjoyed having this room remarked 'Gee, those Nannies sure knew how to live!'

Kitchens are the heart of any house, and here they are modern and practical giving Robert de Ville, who is the chef, and his staff, a cheerful working environment. Here he produces the most delicious English dishes with Continental touches using fresh British produce whenever possible. Every meal is enhanced by the well chosen wine list which is listed by grape variety rather than country of origin, making it much more user friendly. Home-made afternoon tea is one of the delights of Heddons Gate, with fresh scones, jam, cream, cucumber sandwiches and home-made cakes. The hotel is located in the Exmoor National Park in an isolated woodland setting 400 feet up on one side of the Heddon Valley belonging to the National Trust, with fine country views across to Holdstone Down (1200 ft). Steep footpaths lead from the hotels 20 acres to the sea at Heddons Mouth, three quarters of a mile away and to the spectacular hog backed cliffs of the Exmoor Coast. Truly a wonderful place to stay.

USEFUL INFORMATION

OPEN; *From end March-beginning Nov*
CHILDREN; *Preferably over 10 years*
50% discount when sharing parents room
CREDIT CARDS; *Amex/Master/Visa*
LICENSED; *Resident/Restaurant*
ACCOMMODATION; *11 en suite*
in main building. 3 'cottage suites' in lodge

RESTAURANT; *English with Continental touches. Fresh produce whenever possible*
BAR FOOD; *Not applicable*
VEGETARIAN; *Yes but please discuss*
DISABLED ACCESS; *Cottage suites*
GARDEN; *20 acres of woods & lawns*

NEWBRIDGE HOTEL
Northam, Bideford,
Devon EX39 3QA
Tel: 01237 474989

The historic town of Bideford in North Devon is the perfect spot for this 1850's Georgian Hotel. Situated in 2 acres of gardens, this beautiful house has been extensively refurbished and tastefully decorated in keeping with the period of its building. Anthony Johnson is your friendly host, and is to be congratulated on the quality and standard of services provided. The ten bedrooms are all en suite, with TV, direct dialling, refreshments tray and full central heating. Each room is charmingly decorated and has period furniture throughout, and is snug and engaging in character.

The lounge is a comfortable, cosy room in which to relax and unwind after a day's entertainment, and perhaps discuss the next item on the agenda! Talking of agendas, this is a capital place for conferences , and even weddings or functions which are well catered for. The bar is fully licensed and 'mulling' over a glass of something may be the perfect end to the perfect day. The restaurant caters for breakfast, lunch and evening meal. It is an enticing room with its crisp table cloths, candles and very pretty decor. The food is excellent; all freshly prepared and of the highest quality, with a varied menu to suit all tastes. There are some interesting items on the menu too, such as 'Surf and Turf'. which is a fillet of beef and pork grilled together with halibut and salmon and served with a garlic sauce. It definitely makes the choice less difficult, doesn't it - that's four items on the menu all in one! Sounds delicious and is only one of a thoughtful, diverse array of dishes. A favourite must be Shark Steak which is described on the menu as being caught by 'a fast swimmer'! The service is good and each meal is served by a friendly, cheerful staff, who are determined you will have a good time.

Bideford is a great town with an historic port and market. It is a haven for yachting, wind surfing and all water sports. The art gallery is worth a visit to see its paintings, model ships, pewter and ceramics. There are many quality shops and a pleasant day can be spent strolling around this town. If you wish to venture further afield then you are only a stone's throw from Exmoor and Dartmoor, with a wild untamed beauty that only the moors seem to capture. The North Devon coast can be savage and rugged in places and has hardly changed since the time of smugglers and excise men! But then walking along cliff tops and sand dunes will quickly bring you to golden sandy beaches with the waves lapping at the shoreline. The cities of Exeter and Plymouth are also within driving distance if you feel the need for big city life. A congenial host, good food, comfortable accommodation and access to the beauty of one of England's most dramatic counties - what more could you ask for?

USEFUL INFORMATION

OPEN *All year*
CHILDREN *Welcome*
CREDIT CARDS *All major cards*
LICENSED *Full*
ACCOMMODATION *10 rooms en suite 5dbl 4tw, 1*

RESTAURANT *Excellent menu*
VEGETARIAN: *Catered For*
DISABLED ACCESS *No*
GARDEN *2 acres lawn & shrub*

DENHAM FARM AND COUNTRY HOUSE,
North Buckland, Braunton,
North Devon EX33 1HY

Tel/Fax: 01271 890297

This exceptionally nice farm and country house seldom fails to make guests return year after year making it their second home. This is not just because it is comfortable and the food is good, it is because, Tony and Jean Barnes who own and run Denham have that intangible ability that makes them relate to everyone who comes here and offer them old fashioned courtesy within a warm friendly atmosphere. They both have keen senses of humour and clearly enjoy people. Denham will make you feel relaxed, pampered and secure from the moment you arrive. It is situated in the unspoilt hamlet of North Buckland where only the country sounds share the silence. The 160 acre beef and sheep farm is off the beaten track. Here you can revel in the simple joys of the countryside, see the first buds of spring, enjoy the flower laden hedgerows in summer, walk the country lanes as the autumn leaves fall and marvel at the beauty of nature when the first signs of frost announce the arrival of winter. It is a wonderful place for a holiday at anytime of the year. Whilst enjoying this peaceful environment you are nonetheless close to many other attractions. Within walking distance is the village of Georgeham where Henry Williamson the author of 'Tarka the Otter' lived for many years. A short drive will take you to Croyde with its quaint thatched cottages and rolling waves for surfing. Miles of golden sands reach to Woolacombe and from Saunton Sands you can wander on to Braunton Burrows a National Nature Reserve. These are just a few of the delights surrounding Denham.

Within the house the beautifully decorated furnished bedrooms are all en suite with colour television and a generously supplied beverage tray. Each room has a wonderful collection of plates and is distinctive in character. There is a warm, comfortable lounge with a huge open log fire and right next to it is the attractive bar; a great meeting place at night where guests gather to discuss the day and the plans for the morrow whilst sipping a drink and eagerly anticipating the excellent dinner which they know will be forthcoming. Jean is a wonderful cook. Her breakfasts with several choices will set you up for the day and at night her menus are wholesome and mouth-watering using fresh produce. Her desserts are memorable! Jean will happily cater for vegetarians or for special diets given prior notice. In addition to the rooms in the house, the Barnes have two self-catering cottages, both delightful and well appointed. Barley Cottage can sleep eight and Old Granary is perfect for 2 or 4 - Guests in the cottages can also enjoy meals in the farm or have them prepared in the cottages.

USEFUL INFORMATION

OPEN; *All year except Christmas*
CHILDREN; *Welcome*
CREDIT CARDS; *Master/Visa*
LICENSED; *Yes*
ACCOMMODATION; *10 rooms en suite*
2 self-catering cottages

DINING ROOM; *Home-cooked, traditional Farmhouse.*
VEGETARIAN; *By arrangement*
DISABLED ACCESS; *No*
GARDEN; *Yes*

COURT BARN COUNTRY HOUSE HOTEL
Clawton, Holsworthy,
Devon EX22 6PS

Tel: 01409 271219 Fax: 01409 271309

This delightful Country House Hotel is in a class of its own for several reasons. The first impression as you turn into the drive is one of peace and beauty. The five acres of gardens with a frame work of mature trees look out over unspoilt countryside and stand next to the 12th century church. Built as the 'Sanctuary' around the 16th century, Court Barn was partly rebuilt in 1853 retaining its charm and adding Victorian elegance. It could not be a better place in which to stay for those who want to escape from the outside world and who will enjoy the quietude and totally relaxing atmosphere that Robert and Susan Wood, the owners, have created within the house. They have old-fashioned values of quality, comfort and hospitality and offer this to their guests at prices you remember years ago!

The two lounges have deep comfortable chairs and each is decorated in soft, muted tones. A crackling log fire in at least one of the lounges all year round enhances the relaxed atmosphere of Court Barn. The two dining rooms are equally attractive. The small, elegant dining room is used for breakfast - a meal long remembered by those who stay here. The restaurant, open to non-residents, is furnished with antiques, has pretty table settings with gleaming silver and sparkling glasses. The delicious five-course dinners are prepared from fresh, quality food and the changing menu is imaginative, complemented by a choice of some 375 wines from the award winning list. Whilst on the subject of food Court Barn serves a delectable afternoon tea, recognised with an AA Rosette and the Tea Council 'Best Teas in Britain Awards'. The eight en suite bedrooms, one of which has a four-poster, are beautifully appointed and have everything needed to ensure a restful night in preparation for the excitement of exploring the surrounding countryside. Close by there are Blue Flag beaches, nature trails, cycle trails, National Trust and National Parks. No one could possibly be disappointed in Court Barn.

USEFUL INFORMATION

OPEN; *All year*
CHILDREN; *Welcome*
CREDIT CARDS; *All major cards*
LICENSED; *Yes. Award winning wine list*
ACCOMMODATION; *8 en suite rooms*

RESTAURANT; *Delicious, imaginative menu*
VEGETARIAN; *Catered for*
DISABLED ACCESS; *No special facilities*
PETS; *By arrangement*
GARDEN; *5 acres of park-like grounds*

THE VICTORIA HOTEL

27-29 Victoria Road,
Dartmouth,
Devon TQ6 9RT

Tel: 01803 832572

In 1993 Annie Glanfield, fresh from the world of film and television, acquired The Victoria Hotel and with the same unerring eye that made her so successful as a Location Production Manager for major Film Studios overseas and UK based, she tackled the task of restoring, converting and recreating the hotel which has served the public for well over 100 years. The result is somewhere that is very special. Wonderful for someone who wants total comfort combined with a great atmosphere, good food and the friendly atmosphere that pervades the whole hotel with its lively bars.

Everyone of the ten bedrooms has been completely refurbished and the rooms are now attractively furnished, the walls have fine paintings and prints and antique timber head boards adorn the comfortable beds, and are complete with every facility including television, direct dial telephones and a beverage tray. There is a full laundry service if required. Everywhere there is a very high standard which would be hard to equal in a 5 Crown establishment. It is not just the quality, it is an eye for colour and detail which is apparent wherever you go in The Victoria. The restaurant has an excellent reputation and specialises in locally caught sea food as well as freshly cooked organic regional produce. The head chef and his brigade are committed to the task of providing some of the best food you will find in this part of Devon. If one had to describe the menu succinctly one would say Traditional English with Continental influence and cooked with flair. For those not wanting the formality of a meal in the Restaurant, there are two friendly bars which offer a choice of food, traditional beers and fine wines. In fact The Victoria has something to offer everyone whether it is local people who are regulars or the influx of visitors in the summer. Equally there are those who choose to come to Dartmouth out of season to enjoy its beauty, take in its history and use it as a base to explore the area without the hassle of quite so much traffic. Special winter bargain breaks are available at very reasonable prices.

USEFUL INFORMATION

OPEN; All Year
CHILDREN; Restaurant only
CREDIT CARDS; Yes except Amex/Diner
LICENSED; Full On
ACCOMMODATION;7db1 3 tw all en suit
PETS; By arrangement

RESTAURANT; Specialises in fish but has a fine reputation for all its food
BAR FOOD; Excellent choice
VEGETARIAN; Always a choice
DISABLED ACCESS; Not suitable

GREAT LEIGH FARM
Doddiscombeleigh,
Exeter
Devon EX6 7RF

Tel:01647 253008 Fax: 01647 252058

If this book was dedicated to the unusual then Great Leigh Farm or should we say Great Leigh Chicken House, would take a prime position. It is a working farm situated in the lushness of the Teign Valley, nothing unusual about that but the bedrooms have been created out of old hen-houses in which the chickens used to run freely. The conversion is stunning in its simplicity and comfort. Each room is a bed-sitting room complete with its own bathroom en suite and the modern requirement of a colour television. There is warmth and comfort within the beamed ceilings and stone-walls. Each room has a fairly dominant colour scheme which is just right for the building. You eat in the main farmhouse in a friendly atmosphere and there is also a charming sitting room. The hen-houses make Great Leigh different but what really attracts people is the hostess Marie Citroen, who is a lively, vibrant and determined lady who cooks fantastic meals with an eclectic menu that is well nigh faultless. Maria's cooking philosophy is that food should be 'fresh and fun'. Her ingredients are all locally produced or farmed, with many of the vegetables, fruits and herbs picked from her own garden. Not only do you have an enormous and delicious breakfast but dinner is available as well. Maria is a dentist by profession and spent many years working in Australia during which time she managed to fit in running her appropriately named 'Alternative Fillings' restaurant very successfully. Her dream, however, was to own and run a guest house in England. This she has achieved with the help of her sister Angela and Angela's husband Colin Edwards. Colin runs the farm whilst Angela is Maria's right hand. It is a very happy arrangement and between them they make a stay here memorable. Rumour has it that Maria is planning to open an Aussie-style restaurant in one of the Great Leigh barns. Most people who know her are sure she will. To reach Great Leigh, hidden in the lushness of the Teign Valley take the B3193 to the A38 between Chudleigh Knighton and Exeter and make for the village of Doddiscombeleigh and then right at the Nobody Inn

USEFUL INFORMATION

OPEN; *All year*

CHILDREN; *Over 14 years*

CREDIT CARDS; *All major cards*

LICENSED; *No. Bring your own wines*

ACCOMMODATION; *Bed-sitting rooms with Private bathrooms en suite*

DINING ROOM; *Exciting, faultless food*

VEGETARIAN; *Catered for*

DISABLED ACCESS; *Not really suitable*

GARDEN; *Yes + 170 acres to explore*

PETS; *Yes, by arrangement*

ST OLAVES COURT HOTEL,
Mary Arches Street,
Exeter,
Devon, EX4 3AZ.

Tel : 01392 217736
Fax : 01392 413050

There are many accolades to this charming hotel and restaurant, from AA and RAC, to Egon Ronay and Johansens, but the finest must be that those who visit, return again and again to enjoy the hospitality and friendliness of one of Devon's top hotels. Situated 400 yards from the Cathedral in the appealing city of Exeter, this walled, private Georgian mansion has become one of the most loved establishments of visitors and locals alike. Whether you are visiting the city on holiday or business, or arranging that special meeting of clients, then St Olaves Court Hotel can cater to your requirements. Your hosts, Raymond and Ute Wyatt, ensure a quality and service that would be difficult to surpass, and the warm, cosy feeling of this hotel makes it a luxury 'home from home' on any occasion.

There are fifteen bedrooms for visitors, all delightfully furnished and equipped to very high standards. Each room has colour TV, phone, trouser press and hospitality tray and some have Jacuzzi baths. All are en suite and exude the comfort and restful allure that only top quality can display. There are handsome antique pieces alongside tasteful modern furnishings, and the unfussy splendour of these rooms ensure a restful night and pleasant dreams. Breakfast is a traditional English meal and vegetarians are catered for. The evening meal is candlelit, giving atmosphere and intimacy to a wonderful experience. Goldsworth Restaurant is the finest in Exeter, and serves superb European cuisine. Couple this with the service and hospitality, and you have the recipe for an evening that will remain in your memory for a long time. The soft Georgian colours of grey, green and ochre lend a peace and harmony to the occasion, and a pre or after dinner drink in the lounge will just complete a delightful picture.

Exeter is an excellent centre for visiting the many attractions in the surrounding area. Dartmoor and its haunting beauty is nearby and is excellent for walking or riding. The beautiful coastlines of the Devon beaches will have you reaching for your camera or sketch pad, and water sport enthusiasts will find a host of activities to enjoy. There are many National Trust properties to visit, and those steam railway enthusiasts will not be disappointed by the Dart Valley trains. Exeter itself is a beautiful city with its many shops and places of historical interest, including the lovely Cathedral.

USEFUL INFORMATION

OPEN; All year
CHILDREN; Welcome
PETS; Welcome
LICENSED; Restaurant & residential
CREDIT CARDS; All major
ACCOMMODATION; 15 en suite rooms:, 11 dbl 3 twin, 1 sgl.

RESTAURANT; Superb cuisine
VEGETARIANS; Catered for
DISABLED ACCESS; Yes (3 steps)
GARDEN; Walled & private

THE EDWARDIAN,
30/32 Heavitree Road,
Exeter,
Devon, EX1 2LQ.

Tel : 01392 254699
Fax : 01392 276102

This hotel has many accolades, such as Which, and is the only AA four -Q- rated establishment in Exeter, but the best of all must be from the guests who have stayed here and who return again and again to this haven of hospitality. This exquisitely decorated hotel is a 'home from home', with the charming owners, Michael and Kay Rattenbury, ensuring your stay is a most pleasant experience. Each of the bedrooms is very individually decorated and prettily furnished; with rooms having either four-poster, antique brass, wrought iron or period wooden bedsteads. All are en suite, apart from the one single room, and all have excellent facilities of colour TV, hospitality tray, individually controlled heating, hair dryers and direct-dial telephones. There is a beautifully appointed lounge for guests to relax in, and the dining room caters for up to 22 persons. Although Michael and Kay do not cater for evening meal, they are only too happy to point you in the right direction, as there is a wealth of hostelries and eating establishments in the area. Breakfast is cooked to order and can be full English, continental or vegetarian if desired. This is a beautiful home with its Edwardian and Victorian furnishings, and a loving collection of handsome china and porcelain.

Michael and Kay come from many generations of Devonshire 'folk', and have a great deal of information about the area. There is a good collection of books in the lounge giving local information, but they can still give you an insight to many local facilities. Dartmoor is close by, and this is an excellent place from which to explore this lovely, haunting moor. The Pyramid Leisure centre is only 50 yards from the door, and there is even a dry ski slope close by for those enthusiasts. (Personally, I find snow a lot softer). Exeter city is a beautiful place to explore and the wonderful cathedral is 11th century in parts. There is a great deal of history in this city, and much fine architecture.

The Edwardian is open all year round, and if not on holiday, this is the perfect place to stay while on business, as the relaxing atmosphere and congenial company can only enhance any stay in this fine city. Michael and Kay are the perfect hosts, and this is the perfect hotel.

USEFUL INFORMATION

OPEN; *All year*
CHILDREN; *Welcome*
PETS; *Welcome*
LICENSED; *No*
CREDIT CARDS; *All major cards*
ACCOMMODATION; *13 rooms: 12 en suite; 3 four-poster dbls, 5 dbl, 2 twin, 1fmly & 2 sgl.*

RESTAURANT; *Breakfast cooked to order*
VEGETARIANS; *Catered for*
DISABLED ACCESS; *Not really*
EVENING MEAL; *No*

THE OLD VICARAGE

Starcross,
Exeter EX6 8PX
Devon

Tel/Fax: 01626 890206

Maggie and Mervyn Hayes have made the Old Vicarage into a charming home to which they welcome guests. They are genuinely caring people and it would be hard not to relax under their roof. The house is interesting in its own right. It has withstood the wear and tear of almost four hundred years during which it has been a farmhouse and then became Church property providing a home for the incumbent vicar and his family. Situated eight miles south of Exeter on the A379 coastal road, the Old Vicarage is ideal as a base to enjoy discovering the many and varied aspects of Devon which appeal to the visitor in all seasons. You are invited to select your accommodation from one of the five bedrooms, all with names applicable to the area. The Woodbury Suite is a spacious double en suite room with exposed beams and a child's room with a single bed off the main bedroom. The Exe Room is another double-bedded room with en suite shower and toilet. Warren is a twin-bedded bay windowed room with en suite shower and toilet, Haldon is a twin bedded room with a shower-room and toilet on the same floor. This can also accommodate a third single bed. Finally Mamhead is a double room with a shower room and toilet on the same floor. They are all attractively furnished, very comfortable and have wonderful views. The cosy Lounge and Breakfast Room both have log fires in winter and television with books, maps and a variety of board games, cards, jigsaws and reading material. Breakfast is a feast and will certainly set you up for a day's exploration. No evening meals are served but there are many good eateries nearby.

From the Old Vicarage one can explore the historic Cathedral City of Exeter, visit Powderham Castle, just a half mile away whilst within an hour you can be in any of the resorts from Exmouth to Torbay. Quaint villages, forest walks, cliff walks, theme parks, formal gardens, steam trains, animal farms, wind surfing, pony trekking, cream teas - the choice is never ending and cannot fail to please everyone. The Exe Estuary is a birdwatcher's paradise. Golfers will enjoy the challenge of nearby clubs.

USEFUL INFORMATION

OPEN; *All year*
CHILDREN; *Welcome*
CREDIT CARDS; *None taken*
LICENSED; *No*
ACCOMMODATION; *5 rooms*
mainly en suite

DINING ROOM; *Excellent breakfast*
No evening meals
VEGETARIAN; *Catered for*
DISABLED ACCESS; *no special facilities*
PETS; *By arrangement*
GARDEN; *Yes*

COMBE HOUSE

Gittisham,
Nr Honiton,
Devon EXl4 0AD

Tel: 01404 42756
Fax: 01404 46004

Turning into the winding drive through magnificent parkland will give you your first glimpse of one of England's oldest country mansions, now a superb Country House Hotel. Combe House, is a 16th century Elizabethan mansion, set in a 3,000 acre country estate. With views over the Blackdown Hills it stands at the head of a secluded valley, supremely peaceful and yet it is only two miles from the A30 London to Exeter road and the nearby market town of Honiton. Combe has been home to many illustrious families - Nicholas Putt, an active Royalist was taken from the estate by Cromwell's soldiers. The Putt family through the generations have made many alterations to the house and the village of Gittisham - the Markers are the present owners. John Boswell, a direct descendant of James Boswell, the biographer, and his wife, Therese, a talented artist and sculptor, whose delightful work is to be seen throughout the house, first came to Combe in 1970, since when they have worked unceasingly to create an hotel that they themselves would like to stay in. Today they are ably assisted by their son. To claim success is an understatement; they have achieved total grace and comfort combined with excellent service, wonderful food, fine wines, every facility and the glory of the past. Combe House is a mecca for many of the legal fraternity attending the law courts in Exeter. They enjoy the tremendous sense of relaxation that permeates the house and find pleasure and fun in the small, friendly bar with its fascinating sporting pictures, where John Boswell is frequently the barman! Staying, lunching or dining at Combe is to be pampered in the nicest possible way. Nothing ostentatious but every room has its own character and the beautiful dining rooms, slightly theatrical in appearance, when candlelit, are quite special.

USEFUL INFORMATION

OPEN; *All Year.*
PETS; *Welcome*
CHILDREN; *Most welcome. Cots*
CREDIT CARDS; *All major cards*
LICENSED; *Residential Restaurant*
DISABLED ACCESS; *2 rooms from garden*
ACCOMMODATION; *15 rooms en suite*
not suitable for wheelchairs

RESTAURANT; *Dinner à la CarteFrench cuisine*
BAR LUNCHES; *Mon-Sat*
Suppers Traditional
Sunday Lunch
VEGETARIAN; *Various dishes*
GARDEN; *Extensive. Croquet Lawn*

GLEN TOR HOTEL
Torrs Park,
Ilfracombe,
North Devon EX34 8AZ

Tel: 01271 862403

This well situated hotel stands at the foot of the famous Torrs Walk and is only a few minutes walk to beaches, shops and entertainment, including Golf Course and Heated Indoor Swimming facilities. The owners, Tony and Joan Wright and Wendy Dunlop-Jenkins are talented, efficient people who have made Glen Tor something special. In the last eighteen months it has been totally redecorated and renovated and the result is a charming, comfortable establishment that probably resembles a country house rather than a seaside hotel. Glen Tor is open all the year and in many ways it would be even better to spend a winter, autumn or spring break here rather than a stay in the holiday season. What is for certain is that you will be pampered in the nicest possible way whatever time of the year you decide to visit. The house, built at the turn of the century is gracious and the rooms have high ceilings and that sense of spaciousness that is a part of the architecture of the day.

There is a cosy bar with a lounge and a quiet room to which one may escape at any time of the day. In the bar you will find guests chatting over the expeditions of the day and enjoying a drink or two from the well-stocked bar before dinner. Dinner is served in a graciously appointed dining room. The well chosen menu offers choices, sometimes traditional and frequently more exotic fare. Everything is freshly cooked and prepared from produce of the highest quality. The wine list has been well chosen to complement the food. Vegetarian meals are a speciality of the hotel and they will be more than happy to prepare special diets if required. Packed lunches can also be supplied upon request. An excellent and comprehensive breakfast is served every morning. In the bedrooms which are all ensuite or have private bathrooms, you will find all sorts of extra touches for your well being. As well as colour & Satellite TV, a hostess tray and hair driers, there are shampoos, soaps and shower caps. The Premier Suite has its own private south facing balcony with lovely views.

This is an ideal hotel for ramblers, golfers, anglers etc and for those who want to enjoy the staggering coastal beauty of North Devon and the magic of Exmoor as well as the breathtaking surrounding countryside.

USEFUL INFORMATION

OPEN; *All year*
CHILDREN; *Welcome*
CREDIT CARDS; *None taken*
LICENSED; *Yes*
ACCOMMODATION; *9 rooms*
All en suite except for 1 sgl

DINING ROOM; *Comprehensive & varied*
VEGETARIAN: *A speciality menu*
DISABLED ACCESS; *No special facilities*
PETS; *Yes*
GARDEN; *Yes + Patio*

THE TERRACE

Tapas Bar & Fresh Food Restaurant,
62 Fore Street,
Ilfracombe,
North Devon EX34 9ED

Tel: 01271 863482

The Terrace is certainly an unexpected bonus for anyone visiting Ilfracombe and an oasis for local people. The Tapas Bar is continental in both style and atmosphere, whilst the Restaurant is the epitome of Victorian elegance in subtle creams, greens and gold. The eccentric angles of the room and the beautiful original plaster friezes give the clues to its past as a Victorian tea room. In the Tapas Bar you will find International dishes such as cheese fondue, spicy Greek kebabs, Basque squid, Aioli Crevettes and Fajitas to name but a few, with an impressive collection of International beers, wines and spirits. In the summer months from mid-morning till late the bar serves, Italian coffees, Devon cream teas, home-made ice creams, sorbets, Tapas and bar drinks. For the uninitiated Tapas are a selection of small dishes and it is suggested that 1 dish per person should be ordered as a snack or 2-3 or more per person for a meal. The Restaurant operates in the evenings only. Pre-dinner drinks are served in the Colonial style lounge whilst you peruse the short menu of imaginative dishes cooked with flair and passion. The emphasis is on fresh produce prepared with an unfussy approach, everything is fresh from the locally caught fish, which feature strongly during the summer, prime Devon meat and poultry, and Exmoor game when in season, through to the herbs, fruits and vegetables. For vegetarians there are excitingly different options and for the sweet toothed the desserts can only be described as wickedly delicious! To complete your dining experience the Restaurant wine list offers an array of personally selected armagnacs, calvados, ports and other international liqueurs.

1997 has seen the launch of the Terrace Conserve & Preserve Company supplying many local retailers and of course the restaurant, with a wide range of fruit conserves, pickled preserves, flavoured oils and vinegar's.

USEFUL INFORMATION

OPEN; *Tapas Bar: May-Oct:12noon-11.00 7 days Winter: Tues-Sat 6-1 1pm*
RESTAURANT; *June-Sept 7pm-late 6 days Winter: Thur-Sat 7-late*
Closed Mondays. Closed Christmas to beginning Feb
CREDIT CARDS; *All major cards*   **VEGETARIAN;** *Interesting dishes*
LICENSED; *Yes*   **DISABLED ACCESS;** *Yes*
ACCOMMODATION; *Available on Request*

ERMEWOOD HOUSE HOTEL,
Ermington,
Ivybridge,
Devon, PL21 9NS.

Tel : 01548 830741

Ermewood House is a former rectory owned by Mike and Claire Loseby, which overlooks the pretty River Erme. Located in perhaps one of the most scenic parts of England, this haven of peace and tranquillity allows you 'time off' from the outside world, and leaves you feeling refreshed and ready to continue with the daily trivia. South Hams has much to offer the visitor with lots of unspoilt beaches, scenic countryside, and the hauntingly beautiful Dartmoor on your doorstep. Walking and riding are both great pastimes here, but there are many other activities available for you to enjoy. The historic city of Plymouth is a short drive away with its charming Barbican, a wealth of shops, restaurants, and night spots, and the excellent Theatre Royal. Exeter and Totnes are also within driving distance, as are the more crowded resorts of the English Riviera and Paignton. There is something for everyone in this area, and this is the perfect spot from which to visit many of the local attractions.

Ermewood House is a superb country house, situated on the fringe of the picturesque village of Ermington, which combines good quality with a lot of style. Mike and Claire are the perfect hosts and extend a warm welcome to all their guests - the combination of unobtrusive service and cheerful hospitality is the key to this excellent family run hotel. All ten bedrooms are en suite, fully central heated and offer facilities such as colour TV, radio, hair dryer and a hospitality tray. Each is delightfully decorated and has stunning views over the open countryside. An evening meal is available in the restaurant, and is mainly traditional English cooking, making use of the good local produce where possible. The menu changes daily, and vegetarians are catered for. The wine list offers a good variety from around the world, and is reasonably priced. After dinner you can relax in the comfortable guest lounge which opens out onto the terrace, and perhaps plan your next days activities, or just enjoy the view. This is a relaxing, comfortable hotel, which although has very high standards, extends a warm welcoming atmosphere which immediately makes you feel at home.

USEFUL INFORMATION

OPEN; All year
CHILDREN; Over 12 years welcome
PETS; No
CREDIT CARDS; All major cards
ACCOMMODATION; 10 bedrooms en suite.

RESTAURANT; Excellent daily menu
VEGETARIAN; Catered for
DISABLED ACCESS; Partial
BAR; Yes

HEALE FARMHOUSE

Liftondown,
Devon PL 15 9QX

Tel: 01566 784869

The 16th century listed Heale Farmhouse is to be found between Liftondown and Launceston almost on the borders of Devon and Cornwall. The River Carey runs through the grounds and at night the stunning view of the floodlit Launceston Castle can be seen from the front rooms. It is a beautiful spot and the house lies in a lovely valley conveniently between Dartmoor and Bodmin Moor and is approximately 18 miles from the North Cornwall coast.

The house is the family home of John and Judith Edgley and is one of the most welcoming places to be found anywhere in Cornwall. Over almost a quarter of a century they have been caring for guests, many of whom have become friends having stayed here quite regularly. Between them, John and Judith have created such a happy atmosphere in the house that you cannot possibly feel anything but comfortable and relaxed within its walls.

There are four attractively furnished guest rooms, one of which is en suite and the other three share two private bathrooms. Each bedroom has a radio, hairdryer and a well supplied beverage tray. It is so peaceful that it would be hard not to enjoy a restful night and wake up in the morning to the sounds of the countryside and probably the tantalising smell of fresh coffee brewing ready for breakfast. Breakfast is a meal which is quite memorable with everything freshly cooked, free-range eggs and organically home grown produce. There is a wide range of cereals and fruit juices and a choice of several variations in the full farmhouse breakfast.

This is an ideal house for vegetarians. Judith specialises in Vegetarian dishes. An evening meal is available when booked in advance in which everything is home-cooked and with plenty of home-grown vegetables. In addition to the cosy separate dining room there is also a comfortable guests' sitting room.

There are many places to explore within easy distance and the spacious, rambling garden with the river running through it, is very pleasant for an evening stroll.

USEFUL INFORMATION

OPEN; *All year*
CHILDREN; *Welcome*
CREDIT CARDS; *None taken*
LICENSED; *No. Wine available*
ACCOMMODATION; *4 rooms,*
1 en suite 2 private bathrooms

DINING ROOM; *Good, farmhouse breakfast*
Home-cooked evening meal available
Organic vegetables and produce
VEGETARIAN; *A speciality*
DISABLED ACCESS; *Not suitable*

SOUTH HARTON FARM

Lustleigh,
Newton Abbot,
Devon TQ13 9SG

Tel: 01647 277216

The address of this enchanting farmhouse is misleading. The Lustleigh bit is correct but once having reached the village at the junction opposite the post office you need to turn left and follow the road up the hill to 'Rudge Cross' a steep 'T' junction. Turn right, signposted the Cleave, North Bovey. Follow this road for approximately 1 mile. South Harton drive entrance is on the left, proceed to the top of the drive go through the archway and there is the farmhouse. The house dates back to the 16th century and is typical of Devon thatched houses with open fireplaces, beamed ceilings and large rooms, but its much more than that. It wanders going up a few steps here and down some winding ones there, creating a charming, warm-hearted atmosphere which is enhanced by the friendliness of the owners, Mike and Myra Ellicott. There are stunning views and for birdwatchers it is heaven sent - woodpeckers strut about the patio and buzzards live in the trees. Fishing in the river and reservoir, inspiring walks and exploring Dartmoor or the coast will give you plenty to do. Mike Ellicott is more than willing to drop you off at the beginning of your walk and pick you up again at a designated point.

USEFUL INFORMATION

OPEN; *All year*
CHILDREN; *Very welcome*
CREDIT CARDS; *No*
ACCOMMODATION; *1 dbl en suite with bath*
1 twin ensuite shower room, 1 twin with
adjoining bathroom

DINING ROOM; *Good, wholesome*
Farmhouse fare
VEGETARIAN; *By arrangement*
DISABLED ACCESS; *No*
GARDEN; *Farm, patio*
PETS; *Well behaved - by arrangement*

THE CLIFTON AT PAIGNTON,

Clifton Hotel,
9-10 Kernou Road,
Paignton,
South Devon TQ4 6BA

Tel/Fax: 01803 556545

Just a few yards from the sea at Paignton, and in a completely level location close to the shops and stations, the totally non-smoking Clifton offers what one always hopes to find in a comfortable, family run hotel. Primarily one wants to feel welcome and secondly relaxed and this is what Freda Dwane and her partner Steven Bamford achieve admirably. The hotel is open from March to November and for Christmas and, as it is centrally heated throughout, it is ideal for those who enjoy getting away for short breaks in the off seasons knowing that they can enjoy a walk across the beach or the front without the crowds that are to be found in summer. On the other hand the liveliness of Torbay in the summer months with its various attractions, including theatres, is very enjoyable. What Paignton and Torbay do enjoy is a very mild climate which makes anytime of the year ideal for a holiday.

The hotel throughout is furnished with a desire to ensure everyone is warm and comfortable. All the bedrooms are en suite or with private facilities and there are some family size bedrooms. Every room has colour television and that blessing, a hostess tray. In the attractively laid dining room, where the smell of freshly brewed coffee awaits you, you will be served a full English Breakfast which is generous in portion and has several choices, as well as all the toast, butter and preserves you could possibly want. A packed lunch is available to order for your day out exploring the area, or snacks can be served on the patio or in the bar if you prefer. The dining room is transformed at night by candlelight to compliment the superb five-course dinners which are lovingly prepared by Steve using the very best of local produce. The end product is a quality meal one would hardly expect for the very small price which is charged. That together with a very reasonably priced wine list, makes for a most relaxing evening. Coffee is served in the lounge after dinner where you have the opportunity of exchanging, with other guests, tales of your days adventures.

USEFUL INFORMATION

OPEN: *Mar-November & Xmas*
CHILDREN: *Welcome. Family rooms*
CREDIT CARDS: *Visa*
LICENSED: *Yes*
ACCOMMODATION: *15 rooms*
12 en suite, 3 with private facilities
STRICTLY NON-SMOKING

DINING ROOM: *Good home-cooked*
International fare
VEGETARIAN: *Catered for*
DISABLED ACCESS: *No*
GARDEN: *Patio*
PETS: *No*

THE BABA INDIAN RESTAURANT

134 Vauxhall Street,
The Barbican, Plymouth
PL4 0DE
Tel: 01752 250677 or 256488

Plymouth has many Indian Restaurants but without doubt this is one of the best for a variety of reasons not the least being the owner, Baba, Laskar, who runs it under his own personal supervision. This is a man who spent many years learning his trade before he ventured into ownership. There is no job in the restaurant that he cannot personally undertake, and will do so if the need arises. This keeps his friendly and efficient staff constantly on their toes seeing to the needs of the customers. Many customers are regulars who would not consider going anywhere else. They enjoy both the food and the ambience that has been created. The restaurant is a long, panelled room set within one of the oldest buildings in Plymouth. Furnished in a rich style, the warmth of the panelling combined with the deep red tablecloths, sparkling silver and gleaming glass, has just the right atmosphere in which to enjoy a meal. The wide ranging menu will invite you to taste flavours that are as varied as the climate of India and as exotic as its people. Fragrant spices, pungent and warm spices, from the four corners of the country are delicately blended in meticulous proportions to create the dishes of your choice. Each dish will 'have its own distinctive flavour and aroma which cannot come from any Curry Powder but from spices which have to be separately prepared each day afresh for each individual dish. The blending and preparation of spices is a centuries old craft, indispensable to Indian cuisine and one that Baba has perfected. It is no easy matter to select dishes from the menu - everything is tempting but your waiter, or Baba himself, will happily recommend dishes to suit your taste and temperature! For wine lovers there is a well chosen list at sensible prices - the house wine is more than acceptable. Beers, spirits, sherries, port, vermouth and liqueurs are all available. An evening at Babas will long stay in your memory but probably the 9 Course Banquet held every first Tuesday in the month once sampled would never be forgotten! There are two sittings, one at 6pm and the other at 9pm and booking is essential. If perchance you cannot go to the restaurant and live within striking distance there is an excellent Take Away Service delivered free of charge within four miles for orders over ten pounds.

USEFUL INFORMATION

OPEN; *Sun-Thurs 5pm-midnight Fri-Sat 5.30-lam*
RESTAURANT; *Superb Indian food Wide ranging choice. also English dishes*
Every Sunday Family Buffet l2noon-6pm
Every first Tuesday of the Month 9 course Banquet
First sitting 6pm Second sitting 9pm Bookings only
VEGETARIAN; *Several dishes*
CREDIT CARDS; *All major cards*
DISABLED ACCESS; *Yes*
CHILDREN; *Welcome*

THE PLUME OF FEATHERS INN

The Square, Princetown,
Tavistock,
Devon PL2O 6QG

Tel: 01822 890240

The Plume of Feathers is situated in the moorland village of Princetown, which is Dartmoor's main village. On the outskirts of Princetown, is the world renowned Dartmoor Prison. Completed in 1809 it was built by American and French prisoners of war to provide them with accommodation. It is a forbidding, austere; grey and unwelcoming building in total contrast to the warmth and genial atmosphere of the Plume of Feathers. Owned and run by James Langton for the last 25 years, it has a reputation which reaches out all over the world. Built in 1785 it is Princetown's oldest building with copper bars, log fires, oil lamps and an ambience all its own. It retains many of its original features - slate floors, exposed beams and granite walls.

This is a pub beloved by people who come from quite a distance to join the fun and hospitality. With live music on Sunday lunchtime there seems to be something happening all the time, attracting all age groups. You can stay in the Inn in comfortable rooms, pitch your tent or park your caravanette in the space behind the pub which has a toilet block and free showers. The 'Alpine Bunkhouse' and new additional bunkhouses provide 42 comfortable beds arranged in dormitories of 10, 4 or 2 bunks, with showers, hot and cold, toilets, excellent facilities and day room.

Food is served throughout the week and the standard is excellent. There are bar snacks of all kinds with 'Daily Specials'. Try the 'Plume Special' - an enormous mixed grill. Every morning, Sundays included, the Plume serves breakfast for those on the camp site or in the bunkhouses. Good value, good fun, The Plume is there to enjoy.

USEFUL INFORMATION

OPEN; *Mon- Sat: 11-11pm*
Sun: 12-10.30pm
BAR FOOD; *Wide variety .Daily specials*
VEGETARIAN; *Selective menu*
ACCOMMODATION; *B&B + Bunkhouse*
and Campsite
GARDEN; *Adventure Play Area &*
Beer Garden

RESTAURANT; *Large selection Inn food*
CHILDREN; *Families room & menu*
CREDIT CARDS; *All major cards*
LICENSED; *Full Licence. Real Ales*
DISABLED ACCESS; *Ramps, toilets*

DEVON TOR PRIVATE HOTEL
Devon Road,
Salcombe, South Devon TQ88HJ
Tel: 01548 843106

Christina and Malcolm Barlow have made many friends since they came to the Devon Tor Private Hotel. Firstly, of course, because they are likeable people who genuinely enjoy their guests and secondly because they have found the right formula which makes people write things in their visitors book such as 'It's like being at home - but without the work'. Many people who stay here are regulars and would not dream of going anywhere else, first time visitors soon find themselves among friends and becoming almost proprietorial about 'their' hotel! The Barlows philosophy is that Devon Tor has to be the kind of hotel that they would like to stay in themselves. It is small enough for them to be able to keep this personal touch and as for the rest you will find every room beautifully decorated and in excellent order. The six ensuite bedrooms are superbly appointed with pretty floral linens, wall papers and lovely pine beds, colour TV, alarm/radio and a well supplied hostess tray. Hair dryers, an iron and ironing board are available on request. The bathrooms are stunning with 'Heritage' Porcelain and gold taps. The views over the estuary from every bedroom and bathroom is breathtaking. The reception rooms are equally delightful with drapes in the Laura Ashley style and elegant, but comfortable furniture. The whole atmosphere is warm and welcoming and ensures you relax. Much as the Barlows love children they have found that young ones under the age of nine tend to disturb their guests. Dogs are definitely taboo.

Food is all important and while you are enjoying an excellent meal in the dining room, it is enhanced by the view over the magnificent estuary, alive with activity during the holiday season, over the sandy beaches of Mill Bay and Sunny Cove with the English Channel beyond. Every meal is prepared with fresh produce, meat, fish and vegetables. Everything is home-cooked and the portions are more than generous. Special attention is paid to those who have specific diets. One of the most pleasant aspects of the Devon Tor is the terrace, where people gather to have a drink in the evenings, chatting with friends, old and new. It is here too that Barbecues are held on summer evenings. The wine list complements the food, it is not vast but it has been chosen to cover most tastes and pockets.

Few people will need telling how beautiful Salcombe is, certainly one of Devon's most picturesque resorts and famous for bathing from safe, sandy beaches. For sailing, fishing, windsurfing, golf and coastal or woodland walks amidst a rich variety of wild flowers and birds. From the Devon Tor you are less than ten minutes walk from the town and its ferries and in easy walking distance of North and South Sands.

USEFUL INFORMATION

OPEN; *All year except Christmas*
CHILDREN; *Not under 9 year*
CREDIT CARDS; *None taken*
LICENSED; *Yes*
ACCOMMODATION; *6 en suite rooms*
PETS; *No*

DINING ROOM; *Good home-made fare using Fresh fish, meat & Vegetables*
VEGETARIAN; *Catered for + special diets*
DISABLED ACCESS; *No*
GARDEN; *Patio overlooking estuary*

THE KINGSWOOD HOTEL,
Esplanade,
Sidmouth,
Devon EX10 8AX

Tel: 01395 516367 Fax: 01395 513185

There are many architectural gems on the Esplanade in Sidmouth but what makes The Kingswood Hotel stand out amongst them is the sheer floral beauty of the colourful hanging baskets and tubs burgeoning with flowers throughout the season. Sidmouth itself is always a contender for the 'Britain in Bloom' competition and without doubt the Seward family who have owned this very nice, comfortable hotel for over 40 years, are behind the competition and lead by example.

The Kingswood was formerly part of the Victorian Spa Baths and looks out over the Esplanade to the sparkling sea beyond. Although the hotel has every modern comfort, every effort has been made to retain the charm, elegance and standard of service of that bygone age. It is essentially an hotel for those who enjoy peace and quiet and who appreciate the firm non-smoking policy. Every bedroom has en suite facilities with colour TV, direct-dial telephone and a generously furnished beverage tray. Some of the bedrooms have balconies overlooking the sea where one can sit and soak in the sun, read the morning papers or relish the opportunity of reading a book. Having enjoyed a restful nights sleep one comes down to breakfast in the morning refreshed and ready to enjoy the excellent breakfast with its many choices. Snacks are available at lunchtime and can be eaten in one of the lounges or on the patio. Dinner at night is a meal, beautifully prepared, using seasonal, fresh, local produce and accompanied by a well chosen wine list. There are always choices at every course.

Although the hotel has no bar it does have a full restaurant and residential licence, with drinks served on the patio or in the lounge. There is a private Car Park at the rear of the Hotel in which you can reserve spaces. For those who find the stairs difficult the Kingswood has a modern passenger lift serving most rooms from ground to second floor. The Kingswood has a deserved reputation and it is somewhere that once visitors have discovered its welcoming informality and friendliness, tend to return time and time again.

USEFUL INFORMATION

OPEN; *All year*
CHILDREN; *Welcome*
CREDIT CARDS; *Visa/Mastercard*
LICENSED; *Restaurant & Residential*
ACCOMMODATION; *26 en suite rooms*
PETS; *Accepted by arrangement*

DINING ROOM; *Excellent home-made fare Snacks on patio or in lounge*
DISABLED ACCESS; *Passenger lift*
VEGETARIAN; *Upon request*
GARDEN; *Patio. Car Park at rear*
A NON-SMOKING HOTEL

THE ROYAL YORK & FAULKNER HOTEL,

The Esplanade,
Sidmouth, Devon EX10 8AZ
Tel: 01395 513043/513184 Fax: 01395 577472

Sidmouth is unique. It has never forsworn the elegance of the Regency period when it first came to prominence as a seaside resort for the fashionable throng. Beautiful, elegant houses were built, hotels were created to offer the visitors the highest standard of hospitality. The stunning sea views, the comparatively mild climate and the affluent air of the little town have not changed with the centuries and today's visitors are welcomed with the same good mannered approach. The epitome of this is The Royal York which was Sidmouths first purpose-built hotel and dates from 1810. In 1970 it amalgamated with the adjacent Faulkner and now forms a modern, spacious hotel. It looks out immediately across the road to the esplanade and the beach beyond. Painted white, it glistens in the sun and is highlighted by the pretty balconies on the first floor with their blue canopied roofs. At ground level, colourful hanging baskets add to the restrained gaiety of the building.

From the outside one would not have an inkling of all the amenities within its welcoming doors. Beautifully furnished throughout, the lounges are comfortable, restful places and the tastefully refurbished Faulkner Lounge Bar overlooking the sea is a popular meeting place and offers a selection of freshly cut sandwiches and light lunches every day. Two inter-communicating sea-facing dining rooms offer good food served by a friendly, thoughtful staff. You come down to breakfast after a good nights sleep ready to enjoy the excellent breakfast with its many choices. Later in the day Tappers Bar with its Bistro Style restaurant serves a wide choice of dishes from 12-2 pm every day with a menu that includes locally caught fish and much local produce. Dinner is a restful affair, unhurried and the menu is imaginative and so too is the well chosen, interesting wine list. The 68 en suite bedrooms are all attractively and immaculately furnished. Each room has a colour television, a direct-dial telephone and a hostess tray. They are all light and airy , many with magnificent sea views and the 1st floor front rooms have elegant balconies. Two lifts serve all floors.

What is unexpected in the hotel is the excellence of the award winning leisure facilities. Located in the lower ground floor, the purpose built indoor short-mat bowls rink is popular with bowlers and beginners alike. Adjacent to the bowls rink is a full sized snooker table. The large spa pool with Jacuzzi jets and forced-air inlets, the sauna, solarium and a range of exercise equipment help to keep everyone in trim and give great pleasure. Without doubt the Royal York and Faulkner in the capable and friendly hands of Peter and Rosemary Hook whose family have run the hotel for over fifty years, will give anyone lucky enough to stay there, a memorable, relaxing and restful holiday.

USEFUL INFORMATION

OPEN; *All year*
CHILDREN; *Welcome*
CREDIT CARDS; *All major cards*
LICENSED; *Yes. Comp wine list*
ACCOMMODATION; *68 en suite rooms*

RESTAURANT; *Delicious, fresh fare*
TAPPERS BAR; *Wide ranging lunch menu*
VEGETARIAN; *Catered for*
DISABLED ACCESS; *2 ground floor rooms*
PETS; *Yes but not in public rooms*

THE KINGS ARMS INN

Stockland,
Nr Honiton,
Devon EX14 9BS

Tel: 01404 881361 Fax: 01404 881732
E.Mail: Kings. Arms @ Virgin.Net

With the constant desire to improve this already delightful hostelry, Heinz Kiefer, Paul Divani and John O'Leary continually provide something new. They intend to build more bedrooms and to create more dining space, but if they did nothing at all it would not matter; The Kings Arms is everything anyone could wish for. There is a happy mix of locals who come for the pleasure of drinking in this friendly establishment where the bar has large optics and a remarkable range of Malt whisky, and those who know that the food will be memorable. You have a choice of where to eat or drink. The Farmers Bar is the focal point for drinkers and for those who want a quick meal. The Cotley Restaurant Bar is charming and in The Dining Room you can eat intimately in an attractively furnished room. The exciting Menu with an excellent choice is on the Blackboard in the Cotley Restaurant Bar - specially recommended is the Lamb Sicilian - and is available every evening and at lunchtimes from Monday to Saturday (last orders 1.45pm) when a Snack Menu is also available. Traditional Sunday Lunch is only served on Mothers Day.

There are three guest rooms at present, all ensuite and centrally heated with colour television, telephone and tea and coffee making facilities. Well behaved and fully house trained animals are allowed in the garden, guest rooms and the Farmers Bar except where food is being served. The Garden and the Patio are delightful and just the place for a drink on a warm day. When not reserved for functions or Skittle matches (August -April), children are welcome to play in the Terrace Room providing they are under adult supervision and they can also sit with adults in the adjacent lounge. The Kings Arms is an inn to be enjoyed and certainly remembered.

USEFUL INFORMATION

OPEN; *7 days all year 12-3pm/6.30 to 11pm* **RESTAURANT;** *Delicious,imaginative food*
Sun: 12-3pm/7 to 10.30pm Xmas Day 11-1pm only **BAR FOOD;** *Wide range*
CREDIT CARDS; *Mastercard/Visa etc.* **VEGETARIAN;** *Yes + special diets*
LICENSED; *Yes. Great choice Malt Whisky* **DISABLED ACCESS;** *No facilities*
ACCOMMODATION; *3 en suite rooms* **GARDEN;** *Yes + Patio.*
PETS; *Well behaved permitted apart from food areas*

HUNTSHAM COURT,
Huntsham,
Nr Tiverton,
Devon EXl6 7NA

Tel: 01398 361365 Fax: 01398 361456

Mogens and Andrea Bolwig invite you to be entertained Huntsham style! You may rest assured if you accept the invitation that it will be an unforgettable and memorable experience. The house is a beautiful Victorian building with large rooms, tall ceilings, splendid arches, vast windows and has about it that sense of somewhere lost in time. It is certainly hidden away in a pretty spot that is not exactly anywhere yet is only a few miles from Tiverton and 10 minutes from the M5. It is definitely the place for those who want to leave the world for a while. Maybe you need to be a trifle eccentric to stay here but it is not a requirement. A weekend will seem like a country house party that might have taken place early in the century when gracious living was the order of the day and no one had even heard of television. It is relaxed and very friendly. You cannot miss breakfast which is a splendid meal because you can have it whenever you are ready. You cannot lose your room key because there are none, and as you are your own barman, the bar is never closed! The only contact you have with the outside world is an old fashioned radio.

The days pass in a blissful awareness that your every need is catered for. You can walk, ride, shoot a few clay pigeons, ride one of the bicycles left lying about in the outbuildings, hit a tennis ball or simply wander in the grounds. The library is a good hidey-hole and the vast sitting room is full of comfortably big chairs and sofas. Music is of great importance at Huntsham. You may choose to play one of the odd brass instruments that are to be found alongside the 3000 strong record collection. There are endless things to do. All the bedrooms are named after composers which seems very appropriate and in keeping with the Bolwigs love of music. Each is totally individual and has a vast Victorian bath in a bathroom that is the size of any normal bedroom! Dinner is the highlight of the day. You dine round one single table, beautifully appointed, on food that is incomparable. You may find that even before dinner you are mildly mellow as a result of Mogens taking you below to the cellars to choose the evening's wine, and sample a bottle or two. What is so special about the whole Huntsham experience is the excellence of the company, its totally different way of life, the wonderful food and wine, the great conversation and the opportunity to meet the Bolwigs who rescued Huntsham when it was just about derelict and fine tuned it into its present, wonderful state. One should point out that it is an accepted place for companies to use for conferences, small seminars and meetings that they do not wish the world to know about!

USEFUL INFORMATION

OPEN; *All year*
CHILDREN; *Not really*
Only families for Group Hire
CREDIT CARDS; *All major cards*
LICENSED; *Yes. Fine cellar*
ACCOMMODATION; *14 bedrooms*

DINING ROOM; *Superb food at any meal*
VEGETARIAN; *Catered for*
DISABLED ACCESS; *Not suitable*
GARDENS; *Yes. Croquet, tennis etc*
PETS; *No*

THE ABBEYFIELD HOTEL,

Bridge Road, Torquay,
Devon, TQ2 5AX.

Tel : 01803 294268
Fax : 01803 296310

The Abbeyfield Hotel is a comfortable, friendly hotel, run by Diana and Llewellyn Jones who treat their guests as friends, and ensure a high standard of comfort and relaxation for everyone. The Abbeyfield has eight comfortable bedrooms which are well furnished, and have facilities such as TV and a hospitality tray of tea and coffee. Other items are available on request. Most rooms are en suite, and all are individually decorated in a charming manner. An evening meal is available, and is good, wholesome, home cooked fayre. Vegetarians and special diets are cheerfully catered for upon request. There is a cosy bar for guests, where you can enjoy a quiet drink before or after dinner, perhaps planning your next days activities. Bar snacks are also available, and this is ideal if you just want something light in the evening. This hotel has a lovely 'home from home' atmosphere, and is in the ideal spot for the many delights of Torquay and the English Riviera.

Torquay is an ideal haven for that family holiday, and Diana and Llewellyn cater very well for children of all ages. The surrounding area is full of activities that the whole family will enjoy : bowling, tennis, diving, sailing are just some of those on offer, and the hotel is just 200yds from the Torquay train station if you wish to venture further afield. Shops, restaurants, night clubs and pubs are all only a few minutes walk away, but the hotel is situated in a quiet spot so that your nights slumber is not disturbed by all this activity! There are many places in the surrounding area to visit, the cities of Plymouth and Exeter within a car journey, and the beautiful Dartmoor just waiting to be explored. Historically there is much of interest, with a castle at Paignton (Compton), and at Dartmouth, Mount Edgecombe House at Plymouth, and the beautiful cathedral in Exeter city centre to mention just a few. But even if you never leave Torquay, you will be dazed by the beauty of the place, the fine gardens and swaying palm trees, lovely walks along the beach, the friendly locals - this is a place that has it all - the rightly named English Riviera, and the perfect family hotel to compliment your stay in Britain's most famous holiday resort.

USEFUL INFORMATION

OPEN; *All year (inc Xmas)*
CHILDREN; *Most welcome*
PETS : *By arrangement*
LICENSED; *Full*
CREDIT CARDS; *All major*
ACCOMMODATION; *8 rooms -*
6 en suite 5 dbl, 1 twin, 1 fml & 1 sgl.

RESTAURANT; *Good home cooking*
VEGETARIAN & SPECIAL DIETS; *Yes*
DISABLED ACCESS; *Yes, 2 ground floor rooms-subject to prior arrangement*
BAR SNACKS; *Yes*

KELVIN HOUSE HOTEL,
46, Bampfylde Road,
Torquay, Devon TQ2 5AY

Tel: 01803 297313

Kelvin House is a quiet hotel situated in a quiet tree-lined road and just a pleasant short walk through Torre Abbey Gardens to the Seafront, Harbour and Marina, the English Riviera Centre with its vast range of entertainment, and the shops. Built in Victorian times it is a fine example of the architecture of the day. The Victorians were past masters at making their rooms spacious and with high ceilings creating a light and airy feeling throughout the building. Much has changed since those days but little has been lost of the architectural features. Kelvin House is owned and run by the Canning family with Dee cooking the excellent meals and daughters, Charlotte and Alysia looking after the front of the house whilst father, Geoff, takes care of all the many tasks incumbent on running a hotel that is kept to a very high standard. Between them they have created a delightful atmosphere and everyone who comes here to stay immediately feels at home and relaxed.

The hotel has eight en suite bedrooms, all attractively furnished, warm and comfortable. Each room has television and a generously supplied hostess tray. Downstairs the lounge is elegantly furnished and the pleasant dining room is an ideal place in which to start the day with a full, traditional English Breakfast offering several choices and always freshly cooked. The optional, excellent home-cooked evening meal with its varied menu and scrummy desserts is also served here. Kelvin House is licensed so one can enjoy wine with meals and also perhaps sit on the sun terrace enjoying a drink before dinner. In cooler weather the friendly, well-stocked bar is a great meeting place. Open all the year, Kelvin House is centrally heated, and somewhere that many people come to for an out of season break. The mild climate makes Torbay particularly attractive in the winter or early spring.

There is always plenty to do and see in the Torbay area. In the summer the beautiful gardens always draw comment and throughout the year there is a variety of entertainment as well as many leisure activities. The Canning family will be happy to help you plan your days out if you wish them to. They are a caring family and do their utmost to make sure all their guests have an enjoyable stay, and very importantly, want to return.

USEFUL INFORMATION

OPEN; *All year*
CHILDREN; *By arrangement*
CREDIT CARDS; *Visa/Master/Euro*
LICENSED; *Yes*
ACCOMMODATION; *8 ensuite rooms*

DINING ROOM; *Traditional English Fare, home-cooked.*
VEGETARIAN; *Catered for & Coeliac*
DISABLED ACCESS; *Not suitable*
PETS; *By arrangement*

MELBOURNE TOWER HOTEL

Solsbro Road,
Torquay Devon TQ2 6PF

Tel/Fax: 01803 607252

This Grade II Listed hotel really does have a tower which reputedly was used as a place of inspiration for Victorian poets! Whatever it might have been it certainly adds a distinguishing touch to the facade of the hotel today. Owned and run by Tricia and Barne it has recently been totally and very attractively refurbished. Always a house of distinction it now adds comfort to its reason for guests staying here and coming back time and time again. The Victorian architecture and features are still there but every modern convenience has been added wherever possible without destroying its Victorian charm. The eleven spacious rooms, some with sea views, are all centrally heated and mostly en suite with colour TV and a generously supplied beverage tray. Family rooms are available with child listening intercom and special children's rates.

The imaginative food starts with a great English breakfast offering several choices and all freshly cooked. Dinner has a menu devoted to traditional English, home-cooked fare, with additional influences from around the world. The ingredients are always fresh and as much local produce is used as possible. The breakfast sausage is specially made for the hotel. The small, well chosen wine list, perfectly complements the meal. The lounge and the bar are cosy places in which to relax or enjoy a drink. For those particularly lazy days or evenings you can while away the time on the paths and terraced lawns of the well-stocked and mature gardens.

Melbourne Tower is in the heart of Torquay, yet only 400 yards from the beach and is an ideal base for exploring the beautiful Devon countryside. Daily tours can be booked close by, to Dartmouth, Widecombe-in-the-Moor, Becky Falls, Plymouth, Exeter and Lands End as well as many more exciting places. Close at hand is the famous picturesque village of Cockington, the Model Village at Babbacombe, Paignton Zoo, the quaint olde-worlde fishing village of Brixham, and the Dart Steam Railway. For the more adventurous, boat trips, deep sea fishing, wind surfing, golf and bowls are all available locally.

USEFUL INFORMATION

OPEN; *All year*
CHILDREN; *Welcome*
CREDIT CARDS; *All major cards*
LICENSED; *Yes*
ACCOMMODATION; *11 rooms mainly en suite*
PETS; *No*
AMPLE PARKING

DINING ROOM; *Good home-cooked traditional Fayre*
BAR FOOD; *Not applicable*
VEGETARIAN; *Catered for*
DISABLED ACCESS; *By arrangement*
GARDEN; *Yes*

THE PALACE HOTEL
Babbacombe Road,
Torquay TQ1 3TG
Tel: 01803 200200 Fax: 01803 299899

Without doubt this has to be one of the finest hotels in the West Country and one which is privately owned, personally managed and has an enviable reputation for the limitless care and attention lavished on its guests. It is attention that is quietly unobtrusive. The hotel has a fascinating history which started in 1841 although it did not become an hotel until August 1921 and since that date it has been synonymous with the highest standards of cuisine, accommodation and hospitality.

Set above the charming Ansteys Cove one hardly needs to leave the environment of the hotel and its 25 acres of magnificent landscaped gardens and grounds; a feature of which The Palace is justly proud and being floodlit at night provide the perfect place for an evening stroll, to have a complete holiday! The indoor and outdoor sports facilities are second to none and available at no additional expense. They provide a wide range of both energetic and more leisurely activities to suit the mood, all of which are set within the grounds. You can play golf on the 9 hole par 3 golf course, tennis on the six tennis courts; two indoor and four outdoor. There are two squash courts, a heated indoor swimming pool and a heated outdoor swimming pool, a snooker room, a table tennis room, saunas and croquet. Professional coaches are on hand to offer individual tuition, and sports equipment hire is available at nominal cost. Adjacent to the grounds are the secluded, picturesque beauty of Ansteys Cove and the glorious coastal walks which may be enjoyed throughout the year as a consequence of Torquay's temperate climate. A little further afield there are quaint harbours, picture postcard villages, zoological and wildlife attractions; smugglers coves and beaches; with the magnificent untamed wilderness of Dartmoor National Park.

All the en suite bedrooms are beautifully appointed and have telephone, colour television, radio, hairdryer and beverage making facilities. There are luxurious suites which overlook the gardens and those on the first floor have balconies. Every meal is an occasion to savour. The Chefs are dedicated to create for you the ultimate in English and French cuisine. A La Carte, Table d'hote, vegetarian or dietary - whatever your desire - all are prepared from the very highest quality fresh local produce. Light meals are available from the lounges, whilst in the summer a barbecue buffet is served on the terrace. It is truly a wonderful hotel and a privilege to stay there.

USEFUL INFORMATION

OPEN; *All year*
CHILDREN; *Welcome*
CREDIT CARDS; *All major cards*
LICENSED; *Full*
ACCOMMODATION; *Ensuite rooms And suites, some with balconies*
PETS; *Guide dogs only*

RESTAURANT; *Superb cuisine*
BAR MEALS; *Light meals available in lounges*
VEGETARIAN; *Yes & dietary*
DISABLED ACCESS; *Yes*
GARDEN; *25 acres beautiful landscaped gardens and grounds. Leisure facilities Outdoor and indoor.*

THE PALMS HOTEL

537 Babbacombe Road,
Torquay, TQl 1HQ

Tel/Fax: 01803 293970

This friendly, unpretentious hotel has been the base for many guests over the years who have found all it has to offer is everything they wanted to make a holiday on the English Riviera perfect. In the capable hands of Paul Bonner and Phil Vinnicombe it is well run, spotlessly clean and has a welcoming, easygoing atmosphere which makes it easy for people to relax. You will find The Palms Hotel in one of the best positions in Torquay, opposite the lovely Torwood Gardens and only about 300 yards from the bustling Harbour, the Beach and Torquay's excellent shopping centre. For those who enjoy entertainment, the Princess Theatre, the Babbacombe Theatre and the English Riviera Centre all have excellent shows throughout the season and are within easy distance of the hotel.

The hotel has 10 well appointed ensuite bedrooms each with colour TV, Hostess trays and Hair dryers. Children are very welcome over the age of five and for them there are reduced rates. In the pretty Dinning Room a full English breakfast is served every day with several choices and generous in portion. You can choose whether to have an evening meal or not. If you do you will find everything is home-cooked and quite delicious with an ever changing menu. The friendly bar is just the place for a drink in the evening before dinner or perhaps after returning from an evening out at the theatre. One of the nice things about The Palms is that you are welcome to come and go as you please with access to your rooms at all times. Centrally heated the hotel is especially good for short breaks early and late in the season when there are special rates.

Most people find there is enough to keep them happy in Torbay but beyond that is the awesome majesty of Dartmoor, the historic cathedral city of Exeter, Totnes reputed to be the oldest borough in the country and the maritime city of Plymouth. You can take boat trips, sail, windsurf, play golf and enjoy many other sporting activities if you wish.

USEFUL INFORMATION

OPEN; *All year*
CHILDREN; *Over 5 years*
CREDIT CARDS; *Yes*
LICENSED; *Yes*
ACCOMMODATION; *10 en suite rooms*
PETS; *No*

DINNING ROOM; *Excellent full English breakfast*
VEGETARIAN; *Catered for*
DISABLED ACCESS; *Not suitable*
GARDEN; *Patio*

SPRINGFIELD HOUSE

Tuckenhay,
Totnes,
Devon TQ9 7EQ

Tel: 01803 732225 Fax: 01803 732843

Springfield House dates back to 1760 and is owned by the friendly Viv Whybrow. This is a delightful place which seems to excel in the hospitality industry. Everything has been very well thought out to ensure the comfort and relaxation of the guests. All rooms are traditionally furnished and have hair dryers, bath robes, tea and coffee as standard. Breakfast is served in your bedroom between 8 and 10am, and the choice is really excellent. From a Champagne Breakfast to a New York breakfast, which includes fruit juice, home-smoked salmon with cream cheese, chopped hard boiled eggs and fresh bagels, followed by oven fresh croissants and preserves. Does this sound delicious? Well this is only a sample of what is on offer. During the summer, breakfast is also served in the garden or on the terrace overlooking the valley. The walled garden is private and very pleasant. There are views over Bow Creek to the River Dart beyond. Spend some time in the heated outdoor swimming pool or relax with a Jacuzzi and sauna. There are some resident guests at the hotel who will be only too pleased to enjoy your company: four donkeys, a Shetland, four Labradors and two peacocks. But be careful, they are inclined to invite themselves on a stroll to the local pub and are not very good at paying when it is their round! There are two pubs in the hamlet of Tuckenhay, one of which is just at the bottom of Springfield's drive. Both are within walking distance and a pleasant evening can be spent at either. Viv will recommend some eating places, all in the local vicinity. Springfield is one of those charming informal places with an air of civilisation which has been appreciated by such guests as Sir Clement Freud, who praised it in his column in The Times. Tuckenhay is a river side hamlet located between the medieval town of Totnes and the ancient port of Dartmouth. It is an ideal location for touring, with the mystery and seduction of Dartmoor within access and many excellent beaches close by. The steam trains of Dart Valley are something not to be missed, or perhaps a trip on the River Dart appeals. Salcombe, Kingsbridge and Torbay are all a short drive away. Viv is only too happy to advise and help you plan your trips, and a more pleasant stay would be difficult to imagine.

USEFUL INFORMATION

OPEN; All year
CHILDREN; Under 12 years by arrangement
CREDIT CARDS; None taken
LICENSED; No
ACCOMMODATION; 3 ensuite rooms
PETS; By arrangement

DINING ROOM; Wonderful breakfasts
Evening meals by arrangement
VEGETARIAN; Catered for
DISABLED ACCESS; Not really
GARDEN; Yes, with heated swimming pool

BUCKLEIGH LODGE,
Bay View Road,
Westward Ho!
North Devon EX39 1BJ

Tel: 01237 475988

Buckleigh Lodge has the gracious look that Victorian country houses acquire. It is situated above the village of Westward Ho! and five minutes walk downhill to the sea, with 3 miles of sandy beach and breathtaking cliff walks. Westward Ho! is historically interesting in its own right, not because it has been there for centuries but because after Charles Kingsley wrote his popular novel of this name about the seafaring folk of Bideford, Northam and the surrounding district, the name was adopted from his title. Behind Westward Ho! looms Kipling Tors named after Rudyard Kipling who went to school at the old United Services College and started his writing career here. His novel Stalky and Co. tells the story of his school life and his adventures on Kipling Tors. Golfers on the Royal North Devon Course are sometimes surprised to see sheep and horses grazing happily on the links. It is their right to do so because Edward VII who played here gave their owners 'Commoner's rights'. The thrill of exploring Dartmoor and Exmoor is made possible because it is within easy reach of the house and so are the picturesque villages of Clovelly and Hartland. Surfing, windsailing, horse riding will please the energetic.

Malcolm Wise and his wife Kim own this friendly welcoming house and run it happily, informally yet never lacking professionalism. The en suite bedrooms are attractively furnished and have tea/coffee making facilities as well as colour television. Three of these rooms have panoramic views across the Tay. When you come down to breakfast in the morning your nostrils will be assailed by the smell of freshly brewed coffee and the tantalising smell of bacon. The whole meal has many choices, is always freshly cooked and very generous. Something to linger over before you take off for the day. A beautifully cooked three-course evening meal complemented by a good choice of wines is optional but should not be missed. People tend to gather in the lounge bar for a drink before dinner and frequently a night cap afterwards; it is an opportunity to share the pleasures you have discovered and learn about new ones. Open all year, the house is centrally heated and as welcoming in the Autumn, Winter and Spring as it is in the summer. In fact many people enjoy the more peaceful times when the main holiday season is over.

USEFUL INFORMATION

OPEN; *All year*
CHILDREN; *Welcome*
CREDIT CARDS; *None taken*
LICENSED; *Yes, Residential*
ACCOMMODATION; *En suite rooms*
GARDEN; *Yes*

DINING ROOM; *Excellent breakfast, optional 3 course dinner*
VEGETARIAN; *Catered for*
DISABLED ACCESS; *No special facilities*
PETS; *No*
PARKING; *Ample*

ROCKHAM BAY HOTEL

Mortehoe, Woolacombe,
North Devon EX34 7EG

Tel: 01271 862002 Fax: 01271 870107

Mortehoe is one of North Devon's most charming villages, surrounded by National Trust Land, yet just a mile and a half from the Blue Flag beach of Woolacombe. Colin and Bridget Boxshall have created a wonderful, warm atmosphere in their Rockham Bay Hotel where visitors having once discovered its comfort and hospitality tend to return again and again. The hotel is run impeccably but with the degree of informality that is so important to people taking a holiday or a short break. There are 26 bedrooms all of which are en suite and many have views down the valley to the sparkling blue sea beyond. Furnished with style but with the emphasis on comfort, each room has colour TV, tea and coffee making facilities, direct-dial telephones and hair dryers.

Food is a vital ingredient in the success of any holiday and great care is taken to provide an appetising menu which caters to all tastes. Having had a good nights sleep you will come down in the morning to the sunny dining room where breakfast is served. This is a meal that will set you up for the rest of the day. You have a choice of a full English or Continental breakfast with a selection of dishes on offer. In the evening a sumptuous four course evening meal is served with choices at every course and all home-cooked and using as much local, fresh produce as possible. Vegetarians and guests with dietary needs are well catered for with prior arrangement. You may well be tempted to sample the delicious Devon cream teas which are served both in the hotel and around the outdoor heated swimming pool with a sun patio sheltering it on all sides. In fact snacks and refreshments are available daily. The friendly Lounge Bar is the focal point in the evenings and it is here that a variety of entertainment is also provided most nights.

Picturesque walks are plentiful, with the North Devon Coastal Path just yards away from the hotel. Horse riding, Golf and Surfing are also available locally. Barnstaple, the capital of North Devon, Bideford with its historic Quay, Clovelly with its famous cobbled streets and Lynton and Lynmouth with their unique Cliff Railway are all within easy driving distance.

USEFUL INFORMATION

OPEN; *All year*
CHILDREN; *Welcome*
CREDIT CARDS; *Visa/Master/Amex*
ACCOMMODATION; *26 en suite rooms*
Short breaks at special rates available
PETS; *Yes*

DINING ROOM; *Traditional English fare*
VEGETARIAN; *Catered for + other diets*
LICENSED; *Yes*
DISABLED ACCESS; *No special facilities*
GARDEN; *No but heated tdoor swimming pool with sheltered patio*

THE WATERS FALL HOTEL

Beach Road,
Woolacombe,
Devon EX34 7AD
Tel: 01271 870365

Robert and Margaret Howson are the fairly recent owners of The Waters Fall Hotel which has spectacular views of the sandy beach and the unspoilt countryside from all the public rooms and the majority of the 16 bedrooms. What it lacked when they took over was that intangible something that produces the delightful, friendly informal atmosphere it now has. They have completely refurbished throughout breathing new life into all the rooms with the pretty decor, the attractive drapes and floor coverings and comfortable chairs everywhere. The lively bar has become the meeting point for guests in the evening; somewhere you meet old friends and rapidly make new ones. The Restaurant is light and airy and has a stunning view across the lawns to the sea. The bedrooms have been carefully planned and equipped to make sure that they are both restful and comfortable. They all have ensuite bathrooms, colour TV and a generously supplied hostess tray. Some of these bedrooms have balconies overlooking the sea and one really needs to book early to get one of these. Waking in the morning to the sounds of the countryside and the distant murmur of the sea, it is quite magical to step out onto the balcony and drink your morning tea seated at the table put there for your pleasure.

The Restaurant, which is open to non-residents, provides you with a splendid breakfast, freshly cooked to your choice. In the evening the Table d'Hote menu offers choices at every course and for the more discerning palate there is a delightful ALa Carte Menu. There is a choice of interesting and sensibly priced wines to complement the meal.. With plenty of level parking in 2 acres of grounds there is nothing lacking to make a perfect holiday or a short break. If you are a surfer you will discover the hotel is well known for its Surfrider Action Holidays which were featured on TV.

This is a beautiful corner of Devon and within twenty miles you can find the steep wooded valleys of Exmoor with its wild ponies, busy market towns, thatched villages for cream teas and wonderful beaches. It is essentially unspoilt and beautiful at anytime of the year. Springtime is a delight with Primroses and Bluebells and often the warmest climate in Britain. Autumn offers quiet beaches, coastal paths to walk and good golf courses. Good times for lower prices and special offers.

USEFUL INFORMATION

OPEN; *March to November*
CHILDREN; *Welcome*
CREDIT CARDS; *All major cards*
LICENSED; *Yes*
ACCOMMODATION; *16 en suite rooms*
GARDEN; *2/1/2 acres*

RESTAURANT; *Open to non-residents*
High standard traditional fare
VEGETARIAN; *Comprehensive*
DISABLED ACCESS; *Partial*
PETS; *Yes*

Chapter 5

DORSET & WILTSHIRE

INCLUDES

Chapter 5

DORSET AND WILTSHIRE

There is something both comforting and timeless about the County of Dorset: the smoothly rounded hills and convexities have a passive and ancient solidity that soothes and reassures. 'Here I stand and ~ here I be' might well be the motto of a landscape that has sustained Man since his earliest days, from the cliffs, coves and shingle of the coast, the whin-clad heaths, the hills and dales and woodlands of the hinterland. The configuration is so attractive and so varied that it might almost be taken as an epitome of the scenery of Southern England.

It is an intensely rural county, averaging rather more than one acre per inhabitant and is not disturbed by motorway or major road works. There is only one major conurbation, that of Poole and Bournemouth, with the remainder of the population residing mainly in the numerous small market towns and countless villages and hamlets whose names have a resounding ring out of all proportion to their size and present day standing; Rime Intrinsica, Melbury Osmond, Toller Porcorum, Chaldon Herring and Tarrant Gunville. The names, the people and the scenery have inspired writers and artists over the centuries.

In common with many other such rural areas, early settlements seem to have proliferated along the banks of streams and rivers, hence the numerous Winter bournes, Wimbornes, Piddle, Puddles, Tarrants Cernes, Chars and Weys. The great expanse of enclosed water that is Poole Harbour provided the county's earliest sheltered port, and one that remains of great economic importance to this day.

My tour began in the extreme south-west in the delightful little town of **Lyme Regis** close to the boundary with Devonshire. Once an important harbour and protected from prevailing south-westerly winds by the massive breakwater known as the Cobb, Lyme Regis was granted its royal status by Edward I in 1284, during his wars against the French. The first recorded settlement was nearly 600 years earlier when Cynewulf, King of the Saxons granted rights to the monks of Sherbourne for the production of salt. However, Lyme Regis is also renowned for its prehistoric associations; in 1811, Mary Anning, a carpenter's daughter, found the 30 foot skeleton of an ichthyosaurus in nearby cliffs, and ever since the area has been a happy hunting ground for the fossil collector. The 12-year-old Mary and her unpronounceable discovery did well out of the find; the reptile ended up in the Natural History Museum in London and Mary received twenty three pounds for the fossil, a small Government annuity and a window dedicated to her memory in the parish church.

The town is enchanting, set on the shore surrounded by a backcloth of high steep hills and with houses and shops set around narrow winding streets. It is a deservedly popular seaside resort, a role that replaced smuggling as a local and profitable pastime in the late 18th century. Jane Austen gives a vivid portrayal of the town in her novel 'Persuasion' written in 1815:

'....as there is nothing to admire in the buildings themselves, the remarkable situation of the town, the principal streets almost hurrying into the water, the wall to the Cobb, skirting round the pleasant little bay, which in the season is animated with bathing machines and company, the Cobb itself, its old wonders and new improvements, with the very beautiful line of cliffs stretching out to the east of the town, are what the stranger's eye will seek; and a very strange stranger it must be, who does not see charms in the immediate environs of Lyme, to make him wish to know it better.'

I disagree with the eminent novelist's opinion of the local architecture, but wholeheartedly endorse the rest. The Lyme Regis of today is cheerful and bustling, with numerous events and attractions to divert the visitor. As might be expected the town's two museums, **The Philpot Museum** and **Dinosaurland**, make a great feature of fossils, although there are many other exhibits of local interest. **The Lyme Regis Experience** is an award winning multi-media exhibition of the town's history as seen through the eyes of a Town Crier (Lyme has had a Crier for the last 1,000 years) while matters nautical and piscatorial are displayed at the **Lyme Regis Marine Aquarium.**

Some two miles or so to the east is another attractive community popular with holidaymakers, **Charmouth**. The wide main road through the village was first laid by the Romans on the foundations of an ancient pack-horse trail and after their departure, Charmouth was favoured by the Saxons. The stream that ran down from the high hills into the valley and across the sand and shingle to mingle with the waters of the Channel, was a principal attraction to these early settlers. It also attracted rather more unwelcome attention from the marauding Danes and the shore and immediate hinterland were the scene of a number of bloody clashes. After the Conquest, William's half-brother, the Count of Mortain, held the lordship, and the Domesday Book valued the community at 60 shillings. In the 11th century it passed into the hands of the monks of Forde Abbey and it is believed that, when visiting Charmouth for the purposes of collecting rents, they stayed at the Queen's Arms. Catherine of Aragon also stayed here in 1501, on her way to marry Arthur, brother of Henry VIII. A further and rather more dramatic royal connection was established 150 years later when Charles II stayed while making his escape after the disastrous Battle of Worcester. Disguised as a servant, the King waited in vain for a local mariner, one Stephen Limbry, to arrive with his vessel in order to take passage to France. Unfortunately Limbry's wife, evidently a domineering woman who put caution before patriotism, had read a proclamation to the effect that the penalty for harbouring, aiding and abetting Charles Stuart would be extremely unpleasant, indeed terminally so; thus, whilst Charles and his small party fretted on the shore, the intrepid sailor was unable to help - his wife having locked him in a room and taken his trousers! Inevitably the news of the King's presence leaked out and the royal party was forced to flee eastwards.

The ancient highway became of increasing importance, linking the county towns of Exeter and Dorchester and the handsome Georgian and Regency buildings bear witness both to the popularity of the village as a coaching stop, and to the attractions of the area as a resort. Some of this history can be seen reflected in the displays at the **Charmouth Heritage Coast Centre**, together with exhibitions of fossils, geology and wildlife.

The lovely coast and inland scenery, combined with these small seaside communities, offers the holidaymaker a glimpse of more certain and simple pleasures and it is hardly surprising that families return year after year. Neighbouring **Chideock** has much the same atmosphere, albeit on a smaller scale; the houses here also line the hillside but the thatched cottage, rather than the grander Georgian and Victorian buildings of Charmouth, predominates. The happily named Duck Street leads to the tiny seaside hamlet of **Seatown**, where the small River Winniford flows into the sea. The tittle beach is dominated by the highest cliff of the South coast, **Golden Cap**, 618 feet above sea-level. Now under the stewardship of the National Trust, the gorse-clad cliff was the look-out post for an 18th century smuggling gang based in Chideock.

The village once boasted a castle in the shape of a fortified manor house built by Sir John de Chidioke in 1379. His descendants in the form of the Arundell and Weld families have held the Lordship of the Manor to this day, but the castle has long gone. All that remains is a mound surrounded by part of the moat. On the excellent principle of 'waste not want not', the bulk of the castle was incorporated into new or existing buildings in the village. One of these is the most appealing thatched pub, The George Inn in the High Street. Here you can get very good pub food, freshly prepared at family prices.

Apart from the obvious enjoyment to be had beside the sea, this western most area of Dorset has a multitude of attractions inland; historic sites, lovely walks, pretty villages, friendly pubs and stately homes. **Whitchurch Canonicorum**, two miles inland from Charmouth, has a link with those Viking raiders of long ago; the 13th-century Church of St Candida and the Holy Cross contains the tomb of the saint, also known as St Wita, and who is thought to have been a Saxon woman slain in a raid. The tomb has two fold interest, in that it is one of the few where the relics have lain virtually undisturbed and it was built with 'healing holes', three oval openings into which an affected limb could be placed.

It may be that the saint met her tragic end at **Coney's Castle**, where great earthen-works mark the reputed site of a battle between the Danes and King Egbert. **Pilsdon Pen** also bears evidence of a far earlier culture with Iron Age earthworks to be found on the bare top of the highest hill in Dorset, at 909 feet a landmark for half the county and one that offers the most wonderful views.

Further north **Thorncombe** clings to a steep hillside close to the border with both Devon and Somerset, and between the village and the Somerset town of **Chard** lie the lovely buildings of **Forde Abbey**. Started at the beginning of the 12th century, the Cistercian monastery was not fully completed for another 300 years. To avoid destruction at the Dissolution, the Abbot handed the Abbey over to the King. It has been a family home since the 17th century when Sir Edmund Prideaux, Attorney General to Cromwell, commissioned Inigo Jones to convert it into a private house. Set beside the River Axe in some 30 acres of beautiful gardens, the house and monastic buildings contain remarkable tapestries, furniture and pictures.

To the east across the high rolling hills, lies the rambling village of **Broadwinsor**, reputedly the highest in Dorset, and close to the lovely wooded crest of Lewesdon Hill. Charles II stayed the night here after his failure to set sail from Charmouth; once again he had a narrow escape as the Parliamentarian soldiers were diverted by the sight of one of their camp followers giving birth. There are a number of 17th and 18th century cottages, a Perpendicular church and The White Lion Inn, an attractive and friendly pub with a justly popular restaurant.

To the south lies the principal market town for the area, **Beaminster**. The pleasant little town has had more than its share of bad luck, having been virtually destroyed by fire in 1644, 1684 and 1781; nevertheless, it retains a cheerful and friendly atmosphere and still possesses some fine buildings. Steep hills surround Beaminster and the little River Brit runs beside the main street with its handsome 18th-century buildings. There is a good-looking pinnacled market cross and a picturesque little 17th-century Almshouse. The large church, with its imposing 16th century tower is indicative of a large and prosperous community; the manufacture of linen and woollen cloth was the basis of this wealth. The town was also at the centre of an area which produced the famous 'Blue Veins' cheese, the 'blue veins' being produced by stirring the milk with a piece of old horse-harness - or so the story goes.

Parnham House is world-renowned as the home of the John Makepeace furniture workshops, where innovative use of wood and the highest standards of woodworking skill reign supreme. The house dates from the Middle Ages, was rebuilt in Tudor times and further altered by the great Regency architect John Nash. For 500 years it was the home of the Strode family, who are remembered in the church at Beaminster, and within the park there is the grave of Lieutenant Rhodes-Moorhouse, the first airman to be awarded the Victoria Cross. The Makepeace family have restored both house and gardens and the result is superb. There are also numerous events and exhibitions connected with the arts.

Not far away, is another house with lovely grounds, **Mapperton House** is perhaps the most beautiful manor house in Dorset and is set beside terraced gardens through which water gently flows. The house which dates back to Henry VIII, is of grey-yellow stone, which glows a deep golden colour in the sunlight. Handsomely ornamented, it stands beside its own small church and rectory. A few estate cottages complete the community. It is serene and timeless; qualities to be found throughout the county, but particularly in this region where the hills seemingly enfold and enclose minute communities guarding themselves against intrusions of the modern world.

To the north east of Beaminster is the small village of **Chedington** and here you will find one more of Dorset's beautiful mansions, now a hotel. Chedington Court is memorable and the view from the house and the balustraded terrace is probably one of the most magnificent in the South of England. The 10-acre gardens are noted for their beauty, particularly in Spring when the bulbs and wild flowers offer a glorious spectacle. Under the giant gnarled 1000-year-old yew tree, the lichen-encrusted tombstones rest serenely as a witness to the spot where the village church, probably of Saxon origin, once stood. The hotel has a par 74, nine-hole golf course a mile away. Delightful place to stay.

Bridport was a town in Saxon time and was granted its first charter by Henry III, but although it has a number of fine buildings and a wealth of character, the town is far from being stuck in the past. The town has long been known for its net and rope-making industries and the wide pavements of the main street were once rope-walks, where the raw materials were laid out to dry then twisted together. The trade is an ancient one; by the time of Elizabeth I it was claimed that all the ships of her fleet were rigged with cordage manufactured in Bridport utilising the hemp and flax that was grown locally. Today's trade utilises mainly synthetic materials and its products are exported all over the world.

The town has now been bypassed which has considerably eased congestion in the handsome main street where no two buildings are quite alike and the brick and stone Town Hall, complete with stately cupola, presides over all. Almost inevitably, the fugitive Charles Stuart spent a night here, once again escaping by the skin of his teeth. Other than a little half hearted bickering during the Civil War and a minor incident during the Monmouth rebellion. Bridport has kept its head down over the centuries and quietly and consistently prospered - an unusual record for what is after all an industrial town. **The Bridport Museum** in South Street tells the story of the town and its surroundings.

The 'minor incident' during the rebellion was perhaps not so minor as far as one Edward Coker was concerned, for he was shot and killed in The Bull Inn, a fine 16th century coaching inn in East Street. The window through which he was shot has been closed ever since. I have stayed many times in The Bull and always very happily.

To the east **Burton Bradstock**, a pretty village tucked away from the sea by a low ridge, lies close to the beginning of the extraordinary **Chesil Beach**. One of the great wonders of England's coastline, the Beach is some 15 miles of blue-clay reef covered with an immense coating of shingle, more than 40 feet high in parts. No expert has yet produced a convincing theory as to why the pebbles get progressively smaller the further west along the Beach one goes. Behind Chesil Beach is the Fleet, a brackish and reed-fringed lagoon.

North-east of Bridport, the narrow roads lead over the hills to **Powerstock**, a delightful village nesting beneath the 800-foot-high Eggardon Hill; where, from the massive earthen ramparts of an Iron Age fort on the top, excellent views are to be had of the surrounding countryside. A grassy mound in the village marks the place of some remains of a later fortification, a castle that was built during the anarchy of King Stephen's reign and much improved during that of John. It has been suggested that this was built on the site of a manor house belonging to the Saxon King Athelstan. Certainly Powerstock was once a far from insignificant place, and the Norman church contains the most elaborate chancel arch in the county. The Kings and Barons and all their panoply have long gone, leaving a contented rural community of attractive dwellings and a thatched and hospitable pub, The Three Horseshoes.

I have always liked this area and to stay at The Manor House in West Bexington, on the coast road between Bridport and Weymouth, is ideal for anyone wanting to enjoy this extraordinary coastline. This ancient manor house snuggles in a pocket of tree-and-garden on a gentle slope, just a saunter from the great sea-washed sweep of Chesil bank. An old stone building, mellowed by the nine centuries of sun and sea, it dates back far enough to have gained a starred rating in the Domesday Book - but comforts and facilities have been considerably improved since then, without sacrificing the ancient charm.

The gorse-laden heights overlooking Chesil beach are studded with reminders of far earlier civilisations; barrows, standing stones and circles mark the last resting place of forgotten tribal chieftains. **Abbotsbury** has a reminder of those pagan times in the survival of an ancient custom, Garland Day, held on May 13th. Thought to be a survival of sea-god worship, two garlands are carried through the village and one cast into the sea. The village is one of the loveliest in the county. Its narrow streets lined with mellow-stone cottages, many of them thatched. The Benedictine Abbey was founded in the 11th century and survived for 500 years until its destruction during the Dissolution. All that remains are the nave and part of the gate-house, but some idea of the Abbey's wealth may be gained by the magnificent **Tithe Barn**, which is over 270 feet long, and one of the largest in England. St Catherine's Chapel was built in the 14th century and stands on a hill to the south of the village. It is small and simple, with massive walls that have withstood the countless Channel gales; a sailor's chapel that acted as a landmark for those at sea and look-out tower for those anxiously waiting on shore.

Abbotsbury has had but three owners in its long history. First there was Orc, a steward of King Canute, and it was he and his wife, Thola, who established the Abbey. After the Dissolution, the village passed from the Church to the Strangways, Earls of Ilchester. The village suffered grievously during the Civil War; cottages were set alight, the royalist Strangways' mansion was burnt to the ground and the pulpit of the parish church still bears bullet-holes received during a short but bloody battle, described by the Parliamentarian commander as being 'a hot bickering'. A masterful understatement.

The Abbotsbury Sub-tropical Gardens have a wonderful display of rare and tender plants laid out around a walled garden with the added protection of a shelter-belt of trees. They were first laid out in 1760 and provide a stunning display of exotic blooms. **The Abbotsbury Swannery** dates back to the days when the monks reared swans for meat. Now the swan-herd cares for around 1,000 mute swans, plus innumerable wild-fowl, and his concern is that of a naturalist rather than that of an epicure.

Just outside Abbotsbury at **Portesham**, the Millmead Country Hotel and Restaurant is a family-run establishment offering a genuine welcome which immediately communicates to the visitor that their comfort and needs are paramount. The service is personal, the staff friendly and the food of a very high standard. There are 6 en suite rooms.

The eastern end of Chesil Beach runs into the massive rocky outcrop of Portland, the 'Gibraltar of Dorset' although, sadly about to lose its Naval role. Its great harbour and narrow isthmus connect it to the ancient town and port of **Weymouth**. A seaport since Roman times, the small harbour is still busy with fishing boats, yachts and cross-channel ferries, including the futuristic-looking speed catamarans that in the past few years have been introduced on the Channel Islands route. Weymouth is also a cheerful seaside resort, with a beautifully protected sandy beach, deservedly popular with families.

The area around the shallow bay is attractive with an esplanade, where the variety and irregularity of the buildings make for a view that is both comforting and good-looking. An 18th-century wine-merchant's shop (which doubtless provided liquid encouragement to some of those early sea-bathing pioneers) has been converted into Sabretes restaurant, where local fish and shellfish are rightly featured on the menu.

Dorchester, the county town is fascinating but has a colourful and sometimes violent past. Its Roman origins are indicated by the layout of its main street, the square outlinings of the town wall which ran where now there are tree-lined walks and the remains of a magnificent villa behind County Hall, which reveals some of the original mosaics and the hypocaust, or central heating system. Just south of the town, at **Maumbury Rings**, an ancient 'henge' type monument of the stone circle variety was adapted by the Romans as an amphitheatre; it is a gruesome fact that the public gallows stood here until well into the 18th century.

Modern Dorchester contains a variety of domestic architecture from all ages, but no one style dominates. Perhaps one of the reasons for this was the sporadic outbreaks of fire that, over the centuries, forced the townspeople to adopt an almost continuous policy of reconstruction. The most notable of these fires began in August 1613, when most of the populace were busy harvesting in the neighbouring fields. Over 300 houses and two out of three churches were destroyed.

The Civil War caused great hardship but little material damage. A few decades later, the disastrous Monmouth Rebellion was to lead to further suffering, when on September 3rd, 1685, Judge Jeffreys opened his Bloody Assizes, trying those accused of complicity in the Duke's cause. Nearly 250 years later, the town was the scene of another famous 'trial', when six farm labourers from Tolpuddle were sentenced to seven years, transportation for attempting to form a trade union.

Dorchester is a friendly town with plenty to see and do; the excellent **Dorset County Museum** in West Street contains a wealth of material of all kinds. Naturally, there is a large section devoted to Dorset's most famous literary son, Thomas Hardy. In **Higher Bockhampton**, the National Trust has preserved his birthplace, the simple thatched cottage built by his grandfather and referred to as **Hardy's Cottage**. Other museums in Dorchester include **The Dorset Military Museum**, situated in the Keep. In High West Street, the **Tutankhamun Exhibition** is an accurate recreation of one of the world's greatest archaeological discoveries, complete with the great golden coffin, and at Icen Way the visitor is encouraged to go back even earlier in time by visiting **The Dinosaur Museum**.

You will find several Winterbournes' surrounding Dorchester, each attractive in its own right but I am particularly fond of **Winterbourne Abbas** largely because of The Coach and Horses, a fine old coaching inn, likely to have given shelter to the infamous Dick Turpin and his horse, Bess. Certainly it is an establishment full of history and character. Naturally it has a ghost! It is a true pub, welcoming, friendly and offering value for money food from a wide ranging menu. 5 en suite bedrooms make it an ideal, sensibly priced base.

If you head north from Dorchester along the A352, you will pass through the old and delightful village of **Cerne Abbas**. Lying in a chalk-lined valley and once more of a town than a village, the community's wealth was originally derived from the Benedictine Abbey, first established by the Saxon Ethelrnaer, Earl of Cornwall, in AD 987. The Dissolution brought the usual destruction and the only obvious remains are the handsome gate-house, guesthouse and tithe barns. The lovely 15th-century church has a buttressed tower, a   later-Norman chancel and some early heraldic glass. However Cerne Abbas is probably best known for the enormous pagan figure of a priapic giant carved into the turf on the chalk hillside. His origins are unknown; local legend has a David and Goliath account of a local shepherd boy killing the giant while he slept on the hill, whereupon the villagers immediately rushed up and marked the outline of the massive corpse, some 180 feet from head to toe. He may be Neolithic or he maybe the god, Hercules, carved by Roman soldiers; no one seems quite certain, although there is a strong belief that fertility is assured by spending the night on the giant phallus! Whatever the truth, the giant's outline still lies on the hillside, surrounded for miles around by the stone pillars and earthen mounds of earlier and more superstitious times. In this rounded and hilly landscape, a turn away from the main roads brings the traveller, by way of narrow twisting lanes, to tiny settlements and hamlcts and one has the feeling that even in the 20th century, the ancient ways are given more than passing acknowledgement.

Minterne Gardens at **Minterne Magna**, are a series of beautifully landscaped gardens which utilises lakes, cascades, streams and pools to show off a wonderful array of trees, shrubs and plants. Nearby is the village of **Evershot** where excellent accommodation can be found at **Rectory House**.

Before reaching **Sherborne**, the road runs down to what Hardy called 'the Vale of Little Dairies', Blackmoor Vale. In comparison with the chalk downland grazing, this is rich, lush countryside and many dairies still survive, albeit somewhat larger than in Hardy's day.

The land begins to rise as one approaches what is rightly claimed as Dorset's loveliest town, Sherborne. An old town of charm and character, it abounds in fine buildings set beside curving little streets. The learned St Aldhelm founded the Abbey and School in the 8th-century, and to our good fortune both have survived to this day, the school being refounded by Royal Charter after the Dissolution. **Sherborne Abbey**, as seen today dates principally from the 15th century, although evidence of its Saxon and Norman predecessors clearly remain. The delicate stone fan-vaulting is beautiful and intricate and the local yellow stone from which the building is constructed lends a feeling of warmth and mellowness to the magnificent interior. The people of Sherborne showed great far-sightedness when they bought the Abbey, the grounds, about it, the lead, the bells, and other fittings' for the sum of three hundred pounds. Many of the abbey's old monastic buildings have been incorporated into the school, which rambles around much of the southern half of the town with its numerous halls, houses and playing fields.

The town, and indeed the surrounding area, are full of the most marvellous treasures and attractions. **Sherborne Museum**, in the old Abbey gate-house holds items of local interest. The actual castle was built between 1107 and 1135 by Roger, Bishop of Salisbury, and if the construction of a fortress seems a somewhat un-ecclesiastical act, it should be remembered that Bishops in those days were not 'all gas and gaiters.' Between AD 871 and 933 , three Bishops of Sherborne fell in the battle against the Danes.

The castle passed into the ownership of Sir Walter Raleigh in 1597, but he was not to enjoy ownership for long, being indicted for treason in 1b03. Nevertheless, he left his mark; evidently deciding that the massively built stone castle offered little in the way of home comforts, he therefore initiated the building of a more suitable abode almost immediately adjacent to the grim fortress. Thus Sherborne has not one, but two 'castles', **Sherborne old Castle** and later **Sherborne Castle**. The old castle remained as a defensive position until the Civil War, when it was stormed by the Parliamentarians under General Fairfax and destroyed. The new castle, originally known as The Lodge, is owned by the Digby family who have been there ever since Sir John Digby was awarded the estate by James I in recognition of his services as Ambassador to Spain. The Digbys utilised much of the ruins of the old castle to enlarge and enhance the house, and later employed Capability Brown to landscape the area around the two castles. The lake, waterfall and lovely gardens are the result, while the interior of the house is in restrained elegance, with notable collections of furniture and porcelain.

To the west of the town, close to the border with Somerset, lies another lovely home, **Compton House**. This 16th-century building is at the heart of a unique enterprise; for thirty years it has been the home of **Worldwide Butterflies**, where a variety of habitats provide settings for butterflies and moths from all over the world. In conjunction with this amazing programme of conservation and breeding is **Lullingstone Silk Farm**, which has provided the silk on many Royal occasions.

Milborne Port, to the east of Sherborne, provides an ideal base for those who wish to stay and take their time to visit the numerous attractions that exist on either side of the county boundary. The Queens Head, in the High Street is everything an inn should be; comfortable, hospitable and atmospheric. The small town has a church that is a good mix of Saxon and Norman, and an old Guildhall, a reminder of times when Milborne Port was the third largest town in Somerset (to confuse matters its postal address is in Dorset) and once noted for the large number of mills it possessed. At the eastern end of the village stands a handsome Queen Anne Mansion, **Venn House**.

Just to the south is the intriguingly named village of **Purse Caundle**. Amazingly this delightful community was described at the beginning of this century as a 'poor village...where most of the thatched roofs of the cottages have been replaced by corrugated iron, the churchyard in a ruinous condition...' All is now well, with the lovely 15th-century church possessed of an unusual panelled chancel arch, and the beautiful Elizabethan **Purse Caundle Manor** lying close beside the 'clear stream' that goes on to feed Sherborne lake. The manor has a most attractive garden, a great hall with minstrel's gallery, and an interior well, dug in case of siege.

Then a little to the east is the pretty village of **Marnhull** where the Old Lamb House at Walton Elm should be on everyone's visiting list. Run by two delightful people, Jenny and Ben Chilcott, there is no one who will not feel welcome.

The ancient Saxon town of **Shaftesbury** is claimed to have more history in one square mile than any other settlement in ancient Wessex: a claim the visitor can well believe. For all that, it is far from being a fusty old museum of a town, being bright lively and cheerful. A museum, although far from fusty, is to be found by the Abbey Ruins, and is a sensible place to begin to understand the story of the rise and fall of this once important town. It was a settlement of some stature when Alfred the Great founded the Abbey, on the site of a Roman temple, in AD 880, appointing his daughter Ethelgiva as the first Abbess. Less than 100 years later the remains of King Edward the Martyr were re-interred here and his tomb soon acquired a reputation for miracles. Canonisation and a shrine soon followed and both abbey and town settled back to enjoy a long period of prosperity. To the medieval community, possession of a saint's relics was virtually a licence to print money. Pilgrims made offerings, they had to be fed and sheltered to say nothing of being sold souvenirs of their visit. The town and the Abbey mutually prospered for over 500 years. There was a popular saying in the Middle Ages that illustrates the extent of this prosperity; it was said that if the Abbot of Glastonbury married the Abbess of Shaftesbury then their son would be richer than the King of England. Perhaps this bawdy jest was unpleasantly close to the truth; when the Dissolution came, destruction seems to have been both swift, savage and thorough, leaving little of the 10-acre Abbey site standing. The suffering was severe and it was not long before the burgesses were to plead 'that the Towne had grown about two hundred pounds in debt; there are over 300 begging people to be relieved and not above 30 householders in all the town to give relieffe.' The town was then reduced to button-making as a principal source of income, but after a century or so in the doldrums, its fortunes revived although never to the greatness of the past. Shaftesbury is now a peaceful market town, but the glories of the distant past, the Abbey, the two mints, the hospitals, the Guildhalls and eight of the dozen churches have long gone. There is an odd footnote to the story of the savage rending of the great Abbey. In 1931 a lead coffin was discovered during excavation which probably contains the remains of the saintly Edward. For some strange reason, these remains are now in the possession of the Russian Orthodox Church in Surrey and the great stone altar tomb that was erected as recently as 1992 to the martyred king's memory, lies sadly empty.

The town today is still an important market centre and has expanded to take advantage of its position and the talents of its population. Nevertheless, from both the physical and historical viewpoint it is still extremely attractive and, in places like the steep, cobbled Gold Hill with its wonderful views and varied architecture, quite enchanting. It has to be said though, that particular view is oddly familiar to many since it is a favourite with art directors and has been used in television drama as well as numerous advertising campaigns.

The handsome Georgian appearance of **Blandford Forum** owes everything to a great fire and two Bastards; the town was almost completely destroyed in 1731 and restored by two talented architects with that unfortunate surname. Lovely to spend time in, and in Barnack Walk there is an excellent coffee house, Scruples, where you can seek refreshment after admiring the town's architectural glories. However it is entirely appropriate that Blandford in the heart of Hardy's Dorset should have a jewel in its crown, for that is how one would describe La Belle Alliance in Whitecliff Mill Street. Essentially a restaurant where one can dine at night or lunch an a Sunday, it also has six en suite rooms with full facilities and designer interiors. The owners set out to make this a place where diners and guests of the hotel can find tranquillity and relaxation. With accolades from the Michelin red guide, Egon Ronay, Ashley Courtenay, the Good Food Guide and many more, without question they have achieved their goal.

The River Piddle lends its name to the villages east of Dorchester known collectively as the Piddles and Puddles. **Tolpuddle** is celebrated for its association with the ill-treated farm workers of 1831. Public outcry forced the Government to pardon six men, but it took time far the message to reach Australia and one of the Martyrs only found out by sheer luck; four years later on a remote sheep station, he read of his pardon in an old and discarded newspaper.

Piddlehinton has a good Perpendicular church and two fine houses in Glebe Court and Muston manor, while **Piddletrenthide's** church is of Norman origin with the village school sporting gates that once graced Westminster Abbey; the gift of a local man who became a famous London jeweller. **Puddletown** has a superb medieval church with box pews, a musician's gallery and tombs and memorials of the Martyn family. In 1485 Sir William Martyn, whose family had lived in the area since the beginning of the previous century, built a fine house on the site of a Saxon king's palace. The king was Athelstan and the house was named Athelhampton, one of the finest and most interesting medieval houses in the country.

The heathland country of which Thomas Hardy was so fond begins just to the south of Puddletown and runs eastward to the Hampshire border. 'Majestic, watchful and haggard', it is now considerably reduced from the hundreds and thousands of acres it once covered; now there is probably 15,000 acres existing in pockets between cultivated land and new developments. Its sombre, bracken and heather clad beauty makes it an ideal habitat for plants and flowers and birds such as the Dartford Warbler, the red-backed shrike and the honey buzzard.

Bovington Heath has been the site of an army camp since the First World War, and the **Tank Museum** must be the most complete collection of armoured fighting vehicles in existence, containing over 260 such vehicles from 23 countries. As is so often the case, the surrounding ranges that stretch down to the coast, have become a haven for wildlife, including many rarities: paradoxically, they would seem to thrive on the occasional doses of high- explosive shelling and track-trampling, whilst full-time human intrusion would doubtless lead to the need for far more careful environmental management. Public access is allowed at certain times of the year and it is well worth visiting this most lovely part of the county to enjoy the magnificent, unspoilt, coastal scenery and the high heath.
The narrow chalk ridge that divides the sea from the heath has many notable beauty spots, the best known being the nearly circular **Lulworth Cove**. The coastline here has been carved into fantastic shapes by the ceaseless motion of the sea, and just to the west, a great natural arch of limestone projects out into the water at **Durdle Door**.

The coastal region to the east here is known as the **Isle of Purbeck** although not an island in the strict geographical sense, in times gone by it was an area that was cut off from the remainder of Dorset by virtue of bog, stream and forest. The Purbeck Hills, once quarried for marble, are cut at Corfe castle, the principal site for the peninsula. The mellow stone and brick cottages huddle around the foot of a steep hill, crowned by the dramatic ruins of the castle itself. The remains are Norman, but long before they began construction of the great stone fortress, a Saxon hunting lodge existed here. In 978, the young King Edward called at the lodge, having been separated from his companions of the chase. The lodge was then occupied by his step-mother Elfrida and his half-brother, Ethelred. As Edward bent from the saddle to receive a goblet from Elfrida, she stabbed him in the back. The horse bolted dragging Edward's lifeless body with it and thus the young and unprepared half-brother Ethelred gained the throne of England and the title of the 'Unready'. The late king's body was laid to rest in a nearby hovel, guarded by an old, blind woman who kept vigil. During the night, her sight was miraculously restored and so began the long succession of events that was to end with the eventual canonisation of Edward who was eventually buried in Shaftesbury Abbey.

Corfe Castle was begun in the 1080's and expanded over the centuries. King John made much of the place, which is understandable; given his undoubted unpopularity, any large remote and easily defended castle must have been immensely appealing. He kept his crown, his ill-gotten treasure and his unfortunate prisoners at Corfe, few of whom were ever seen again. Over the centuries the castle has dominated the surrounding countryside and seems to have been used principally as a barracks and military store until, in 1643, it was besieged by Parliamentarian troops. The castle was then in the possession of Sir John Bankes, who was away fighting with the King. In his absence, Lady Bankes led a spirited and successful defence, commanding a garrison composed almost entirely of the domestic household: children, maids, cooks, old and infirm men-servants, who were unable to accompany Sir John, scullions and washer women. Despite the best efforts of the besiegers, with 'canon, culverin and saker', the spirit of the defenders and the high stout walls were not breached during a period of some five months. Sadly a second siege did not end so happily; a traitor crept down and opened the gates one night and a month later, immense amounts of gunpowder were expended in order to 'slight' or reduce the castle to the ruins we see today.

The ancient little village has a lovely old church that was built in memory of the murdered saint and king, and a fine inn, that dates back to the 1300's and whose name was changed from the Ship Inn to that of Bankes Hotel, in memory of the gallant chatelaine.

The great white cliffs of Durlston guard the attractive little resort of **Swanage**, once the principal port for the shipping of Purbeck stone and marble. The first of England's great series of naval victories is commemorated by a granite column on the front; in AD 877 King Alfred's little fleet defeated that of the Danes in Swanage Bay. The sandy beach and sheltered waters of the Bay and that of neighbouring Studland make the area ideal for the family holidaymaker. Swanage is justly popular and the town is attractive and welcoming; apart from water-sports of every variety and the obvious attractions of the area, there is a fine parish church, built in the 13th-century and sited next to the Millpond, the steam engines of **The Swanage Railway**, the **Tithe Barn Museum** and numerous pubs, hotels and restaurants.

The northern side of Purbeck is bounded by the huge natural expanse of **Poole Harbour**, whose perimeter, laid in a straight line, would stretch for some 95 miles! The oldest community on the shores of this great lake-like harbour is **Wareham**, at the western end. An important port in Saxon times, it was always being attacked by the Danes and then by the Roundheads who destroyed the Norman castle. Long before then the town suffered a terminal decline with the silting up of the River Frome, attacks by pirates, plague and a succession of fires, the worst destroying over 140 buildings in 1762. The town fared no better during the Monmouth Rebellion, with some of the citizens being brutally dispatched by the dreadful Judge Jeffreys. It is hard to see what this attractive and friendly little town ever did to encourage such a chapter of disasters. Some of Wareham's misfortunes were instigated by the piratical inhabitants of Poole, who appear to have been somewhat jealous of their sister town's early success. Apart from being objectionable to their neighbours, piracy and smuggling were just two trades that came naturally to the fine seamen from the northern part of the harbour. Today it is highly respectable and very busy, a seaport specialising in cross-channel traffic, and a paradise for yachtsmen, with marinas, boatyards and slip-ways spread around a waterfront first used by the Romans.

Poole has become almost as one with its neighbour to the east, **Bournemouth**, but still retains a strong streak of individuality; besides being a port it is a major residential centre, a light industrial centre and a recreational centre. There are two excellent museums. **The Waterfront Museum** and the **Guildhall Museum** and the delightfully restored **Scalpen's Court**, a medieval merchant's house. On the Quay, **Poole Pottery** has an international reputation, while the revamped and pedestrianised High Street has a modern indoor shopping centre and a wide variety of shops, pubs and restaurants.

Within the harbour, boat trips are available to such attractions as **Brownsea Island**, a nature reserve and bird sanctuary where Baden Powell held his first scout camp. If the weather is unkind then the **Tower Park** is a vast indoor complex housing such diverse activities as bowling and ice-skating, together with water-slides, cinema, shops and restaurants.

Bournemouth is a town full of hotels and places to stay, which concentrates on the caring for tourists and business people. It is many things to many people depending on what you are looking for. Bournemouth offers excellent opportunities for those who love concerts and the theatre.

To the north of the conurbation of Poole and Bournemouth is historic **Wimborne** Minster where the great twin towers of St Cuthberga stand on the site of an 8th century monastery. The town is an attraction in itself with an award winning local museum to tell its story in **The Priest's House Museum**. Other places of interest are the lovely **Knoll Gardens**, a six acre site of rare and exotic plants, and, to the south of the town, the **Georgian Merley** House, with its fascinating model toy collection, and **Merley Bird Gardens**, with avians ranging from parrots to penguins. Just outside Wimborne is **Horton** with Horton tower, known locally as Sturt's Folly, the scene of the cock fight in the film 'Far from the Madding Crowd'. Here is **Drusilla's Inn** which dates back over 300 years and has genuine old oak beams to prove it! It is bursting with character and not the least is the owner, Roger Kernan, whose outgoing personality spreads its warmth among his regulars and rapidly reaches out to embrace newcomers making them feel at home instantly. Good food, good wine but no accommodation.

A link with the epic siege of Corfe can be found west of the town at **Kingston Lacy**, a National Trust property included in the vast estate left to the nation by Henry Ralph Bankes. The estate included Corfe and the 17th century house at **Kingston** with its wonderful pictures and grounds. The road running to the north-west has a magnificent avenue of beeches skirting the immense earthworks of Badbury Rings. Legend has it that this was the site of one of King Arthur's great battles and that somewhere, buried beneath the great grassy ramparts, there lies a solid gold coffin.

The deer that were once so prized by Saxon and Norman nobility still graze amongst the woods and coverts in this lovely part of the county. In the neat village which delights in the enchanting name of **Sixpenny Handley**, the cheerful Roebuck Inn is a reminder that the descendants of those noble animals are around; as too, are the descendants of those who hunted them so long ago. Somehow, this seems only right in an ancient county possessed of timeless charm.

This part of the chapter is concerned principally with Wiltshire and the great open downlands of Salisbury Plain, the more wooded folds to the south-west where Cranbourne Chase enters the county town of Salisbury. It is a landscape full of interest and of rare charm: always changing with weather and seasons. I think I can fairly claim to know this part of Wiltshire well, I have been here many times and found it to be a part of England that repays attention for there is always something new to do and see, same little undiscovered corner or unexpected delight of a view.

The true inhabitants are unhurried rather than slow, thoughtful rather than thick. Their character has been shaped by the countryman's compromising attitude to the seasons and the weather, yet they don't lack for native wit. True Wiltshiremen are known as 'Moonrakers' after two of their number were challenged one moonlit night, raking the surface of a village pond with hay-rakes. Their explanation for this strange activity was that they were trying to retrieve 'they gurt yaller cheese', pointing to the reflection of the moon in water. The interrogators rode away laughing and tapping their heads; but the last laugh was on them, for they were excisemen, and unknown to them, the pond contained smuggled casks of brandy! There 'bain't no flies' on a Moonraker, as the over-confident outsider can find to his cost. The story has echoes in other counties associated with the free-trades, but in Wiltshire it rings the truest.

The countryside that runs into the south-west of Wiltshire towards Salisbury in medieval times was heavily afforested but now it is a region of chalk downland divided by the valleys of the Ebble and the Nadder. The clear waters flow by some of the most lovely little villages and hamlets in the county, often settlements of great antiquity that lie tucked into folds of the hills and protected by woodland. This is delightful country and an area that repays the peripatetic wanderer in full.

Ebbesbourne Wake is a rambling village to the south of White Sheet Hill. Thatched cottages cluster around what was once an important cattle drover's trail and the friendly Horseshoe Inn is everything a village pub should be. Continuing eastwards via **Fifield Bavant** with its miniature Norman church, the valley floor begins to broaden by the time one reaches the 'capital' of the stream-set villages, **Broadchalke**. The Ebble provides nourishment for watercress beds and the 17th century antiquarian and folklorist John Aubrey, for part of his life a landowner and churchwarden here, recorded fondly that...'The water of this stream washes well and is good for brewing. I did put in craw fish but they would not live here: the water is too cold for them.' The 15th-century village pub, The Queen's Head Inn', is more than worthy of a mention.

On the northern side of White Sheet Hill there are two castles with the name of **Wardour**. Strictly speaking, neither are true castles: **Old Wardour Castle** was more akin to the fortified chateaux of France and was a tower house of octagonal shape. Its defensive capability was proven in 1634, when the elderly Lady Blanche Arundell, commanding a force of twenty five men and some dozen or so womenfolk, held out against a besieging Parliamentarian force of 1,300. The siege lasted five days and nights and was ended when Lady Blanche negotiated an honourable surrender. The Parliamentarians reneged on the conditions, imprisoned the gallant defenders and looted the castle. When her son, Lord Arundell heard the news, he became the besieger but at great cost; in order to force a conclusion to the siege, he had no option but to blow up his own inheritance. In 1776, the family built a new house within sight of the romantic ruins of the old. **Wardour Castle** is a rather austere Palladian mansion designed by James Paine for the eighth Lord Arundell, which became a school after the Arundell family's tenure came to an end.

Lady Blanche was buried, as were so many Arundells, at **Tisbury**. Rudyard Kipling's parents are also buried there, in the graveyard of the lovely church beside the river. The village cum small town lies on a steep slope leading down to the Nadder and in times past was considered inferior to its neighbour to the north, **Hindon**, because it had neither fair nor market. There is a magnificent Tithe Barn, beside the 15th-century Place House, which once belonged to the Abbey of Shaftesbury.

Hindon, having made the most of its past glories, has settled into comfortable and well to-do retirement amongst the downland. The broad High Street, flanked by many charming cottages and houses in the Georgian style, is a reflection of the medieval village's origins as a planned settlement by the Bishop of Winchester. In the past it had both bailiff and burgesses, a weekly market, two annual fairs and sent two members to Parliament: the Georgian appearance is the result of a terrible fire in 1752, which destroyed nearly two-thirds of the village. There are two excellent pubs facing each other, The Lamb Inn and The Grosvenor.

The surrounding countryside and villages are a delight to the curious visitor. **Chilmark**, where the best of the beautiful creamy-lime stone was quarried, has a wealth of lovely houses built of the same material; the stone being first utilised by the Romans and later in the construction of **Salisbury Cathedral** and then **Wilton House**. A stream running through the village is spanned by a delightful little stone bridge and the Early English church has a broad spire. **The Teffonts, Teffont Magna and Teffont Evias**, are charming. Many of the cottages in the latter have their own little stone bridge giving access across the stream from front door to street. **Teffont House** is a handsome mansion dating from the reign of Henry VII, whilst **Fitz House**, in Teffont Magna is a pleasing 16th-century farmhouse and has delightful gardens. Close by the village is 130 acres of the Wessex Shire Park and Country Centre. To the south of the A30 at Fovant, there are some moving examples of 20th century graffiti; the huge regimental crest carved into the chalk hillside by soldiers undergoing training during the First World War. Sad to reflect on how few have returned to see their handiwork, and how few of those regiments have survived. **East Knoyle's** chief claim to fame is that it was the birthplace of Sir Christopher Wren, who was far from being the only talented member of that family; the ornate plaster-work in the chancel of the parish church was designed by his father, the rector of the parish.

I have no idea what an annual income of one hundred thousand pounds would be worth today, but it must be well in excess of a million or more; near to the villages of **Fonthill Bishop** and **Fonthill Gifford** lies Fonthill Park, where a great English eccentric, William Beckford provided employment for so many to say nothing of entertainment for all. He inherited his vast fortune at the tender age of ten, travelled widely (accompanied by a large personal staff, which included his own personal orchestra and an advance party, whose joy it was to ensure that the rooms in each inn that he stayed in were repapered and decorated), took an intense interest in the Orient and wrote a well-received book on the subject; and retired to the family estates at Fonthill in 1799 to indulge a new-found passion for building. He lived here until the 1820's with only his doctor, heraldic adviser, a Spanish dwarf and four dogs for company: during this time he commissioned the architect James Wyatt to build him an entire mock medieval abbey, complete with a 300 ft tower. Due to Beckford's impatience, the immense building suffered a number of collapses owing to the poor materials and hurried workmanship, but even when the money began to run out, he never changed his ways. He calmly sold the fantastic creation on which he had spent millions and over 20 years of his life, and retired to Bath - where he promptly built another, if slightly smaller, tower at Lansdowne Crescent. He was buried there in 1844, in a pink granite sarcophagus, alongside the marble tomb of one of his dogs.

The undulating downlands to the north contain two of Wiltshire's most famous stately homes. The first is the mansion of **Stourhead**, where the famous gardens contain the source of the meandering River Stour. Now administered by the National Trust, there has been an estate here since Saxon times. The Stourton family held it for several hundred years; their long tenure marred by a regrettable incident in the 16th century when one of their number was hanged at Salisbury market place for murdering two men; a father and son. Since the guilty party was a baronet, the instrument of execution was not the usual hempen noose but a 'halter of silke'. In 1714 the estate was sold to the Hoare family, goldsmiths and bankers. The chief glory of Stourhead are the grounds; the talented Henry Hoare was inspired by the Grand Tour of Europe and devised a delightful series of romantic gardens surrounding the lake, complete with temples and a grotto sheltering amongst the magnificent specimen trees. King Alfred's Tower, a brick folly, gives fine views over three counties and is said to mark the spot where King Alfred defeated the Danes in AD 879.

The Hoare family continued to enhance both house and estate until, following the loss of their only son in the First World War, the late Sir Henry Hoare generously donated it to the National Trust. There is a sad but touching postscript to the story when Sir Henry and his wife, having given away their beautiful property to which they had devoted most of their lives, died within two hours of each other.

The road north runs through **Maiden Bradley**, an attractive village and centre of a large parish, where the old ceremony of beating the bounds was accompanied by cart loads of cakes and ale. Any stranger encountered by the villagers during this hilly perambulation was offered hospitality then stood upside down in a shallow hole and beaten with a shovel in order that he might remember the parish boundary (and undoubtedly avoid it in future).

The second great stately home stands just to the north and close to the Somerset border. **Longleat**, a palatial Elizabethan mansion set in wonderful grounds landscaped by the inimitable Capability Brown, is perhaps the best-known such house in the country. Until the Dissolution it was the site of a medieval priory, the great house that replaced it was built by Sir John Thynne and has remained in the hands of the same family ever since. During the late 19th century it was redecorated in Italian Renaissance style with elaborately painted ceilings. Some idea of the scale of the house can be gained by the fact that it has seven libraries housing over 40,000 volumes! Today it is a major tourist attraction with its Safari Park and many other diversions.

Wiltshire takes its name from the West Saxons who settled in the valley at Wilton, the 'farmstead beside the banks of the Wylye.' Although now a small but well-to-do town, **Wilton** was once capital of Saxon Wessex. Alfred founded an abbey here and there was a royal palace. The Dissolution saw the Abbey in the hands of Sir William Herbert, first Earl of Pembroke, and the estates have remained in the possession of that family ever since. Sir Virilliam demolished the Abbey and asked his friend Hans Holbein to design him a house utilising much of the remains. Sadly a fire destroyed much of that great house in 1647, but happily the great Inigo Jones was on hand to rebuild. The result is one of the most magnificent and dignified stately homes in the county. The furniture, objets d'art and pictures are superb; the latter include works by Rembrandt, Ruben, Tintoretto, Reynolds and Van Dyck.

There is a triumvirate of ancient and important dwelling-places close to where the three valleys of the Wyle, Nadder and Ebble meet, and their histories are all intertwined. The oldest recorded site is that of **Old Sarum**, a 56-acre earthwork on a rise north of Salisbury. Of Iron Age origin, it was appropriated by the Romans and later became a Saxon fortified town, important enough for King Edgar to hold a parliament there in AD 960 and to have a mint. The Normans, probably by virtue of its raised and protected position, made a great to-do about the place using it as an administrative headquarters and building a citadel and cathedral. It was here in 1086 that William held council to establish the feudal system and to initiate the compilation of the Domesday Book. However by the beginning of the 13th-century all was not well within the ancient ramparts; friction between the soldiers and the clergy, coupled with cramped conditions and shortage of water led to Bishop Richard Poore seeking a new site for the cathedral. Naturally he went first to Wilton, since it was the nearest community of size and importance, but the Abbess objected strongly to the thought of a rival religious foundation. Eventually Bishop Poore selected a site where the Wylye, Nadder and Avon met amongst lush green meadows. Legend has it that the spot was chosen by losing an arrow from the ramparts of Old Sarum. The archer must have been an exceptional man, doubtless aided by a northerly gale, for the new site is some two miles from the old!

Under the direction of Elias of Dereharnn, rightly described as an 'incomparable artificer', building proceeded apace. The stone, which has weathered over the centuries to a lovely greeny-grey, was quarried and carted over the rutted lanes from Chilmark to new Sarum, or Salisbury, where the master-masons gave it is final shape before it was hoisted into position. The building was completed in the remarkably short time of forty years and is consequently an almost perfect example of Early English throughout. Almost certainly, Elias was aware of the problems that beset another cathedral, Winchester, which was also built on marshy ground and whose central tower had collapsed in 1107, for he left the construction of the elegant spire to his successors in the next century. By that time the people of Old Sarum, who appeared to have sided with the Bishop against the uncouth soldiers, had deserted the old hill fort and settled around the new cathedral. There was nothing haphazard about this settlement; the new town was carefully planned from the start with the streets neatly laid out in a grid system which lasted almost untouched until the present century. There were numerous water-channels which led to the medieval nickname 'The Venice of England' and it may be that the drainage effect of these channels gave Bishop Wyvil and his architect, Richard of Farleigh, the confidence to add the audacious and elegant 404 ft spire in 1334. Aware that vibration is the cause of collapse, the master-builder housed the peal of bells in a separate campanile, or bell-tower. Over 400 years later, it was left to the 18th-century architect James Wyatt to add, or subtract, the finishing touches. He was much criticised at the time far his ruthlessness, but it is to him that we owe the purity and beauty of what, externally, is the most beautiful cathedral in the country. Wyatt demolished the campanile, cleared away the jumble of tombstones in the graveyard and laid out the great sward of mown grass that surrounds the building. He removed much of the ornate that was within, including much of the early glass; the result is the austere Gothic nobility of the original craftsmen, who dared in those far off times to construct such a great and lofty edifice on marshy ground; their decision must have been an act of faith in itself.

The great spire is a landmark from far and wide and every year thousands come to wonder and pay homage to those old master-builders. Glorious as the building is, with its great cloisters, massive Purbeck pillars, lovely choir vaulting, copy of Magna Carta and ancient clock (1386 - and still ticking!), it has to be said that part of its attraction lies in its incomparable setting. The Close is rectangular in shape, surrounded by an intact medieval wall, with a wonderful collection of buildings and houses, some contemporary with the great church, others fine examples of Queen Anne or Georgian. Three of these are not only fine examples of the architecture of their day but also excellent museums. A 13th century house, The Wardrobe, so named because it was once used for storing clothes belonging to the Bishop and his entourage, is now the home to **The Museum of the Duke of Edinburgh's Royal Regiment**. The Regiment was formed in 1959 by the amalgamation of the Wiltshire and Berkshire Regiments and the museum contains a fascinating collection of the historical items, relating to 250 years of military history. The King's House is a 14th century building housing the award-winning **Salisbury and South Wiltshire Museum** with a fine collection of archaeological and historical artefacts. The classic facade of **Mompesson House**, built in 1701, conceals a fine collection of glassware and furniture together with a delightful garden.

That famous man of Wiltshire, Sir Christopher Wren was responsible for a number of The Close houses together with the Matron's College, just inside the High Street Gate. It is rumoured that this handsome dwelling for 'widows or spinster daughters of departed clergy' was built at the instigation of Wren's friend Bishop Seth Ward because, when a young curate, he had been rejected by a young lady who subsequently married another cleric. On his death she was left in poverty and by building the College, Bishop Ward assured the comfort of his lost love for the rest of her days.

Salisbury thrives and even outside the timeless area within the Close Wall, has much to offer visitors although, in adapting the medieval city to the demands of the internal combustion engine the planners did the city no great favours. Its charm, as in all old communities is discovered in both the unexpected and the familiar; turn a corner and there is a street almost unchanged since the Middle Ages, the houses jutting towards each other and each uniquely individual. Walk along a path in the meadows beside the ever flowing river and there is the great tapering cathedral framed by trees and sky; the same view that inspired John   Constable nearly 200 years ago. The business acumen that brought such financial rewards to the city of New Sarum is reflected in the splendid town houses of its merchant venturers; two of the greatest of these were John Halle and John a'Port, and the same acumen has seen these great timber-framed houses continuing to play a part in the economy of the city by being turned into, respectively, a cinema and a shop. The old market place where much early wealth was generated, felons hung and heretics burnt, is still large and faces that handsome Gothic Guildhall, but the agricultural market has long moved to purpose built premises. The medieval poultry cross stands nearby and is still surrounded by stalls on market day; overlooked by several buildings of equivalent age. high quality shops and high quality craftsmen still trade in the shadow of the spire. Still, in the sense of peacefulness and continuity, is a word that can easily be applied to the city.

The traveller of long ago had a wide range of choices where hospitality was concerned and, as might be expected, little has changed. The Red Lion in Milford Street was built in the 13th century, reputedly to house the draughtsmen working on the cathedral. The original building now constitutes the main body of the hotel which includes the lounge, reception and part of the restaurant. Further wings have been added over the centuries to form the creeper-clad courtyards which are such a renowned feature of the inn. The Red Lion is probably the longest running purpose built hotel in the country and has never been better than it is today. Wonderful place to stay or eat.

At 206 Castle Street Milford Hall Hotel is a rare experience. Most visitors, already in awe of the majesty of the cathedral, cannot believe their good fortune in finding a gem like this. With its two contrasting but carefully harmonised faces - the graceful Georgian mansion which fronts Castle Street and the modern extension set in the grounds of the old house, and echoing its perfect proportions, it represents a new concept in hotel comfort, convenience and value.

A cathedral city always attracts the arts and Salisbury is no exception; there is a festival in September, music in the Cathedral and the Guildhall, exhibitions in the Arts Centre and live theatre at the excellent Playhouse. There is an attractive and well patronised racecourse whilst virtually all forms of recreation and sport are catered for in and around the city.

Two attractive villages close to Salisbury have particularly pleasing hostelries. At **Broadchalke,** a conservation village standing in a valley of outstanding beauty, the 15th century Queens Head Inn, full of beams and a splendid inglenook offers good, traditional fare including seasonal game dishes such as Pheasant and Bacon Pie, Jugged Hare or Rabbit. You can also stay here in 5 en suite, motel-style rooms. Ideal for those wanting to tour and not stay in the city.

The Crown Inn at **Alvediston** is also 15th-century and is a Grade II Listed freehouse nestling between the hills of the beautiful Chalke Valley, an area of outstanding beauty beloved by walkers, those who enjoy shooting, fishing and riding, and by those who just like to be amongst wonderful scenery in a peaceful backwater. An excellent International menu, a well chosen wine list and 3 charming en suite bedrooms make the inn another great choice for a break or just to sample the delicious food. Wiltshire was once the home of the Great Bustard, a large turkey-like bird which features on the county's coat of arms, and which became extinct towards the end of the 18th-century. Near Porton, a Ministry of Defence research establishment, a 10 acre site was set aside in an attempt to breed imported bustards, and it is in these restricted areas that many rare forms of flora and fauna can survive, including a relative of the bustard, the stone curlew. Incidentally the bustard was probably the first bird to have its eggs protected by law; as early as the reign of Henry VIII, it was an offence and punishable by the heavy fine of 20 pence. Considering that half of the sum went as a reward to any informer, there should have been a considerable incentive to protect the bird.

Ancient yews with Druidical associations and reputed to be haunted overlook the quiet little village of **Cholderton**, which has an unusual church and owes its existence to the hard work and perseverance of the Rev Thomas Mozley, vicar of the parish in the 1840's. The original was described as being 'small mean and dilapidated', so the vicar proposed to build anew and be responsible for the financial arrangements. It cost eleven pounds to have the church demolished and the new one cost six thousand pounds, five thousand of which the vicar provided, earning it from writing. The church was consecrated in the name of St Nicholas in 1850.

The Cholderton Rare Breeds Farm has many rare and not-so-rare examples of domestic animals. Poultry breeds such as the Jersey Giant scratch the ground alongside Ronaldshay sheep, which have learnt to survive on seaweed. Opposite the village hall, the thatched and hospitable Crown Inn is justly popular.

A couple of miles or so to the west is the small town of **Amesbury**, where a fine Palladian style bridge crosses the River Avon. It is a town with a history and today it is a bustling little town, providing shopping facilities and accommodation for many of the modern military establishments that lie around. The great expanse of the Plain to the north and west is the principal area where the weaponry and soldiers of today exercise to protect our civilisation - but surrounding Amesbury are the mysterious relics and memorials of civilisations of which we know little. The best known of these is, of course, Stonehenge. Viewed from the main road, the stones appear insignificant against the sky line; approach closer and they became massively impressive, the largest weighing some 50 tons. The image is so familiar to us we almost take it for granted until closer contact with its scale and brutal bulk begins to impress our consciousness, together with an almost indefinable sense of wonder and awe. We are so used to giant edifices of the 20th century, such as tower blocks and great bridges, that it takes a moment or two to redefine our sense of proportion; today's constructions are not really the product of man but the products of man's machines, his steel mills, the earth-moving machinery and his cranes. Stonehenge was constructed by man in concert with nature, using only that which he found around him.

Gazing at the marvellous circle of upright stone with their huge lintels, the questions that come to mind are Who, When, Why and How? the answers range from the wildly fanciful to the reasoned and scientific, but it must be admitted that even the soundest of answers is but theory and there are still great gaps in our knowledge when it comes to a matter of actual fact. The Who is obviously tied in with the When and archaeology tells us that Stonehenge was built, in several stages, somewhere between 1900 and 1500 BC. The first people involved were Bronze Age settlers and in the initial stage of construction the stones came from Marlborough Downs some 20 miles to the north but later stages involved the Beaker people (named after their pottery artefacts) who arrived from the Continent around 1700 BC. Additional stone was brought all the way from South Wales; some old bluestones weighing four tons apiece were quarried from the Preseli Mountains in Pernbrokeshire, over two hundred miles away.

Why? There is an almost overwhelming amount of evidence and a general consensus among scientific bodies that the massive construction is a form of observatory and astral 'clock' to keep track of the seasons and to make astronomical predictions with regard to the sun and the moon. It follows (theoretically of course) that any person or persons who possessed such useful knowledge would be of great importance to the rest of the community.

The actual logistics and techniques of construction are certainly answered; quarrying was done by using the simplest of tools and by applying heat in the form of fire, immediately followed by cold in the form of water, thus causing the rock to split. Transport was by means of raft, pure muscle power and rollers made from logs and the stones were erected by digging a hole close to the base and then levering and pulling the stone upright. Lintels were raised by building a timber or earthen ramp and dragging the stone up.

That all sounds straightforward and practical but another dimension is added when Stonehenge is placed in context with the surrounding countryside, for dotted all around are the humped earthworks that mark the graves of our prehistoric ancestors. There are ancient trackways that seem to run towards the site from every point of the compass and there are great earthworks that mark ancient camps and settlements. Then there is the fact that what we see of Stonehenge are only the remains of what was originally a far larger and more sophisticated structure. The only thing we can be certain of is that the mysterious stones were of great importance and attracted the interest and respect of our ancient ancestors over a considerable period of time; in fact it still continues to do so. Sadly, this has meant that the site is surrounded by barbed wire and approach is strictly controlled. Since there were also large circular earthworks surrounding the original construction, might it be that the ancient priests or astronomers were as sorely afflicted by the lunatic fringe as English Heritage and the Wiltshire constabulary are today?

The high ground of the Plain is divided from the richer and lower soil of northern Wiltshire by the road that runs from Westbury to Upavon. Protected by the bulk of the downland, numerous villages, hamlets and farmstead are spread along the road. Solidly prosperous, **Westbury** made its money from cloth-weaving, glove-making and later from foundries exploiting a seam of iron-ore that was discovered nearby. On the heights above is the 23-acres site of Bratton Castle, a massive and ancient earthwork hill-fort whose presence gives some credence to the theories about that battle of so long ago.

Bratton, like Westbury, also had a flourishing iron-works and specialised in agricultural implements. There is a delightful 13th-century church perched on the steep hillside with over a hundred steps leading upwards. **Edington's** past is reflected in its great church built between 1352 and 1361 whilst **Erlestoke** has a connection with the legendary Dick Turpin for Tom Boulter, a highwayman whose exploits were often attributed to Turpin, stole a horse here - and its name really was Black Bess!

Devizes lies not far to the north and close to the geographical heart of Wiltshire. It is a pleasant small market town with a remarkably short history by county standards; the Normans first established a castle here in 1484 and a settlement quickly gathered around it. There is little but earthworks remaining now since the Parliamentarians razed the structure to the ground during the Civil War. There are two attractive Norman churches, a thriving market and a great many interesting and picturesque old buildings including The Bear Hotel, an old coaching inn.

The little town which lends its name to the Vale, **Pewsey**, was founded in Saxon times and also has a church with a splendid roof, parts of which came from an old Augustinian priory. The altar rail is made from timbers of the San Josef, a Spanish man o' war captured by Lord Nelson. Pewsey is a friendly and cheerful little town with good buildings and a fine statue of King Alfred gazing across the River Avon from the crossroads, a reminder of the time when the community was owned by Saxon kings.

The little villages drowsing in the vale have an individual charm and the richness of the surrounding soil has contributed much to their secular as well as ecclesiastical well-being. It was not only the church and land-owners who profited; for example, the annual accounts in 1576 for The Woodbridge Inn show a very handsome income of thirty nine pounds for dealing in 'wool and ale'. Set in rich meadow pasture beside the Avon, the hospitable pub at **North Newnton** no longer deals in wool, although the ale is as popular as ever.

To the north-west, via the causeway, is the pleasant village of **Burbage**, once totally surrounded by the Savernake Forest. Nearby Wolfhall was the home of the Seymours, hereditary wardens of another once vast forest, a favourite hunting ground of Norman kings. It was at Wolfhall that Henry VIII met and courted Jane Seymour, his future queen, who died later in childbirth. An 18th century coaching inn, The Bullfinch, was once a centre for a great deal of horse-trading some two centuries back, for the animals were not only required for the coaching trade but also for pulling the narrow boats on the canal. Half a mils from Burbage Wharf is the Bruce Tunnel, which is some 1500 feet long; horses were not used here since the boats were pulled through by hand using chains along the tunnel wall.

On the edge of Savernake is another of those ancient burial mounds known as Barrows; this particular one is believed to have been the resting place of Merlin the wizard (Maerla), and the conjunction of the names has been taken by the town that lies alongside; **Marlborough.** A handsome and popular town with fine, predominantly Georgian architecture lining the immensely wide main street. Where cars are parked down this street today, market stalls and livestock were tethered in the past. In fact life in this cheerful town often seemed to be little short of one great long street party. Because of the town's past importance as a staging post on the main London-Bristol road, the modern 'partaker of conviviality' is well provided for at the many coaching inns that have survived, such as the 17th century Lamb Inn in the Parade.

The road to the west passes through small rural communities in the Downs containing many a delight so typical of Wiltshire, sites where the historic and the pre-historic site peacefully side by side. **Fyfield** has a 13th century church with a splendid 15th-century tower, complete with pinnacles and gargoyles. Half a mile away are the strange stones that comprise Devil's Den, actually the remains of the stone-framed burial chamber that was once covered by a barrow, or mound. At first glance, **Avebury** appears little more than a picturesque downland village with an attractive grouping of part saxon church, the gabled Elizabethan **Avebury Manor,** thatched cottages and farmsteads - and then one notices the stones. Massive weather wrought lozenges of sandstone, many weighing more than 40 tons, stand upright in groups, around and amongst the village.

Avebury Stone Circle pre-dates Stonehenge by some two centuries and differs particularly in that the great stones are undressed; called sarsens (a local corruption of 'saracen' or foreign) they are found locally on the Marlborough Downs. They surround the village, contained within the remains of a large earth ring, some 1200 feet across. The Stone Circle is by no means the only prehistoric site in the area, and by no means the most mysterious. A 50 ft wide avenue of megaliths nearly a mile long, once led to an older site named the **Sanctuary,** near the village of **West Kennett**. The stones here have long vanished but, once again, patient archaeological detective work has established their positions. On the southern flank of Avebury is probably the strangest object of all, the vast conical earthwork of **Silsbury Hill**; an earthen pyramid, 130 feet high whose base covers a staggering five and a half acres, large enough to fill Trafalgar Square and reach three quarters of the way up Nelson's Column. Described as the largest man-made mound in Europe, its purpose and origins are obscure. All that we know is that it was built over 4,000 years ago that a million cubic yards of chalk were excavated and, given the simple tools of the period, would have taken 500 people ten years to build! Local legend has it that a certain King Sil or Zel, is somewhere buried beneath the mound, upright on his horse and clad in a suit of gold armour.

There is no doubt it can be extremely breezy up on the downs and it has been suggested that specialised forms of miniature tornadoes or whirlwinds are responsible for a phenomenon known as Corn Circles, strange geometric shapes that appear in the great cornfields around this area. Although occasionally seen elsewhere in the country, this part of Wiltshire appears particularly susceptible during the summer months. Inevitably, fanciful theories have been produced linking the shapes with the ancient stone circles, or even with aliens from outerspace. Undoubtedly some are the work of hoaxers but others are not so easily explained although cosmic doodling seems highly unlikely.

The River Kennett flows to the east from Marlborough, maturing from stream to trout-stocked river and entering Berkshire at **Chilton Foliat**. A pretty little village of timbered cottages, Georgian houses and a 13th-century church, it lies across the river from **Littlecote**. The Romans built a splendid villa here in AD 170 and the 3-acre site with its lovely mosaic can now be seen. The location has obviously long appealed to those with a deep purse, for the villa is in the grounds of the lovely **Littlecote House**, which dates back to the 15th-century. The situation is delightful, although regrettably not equalled by the personality of one or two of the owners; five ghosts are reputed to haunt the house, one being the exceptionally unpleasant 'Wild' Darrell, a 16th-century physchopath, who threw his own new-born baby onto the fire. He escaped legal retribution probably because a relation of his was the Attorney General, but later broke his neck out hunting. It is said that the baying of ghostly hounds, in full cry after his soul, can still be heard in the grounds. The house is an excellent example of a Tudor manor and contains a notable collection of Civil War artefacts and armour, also some fine furniture and works of art.

Just between Marlborough and Hungerford lies the little hamlet of **Froxfield**. Here you will find the delightful Pelican Hotel, a great spot to pick as a base for visiting the surrounding attractions. It is well worth the five minute drive over the border to **Hungerford** where the river flows into the Kennet and Avon canal. It is an ancient and attractive town with gaily painted canal boats tied up along the banks. Renowned for the quality of its antique shops, it is also famous for its Hocktide celebrations, an ancient ceremony that takes place on the Monday and Tuesday of the second week after Easter. It is thought that the celebrations, known locally as 'Tutti Day' commemorates the defeat of the Danes by Ethelred in 1002. The ceremonies are complex and ritualistic but it is the Tutti men, with their long staves garlanded with flowers, known as 'Tutti Poles', who appear to have the most fun; they have the right to visit certain houses and demand a penny and a kiss from the ladies within - even if they have to climb through a window to do so!

A reminder of this ancient rite is to be found in the High Street, in a 15th-century building, The Tutti Pole is a restaurant popular with visitors and locals, not to mention the immaculately turned out trainee nannies from the famous Norland Nursery College. There is something pleasantly other-worldly about Hungerford.

The M4 motorway effectively chops off the flatter lands of the northern tip of the county and contains the great mass of **Swindon,** the largest industrial town in Wiltshire. It was the railway that brought prosperity here and although the great locomotive works have been phased out, Swindon remains one of the principal termini far goods and passengers and the great days of the GWR are remembered in the **Great Western Railway Museum** in Faringdon Road, which has a comprehensive display of old locomotives and railway memorabilia. Just opposite is **The Railway Village** house, a perfectly restored foreman's house from the turn of the century. Both exhibits are situated within the area known as the Railway Village, a model community built by GWR for their workers.

The River Thames, although little more than a stream, takes a meander into the extreme north of Wiltshire, running under **Cricklade** High Street. It is hard to believe that the choleric Cobbett once fulminated against this charming and ancient little town, saying that it was a 'villainouse hole, a more rascally place I never set my eyes on'. Once again his blood pressure had been raised by Cricklade's role as a 'Rotten Borough', although the inhabitants had little objection since it was the custom of their prospective candidates to visit poor voters, purchasing their support by offering them ridiculous prices for useless articles, such as ten shillings for a piece of coal or three pounds for a bent poker! Cricklade's church dedicated to St Augustine is a handsome confection of medieval styles, beginning with Saxon and ending with a Tudor tower, the gift of the Duke of Northumberland in 1553.

Another ecclesiastical establishment although far greater in terms of scale, influence and enterprise, was situated to the west at **Malmesbury**. A handsome small town, situated on a rocky outcrop above the waters of the Avon. It was a borough before Alfred the Great reigned and **Malmesbury Abbey** was first established in about AD 680 by St Aldhelm. The saint appears to have been a jovial character, something of a charismatic, who could attract an audience by means of popular songs and jests, then switch to religious matters without losing their attention. Much loved by the townspeople, he is said to have built the first organ in England in the Abbey, 'a mighty instrument with innumerable tones, blown with bellows and enclosed in a gilded case.' Two centuries later, another great man appeared on the scene who was to become equally popular with the inhabitants. King Athelstan was the favourite grandchild of King Alfred. His affection for the town seems to have come about because of the support he received during the battle of Brunanburh, in which he defeated the Danes. No one is exactly sure where this took place but it obviously cannot have been far away, for Athelstan rewarded Malmesbury by rebuilding the Abbey and gifting the town with some 500 acres of land, ownership of which has continued through the generations to this day.

South of the M4 lies a mecca for tourists to this area of the county. **Castle Combe** is almost impossibly pretty, with its immaculate grouping of houses of golden Cotswold stone, thatch and tiles, trout laden stream, church, old market cross and manor house, set below wooded hills, where a castle once stood. It looks like a film set, indeed it has been used as one but its original prosperity came from weaving.

Calne to the east of **Chippenham** is also beholden for its prosperity to the weaving industry which ended with the Industrial Revolution. Since it has become famous for bacon-curing and the production of sausages and pies. This came about through the enterprise of a local family of butchers, the Harrises. At the time, the town was on the principal route for livestock being driven from the West to London and among the animals were large quantities of Irish pigs, having been off-loaded at Bristol. The Harris family realised that if they bought the pigs at Calne before they became weary and lost weight on their long trot to London, then the pork would be of superior quality. From 1770 until the 1980's, their factory dealt with literally millions of those versatile beasts of whom, it is said, 'everything can be used except the grunt'. Economic and regulatory factors conspired to close the factory and the only memorial to this once great business that made the name of Calne synonymous with bacon, is a bronze pig by the small shopping precinct.

Two miles to the south-west is the great estate of **Bowood**, home of the Marquesses of Lansdowne since 1754. Robert Adam spent eight years enlarging and improving Bowood House while Capability Brown was at work on the gardens and glorious parkland. The house has fine collections of sculpture, paintings and costumes. The real glory is the setting; the wonderful park and gardens, over ninety acres of which are open to visitors.

Lacock Abbey was founded in 1232 by Ela, Countess of Salisbury, the grieving widow of William Longspee. An Augustinian order flourished there until the Dissolution, when it fell into the hands of one William Sharington, a man who was described as being of dubious character. Fortunately he also had excellent taste and did not go in for the large scale demolitions that most of the ecclesiastical property developers of that time seemed to enjoy. Indeed such additions that he did make were well executed and in perfect harmony with the preserved Abbey. The Talbot family were fine stewards of both the Abbey and Lacock until in 1944, Miss Matilda Talbot presented both with 284 acres of land to the National Trust. There is no building later than the 18th century in the winding streets of grey stone and half timbered cottages. The Perpendicular church, dedicated to St Cyriac, has an elegant interior and a beautiful east window. The George is one of the oldest continuously licensed pubs in England while The Sign of the Angel dates back to the 14th century. A stone barn contains a museum dedicated to William Fox Talbot, pioneer of photography. One cannot help but wonder what he would think of his invention now as yet another coach load of tourists arrive with motor-driven, self-focusing cameras at the ready.

Once again it was wool that provided the wealth for Bradford-on-Avon. It is hard in these days of man-made fibres and multi-national fashion corporations to appreciate just how important fleece was to medieval life; suffice it to say that there were no other fibres that were so adaptable or so economical to produce and that the best wool came from the backs of English sheep raised on the chalk downlands. An indication of the little town's one-time importance in this vital trade is the fact that the Yorkshire wool and textile town of Bradford was named after it. The Wiltshire Bradford is an eminently picturesque town perched on the sides of a ravine through which the Avon flows westwards. The town's most precious treasure must be the little Saxon Church of St Lawrence. Oddly the church was 'lost' for centuries as the Normans had built a larger church almost adjacent, making the smaller building redundant. In the middle of the last century, the Vicar of Bradford was looking down on the town from the hillside and thought he recognised the outline of an ecclesiastical building amongst the jumble of roofs. He did some research and discovered St Lawrence. Now, the old and the new are grouped together with a magnificent tithe barn some 1b0 feet long and 30 feet wide, which dates from early in the 14th century and would have held the harvests of the Abbey of Shaftesbury. The lovely honey-coloured stone from which many buildings in the town are constructed lends a mellow richness to a scene that is brought alive by the river wending its way through.

Just to the east of Bradford on the little B3107 is the village of **Holt** with a delightful 16th century inn, The Toll Gate which is well worth seeking out. It is a welcoming freehouse with regular visits from the Holt Morris Dance Team, and live Jazz on the first Friday of each month. Delicious and varied food is served daily and Barbecues are quite frequently on offer. On Sundays you would be well advised to book a table for the traditional lunch.

South of Bradford is **Trowbridge**, the administrative centre of Wiltshire. Here too the wealth came from wool but a variety of industries took over and today the town thrives. The church begun in the 13th century and rebuilt in the 15th, claims to have the finest spire of any parish church in the county. Trowbridge Museum in the Civic Hall, is an excellent example of a town museum, recording the life and times of the community.

Heading south and within sight of the White Horse at Westbury, the gentle countryside seems so peaceful and idyllic, the villages so friendly and welcoming, that it is hard to imagine what life must have been like when the ancient Anglo-Saxon chronicler set down his despairing account of anarchy and misrule. Yet many of the small communities one drives through existed then and it is a tribute to the spirit and purpose of their inhabitants that they survived.

At **Hawkeridge**, there is a fine example of those characteristics that brought the countrymen and women of Wiltshire through the worst of times to the best of times. It is not the saga of a wealthy wool-merchant or rich clothier who became landed gentry, but a rather more modest account; in 1851, Mr Ephraim Dole and his wife Sarah, invested their savings into converting three labourers' cottages into an ale house. Nearly one hundred and fifty years later The Royal Oak is still going strong, complete with skittle-alley and dining room. Just goes to show that 'there ain't no vlies on Wiltshire volk...'

CHEDINGTON COURT HOTEL & RESTAURANT,

Chedington, Beaminster,
Dorset DT8 3HY
Tel: 01935 891265

Chedington Court is somewhere where one lets time go by and where you revel in its beauty, not only externally but internally as well. From the moment you turn into the lane leading to Chedington, the feeling of expectation heightens as the panoramic view of the Vale of the River Parrett unfolds to the West. Chedington Court appears between a framework of ancient beeches and one sees just how glorious this 19th-century house is with its lovely mellow stone with a clematis or two reaching up towards the sky, mullioned windows and a welcoming, gracious porch. The view from the house and the balustraded terrace is probably one of the most magnificent in the South of England. The 7-acre gardens are noted for their beauty, particularly in the Spring when the bulbs and wild flowers offer a superb spectacle. Flights of steps and paths lead to sweeping lawns, ponds, the grotto and water gardens, which blend magically with the landscape beyond. Under the giant gnarled 1000-year-old yew tree, the lichen encrusted tombstones rest serenely as a witness to the spot where the village church, probably of Saxon origin, once stood. The massive sculptured hedge, mature trees and shrubs give the garden an air of solemnity and peace and attract large varieties of birds, butterflies and wild life.

The interior is delightful, beautifully furnished, comfortable warm and very friendly. It has that indefinable air of well-being that comes when an establishment is run by people who not only know their business but have a great love for it. The mixture of stone fireplaces, old Persian rugs, fine brass fittings and antique furniture add to the beauty of the whole. The reception rooms are especially attractive with crackling log fires on chilly evenings. Here you can relax in the comfort of the deep armchairs, and enjoy the masses of books left there for your use. Staying here is like staying with friends in a country house. Supremely relaxing.

The ten spacious bedrooms, all en suite, are individually furnished with pretty drapes and fine furniture and most have extensive views of the gardens. It would be hard not to enjoy meals in the light and airy dining room where, at breakfast, the perfumes of jasmine and mimosa drift in from the conservatory. Chedington Court is renowned for its food. Dinner is memorable with a choice from a short but ever changing menu. The chefs prepare everything freshly using well chosen raw materials and turning them into exciting and often innovative dishes. The acclaimed wine list with wines from across the world, many of them half bottles, complements the food perfectly. Vegetarians and special diets are catered for. The attentive service is both friendly and unobtrusive. Open to non-residents this must be a place to dine if you are in the neighbourhood

USEFUL INFORMATION

OPEN; All year except January
CHILDREN; Welcome
CREDIT CARDS; All major cards except Diners
LICENSED; Yes. Acclaimed wine list
ACCOMMODATION; 10 en suite rooms
GARDEN; 7 acres of beautiful gardens

RESTAURANT; Excellent. Featured in all major food guides. Open to non-residents
VEGETARIAN; Catered for
DISABLED ACCESS; Limited

SYDNEY HOUSE HOTEL
6 West Cliff Road,
Bournemouth, Dorset BH2 5HY
Tel/Fax: 01202 555536

Barbara and Eddie McVeigh are the resident proprietors of this comfortable, friendly hotel built in 1874, which is ideally situated on the West Cliff just 150 yards from the beach and just a few minutes from Bournemouth's International Centre with its superb leisure pool and tap flight entertainment throughout the year. From Sydney House you can also reach the Pier, Central Garden and Bournemouth's excellent shopping centre. This is the sort of hotel where guests return regularly knowing that they will be well cared for and made extremely welcome. Families on holiday find Sydney House ideal with its facilities and relaxed, informal atmosphere. Many couples come here for off season breaks when there are special reductions for Senior Citizens. Conference delegates are also offered a special reduction.

Furnished attractively throughout, there are 14 bedrooms all en-suite and complete with colour television and a well supplied beverage tray. The Hotel has a friendly licensed bar, ideal for a drink at the end of the day. Breakfast is a substantial meal with several choices and in the evening the home-cooked meal is delicious. Sandwiches and snacks are also available either to eat in or take away. Sydney House also has Tea Rooms which are open to non-residents and where you can get a super Dorset Cream Tea. The scones are home-made, fresh and decidedly moreish. Barbara McVeigh is extremely good at helping people to plan their days and she and Eddie have their own PSV transport with which they provide specially organised tours custom tailored to the current guests interests - a great way of seeing Dorset.

USEFUL INFORMATION

OPEN; All year
CHILDREN; Welcome
CREDIT CARDS; Visa/Mastercard
LICENSED; Yes
ACCOMMODATION; 14 en suite rooms
PETS; Yes

DINING ROOM; Good home-cooked fare. Local Produce.
TEA ROOMS; Wonderful Dorset Cream Tea Open to non-residents
VEGETARIAN; Catered for
DISABLED ACCESS; No special facilities

THE MILL HOUSE.
Bradford-on-Avon Marina,
Bradford-on-Avon
Wiltshire BA15 100

Tel: 01225 862004

This interesting Family Restaurant and Bar absorbs the atmosphere of canal life. Brightly and artistically painted boats lie tied up alongside the restaurant and not far off the canal traffic creates enormous interest for people lucky enough to have discovered this very different eaterie. There is nothing olde worlde about The Mill House. It is very much a product of our times but within its walls there is an ambiance of well-being and happiness which communicates itself to the many people who have discovered it. Open all the year round, it provides warmth, comfort and good food in the winter months as readily as it does in the summer, although the latter is obviously busier. As well as the many visitors who come to the interesting small town of Bradford-on-Avon, the restaurant has a regular clientele from local people and those who live in the surrounding areas who have found that not only can one eat well here, but have fun also.

Seating some 150 people altogether, the menu in the restaurant has been designed to tempt most palates. It is firmly traditional English in content in the main with many tried and trusty favourites available but there is also an Oriental selection on offer. The speciality of the restaurant is undoubtedly the succulent steaks of all kinds, procured from local suppliers and cooked in whatever manner you wish. It maybe you like sauces with steak, it may be you prefer your fillet steak just simply grilled and medium rare. Whatever way you order, you will find it comes to table beautifully garnished and cooked to perfection. The portions are very generous and the prices sensible. The Mill House has an extensive wine list with wines from around the World, again at prices to suit every pocket. Vegetarians are catered for and there are meals for children.

Many people come down to the Bradford-on-Avon Marina just to enjoy the sights and to explore the history of the canal but few will resist the gastronomic pleasures of the Mill House once they have discovered its worth. The Management and the Staff are friendly, welcoming and quietly efficient.

USEFUL INFORMATION

OPEN; *All day. Every day*
CHILDREN; *Welcome*
CREDIT CARDS; *All major cards*
LICENSED; *Yes*
GARDEN; *Yes. Outside Play Area*

RESTAURANT; *Traditional English fare and an Oriental Selection*
VEGETARIAN; *Catered for*
DISABLED ACCESS; *Yes*
PETS; *No*

THE BULL HOTEL
34 East Street,
Bridport,
Dorset DT6 3LF

Tel/Fax: 01308 422878

Bridport has been bypassed and now you can really enjoy the flavour of this old market town, where, on Wednesdays and Saturdays, colourful market stalls line East Street. Behind the bustling activity of the market, The Bull Hotel stands as it has done since the 16th-century, waiting to open its welcoming doors to travellers from all parts of the world as well as the regular stream of local people who regard the Bull as their second home!

This is a comfortable hotel to stay in. The restaurant offers excellent traditional fare with a slight Continental influence, and in the Long Bar just off the courtyard you will find not only good ale, good bar food but quite often live music which may be Jazz, Folk or Blues. This bar was once the stables for the coach horses and makes a very attractive place in which to drink.

I have stayed here many times over the years and I can remember listening to George Melley and at one time George Chisholm accompanied by Stephan Grapelli. Today traditional New Orleans Jazz takes place once a month and the Fringe Folk Club meets every Tuesday. Sometimes there are musical events on a Friday and Saturday. The atmosphere of The Bull is something one never forgets; its fabulous. Standing in the courtyard one can almost hear a coach and horse pulling in and the ostlers running out to hold tired animals and help the passengers to alight before they went into the welcoming comfort of the inn. Modern day customers arrive by car and having parked stroll through the courtyard to the Bull and its amenities, or indeed, in good weather enjoy them alfresco. The bedrooms have been carefully modernised and most of them are now en suite, but not one iota of the character of the building has been lost; the resident owners, Ray and Frances Buzza have seen to that.

USEFUL INFORMTION

OPEN; *10-3pm & 6-11pm*
CHILDREN; *Yes. Cots & Highchairs*
CREDIT CARDS; *All major cards*
LICENSED; *Full. Cask Ales*
ACCOMMODATION; *23 rooms mainly en suite. Car park at rear - 23 spaces*

RESTAURANT; *Traditional, high standard*
BAR FOOD; *Freshly prepared, wholesome*
VEGETARIAN; *Yes, at least 10 dishes*
DISABLED ACCESS; *Achieved by many*
GARDEN; *Courtyard, terrace facing south.*

FAIRFIELD FARM,

Upper Wraxall,
Chippenham, Bath,
Wiltshire SN14 7AG

Tel: 01225 891750 Fax: 01225 891050

Upper Wraxall is a small, contented village tucked away in the Wiltshire countryside, yet conveniently close to the M4, the town of Chippenham and the incomparable city of Bath. This is where Mrs Julie McDonough has her lovely house, Fairfield Farm. Built in 1901 it is a very substantial property with large windows that look out across the sizeable, well-tended garden which abounds with colourful flowers, shrubs and has a well manicured lawn, which is much in use during the summer for Badminton and Barbecues which are always great fun.

Inside the house the large airy rooms with their high ceilings are both welcoming and gracious. Everywhere you will find fresh flowers which highlight the attractive decor. The guests sitting room has a television and deep, comfortable sofas and chairs into which you are invited to sink and relax after a busy day, perhaps to read a book, a newspaper or chat to your fellow guests. The bedrooms, 1 double and 1 twin, have their own private facilities, clock-radio, hairdryer and a complimentary tea and coffee tray. In the morning, refreshed after a peaceful night's sleep you will come down to a delightful dining room where you will be served a scrumptious farmhouse breakfast, cooked to perfection on the Aga. Vegetarians are catered for as well, with yoghurts, fruit, cereals and plenty of toast. There are no evening meals but Julie will point you in the direction of a number of restaurants in Chippenham where you will find food to suit every taste and pocket. A very warm and friendly atmosphere awaits you at this English Tourist Board '2 Crowns Commended' Farm.

Fairfield Farm makes an excellent base for anyone wanting to explore Wiltshire, seek out Stately Homes or venture into the magical city of Bath where there is so much to see. Julie not only cares for those on holiday but takes special trouble over those who come to the area to work or on business. For them Fairfield Farm definitely becomes a home from home.

USEFUL INFORMATION

OPEN; *All year*
CHILDREN; *Welcome*
CREDIT CARDS; *None*
ACCOMMODATION; *1db 1 tw both en suite*
Special Rate; *Two nights or more*

DININGROOM; *Excellent farmhouse breakfast, No evening meal*
VEGETARIAN; *Catered for*
DISABLED ACCESS; *No*
GARDEN; *Beautiful Gardens*
PETS; *No*

WHITEWAYS,
Nimlet, Cold Ashton,
(A46 Nr Bath)
Nr Chippenhan,
Wiltshire SN14 8SJ

Tel: 01225 891333

You will come to the quiet, friendly village of Cold Ashton via the A46 to Bath. It is right on the Gloucester/Wiltshire border and is full of attractive cottages and houses. Linda Pike owns Whiteways, one of these fine houses and it is here she welcome guests into her home, making them feel comfortable and relaxed immediately and ready to enjoy all that Whiteways has to offer.

The house is charming, beautifully and tastefully furnished, and decorated in a style which is absolutely right for the house. From almost every window there are stunning views out across the rolling countryside. The garden is lovely and well-tended, here you can sit out and admire the views. The 3 attractive and well-appointed bedrooms, 1 double and 2 twin-bedded rooms, are all en suite. The beds are so comfortable that one does not want to get up in the morning even if the day promises some wonderful excursions. Having decided to rise you will come down to one of the best breakfasts to be found in the county. Linda is a wonderful cook and serves a traditional full English breakfast which is so large in size you can almost hear the plate groaning! Being so close to Bath, it is there you will probably want to eat in the evening. This magical city with its superb Abbey will enthrall anyone who has not been there before and always provide some new gem to discover for those who are returning for yet another visit.

Bath is just one of the many places to explore within easy reach of Whiteways. There are several Stately homes, a host of small villages, welcoming country inns and much more. Linda has many people who stay with her when they come to Bath on business and she welcomes businessman or visitor with the same genuine warmth.

USEFUL INFORMATION

OPEN: *All year*
CHILDREN: *Welcome*
CREDIT CARDS: *None taken*
ACCOMMODATION; *1dbl 2tw all en suite*
  Special rates for long stays

DINING ROOM; *Excellent breakfast*
VEGETARIANS: *Catered for*
DISABLED ACCESS: *No*
PETS: *No*
GARDEN: *Beautiful*

THE MANOR HOTEL

West Bexington,
Dorchester, Dorset
DT2 9DF

Tel: 01308 897 616 Fax: 01308 897035

The Manor Hotel is the ancient Manor House of Bessington, now West Bexington, in Dorset. It snuggles in a pocket of tree-and-garden on a gentle slope, just a saunter from the great sea-washed sweep of Chesil Bank. An old stone building, mellowed by the nine centuries of sun and sea, it dates back far enough to have gained a starred rating in the Domesday Book - but comforts and facilities have been considerably improved since then, without sacrificing the ancient charm.

West Bexington dips a toe in the sea close by Swyre - itself a stone's throw from the old rope-making town of Bridport, and is a meandering drive off the old coast road linking Lyme Regis to Portland; a road which has an almost unfair share of scenic grandeur. Breast the climbing road to meet the sudden revelation of the old Abbey of Abbotsbury, saffron with sunshine against a backdrop of velvet green, and you'll know what 'breathtaking' truly means. The oak-panelled Manor offers a choice of rooms redolent of country gardens, sea and crisp fresh linen. The original stone-lined cellar now earns its keep as a friendly bar with an imaginative bar menu on offer, and the dining room boasts cuisine conjured by a master chef of skill and imagination, which has gained a reputation that is not allowed to diminish. The flowered garden is beautiful and provides a safe paradise for children with its merry mixture of swings, slides, climbs, clambers and anything else which can be thought up at any one time. The garden also provides a wonderful setting for wedding photographs - The Manor Hotel is licensed for marriages and everything is done to make a wedding day wonderful and memorable. For people wanting a place of rest, the hotel could not be better, here you can listen to the constant sea murmuring all up and down the length of Chesil Bank. Within easy reach are the great sandy stretches of Weymouth, Charmouth and Lyme Regis.

Historic towns abound, historic houses and gardens await. Nothing is too much trouble for the owners, Richard and Jayne Childs, to ensure you have a perfect holiday. The hotel is open to non-residents.

USEFUL INFORMATION

OPEN; *11-11pm Mon-Sat. 12-3pm & 7-10.30 Sun.* **RESTAURANT;** *All fresh produce*
CHILDREN; *Yes. Cots. Baby listening* *Fish & Game. Sweets home prepared*
CREDIT CARDS; *Visa/Master/Amex/Diners* *Open to non-residents*
LICENSED; *Full On* **BAR FOOD;** *Wide selection*
ACCOMMODATION; *13 en suite rooms* **VEGETARIAN;** *Always 6 dishes*
Licensed for marriages **DISABLED ACCESS;** *No facilities*
GARDEN; *Flower filled. Play area. Safe*

RECTORY HOUSE
Fore Street,
Evershot, Dorset DT22 0JW

Tel/Fax: 01935 83273

Evershot will be familiar to readers even if they have never been to this beautiful village in an area of outstanding beauty. Jane Austen's 'Emma' was filmed here and Thomas Hardy featured it as 'Evershead' in his 'Tess of the d'Urbervilles. Little has changed in Evershot over the centuries and it gives one a sense of stepping back into the past. The High Street for example apart from the names of the shops, has changed not at all. The whole area is entrancing and ideal for a holiday. The village lies one mile and three quarters from the A37 main Yeovil-Dorchester road. It has its own inn, bakery, shop and post office. Nearby, many beautiful walks may be taken. There is so much to see. The lovely Melbury Park is close by at Melbury Osmond, and fishing, riding and sailing facilities are available at Sutton Bingham. Sherborne Castle and its beautiful Abbey, The Cerne Giant, Yeovilton Air Museum, Compton House Butterfly Farm and the Mute Swan Colony and Sub-tropical Gardens at Abbotsbury, are all within easy distance.

In Fore Street you will find Rectory House, an 18th-century listed building of great charm which is the home of Angela and Denis Carpenter. These two friendly, welcoming people invite you to share their comfortable home with its fragrant rooms, antique furniture, deep pile rugs, fresh flowers and home-cooked food. You will enjoy the garden with its huge copper beech tree and relax after dinner with coffee in the delightful and spacious lounge. The house has been furnished and decorated with loving care and an eye for style and detail. There are some splendid oil paintings which are frequently a talking point. The six bedrooms, four double and two twin are all en-suite. Each room has television and a generously supplied beverage tray - always a boon to the traveller.

You will be fed on traditional English fare of a very high standard, using as much local produce as possible. The menu is designed to tempt everyone's culinary tastes. Whilst there are no specific dishes on the menu for vegetarians, they can always be produced if asked for in advance. The house has a wine licence and the small but well chosen list compliments dinner perfectly. Breakfast is a feast with a choice. Rectory House is a No Smoking Establishment, open from February to November. Pets are not permitted, but Flossie, the resident collie, will be pleased to welcome you with her yellow 'Frisbee'.

USEFUL INFORMATION

OPEN; *February to November*
CHILDREN; *Not suitable*
CREDIT CARDS; *All major cards*
LICENSED; *Residential*
ACCOMMODATION; *6 en suite rooms*
PETS; *No*

DINING ROOM; *Delicious home-made fare*
VEGETARIAN; *With prior notice*
DISABLED ACCESS; *Ground floor room but no special facilities*
GARDEN; *Spacious. 1-acre beautifully kept*

PELICAN HOTEL AND RESTAURANT
Froxfield,
Wiltshire SN8 3JY

Tel: 01488 681193

The charm of the 17th century still lingers in the Pelican Hotel. The hotel acquired its name because of 'The Pelican Coach Company' which ran a stage coach service between Devizes and London and called here to pick up passengers and to allow time for refreshment for those who were already aboard. How glad they must have been to see the welcoming portals of The Pelican which is as welcoming today as it was in those far off days. The hotel is full of interest with low ceilings, beams, uneven floors and a sense of history reinforced by the fact that Charles I is reputed to have stayed here before the Battle of Donnington. One wonders in which of the 5 bedrooms, possibly the one with the four-poster! The hotel is reputed to have a friendly ghost who makes his presence felt by uttering odd noises!

The Pelicans very friendly, welcoming atmosphere attracts many people from far and wide. You will find regulars supping in the bar and exchanging friendly banter. Others looking at the exciting menu before they adjourn to the Restaurant for a meal. The Restaurant is an attractive room, beautifully appointed, with fresh flowers on every table, gleaming silver and sparkling glasses. The À La Carte menu is based on Modern English and European dishes, cooked by experts and superbly presented. The staff are caring and thoughtful, as they are throughout the hotel. Bar Food is available every day and you will see Blackboard Specials with many tasty dishes to tempt you.

Fine pine antiques mixed with tasteful modern furniture fill the rooms and together with attractive, colourful drapes, give the whole hotel an air of well-being. The five bedrooms are all en-suite and in each you will always find fresh flowers, television and a hospitality tray. The Pelican's garden runs down to the river, although at this stage it is really more of a pond! However the garden is a delightful place in which to sit and have a drink on a summer's day. From the hotel you can go boating on the canal, fish, walk, ride or play golf. There are several battlefields closeby and the famous White Horses at Amesbury are not far off. Something you should not miss is a visit to Spackmans in Hungerford's High Street, which belongs to The Pelican. It is a superb delicatessen and quite justifiably is known as 'The Harrods of Hungerford'. Here you will find everything from exotic preserves to Vintage Port and Quails' Eggs. If you should happen to be in Little Bedwyn, Berkshire you should also go to The Harrow Inn, a delightful place, under the same ownership.

USEFUL INFORMATION

OPEN; *11-3pm & 6-11pm*
All day Saturday & Sunday
CHILDREN; *Welcome*
CREDIT CARDS; *All major cards*
LICENSED; *Full On*
ACCOMMODATION; *5 en suite rooms*

RESTAURANT; *Modern English & European*
BAR FOOD; *Good menu. Daily Specials*
VEGETARIAN; *Always a choice + Vegan*
DISABLED ACCESS; *Only in Bar & Rest.*
GARDEN; *Yes. River frontage*
PETS; *Yes*

THE HARROW INN

Little Bedwyn, Nr Hungerford,
Wiltshire SN8 3JP
Tel:01672 870871 Fax: 01672 811231
email :josher@globalnet. co. uk

The small hamlet of Little Bedwyn is tucked away on the Eastern edge of the Vale of Pewsey, on the Wiltshire/Berkshire border. Little Bedwyn is ideally situated to explore the local area's attractions. Wiltshire is an extremely old part of the country, and Stonehenge, Avebury and Silbury Hill are close by. The Kennet and Avon Canal is a couple of hundred yards away from the Inn, and offers boating, fishing and good walking. Within easy reach are the antique shops in Hungerford and Marlborough, with Bath a little further away.

Dating from the 19th Century, the Harrow Inn is full of character and has the authentic atmosphere of a village Pub, something that is appreciated by the many people who treat it as their local - even if they live some distance away. Michael Chinner, the Chef and Landlord, is ably assisted by his staff, who go out of their way to give a warm and courteous welcome. The decor in the Inn is warm and country style, which emphasises the attraction of the Inn itself. Upstairs there are two Bed and Breakfast rooms with full en suite facilities. The rooms also have televisions and tea and coffee making facilities. Breakfast the next morning is sumptuous!

The Restaurant seats 25 in comfort and style, and the food is delicious. The menu is comprehensive in style and price offering something for everyone and every budget. Typically dishes range from Spicy Thai Prawns to a Traditional Roast Beef lunch on Sunday. All the food is freshly cooked and is presented in a relaxed, informal 'bistro' style. The Restaurant Wine List features wines from 6 different countries. Additionally, their Premier Wine List offers a select range of fine wines which are very competitively priced.

If you have ever wanted to sample a bit of the 'real' England, this is a perfect opportunity.

USEFUL INFORMATION

OPEN; *11-3pm & 6-11pm*
CHILDREN; *Welcome*
CREDIT CARDS; *Visa/Master/Switch*
LICENSED; *Full On & Off*
ACCOMMODATION; *2 en suite rooms*
GARDEN; *Yes*
PETS; *Yes, by arrangemant*

RESTAURANT; *Modern English. wide choice of dishes at varying prices*
VEGETARIAN; *Yes, also special diets by arrangement*
DISABLED ACCESS; *Ramp access to Inn but not to toilets*

LONDON HOUSE RESTAURANT

Market Place,
Pewsey, Wiltshire SN9 5AB
Tel: 01672 564775 Fax: 01672 564785

Saxon Pewsey stands in the shadow of one of the most famous white horses, perfectly located at the head of the Vale. It is a quiet village, basking in its proud history - it came to eminence in the days of King Alfred the Great, infamous for burning the cakes, and his statue now stands guard in front of the elegant, listed Queen Anne building, London House. Recently London House has undergone total renovation without losing any of the classic style of the Queen Anne period. Now it is one of the finest restaurants in Southern England providing an elegant and comfortable environment in which to enjoy the finest food and wine. It is an unforgettable dining experience. However that is not all, because what they have achieved at London House is a wonderful ambience and environment in which to enjoy the food, the wine and the conversation amid perfectly appointed rooms. It may be you have just come here to lunch or dine with friends or maybe it is a special occasion, a wedding reception or large dining parties, in which case London House will offer you the Kennet and Avon Rooms. These can accommodate from eight to thirty guests, seated in comfort, more if you prefer less formality. These rooms are also ideal for meetings and conferences. There is a choice of two syndicate rooms or one large conference area, fully equipped and beautifully furnished. Conference equipment can be supplied.

For sure you will receive the most attentive service to be found anywhere and the food is unsurpassed. The menu has a French flavour and regular, unique monthly specialities feature authentic examples of International cuisine. The London House team pride themselves on searching out the best of local produce to ensure the highest standards are always maintained. The wine list matches the excellence shown throughout this superb restaurant. There are wines representing the best from the Old and the New World. There are wines to suit every taste and pocket and to match every dish. To find such a wonderful place in such a beautiful village as Pewsey, is one of life's great rewards.

USEFUL INFORMATION

OPEN; *All year Mon - Sat.*
CHILDREN; *Welcome*
CREDIT CARDS; *All major cards*
LICENSED; *Yes. Outstanding wine list*
VEGETARIAN; *Special menus always available*

RESTAURANT; *Superb French style cuisine with a French, European & International flavour.*
No smoking in the dining room

SWAYNES FIR FARM

Grimsdyke, Coombe Bissett,
Salisbury,
Wiltshire SP5 5RF

Tel: 01725 519240

Situated seven miles from Salisbury on the A354 Salisbury to Blandford Road, Swaynes Firs is a small but active farm where beef cattle are kept with horses and a large variety of poultry. To those with an interest in the past Swaynes Firs is fascinating because The Grimsditch runs through the farm and is thought to have been constructed in the Bronze Age (1,000 BC to 500 BC) for farming purposes and as a tribal boundary ditch. It is also known locally as Grims Dyke or Devils Ditch.

The farm house is so attractive with its white bay windows and pretty colour schemes inside. The rooms are spacious and have lovely views overlooking the countryside. There are three bedrooms all en suite and with beverage trays as well as television. The large dining room welcomes you when you come down to a plentiful breakfast, either traditional English or whatever you wish for. It is always cooked to order. Plenty of fruit juices and cereals to start with, and a never ending supply of toast together with freshly brewed coffee or tea complete a meal which will set you up for the day. No evening meals are served here but there are plenty of eating houses in the vicinity; enough to suit everyone's taste and pocket. The large garden has ornamental duck ponds which you can see from the dining room windows. It is quite entertaining to watch the ducks cavorting whilst enjoying your breakfast.

There is a summerhouse and you will see Peacocks and Bantams strutting about the lawns whilst the geese and hens hold court in the adjacent paddocks. A happy house and one from which you can easily reach Salisbury Cathedral, Old Sarum, Wilton House, Stonehenge and many other historical and ancient sites.

USEFUL INFORMATION

OPEN; *All year*
CHILDREN; *Welcome*
CREDIT CARDS; *None taken*
LICENSED; *No*
ACCOMMODATION; *3 rooms en suite*
PETS; *Yes*

DINING ROOM; *Full English breakfast with options*
VEGETARIAN; *Catered for*
DISABLED ACCESS; *No*
GARDEN; *Yes, spacious with wildlife*

COURTLEIGH HOUSE,

40 Draycott Road,
Chisledon,
Swindon,
Wiltshire SN4 0LS

Tel: 01793 740246

Swindon is the largest town in Wiltshire, and was built on the prosperity of the Great Western Railway. The Railway Museum is housed in a former Wesleyan Chapel and provides hours of thrilling entertainment for Railway Buffs with exhibits from the days of steam to present times. Swindon is blessed with good shops which will tempt you to get your credit cards out and there are some good pubs and restaurants where you are sure to have a pleasant meal.

It is just outside Swindon in the quiet village of Chisledon, that Ruth Hibbered has her country house to which she welcomes guests. Ruth is a very friendly lady who goes out of her way to make you feel at home. On arrival you are welcomed with tea, coffee and home-made biscuits and cakes. The house is furnished in a Regency style which compliments its age. The bedrooms are delightful, light, airy and very comfortable, with the added privacy of en suite facilities, colour TV, a tea and coffee tray and fruit. The views from the rooms are of are of beautiful open countryside.

The breakfast at Courtleigh House is plentiful and memorable, starting with fruit juices and cereals and progressing to a freshly cooked and delicious traditional   English meal in which you have a choice of fried, scrambled, poached or boiled eggs which are fresh and free range. Evening meals are not available but Ruth Hibbered will happily advise you about the restaurants, pubs etc. The garden is very large and well kept with a hard tennis court which you are welcome to use if you wish.

Courtleigh House is convenient for the M4, Marlborough, historical Avebury, Bath and the Cotswolds with a plethora of fine stately homes and gardens as well.

USEFUL INFORMATION

OPEN; *All year*
CHILDREN; *Welcome*
CREDIT CARDS; *None taken*
ACCOMMODATION; *2 en suite rooms*
PETS; *No*

DINING ROOM; *Breakfast only*
DISABLED ACCESS; *Not really*
GARDEN; *Beautiful, large. Hard tennis court*

PREMIER HOTEL
121 The Esplanade,
Weymouth,
Dorset DT4 7EH
Tel: 01305 786144

The Premier Hotel has the good fortune to have a prestigious sea front location which offers an all embracing view across Weymouth Bay. That is one good reason for staying here but more importantly it is the warmth of the welcome and the friendly atmosphere which pervades this efficiently run Hotel. Sue and Mike Beaumont, the resident owners, endeavour to ensure their guests relax and feel at home. They succeed admirably; there are few people who, once having discovered the Premier, do not have the desire to come back.

Recently re-decorated and with new carpets and bedlinen, the modern bedrooms with en-suite facilities with double/twin and family rooms, are comfortable and welcoming. Each bedroom has colour television and a generously supplied tea/coffee tray. Food is important at all times but when one is on holiday it takes on even greater meaning because one can relax over an unhurried breakfast or dinner. Breakfast at the Premier is a typical traditional English meal, with a wide choice to suit all tastes. Vegetarians are well catered for. At dinner, the freshly prepared food is beautifully cooked and presented from a menu that is varied and comprehensive. The residents bar is a popular meeting place in the evening and there is also a comfortable lounge with colour television. Car parking is situated in the street to the rear of the Hotel, as well as public car parks closeby.

The Premier is central to all amenities including coach and rail stations, also the town centre with its many interesting shops, tea houses and restaurants. The sheltered sandy beach is ideal for children and boating in the bay is safe. There are many and varied outdoor pursuits in the area and Mike will be only too happy to supply the information.

USEFUL INFORMATION

OPEN; *1st March-31st October*
CHILDREN; *Welcome*
CREDIT CARDS; *Visa/Master*
LICENSED; *Yes*
ACCOMMODATION; *Available:*

RESTAURANT; *Traditional English Fare*
VEGETARIAN; *Catered for*
DISABLED ACCESS; *No, but welcome*
GARDEN; *No*
PETS; *No*

Twin rooms / Family rooms / Double rooms all en suite.
Twin & Double rooms not en suite

THE SWAN INN & LODGE,
1 Rodden Row,
Abbotsbury,
Weymouth, Dorset DT34JL

Tel/Fax: 01305 871249

Abbotsbury is deep in the heart of Thomas Hardy country and world renowned   because of its beautiful and fascinating Swannery which attracts visitors from around the world. The appropriately named Swan Inn with its adjoining Guest House is a sturdy building of mellow Dorset stone which has been in the capable hands of the Roper family for well over quarter of a century. You will discover that Graham and Sue have excellent assistance in running this friendly establishment from various members of the family. It is one of those places that have a refreshing informality about them but with an underlying efficiency that makes everything run like clockwork. Known for its food and hospitality, the Swan is equally well known for the beauty of the garden which consistently wins prizes and in summer is a riot of colour. Great place for good fun Barbecues in the summer. Chairs, tables and gaily coloured umbrellas make it a delightful place in which to drink or eat when the weather is kind.

Food is all important and the menu provides something for everyone from a full menu to a freshly cut sandwich. Steaks are one of the specialities of the house and cooked to your requirement. There are home-cooked Daily Specials and a range of tempting home-produced desserts. In the Lodge there are 5 bedrooms. 2 of which are en suite. There are tea and coffee facilities in every room and colour television with remote control teletext. A private Television Lounge is provided for guests. It is unpretentiously furnished but like the pub, it has a happy atmosphere. Children and pets are very welcome. Abbotsbury is well situated for anyone wanting to explore the Dorset countryside or enjoy the fine beaches. There are many places of interest within easy reach.

USEFUL INFORMATION

OPEN; *Winter 11-3pm & 6-11pm*   **RESTAURANT;** *Not applicable*
Summer: All day
CHILDREN; *Large family room & garden*   **BAR FOOD;** *Wide range. Good value*
CREDIT CARDS; *Master/Visa*   *Daily Specials*
LICENSED; *Full On & Off*   **DISABLED ACCESS;** *Yes*
ACCOMMODATION; *5 rooms, 2 en suite*   **GARDEN;** *Prize winning. BBQ*

PEACEHAVEN GUEST HOUSE

282 Sopwith Crescent,
Merley,
Wimborne,
Dorset BH21 1XL

Tel: 01202 880281

If you are looking for somewhere to stay that is quiet and tranquil yet within easy reach of places like Bournemouth with its wonderful beaches, theatres and night life then Peacehaven Guest House lives up to its name exactly. This lovely bungalow is situated on the outskirts of Wimborne and surrounded by an attractive and well maintained garden, full of flowers, shrubs and in summer a plethora of hanging baskets. In addition to Bournemouth, Poole and Wareham as well as the New Forest are within easy reach. Fishing, golf, water sports, coastal and country walks are just a few of the activities for the energetic. For lovers of history there are some wonderful Stately homes and gardens as well as the magnificence of Salisbury Cathedral within striking distance.

Peacehaven is immaculate, comfortable and warm. The owners, Margaret and Len Justice are friendly, welcoming people who enjoy their guests and do their utmost to ensure they have a comfortable, happy and memorable stay. The standard of accommodation is high, the cosy bedrooms have attractive linen and curtains, television and a hostess tray, plentifully supplied with tea and coffee. In the morning you wake to the tantalising smell of fresh coffee brewing and the breakfast you are offered is delicious. Freshly cooked to your order, it starts with fruit juices and cereals and there is always plenty of toast and preserves. Vegetarians are catered for if need be. Open all the year, the bungalow is warm in winter and cool in summer. An ideal place in which to stay for anyone on holiday, taking a short break or working in the area. There are good pubs closeby which offer an exciting range of food.

USEFUL INFORMATION

OPEN; *All year*
CHILDREN; *Welcome*
CREDIT CARDS; *None taken*
LICENSED; *No*
ACCOMMODATION; *1dbl 1tw*
NO SMOKING;

DINING ROOM; *Traditional English breakfast*
VEGETARIAN; *Catered for*
DISABLED ACCESS; *No*
GARDEN; *Yes. Very attractive*
PETS; *No*

Chapter 6

GLOUCESTERSHIRE, OXFORD, THE COTSWOLDS.

INCLUDES

Chapter 6

GLOUCESTERSHIRE, OXFORDSHIRE & THE COTSWOLDS

The City of **Gloucester** makes a wonderful springboard for this chapter which will take me to some of my favourite places in the whole country. They say that 42 Kings have visited the city, to say nothing of Queens, Princes, Princesses and other Royal personages. The Saxon Kings had their own royal palace here, giving the name to the district of Kingsholm. Gloucester owes much to one Saxon 'royal' Aethelflaeda, daughter of Alfred the Great, who undertook the restoration of the city after its period of decline.

We have to thank a Christmas Witan (Parliament) for the commissioning of the Domesday Book by William the Conqueror in or around the Abbey church of St Peter in 1085. Gloucester's own entry described the City as a prosperous town of some 3,000 souls. William built a castle at the south-west corner of the old Roman town. Henry I built another, while Henry II gave Gloucester their very long line of Royal Charters. Henry III was crowned in Gloucester Cathedral and no other coronation has taken place outside Westminster since. Richard III's most famous entry into the City was a triumph. Gloucester had supported him during the Wars of the Roses and in 1483 he rewarded Gloucester by granting them Letters Patent. Henry VIII brought Anne Boleyn here and Elizabeth I gave the City the status as a port. It was the arrival of the Stuarts that upset Gloucester's long and happy association with the Royals.

Charles I was denied entry although he tried hard to gain access. It rained that August of 1643 and the two young princes, later Charles II and James II were kept within the walls of Matson House by the weather and also as protection against possible kidnappers. Given the humiliation of their ignominious retreat, and the sheer boredom of their confinement it was not very surprising that Gloucester was not their favourite place after the restoration or that Charles took his revenge by reducing the boundaries and ordering the destruction of the City Walls. Good relationships have been continued with the House of Windsor and in 1988 the Prince of Wales opened the magnificent **British Waterways Museum.**

Gloucester sits in an enviable position and is able to claim it is part of the West Country as well as being in the Heart of England. Whichever it chooses to be it is bustling and prosperous. A wonderful base from which to explore so many places. Close to the Cotswolds, no distance from the Severn Vale, and a short drive to the Royal Forest of Dean. Wherever you are in the city you cannot miss the Cathedral.

Whatever one's opinion of the less than sympathetically developed City of Gloucester nothing can detract from the magnificent grandeur of the body nor the glorious symmetry of the cathedral tower. Inside it has so much beauty that one is left almost bereft of speech and it takes a while to re-adjust to the hurly burly of the twentieth century when you leave its hallowed portals. Royal events have regularly taken place and in 1216 following the sudden death of King John at Newark on the 28th October, his son, a mere nine years old, was crowned at the abbey church and became Henry III. If you look you will see there is a Victorian window in the south aisle of the nave which commemorates the event. It seems to indicate that he was crowned not with a crown but his mother's bracelet.

The great round columns of the nave lead us to the choir where the beauty is so wondrous it is almost miraculous. There are soaring columns, a great lierne vault and the largest stained glass window in England which somehow has survived six centuries, and is still full of superb l4th century glass. It is known as the Crecy window because it was probably a gift of Lord Bradstone who fought with his friend Sir Maurice Berkeley, at Crecy in 1346, and he too is commemorated. The window shows the coronation of The Virgin, the twelve apostles surrounded by saints and under them abbots of Gloucester and bishops of Worcester. There are flying arches and angelic musicians form the bosses in the vault above the high altar. There are no adequate words to describe the beauty. It is for you to see and make up your own mind.

Gloucester Cathedral is a favourite of mine and in amongst its stunning beauty there are some very simple and moving things to see as well. For example, only a few steps away from the tomb of Edward II, perhaps the finest of all royal effigies, is a very different piece of stonemasonry - a tiny cross, obviously fashioned by a loving but amateur hand. This is the cross of Colonel Carne VC, carved with a nail in the Chinese prison camps by the brave and valorous Commanding officer of the Glorious Gloucesters, who preferred to go into captivity with his men rather than escape to freedom after the heroic battle at Solm-ri on the Imjin River during the Korean War in April 1951.

With a love of things ecclesiastical it would be a pity not to take a look at Gloucester's fine churches. There is an old saying which is supposed to relate to the amazing number of churches in Gloucestershire. 'As sure as God's in Gloucestershire'; something that certainly applies to the number and variety in this county capital. At the north-west corner of the Cathedral precincts, is the Green of **St Mary's Square** which has a massive memorial to the martyred Bishop Hooper and it also has a pleasant church St Mary de Lode which just might be the site of one of the earliest places of Christian worship in Britain. Just a stroll from the cathedral is the ruined priory church of **St Oswalds** which is Gloucester's oldest building. English Heritage have the care of **Blackfriars**, the most perfectly preserved example of a Dominican Friary in Britain. **Greyfriars** is a fine example of an early l6th century Franciscan Friary, ruined after the Dissolution. It forms a most dramatic backdrop to the delicate beauty of **St Mary de Crypt** church and the modern architecture of **Eastergate Market.**

Llanthony Priory has undergone a massive programme of restoration after years of neglect. Probably the most intriguing of all Tourist Information Centres in the country is housed in **St Michaels Tower,** all that is left of a medieval church. No less than seven mayors of Gloucester are buried in **St John's** in Northgate Street, founded by the Saxon King Athelstan in about AD931 and later rebuilt by the Normans. The pulpit is all that remains of the original 'three-decker' from which both George Whitfield and John Wesley are known to have preached.

Gloucester is a multi-racial city and many new churches have been welcomed into it. The buildings have certainly added a new, handsome and spectacular dimension to the architecture of the city. None of these is more remarkable than the **Mosque Jama**, which adds its own distinctive spire and dome to the eastward skyline of the Barton area.

One of my favourites is the delightful, tiny Mariner's church which is incorporated into the redevelopment of **Gloucester Docks**. It is a Victorian foundation, provided for the spiritual well-being of the sailors and dock workers, who perhaps felt uncomfortable in the town churches. Gloucestershire poet and composer, Ivor Gurney, was choirmaster here for a while. You could travel all over Britain and Europe to-day and see nothing quite like Gloucester Docks. They represent a resource of national importance and one of England's most exciting new tourist attractions. Charles Dickens description of the port in days gone by will explain succinctly, what it was like.

You will see, suddenly appearing, as if it is in a dream, long ranges of warehouses, with cranes attached, endless intricacies of dock, miles of tramroad, wilderness of timber in stacks, and huge, three masted ships, wedged into little canals, floating with no apparent means of propulsion, and without a sail to bless themselves with.'

That was Gloucester Docks at the height of their wealth and prestige. Now where dockers and mariners once toiled and strived, tourists can sit and stroll at leisure. Where grain, salt and timbers were stored, there are bars, restaurants an antique centre and three museums. Dickens 'long range warehouses' have been restored to their former glory and this is only one part of the miracle that has occurred. A decade or so ago public opinion was so strong that the acres of dereliction which existed were nearly demolished with the objective of starting something new from scratch. Fortunately there was an acceptable alternative made possible by British Waterways Board and the Gloucester City Council, and so now we are able to see the most complete example of a Victorian Dockland in existence anywhere in the world. The Docks are a mecca for film and TV companies who have used the Dock as a period setting on many occasions including the memorable 'Onedin Line'. One could spend at least a day exploring Gloucester Docks taking in everything from the exciting **National Waterways Museum**, The Regiments of Gloucestershire Museum, The Robert Opie Collection- Museum of Advertising and Packaging or '**Merchants Quay** a new green steel and glass pavilion on the edge of the main dock basin which forms the heart of dockland shopping. Here you can hire a ball gown, buy a postcard, enjoy a cup of freshly ground coffee with a doughnut, have a pizza or relax with a pint looking out across the water from Doctor Foster's Public House and Restaurant.

Exploration inevitably produces a thirst and Gloucester is full of historic inns. In Northgate Street is The New Inn built around 1450 to accommodate pilgrims visiting the tomb of Edward II. You can stay here as people have done for the last 500 years. It has a fine galleried courtyard which is a wonderful spot for a quiet drink on a sunny morning. The Fleece Hotel on Westgate Street can claim to be one of Gloucester's oldest inns, dating from the 16th century. Here you can stay in comfort, dine on delicious food and take a drink in an old cellar bar that was known as 'The Monks Retreat'. Supposedly there was a tunnel that ran from here directly to the Crypt of the Cathedral for the benefit of the monks!

Cheltenham three hundred years ago was just an ordinary village and not the elegant place we know today. The story of how it became a Spa is undoubtedly far fetched but nonet heless an enjoyable thought. A resident watched a flock of pigeons who appeared particularly healthy. Daily they came to drink from the same spring. Samples of the water were taken and it was found that it had health giving minerals. This brought people flocking to the town to gain the same benefits as the pigeons and so the Spa town was born. You may not believe it, but Cheltonians do - they have seen fit to include a pigeon on the town's crest. By the end of 1783 the first Pump Room was established and it attracted such distinguished visitors as George III and the Duke of Wellington. There is no question that the waters were beneficial and still are.

Today you can take the waters at the **Town Hall** as well as the Pittville Pump Room which has to be the most notable of all Regency buildings. The whole town has an air of elegance with its fine crescents and distinguished mansions. The Regency Promenade, laid out in 1818, must be one of the most gracious thoroughfares in Britain. It was built as a carriage drive leading from the High Street up to the Spa, now the site of the impressive Queens Hotel.

Cheltenham is a town of Flowers and has many times won awards in Britain in Bloom Competitions. You need go no further than **The Imperial Gardens** in the heart of the town to enjoy wonderful floral displays. Two museums are worthy of your attention. **The Gustav Holst Birthplace Museum** and **The Cheltenham Art Gallery and Museum**.

People come to Cheltenham for many reasons but probably more for the horse racing at the Cheltenham course, one of the prettiest in the country. As every meeting comes around so the town fills up, every hotel is full for miles around and the whole place seems to become preoccupied with the sport of kings. It creates a wonderful atmosphere. Where to stay? Without doubt the elegant, beautifully appointed Hotel on the Park on Evesham Road would be my first choice. It has a charm which surrounds you from the moment you enter its portals. Expensive yes, but worth every penny. There are hotels and guest houses galore catering for every taste and every pocket.

Who could not love **Tewkesbury**. Situated where the Avon meets the Severn, it is the northern gate to the Cotswolds. It grew up around the Abbey, first founded in the 8th century, one of England's most magnificent Norman churches which was saved from sacking at the time of the Dissolution when the townspeople decided to buy it. It cost them the vast sum of £453! Everything about it is so beautiful. Each time I visit, I find something new but perhaps the superb Quire windows - seven of them, all of which have l4th century stained glass, and the dazzling splendour of the Beauchamp Chapel, are my favourites.

Tewkesbury prospered particularly in the l5th and l6th centuries as you can see from the fine buildings. To see what such a home would look like inside do visit **The Little Museum** in Church Street which was built in 1450 and restored in this century. It is simply furnished in solid oak. Open Easter-October Tuesday-Saturday from l0am-5pm.

We have King Canute in 1016,to thank for the glorious 27,000 acres which today make up the Forest of Dean. He decreed this should be a royal hunting ground. It is a world of its own with beauty spots, picnic areas, walks, trails, camping sites and a myriad of other activities. It is magical, mysterious, tranquil and yet still it is a source of industry in coal mining and timber. Beneath the tree clad hills, Britain's free miners continue to dig for coal. Quarrying for stone is still active and the last of the stone-cutting factories can be found at **Cannop**.

To understand more of the past, a visit to **Clearwell Caves** near **Coleford** will help and fascinate at the same time. Eight caverns are open to the public in addition to which there are excellent geographical and mining displays which bring home, with clarity, the dangerous and courageous lives our miners have always led. You will be taken on a guided tout into the Bat Chamber, which is the home of the hibernating Greater and Lesser Horseshoe Bats in the winter. Since the cessation of mining calcite has grown everywhere and it provides a beautiful backdrop. As you progress through Old Churn, 100ft below the surface, here you are at the deepest point open to the public. It brings home the labour involved in bringing the ore to ground level. I thought about my nine year old grandson and realised that boys not much older were expected to manhandle the loads which could well weigh 70lb a time.

Nearby is a charming place, **Puzzle Wood**, which was created out of some open cast iron workings which were left to gather moss. In the 19th century it was landscaped creating a puzzle path with steps, seats and bridges. You can take picnics here in the very pretty garden. Open daily except Mondays from Easter until October 31st.

Is the Forest more beautifully clad in spring or autumn? I do not know; either is wonderful. The spring has the joyous arrival of the soft green unfurling leaves when the ground is carpeted with bluebells, but autumn is a delight to the eye when the Larch turns to russet gold. Wildlife abounds with deer and badgers leading a protected life. Forest sheep thrive and munch their way through the pasture. At **Nagshead** near **Parkend** you will see birds of all kind in the reserve. Peregrines dominate the scene coming from their breeding ground in Symonds Yat Rock in Herefordshire.

The Forest is encompassed by three rivers; the mighty Severn, the Wye and the little Leadon. The Severn Valley has everything. It is fertile and full of orchards. Drive along and you will be invited to stop time after time to select fresh fruit, vegetables or flowers from wayside stalls. The Severn Bore is known by most and if you want to see it at its most spectacular then **Newnham** will provide you with a grandstand view. For those who have not met this natural phenomenon before, it is caused by the river flowing seawards and meeting the incoming tide from the Bristol Channel. In the late spring or autumn it reaches its greatest height causing a wave sometimes as high as 10ft. Lesser bores happen throughout the year and give an endless challenge to surfers and canoeists.

On the southern edge of the Forest is **Lydney** with its beautiful **Lydney Park Gardens**, set in a valley, full of rhododendrons, azaleas, flowering shrubs, trees, magnolias, and in the spring, daffodils. There is a Roman Temple site and a museum. The park is home to a herd of deer. You are welcome to picnic if you wish. Open Sundays and Wednesdays from the end of April until mid June from 11-6pm.

Cinderford and **Coleford** are the two main towns in the Forest, aptly called because of their connection with coal. I found Cinderford interesting more because of its people than its architecture. Coleford may not be so pretty but it is surrounded by picturesque villages which are a pleasure to explore. Choose either **Newland** or **Broadwell** and you will have chosen well Newland has The Ostrich Inn which dates back to the 13th century when it was a hospice for the workers building 'The Cathedral of the Forest'.

The Dean Heritage Centre at Camp Mill, **Soudley**, near Cinderford on the B4227, will provide you with a wealth of information and understanding about the Royal Forest. If you are more interested in visiting places you may enjoy **Littledean Hall,** which is 2 miles east of Cinderford. The family owned house is renowned for its claims to ghostly hauntings. The site was originally used by the Romans and the remains of a Roman temple were found there in 1984 and identified as Springhead Temple. It is now the largest restored ground plan of such a temple in Britain. Legends abound about Littledean Hall. Most of it seems to stem from 1664 onwards. Tragic events in the dining room led to poltergeists being active. A servant is said still to haunt the landing outside his bedroom. On another occasion two members of the family fell in love with the same woman and ended up shooting each other at the dining table. They have not yet found rest! Phantom blood stains appear alongside the fireplace where two officers of the King died in the Civil War. Finally in amongst this motley collection of ghosts, is a monk who came to give Holy Communion to the family in the days when Catholicism was illegal. No one has slept in the Blue Room with its four-poster bed since the 1950's because sleep is disturbed by the sound of footsteps and the clashing of swords! Exciting isn't it? You can visit daily from April to October 10.30am-6pm.

St Briavels Castle southwest of Coleford is also interesting. What is left is the remains of a 12th century castle adjacent to a Norman church. It stands high above the Wye valley amid glorious scenery. The church is a beautiful example of Norman and Early English architecture. It is open 10am-dusk daily. There is an amusing custom which takes place in the village after evensong on Whit Sunday. Bread and cheese is thrown by a local forester towards the people and it is considered a good omen for the year if you catch a piece. It is a 700 year old custom which used to take place in the church.

It would be a pity not to visit **Newent**, a bustling market town, which has so much that is delightful. **The Shambles** was once a slaughterhouse but has been turned into a museum of Victorian life completely furnished in the period. Behind the house is a cobbled square with a blacksmith and a carpenters shop. It is open from Easter to October from 10am-6pm except Mondays. It has a licensed restaurant which serves light lunches, teas and coffees.

If you are interested in Vineyards then two miles north of the village is one that produces a well known English wine, **The Three Choirs Vineyard**. It is best to visit between May and October but it is open all the year from 9am-5pm.

The Butterfly Centre in Newent is a great attraction. It has a tropical butterfly house, menageries, aquarium and a natural history exhibition. On the B4216, just outside Newent, is **The Falconry Centre**, where eagle and falconry displays are given providing the weather is kind. Open from February to November daily except Tuesdays, 10.30-5.30pm.

A birds eye view of The Cotswolds is all that I am able to give you in the permitted space. At worst it will whet your appetite to know more and at best it will instil in you a little of the sheer joy the area has given me over many years.

The Cotswold Hills extend from near Bath in Avon across to North Oxfordshire and part of Northamptonshire. At first their wooded slopes descend steeply to the Severn Vale. Later however they shake off the trees as they roll towards the Midland plain. Near Cheltenham and again above Broadway, they reach heights of over 1000ft. Drystone walls, towns and villages built of mellow stone or that silvery-grey limestone which shimmers in the light, characterise the Cotswolds. The wool industry, once the wealth of this area has gone into decline but sheep continue to roam the hills, and cloth is still woven around Stroud.

There are two good places to stay close to **Stroud.** One is The Crown Hotel and Restaurant, at **Frampton Mansell**, a small hamlet off the Cirencester to Stroud road. Tucked away in a corner you will find this picturesque pub looking out over a magnificent valley. Parts of this fascinating building date back to 1595 which is evidenced by the thickness of the walls, the low ceilings and sloping floors. A wonderful, crackling open fire and the warmest of welcomes greet you. The other suggestion is Ashleigh House at **Bussage**, which has no pretensions of grandeur but is just a very well appointed house.

For the ardent walker there are almost one hundred miles of footpath which will take you through ever changing scenery, sometimes climbing steeply or descending abruptly, following the escarpment for much of the time. It will never fail to delight you as you walk along beside burbling streams, over rickety bridges, through woods and in and out of 'kissing gates'. You will sometimes find yourself on a golf course and the next moment wandering through fields of corn. There are long barrows, hill forts and picturesque   Cotswold villages. The route will take you from Kelston Round Hill near Bath through Tormarton and the Sodburys, Nibley Knoll and Stinchcombe Hill. Close to Nibley Knoll, the village of **North Nibley**, a quiet place just off the M5 you will find The Black Horse Inn, a traditional country pub with an enormous welcome, comfortable bedrooms and excellent food at very reasonable prices. I tasted one of the best home-made Mushroom Soups I have ever had here. A little way off, Drakestone House near **Dursley**, a member of Wolsey Lodges, is the perfect place to stay if you want to be pampered.

The route continues to Freocester Beacon, Painswick Hill Fort, Cooper's Hill and Birdlip by the Devil's Chimney high up on Leckhampton to the highest point in the Cotswolds at Cleeve Cloud and then down to Winchcombe, the ancient capital of Mercia. Not far on is Hailes and then another climb to Beckbury Camp. Down again to Stanway and Stanton and on to Broadway and so to Chipping Camden. Much too long a trail for most of us but you can join it anywhere along the way.

I started my journey more sedately by visiting **Bishops Cleeve** just two miles outside Cheltenham where, near the racecourse, there is a charming thatched pub, The King's Head, which I always enjoy. **Winchcombe** next which wreaks of history. The town grew round its abbey in the 8th century but almost nothing remains, except for part of the gallery which you can see in The George Inn, another fine establishment. By the 16th century Winchcombe was revelling in the wealth brought by the tobacco industry. Fine houses were built and the character of the town was born. If you go into the **Folk Museum** at the Town Hall you can discover all about it. Winchcombe also has Britain's oldest private railway museum. It is a fascinating collection of railway memorabilia including one of the country's largest collections of cast iron and lineside notices. Winchcombe Railway Museum is open daily from 1-6pm.

It would be sacrilegious to miss a visit to **Sudeley Castle** which is close to Winchcombe, just off the A46. It is rich in history and contains some fine art treasures. The grounds are beautiful and include an Elizabethan garden, and there are regular Falconry displays. You will need to allow some considerable time here if you are to get the most out of it.

Nestling peacefully in its sheltered wooded valley, the village of **Temple Guiting** is one of the Cotswold's best-kept secrets. Its close neighbour **Guiting Power** is a village of simple, uncontrived beauty; its typically Cotswold cottages with gables and stone-tiled roofs converge upon the sloping mound of the village green in a perfect grouping. Further down river **Windrush** village sits on a steep slope overlooking its river namesake. A small triangular green is surrounded by attractive cottages and one of the most fascinating village churches; the beaked and bearded head carvings around the Norman South porch are grotesque but still stand out despite the passing of eight centuries.

Upper and Lower Slaughter close to Stow-in-the-Wold, I find to be beautiful and breathtaking but almost too perfect. Both have excellent, expensive, superbly run hotels and many lovely houses.

Hailes Abbey is a beautiful medieval abbey lying in ruins but with a romanticism about it that makes it a must for visitors. Then there is **Stanway House,** a golden Jacobean manor, just to the north east of **Hailes,** which demands your attention. The house has only changed hands once in the last 1300 years or thereabouts. And so to **Snowshill** just west of the tiny hill-top village of **Bourton-on-the-Hill** with its church that has a fine Norman south arcade. **Snowshill Manor** is a charming Tudor house with a 17th-century facade. It has an incredible mixture of displays inside. Anything from weavers and spinners tools to Japanese armour and musical instruments. The owner filled up the house so much with his collections that he had to move to an adjoining cottage. His name was Charles Wade and his coat of arms bears the motto 'Nequid Pereat' -'Let Nothing Perish'!

South of Bourton is **Sezincote**, famous for its house and garden. The house was remodelled by a wealthy 18th-century Nabob, Sir Charles Cockerell. He loved all things oriental and had his house constructed in Indian style with oriental gardens. So impressed was the Prince Regent when he came to stay in 1807 that he decided to use a similar design for his own Brighton Pavilion.

Broadway, unfortunately for those who love it, has become almost too popular. It is so attractive that it brings people from all over the world to savour its loveliness only to find that the overcrowding disguises its true beauty. See it early in the morning or just as evening is drawing on and you will see the real Broadway. There can be very few people who have not heard of The Lygon Arms one of the country's leading inns. A place of charm, character and furnished quite beautifully with genuine country furniture. It goes without saying that the food and the hospitality are superb. Stay there and you will be cocooned in comfort.

One of the great Cotswold wool towns in the Middle Ages was **Chipping Camden**. It is one of my most favourite Cotswold towns and well worth visiting if you want to see a flawless example of a 'wool church'. It represents the wealth of the time, and piety thrown in for good measure. It has a splendidly decorated West tower, tall nave arcades with light that floods from the clerestory and window over the chancel arch. The church is open from 8am-until dusk. **The Woolstaplers Hall**, which was a 14th-century merchant's house, now holds a wonderful collection of things pertinent to the history of the town. Traditions dating back to 1612 are still celebrated annually in the form of Scuttlebrook Wake and Robert Dover's Cotswold Olimpick Games, whose disciplines include the ancient and honourable sport of shin-kicking!

The whole of the main street is full of lovely mellow buildings and amongst them is Seymour House Hotel, a place of tranquillity, charming, friendly service, wonderful food in a restaurant that just delights the eye and whets the appetite for what you instinctively know will be a memorable meal. It is a hotel to which guests return with the greatest regularity - fully understandable.

Gardens always attract me and right in the High Street is the **Ernest Wilson Memorial Garden** which opens daily. It is in memory of Ernest Wilson who was dedicated to the study of Chinese and Japanese botanical specimens. Two other gardens are quite near the town, **Hidcote Manor Gardens** lying 3 miles to the northeast, was created early this century by a noted horticulturist, Major Lawrence Johnstone. He strove successfully to build a series of formal gardens separated by walls or hedges of different species If you are there in July you may be lucky enough to catch a performance of a Shakespeare play which takes place in the grounds.

189

Kiftsgate Court is right by Hidcote and is full of unusual plants and shrubs as well as a wonderful display of hydrangeas.

Blockley comes under the heading too of villages you should not miss. It is probably the most unspoilt of all the Cotswold villages. It suffered, like so many others, from the decline of the woollen industry but it was saved by the continued production from its eight silk mills. Many of the houses on Blockley Brook at the southern end of the village were once mills. It has a collection of genuinely ancient inns which will provide you with food and particularly good Real Ale. It is the sort of place that will have your cameras hard at work.

Another small town with much character is **Moreton-in-the-Marsh**. It is right on the Fosseway and has a High Street full of splendid 18th and 19th-century buildings among them the former manor house in which Charles I sheltered during the Civil War. Although not one of the principal markets during the heyday of the Cotswold wool trade, Moreton now claims the largest open-air street market in the Cotswolds. Every Tuesday, thousands of visitors arrive by coach, car and train, to browse around the 200+ stalls.

Just outside the town in **Upper Oddington**, a peaceful hamlet, is a 16th-century pub of Cotswold stone, The Horse and Groom, owned and run by Graham and Phyllicity Collins. This couple are comparative newcomers to the Cotswolds but have rapidly been taken to the heart of the regulars and at lunchtime you will always find local people standing at the bar enjoying a drink and a chat. From there you could sally forth to visit **Batsford Arboretum** just one mile west of Moreton. It has the largest private collection of rare trees in the country, planted in the 1880s by Lord Redesdale when he returned from his Embassy posting in Tokyo. The views are stunning and the magnolias and maples stand out in my mind as being especially wonderful.

Wandering along the small roads from Upper Oddington or from Stow you will come to the peaceful, pretty village of **Bledington** complete with its village green. It is the sort of place that makes you feel at peace with yourself and to add to that enjoyment is The Kings Head Inn, one of the nicest hostelries in The Cotswolds. Staying here would recharge anyone's batteries. Every bedroom is individually furnished and en suite. Excellently situated too for a weekend's Cotswold exploration. There are even those who will drive down from London and spend the day here, revelling in the countryside and then, after a delicious early dinner, returning to London feeling totally refreshed.

High on a hill beside the Roman Fosse Way is **Stow-on-the-Wold**. It was a centre for wool in medieval times and today is a picturesque town which will give you a great deal of pleasure. The big square, complete with its old stocks seems to encompass the whole life of the town. The busy shops, with a preponderance of antique shops, a wealth of pubs, eating houses and hotels all make for the hustle and bustle of a well kept, well loved place. I love the different shapes and sizes of the buildings which dominate the square. The Old Stocks Hotel is one of my favourites with its friendly welcome, slightly odd shaped rooms and overall feeling of homeliness. In Digbeth Street is The Royalist Hotel which features in the Guinness Book of records as the oldest inn in England dating from AD947. Behind its 1615 facade stands the original oak framed structure erected in the 10th century, the roof being supported by a five bay open braced collar beam truss. It is full of history with everything from marks to ward off witches and leper holes to a friendly ghost who lives on the ground floor and has been identified as Young John Shellard who died in 1638 age twenty three. He moves between the bar and the cellar without favouritism.

Another village just off the Fosse Way is the incomparable **Bourton-on-the-Water**. It is infinitely photographable and because of this, like Broadway it does suffer from a surfeit of visitors. There are several places to visit, amongst them **The Model Railway Exhibition** which will endear itself to young and old with its 400 sq ft of model railway layouts. At the New Inn in the High Street is **The Model Village** which has been in situ for over fifty years and is a model of the village built in Cotswold stone. Then there is **The Birdland Zoo Garden** with a penguin rockery. If you enjoy cars and cycles from the past you will enjoy **The Cotswolds Motor Museum** which is housed in an 18th century watermill. I can recommend both The Mouse Trap Inn and The Olde Charm in Bourton when you are in need of refreshing the inner man.

Two more places beginning with the letter B are Cotswold favourites of mine. **Burford** which is actually in Oxfordshire is somewhere that rekindles happy memories whenever I go there. Many years ago I used to stay in The Bay Tree in Sheep Street when I was attending the Cheltenham Spring Meeting. It was a wonderful time and from what I can see the hotel has simply grown in stature over the years, adding modern comforts to rooms of all shapes and sizes in this very old building. It is atmospheric and just the place to stay if you want to be pampered. The other place that I discovered this time was the enchanting Angel Inn tucked away in Witney Road. It has taken only a few, but inspired years, for Jean Thaxter to become recognised as the owner of one of the most attractive and exciting small inns in the Cotswolds. Its charm lies in the atmospheric interior which will not have changed much in the 400 years it has been in existence. The food is innovative and imaginative and specialises in fish, game in season and Cotswold lamb. You can stay here as well.

The steep main street leads down to the river Windrush from the Wolds. There is only one way to see Burford and that is on foot. South of Burford is **The Cotswold Wildlife Park** with is expansive enclosures, reptile house and wonderful landscaped gardens. **Bibury** is the second B. In the 17th century it was a famous horse racing centre and home of England's oldest racing club. Take a look at Arlington Row with its picturesque Cottages. **Arlington Mill** is built on a Domesday site. It is a 17th century corn mill, which, with the adjoining cottages, has become a museum with 17 exhibit rooms. It opens its doors from mid-March to mid November daily from 10.30-7pm but only at weekends in the winter. Looking for somewhere to stay then the 17th century Swan Inn is very special. Once a coaching inn, it is full of character, lies by the river and has Fishing rights. Good food and very comfortable bedrooms as well as friendly bars complete the picture.

Northleach is very special because of its church mainly which dominates the small town. It is magnificent, built in the 15th century when the woollen industry was at its height. The south porch has original statues under canopied niches, great crooked pinnacles and a stair turret crowned with a delightful spirelet. It is open daily from 9am-dusk.

On a steep sided tributary of the Coln is **Chedworth**, a picturesque village, which sits on either side of a steep valley making the cottages appear to be growing out of it. In Queen Street is The Seven Tuns, a true pub giving value for money within its 17th century walls. Outside there is a pretty walled garden which was once the village Pound. Good home-made fare is on the menu. Perhaps a place to visit before or after tackling **Chedworth Roman Villa**. There are several paths and bridleways that lead from the village into the woods and on to the Villa which is often regarded as the finest in Britain. You realise when you see its size, some 32 rooms and separate bathrooms, just how sophisticated the Romans were.

CHAPTER SIX

To the south of the A40 from Northleach to Burford, the Cotswolds are split by fertile river valleys along which villages have grown. The wolds of this southern section are not as well populated as the north. The difference between the populated valley and empty wold is marked. The first valley was cut by the river Leach that flows by Northleach, and in its upper reaches the leak drains bleak wold. It is not as pretty as the Coln nor does it have the character of the Windrush, but it is beautiful and gives its name to **Lechlade,** the town that separates the Cotswolds from the Thames valley. It is a nice small town well known to Thames cruisers for it is the highest point of navigation on the river. There are some fine Georgian buildings and a church whose roof boss above the nave shows two carved wrestlers. It has the look of Lincoln cathedral but nowhere near as grand.

Fairford is somewhere I always try to see for two reasons. The first is the superb Perpendicular church of St Mary the Virgin built at the end of the 15th century by John Tame, a wool stapler and cloth merchant, except for the base of the tower which was built by the Earls of Warwick. Everything about it is wonderful but the greatest glory is the 28 windows of opulently coloured glass, contemporary with the church, which may be the work of Barnard Flower, Henry VII's master glass painter. It is ablaze with colour, a sublime sight unparalleled in any of England's parish churches. In the Market Place there are fine 17th and 18th century houses including the well loved and well established Bull Hotel which sits in a corner by the church. This is the meeting place for people from miles around and it is fun just to listen to the general chatter at the bar whilst enjoying a good, home-cooked meal. Ideal base for anyone to stay wanting to enjoy the atmosphere of an old inn and be well situated for exploring both the Cotswolds and Oxfordshire.

Cirencester is somewhere about which I am never quite certain. I know I love the graceful Georgian buildings in which the town is rich. The church is dazzling and will give you hours of pleasure. It is open in summer from 9.30am-6.30pm. Then there is **The Corinium Museum** in Park Street which contains one of the largest collections of Roman artefacts in the country. If you would rather be out of doors, at the top of Cecily Hill is the entrance to **Cirencester Park**, a wonderful expanse of greenery which is owned by Earl Bathurst. Cars and cycles are not permitted but you can walk or ride to your hearts content, in woodland and parkland laid out in the 18th century by the 1st Earl Bathurst helped by his friend, the poet, Alexander Pope.

South of Cirencester is **Tetbury** dating from 681, one of the most popular Cotswold towns. In spite of being famous as the home of the Prince of Wales at Highgrove House, the town has remained comparatively unspoilt. Both the fine parish church and the Market House of 1655, have been well restored. The town still accommodates a busy general and antiques market every Wednesday and Tetbury is world famous for its antique shops. A walk down the old Chipping Steps leads to Gumstool Hill, site of the ever popular Woolsack races, dating from the 16th century in which teams of men and women race up and down the 1-in-4 hill carrying 65lb woolsacks on their backs!

Westonbirt House and Garden, roughly three miles south of Tetbury, is an excellent place to visit. The Arboretum contains one of the world's finest collection of temperate trees and shrubs. It is a place of startling contrasts. In the spring the magnificent rhododendrons bloom and in autumn the fantastic colour of the leaves are stunning.

I have visited **Chavenage House** twice and enjoyed it each time. It is on the B4014 just northwest of Tetbury. It is an Elizabethan manor house thought to be haunted by Charles I and has Cromwellian associations. It has a great air about it which is intangible but charming. Open from May to September on Thursdays and Sundays from 2-5pm.

192

Oxfordshire's contribution to The Cotswolds is not to be ignored. When I was travelling about the Cotswolds garnering information for this book and drinking in the autumnal beauty of the area I felt that every road led to **Chipping Norton**! Here is a busy town with a sloping main street that appears to be tiered. It has a great deal of character and much to recommend it. I found The White Hart an historic coaching inn, to be much to my liking. It has a quiet dignity about it and at the same time caters for the needs of the town on a daily basis as well as ensuring travellers are well cared for. Not far a way a turning off the A44 onto the B4022 will take you to the sleepy town of **Charlbury** where nothing much ever seems to happen and yet it has a railway line! One of its virtues is this direct line with Paddington which means that visitors can spend a day here, mooch around a bit and take a walk in the sparkling countryside having first sampled the fare at the hospitable Bull at Charlbury.

If you took the A3400 out of Chipping Norton making for Shipston on Stour which is just in Warwickshire, you would find a right turn onto the B4035 which would bring you along a winding road to **Lower Brailes** somewhere I would like you to know about because it is the home of The George Hotel. It is believed that the George was constructed in 1350 to house the masons who built the church of St George. Standing in the bar today one can imagine a time when it would have been full of herdsmen and others attending the market. Much has happened here throughout seven centuries and as one dines on good food and drinks fine wines, it is wonderful to think about the romances and the tragedies, joys and frustrations, and the many suppers that will have been burnt to a cinder whilst their recipients were kept 'on business' in the bar! You are invited to stay here if you wish in one of the well appointed en suite bedrooms.

From here the road meanders along until it comes out at **Banbury**. No longer part of The Cotswolds but very much part of the life of the county. The town is best known for its cakes and its cross of nursery rhyme fame. It disappoints many because here you have a town that dates from Saxon times but few pre-17th century buildings survive. The people of Banbury throughout the ages have always wanted something up to date and in their quest destroyed much of their history. In the 17th century they petitioned Parliament to pull down their great castle so that the stone could be used to repair damage caused to the town by two Civil War sieges. In the 18th century they blew up the church rather than restore it. The original Banbury Cross was destroyed too, in an upsurge of Puritanism 300 years ago. The present cross dates only from 1859. The 'fine lady' of the rhyme is believed to have been a member of the Fiennes family, who still live nearby at Broughton Castle. The ride to the cross was probably a May Morning ceremony.

Down the A4260 from Banbury you will come first to **Deddington** and if you take a left turn there onto the B4031 you will happen upon **Clifton**. Not specially remarkable as a hamlet but it is a must because here I found The Duke of Cumberland's Head. This exciting establishment has all that is required of an inn which has been in situ for three hundred years, and much more. Walk through the main entrance and the smell of the logs burning in the big fireplace plus the air of well being that pervades the atmosphere, and you will recognise that you have found somewhere that will remain in your memory as one of the good things of life. The food is very French with International overtones. The whole place is candlelit at night adding another dimension to this charming establishment.

On again a little further down the A4260 for a few miles until on your right you will see **Duns Tew** signposted. This is where you want to be, in a quiet backwater in lovely countryside and ready to sample the delights of The White Horse Inn. It has welcomed travellers for over three hundred years and the tradition is carried on today. The low beamed ceiling in the bar, the intimate pretty restaurant and the huge log fire all serve to make this a special place. An ideal place for a quiet short break; the rooms situated round the courtyard are all comfortable and en suite.

Just off the Oxford to Swindon road I started an immediate love affair with Fallowfields Hotel at **Kingston Bagpuize**. This is the family home of Anthony Lloyd and his wife. It is a magical place with high ceilinged rooms downstairs and wonderfully spacious bedrooms with vast beds and beautiful drapes and furniture upstairs. It is a house that is loved and everyone who stays there seems to acquire the mantle of well-being it gives out. Most of the vegetables used in the cooking, which is superb, come from the organically cultivated kitchen garden and all other produce is always organic, pesticide free locally grown and reared where possible. Fallowfields grounds are a delight in themselves. Ponies used by Riding for the Disabled stay contentedly in the paddock, a swimming pool lies in one corner and in the summer it is blissful to enjoy a gin and tonic on the lawn. A very special place.

Wantage is a quiet town with cobbled streets and 17th and 18th-century houses. It lies at the foot of the Berkshire Downs in the vale of the White Horse. King Alfred the Great was born here in 849 and his statue stands in the market place. Parts of the church of St Peter and St Paul date back to the 13th century. It has a 15th century hammerbeam roof, some fine wood carvings and the tombs of the members of the Fitzwarren family, into which Dick Whittington married.

To the west through country lanes you come to a little hamlet where it is more likely to see horses than cars. **Kingston Lisle** is super. Not so much because of the houses that make it up but because of the genuine community spirit and above all the love of horses and racing. Lambourn Downs lie to the south and for a long time The Blowing Stone Inn has resounded to the happy chatter of those who love this sport of kings. In the bar you will almost always find people who are involved in the training of race horses. It is a delightful pub, not so much from its appeal when you first see it but because of the comfortable, happy and friendly way in which it is run. It has the wonderful feel of the country about it but in fact if you left the M4 at Swindon Junction 15 you would be there in about fifteen minutes at the most. The food is excellent and there are 3 charming en suite bedrooms. A break here would be great at anytime of the year. For those staying longer than two nights free fishing and shooting are available on the estate which lies alongside the inn.

I have deliberately left **Oxford** until last. So much has been written about it by generations of people. Matthew Arnold's city of 'dreaming spires' bewitches all who come here. It maybe that much of the outskirts is industrialised but it is of no importance. Oxford remains a University town, par excellence, its streets dominated by the stone-built walls and quadrangles of its ancient colleges and in term-time by flocks of black-gowned undergraduates on foot or on bicycles.

The Broad, where that famous Oxford institution, **Blackwell's Bookshop** is to be found, the High, Cornmarket and the narrow lanes leading off them are the centre of university life, and where most of the old colleges, public houses, good restaurants and shops are to be found. In Spring and Summer the University Parks and the Rivers Cherwell and Isis, as the Thames is known here, come into their own. On May Morning at 5am the Cherwell is packed with punts at Magdalen Bridge to hear the Choristers of Magdalen sing a Latin hymn to salute May Day from Magdalen Tower. Something, which once heard will never be forgotten.

Where do you stay? I have chosen three vastly different places. The first is The Randolph Hotel, famous for over a century, looking out over the Ashmolean and onto St Giles. Its public rooms are very special and its bedrooms quite beautiful. Right in the centre of Oxford it is the place to stay. Tea is served daily in their glorious drawing room where you can enjoy the delights of cucumber sandwiches, cakes and scones. If you approach Oxford from the Banbury road, just before entering St Giles, you will find one of the most attractive and delightful hotels in Oxford, The Old Parsonage. Small and intimate it has a high standard of service, all the bedrooms are appointed to the highest standard and the marble bathrooms are exquisite. It is a place Oxford residents use when they want to meet for a drink or a meal. During the summer months the front terrace is open and food and drink is served all day, as indeed it is in The Parsonage Bar throughout the year. The hotel is a favourite with the acting profession. Anthony Hopkins, Debra Winger and Lord Attenborough stayed here while they were making Shadowlands. Dudley Moore, Michael Palin and Diana Rigg have also been guests and it is rumoured that Oscar Wilde graced the hotel with his presence when he was at Oxford.

You may think that my third choice does not come into the same category as The Randolph and The Old Parsonage. It does not profess to do so, but what Parklands Hotel in Banbury Road, offers is a friendly, comfortable and informal establishment where nothing is too much trouble. It is not fashionable and does not ever suggest it is. However reading the visitors book you will realise that there have been hundreds, probably thousands of people who have enjoyed its ambience over the years.

There are many places to visit here in Oxford, but it is the overall beauty of this university town that will remain with me forever and will outweigh everything else - even the majesty of **Blenheim Palace** at **Woodstock.**

THE BELL
Church Street,
Charlbury, Oxfordshire OX73PP

Tel: 01608 810278 Fax: 01608 811447

The Bell is a fine hostelry, built in 1700, which has carried on the tradition of caring for travellers ever since it first opened its doors. It has never been better than today when the character of centuries has been retained but the comforts of the modern day have been sympathetically added to make The Bell one of the most comfortable places to stay in the county. In the Oak-beamed and flagged stoned floor of the bar you will almost always find regulars enjoying a drink from the well-stocked bar or having an excellent bar snack lunch from a menu that is wide ranging, well presented and sensibly priced. In the elegant, cosy restaurant, the menu is innovative and the choice enough to ensure that there will always be something to tempt even the most pernickety palate. Special menus can be created for family occasions and if there are more than eight people in the party, there is a private dining room available. The extensive wine cellar has a wide variety of vintage wines and ports to accompany your meal. A self-contained conference room for up to 55 delegates is fully equipped and there is a small room for up to 15 people. Whatever you need in this hotel you will find the service is friendly, helpful and efficient.

The bedrooms are attractive and well-appointed. Each room is individually furnished and en suite with colour television, direct dial telephone, a hostess tray, hair dryer and trouser press. The gardens set in over an acre of its own grounds tempts many people to stroll on summer evenings and is very popular for pre-dinner drinks. From The Bell there is so much to see and do. You can go horse riding, fishing, shooting, play golf, with nearby facilities for swimming, squash and tennis. Blenheim Palace is within easy reach and so are 'the dreaming spires' of Oxford. It is an area full of charm, romance and beauty and The Bell makes an ideal place in which to stay.

USEFUL INFORMATION

OPEN; *All year, all day*

CHILDREN; *Welcome*

CREDIT CARDS; *All major cards*

LICENSED; *Yes. Extensive wine cellar*

ACCOMMODATION; *13 en suite rooms*

GARDEN; *Over an acre*

RESTAURANT; *Anglo/French dishes From an innovative á la carte menu*

BAR FOOD; *Wide range*

VEGETARIAN; *Catered for*

DISABLED ACCESS; *Not suitable*

PETS; *Yes*

BEAUMONT HOUSE HOTEL,
Shurdington Road, Cheltenham,
Gloucester, GL53 0JE.

Tel : 01242 245986
Fax : 01242 520044

The architecture of the 1850's stands out because of its enlightened and generous features and this is particularly apparent at Beaumont House one of Cheltenham's most delightful small hotels. Situated in Shurdingham Road one is reminded, within its elegant doors, that the 1850's was the time when the traditional Victorian rocking horse was being crafted and the first race meeting was held at the Duke of Ellenborough's Prestbury Park, now the famous centre of the annual Cheltenham National Hunt Festival and steeplechasing. The Whole house feels as though it is still living in the past and that adds to the sense of well-being and restfulness which guests will tell you is the hallmark of a stay here. Cheltenham itself adds to this feeling with its fine Regency buildings and the knowledge that the glorious Cotswolds are only a little way away as well as Bath, Bristol, Stratford-upon-Avon or Oxford less than an hour by car.

The whole house is furnished in style but with the accent on comfort and relaxation. The gracious lounge with its long windows looking out over the garden is the perfect place to curl up and read a book, enjoy a quiet evening drink or have a cup of the hotel's excellent coffee. The pretty dining room also has views of the garden, the walls and the drapes are both soft coloured and each table is attractively appointed with linen clothes and bone china. Here you will be served one of the best breakfasts in Cheltenham and enjoy a deliciously cooked dinner, if that is your wish.

Upstairs there are sixteen en suite rooms, each individually decorated and some with fourposters. All the curtains and drapes are colour co-ordinated and the whole effect is one of tranquillity in which to have a good night's sleep. Every room has a hostess tray, direct dial telephone with radio alarm clock and colour TV with satellite; some rooms have video recorders. The hotel without a doubt offers good, old fashioned values allied to a cheerful friendliness and quiet, efficient service

USEFUL INFORMATION

OPEN; *All year*
CHILDREN; *Over 10yrs welcome*
PETS; *No*
CREDIT CARDS; *All major cards*
ACCOMMODATION; *15 en suite rooms;*
9 dbl, 4 twin, 2 sgl.

DINING ROOM; *Excellent quality*
VEGETARIANS; *Catered for*
DISABLED ACCESS; *No*
LICENSED; *Full*
GARDEN; *Lovely grounds & private parking*

MONTPELLIER HOTEL,
33 Montpellier Terrace,
Cheltenham,
Gloucestershire, GL50 1UX.

Tel : 01242 526009

Situated in a lovely part of Cheltenham, the hotel overlooks the Montpellier gardens and tennis courts. Shops, inns and restaurants are only a two minute stroll away, and this is a most fashionable area to be located. The hotel is a Grade II listed building which dates back to the 18th century, with a character and warmth that will have you immediately relaxed and 'at home'. Pat and Steve Mylnarski are your hosts, and endeavour to provide the type of service and hospitality, that will ensure your return time and time again!

The furnishings and fabrics are of modern design, having recently been improved and updated, and the warmth and ambience of this fine establishment shines through in the friendliness and attentiveness of your hosts. There are five bedrooms all en suite, delightfully decorated, with all the necessities including colour TV, radio, and hospitality tray. The dining room provides a generous English breakfast and an evening meal can be arranged. Vegetarians are catered for and there is a variety of bar snacks on offer. The bar is fully licensed and what better way than to relax here, enjoy a pre dinner drink, and chat about your days activities. This is a charming 'home from home', with congenial hosts and superb accommodation.

Cheltenham is a great place to stay with it's variety of shops, architecture, and arts. This is home of the 'races' and also the parks and gardens are a delight to behold. Cheltenham has won the 'Britain in Bloom' award many times. It stages festivals of music, sport and culture, and is visited by many on these occasions. Horse riding is available and there are many golf courses nearby. The Cotswold villages and towns are less than a thirty minute drive away, and for those walking enthusiasts the area is perfect. It is a beautiful part of the country, with a diversity to suit all, and having the advantage of being close to many things and places of interest. Oxford, Stratford-upon-Avon are just two of the wonderful places to visit (about an hours drive), and here you could visit Royal Worcester Porcelain factory (Oxford), or the Shakespeare Theatre. There is a wildfowl trust at Slimbridge, and National Trust properties include stately homes and gardens.

USEFUL INFORMATION

OPEN; *All year*
CHILDREN; *Welcome*
PETS; *No*
LICENSED; *Full*
CREDIT CARDS; *None taken*
ACCOMMODATION; *5 en suite rooms.*

DINING ROOM; *Generous fayre*
VEGETARIANS; *Catered for*
DISABLED ACCESS; *No*
BAR SNACKS; *Available*
GARDEN; *No, but overlooks beautiful public gardens.*

THE GEORGE HOTEL

High Street,
Dorchester-on-Thames,
Oxfordshire OX10 7HH
Tel: 01865 340404 Fax: 01865 341620

Originally associated with the medieval abbey opposite, The George Hotel has been the haven for travellers since the end of the 15th century. It is the oldest building in the village and one of the oldest inns in the country. Throughout the centuries it has been restored but has never lost its sense of old world charm which has been preserved throughout. All sorts of famous people have stayed here including aristocrats like Sarah Churchill, the first Duchess of Marlborough whilst in more recent years the author D.H. Lawrence. There is also a friendly female ghost, who has been seen and leaves a musty smell! The character of the hotel with its oak beams and uneven floors is enhanced by the aged oak furniture, brightly polished brass and a varied collection of prints and antiques. Quintessentially English, this beautiful timber-framed inn could not be a better place to stay whether one comes for business or pleasure. The bedrooms are very special with a choice of the rather grand rooms with four-poster beds or the cosy rooms beneath the oak beams, low ceilings and leaded light windows. With great care the comforts of this century have been added which have provided en suite bathrooms in every room. Tea and coffee making facilities as well as colour television are there for your comfort and leisure and the added touch of fresh flowers is delightful..

Renowned for its food The George has an elegant restaurant with an attractive water garden setting. The master chef is talented and inspired and using the freshest ingredients and herbs from the hotel garden, produces memorable dishes. The George is renowned for its Sunday lunches. The cosy bar, complete with inglenook, is a friendly meeting place and equally enjoyable for a quiet relaxing drink by oneself. It, too, has a good Blackboard menu. Two rooms in a self-contained annexe offer ideal surroundings for business meetings or for wedding receptions - which are highly popular because, apart from the elegant surroundings and superb food, the service is perfection.

Dorchester-on-Thames in the heart of the Thames Valley is in an area in which there are many fascinating towns, villages and historic homes. The Cotswolds, Woodstock and Stratford-upon-Avon are to the north and Henley, Windsor and London to the south east. Oxford and the magnificent Blenheim Palace are just a short drive away.

USEFUL INFORMATION

OPEN; *All day, all year*
CHILDREN; *Welcome*
CREDIT CARDS; *All except Diners*
LICENSED; *Full On. Fine wines*
ACCOMMODATION; *18 en suite rooms*
GARDEN; *Yes*

RESTAURANT; *Superb food in elegant surroundings*
BAR FOOD; *Home-cooked fare*
VEGETARIAN; *Always a choice*
DISABLED ACCESS; *Yes*
PETS; *Yes*

OWLPEN MANOR
Owlpen, Near Uley,
Gloucestershire GL11 5BZ
Tel: 01453 860261 Fax: 01453 860819

Uley is a pretty weaving village situated between Tetbury, Stroud and Dursley and Owlpen is set in a valley half a mile east of Uley, off the B4066. Owlpen has been described as a 'Gloucestershire Shangri-La' where those in the know come year after year for absolute peace and seclusion. It is an apt description but barely scratches the surface of what this beautiful Tudor Manor house is all about. Owlpen has long been recognised as one of the most romantic small manor houses in the West of England. The Tudor manor - with its magnificent yews and clutch of medieval outbuildings - is set in its own remote and picturesque wooded valley, under the edge of the Cotswolds. Inside are a unique series of wall-hangings and arts and crafts, while outside the gardens and valley provide hours of beautiful walks.

You have the choice of staying in the house in historic bedrooms and in unbelievable luxury. The sense of 900 years of history is all about you and it is quite wonderful. The other, equally delightful choice is to stay in one of the dreamy cottage hideaways which lie scattered along the valley. Several of these enchanting cottages are 'listed' period buildings. There are snug medieval barns and byres, a watermill first restored in 1464, the Court House of the 1620's, weaver's and keeper's cottages, and even a traditionally built modern farmhouse. It is all very exclusive and very private. In each cottage, the owners, Nicholas and Karin Mander, have created the subtle intimacy and feeling of a well-loved home, kept in first class order. They have taken the trouble to furnish the cottages individually, blending traditional and contemporary designs with antique furniture and nick-nacks, prints and plants, all in co-ordinated interiors. Each cottage is fully equipped with everything you could wish for.

The Cyder House, has been restored and has become a charming Licensed Restaurant with an atmospheric setting serving home-cooked lunches, traditional cream teas and gourmet dinners. Opening times do vary and it is wise to book a table in advance. The food is superb and the speciality is home-reared pheasant and beef. A great place for private parties, weddings and conferences.

Owlpen Manor once having been visited will remain in your mind as an unforgettable memory - something to be savoured and treasured.

USEFUL INFORMATION

OPEN; *All year*
CHILDREN; *Welcome*
CREDIT CARDS; *All major cards*
LICENSED; *Restaurant, yes*
ACCOMMODATION; *Bed and Breakfast in house. Self-catering cottages*

CYDER HOUSE RESTAURANT; *Delicious food. Home-reared pheasant & beef a speciality*
DISABLED ACCESS; *By arrangement*
GARDEN; *Superb grounds*
PETS; *In cottages by arrangement*

BLACK HORSE INN,
North Nibley,
Nr Dursley,
Gloucestershire GL11 6DT

Tel: 01453 546841 Fax: 01453 547474

The 16th century Black Horse Inn is a true Gloucestershire village inn which opens its welcoming doors with the same friendliness to strangers as it does to those who come in regularly for a pint and a chat, a good meal or a game of dominoes - the inn takes the latter seriously and fields a team in the local league. You will find it on the B4060 midway between the old market town of Dursley and Wotton-under-Edge nestling among the slopes of the Cotswold escarpment in North Nibley. The village is reputed to be the birthplace of William Tyndale who first translated the Bible from Latin into English and was subsequently burned at the stake as a heretic. Tyndale's Monument built in his memory stands vigil above the Inn on the summit of Nibley Knoll from which there are stunning views of the Malvern Hills, the Severn Vale, Severn Bridge and Forest of Dean.

What strikes one most as one enters the inn is the old world charm. The Bar and Restaurant have an intimate atmosphere with low ceilings and a profusion of oak beams, inglenooks and brass work. There are six comfortable and homely bedrooms, four with en suite facilities. All the rooms have a colour TV, telephone and beverage-making facilities. A full English breakfast is included in the very reasonable price. In fact all the prices are designed to please your pocket. An extensive lunch-time and evening menu offers a whole range of good home-cooked dishes from light bar snacks to full á la carte meals prepared to order. At weekends special rates are on offer for those wishing to explore the area or just relax in this peaceful corner of England.

USEFUL INFORMATION

OPEN; *All Year. 12-2.30pm & 6-11pm*
Sunday: 12-2.30pm & 7-11pm
CHILDREN; *Permitted if eating*
CREDIT CARDS; *All major cards*
LICENSED; *Full On*
ACCOMMODATION; *6 rooms 4 en suite*
PETS; *No*

RESTAURANT; *Wide range. High standard Home-cooked. Inexpensive*
BAR FOOD; *Extensive range. Home-cooked*
VEGETARIAN; *2 dishes daily*
DISABLED ACCESS; *Bar & Restaurant. Not accommodation*
GARDEN; *Beer Garden. Large Car park*

HOLMWOOD

Shiplake Row,
Binfield Heath,
Henley-on-Thames,
Oxfordshire RG9 4DP

Tel:0118 947 8747 Fax: 0118 947 8637

Holmwood is a large and very beautiful country house just three miles from Henley-on-Thames. The house faces south and has some stunning views over the Thames Valley. Covered with clematis and wisteria in parts, the house is the home of Brian and Wendy Talfourd-Cook who welcome their guests throughout the year and ensure that their stay is memorable. Inside, the house has impressive reception rooms with carved marble fireplaces and carved, polished mahogany doors and a galleried hall. The large drawing room with welcoming log fires crackling in the hearth on cold days, is available at all time to guests. The elegantly furnished bedrooms with mainly antique and period furniture, all of which have bathrooms en suite, are spacious and very comfortable. Each room has colour television and tea and coffee making facilities. Holmwood is open all the year for Bed and Breakfast but does not serve dinner. You will find that the surrounding area is full of restaurants and pubs serving good food.

The gardens of Holmwood are particularly beautiful. There are four acres with extensive lawns and many fine specimen trees including Cedar, Wellingtonia, Beech, Oak, Lime, Hornbeam, Chestnut, Magnolia and Wisteria, together with Rhododendrons, and in spring, banks of daffodils and bluebells. Beyond the gardens are another 26 acres of paddocks and woods. It is such a tranquil place and quite idyllic to stay in for anyone who enjoys and appreciates a house and home of this quality. It is no wonder that Emily Tennyson spent the night here before her wedding to Alfred, Lord Tennyson, and here Algernon Charles Swinburne composed many of his poems in the peace of the Oxfordshire countryside.

Business people have come to appreciate Holmwood because it is ideal for small functions and meetings, where in complete confidence matters can be discussed in a relaxed atmosphere and be uninterrupted by pressures of the work place. Fax, Photocopier and Word Processor are available.

USEFUL INFORMATION

OPEN; *All year*
CHILDREN; *Not under 12*
CREDIT CARDS; *None taken*
LICENSED; *No*
ACCOMMODATION; *2tw.2dbl 1sgl*
All with private bathrooms en suite

DINING ROOM; *Excellent breakfast only*
VEGETARIAN; *By arrangement*
DISABLED ACCESS; *Partial. Lift available*
GARDEN; *Superb, beautiful 4 acres + 26 acres*
PETS; *No*

THE PEACOCK HOTEL & RESTAURANT

Henton, Nr Chinnor,
Oxfordshire OX9 4AH

Tel: 01844 353519

Quiet and secluded the 16th century Peacock Hotel is a small country hotel with 20 bedrooms set at the foot of the Chilterns. It is close to Thame, Princes Risborough, High Wycombe, Oxford, Henley, Marlow and Aylesbury as well as being only 45 minutes from London by the M40 where you leave the motorway at junction 6. So many people have found The Peacock a restful haven over the years. Visitors come because of its delightful, surroundings, the comfort offered and the excellence of the food but they have also found that it is the perfect location for small business meetings for companies in this area.

The outside of the hotel is charming but it is the inside that will delight you with its harmonious collection of ancient and modern furnishings to the highest standard. It is cosy, intimate and welcoming, with a staff whose pleasure it is to ensure that your stay is a happy one. The Restaurant opens 7 days per week at lunchtime and in the evening. Business lunches are well known in the district for their excellence and for the speed of service when it is necessary. On Sundays at lunch the atmosphere changes from the urgency of a working day to the pleasure of relaxing over a traditional Sunday roast or enjoying the excellent á la carte menu which offers a wide choice. Dinner is equally relaxed and the food delicious with a range of starters that major on fish and seafoods but also offer the vegetarian a choice. Whether you choose from the á la carte menu or opt for the imaginative table d'hôte menu you will be served with a meal that is memorable. If you prefer to have a meal in the Bar you will find that equal attention has been given to providing a wide ranging menu with something to please everyone.

The 20 bedrooms all have private bathrooms, colour satellite television, telephones, tea-making facilities and some feature four-poster beds. There is an executive room with lounge area and spa bath, also the Chiltern Suite. Recently the hotel has added an excellent outdoor heated swimming pool.

USEFUL INFORMATION

OPEN; *All year*
CHILDREN; *Yes*
CREDIT CARDS; *All major cards*
LICENSED; *Yes*
ACCOMMODATION; *20 en suite rooms*
PETS; *By arrangement*

RESTAURANT; *Excellent menu.*
Open to non-residents
BAR MEALS; *Good range, sensible prices*
VEGETARIAN; *Several choices*
GARDEN; *No. Heated outdoor pool*

BOWOOD HOUSE HOTEL,
238 Oxford Raad,
Kidlington, Oxford OX5 1EB
Tel: 01865 842288 Fax: O1865 841858

This interesting hotel built in the 1950's is splendidly situated for anyone with business in Oxford or simply there to enjoy the 'dreaming spires' and all the other wonderful facets of this charming, very busy city. You will find Bowood House on the A4264 in the village of Kidlington, just 4 miles from Oxford's city centre. Kidlington is purportedly the largest village in Britain but with a population of 18,000 and a thriving business community, it is in effect a small town. Nonetheless it still has a village atmosphere and some interesting historic buildings.

Within Bowood House there are ten en suite bedrooms and then another twelve have been built on the motel basis with separate entries. Whichever you choose you will find them well appointed and immaculate and with far more individual character than one might expect from a comparatively modern building. Each room has a colour television, direct dial telephone, a trouser press, hairdryers and a hostess tray. The hotel, in the capable hands of the owner, Hans. D. Otto, has a well earned AA and RAC listing as well as BTA Commended.

One of the pleasures of staying in this small hotel is the friendly atmosphere which prevails throughout. It is somewhere that guests can relax in the very comfortable lounge or enjoy a drink in the well-stocked bar - a particularly pleasant occupation after a busy day exploring or on business. The restaurant offers a very comprehensive breakfast menu and the Table d'hôte or Á La Carte menu entices one at night to linger over the good food on offer and perhaps enjoy wine from the well chosen wine list. The chef is sympathetic to anyone with dietary needs and is also aware that many people prefer simple grills to the more adventurous dishes he enjoys creating. It should be noted that the restaurant is closed on Sundays but that does not pose a hardship, Oxford and the surrounding areas have many good eateries.

Bowood House is an excellent base from which to explore the many exciting places within easy reach such as Woodstock, Blenheim Palace, the home of the Duke of Marlborough, and Bladon, the last resting place of Sir Winston Churchill. Both Stratford-upon-Avon, Warwick and the Cotswolds are within striking distance.

USEFUL INFORMATION

OPEN; *All year, 24 hours*
CHILDREN; *Yes.*
CREDIT CARDS; *Visa/Master/Amex*
LICENSED; *Yes*
ACCOMMODATION; *22 en suite moms*
CAR PARKING; *Ample parking at rear*
GARDEN; *Yes*

RESTAURANT; *Comprehensive Breakfast Menu*
Table d'hôte 8c A La Carte evening menu
BAR FOOD; *Freshly cut sandwiches*
VEGETARIAN; *Yes + other diets*
DISABLED ACCESS; *Yes*
PETS; *Yes*

CONYGREE GATE COUNTRY HOUSE HOTEL

Kingham,
Oxfordshire OX7 6YA

Tel: 01608 658389

It is only recently that Judy and David Krasker-McDermott have become the Proprietors of the Grade II listed, Conygree Gate Hotel, which started its life as a Cotswold stone farmhouse in the 17th century. They quite obviously love this beautiful house and are more than happy for you to share its beauty, its elegance and its quiet comfort. The house is full of character with a flagstone hall, creaking floorboards, oak beams, odd shaped bathrooms and much more to intrigue you. Since their arrival, Judy and David have been busy implementing some of their exciting ideas for the house. They have redecorated the dining room in spectacular fashion and one of the lounges and in doing so have discovered the original flagstones in the hall. The garden too has come into their baileywick and there they have found several old roses which with their greenfingered touch will be coaxed into bloom each summer. Conygree Gate Hotel is responding to the Krasker-McDermott's loving attention and everyone who comes to stay feels part of the house.

The food served in the newly decorated dining which is open to non-residents, is in the inspired hands of Andrew Foster, a young and ambitious chef. He favours fresh, local produce to produce beautiful dishes which demonstrate his classical training and love of uncomplicated, brilliantly executed flavours. Dinner is really memorable and in the morning a sumptuous, freshly cooked breakfast awaits you.

Each of the 9 bedrooms has either en-suite or private bath or shower, colour television and tea and coffee making facilities. Ground floor rooms are available and pets are welcomed. All of the bedrooms are non-smoking.

The Krasker-McDermott's main priority is to understand what their guests want and they make every effort to meet any requirements they may have. While you are staying with them in the Cotswolds they would be glad to organise and book excursions, advise on local walks and cycle rides and point you in the direction of antique shops. Conygree Gate Hotel with its friendly, relaxed atmosphere and peace and quiet is everything anyone could wish for at anytime of the year.

USEFUL INFORMATION

OPEN; *All year*
CHILDREN; *Yes over 10years*
CREDIT CARDS; *All except Amex*
LICENSED; *Yes*
ACCOMMODATION; *9 en-suite rooms*

DINING ROOM; *Imaginative, innovative food*
Open to non-residents
VEGETARIAN; *Upon request*
DISABLED ACCESS; *Yes. Ground floor rooms*
GARDEN; *Beautiful grounds*
PETS; *Yes*

THE COTSWOLD LODGE HOTEL

66a Banbury Road,
Oxford OX2 6JP
Tel: 01865 512121 Fax: 01865 512490

Built at the turn of the century The Cotswold Lodge Hotel is situated in a quiet conservation area, just half a mile from the city centre, making it the ideal place for those wanting to explore the ancient city centre of Oxford renowned for its 'dreaming spires' its splendour and charm. There are a number of guided tours available, or you can wander the pick of College buildings at your leisure. The University Parks which are no more than two minutes walk from the hotel are great for those wanting to stroll in tranquil surroundings.

The Cotswold Lodge has an enviable reputation for its hospitality and food, whether it is for those who come to stay on holiday or those who have found the hotel an excellent base for business purposes. Conferences, whether residential or non-residential are superbly run and give the company and its delegates everything they need. This also applies to wedding receptions which have become a speciality of the hotel. Over the past 20 years The Cotswold Lodge has become the place to be for such a great occasion. They can cater for up to 150 persons and the attention to detail which ensures the bride and groom have a wonderful day, is unsurpassed.

The 52 bedrooms are all different and all with private bathrooms, colour television, telephone, hairdrier, tea and coffee making facilities. Each has delightful furnishings and is the epitome of comfort. The elegant and attractive Dining Room provides the perfect setting for meals whether it is lunch or dinner. The talented Chef produces an ever changing menu and always a wide choice whilst the wine list compliments the food. During the winter months log fires enhance the cosy atmosphere of The Lounge Bar which is popular with both residents and non-residents who find it an ideal venue for meeting their friends.

USEFUL INFORMATION

OPEN; *All year*
CHILDREN; *Welcome*
CREDIT CARDS; *All major cards*
LICENSED; *Yes. Fine wine list*
ACCOMMODATION; *52 rooms with private Bathrooms*

DINING ROOM; *High standard with an ever changing menu. Open to non-residents*
VEGETARIAN; *Catered for*
DISABLED ACCESS; *No special facilities*
GARDEN; *Yes*
PETS; *By arrangement*

MANOR HOUSE HOTEL,

High Street,
Moreton-in-Marsh,
Gloucestershire GLS6 OLJ
Tel: 01608 650501 Fax: 01608 651481

This typically mellow, honey coloured stone building is the epitome of all that is beautiful in the Cotswolds. The Manor House stands quietly back from the busy High Street, which has one of the most extensive street markets in the world on Tuesday each week. There are few people who can resist its charm which is as great inside as it is out. It is a hotel which is popular with visitors and business people alike both for its comfort and hospitality and because of the easy access by road and by regular Inter-City rail services. It is less than two hours from London; Stratford-upon-Avon with its world renowned theatre and delightful choice of shops is just 25 minutes as are the spa towns of Cheltenham and Leamington. Not too far away is the incomparable city of Bath and the dreaming spires of Oxford.

Every bedroom has a private bathroom. Each is attractively, individually and luxuriously furnished with wonderfully comfortable beds, direct-dial telephone, colour TV, in-house video and a beverage tray. In the Mulberry Restaurant you will find the food memorable starting with a delicious breakfast which offers all manner of interesting things. At night dinner is eagerly anticipated and never disappointing. The talented chefs provide dishes to suit every ones taste and you may choose from the Table d'hôte or the Á la Carte menu. Sunday Lunch is a popular occasion and one for which it is advisable to book. The service is quiet, unobtrusive and efficient, as indeed it is throughout the Manor House.

The Mulberry Restaurant gets its name from the centuries old Mulberry tree in the beautifully maintained gardens; gardens that contain many unusual plants which make it a delight at any time of the year. To sit in the garden with a drink before dinner on a summer's evening is perfect. If the weather demands that you stay indoors you will find the bars and lounges with their crackling log fires just the place to be.

The Manor House has its own indoor heated swimming pool with spa bath and sauna together with changing rooms and, of course, a constant supply of clean cossetting towels. But the Manor House is not just a place to relax. A superb custom built conference venue is designed so as not to intrude in any way upon the activities of other hotel guests. It is ideal for meetings or seminars from 2-100 delegates and has every modern facility. Wedding receptions are one of the success stories of the Manor House and can accommodate up to 108 guests with a licence to hold ceremonies on the premises. The staff ensure that the day is very special and the gardens are superb as a background for the photographs.

USEFUL INFORMATION

OPEN; *All Year*
CHILDREN; *Welcome*
CREDIT CARDS; *All major cards*
LICENSED; *Yes. Fine wines*
ACCOMMODATION; *Luxurious rooms*
With private bathrooms

RESTAURANT; *Award winning cuisine*
VEGETARIAN; *Catered for*
DISABLED ACCESS; *No special facilities*
GARDEN; *Beautiful gardens. Heated in door Swimming pool*
 PETS; *Guide dogs only*

THE LONDON HOTEL
30-31 London Road,
Stroud,
Gloucestershire GL5 2AJ

Tel: 01453 759992 Fax: 01453 753363

This quiet, dignified hotel in the centre of Stroud has catered for travellers for many years and is now in the competent, friendly hands of Betty and Roger Giffard. Here you may stay in a 200 year old building which has been brought tastefully into modern times. Throughout the hotel you are aware of the high standards both in furnishing and cleanliness that are demanded by the Giffards. It is a warm, welcoming environment in which anyone would be pleased to stay whether on business or on holiday in this lovely part of the country. You can fish, play golf and within five minutes drive, walk on the Downs. The historic city of Gloucester with its magnificent cathedral and fascinating dock conversion is only a little way away.

Within the hotel there are twelve well appointed bedrooms, each equipped with television, direct dial telephones and beverage trays. Downstairs the pretty restaurant is rapidly gaining a name for the excellence of its food. The presentation is exquisite and matched by the flavours of the a la carte menu. Six starters begin the dinner menu. You might choose Blackened Chicken Salad, with roasted peppers or a delicious concoction of Smoked Haddock and Welsh Rarebit. The main course always has superb, succulent steaks and probably young English Rack of Lamb, served in its natural juices, or there may well be Barbary Duck Breast in a sweet and sour sauce with savoury rice. The vegetables will always be fresh and seasonal. Indeed, emphasis is laid on all the dishes being prepared from locally purchased produce and therefore subject to availability. Follow this with some delectable home-made desserts and you have had a meal fit for a Queen. Vegetarian dishes are always on the menu and special diets can be catered for at notice. The accompanying wine list is well chosen and has some interesting wines from around the world.

The comfortable lounge bar with its warm, informal atmosphere provides a full choice of draught and bottled beers, wines and spirits. Dinners, wedding parties and other special occasions all come within the services the hotel offers and the location of the Hotel makes it a convenient meeting place for business people.

USEFUL INFORMATION

OPEN; *All year round*
CHILDREN; *Welcome*
CREDIT CARDS; *All major cards*
LICENSED; *Full On. Fine wines*
ACCOMMODATION; *12 rooms*
8 en suite.

RESTAURANT; *Delicious food.*
Traditional and very high standard
VEGETARIAN; *Always available*
+ special diets
DISABLED ACCESS; *Not suitable*
PETS; *No*

You are politely requested not to smoke in the Dining Room.

LAMPET ARMS
Main Street,
Tadmarton, Oxfordshire OXt 5 STB

Tel: 01295 780260/780070

Built as a private house by a Naval Officer, Captain Lampet for his Mother in 1840, the Lampet Aims became a hostelry in 1860 and was then known as The Red Lion. It was not until 1906 that it became The Lampet Arms, a Freehouse which has grown in reputation throughout the years and never been better than today in the capable, friendly hands of Tim and Jane Howard. Its attractive white Mock Tudor front leads into an attractive bar, much used by local people and by those who come from further afield to enjoy the excellent food for which The Lampet has such a high reputation.

What strikes one most about this congenial inn, is the relaxed atmosphere and the sense of well-being that pervades the whole of the building, This stems from the Howards who have the knack of making everyone feel welcome and whose high standards in every department never falter. All sorts of interesting features attract ones attention including the amazing collection of Foreign Bank Notes above the bar. One can eat either in the restaurant from a well chosen, imaginative a la carte menu in which seasonal local produce features largely, or in the Bar where the traditional snacks are available as well as some exciting and very tasty dishes from the Blackboard. The Howards enjoy wine and this is apparent in the wine list which includes wines from around the world.

Situated on the B4035 Banbury to Shipston-upon-Stour road, The Lampet Arms is an ideal base from which to set out to visit some of the many National Trust properties nearby. Broughton Castle where Charles I took refuge during the Civil War is closeby and there are many attractive small villages and towns within easy distance. The Lampet Arms has 4 charmingly furnished, ensuite bedrooms all of which have television, telephones and beverage trays. You will be cossetted, well fed and made extremely welcome.

USEFUL INFORMATION

OPEN; *11-3pm & 6-11pm*
CHILDREN; *Over 5 years*
CREDIT CARDS; *All major cards*
VEGETARIAN; *Always a choice*
LICENSED; *Full On*
ACCOMMODATION; *4 ensuite rooms*

RESTAURANT; *Excellent ÁLa Carte menu*
BAR FOOD; *Wide range. Blackboard specials Seven cask ales*
DISABLED ACCESS; *Not really suitable*
GARDEN; *Beer Garden*
PETS; *No*

FOLLY FARM COTTAGES

Malmesbury Road,
Tetbury,
Gloucestershire GL8 8XA

Tel: 01666 502475 Fax: 01666 502358

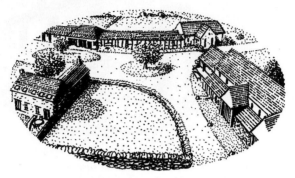

*In one's dreams sometimes one sees the perfect holiday retreat. Dreams seldom become reality but Folly Farm Cottages provide the idyllic choice for a peaceful week or two, a long weekend, or a home from home base during a business trip. These lovely old Cotswold stone cottages have been converted from the time mellowed workshops, byres and wool stores of the original Folly Farm, which dates back hundreds of years. Their names reflect a fascinating past, **Churn Cottage, Kiln Cottage, Middleyard Cowbyres and Barnend, The Weigh House and Wheelwrights, Cider Loft, Bull Pen,** and last but not least, **Folly Cottage,** which Beatrix Potter's 'Mrs Tiggy Winkle' would have loved. They are beautifully furnished, equipped with everything you could wish for, will sleep anything from 2-8 people and some cottages are especially suitable for the disabled and the elderly.*

***Folly Farm** is a working farm, with a large herd of dairy cattle and is situated just five minutes walk from historic Royal Tetbury, an authentic Cotswold town famous for its Wool Market Hall and fine church, built by the wealth of the wool trade. Superbly situated for the Cotswolds, within easy reach of Cheltenham, Bath, Stratford-upon-Avon with several castles and cathedrals begging to be explored. Within the house there are four en suite guest bedrooms with Television and a beverage tray. A Continental Breakfast is available every morning. The house, like the cottages, is the epitome of comfort.*

*Finally **The Great Tythe Barn** has four meeting rooms, catering facilities, and with the flexible accommodation available makes it a unique venue for conferences, formal occasions, large parties, family reunions, or simply weekends away. Close to the M4/M5 motorways. Heathrow 1 hour.*

USEFUL INFORMATION

OPEN; *All year*
CHILDREN; *Welcome*
CREDIT CARDS; *All major cards*
PETS; *In Cottages by arrangement*
ACCOMMODATION; *Self catering cottages*
4 en suite guest rooms in house
Great Tythe Barn available for conferences, parties etc.

BREAKFAST; *Continental only for guests staying in the main house*
DISABLED ACCESS; *In some cottages*
GARDEN; *Yes*

ORMONDS HEAD COACHING INN,

Long Street, Tetbury,
Gloucestershire GL8 8AA

Tel: 01666 505690

Tetbury is a small Cotswold market town steeped in history with a plethora of fine old buildings, in amongst which is the mid 17th century Ormonds Head Coaching Inn. With some three hundred odd years of caring for travellers and never better than today, the inn is charming, atmospheric and full of character. Old beams, uneven floors and low ceilings are as they must have been centuries ago. Lyndon and Judy Booth are mine hosts. They have not been here very long but their stamp is rapidly appearing on all that happens much to the delight of the locals who enjoy coming here for a good pint of ale and to chew over the happenings of Tetbury. They are never at a loss for conversation because apart from the many antique shops which attract visitors, the Royal connection with Prince Charles's home, Highgrove House close by, never fails to be a topic of discourse.

The bars are comfortably furnished and the restaurant with its thirty covers is small enough to produce the intimacy that people enjoy. Throughout Ormonds Head the furnishings are tasteful, of a very high standard and welcoming. The food which one could describe as broadly based is still traditional with an emphasis on quality and price - the latter is something the Booths regard as very important. Every day there is a Blackboard which tells of Daily Specials, which are both tasty and generous in portion. On Sundays there is an excellent traditional lunch at an unbeatable price for such a good meal.

There are 20 attractively furnished bedrooms, all of which are en suite and each has colour television and tea and coffee making facilities. It is a delightfully informal place to stay but that does not mean that Ormonds Head is not professionally run - that is evident.

USEFUL INFORMATION

OPEN; *All year*
CHILDREN; *Welcome*
CREDIT CARDS; *All major cards*
LICENSED; *Yes*
ACCOMMODATION; *20 rooms en suite*

RESTAURANT; *Traditional fare- value for money*
BAR FOOD; *Wide range, home-cooked*
VEGETARIAN; *Always on the menu*
DISABLED ACCESS; *Partial & by arrangement*
PETS; *No*

THE PLAISTERERS ARMS

Abbey Terrace,
Winchcombe,
Gloucestershire GL54 5LL

Tel: 01242 602358 Fax: 01242 602360

To find an 18th century inn built of Cotswold stone with a split level arrangement of its bars, is very unusual. It adds to the charm of this old inn rather than detracts and the olde worlde architecture plus the sloping floors and heavy beams builds up a splendid atmosphere which is enjoyed by all the people who have beaten a path to its friendly door over the years. David Gould is mine host and his cheerful presence allied to the friendly efficiency of his staff makes sure everyone is welcome.

Set in the heart of the historic Cotswold town of Winchcombe, The Plaisterers is a focal point of community life and every day you will find regulars enjoying a drink and some spirited conversation in the bar. Food is all important and the extensive menu has something to suit everyone's palate whether it is a Bar Snack, a Pub Lunch or a more sophisticated evening meal. Basically the food is traditional English but that does not prevent there being an excellent Curry and some other interesting and sometimes exotic dishes. Everyday Daily Specials are on the Blackboard at lunch time and for those who just want something light, freshly cut sandwiches or generous Ploughman's Lunches are readily available. In the summer the pub's lovely garden and terraced patio area provide an ideal place to relax after a day out.

This is a comfortable hostelry and would make an ideal base for anyone wanting to stay awhile in order to explore the wonderful countryside around and about, go deeper into the Cotswolds, take a look at some of the charming villages or make for Cheltenham with its fine buildings and superb racecourse. The Plaisterers has three double, one twin and one family room, all ensuite and all well appointed with colour television and tea and coffee making facilities. You will be made very welcome and the breakfast in the morning is as good as any you will find in the county.

USEFUL INFORMATION

OPEN; *All year*
CHILDREN; *Welcome*
CREDIT CARDS; *All major cards*
LICENSED; *Full On*
ACCOMMODATION; *5 en suite rooms*
PETS; *By arrangement*

RESTAURANT; *Traditional English fare*
BAR FOOD; *Wide range, good value*
VEGETARIAN; *Daily choices*
DISABLED ACCESS; *Partial by arrangement*
GARDEN; *Lovely. Terraced patio*
PARKING; *Ample free parking*

SHIPTON GLEBE

Woodstock,
Oxfordshire 0X20 1 QQ

Tel: +44 (0)1993 812688 Fax:+44 (0) 1993 813142
Email: Phase@Patrol.I-way. co.uk

There are few lovelier and more serene houses in Southern England than Shipton Glebe. It stands in 9 acres of beautifully laid out gardens which delight all those who have the good fortune to stroll in them whilst staying here. The house is the home of Mr and Mrs Brian Bevan, two friendly and welcoming people who genuinely enjoy the visitors who stay with them. Many of them become so attached to the way of life at Shipton Glebe that they make a bee line for the house whenever they can get away, Throughout Shipton Glebe which was built in the gracious manner of architecture some two hundred years ago, the furnishings delight the eye. Mrs Bevan has an eye for colour and design and the mix and match of pretty fabrics, the wall decor, the carpets and the lighting make a splendid background for the fine antique pieces which are to be seen everywhere mingling harmoniously with those of more modern times. Every room is spacious, high ceilinged and light. The bedrooms have large, comfortable beds and all three rooms have their own well appointed bathroom. Each bedroom also has colour television and a generously supplied beverage tray. In the morning you come down to the elegant dining room to enjoy a delicious, freshly prepared breakfast with several choices. There are evening meals by prior arrangement but you will find any number of excellent eateries in the vicinity. Shipton Glebe is on the A4095 just one mile from Woodstock and 6 miles from Oxford. It could not be better situated for anyone wanting to enjoy the countryside, visit the glorious Blenheim Palace, or explore Oxford itself. You can walk, fish, ride, shoot or play golf or maybe you might find it simply more relaxing to enjoy the garden at Shipton Glebe, use the Golf practice facility or lounge in the Conservatory overlooking the garden. One thing is certain, whether you stay at Shipton Glebe because you are on business locally or enjoying a holiday, you will find by the time that you leave, you feel refreshed and ready to return to the hurly burly of modern day life.

USEFUL INFORMATION

OPEN; *All year*
CHILDREN; *Over 12 years*
CREDIT CARDS; *Visa/Master*
LICENSED; *No By arrangement*
ACCOMMODATION; *3 ensuite rooms*

DINING ROOM; *Excellent breakfast*
VEGETARIAN; *Upon request*
DISABLED ACCESS; *Yes. One room*
GARDEN; *Yes. Golf practice facility*
PETS; *By arrangement*

Chapter 7

HAMPSHIRE

INCLUDES

Chapter 7

HAMPSHIRE

Surely one of England's finest counties, Hampshire, in ancient times, had thickly wooded downland in the northern half which must have been something of a porcine paradise for the hirsute and thick-set wild boar, rooting amongst the myriad oaks in a never-ending quest for acorns and other such delicacies. No true son of the county has ever objected to the sobriquet of Hampshire Hog, first given it by Michael Drayton, Polyalbion 1622 when he wrote 'Hampshire, long for her, hath had the term of Hogs'. The long-vanished beast represented those qualities of independence, nimbleness and strength that has enabled the area to cope and come to terms with both invasion and innovation. Romans, Danes, Saxons and Normans found the rolling countryside much to their liking, whilst in recent times, industry and urban development have stamped their mark on the landscape. Nevertheless, adjacent to the roar of the motorway and the bustle of the conurbation's, there exists a seemingly tireless world rich in history and bucolic charm.

An apt example of this happy balance is to be found in and around the county town of **Winchester**. The M3 noisily snakes its way past to the east of the town, cutting a giant's furrow through the chalk downs. Motorways may not be the most attractive of man's creations, but they are far from being the worst; merely the 20th century equivalent of the railway; bringing life and prosperity, even in recessionary times. The controversial final section of the M3, linking London with the port of Southampton south of Winchester comes close to the village of **Twyford**. Here Benjamin Franklin, the American statesman, wrote his memoirs, Thomas Hughes, the author, taught at the local school while Alexander Pope, the poet, lampooned the masters and was expelled.

Excavations have revealed that Man had been settled in the area since the Iron Age, but it was the Romans who did most to establish the early foundations of Winchester. Under their direction it grew to become an important fortified market town, but greater things were in store for the place then named Venta Belgarum; the Saxons, and their successors, the Normans, together with the introduction of Christianity, ensured that the town became a city. A city, moreover, that was to become the Capital of Wessex and ultimately that of England itself.

King Alfred re-established Winchester after his defeat of the invading Danes. Arguably the greatest of all English Kings, he brought the city out of the Dark Ages and made it a centre of religion, learning and the arts. His statue dominates The Broadway, close to the remains of the Benedictine nunnery that he founded in conjunction with his wife. After the Saxon kings, William the Conqueror, always one with an eye for the main chance, also made the city his capital. From here, his clerks and soldiers set out on the first census, the compiling of that great survey, the Domesday Book. First known as Liber Wintoniensis (the Book of Winchester) the massive list of entries contain one surprising omission - that of Winchester itself. It is thought that this was because the city enjoyed tax exemptions due to its royal connections.

Winchester's position as the capital of England continued for a century or so, until supplanted by Westminster (London) and it is interesting to note that the population during the peak of its prosperity in 1150 was listed as 8,000 - a figure that was not reached again until after 1820!

The County Town of Hampshire is therefore rich in historic associations and remains with a wealth of fine old architecture but one feels far from being trapped in a time-warp or historical 'experience'. The city bustles and flourishes; there is room for both tourist, citizen and trader. Much of the city centre has been set aside for pedestrians and it is a real pleasure to wander amongst the thoroughfares and narrow medieval side-streets, enjoying the wealth of shops and buildings, yet never being far from greenery or running water, for the River Itchen, one of the finest of trout rivers, flows rapidly through the city towards the water-meadows to the south.

The great grey **Winchester Cathedral** dominates; at 556 feet it is the longest medieval church in Europe. Magnificent and awe-inspiring, it was founded in 1079 and consecrated in 1093. Over the centuries it has become a graceful melange of styles, reflecting the energy, determination and skill of those who built 'to the greater glory of God'.

Savaged by the Puritan Parliamentarians during the Civil War (as was much within the city), the Cathedral nevertheless has retained much in the way of furnishings, relics and memorials. The Library is the oldest in Europe and contains the wonderfully illustrated 12th-century Winchester Bible, whilst the choir-stalls are thought to be the oldest surviving in England, dating from 1308. The misericords are carved with medieval flair and humour - there is even a representation of a family of musical pigs! Early wall-paintings are to be found in many of the chapels and the cathedral treasury has a superb display of church silver. Although Cromwell's men destroyed many royal tombs and memorials, the large tomb in the chancel is reputedly that of William Rufus (1087-1100), the unlamented king who met with a mysterious hunting accident in the New Forest. The cathedral was also a site of pilgrimage for those who revered the memory of St Swithun, who died in AD 862. I have often thought that he and not St George, should have been the true patron saint of England because of the fact that the name of Swithun, or Swithin, will always be associated with our most notable climatic characteristic - that of rain. The story goes that he was buried, according to his wishes, in a grave under the open sky where his fellow men could walk upon it and the rain could fall freely. However, after he was canonised it was thought more fitting that the bones should rest within the Minster which preceded the cathedral. Legend has it that his sadness at being thus confined expressed itself in the form of 40 days of rain; hence the origin of the superstition that if it rains on the anniversary of the day his grave was disturbed, July 15th, it will continue for the said period.

The broad lawns and fine buildings of the Close set off the ancient Cathedral to perfection. To my mind, one of the greatest glories of English cathedral liturgy is to be found in its music and Winchester's choristers are trained at the Pilgrim School, with its fine Pilgrim's Hall, worth visiting for its magnificent hammerbeamed roof that dates back to the

217

early 14th century. Education has long been an integral part of ecclesiastical life and in 1382, Bishop William of Wykeham founded Winchester College which is to be found south of the Close. 600 years later, the school is still going strong and using many of the same buildings. The original foundation provided for 70 'poor and needy scholars' and although they have been joined by some 600 fee-paying pupils known as 'Commoners', the tradition continues.

Charity of a different kind was and still is, dispensed by the Hospital of St Cross which was established in 1136. The pensioners who reside within this, the oldest charitable institution in the country, are often to be seen about the city wearing their distinctive black or red gowns. The traditional 'Wayfarer's Dole' of bread and ale can still be claimed by visitors at the Porter's Lodge, just part of this wonderfully complete range of medieval buildings that lie to the south of Winchester.

With a long tradition of hospitality the city has much to offer the visitor and rather more substantial fare than the Traveller's Dole can be found in the many hostelries and restaurants. Sight seeing can work up quite an appetite and I therefore enjoyed my visit to The Elizabethan Restaurant, situated in the picturesque Jewry Street. Housed in a building that is certainly 16th century, if not earlier, the restaurant offers a wide range of Anglo-French cuisine and is ideally positioned for those exploring the city centre.

One of the delights of Winchester is that the centre is laid out in a grid - possibly influenced by the original Roman planners - and therefore finding one's way around is a relatively simple business. South of the Jewry and set back from the High Street, is the Great Hall dating back to the beginning of the 13th century and once part of Winchester Castle. The Hall is the only part of the Castle, which was slighted - made unfit for military use, during the Civil War. The splendid and impressive old building is divided into a nave and aisle by two rows of Purbeck marble columns and is considered by man to be second only to Westminster Hall. On the west wall hangs a magnificent Round Table of unknown origin. It was first mentioned in the middle of the 13th century when it was described as being of 'great age'. In 1522, it was decorated to commemorate a meeting between Henry VIII and Charles V of Germany and Spain - but inevitably its age and shape lend itself to rumours concerning the legendary King Arthur........

Although Winchester places a strong emphasis on preservation and heritage, its real charm comes from the fact that it possesses a past that is truly alive; clerics still tread cloisters, scholars are still in the school-room and quadrangle, soldiers stamp the parade-ground and traders hawk their wares in the market place.

Skirting the north of Winchester and heading east, I crossed over the M3 and almost immediately found myself in fine countryside. Woods and coverts speckled the broad acres of rich plough and pasture through which ran the gin-clear waters of the Itchen. My first stop was at **Alresford** (pronounced Allsford), a delightful predominantly Georgian town, who's fortunes were founded on the 14th century wool-trade. In more recent times, the inhabitants turned to the cultivation of watercress and because of the importance of this industry, the Mid-Hants railway became known as the **Watercress Line**. A victim of Dr Beeching's now infamous cuts, the railway has been happily restored by dedicated individuals and is now one of Hampshire's most popular - and most useful - attractions. The steam railway runs via Ropley, Medstead and Four marks to the market town of **Alton.** The journey is a sheer delight and the company offers numerous week-end events and attractions besides the return service.

South of Alresford, I came across another example of 'living history'. At **Tichborne**, the Tichborne Dole, in the form of a gallon of flour, bread or money has been handed out yearly to each deserving adult since the 12th century. It is said that this custom originated with the dying Lady Isabella who begged her husband, Sir Roger Tichborne, to grant her enough land to provide for the sick and the needy. In reply, Sir Roger, a chauvinist if ever there was one, took a flaming brand from the fire and told his sick wife that 'she could have as much land as she could crawl round before the flame was extinguished'. Astonishingly, she managed to cover some 23 acres before the brand burnt out, and the land thus enclosed is known to this day as The Crawles. Tradition has it that tragedy will befall the family if Lady Isabella's request for the Dole is ever ignored, and, amazingly, on the few rare occasions that this has happened, the consequences have been singularly unpleasant.

Tichborne Church is unusual in that it contains a rare example of a Catholic chapel within an Anglican church.

Both Tichborne and its neighbour **Cheriton** (reckoned to be the last place in England where truffle hu nting took place) are extremely attractive communities with a convincing blend of vernacular architectural styles and materials; snuggling into the landscape with an air of contented continuity and permanence. The peacefulness is deceptive, for on the 29th March 1644, near Cheriton Wood, the Royalists and Parliamentarians clashed in bloody battle, 20,000 men were involved in what turned out to be a decisive victory for the Parliamentarians under Sir William Waller, but it was not only the soldiers who were to suffer. The fleeing Royalist troops set fire to medieval Alresford and casualties were heavy.

The battle is re-enacted yearly (with minor casualties and without razing any local towns or villages) a short distance from the original site, close to The Jolly Farmer pub by the A272 Winchester-Petersfield road. The good food and fine ales are as popular with the 'combatants' as they are with locals and visitors.

It is difficult when writing a guide to this part of the world to avoid the over-use of the word 'attractive'. So many of the small villages and hamlets nestling in the chalk downland catch the eye and are worthy of mention; not necessarily because they are linked with historical sites or notable personages, or because they possess a fine church or noble house, but simply because of their charm and character - their very individuality attracts. Six miles along the A272 from Cheriton I turned south to visit **East Meon** a village which to me, represents the epitome of the Hampshire downland village.

Izaak Walton fished the trout-rich waters of the River Meon which rises from the chalk not far from the village to run under and beside the main street. A good and God-fearing man, he doubtless worshipped in East Meon Church, one of the finest Norman buildings of its type and set to perfection, built above the village in what was once a bishop's deer park. The beautiful mellow stone-work contains a Tournai marble font, wonderfully carved, and an unusual stained glass window depicting the patron saints of all the allied countries that took part in the First World War. The Court House south-east of the church is said to have been built about 1400 but the origins of the village are obviously far earlier, and reputedly it was the first community to be mentioned in the Domesday Book. Ye Olde George Inn has charm, character and comfort complementing the warm welcome and excellent cuisine; old Izaak may have been a Puritan but he was no kill joy and I have no doubt he would have enjoyed the inn.

Loathe to return to the main roads, I meandered roughly south-east where the landscape is dominated by the imposing mass of **Buster Hill.** At nearly 900 feet, it is the highest point in the western end of the South Downs and is contained within **The Queen Elizabeth Country Park** jointly administered by Hampshire County Council and the Forestry Commission. It is an admirable example of how an area can be successfully managed to incorporate a multitude of quite difference interests, Recreation, Forestry, Conservation and Education all take place within the 1,400 acres which is liberally strewn with nature trails, bridle ways and woodland walks. I was fascinated by a modern reconstruction of an Iron Age farm of around 300BC, partly based on information gathered from local   excavations. Crops of the period are grown here and it was intriguing to learn that the prehistoric varieties of wheat produce have nearly twice the protein content of to-day's. Not only that, but the experiments have shown that yield per acre would have been not far off our modern figures - so much for selective breeding and genetic engineering!

Keeping to my policy of byways in preference to highways, I have to confess I got slightly, but pleasantly, lost trying to make my way north to Petersfield and ended up slightly to the west of the town at **Stroud.** At the very hospitable and recently refurbished Seven Stars Inn I enjoyed a drink and marvelled at an imaginative menu which included guinea fowl, grouse and shark steak. It is astonishing to reflect that when I first started writing guide books the culinary expertise found in the vast majority of pubs would hardly run to a cheese and pickle sandwich. Times have definitely changed for the better.

Petersfield is a handsome market town that has much to offer, but has suffered heavily since the introduction of the internal combustion engine; too many people pass through and never stop to investigate. In a sense, it was ever thus since the town sits astride the main Portsmouth to London road and was an important coaching stop long before the car was invented.

In the square, there is a heroic statue of William III on horseback dressed for some odd reason as a Roman emperor. The church is a fine Norman edifice, one of the finest in the county, and the best of the domestic architecture Georgian, a style continued along with more rustic examples, around the corner in the delightful area known as The Spain. To the east of the town and ancient heath-land, containing several Bronze Age barrows or burial chambers, provides amenity land, including a large boating-lake and golf course.

North of the town, there is some of the finest scenery to be found in the South of England. Around **Steep,** and further north at **Selborne,** the remarkable landscape features great beech 'hangers'; great clumps of mature trees hanging (hence the name) precipitously over almost sheer chalk inclines that run down to a base of greensand rock. Known as 'Little Switzerland', it is an area of great beauty and contrasts favourably with the more serene charms of the Meon Valley.

All Saint's Church, Steep, part Norman, part Early English is reached by way of a marvellous yew arch running from the lych-gate and there is a memorial window to Lawrence Whistler dedicated to the memory of Edward Thomas, the poet who was killed in France in 1917. Eastwards past the church and down the hill is to be found the countryman's ideal; pub and cricket-pitch in close proximity. The snug Harrow Inn, low beamed and serving beer from the barrel is everything a rustic pub should be without being twee or pretentious.

The landscape changes yet again as one moves northwards along the border with

Sussex and Surrey. Vast areas of sandy heath-land studded with wood and copse denote that these were tracts of forest. (Timber was felled here from earliest times) first for fire-wood, then for smelting and later for building. In the 14th century, wood for another magnificent hammer-beam roof, that of Westminster Hall, came from here and in the 17th and 18th centuries trees were felled by the thousand to provide the 'wooden bulwarks of England' - the ships of the Royal Navy. The resultant heath became a notorious haunt for the highwaymen and cut-throats, intent upon rich pickings to be found on the main coaching route, now the mainly dual-carriageway A3, running from Portsmouth to London.

Justice in those days was both summary and savage, and at **West Liss**, the local pub, The Spread Eagle, was the venue for the local court. The old oak tree on the small green opposite is still known as 'The Stocks Oak'. In these more gentle times a warm welcome rather than a whipping lies in wait for the weary traveller.

The Forest of Liss was succeeded to the north by the Forest of Woolmer at **Greatham**, one of the native trees of this healthy land lends its name to a cheerful hostelry, The Silver Birch Inn. Appropriately a large and handsome example of Betula Pendula stands in front of the building - possibly the largest pub sign in the country? The Inn, though late Victorian, is interesting since it reflects another facet of the changing face of this part of the county. When first constructed it was used for a while as an officer's mess for the Army had realised the value of vast expanses of heath even if nobody else had. Military camps are still to be found in the area the result of a natural expansion caused by two World Wars and the close proximity of the home of the British Army, **Aldershot,** which lies in the north-eastern corner of Hampshire some dozen or so miles away.

From Greatham, I headed north-west to that Mecca for all English naturalists, **Selborne.** The country reverts to downland and the village lies, tucked under a steep escarpment, with a great beech hanger spread along its edge. Selborne was the birthplace and home of Gilbert White (1720-93), four times curate of the church and author of that delightful classic, 'The Natural History and Antiquities of Selborne'. Published in 1789, it is based on his forty years of observations of the wildlife, plants and habitat found in the immediate vicinity. The book, in the form of letters to interested parties, has a singular freshness and charm which reflects the enthusiasm and character of the man. His old home, The Wakes, contains much relating to his studies, and also houses collections belonging to a later owner, the explorer Francis Oates, uncle of Captain Lawrence Oates who perished with Scott on the expedition to the South Pole in 1912. The joint exhibitions are housed together as **Gilbert White's House and Garden** and **The Oates Exhibitions.**

Selborne Church dates from about 1180 and has a memorial window dedicated to its former curate showing St Francis and the 82 birds mentioned in White's book. White himself is buried in the graveyard under a simple stone inscribed 'GW, 26th June 1793.'

Leaving the lovely Selborne area, where the National Trust has done so much to preserve and maintain the landscape, other literary and botanic connections are to be found just a few miles further north. At **Chawton**, Jane Austen's House provides an insight into the life led by the novelist and her family from 1809 until 1817, while she wrote or revised her six great novels. The delightful garden contains many old fashioned varieties of flowers and visitors are welcome to picnic on the lawns. Nearby **Alton**, a busy and good-looking market town, is home to **The Curtis Museum** named after William Curtis who founded the Botanical Magazine. As well as exhibits relating specifically to Curtis, the museum possesses excellent displays relating to local industry and crafts, and all manner of historical exhibits including the exquisite Alton Buckle, a 1500 year old item of Saxon jewellery. There are also exhibitions of children's toys and games, silver and pottery.

The Parish Church of St Lawrence, with its Norman tower and 15th century additions, is situated at the highest point of the town and, in December 1643 was the scene of a vicious clash between the Parliamentarians and the Royalists. With Alton lost the Royalists retreated to the church under the command of one, Colonel Boles. Boles, determined to fight to the last, died in the pulpit. Bullet holes are still visible in the old oak of the south door.

Since I elected to explore the more rural areas of North Hamphshire, I made my way across country to the north-west, avoiding the conurbation's of Farnborough, Aldershot and Basingstoke. Although there is much of interest in and around these areas, and there are some great places to stay including the **Basingstoke Country Hotel** near **Hook** just outside Basingstoke, overspill from London and commercial and industrial development obscure much of the original flavour of the county.

My destination was amongst the high wooded downland that lies close to the border with Berkshire and to the south of Newbury. Trees fringe wide expanses of chalk soil either under cultivation or down to rich pastures. This is a county of quiet wealth and great estate, with small villages, hamlets and farms scattered across the countryside.

At Highclere, I stayed at another inn also named after a well-known native tree the delightful Yew Tree Inn. For over three and a half centuries the traveller has found a warm welcome within its portals and I was no exception.

A steep climb up **Beacon Hill** is worthwhile for the splendid view over the Downs. The summit is crowned by an Iron Age hill-fort and the grave of the fifth Earl of Caernarvon, who with Howard Carter, led the expedition to find the tomb of Tutankhamum. The Earl's palatial home **Highclere Castle** lies close to the foot of the hill surrounded by lovely parkland laid out in the inimitable 'Capability Brown' style. The Castle, the largest mansion in the county, was rebuilt in the middle of the last century and is renowned for the richness and variety of its interior decoration. Treasures on display include Napoleon's desk, a fine collection of paintings by Old Masters and Egyptian relics found by the fifth Earl.

On the subject of decoration, I recommend a visit to the Sandham Memorial Chapel, **Burghclere**, to view the paintings by Stanley Spencer (1891-1959). They are considered to be amongst the most important of modern English murals. They reflect on the futility and horror of war and were painted between 1926 and 1932; the chapel was built in memory of Lieutenant H.W Sandham who died in the First World War.

The largest of the 'cleres' is **Kingsclere**, at the foot of Watership Down - made famous by the author Richard Adams. His hero was a rabbit, but for many years mine was a horse the great Derby winner, Mill Reef. He was trained at Kingsclere and throughout the area, studs and racing stables breed and train in an endeavour to produce another such equine star.

I mentioned earlier the sporting propensities of the Hampshire character and it is interesting to note that the chalky downland acts as a common link between the three most popular pastimes. Cricket had its origins in the South Downs, racing is a major industry in the North Downs, whilst the clear flowing rivers that provide the setting for so much classic fly fishing have their beginnings deep under the calciferous hills. These high downs of the northern part of the county, with their steep valleys and wooded slopes, are little populated and have a quiet charm of their own. One small river, the Swift, rises at **Upton** in the heart of this lovely country, some ten miles to the west of Kingsclere. The village pub, The Crown Inn, is a small hospitable establishment, and an ideal base for fishermen, racing enthusiasts or simply for those who enjoy this most lovely part of England.

The most notable of Hampshire's rivers is The Test, and seven miles south of Highclere lies the attractive and ancient town of **Whitchurch**. Here the fast running alkaline waters once served both sport and industry, providing power for silk-weaving and at nearby **Laverstock**, for the manufacture of banknote paper. Both industries have survived and **The Silk Mill** is beautifully preserved and open to the public with a shop well worth visiting. The banknote contract with the Bank of England dates back to 1727 and continues to this day.

The countryside around is lower and the contours far gentler than that of the Downlands. The Test makes its way west and south passing through **Hurstbourne Priors,** where the graveyard marks the last resting place of one of the best-known fly-fishing authors, Richard Plunkett-Greene.

The nearby town of **Andover** is representative of much of the change occurring within the County in recent times. It is a busy place today where not so long ago it was said that dogs sleeping on the pavements would look up in surprise if anyone passed by! The area has been home to man since ancient times: at **Danebury**, together with some fascinating reconstruction's and audio-visual displays.

Rural attractions abound; two local favourites with all ages are **Finkley Down Park Farm** and **The Hawk Conservancy**. Finkley Down breeds a wide variety of rare and not-so-rare farm animals and has displays of farm machinery and implements from across the centuries. Near **Weyhill,** once the scene of a great autumn fair where 140,000 sheep were recorded as being sold in one day - and not only sheep. Thomas Hardy's famous scene in 'Mayor of Casterbridge' where Henchard sells his wife at auction was based on a thinly disguised Weyhill.

Thatch is common throughout the area and doubtless owes its origins to the readily available supply of reed from along the river banks. The splendidly named **Wallops** (the name means, rather disappointingly, 'valley of the stream') also have a wealth of thatched   cottages. Strung along the valley of the Wallop Brook, the three villages retain a wealth of character and tradition, with **Nether Wallop** being noted for its fine Saxon wall paintings in the church. **Over Wallop** for a magnificent 15th century font, and **Middle Wallop** for its Museum of Army Flying. This award winning museum houses an unique collection of flying machines, equipment and displays depicting the history of Army Aviation since the end of the last century from balloons and kites to the latest in helicopters.

It is a truly lovely part of England with plenty of footpaths for the walker and bridleways for the rider. At **Stockbridge**, The Test flows under the London to Salisbury road and the wide main street reflects its past as a drover's town. On the Houghton road is Drovers House with an inscription on the front in Welsh meaning 'seasoned hay, tasty pastures, good beers, comfortable beds'. Once an infamous 'rotten borough' where, in 1790 the enormous sum of ,20,000 was spent between a Captain Luttrell and a certain Lord Inham in order to bury the vote, and a town that gained certain notoriety when Edward VII attended races with his mistress, Lily Langtry. Stockbridge is now a quiet and peaceful spot. From an inspection of the local shop fronts, antiques and fishing would seem to be the two main sources of income.

My journey around North Hampshire ended close to where it began, just a few miles to the ancient capital of Wessex. In 1201, a group of followers of St Augustinian established a priory in one of the most idyllic situations imaginable. **Mottisford Abbey** became a private house after the dissolution and work over the centuries has resulted in the present handsome Georgian south front, perfectly complemented by the wonderful gardens that sweep down to The Test. Green lawns are shaded by great trees and the celebrated rose garden contains the National Trust's collection of old-fashioned roses. It has to be said that this is the most harmonious setting of any house in England.

First impressions of South Hampshire can be misleading, particularly for those travelling through on the East - West axis. The received image from motorway and main arterial road is one of population where cities, towns and villages seem to have combined to create one vast urban sprawl. From Cadnam, to the west of Southampton, to Emsworth, on the Sussex border, communities appear endlessly linked by commercial developments, industrial parks and housing estates. Don't be fooled by all this for, although untidy ribbon development exists along many main roads, behind it lies much of beauty and interest. Areas where grazing animals far outnumber people, where little seems to have changed for centuries, and where the visitor can feel as remote as anywhere in England. To properly explore the south of the county with its immense wealth of varied scenery and historical connections and assets could literally take months.

The most obvious example of how deceptive first impressions can be is to be found in the western-most part of the county. A spur projects into Wiltshire and Dorset and within this small area the landscape includes chalk-downland, river valley, wooded slopes and pasture. At the extreme west of the whole county is **Martin Down**, a National Nature Reserve. This area is noted for the variety of its flora and fauna; rare orchids and grasses share the close-cropped sward with uncommon butterflies such as the silver-spotted Skipper and the Adonis blue, Bronze and Iron Age remains show that man has appreciated these high open lands since earliest times. Later came the Romans and remains of one of the largest villa and farm complexes ever discovered in Britain are to be found displayed close to **Rockbourne.** This most attractive village, again little more than a single street, has the deserved reputation of being one of the prettiest villages in the county with several cottages of 'cruck' construction - an early medieval form of the A-frame.

At nearby **Whitsbury**, the local racing stables are home to that most endearing horse, Desert Orchid, who won the King George VI Cup, the Irish Grand National and the Cheltenham Gold Cup. His health has been drunk many a time in the cheerful and hospitable Cartwheel Inn, a pleasant mellow brick building which started life as a barn in the early 1800's.

Breamore's (pronounced Bremmer) attractions date from earlier ages. The little, predominantly Tudor village, has an excellent Saxon church, dating from the early 10th century. The ancient inscription over the south transept has been interpreted as 'Here is manifested the Word unto thee'. Breamore House was completed in 1583 and is a gabled Elizabethan building housing a fine collection of pictures, tapestry and furniture. Behind the house, through dense woodland of ancient yews, is evidence of a far older civilisation, although just how old, no-one seems quite certain. This is the Miz-Maze, a series of elliptic circles leading to a central mound. Most guide-books describe it as being of medieval construction, representing the tortuous path to Paradise; but strangely, there are no contemporary accounts of its construction or even of its existence. It may be that the Maze is of earlier, perhaps Druidical, origin.

Damerham to the south of this most attractive little outpost of Hampshire, lies in the narrow valley of the River Allen. St George's church has a massive square Norman tower with a carving over the south doorway depicting the legend that the saint appeared before the Crusaders at the Battle of Antioch in 1098, thus inspiring them to beat the Saracens. The Compasses Inn is a fine old coaching house dating back to the l6th century, and the high standards of accommodation and hospitality make it an ideal venue from which to explore this enchanting area.

The River Avon noted for the variety of its fishing (particularly its fine, though sadly declining runs of salmon) runs southward, marking the eastern boundary of the county spur. The A338 from Salisbury to Bournemouth follows the river for much of its course, passing through the attractive towns of **Fordingbridge** and **Ringwood**.

This stretch of the river runs close to the small village of **Ellingham**, where, in the graveyard of St Mary's Church, lie the mortal remains of Dame Alicia Lisle and her daughter, Ann Hortell. Dame Alicia, who lived nearby at Moyles Court, was executed at the age of 71 on 2nd September 1685. Her crime was to give shelter to two men after the Battle of Sedgemoor, but her trial and sentence were a travesty. Tried by the infamous and foul-mouthed Judge Jeffreys, who bullied and intimidated the jury, she was sentenced to be burnt at the stake but there was such an outcry from the crowd within and without the Great Hall of Winchester, that this was altered to the less agonising - but every bit as brutal - death by beheading. After her execution, her body was taken to Ellingham, accompanied by hundreds of men on foot, walking in homage to a brave and noble lady. Four years later by Act of Parliament, the conviction was annulled on the grounds that 'the verdict was procured by menaces, violence and other illegal practices of Lord Jeffreys.'

Ringwood a cheerful market town, also has links with the sad fate of Dame Alicia, for Sedgemoor marked the end of the Monmouth rebellion, and the Duke of Monmouth, pretender to the Throne, was caught hiding in a ditch close to the town at Shags Heath. Before being taken to London for trial and execution, he was imprisoned in a house in West Street which is now named after him. Tourism plays an important part in the town's economy and angling is a major attraction. Many of the hotels cater specially for those enthusiasts who travel from all over the country to fish the Avon and its tributaries; the 250 year old Lamb Inn on the outskirts of the town, is no exception and offers the visitor warm and friendly hospitality with early breakfasts for those who wish to be beside the water for first rise.

Ringwood lies on the western edge of another great area of natural beauty within this county of contrast - **The New Forest**. It is an area of over 90,000 acres of heath and mixed woodland with an abundance of wildlife. Paradoxically it is the oldest of the forests of England but that is simply because the word 'forest' is of Norman origin; it means an area set aside for hunting and the New Forest was the first of these preserves to be created by William the Conqueror. Savage penalties were exacted on those who broke the forest laws; at one time a person could be blinded for merely disturbing deer, whilst death was the automatic penalty for poaching. The modern day visitor may like to be assured that the passing of the centuries have seen extensive modification of these draconian measures;

apart from occasional necessary culling the deer are left in peace while the tourist can wander freely through much of the beautiful country. Nevertheless, much of the administration of the Forest is still in the hands of an organisation, the Verderers, which dates back to the Middle Ages. There are three distinctive habitats within the forest boundaries. The high heathlands, covered with heather and gorse together with Scots pine and birch, give a somewhat barren impression - particularly to the motorist travelling along the main east-west route of the A31. However the lower slopes and better drained land provides true forest in the modern meaning; superb traditional woodland planted with oaks, yew, beech and thorn, producing in the summer great sweeping canopies of foliage. Finally there is the marsh land where white cotton-grass conceals the bogs and where alder and willow grow.

Amongst this vegetation can be found all manner of wildlife, from grouse on the high heath to the four varieties of deer (Red, Roe, Fallow and the tiny Sika) who favour the woodland. Domestic animals, their numbers strictly controlled by the Verderers, graze amongst the trees and shrubs. These include cattle, pigs, donkeys and the celebrated New Forest ponies. Mention was first made of wild 'horses' at the time of King Canute (1017-35) while some believe them to be descendants of the Jennets, the small Spanish horses which swam ashore from the wrecks of the Spanish Armada in the 16th century. Many of them are employed in the numerous riding stables and schools to be found within the forest.

Leisure is the principal 'industry' of the New Forest and much has been done to encourage its development. Picnic areas, camping sites, trails, drives and paths are to be found throughout, and hotels, boarding houses, inns and pubs all do their very best to make the visitor welcome.

'Badgers Wood' is the meaning of **Brockenhurst**, a village that grew in popularity with the arrival of the railway in 1847. It has a fine Norman church with many memorials; one of which is of particular local interest. 'Brusher' Mills, who died in 1905, earned his nickname because he brushed the cricket pitch at Balmer Lawn between innings. Of singular appearance, with a grey beard, long coat and furry hat, he made his living by catching snakes, mainly adders, with his bare hands. It is said he was never bitten because he drank a bottle of rum a day, and never washed! Undoubtedly he would have approved of his other memorial in the village, a pub named **The Snake Catcher** - although I doubt whether the customers would have enjoyed his company.

*Tea though ridiculed by those who are naturally coarse
in their sensibilities. Will always be the favourite
beverage of the intellectual.'*
Thomas de Quinrxy 1785-1859

Although I have no pretensions to be an intellectual, that quote on the cover of the tea menu of The Thatched Cottage Hotel gives one an indication of how seriously this charming little family hotel takes its reputation as a mecca for those in search of the perfect afternoon tea - another is the fact that the menu runs to four pages! Excellent place to dine and stay as well.

A couple of miles to the south of Brockenhurst lies **Boldre,** one of the best looking villages in the New Forest, where the thatched cottages spread out along numerous country lanes. The Red Lion has been dispensing ale since the 1600's and is very much part of village life. It is frequented by many yachtsmen who sail out of Lymington who love the pub's atmosphere and are not averse to the wholesome, home-cooked, old fashioned English food. The church is a happy mixture of Norman and early English, but is most celebrated for having been the living, from 1777 to 1804 of William Gilpin. Gilpin was a contemporary of Gilbert White, and like him, a writer and a naturalist. He must have also been something of a saint, for he recorded, on first arriving in the parish, that the village was 'utterly neglected by the former pastor, and exposed to every temptation of pillage and robbery from their proximity to the deer, the game, and the fuel of the forest, these poor people were little better than a 'herd of bandits'. Thirty years later, the 'herd of bandits' clubbed together to erect a memorial within the church to Gilpin's memory, a tribute earned by remarkably few vicars in English village history. There is also a memorial to the ship's company of the battle-cruiser HMS Hood, sunk in May 1941; the 1406 officers and men are remembered in an annual service.

In her 18 years in commission HMS Hood frequently sailed through the narrow patch of water that guards the western entrance to the Solent. **Hurst Castle**, built at the end of a shingle spit less than a mile from the Isle of Wight, was built by Henry VIII with a formidable armament of 70 guns. It can be reached on foot from **Milford on Sea**, a small but popular resort, or by ferry from the little harbour of **Keyhaven.** To the west of Milford on Sea is **Barton on Sea,** next to New Milton and just 6 miles from Lymington. Right on the cliff tops approximately 75 ft above the sea and with spectacular views, is the Ventana Hotel, now a pub and restaurant with a limited bed and breakfast operation. A Friendly place with good food.

Situated just outside Lymington Town and within the New Forest National Park is the little village of **Hordle** where The Gordleton Mill Hotel and Provence Restaurant should not be missed. This delightful 17th century water mill house has been sympathetically extended and refurbished. It has a quite spectacular riverside location with five and a half acres of ground on the banks of Avon water. It is quite idyllic, the seven bedrooms are exquisitely furnished, in the summer, breakfast and luncheon are served on the terrace. Dinner is a gastronomic experience.

The mud flats and marshes run eastward to **Lymington**, an attractive market town whose popularity attests to its position by the water and close to the southern fringes of the New Forest. Now a popular yachting centre, its elegant streets lined with nautical boutiques and smart hostelries while every inch of shore-line appears dedicated to the parking of cars and the mooring of boats, it is hard to visualise this chic little town as being the great trading port that it once was. Its origins are ancient; it has one of the oldest charters in England, dating back to 1150. In 1345, the town contributed nine ships and 159 men to Edward III for the Battle of Crecy, and in the same year exported 32,000 bushels of salt and imported nearly 40,000 gallons of wine. By the 17th century, coal had become a major import while the 18th century saw the beginnings of trade with Newfoundland, while maintaining strong links with America, the West Indies and Scandinavia. The production of salt was a local industry first mentioned in the Domesday Book and continued until the middle of the 19th century.

Although the present facade of Lymington would appear smart and leisurely, its trading past has far from disappeared; the international reputation of its yacht designers, boat builders, sailmakers and marine electronics manufacturers contribute significantly to the national export market, albeit in a less obvious manner than when the quays and warehouses bustled with rude life. The only commercial shipping that survives comes from the operation of the Lymington-Yarmouth ferry and a handful of fishing boats.

On the outskirts of the town, I was fascinated to discover a small museum situated in the old toll-collector's cottage behind The Tollhouse Inn - a good example of diversification!

Some five miles to the north-east, set in the Forest and at the head of a lovely stretch of river, lies **Beaulieu** (the beautiful place), founded by Cistercian monks more than 750 years ago. The Abbey has been referred to as King John's Good Deed since it would appear that he quarrelled with the then-powerful Order; then, whether caused by over-indulgence or excessively guilty conscience, dreamt that he had to make amends. Whatever the truth, the Bad King contributed generously to the Abbey's endowment. Under the direction of the French monks, clad in their simple white habits, land was cleared, quays built and foundations dug. It was a tremendous task, since the stone had to be shipped in from Binstead, on the Isle of Wight, and Purbeck, in Dorset. In 1246 the Abbey was finished and dedicated by the Bishop of Winchester in the presence of Henry III. For nearly 300 years the monks lived their simple life of contemplation and prayer while the lay-brothers   laboured on the rich estates but the dissolution of the Monasteries saw the largest of the Cistercian abbeys reduced to little more than a romantic ruin. One reason for this especially harsh treatment may have had its roots in the fact that Beaulieu was a noted sanctuary and was a place of refuge for many, including Margaret of Anjou, the Countess of Warwick and Perkin Warbeck. Another may have been the fact that the Cistercians gave no allegiance to the Bishops, recognising only the authority of the parent Abbey at Citeaux, in France. Thomas Wriothesley, first Earl of Southampton and ancestor of the present owner, Lord Montagu, took over the Abbey and retained only the Great Gate House (now known as Palace House), the porter's lodge, the cloisters, the lay brother's dormitory and the refectory, which has long served as the parish church. The Abbey may have been reduced to ruins but its remains are still singularly beautiful and well-kept. The second Lord Montagu did much to preserve and his successors have carried on the tradition in like manner.

Beaulieu, apart from its attraction as the site of a great religious house, lovely situation and immaculate small village, is also home to the splendid **National Motor Museum**, which was founded by the present Lord Montagu in memory of his father, a pioneer motorist.

Downstream from Beaulieu, lies the neat little community of **Bucklers Hard,** a single wide street of Queen Anne cottages that runs down to the river. Originally created by a Montagu for the importation and refining of sugar, political events in the West Indies made the development obsolete. Instead the site became one of the most famous naval shipyards in Britain, building many of the Royal Navy's most famous ships, including Nelson's   favourite command the Agamemnon. Today yachts moor where ships grew on their slipways and the **Maritime Museum** at the top of the village recounts its past glories. The street was wide enough to roll mighty oak trunks down under the stern direction of the master ship-builder, Henry Adams, and his house is now a delightful small hotel and restaurant, The Master Builders House.

Exbury Gardens, on the opposite bank of the river, are made up of 200 acres of the most stunning displays of shrubs, trees and flowers. Particularly beautiful are the spring-time displays of the noted Rothschild collection of rhododendrons, azaleas, magnolias and camellias.

Returning to the heart of the New Forest, a meandering cross country drive brings me to its capital **Lyndhurst.** This pleasant little town is the administrative centre of the Forest; the Verderer's Court meets six times a year at the Queen's House, which is also headquarters of the Forestry Commission. At **The New Forest Museum and Visitor Centre**, an excellent introduction to the history, customs, traditions, flowers and fauna of the area is provided through the medium of displays and audio-visual presentations.

The Church of St Michael, a splendid Victorian-Gothic confection with a small 13th century chapel denoting its origins is well worth a visit for the remarkable wall painting and the glass by William Morris to a design by Burne Jones. The painting is by Lord Leighton and depicts the Parable of the Ten Virgins. The artist used local people as his models and it is a large and striking work. Another model, although in the literary sense, lies buried in the churchyard; Alice Liddell was the inspiration for the central character in Lewis Carroll's Alice in Wonderland.

Sir Arthur Conan Doyle, although best known for his Sherlock Holmes stories, also wrote many fine historical novels. He lies buried some two miles north of Lyndhurst, in the idyllic little village of **Minstead.** His principal characters in 'The White Company' becomes the splendidly titled Socman of Minstead and Doyle obviously had much affection for the place for he and his wife spent several years there.

The church is a delightfully domestic building, almost cottage-like. The interior gives much the same feeling with a double tier of galleries and two extraordinarily comfortable box-pews - one still with its own fireplace. Just the place for a quiet doze during the vicar's sermon!

To my mind, Minstead is the perfect New Forest village and perfection of another kind is reflected in the sign outside The Trusty Servant Inn. It is a copy of a 17th century picture hanging in Winchester College and depicts a man with a pig's head, the snout padlocked, and with the ears of an ass. His feet are those of a stag while he holds his right hand open and holds a shovel, pitchfork, broom and griddle-iron in his left. A sword is on his hip and a shield on his shoulder. Take a look at it - you will enjoy the original inscription under the picture.

Heading eastwards, after the peace and tranquillity of the forest glades, the heavy traffic rambling towards **Southampton** comes as an unpleasant shock. The city, much of it modern, appears initially as an industrial sprawl, with pylons marching along the low marshy ground towards the tall cranes that indicate the presence of the docks. Further investigation of this unprepossessing facade is richly rewarding; Southampton is a city that rewards the inquisitive - its history is ancient and its treasures many.

The port was and has been of premier importance in wartime; as long ago as the 14th century soldiers embarked here to fight at Crecy and Agincourt. The Crimean and Boer Wars, the two World Wars and the Falklands Campaign all made extensive use of Southampton. During the Second World War, enemy bombing severely damaged the town; much of the historic High Street was destroyed and altogether 3,500 buildings were lost. The recovery was remarkable and the granting of city status well-deserved.

Although the M27 and its associated developments are essential to the livelihood of this area of the country, there is no doubt that the great swathe of countryside that it occupies is lost to us for ever; nevertheless charming pockets of rural calm are to be found with little trouble and often lie remarkably close to the busy motorway. **West Wellow** is just such a place, where a welcoming old coaching inn, The Red Rover, stands beside the

Southampton to Salisbury road. The great nursing pioneer Florence Nightingale once lived at Embley Park, now a school, and is buried in nearby **East Wellow** churchyard. St Margaret's Church there has 13th century wall paintings and also carved Jacobean stalls and pulpit. The Church of St Leonard at neighbouring **Sherfield English** is in delightful contrast; built in 1902, it is an ornate structure of brick and stone with a richly detailed interior and Art Nouveau windows.

In the early Middle Ages, vineyards were commonplace in England, but with the marriage of Henry II to Eleanor of Aquitaine and the acquisition of the wine-rich country of Bordeaux, they began to fade out and it is only in recent times that viticulture has been revived. The chalky soils and mild climate of Hampshire has proved ideal for this venture and a visit to the Wellow Vineyards is recommended. Guided tours can be arranged and the wine bar sells a number of English and foreign wines besides their own produce.

The River Test flows through the town of Romsey, where it once provided the power of milling and water for the many breweries. The town grew around **Romsey Abbey**, founded in AD907 by Edward the Elder for his daughter, Ethelllaeda. Sixty years later it was re-founded as a Benedictine nunnery by King Edgar. The abbey church was begun in the early part of the 12th century and construction continued over the next hundred years; it is second only to Durham Cathedral as the finest Norman building in England.

The peaceful tranquillity of the abbey is in cheerful contrast to the bustling little market town surrounding it. Some idea of the town's history can be gained in **King John's House**, a 13th century stone upper-hall house containing a small museum. Tudor, Georgian and Victorian domestic architecture are to be found throughout the town centre and the local Preservation Trust has done an excellent job.

As important as the abbey, was the inn required to service the many travellers who came to Romsey, and The Abbey Hotel which you see today was built in 1880 on the site of its medieval predecessor. The original cellars and an underground passage to the Abbey are still there and play home to a ghostly nun whose strict observance of the vow of poverty makes her turn off the gas with regularity. Her performance does nothing to detract from the convivial and warm atmosphere upstairs.

Broadlands, to the south of the town, once belonged to the Abbey. The Palladian style mansion was remodelled for the Palmerston family (a statue of the third Viscount who became Prime Minister stands in Romsey market place) by Capability Brown, who also laid out the surrounding parkland. It was later the home of Earl Mountbatten until his tragic death, and the stables have been converted to an exhibition of his life and career.

From Romsey it is only a short journey to view the **Hillier Arboretum** at **Ampfield,** a world-renowned display of rare and beautiful plants set in 160 acres together with a magnificent collection of trees and shrubs.

> *Botley is the most delightful village in the world..it*
> *is in a valley. the soil is rich, thick set writh woods;*
> the farms are small, the cottages neat.... ,

So wrote the writer and reformer William Cobbett (1763-1835), who farmed at **Botley,** to the east of Southampton. Much has changed since he penned those words but the large village still retains a rural atmosphere. An important market was held here for many years and at one time there were fourteen inns catering to the coach and carriage trade. Two of these still survive, The Bugle and The Dolphin, as does the mill, the only one in Hampshire to be listed in the Domesday Book and still working. Until the 1930's, small trading vessels would come up the River Hamble to Botley to load timber and corn.

I think Cobbett would have approved of the **Upper Hamble Country Park** to the south of Botley. This is a clever blend of working farm and preserved wood and marshland; bridle paths and walkways allow almost unlimited access and the traditional farm buildings house livestock as well as displays of old farm machinery.

The lower reaches of the Hamble River must contain more yachts than any other waterway in the world. A forest of masts bristle upwards from marinas and moorings that run the entire length of the river, from Swanwick Bridge to the river mouth. At first sight it hardly seems possible for any of them to move, but on closer inspection a reasonably wide channel is revealed, running up the middle of the rows of moored pleasure craft. Like Lymington, the industry on, and alongside the water is yachting and from the boatyards have come many notable vessels, including America's Cup yachts and record-breaking power boats. Two pubs, The Jolly Sailors at **Burlesdon,** and The Bugle at **Hamble,** are ideally situated for eating and drinking and watching life on the river go by. Both villages were once renowned for ship-building and The Elephant, Nelson's ship at the battle of Copenhagen was built next to the Jolly Sailors; the boatyard that still exists there proudly carries the same name.

Netley was once at the heart of a row between Florence Nightingale and the powers that be because she discovered that the Royal Victoria Military Hospital, built in 1863 for casualties from the Crimean War, was completely useless. Somehow two sets of plans had been drawn up at the same time and the one designed for the orient had been used here and the English-style ones sent abroad. This resulted in the hospital being built the wrong way round; the wards should have overlooked the shipping lanes and the wooded skyline; instead they faced inland. The worst offence in Florence Nightingale's eyes was the unwieldy building which was hard to administer. The hospital was demolished in 1966 and only the chapel now stands. Cistercian monks built their abbey at Netley about 1239 but all we can see today is a graceful ruin with some delightful arches and windows topped with delicate tracery. Netley Marsh does have The White Horse however in Ringwood Road - the epitome of a traditional English village pub. Real Ales hold pride of place - there are eight of them. The food is home-cooked and tasty with one of the best steak and kidney pies in the county.

Of course, the name of Nelson will always be associated with one ship in particular, that of HMS Victory, both she and many other links with the Royal Navy are to be found less than ten miles to the east at **Portsmouth**. 'Pompey', as it is affectionately known to both servicemen and natives alike, is situated on a peninsula that projects southwards between the two natural harbours of Portsmouth on the western side and Langstone to the east. Like its civilian counterpart, Southampton, Portsmouth enjoys certain natural advantages; there is deep water throughout a large part of the harbour, the Isle of Wight offers shelter from much of the channel weather and the narrow entrance is easily defended. These assets were first recognised by the Romans, who ignored the site of the present day Portsmouth and sailed right up to the top of the harbour, landing at Porchester. Here they built Portchester Castle, the best preserved Roman fortress in northern Europe.

Portsmouth as a community had a relatively late beginning and a somewhat shaky early history. Originally there was a small trading settlement at the mouth of the harbour at what is now known as the Camber area. Then, in about 1180, a local landowner began to develop the area which is now the city centre. A chapel was built to the memory of the recently-murdered Thomas á Becket; that site is now where the present cathedral stands. Richard I granted the first charter in 1194 but even by the 14th century Portsmouth was hardly more than a village relying mainly on agriculture. The area that was to become the Royal Dockyard was little more than mud-flats, although there had been some attempt at ship-building and repairing, albeit in a somewhat half hearted way. The little township suffered grievously from the raiding French, being razed to the ground on at least one occasion. Not until the accession of Henry VII (1457-1509) did things begin to change, with the establishment of a dry dock and a number of defensive measures. Henry VIII (1491-1547) did much to continue this development by expanding the Navy and building **Southsea Castle** on the southern tip of the peninsula. His innovations were tested in 1545 when the French set out to revenge the recent capture of Boulogne by the English. Their plan was to defeat the English Navy, consisting of some hundred ships, and take the Isle of Wight to act as a bridgehead to invade the mainland. Their force of 150 ships and 60,000 men waiting nearby in additional transports, met with the English just off the harbour mouth. The Battle of Spithead, with Henry watching from Southsea Castle, ended in defeat for the French. Lost during the action, probably because her gun-ports were not secured while manoeuvring, was the Mary Rose, which turned over and sank, taking her entire crew of 700 with her.

Portsmouth, and to some extent the Royal Navy itself, then fell into decline, which was only to be ended after the Civil War; the Royal Navy declaring for Cromwell while the town remained loyal. If this sounds odd, it should be remembered that one of the major factors which ultimately turned Englishmen against the crown was the subject of the Navy and finance.

Under Cromwell, and later Charles II, the fortunes of both the Navy and Portsmouth were restored. Over the years the dockyard expanded to provide all the facilities required. By the 18th century, the town was entirely dependant on the Royal Dockyard. After the Napoleonic Wars there was a brief period in the doldrums, but the fruits of the industrial revolution, the demands of Empire and European expansionism soon brought that to an end. Steam was introduced and iron-clad ships constructed; the humble sailor was becoming a technician and shore-establishments were built to provide him with an education. With much of the Fleet serving in the far-flung waters of the Empire, it was felt that Portsmouth might be vulnerable to attack - particularly from our old enemy, the French. A mighty ring of fortresses were built to surround the entire area, from Gosport on the western side of the harbour, running right along the crest of Portsdown Hill to the north, and down to Farlington, at the head of Langstone Harbour. Out in the Solent four massive sea-forts were built of granite and clad with armour plating. Portsmouth became the most heavily defended city in Europe. Both World Wars served to emphasis the strategic importance of the city, but the much vaunted land defences were of little use, being utilised for headquarters, stores and barracks. Like Southampton, both Gosport and Portsmouth were heavily bombed, with much of the heart being torn out of the city and yet, phoenix like, they have arisen from the ashes of their past and look to a new, and perhaps not so defence-dependant future. The Royal Navy is now smaller and more compact, ships are no longer built in the Dockyard and personnel have been drastically reduced. New industries, no longer related to defence have moved into the area and the harbours used by cross-channel and merchant shipping as well as the sleek grey warships. The city has made a determined effort to find itself a niche by promoting itself as 'the City of Maritime Heritage' and its assets in this area are unequalled.

Undoubtedly the best place to start a tour of the city and its heritage is at the **Royal**

Dockyard which houses three of the world's major maritime attractions as well as an excellent museum. Here we have **HMS Victory**, the **Mary Rose, HMS Warrior** and the **Royal Naval Museum.** Other aspects of Naval and Military life are displayed in Fort Nelson near Fareham, the splendid **Royal Marines Museum** in Eastney Barracks on the Southsea front, **The D-Day Museum** which is adjacent to Southsea Castle, and **The Royal Naval Submarine Museum** across the water in Gosport (a good excuse to get afloat and see something of the harbour itself.

The Camber, the original port within the natural harbour, is surrounded by **Old Portsmouth,** an attractive area that had a lewd reputation in years gone by. The streets are quiet where once the drunken jacks did their roistering and the drabs and bawds no longer call from the windows to promote their trade. It is something of an oasis amidst a rapidly changing world, with good-looking, principally Georgian housing, although there are traces of far older construction. Finally there is the cathedral, quite unique among its fellows, since it has only recently been finished, but it is also made up of three distinct periods; 12th century, 17th century and 20th century. Somehow the great building seems to represent an apt simile for the city itself; it is organic, its growth has been untidy and inconsistent, yet it is intensely alive with an eye to the future as well as to the past.

North of Portsmouth there is no difficulty in finding ones way back into rural charm. One moment it is all hustle and bustle with coaches, lorries and cars shooting past, while the next moment the scenery changes to narrow lanes, rolling green fields and small rural communities. The London-bound A3 takes one past **Horndean**, where the local brewery, Gales, is renowned for its quality beer. A pleasant meandering drive brings one to **Hambledon** an isolated red-brick village celebrated as the early home of cricket, and in recent times, for the vineyards planted on the chalk slopes behind the village. Once a market town, the village has some charming houses and a medieval church built on Saxon remains. Cricket actually began some two miles to the north east on **Broadhalfpenny Down**, where Hambledon Cricket Club was the parent of the celebrated Marylebone Cricket Club. Hambledon's finest moment came in 1777; they played All-England and beat them by an innings and 168 runs. It is interesting to note that they played for the huge sum of a thousand guineas!

The Bat and Ball retains the area's close links with the game and contains any interesting momentoes. A stone pillar erected on Broadhalfpenny Down itself records the fact that cricket was played there from 1750-87. West of Hambledon lies the Meon Valley with many small and attractive villages and hamlets; an area that is largely unspoilt and of serene beauty. At **Corhampton**, there is a delightful simple Saxon church, built about 1035. The rare Saxon sundial on the south wall is divided into eight sections, because it was their custom to separate the day into eight 'tides' of three hours each; it was the Normans who introduced the 24 hour sundial. The interior contains some equally rare 12th century wall paintings, some of them depicting scenes in the life of St Swithun. In the churchyard there is an enormous yew and a late Romano-British coffin.

The furthest point east in Hampshire is **Emsworth** where my tour ends. Once upon a time Emsworth was noted for its oysters but in the beginning of the 19th century it was dealt a body blow, when oysters supplied for a banquet in Winchester, were found to carry typhoid, resulting in a lot of deaths. Those days are long gone and this busy little place has become a yachting centre with excellent facilities for boat building.

Hampshire is full of unexpected beauty, hidden history and friendly people.

THE GOLDEN POT,
New Odiham Road,
Alton, Hampshire GU34 4DJ

Tel:01420 84130 Fax:01420 85235

This is a pub with a difference! A warm, vibrant place to visit which one rapidly recognises is down to the landlord, Helen Kaye, who owns and runs The Golden Pot with the aid of her daughter, Ann-Marie who is the Chef, and with help from her husband whenever it is needed - he is immensely supportive but has another job as well. Helen had worked for the previous owners and enjoyed what she did but always felt there was immense scope for improvement. Since she took over the whole place has become lively, trade is up and the locals who regularly frequent the bar obviously approve of the present regime. They come to chat and frequently to play Skittles. One might say that Helen and her family have put the Golden Pot on the map but in fact it is the only pub to be genuinely included in the local ordnance survey map.

Built about 100 years ago the pub has a delightful atmosphere and in the bar and dining room there are all sorts of interesting trinkets and bric a brac which makes the place homely. The food is traditional English with one or two surprises. Home-cooked, sensibly priced and generous in portions you will find an excellent Chicken Curry, a mouth-watering Steak and Kidney Pie, Sizzling Cantonese Prawns and lots of other delicious dishes on the menu. In addition there are always excellent steaks cooked as you request as well as an enormous Mixed Grill. Every day the Blackboard displays the Daily Specials. If you want a Bar Snack you will find the menu wide and varied including an 'All Day Breakfast'. Fresh sandwiches, Burgers, Ploughmans, Giant Yorkshire Puddings with rich Onion Gravy with the filling of the day, Omelettes and Jacket Potatoes with a whole variety of fillings make sure that there is something for everyone. Rapidly becoming well known and very popular are the Theme Nights which might be Spanish, French or Italian and of course, the excellent, good value Sunday Lunch with all the trimmings.

Helen hopes to build an extension in the next two years and be able to offer accommodation. It certainly would be a very friendly place in which to stay but in the meantime a visit for food and drink will have to satisfy you.

USEFUL INFORMATION

OPEN; *All year* **DINING ROOM;** *Good traditional fare*
CHILDREN; *Welcome* **BAR MEALS;** *Varied menu. Good value*
CREDIT CARDS; *In 1998* **VEGETARIAN;** *Catered for + Special diets*
LICENSED; *Yes* **DISABLED ACCESS;** *Limited*
ACCOMMODATION; *Planned for 1998* **GARDEN;** *Yes & Children's Pets Corner*

GREAT WESTERN HOTEL
Vyne Road,
Basingstoke,
Hampshire RG21 5ND

Tel/Fax: 01256   323883

Basingstoke in the days when the Great Western Hotel was built about 1850, 11 years after the railway first arrived, was a sleepy place. Today it is one of the fastest growing and busiest towns in Hampshire. As its name suggests the hotel is conveniently located next to the railway station and just a few minutes walk to Basingstoke town centre. The town is interesting in its own right with a wealth of historic architecture, the Basingstoke Canal, Haymarket Theatre, Anvil Concert Hall, Willis Museum, excellent Sports   Centre, Ten Pin Bowling, a Multi Screen Cinema, Night Clubs and some wonderful walks.

Roy and Janet Davies who are the owners of the Great Western believe in ensuring the comfort of their guests and at the same time making the prices affordable. The comfortable bedrooms all have colour television, tea and coffee making facilities and an iron and ironing board is available. For those who have an early start or need to be up and about early for business purposes, there are Wake-Up Calls. Packed Lunches are also available. The Pub part of the Great Western is a lively, friendly place with a definite emphasis on sport. Monday is Crib and Quiz Night, Tuesday Darts, Wednesday Sport Night, Thursday Pool League and on Friday there is a Disco with Live Music on Saturday. Sunday is described as a Fun Day and it lives up to its name. Big Screen Sky TV is available throughout the week showing all the top sporting events, including live Carling Premiership football.

Food is all important and the Restaurant is open 7 days a week for Breakfast, Lunch and Dinner. The menu always includes the Special of the Day and a tender, succulent roast as well as things like Chilli, Curry and Lasagne. The aim is to cater for all tastes and appetites by offering traditional home cooked foods at sensible prices.

USEFUL INFORMATION

OPEN; *All day 6.30am-12 midnight*
Bar; *Mon-Wed 11am-11pm Thurs-Sat:11am-midnight*
Sun:12-10.30pm
CREDIT CARDS; *All major cards*
ACCOMMODATION; *Comfortable rooms*

RESTAURANT; *Home-cooked fare*
BAR FOOD; *Yes + Daily Specials*
LICENSED; *Full On/Off*
CHILDREN; *Welcome in Dining area*
PETS; *By arrangement*

THE ROSE AND CROWN

Lyndhurst Road,
Brockenhurst,
Hampshire 5042 7RH
Tel: 01590 622225

The New Forest has many good hotels and hostelries and to our delight The Rose and Crown at Brockenhurst has just been refurbished to the beauty and standard one would expect in a Queen Anne Manor house built about 1710. Eldridge Pope have taken the Inn back into their care and have spent lavishly, but with great taste and flair. Never will you find one of their establishments duplicated in another - something that happens all too often with big chains. Under the skilful, professional management in the hands of Richard Thrift and his wife Melanie, The Rose and Crown will become one of the most sought after venues in the New Forest.

Every room in The Rose and Crown is gracious and cosily furnished in keeping with the age of the house. The decor is soft and restful and the pretty drapes highlight the large windows. There are two bars, a Lounge Bar and a Skittles Bar. The latter adjoins the full length, mapled floor Skittle Alley which provides a great deal of fun for parties in the winter months and is unusual because most Skittle Alleys are less than full length. In the Dining Room, an attractive L shaped room which seats 90 in comfort, the emphasis is on good food, freshly cooked and using as much in the way of local ingredients and produce as possible. A traditional Carvery is a feature on selected days in the winter but every day in the summer. Succulent Roast Beef, Roast Pork with plenty of crackling, and Turkey, grain fed from the local farm, are all accompanied by a selection of vegetables and crisp roast potatoes. Bar Food is also available and one can have anything from a steak to a sandwich. It is delicious fare and reflects the high standard of the Inn. The comprehensive wine list with wines from around the world underlines the quality and choice to be found throughout.

Staying here is a pleasure. There are 14 en suite bedrooms all themed after villages and attractions of the New Forest and each furnished delightfully with comfortable beds, colour television and a hostess tray. The large and beautifully maintained garden is shaded by the largest and oldest spreading Yew Tree you are ever likely to see and attracts many customers to linger under its branches in the warm weather   enjoying the sun, the wine and the food. Well behaved children are very welcome and dogs on leads at the discretion of the management in the bars but never in the rooms or dining room.

USEFUL INFORMATION

OPEN; All year. All day in summer
CHILDREN; Welcome
CREDIT CARDS; All major cards
LICENSED; Full On
ACCOMMODATION; 14 en suite rooms
GARDEN;: Large, beautifully maintained
 of the management

DINING ROOM;: Excellent
well-presented food
BAR FOOD; Wide range
VEGETARIAN; Always a choice
DISABLED ACCESS; Yes
PETS; On leads at discretion

BASINGSTOKE COUNTRY HOTEL

Scures Hill, Nately Scures,
Nr Hook,
Hampshire RG27 9JS

Tel: 01256 764161 Fax: 01256 768341

This truly excellent hotel is situated on the main A30 London Road but set well back from the highway yet with easy access to the motorways and only four and a half miles from Basingstoke. It was once a private country residence but has been skilfully converted into an elegant, modern country hotel, set in four and a half acres amidst the mature woodland and countryside of Northern Hampshire. What is so refreshing about it is the quality of service which starts the moment you arrive. A caring and attentive reception staff greet you making sure you feel both welcome and important - how many times have you been to a hotel where the receptionist barely looks at you and you become simply a room number! The whole staff are efficient, friendly and interested in your well being. In fact the motto of the hotel is 'We go further to make you feel at home'.

Both the standard bedrooms and the suites are individually furnished with great taste and have remote control colour televisions with satellite reception, direct-dial telephone, trouser press, hair dryer, and hospitality trays. Some rooms also offer mini-bar facilities. The menus in the award winning Winchester Restaurant with its quiet elegance, will long be remembered for the delicious flavour of the contemporary English style and traditional culinary classics, and the presentation. As one would expect the wine list offers some outstanding wines. The pleasant Cocktail Lounge is a perfect pre-dinner venue in which to enjoy a drink or simply read a book in the comfortable fireside retreat.

1996 saw the opening of the new purpose built Woodland Suite which offers one of the Hampshire Borders most technologically advanced Conference and Banquet facilities. Superb for business purposes and equally delightful for wedding receptions. The Naseby Suite and an array of private function rooms make it possible to offer facilities for anything from a small number to 200 hundred guests. The attention to detail of the management and staff make absolutely certain that the occasion will run perfectly. The leisure facilities of the 'Club Veranda' provide the perfect environment for exercise and relaxation with the ozone-filtered swimming pool, gymnasium, sauna and solarium. The Basingstoke Country Hotel is ideal for anyone whether on business or pleasure.

USEFUL INFORMATION

OPEN; *All year*
CHILDREN; *Welcome*
CREDIT CARDS; *All major cards*
LICENSED; *Yes. Fine cellar*
ACCOMMODATION; *Suites & standard rooms*
Leisure and Conference facilities

RESTAURANT; *Award winning*
VEGETARIAN; *Catered for*
DISABLED ACCESS; *Yes*
GARDEN; *Yes.*

THE RED LION
Boldre, Lymington,
Hampshire SO41 8NE
Tel: 01590 673177 Fax: 01590 676403
E .Mail.John Bicknell@Dial.Pipex.Com.

Tucked away just a little distance from Lymington, is the pretty village of Boldre where The Red Lion is the centre of village life. It is such a pretty old inn. Built in the 1600's it is full of character, charm and a tangible feeling of well-being born of the happiness that has been spread beneath its roof through the centuries. What strikes one first of all, in the summer months anyway, is the stunning and colourful display of hanging baskets, pots and a flower laden farm cart, which adorn the front of the building. Old fashioned flowers climb up the walls of the porch and provide a delightful country scent as one walks in. Inside John and Penny Bicknell welcome you to their traditional country pub which was once two cottages with stables attached. The Bicknells have been mine hosts here for the last twenty seven years and they have the most amazing collection of memorabilia of every kind adorning the walls, the beams, shelves behind the bars and anywhere else a gleaming piece of copper or a charming old plate can be accommodated. There are brasses, tapestries worked by Penny's mother, man-traps, a collection of chamber pots and all manner of other items which all help to build the cosy, relaxed atmosphere. The bars with their low beams are popular with locals who stroll across the village green to the inn for their pint of well kept ale. Many of them are great characters and many a story is told. One in particular amuses visitors especially. A drunken man insisted on climbing up the chimney but unfortunately got stuck fast and could neither get up nor down. A professional chimney sweep went to his assistance but could not move him, so at last by means of chains he was drawn up the chimney from outside! Yachtsmen who sail out of Lymington are also attracted to the Red Lion because of its terrific atmosphere.

There is no separate restaurant but the food is superb. It is accurately described as 'wholesome, home-cooked, old fashioned English food like Mum used to cook'. Penny Bicknell is the creator of all the interesting, tasty dishes and is assisted by Angie who has been with them for 18 years. There are always 12 starters including a very good home-made soup which ,with a Cottage Roll and butter, is almost a meal in itself. The main course may be anything from a home-made steak and kidney pie to half a local Pheasant, casseroled in red wine and orange juice. One of the most popular dishes is a plate of cold home-cooked Gammon with two poached eggs and a basket of chipped potatoes. There are Basket meals, Ploughman's, sandwiches and a selection for vegetarians. The flower festooned patio and the large garden with an adjoining field makes eating and drinking in the fresh air in summer an added reason for coming to this very nice pub.

USEFUL INFORMATION

OPEN: 11am-11pm all year
CHILDREN: Over 14 years
CREDIT CARDS: All except Diners
LICENSED: Full On
GARDEN: Flower festooned patio
Large garden & field. Tables & chairs
for eating and drinking

RESTAURANT: Not applicable
BAR FOOD: Wholesome, home-
cooked, old fashioned English
VEGETARIAN: 3/4 hot dishes + starters
DISABLED ACCESS: Semi-level

SAILMAKER'S LOFT

5 Bath Square, Spice Island,
Old Portsmouth,
Hampshire PO1 2JL

Tel: 01705 823045 Fax: 01705 295961

This attractive establishment is situated in the heart of Spice Island with its cobbled streets and waterside taverns. The whole area is steeped in history and closeby are the ancient fortifications, where Lord Nelson embarked on HMS Victory before the Battle of Trafalgar. Spice Island is adjacent to Camber Docks, now a thriving fishing port where the very first tobacco and potatoes were landed. From here you can catch a water bus which will take you on a tour of the harbour - one of the best ways of seeing Portsmouth. Like a land bus, it stops at various places to allow you to land and visit the various maritime attractions. From the house you can stroll to many of the City's major sights, including the Dockyard with it's historic ships, HMS Victory, Mary Rose and HMS Warrior. Also closeby are the D-Day Museum, Sea Life Centre, Southsea Castle, from where Henry VIII watched the Mary Rose sink and the Hovercraft terminal to the Isle of Wight.

The Sailmaker's Loft is a great place in which to stay. Small, friendly and family run, it is the epitome of comfort and hospitality. There are three guest rooms, 1 double, one twin and a single. Two rooms are ensuite and also have splendid sea views. All the rooms are attractively furnished and have colour TV, a hostess tray and hairdryers. Breakfast is a delicious, freshly cooked, Spice Island meal which is served from 7.30am although if you need to eat earlier, a Continental breakfast is available from 6.15pm. You can frequently see an array of ships plying their trade, reefers and RORO's, ferries, tugs, warships and yachts, whilst you are enjoying one of the best breakfasts in Hampshire.

You will find The Sailmaker's Loft is close to the Railway Station, Isle of Wight Ferries, Hovercraft and coach terminals and it is just 5 minutes drive to the Continental ferryport. Although there is no evening meal available at The Sailmaker's Loft,. it is unimportant because there are excellent tea-rooms, bistros, restaurants and pubs nearby.

USEFUL INFORMATION

OPEN; *All year*
CHILDREN; *By arrangement*
CREDIT CARDS; *None taken*
LICENSED; *No*
ACCOMMODATION; *3 rooms 2 en suite*

DINING ROOM; *Spice Island Breakfast -excellent*
VEGETARIAN; *Catered for*
DISABLED ACCESS; *No*
PETS; *No*
PARKING; *Free car park closeby*

Chapter 8

HEREFORD & WORCESTER

INCLUDES

Chapter 8

HEREFORD AND WORCESTER

P ulchra Terra Dei Donum' (This fair land is the Gift of God) is the County Motto of Hereford and the more I see of this beautiful land, the truer I know the statement to be. Although Herefordshire is joined with Worcestershire for administrative purposes, the characters of the two counties have little in common. A perfect illustration of this is gained from the viewpoint atop the Herefordshire Beacon in the Malvern Hills. To the east lie the rich fertile lowlands of Worcestershire through which the Severn and Avon wander, whilst to the west, the undulating wooded scenery of Herefordshire extends to the lowering ridge of the Black Mountains, some forty miles away. A further clue to the disparity between the two counties is given by the nature of the viewpoint, for this is the site of that ancient Iron Age fortress known as the British Camp. Although the sleepy rural calm of the region to the east was brutally disturbed by three of the most decisive battles in English history, its western neighbour was engaged in continuous territorial struggle for many centuries and rarely turned to the more peaceful pursuits once the din of battle had died away. Here, people were always on their guard with billhook, sword or spear close to hand and a wary eye cocked to the western horizon. Herefordshire was the last English territory to be seized from the Celtic Welsh by the Anglo-Saxons - and neither race has ever been noted for their expertise in turning the other cheek. Norman intervention hardly helped matters and for generations blood was shed in ambush , foray, raid and battle. Following the example of their predecessors, the Romans, in their dealings with the Scots, the Saxons expended an enormous amount of time and energy in the construction of Offa's Dyke, named after the King of the Mercians and which ran north to south, from 'sea to sea'. Although the great ditch was, in reality, more of an official boundary than a defensive work, fortifications were built and these works were accelerated by the Normans who constructed a chain of castles along the border, known as the Welsh Marches. The barons who com- manded these castles were known as the Marcher Lords and their conduct was not always above reproach. William the Conqueror was evidently a believer in the dictum 'Divide and Rule', for the noblemen he appointed to the Marches were the moist scheming and potentially disruptive in the Kingdom. Far from the intrigues of Court, they were left to their own devices - harrying the Welsh, bullying the Saxons, plotting against each other and generally feathering their own nests (or castles - it is interesting to note that, over the centuries, the number of fortifications built in the county has only been succeeded by those of Northumberland). This was border country where the King's Law was of little import and territory was all.

With such a turbulent history, the casual visitor might be forgiven for imagining the county a gloomy introspective place, much given to brooding over the past injustices and full of ghost-ridden ruins. Nothing could be further from the truth for the region as a whole, including the Welsh border county, has a cheerful, bucolic atmosphere; a land of great beauty where the stranger is welcome, not suspect. Perhaps this owes much to the six 'W's; Wool, Water, Wheat, Wood, Women and Wine (or cider). Herefordshire has long been a rich agricultural county and is famed for its cattle, whose robust constitution have resulted in their export all over the world. The Normans established a wool and cloth industry and sheep still graze the hills and slopes while the many apple orchards contribute to that well known beverage, cider. Beer-drinkers are catered for by the cultivation of hops and the rich red earth produces fine cereal crops. It is still an intensely rural landscape with few great houses - though many are of great age and antiquity - and is, in some senses an almost forgotten region of England with but a few miles of motorway intruding into its south-eastern corner.

This motorway, the M50, is a western spur of the M5 and runs some five miles into Herefordshire before ending at Ross-on-Wye, a delightful market town overlooking the River Wye. Agriculture, light industry and tourism form the basis of the local economy and Ross (from the Welsh ros, meaning a spit of land) is ideally situated for exploring the glorious country of the Wye Valley. Its friendly and welcoming atmosphere owes much to the example set by the town's best loved inhabitant, John Kyrle (1637-1724). Trained as a lawyer, he inherited a small fortune and never practiced, preferring to spend his time and money on good works and acts of great public generosity. He died, a bachelor, at the age of 89, having given all his money away but never incurred a debt. He is remembered as the 'Man of Ross', and among his many philanthropies were the provision of a town water supply, a causeway enabling the bridge to be used when flooding occurred, and a walled public garden, still known as Kyrle's Prospect. He built a summer house in the grounds of his home, now known as Kyrle House, and paid the poor and unemployed to find horse's teeth from animals killed in a nearby cavalry skirmish during the Civil War; these were set into mortar to create a mosaic in the shape of a swan. Kyrle is buried in the Church of St Mary's, and his monument is modest and restrained. Inevitably he did much for the church including the casting of the tenor bell and the rebuilding of the elegant spire which he had raised by nearly fifty feet. He provided help for the needy, aid for the sick, and education for the illiterate and remained a modest and much-loved man.

The little town on its steep rocky outcrop has been a favourite with visitors since the early Victorian era when, as now, the attractions of the surrounding countryside and the excellent salmon fishing brought people back year after year, prompting a testy local parson, Thomas Fosbrooke, to comment in the 1830's that the tourists 'during the summer and autumn poke about the Wye like snipes and woodcocks, and after rummaging through everything, re-emigrate to London'. Around that time, a conscious effort was made to romanticise the town by 'medievalising', constructing walls and a round tower. Thankfully, the soft red local sandstone has eroded fast and what looked uncomfortably twee now looks uncommonly like the real thing. Hotels, pubs and restaurants are plentiful. I was impressed by the enthusiasm and high standards to be found. In Edde Cross Street stands the deservedly award winning Pheasants Restaurant, just around the corner from the unique Button Museum. The high culinary standards of the restaurant are matched by the warmth of welcome, decor and service; limited accommodation is also available. Two hotels I am happy to recommend are The Chase Hotel in Gloucester Road where the brochure states 'That your stay with us is among the more memorable of life's happy interludes is the earnest wish of us all here'.It is an aim that is achieved. Dinner which is open to   non-residents, is an experience of fine food and good service. The cuisine is exceptional. The Chase is, as they promised, memorable. Glewstone Court Country House Hotel is a spacious and elegant Listed Country House set amongst fruit orchards in its own grounds of some three acres with an outstanding Cedar of Lebanon reputed to be the oldest in the West of England. Secluded, yet accessible it is less than half a mile off the A40 three miles from the centre of Ross. It is convivial and friendly. Nothing is too much trouble; children and dogs under control are very welcome! In the High Street, Cloister's Wine Bar, distinguished from the outside by its impressive stained glass windows, is rightly popular with visitors and locals alike for its cheerful atmosphere, good food and drinks.

The Lost Street Museum is a charming, and very well thought out museum in the form of an arcade of Edwardian shops containing all manner of period items including amusement machines, musical boxes, toys, costumes and gramophones. An unusual local industry is candle-making and Ross-on-Wye Candlemakers open their workshop to the public in Old Gloucester Road. Two gardens are worth visiting. Hill Court Gardens and Garden Centre to the east of the town and How Caple Court Gardens to the north, are a gardener's delight.

South of Ross, there are a multitude of attractions to be found as the Wye loops its way round to enter the precipitous limestone gorge known as Symonds Yat, one of the most beautiful and spectacular views in England. The 400 ft high Yat Rock (yat being Old English for a gate or gorge) is a favourite spot to admire the scenic splendour of the Wye curling its way sinuously through the wooded country-side. Peregrine falcons nest in these perilous cliffs and at the bottom of the path from the Rock down to the river there is an unusual man-powered rope ferry.

At **Symonds Yat West**, The Jubilee Park offers a wide range of family entertainment, including a maze, craft shops and a butterfly farm. The Herefordshire Rural Heritage Museum, set in an attractive rural location, houses one of the countries largest collections of historic farm machinery and agricultural implements. Here too is the most peaceful of hotels, Woodlea in a secluded woodland valley and overlooking the famous Wye Rapids. It is beautiful at anytime of the year but perhaps autumn has to be a favourite time when the brilliant colour of the trees is spectacular.

About three miles downstream in the wooded Doward Hills above the river, is King Arthurs Cave where excavations have revealed that its occupancy by man dates back nearly 60,000 years! Five miles south of Ross and upstream from Symonds Yat are the romantic and massively impressive ruins of Goodrich Castle. Goodrich is an entertaining, though somewhat scattered little village and the 12th century castle is sited on a high rocky spur overlooking a crossing of the river. Square in shape with a tower at each corner and surrounded by a moat hewn out of the red rock, Goodrich was besieged by the   Parliamentarians, under the command of Colonel Birch in 1646. Legend has it that Birch's niece, Alice, was inside the castle with her Royalist lover, and that they were both drowned in the Wye whilst trying to escape. Her shrieks of distress can still be heard on stormy nights when the river is in spate.

The castle was slighted at the end of the Civil War, having suffered severe damage during the siege, and some idea of its immense construction can be gained by a contemporary account of the oaken roof timbers which were described as 'without knotte or knarle and being sixty-six feet long and two feet square'. These would have come from the nearby **Forest of Dean**, in Gloucestershire.

The Cross Keys Inn in the village is a welcome stop after walking to the castle and back. A traditional country pub without pretensions, it has comfortable bed and breakfast accommodation with a friendly ghost included at no extra charge!
Heading north-east from Ross on the A449 and lying close to the eastern border of the county is the attractive village of **Much Marcle**, blessed with a fine church of 13th century origins, **St Bartholomews** and two historic houses. By the church porch is a splendid hollow yew with planked seats inside reputed to sit seven. Just over four miles further along the A449 is the delightful ancient market town of Ledbury. Set by the old cross-roads to Tewkesbury, Hereford, Gloucester and Malvern, it has been inhabited since around 1500BC. The church of St Michael and All Angels, Herefordshire's premier parish church was built on an earlier Saxon foundation, and has a Norman chancel and west door, and a magnificent medieval north chapel. The tall and elegant detached spire was built by Nathaniel Wilkinson who was commissioned by John Kyrle to replace the spire at Ross-on-Wye, and a further connection between the towns can be found in the belfry; the bells were presented by the Rudhalls in the 17th century. Their restoration in this century were made possible by John Masefield the poet who was a native of Ledbury, who donated the profits from many of his books towards the work.

The wide main street, flanked by many half timbered houses including the Elizabethan **Feathers Inn** was the scene of a desperate charge by Prince Rupert's cavalry during the Civil War, when a Parliamentarian force was routed. Bullets are still embedded in the church door and in the walls of the **Talbot**, in New Street. Church Lane, cobbled and narrow, offers a delightful period view of St Michaels and opens out into a small close with some handsome houses surrounding the church.

Ledbury stands at the southern end of the Malverns and the beauty of the surrounding countryside has inspired many notable works of art. One of the central works of Early English literature is the poem, 'Piers the Plowman', which has its setting in the area and its author, William Langland (c1332-1400) was probably born in Ledbury. The big church of **Holy Trinity** is particularly notable for the fact that the massive tower is completely detached from the main body of the building. This unusual feature is found more in Herefordshire than in any other county and is thought to have been a defensive measure; a refuge for the villagers when danger threatened.

The south-eastern quarter of Herefordshire is the main hop-growing region, and hopyards, with their trellis-work of poles, wires and strings can be seen throughout the area. At **Bishops Frome**, on the Ledbury to Bromyard road, **The Hop Pocket Hop Farm** is open to visitors interested in a form of cultivation that is regrettably in decline. Drying kilns, hop-picking machines and the hopyards are all open to inspection. Finally, in order to sample the end-product, the splendid **Green Dragon Inn** keeps an excellent cellar of traditional ales on its 400 year old premises.

For those wanting a total escape from the commercial world and the opportunity to stay as house guests in a wonderful house, I wholeheartedly recommend **Grove House** at **Bromsberrow Heath**. To get there you leave the M50 at Junction 2 and follow signs to Ledbury. Take the first turning left signed Bromsberrow Heath. In the village turn right by the post office and go up the hill. The l4th century Grade II Listed house is on your right with a tennis court by the gate. Dinner in the candlelit dining room is the highlight of what will be a memorable visit.

Further information on the history and practices of hop-growing can be found at the **Bromyard Heritage Centre** along with other displays relating to matters of local interest. **Bromyard** sits in a natural bowl amongst rolling downland and was one of the most important towns in Herefordshire long before the Norman clerks started to compile the Domesday Book. It had a Saxon church in AD 840 and the present church of **St Peter** was probably built on the same site in about 1160. The town's wealth came principally from its market and local agriculture- later came an added bonus in the form of its geographical position half way between Worcester and Hereford which led to its development as a coaching centre. Notable amongst the inns catering to this trade was **The Falcon**, whose post-boys wore a smart uniform of white hats, breeches and yellow jackets. Somehow I cannot believe they stayed smart for very long!

The **River Teme** wriggles through the three counties of Herefordshire, Worcestershire and Shropshire in the area around **Tenbury Wells**. A borough since 1248, Tenbury has remained an attractive small market town surrounded by hopyards and apple orchards. Hopes of fame and fortune came its way in the l9th century, with the discovery of saline springs - but the town lacked an entrepreneur of the quality of Doctor Wall at Malvern and the spa never became fashionable - in fact, before it was closed during the First World War, the owners were rather desperately advertising it 'as suitable for the middle and lower classes with every convenience at the lowest popular price'. Potential customers may also have been put off by the somewhat ambiguous remarks made by the wonderfully named Dr Augustus Bozzi Granville, who was quoted as saying 'Immediately upon swallowing half a tumbler of the Tenbury water, a disturbance, or rather a commotion, is set up in the abdomen, which upon repetition of the same quantity of fluid, after a proper interval, will be found, in most cases, to end in a way desirable under such circumstances'. Little wonder the waters never gained great popularity! The incongruous **Pump Rooms** survive, known locally as the 'Chinese Temple' because of the style of architecture. In Market Street, there is **The Royal Oak Hotel**, whose half timbered black and white facade is both complex and attractive. When I was there before Christmas 1994 it was being totally revamped and new bedrooms added.

Two miles to the west at **St Michaels**, there is a splendid family run hotel - but of a quite different type. **The Cadmore Lodge Hotel** is a development which gets better every time I see it. It stands within its own wooded estate which has been laid out to provide golf, fishing and other sporting facilities as well as to encourage conservation and wildlife - a subject very dear to John and Elizabeth Weston, the owners. A new function room had recently been added when I was there just after I had been to Tenbury Wells. It looks out through its glass front onto the lake and is complete with a bar and a dance floor.

Also just outside Tenbury Wells in the little hamlet of **Eastham** is **Robins End**, a lovely old house with a wonderful garden. Here Sarah and Adrian Worsley offer you beautiful   accommodation in spacious, delightfully furnished rooms. They can only take a very few guests and the whole atmosphere is one of a house party at which your hosts are truly delighted to see you.

Leominster (pronounced 'Lemster') lies nine miles to the south-west and is Herefordshire's second largest town, set amongst a gentle landscape of fields, hills and meadows where river, stream and brook wander. The town's fortunes were based on the fine quality of the wool from the local breed of sheep, the Ryeland, an animal that thrives on the poorer grazing to be found on the neighbouring hills and the less fertile outcrops of sandy soil from which the name is derived. The demand for this wool was so great that at one time the fleece was known as 'Lempster Ore'.There are a good mix of architectural styles in the town, principally Jacobean and Georgian, and High Street Church Street and Etnam Street all contain good examples. **The Leominster Folk Museum** is in Etnam Street.

Leofric, Earl of Mercia, and husband of that well-known naked equestrienne, Godiva, is supposed to have given his name to the town with the establishment of a religious order in the 9th century (Leofric's Minster). This is thought unlikely since the order was a nunnery (although he may have hoped his wife would enter and stop embarrassing him) and anyway, the family cannot have been over popular in the area since Leofric's son promptly ran off with the Abbess! A second legend concerns a lion who cornered a Christian missionary but spared the man's life in return for a share of his bread, whereupon the missionary took this to be a remarkably good omen and founded a church on the spot (Leo's minster). The most likely story is rather more prosaic and has no connection with either embarrassed Saxon aristocrats or vegetarian lions: Leominster simply means 'the Church on the Lene' - Lene being the old name for Arrow Valley. Nevertheless, carved into the head of one of the huge pillars of the west entrance to **Leominster Priory Church** are the figures of a monk and a lion.

A thriving market town with a sprinkling of light industry and a large number of antique shops, Leominster stands surrounded by hopyards and apple orchards, and the products of the former find special favour with the landlord of the **Black Horse Coach House**, on the southern edge of town. This is because the attractive old pub brews its own ales. One would have thought the town would be a natural brewing centre because of the availability of hops and water, but this is the town's first brewery since 1926.

Cider orchards along the road heading south to **Hereford**, hint at one of the city's major industries. **Bulmer's** have been making cider in Hereford for well over a century, and their premises in Plough Lane are open for tours and samplings. The contrast with modern automated production techniques with those of yesteryear are enormous, and a visit to **The Cider Museum and King Offa Distillery**, in Ryelands Street, is a real eye-opener.

Any town or city engaged in the convivial pursuits of brewing or distilling has a rather jolly atmosphere, and Hereford is no exception, although its early history would suggest otherwise. Never free of strife until the end of the Civil War in 1651, the city suffered numerous attacks and sieges over the preceding centuries, yet during that time managed to become one of the most thriving medieval cities in England; a centre for both trade and scholarship.

Its tactical importance can be judged by its name, which means 'an army river-crossing'. The Saxons built the earliest defences against the Welsh, who managed to destroy them in 1055, and William Fitz-Osborne, first of the Marcher Lords, built the Castle in 1067. The power of these Lords of the Marches grew rapidly and they were rightly perceived as a threat to the Crown, for their rule was absolute and they commanded large and well-disciplined armies whilst their allegiance was often doubtful. Their weakness was in the fact that they quarrelled with each other as much as they did with Celt or Crown; feudal laws existed in the Marches long after the rest of England had settled down peacefully. One result of this was that the unfortunate citizens of Hereford, and indeed of the entire region, were subject to attack, not only by the Welsh, but by forces of the Crown attempting to break up unwelcome alliances, or simply by rival barons seizing an opportunity to take a neighbour's property. Hereford and its castle were attacked regularly. The last time the castle was rebuilt was in 1402, during Owen Glendower's Welsh revolt. It suffered its final siege during the Civil War and was demolished in 1660 with a large part of the city walls being removed for redevelopment in the 18th century. **Castle Green**, east of the cathedral, bears no trace of the long-suffering fortress which stood guard above the Wye - but does have a monument to a freeman of the city, Admiral Lord Nelson. Unfortunately money ran out so the sixty-foot column has an urn rather than a bust at the top.

Items relating to the turbulent past, as well as to more peaceful interests, such as bee-keeping, can be seen in **The Hereford City Museum and Art Gallery**, in Broad Street.The modern military presence in the city is restricted to the **Herefordshire Regimental Museum** at the TA Centre in Harold Street, and to the discreet gentlemen of the SAS, at Bradbury Lines. Hereford is rich in museums; apart from those already mentioned, there are the Bulmer Railway Centre, for steam enthusiasts, The Churchill Gardens Museum, displaying fine furniture, costumes and paintings of the late 18th and 19th centuries, The St John Medieval Museum, containing armour and other relics relating to the order of St John, and The Old House, built in 1621 and beautifully furnished in period. The area around the old house is a pedestrian precinct and in nearby St Peter's Close weary feet can be rested, thirsts quenched and hunger satisfied at Gilbies Bistro and Bar. A splendidly secluded spot with a distinctly Continental flavour, it has a continually changing menu which the proprietor modestly describes as 'good, but not great' and some real bargains in the wine-list.

The medieval visitors to the city - scholars, men-at-arms, and traders - would have had their numbers swelled by large numbers of pilgrims, visiting The Cathedral of St Mary the Virgin and St Ethelbert the King. The cathedral was begun in the 7th century - in fact, the appointment of the first Bishop of Hereford dates back to that time. A large proportion of the Norman masonry work survives, particularly inside, but the siege and structural collapse in the 17th and 18th centuries led to extensive re-building and renovation. For all this, it is still a wonderfully handsome building, quite small compared to most cathedrals, and full of many unique treasures. Chief amongst these is the Mappa Mundi, a map of the world drawn around 1290 and of great importance because it shows us how the scholars of that time saw their world, both in spiritual, as well as geographical, terms. The medieval draughtsmanship is superb with all manner of beasts, both fabulous and familiar. The Cathedral also has a notable collection of manuscripts and early printed material in the chained Library, including the 8th century Anglo-Saxon gospels still used when Hereford bishops are sworn in.

The choral traditions of the cathedral are long and the origins of the magnificent Three Choirs Festival can be traced back to an 18th century chancellor, Thomas Bisse. To listen to soaring music in such surroundings is surely close to 'the rudiments of Paradise'.

Rather than stay in one of the city hotels may I recommend to you a most unusual and delightful establishment. Steppes Country House Hotel is tucked away at Ullingswick, a hamlet off the A465 between Bromyard and Hereford. It is totally different from every other hotel I have ever visited and is the fulfilment of several years of work by the owners, Henry and Tricia Howland. Furnished beautifully, it has all sorts of unexpected things about it. I fell in love with it as I am sure you will.

South of Hereford the loops of the Wye become even greater as it twists and turns on its way towards Ross-on-Wye. One can only admire the endurance of the salmon as they make their way upstream to their spawning grounds. The river has long been renowned for the quality of its fishing, and the acknowledged Master of the Wye was Robert Pashley, who between 1908 and 1947, caught 9122 salmon weighing an astonishing total of 63 tons! The Wye is still a mecca for fishermen and women and fishing rights nowadays change hands for immense sums of money, although it is still possible to fish for the day for reasonable prices. Salmon fishing with rod and line became really popular in the Victorian era and the number of smart fishing-lodges in the area bear testimony to that fact, and the demand continues to this day. When in season, salmon is often on the menus of the many excellent local pubs and restaurants, as it is in The Cottage of Content ,an aptly named and quite delightful inn at Carey, near Hoarwithy. Atmosphere, service and comfortable accommodation make this a perfect spot for a fishing holiday, but it is equally popular with the many walkers and tourists who visit the area - not to mention the locals.

The church of St Catherine at Hoarwithy is reached by a steep flight of steps and is worth visiting for it is Mediterranean in appearance and even possesses a campanile. Its exotic appearance is due to an eccentric and wealthy vicar who spent most of his fortune on it - even to the extent of importing Italian craftsmen, giving the church its present Byzantine look, and decorating the interior with gold mosaics and lapis lazuli.

The south-western region of Herefordshire and the Welsh Borders was known as Archenfield and stretched from the western bank of the Wye to the long ridge of the Black Mountains, twenty miles away. It remained a Welsh enclave in England for around six centuries until well after the Conquest. Many of the laws and customs remained peculiarly

Welsh until as recently as the present century. An attractive, yet sparsely populated region, with few large villages but a wealth of churches, which point to the fact that this area has had possibly the longest history of continuous Christianity in England.

Welsh Newton is still the scene of a yearly pilgrimage since the graveyard contains the last of Herefordshire's many saints. John Kemble, who was canonised as recently as 1970, was a Jesuit priest who administered to the many Catholics in the area, including the wife and daughter of the man who arrested him for complicity in the popish plot. An innocent and greatly loved man, he was executed in the most barbaric manner at Hereford, in August 1679. He was eighty years old.

At Kilpeck, just off the A465 from Hereford, is the most famous of Archenfield churches, Saint Mary and Saint David. Saxon work remains in the north-east wall of the nave, but the church is principally Norman and the local red sandstone from which it was built has survived the weathers of time remarkably well (exactly where this extraordinary stone was quarried is still a mystery). The real glory of the little church is its carvings; work of the skilled masons who are sometimes referred to as the Herefordshire School, and who flourished during the 12th century. Behind the church can be found the remains, little more than a stump, of Kilbeck Castle, built around the same time that the carvers were indulging their strange fantasies with hammer and chisel, King John visited here a number of times, and it is recorded that a pretty widow, Joan de Kilpeck, offered him a bribe of fifty marks and a palfrey (a small horse) if he would allow her to marry whom she pleased.

It was to the men of Archenfield that England looked in time of strife. From this area came the medieval equivalent of the machine-gun; the long bow, made from yew, and in the hands of a master, capable of piercing though the mailed thigh of horseman and nailing him to the saddle at fifty paces or more. More importantly the next arrow would be on its way within seconds, whereas the cross-bowman would still be tensioning his weapon. Once the major disputes between English and Welsh were settled, it was the bowmen of Archenfield who led the armies in attack and held the rear in retreat.

Men-at-arms of higher rank but of common experience, are remembered amongst the high, sheep grazing hills of Garwuy. These were the Knights Templar, soldiers of Christian belief and noble birth who wore a red sign of the cross on the simple white surcoats that covered their armour. Formed to protect pilgrims on the long and dangerous journeys to and from Jerusalem, they showed great bravery during the Crusades and later founded numerous religious houses throughout Europe. Garway was one of their estates and the church of St Michael is one of only six Templar foundations left in England. It seems strange to think of those grim monastic soldiers, used to the blazing sun and the desert battles with the Saracens, ending their days on these damp hillsides. The place is moving in its simplicity and well worth the meandering drive south.

Harmony in church, chapel or pub is still part of the tradition of Herefordshire, and I was delighted to hear the landlady and her daughter singing most beautifully in the handsome little Bridge Inn at Kentchurch. Lying beside the waters of the Monnow and at the southern approach to the Golden Valley, this 400 year old pub provides excellent straightforward food and everything a good country pub should be.

The Golden Valley gets its name from a justifiable piece of linguistic confusion on the part of the Normans they muddled the Welsh 'dwyr' meaning water with their own 'd'or' meaning gold - hence Golden Valley and the River Dore. Also Abbey Dore, a mile or so from Ewyas Harold castle (pronounced Yewas) on the west side of the valley. This was a great Cistercian monastery until the Dissolution. The remains were carefully restored under the direction of the first Viscount Scudamore, and he and his craftsmen did a most excellent job. The present building possesses a simple grandeur and contains good glass, some interesting glazed tiles and a knightly effigy of the grandson of the founder of the Abbey, Robert de Clifford.

Several centuries later - but sadly no longer - there was a railway in the valley which was described as 'the loveliest and most inefficiently-run line in England', and there is a splendid account of it, written in 1892:

'that most eccentric of lines….where we have seen the linesman, when not engaged in hay-making deeply engrossed in his occupation of weeding between the rails as we waited for the trains which, if we are to believe the tongue of rumour, sometimes fails to put in an appearance, the company's only locomotive having been seized for distraint of rent'.

Those lines may well ring a bell with one or two modern commuters..

Michaelchurch Escley sits tight under the lee of the Black mountains, truly a dark and brooding mass, frequently blue or purple in tint. From these slopes the Celtic warriors of long ago would rush in ambush, only to vanish into the woods and hills when ambush threatened.

The trout laden waters of the Escley Brook run parallel to those of the Mannow, into which it eventually merges, and the area is border country at its best - remote and beautiful. Here the drovers on their way to Hereford market, would stop to water their beasts and refresh themselves at the lovely Bridge Inn at Michaelchurch Escley. A pastoral atmosphere still clings to the l4th century building, sitting in tranquillity beside the brook, and it is a wonderful place to enjoy a drink or a meal.

The road running north alongside the Monnow passes through Craswall with Hay Bluff, the source of the river, rising high over the hamlet. The Order of the Grandmontines, an offshoot of the Cistercian order and named after their founding-house in Limoges, had their abbey here. The remote situation must have suited an order which emphasised strict discipline and reliance on alms and agricultural labour.

The road continues northward, climbing to around 1500 feet, before dropping down through the steep wooded slopes and into Wales at Hay-on-Wye. Hay changed hands several times in its turbulent early years, being burnt down five times, which may account for the fact that there are the remains of two castles in the small town. Hay is known Worldwide for its bookshops. Second-hand books in their millions line the shelves of the castle, the cinema, a garage and shops that once catered for the more mundane demands of the local populace. Rare first editions and fine leather bindings lie in close proximity to heaps of dog-eared paperbacks and bundles of yellowing magazines. Sleepy little Hay woke up to the fact that it is now a tourist attraction in its own right - thanks to the wonderfully eccentric, but undoubtedly shrewd local entrepreneur, Richard Booth, who started the whole idea.

I am going to suggest that from here you seek out Dolbedwyn Farm House which has an official address of Newchurch, Nr Kington, but I have found it easier to find from Hay. You will find it high up in the beautiful unspoilt countryside and it is a Grade II star listed Tudor Farmhouse. In addition to the warmth, friendliness and hospitality of its owners Glyn and Anne Williams, it has an interior of outstanding interest with splendid panelling, beams, stone flagged floors and a superb Jacobean oak staircase. Here you will feel as though you are staying away from the world, you will be pampered and wonderfully fed.

Turning back from Hay towards Hereford, it is worth taking a detour to view the remains of Clifford Castle, whose ivy-clad ruins tower over a shallow bend in the Wye. It was built by Walter de Clifford in the early 1200's and first saw action not long after when it was captured, not by Celt or fellow Norman Marcher Lord, but by Henry III. This unfortunate episode was as a result of Henry's request that Walter's debts should be paid off. Walter's reply was to make the King's messenger 'eat the King's writ, waxe and all', so the incensed Henry promptly sacked the castle. The 'fair Rosamund'; an earlier de Clifford who was the mistress of Henry II, was probably born here. The King kept her hidden from the jealous Queen Eleanor, but eventually the Queen found Rosamund and forced her to drink poison. The Mortimers succeeded the Cliffords, so the old fortress was held by two of the greatest Marcher families.

Weobley (pronounced 'Webley') is where the first tough Hereford strain of cattle, dark red with white faces, bellies and hocks, were first bred on the Garnstone Estate. The village was evidently one of the more successful Norman settlements. Only the castle's earthworks remain today, but Weobley's prosperity is indicated by the wealth of half timbered housing and the large parish church. Weobley is the place where the expression 'pot walloper' was first coined; the term referred to Shropshire tenants of the Marquess of Bath who had the right to vote in local elections providing they had set up their cooking fires in the main street the previous night. Needless to say, during the corrupt political era of the 18th century, His Lordship took full advantage of this strange custom to ensure the successful return of his chosen candidates. Pot-walloping is no more but another tradition, that of fine food and good accommodation, existed in Ye Olde Salutation Inn long before the political chicanery described, and is happily continued to this day. A fine half timbered building in keeping with so much of its neighbours, the inn is set at the top of Broad Street and commands a fine view of the village.

The half timbered black and white theme is continued at Eardisland to the north of the A44. A picture postcard village by the banks of the Arrow, the enchanting Mill Stream Cottage was once the village school and was built in the 1700's at a cost of fifty pounds! Close by was the site of an ancient British settlement, now the site of Burton Court, a Georgian house of 14th century origins which houses a fascinating collection of European and Oriental costumes and curios, together with natural history displays, ship models and a working model fairground.

Almost next door to Eardisland is the beautiful and unspoilt village of Pembridge with a wealth of 13th and 14th century buildings and none more beautiful than The New Inn which is a hostelry of warmth and atmosphere acquired over the centuries. Everything about it reeks of history. It was the Court House before it became an inn and even after that one room was used to administer the majesty of the law. It has two ghosts who refuse to leave. It would be difficult not to enjoy a visit here although you must be warned that the five bedrooms, simply but comfortably furnished, are not en suite and not likely to become so because of the age of the building.

While you are in the village one of the places to visit is Pembridge Terracotta, makers of fine handthrown flowerpots from strawberry barrels to Ali-Baba urns and much more. Just to the south of Pembridge is The Cider House at Dunkertons in the little hamlet of Luntley. Warm, friendly and beautiful you are invited to lunch every day except Sunday, dine on Friday and Saturday evenings, have morning coffee, tea, home-made cakes and biscuits in a restaurant that has been described as the best between Chester and the Channel Islands. Booking for dinner is essential.

Another beautiful house in which to stay, and close to Pembridge is Broxwood Court in the hamlet of Broxwood. Tranquil, beautifully furnished, wonderful gardens, memorable food and plenty to do on the 1200 acre estate, makes this especially good for anyone wanting a quiet break in an elegant, friendly family home.

It really does seem extraordinary that in such an area, outstanding in its natural beauty, combining peace and solitude with the scenery of the hills, woods and rivers, should have been the scene of so much strife - yet reminders lie all around. Wigmore Castle has a connection with Brampton Bryan in that it was briefly owned by the Harleys before being dismantled by Parliamentarian troops, but it was first built by William Fitz-Osborn, Earl of Hereford, and then owned by the Mortimer family. The castle is impressively and strongly sited on a ridge in a most commanding position. It was to this great fortress that Prince Edward fled, before rallying his forces against Simon de Montfort (he had been imprisoned at Hereford and escaped by the simple ruse of challenging his captors to race their horses. When the animals were exhausted, the cunning Prince produced a fresh beast that had been kept hidden by a sympathiser and disappeared in the proverbial cloud of dust).

Of this great family who held the castle, perhaps the most astute and savage of the Marcher Lords, little remains but a tablet in the nearby gatehouse, where once stood an Augustinian abbey: 'In this abbey lies the remains of the noble family of Mortimer who founded it in 1179 and ruled the Marches of Wales for 400 years'. Henry VIII took little notice, even though his mother was a Mortimer, and the tombs vanished with the Abbey. Their name is, however, commemorated a little further down the road where the A4110 intersects the B4362. This innocent looking junction in the valley of the River Lugg, was the scene, in 1461, of 'an obstinate, bloody and decisive battle'. Four thousand men died at what is now known as Mortimer's Cross; the first defeat to be inflicted on the Lancastrians by Edward Duke of York - himself half a Mortimer, and later to become Edward IV. Before the fight began, an extraordinary sight was to be seen in the sky - three suns appeared. We now know that this phenomenon is caused by the refraction of light through particles in the atmosphere, and is called a parhelion, but to the superstitious medieval warriors it appeared as an omen, a sign from God. The Yorkists took the three suns to represent the triumvirate of Edward, Duke of York, Richard, Duke of Gloucester, and George, Duke of Clarence, and the 'sun in splendour became a favourite heraldic badge with the House of York.

Turn to the east at Mortimer's Cross, and you will come to three large houses lying within a few miles of each other, the first of which acted as a rendezvous for the Yorkist forces. The Croft family have lived at Croft Castle since the time of Domesday, with the exception of a break of 177 years - due to some unfortunate debts incurred by an 18th century Croft - and still live there, although the house and the estate is administered by the National Trust. In its present guise the castle is a massive but handsome house with turrets at each corner, and stands in beautiful parkland with an avenue of Spanish chestnut trees - said by some to have been grown from chestnuts carried in a galleon of the Spanish Armada. For all its troubled history, it is a wonderfully peaceful and attractive home. A strong feeling of continuity and service hangs in the air; as exemplified by the memorials in the little church to two more recent members of the family. Both the tenth and eleventh baronets, father and son, were killed while serving with the Herefordshire Regiment in the First and Second World Wars, nearly eight hundred years after their ancestor, Jasper de Croft, was knighted during the Crusades.

The other two houses stand almost side-by-side to the east of the Leominster to Ludlow road. The smallest is Eye Manor, a neat Restoration house, built for a slave-trader and plantation-owner from Barbados, with the exotic name of Sir Ferdinando Gorges. Known as the 'King of the Black Market', he spent a good deal of his ill-gotten gains on the interior decoration, particularly the ornate and well-crafted plasterwork.

Berrington Hall has links with Moccas Court and Brampton Bryan, for the estate once belonged to the Cornewells who sold it to the Harleys in 1775. Thomas Haxley, a prosperous banker, employed Henry Holland, later responsible for the original Brighton Pavilion, to design the house, and Holland's father-in-law, Capability Brown, to lay out the grounds. They succeeded splendidly and Berrington is surely one of the most attractive and elegant Georgian houses in the country. Berrington Hall is now run by the National Trust but from 1901, it belonged to Lord Cawley, and there is a moving memorial in the Norman church at Eye to his three sons, all killed in the First World War.

It is tragic, that they, like their neighbours the Crofts and so many other thousands of Herefordshire's sons and daughters, could not have been laid to rest in the soil of their birth, the land that Henry James described as 'The copse-chequered slopes of rolling Hereford, white with the blossom of apples'.

DORMY HOUSE HOTEL

Willersey Hill,
Broadway,
Worcestershire WRl2 7LF
Tel: 01386 852711
Fax: 01386 858636
Email:reservations@dormyhouse.co.uk

Ingrid Philip-Sorensen, the Managing Director of the Dormy House Hotel is an in-spired leader and her desire to make Dormy House one of the best hotels in the country has almost been achieved. In fact most people staying here would tell you that it is the best. The house itself is charming and set in beautiful grounds - imagine a lovely day and some gentle exercise whilst you play on the professionally prepared putting green or endeavour to master the intricacies of croquet on the velvety top lawn whilst a jug of Sangria or a glass of Pimms is within reach - it conjures up the atmosphere that permeates the whole hotel. Inside this uniquely converted l7th century farmhouse ones first impression gleaned as one comes up the drive, is confirmed. It is warm, friendly and welcoming. Roaring log fires, time-worn leather chairs and deep sofas make the lounges just the place to be on a cold day. There is a friendly Barn Owl Bar where many people meet and eat at lunchtime or at the end of the day, and in the cosy cocktail bar you can take an aperitif before adjourning to the Tapestries Restaurant for dinner. The forty-nine bedrooms all en suite of course, have been individually appointed with a mixture of antiques and traditional pieces enhanced by attractive soft furnishings and many other nice touches give one the feeling of being pampered. The Dormy House Restaurant is superbly appointed and the staff quietly efficient without being obtrusive. The Chef is a talented man and with his brigade conjures up wonder-ful food which has earned the restaurant a deserved reputation over the years. The wine list has carefully chosen wines from the vineyards of the world. It is the sort of restaurant which makes a meal an occasion. For those who want a slightly more informal meal delicious bar food is also available.

Dormy House is licensed for weddings and it makes a superb venue both for the service and for the reception. The attention to detail ensures that the bride and groom, their bridesmaids and families have a day they will never forget. Equally, the specially created Tivoli Room is a state-of-the-art venue for meetings and conferences. Throughout the year there are special events at Dormy House including a Summer Ball, a Jazz Brunch, a Night at the Opera and a romantic Valentine's Break. Dormy Diversions offer you a Sauna or Steam session in total privacy, you can relax in the games room - with pool or bar billiards or keep up your fitness regime using the cardio-vascular equipment in the gym. If you are a walker the hotel's nature trail will provide you with a great deal of pleasure. Maybe you would like to hire one of the hotel's mountain bikes to explore the Cotswold country lanes

Dormy House is situated high above the village of Broadway in a rural setting over-looking thebeautiful Cotswold countryside. Easily found you drive from Broadway up Fish Hill when youreach the top you turn left where it is signed Picnic Area and Saintbury. Continue along this road for about one mile, turn left on the right-hand bend signposted Saintbury - and Dormy House is 100 metres on your left.

USEFUL INFORMATION

OPEN; *All year*
CHILDREN; *Welcome*
CREDIT CARDS; *All major cards*
LICENSED; *Yes. Fine wine list*
ACCOMMODATION; *49 rooms*
with en suite facilities
PETS; *By arrangement*
CONFERENCE FACII.ITIES; *Yes.*
Specially created room with every facility

RESTAURANT; *Superb cuisine*
BAR FOOD; *Delicious bar food available*
VEGETARIAN; *Always a choice*
DISABLED ACCESS; *Yes but no special facilities*
GARDEN; *Beautifully maintained grounds Putting green, Croquet*
SPORTS FACILITIES; *Games Room. Sauna Gym*

Licensed for weddings

DORMY HOUSE HOTEL

Willersey Hill,
Broadway,
Worcestershire WR12 7LF
Tel: 01386 852711
Fax: 01386 858636
Email:reservations@dormyhouse.co.uk

Ingrid Philip-Sorensen, the Managing Director of the Dormy House Hotel is an inspired leader and her desire to make Dormy House one of the best hotels in the country has almost been achieved. In fact most people staying here would tell you that it is the best. The house itself is charming and set in beautiful grounds - imagine a lovely day and some gentle exercise whilst you play on the professionally prepared putting green or endeavour to master the intricacies of croquet on the velvety top lawn whilst a jug of Sangria or a glass of Pimms is within reach - it conjures up the atmosphere that permeates the whole hotel. Inside this uniquely converted 17th century farmhouse ones first impression gleaned as one comes up the drive, is confirmed. It is warm, friendly and welcoming. Roaring log fires, time-worn leather chairs and deep sofas make the lounges just the place to be on a cold day. There is a friendly Barn Owl Bar where many people meet and eat at lunchtime or at the end of the day, and in the cosy cocktail bar you can take an aperitif before adjourning to the Tapestries Restaurant for dinner. The forty-nine bedrooms all en suite of course, have been individually appointed with a mixture of antiques and traditional pieces enhanced by attractive soft furnishings and many other nice touches give one the feeling of being pampered. The Dormy House Restaurant is superbly appointed and the staff quietly efficient without being obtrusive. The Chef is a talented man and with his brigade conjures up wonderful food which has earned the restaurant a deserved reputation over the years. The wine list has carefully chosen wines from the vineyards of the world. It is the sort of restaurant which makes a meal an occasion. For those who want a slightly more informal meal delicious bar food is also available.

Dormy House is licensed for weddings and it makes a superb venue both for the service and for the reception. The attention to detail ensures that the bride and groom, their bridesmaids and families have a day they will never forget. Equally, the specially created Tivoli Room is a state-of-the-art venue for meetings and conferences. Throughout the year there are special events at Dormy House including a Summer Ball, a Jazz Brunch, a Night at the Opera and a romantic Valentine's Break. Dormy Diversions offer you a Sauna or Steam session in total privacy, you can relax in the games room - with pool or bar billiards or keep up your fitness regime using the cardio-vascular equipment in the gym. If you are a walker the hotel's nature trail will provide you with a great deal of pleasure. Maybe you would like to hire one of the hotel's mountain bikes to explore the Cotswold country lanes

Dormy House is situated high above the village of Broadway in a rural setting overlooking thebeautiful Cotswold countryside. Easily found you drive from Broadway up Fish Hill when youreach the top you turn left where it is signed Picnic Area and Saintbury. Continue along this road for about one mile, turn left on the right-hand bend signposted Saintbury - and Dormy House is 100 metres on your left.

USEFUL INFORMATION

OPEN; *All year*
CHILDREN; *Welcome*
CREDIT CARDS; *All major cards*
LICENSED; *Yes. Fine wine list*
ACCOMMODATION; *49 rooms*
with en suite facilities
PETS; *By arrangement*
CONFERENCE FACILITIES; *Yes.*
Specially created room with every facility

RESTAURANT; *Superb cuisine*
BAR FOOD; *Delicious bar food available*
VEGETARIAN; *Always a choice*
DISABLED ACCESS; *Yes but no special*
facilities
GARDEN; *Beautifully maintained grounds*
Putting green, Croquet
SPORTS FACILITIES; *Games Room.*
Sauna Gym

Licensed for weddings

THE CROWN INN AT HOPTON

Hopton Wafers,
Cleobury Mortimer, Nr Kidderminster
Worcestershire DY14 0NB

Tel: 01299 270372   Fax: 01299 271127

Two miles west of Cleobury Mortimer, on the A4117, nestling at the base of Titterstone Clee you find the quiet hamlet of Hopton Wafers and at its margin a lovingly restored 16th Century coaching inn - The Crown. Here one cannot help relaxing: it is a place of peace and quietude well loved by all who cross its welcoming portal. Today, in the efficient hands of Alan and Liz Matthews, it has never been better or more welcoming.

In the 'Rent Room' Bar where tenant farmers once paid their rents to the local squire, you can relax in front of the large Inglenook fireplace enjoying a well kept pint while listening to the banter of the locals, or, noting the highly polished horse brasses and other memorabilia that add to the ambience of The Crown. The Rent Room Bar and Lounge are sympathetically decorated to complement their ancient timber beams and stonework. Select your drink from a wide range of fine wines and spirits, or from the varied cask conditioned draught beers, whilst you ponder the menu.

Well known for the high standard of its food, The Crown prides itself on serving delicious fare, whether in the bar, adjacent lounge or delightful Hopton Poachers Restaurant. In the latter you dine beneath a wealth of exposed beams, warmed by yet another large Inglenook fireplace. It is a great place to have a business lunch, a lively family get-together or an intimate, candlelit dinner for two. The menu is imaginative, extensive and seasonal, using only fresh ingredients, lovingly prepared and attractively presented. The carefully chosen wine list, compiled using a number of local merchants, and a comprehensive selection of fine Vintage Ports, Armagnacs and Cognacs are always available to complement your meal.

For those wanting to stay in this charming hostelry there are 7 en suite bedrooms which have been individually decorated and furnished in cottage style with antique furniture, interesting paintings, prints and objets d'art. All have telephone, remote control colour TV and a hostess tray. Here you have everything you need from the modern world but continue to enjoy the intimacy and personal service of an old, family run, village inn.

USEFUL INFORMATION

OPEN; *All year*
CHILDREN; *Welcome*
LICENSED; *Full On. Fine wines*
CREDIT CARDS; *All major cards except Amex*
ACCOMMODATION; *7 En suite rooms*
GARDEN; *Yes*

RESTAURANT; *Delicious, imaginative fare*
BAR FOOD; *Wide choice*
VEGETARIAN; *Yes*
DISABLED ACCESS; *No*
PETS; *No dogs in bedrooms*

FELTON HOUSE
Felton,
Herefordshire HRl 3PH
Tel: 01432 820366

Felton House has immense character, in a tranquil setting of beautiful gardens, set in the rich agricultural land of Herefordshire. With views to the Welsh hills, the Victorian/ Edwardian character of this house settles nicely in the Herefordshire countryside and Welsh borderlands. For 5,000 years there have been people living in Felton; evidenced by the Bronze Age Woodhenge, the recording in the Domesday Book of 1086, and the church which has been maintained since 1556. Felton House was built in 1851 with the Verger's Cottage (now let for holidays) soon after. The house actually forms the heart of Felton with the rest being made up of 6 farms and cottages. There are approximately 80 people in the parish! Marjorie and Brian Roby arrived in 1977 and have restored the house to it's former glory. Everything is in keeping with it's Victorian/Edwardian heritage and has been thoughtfully and immaculately renovated. Brian takes charge of the gardens, which are just over 3 acres in size, and has extensively remodelled them, planting trees and shrubs, making it a haven of quiet spots where visitors can sit and relax. There is a garden stage which was used between 1919 and 1939 to produce Shakespeare's plays. Actors were local characters including farm labourers and inn keepers daughters. This interesting history is all recorded in the stained glass windows of the local church. Felton House is one of those places you return to time and time again, and recommend to friends. This has everything to do with the hospitality extended by Marjorie and Brian who do all they possibly can to make you welcome. You sleep in an 18th century four-poster bed or an Edwardian brass bed or even a Victorian mahogany half tester! Most rooms have either private bathrooms or en suite shower rooms, and complimentary refreshments are provided. These can also be taken in the garden room, the sitting room, the library or the garden. The dining room is a beautiful relaxing room where breakfast is served and has a history all of it's own. You would have to stay at least two weeks to sample everything on the menu. All tastes are catered for; from full English to Continental to vegetarian. Local fresh produce is used where possible. The local inns, one within walking distance, serve excellent evening meals. A unique service which just rounds off the delights of this country house is the free route planning service that Marjorie and Brian offer. Whether your interest be castles, antiques, food, golf or any other, they will give helpful advice and plan your day (or whole holiday) as you require. This is an excellent holiday retreat with service and surroundings difficult to surpass.

USEFUL INFORMATION

OPEN; *All year*
CHILDREN; *Welcome, baby-sitting service*
CREDIT CARDS; *None taken*
GARDEN; *3 acres, beautifully kept*
ACCOMMODATION; *4 rooms*

DINING ROOM; *Breakfasts for all tastes*
VEGETARIAN; *Catered for*
LICENSED; *No*
DISABLED ACCESS; *Restricted*
PETS; *Welcome*

YE HOSTELRIE HOTEL

Goodrich, Ross-on-Wye,
Hereford HR9 6HX
Tel: 01600 890241 Fax: 01600 890838

Goodrich, with its famous castle is one of the most exciting and beautiful places in the Wye Valley. The 12th century castle is the only remaining fortress in Herefordshire, where its last inhabitant was Charles I during the Civil War. A fascinating place to visit and where better to stay than Ye Hostelrie Hotel which overlooks the castle's walls. Every building in this small village has some historic interest and there is none quite so dramatic as Ye Old Hostelrie Hotel with its pinnacles and tall latticed windows which dominate the small main street.

David and Heather Brown and their son Matthew, own the 17th century Ye Hostelrie Hotel, and they will tell you that as hoteliers, their aim is to make your stay, whether it is for Morning Coffee, Lunch, Dinner or residential, as comfortable, welcoming and friendly as possible. They can make you laugh, respect your privacy or just chat. The choice is yours but you can rest assured that you will leave here with very happy memories and a great desire to return as soon as possible.

Inside, the hotel is attractively furnished with great attention to detail The bedrooms are all en suite and individually decorated, all have colour television, clock radio and courtesy tray. Downstairs the hotel has two restaurants which are tranquil and elegant and in which either the ÁLa Carte or Table d'hôte menu offers genuinely home-cooked fare. The dishes are wide ranging with a great emphasis on locally produced meat, poultry and game. Fish also features largely and Vegetarians are not forgotten. Every meal has been well thought out whether it is a Starter, a main course or a dessert. On Sundays a traditional lunch is served with succulent Roast Beef and all the trimmings, Roast Lamb, or Chicken, with fish for those who prefer it and a vegetarian dish. Fresh Seasonal Vegetables, Roast and Boiled Potatoes and Yorkshire Pudding make the meal complete. There is an extensive Bar Menu available every day and you will find the bar stocks a range of real ales. Many fine wines are also available. Ye Hostelrie Hotel is perfect for a holiday and equally perfect for a Wedding or a Christening, Private Party or Conference. The staff go out of their way to make these occasions run like clockwork and to provide a carefree, happy day for guests or delegates.

You will never be at a loss for something to do or somewhere to go if you stay here. If your interests lie in sporting activities you can go canoeing, walk, climb, pony trek, cycle, play golf, go caving, windsurfing, hang-gliding, shoot or fish. Taking a balloon flight over The Wye Valley is a wonderful way of seeing its beauty and splendour. The bustling market towns of Ross-on-Wye and Monmouth are full of interest. The hotel will provide you with packed lunches to help you get the best out of your day.

USEFUL INFORMATION

OPEN; *All year inc. Christmas*
CHILDREN; *Welcome*
CREDIT CARDS; *All major cards*
LICENSED; *Full On. Fine wines*
ACCOMMODATION; *6 en suite rooms*
PETS; *Yes*

RESTAURANT; *Good home-cooked fare*
BAR FOOD; *Wide range*
VEGETARIAN; *Always a choice*
DISABLED ACCESS; *No*
GARDEN; *Yes*

THE SWAN AT HAY HOTEL

Church Street,
Hay-on-Wye,
Hereford HR3 5DQ

Tel: 01497 821188   Fax: 01497 821424

Hay on Wye is a delightful, small market town on the Welsh border. Few people can resist its charm. It nestles into a calm river valley at the foot of wild mountain scenery and affords anyone who comes here with the pleasure of seeking out the dozens of antiquarian bookshops that have made it the 'town of books' and exploring the maze of streets and alleys that have changed little from medieval times. Within easy reach of Hay there is a wealth of interesting places to visit including the spectacular show caves at Dan-yr-Ogof, the priceless Mappa Mundi in Hereford Cathedral and guided tours of the Royal Welsh crystal factory in Rhayder.

Having explored you will be hungry and thirsty and one doubts if there is a pleasanter place to stay, eat and drink than The Swan at Hay. For centuries there has been a hostelry on this site and the present building dates from 1821. However in 1987 Rosemary and Colin Vaughan bought The Swan and in the ensuing years they have transformed it into a luxurious 3-star hotel without in anyway detracting from the elegance of the building. Inside it is warm, comfortable, beautifully furnished and offers you two different places in which to eat. The Cygnet Restaurant with its gorgeous peony shades has a first class a la carte menu prepared lovingly by talented chefs whose passion is food. Everything is freshly cooked, they make their own bread and cakes, and use fresh local produce and herbs from the garden. Vegetarians have a menu for both eating places. You will find the staff efficient, helpful and very friendly. If you just want to have a drink you may welcome the opportunity to meet up with locals in Drakes Bar. Having eaten here and discovered how good it is, you will probably be more than tempted to stay in one of the very comfortable, beautifully appointed bedrooms - all en suite of course. A Swan at Hay Special Break is available throughout the year.

USEFUL INFORMATION

OPEN; *All year*
CHILDREN; *Welcome*
CREDIT CARDS; *All major cards*
LICENSED; *Yes*
ACCOMMODATION; *19 en suite rooms*
PETS; *Dogs by arrangement*

RESTAURANT; *A La Carte. Delicious*
BAR MEALS; *Daily choice. Traditional*
VEGETARIAN; *Special menus*
DISABLED ACCESS; *No special facilities*
GARDEN; *Yes, 2 tiered, beautiful*

HEDLEY LODGE GUESTHOUSE,
Belmont Abbey,
Abergavenny Road,
Hereford HR2 9RZ

Tel: 01432 277475 Fax: 01432 277597

Of course Belmont Abbey has always had a guest house, or at least guests rooms available for visitors. For the most part these were reserved for visiting monks and male guests. Today Hedley Lodge is a modern, comfortable guesthouse, open to all, offering basic single or the more 'upmarket' twin-bedded en suite rooms. Every twin room has television, direct dial telephones and a beverage tray. The single rooms have access to a TV Lounge, Library and Kitchenette. It has three crowns from the Heart of England Tourist Board and is set in the glorious Herefordshire countryside providing an ideal place for peace and tranquillity. Fr James is the Guestmaster - always there with a welcoming smile and he is ably assisted by other monks who also provide valuable cover and assistance,

Throughout history monasteries have welcomed guests from all walks of life, from kings to pilgrims and the poor. Today many guests come to Belmont to take part in the life and prayer of the monks or to share in some peace and quiet. The Guest House also caters for people who are travelling, sightseeing, working or simply wish to 'get away' for a few days. Hedley Lodge is licensed and the food is delicious, traditional English and plenty of it. It is a contented happy house with few restrictions and always a genuinely warm welcome at whatever time of the year.

Recently a new function room has been added which will hold 200 people for wedding receptions, conferences and other occasions. Well-appointed it is much in demand. You can well imagine what a furore this new venture caused. The thought of monks hosting discos and wild parties in the 'hallowed cloisters' was wide of the mark but the media loved it. Headlines read 'Parties by Prior arrangement' and 'Get the party habit'! It is a delightful setting, the occasions are catered for with great skill and taste. But above all Hedley Lodge provides peaceful, restful accommodation for whatever your needs.

USEFUL INFORMATION

OPEN; *All year*
CHILDREN; *By arrangement*
CREDIT CARDS; *None taken*
LICENSED; *Yes*
ACCOMMODATION; *12 rooms, 8 en suite*
PETS; *No*

DINING ROOM; *Good, traditional English fare*
VEGETARIAN; *By arrangement*
DISABLED ACCESS; *No*
GARDEN; *Yes*

THE MERTON HOTEL,
Commercial Road,.
Hereford HR1 2BD

Tel: 01432 265925 Fax: 01432 354983

This well known and highly respected hotel has a name that originates from the 11th century Bishop of Hereford, Walter-de-Merton. Centuries later the building housed Hereford County's Prison Officer, and then became a Coaching Inn some 140 years ago. With great care and attention to detail, The Merton Hotel has been brought into the modern world, offering every facility expected by today's traveler but retaining the rustic charm, the quiet elegance of the past. It is essentially a friendly place where one feels comfortable and at home. The staff are well-trained and unobtrusively ensure that everyone is cared for.

The hotel has 19 bedrooms each beautifully furnished to a high standard. All the rooms have en suite bathrooms, colour television , direct dial telephone, a hospitality tray and hair dryer with the added bonus of Room service if you choose. Guests also have the use of the Leisure Facilities, which include a fully equipped gymnasium, sauna, steam room and solarium - or aromatherapy session to relieve the tensions after a strenuous days business.

One of great pleasures of staying at The Merton is The Governors Restaurant. A warm friendly atmosphere is the first thing that strikes you but then you become aware of the elegant surroundings, the crisp white linen softened by pink cloths and linen napkins -absolutely right for the enjoyment of a perfect meal. The menu, whether it is Á La Carte or Table d'hôte, is carefully chosen and prepared by chefs who are both imaginative and innovative. The freshest of ingredients are always used. The end result is a delicious meal accompanied by wine from a well-stocked cellar. Recently The Governors was awarded 'Best Restaurant in Hereford' - a well deserved accolade. Celebration dinners, corporate seminars, weddings, conferences for up to 80 are treated with the same meticulous attention as the private dinner for two.

USEFUL INFORMATION

OPEN; *All year*
CHILDREN; *Welcome*
CREDIT CARDS; *All major cards*
LICENSED; *Yes. Excellent wine cellar*
ACCOMMODATION; *9dbl.2tw.8sgl*
PETS; *Yes*

RESTAURANT; *Award winning delicious food*
VEGETARIAN; *Catered for*
DISABLED ACCESS; *No*
GARDEN; *No*

PENCRAIG COURT COUNTRY HOUSE HOTEL

Pencraig, Ross-On-Wye,
Herefordshire HR9 6HR
Tel: 01989 770306 Fax: 01989 770040

This fine Georgian country house set in three-and-a-half acres of gardens, lawns and secluded woodland overlooking the River Wye, was built in 1780 although its foundations date from a much earlier time. Originally occupied by the Rev W. Holt-Beever it later became the home of Sir Humphrey de Trafford and his family who remained in residence until the 1950s. It has the atmosphere of well-being that only well loved homes have and this is enhanced by the manner in which the current owners Mike Clifford, his wife Sue and her sister Jan Bull run the hotel. They have made it a house of character and elegance throughout. It is beautifully furnished with some wonderful pieces including many treasured family ones. You will see attractive arrangements of plates on the walls, fine pictures, a profusion of plants and fresh flowers. The drawing room has that comfortable, lived in air with a fine fireplace and large windows and Grandpa's favourite fireside chair inviting you to curl up by the fire with a book.. The small sitting room has a collection of crystal salt cellars and fascinating family photographs. The charming dining room, which is open to non-residents, has a magnificent oak table which extends to seat up to eighteen people. It is here you will enjoy the sumptuous breakfast and the first class dinners which may be cooked by Mike, Sue or Jan who are all excellent cooks and rise to the challenge of constantly producing traditional English food with a light and sure touch. Everything is fresh and often includes Herefordshire beef, Welsh lamb and Wye salmon. Vegetables and herbs come from the kitchen garden and there are home-made jams and chutneys. Afternoon tea is always a treat when one is staying away and at Pencraig Court you will be tempted by the delicious home-made cakes and scones served in fine china with pretty matching tray cloths. The wine cellar has excellent vintage French wines together with others from around the world - a cellar that equals any in the county.
Most people are fascinated by the patchwork quilts which cover the beds in the individually decorated eleven bedrooms, all of which are en-suite. These quilts were brought from America by Jan, some of which are antique, dating from the early 1800's. The rooms are delightful and full of extra little touches that make guests feel at home. There is colour television, direct dial telephones and a hostess tray in each room. One bedroom is designed for the romantics and furnished to show off a splendid antique four-poster bed with stunning gold brocade covers, drapes embossed with cherubs and stars, and side-curtains of gossamer-fine material decorated with fleur-de-lys. Pencraig will provide you with a wonderful holiday or break, ease the strain if you are on business, at any time of the year. The gardens are glorious in summer and the natural warmth of this lovely old house, assisted by central heating and a log fire in the drawing room, is good to come back to after a crisp winter walk. Sporting parties can enjoy excellent golf, fishing or shooting and dogs are happily accommodated by arrangement.

USEFUL INFORMATION

OPEN; *All year*
CHILDREN; *Welcome*
CREDIT CARDS; *All major cards*
except Amex/Diners
LICENSED; *Yes. Excellent cellar*
ACCOMMODATION; *11 en suite rooms*

DINING ROOM; *Delicious, traditional home-made Food using fresh local produce wherever possible Open to on-residents*
VEGETARIAN; *By arrangement*
DISABLED ACCESS; *No special facilities*
GARDEN; *Yes, wonderful views*

CADMORE LODGE
HOTEL, RESTAURANT & COUNTRY CLUB

Berrington Green, St Michaels,
Nr Tenbury Wells, Worcestershire

Tel/Fax: 01584 810044
E Mail. EAW@cadmorelodge.demon.co.uk.
www.cadmorelodge.demon.co.uk

When Cadmore Lodge first started a few years ago it was plain to see that the owners, John and Elizabeth Weston had excellent plans for its well being. Over the years it has steadily blossomed and today offers something special. John, a Civil Engineer, designed and created the whole venture while Elizabeth is a Wild Life expert and a keen sportswoman. You will find Cadmore Lodge 2 ½ miles west of Tenbury Wells, set in a Private Estate. It's idyllic lakeside setting is a perfect venue for Weddings, Private Parties and Conference with the Lake Room seating 160 guests comfortably. For anyone enjoying sporting activities it is ideal. There is a 16 metre Pool, Spa, Cardio Vascular Equipment and Steam Room as well as Scuba Diving Tuition. A well laid out 9 hole golf course Par 68 (18 holes) 5132 yards, is open to the Public as well as Members. You can fish on two lakes. The first has Fly Fishing for Rainbow and Brown Trout and the second Coarse Fishing. Tennis Courts and a Bowling Green complete the picture. There are special 2 Day Golf or Fishing Breaks. There is much to explore in the area including the historic town of Ludlow just seven miles away and both the cathedral cities of Hereford and Worcester are within 20 miles.

For those who enjoy good food in attractive surroundings, the Restaurant is open daily for Lunches, Dinners and Bar meals. The chefs are not only talented but have flair and imagination and are happy to cater for anything from Gourmet, Á La Carte and Table d'hôte to Grills. The home-made desserts will tempt even the strongest willed. The emphasis in always on fresh local produce. What strikes one most throughout Cadmore Lodge is the warm, welcoming atmosphere enhanced by log fires in winter. There are 13 en suite Double rooms, five of which are Luxury Rooms and 1 single en suite. Every room is beautifully furnished and well appointed with television and a well supplied hostess tray.

USEFUL INFORMATION

OPEN; *8am until after midnight*
CHILDREN; *Welcome*
CREDIT CARDS; *Visa/Mastercard Switch/Amex/Diners*
LICENSED; *Full & Supper License*
ACCOMMODATION; *14 en suite rooms*

RESTAURANT; *High quality, fresh produce*
BAR FOOD; *Good selection, good value*
VEGETARIAN; *Yes. 5/6 dishes daily*
DISABLED ACCESS; *Yes*
GARDEN; *60 acres, walks, patio by lake*

THE WHITE LION HOTEL
Upton-upon-Severn,
Worcester WR8 0HJ

Tel: 01684 592551 Fax: 01684 593333

In 1749 in Henry Fielding's book 'Tom Jones' this hotel was described as 'a house of exceedingly good repute'. Today the wind of change has swept through it with the arrival of two dedicated, professional and enthusiastic hoteliers, Jon and Chris Lear bringing it back to a standard which underlines those words written nearly three hundred years ago. The Lears looked around the White Lion before they bought it and had you been able to read into their minds at that moment you would have seen their brains ticking over so rapidly when they saw the huge potential this ancient establishment offered anyone with imagination and flair. Since they arrived virtually every room has been refurbished, redecorated and exciting changes either already made or in the offing.

Everything that was good about the White Lion has been preserved including the Wild Goose room and the Rose room; both rooms referred to by Henry Fielding. All 10 rooms have en suite facilities, colour TV, direct-dial telephones and radio alarms. Everything in fact to make one comfortable. Downstairs the busy bar is a haunt for locals who enjoy the banter and the great atmosphere into which they readily welcome newcomers. Jon Lear is a talented, inspired chef whose food has already won him a coveted Rosette in the short time he has been here. His Menu, served in the friendly Brasserie majors on English fare with a Mediterranean influence. Here you can have a one, two or a three course meal, a light lunch, in fact whatever you wish. Shortly a Licensed Coffee Shop and Patisserie will be opened, especially to cater for the morning and lunchtime trade and in due course a Continental Type open air Café will grace the back of the hotel - a delightful place to be on a warm day. The Brasserie can be booked for private parties seating up to 45 or 100 buffet style. The advent of the Lears has made The White Lion Hotel one of the best and most popular inns in the area - deservedly so. One looks forward to seeing what other enterprising ideas will stem from them!

History has always played a large part in the life of The White Lion Hotel. In the Civil War Price Rupert's men were incapable of engaging Cromwell's army - they had over indulged in the bar! It is also one of the best stops for walking the Severn Way and, yes, it does have a ghost!

USEFUL INFORMATION

OPEN; All year
CHILDREN; Welcome
CREDIT CARDS; All major cards
LICENSED; Full On
ACCOMMODATION; 10 rooms with
Private bathrooms

BRASSERIE; Superb English fare
with a hint of Mediterranean
BAR FOOD; Daily specials, light lunches
VEGETARIAN; Always a choice
DISABLED ACCESS; Bar & Brasserie
PETS; Well behaved welcome

Chapter 9

KENT & ESSEX

INCLUDES

Chapter 9

KENT AND ESSEX

If one wanted to choose somewhere that spelt out beauty, history, heritage and national pride then **Canterbury** in Kent, the Garden of England, would probably top the poll. It is for this reason that my tour of Kent this time is centred on this great, awe-inspiring Cathedral. You have only to stand back a little and watch the expression on the face of visitors as they see this building of incalculable beauty for the first time. Even for me, having visited it many, many times over many years, I still feel the tingle of excitement course through my blood every time I come here.

Canterbury was welcoming pilgrims 900 years ago and even then it was an ancient city. Three hundred years later Chaucer brought attention to it with his Canterbury Tales. The Cathedral dominates the city and is the spiritual centre for Christians who belong to the Church of England in many countries but the non-believers in the tenets of the Anglican Church are as much addicted to its beauty as anyone else. Thomas à Becket who was murdered within its walls by four knights who heeded Henry II's plea to rid him of 'this low born priest' has been revered as a martyr ever since that gruesome day.

There is so much to see in Canterbury but it is always the Cathedral that takes precedence. The Cathedral was rebuilt in 1067, with a crypt that is the largest in the world. There is the city's spectacular West Gate built in the time of Edward III. There are the medieval remains of the oldest part of the city, the Roman remains of a town house, the ruined St Augustine's Abbey, museums, fascinating lanes and a pedestrianised shopping centre that is hugely attractive. Great writers have always been associated with Canterbury. Its theatre is named after Christopher Marlowe, the 16th century playwright who was born here. Much of the story of Charles Dickens great novel, 'David Copperfield' is set in Canterbury. The House of Agnes in St Dunstan's Street belonged to his heroine. One of our greatest novelists, Joseph Conrad lived near the city and lies in its cemetery. The famous King's School was where Somerset Maugham, novelist and playwright was educated. Kings and Queens, noblemen, scholars, statesmen and men and women of all ranks have been among the city's guests, and they will continue to be until the end of time.

Canterbury's beginnings go back to the Iron Age and oddly enough the damage caused by German bombs in World War II which destroyed almost a third of its buildings, assisted archaeologists. The craters disclosed foundations more than a thousand years old and enabled them to trace its history from the time man first settled there long before Christ.

Over the years I have found that it is beneficial to stay in Canterbury and to alternate my days there by taking a full day in the Cathedral and the following day going out to the Kent countryside and exploring there. Too much Cathedral, beautiful and inspiring as it is, becomes a recipe for mental indigestion and almost being sated with loveliness, making one unable really to appreciate all that one sees.

The Cathedral Gate Hotel at 36 Burgate, is the ideal place to stay, dignified and welcoming, where comfort and hospitality are paramount. Built in 1438 it has stood for centuries between the tranquil haven of the Cathedral, its precincts and the busy commercial life of the city. The site is recorded from Saxon times and linkage with the Cathedral is recorded over a millennium. In medieval times the inn was called 'Sonne Hospice', the name later moving to an inn in neighbouring Sun Street, one of the English tea houses, written about by Charles Dickens. Every room reminds one of its medieval construction with sloping floors, massive oak beams and winding corridors. There is nothing medieval about its comfort however!

The martyrdom of Thomas à Becket is a well known fact and within days of his murder it turned Canterbury into a place of pilgrimage. He was canonised in 1173 and a year later a remorseful King Henry himself made the pilgrimage in an act of penance. The pilgrims were to help make Canterbury one of the richest and most magnificent churches of medieval times.

You may think Canterbury Cathedral holds the record for the number of steps one climbs up and down during your tour of the building. There are steps up the chancel, steps down to the transept and a flight of steps ascending to the pulpit. It is a journey of never ending thrills, stunning architecture, glorious glass and always this awareness that the Almighty is gazing upon us.

There is so much to see. In the Trinity Chapel, the ambulatories, the Corona and the east transepts is the finest 13th century glass in England. The stole screens in the chapel of Our Lady were a gift from the Black Prince. The famous 'Bell Harry' Tower was built at the end of the 15th century and completed in 1503. You will see how this slender, soaring central tower pulls the whole building together the lofty nave, the long straggling choir and retrochoir, the corona, the double transepts. There are those who have been heard to say that the lack of architectural unity makes for a 'higgledy piggledy' appearance but surely this is one of the great charms of this complex building. When it is time to leave my feet are aching and my head bursting with the overwhelming beauty. In my nostrils lingers the very special smell of the Cathedral.

The High Street is an unending source of delight. For example at No.37 there is a 12th century crypt and across the road is The Beaney Institute where archaeological items such as Roman glass, silver and Saxon finds from local excavations are exhibited. Cross over into St Margaret Street and you will find in a former church 'The Pilgrims Way', a fascinating exhibition portraying both the Canterbury Tales and medieval life generally. Just past the Yeomanry War memorial is Queen Elizabeth's Guest Chamber which began as a fifteenth century inn and was modernised in Restoration times. According to legend Queen Elizabeth I was entertained here and there is certainly a Royal monogram in the plaster of a first storey ceiling. And so the delight goes on. Across the River Stour by the King's Bridge is a group of half timbered cottages, the Weavers houses. They were built in the 16th century for the Hugenots who fled from France to escape religious persecution.

In All Saints Lane you will find a beautifully restored half timbered building in All Saints Court. It was originally built in the 15th century. Across the road is Cogan House the only existing early stone house of Canterbury in part remaining. Built about 1200 it has a fascinating history and must be seen. Within is the Tudor Tea Room and Garden where people can sit amidst the roses and apple trees on the lawn and enjoy a meal or walk across the aisled hall into the old Tudor dining room. It really is a wonderful building.

CHAPTER NINE

You will need many days and many walks if you are to uncover all Canterbury's treasures. On each of them you will discover many fresh delights and reminders of past ages. Nothing is farther than twenty minutes from the heart of the city when you take a walk round the city walls which enclosed the original Roman town.

One of the many attractive places outside Canterbury and close to **Faversham** is **Boughton-under-Blean** a pretty village in the hop growing and fertile fruit area of north eastern Kent. It is steeped in history, with a section of Roman Road having been discovered in the village. Chaucer mentioned Boughton in the prologue to the Canon Yeoman's Tale and it was also the scene of the Courtenany Riots in 1838 - the last battle to be fought on English soil. Here you will also find the 17th century Grade II Listed Garden Hotel and Restaurant, a charming 10 bedroomed hotel which you may well prefer to stay in rather than be amidst the bustle of Canterbury. There is an eighteen hole golf course close by.

At **Hernhill** also near Faversham, is **Mount Ephraim Gardens** at the heart of an 800 acre estate comprising the house and gardens, a progressive fruit farm, woodland and grazing, which acts like a magnet to those who enjoy the glory of a garden in a superb setting. The house rebuilt in 1870, but the home of the Dawes family for over 300 years, commands a magnificent view over the woodland park, orchards and the Swale and Thames Estuary. The gardens have a wonderful atmosphere of peace and charm. A word of warning; Mount Ephraim Gardens are not specially set up for disabled visitors as there is limited access for wheelchairs.

Then there is **Forwich on Stour** which was once the port for Canterbury. **Hackington** near the University was once a village in its own right. **Harbledown** appears in the Canterbury Tales as the last village before the destination of the pilgrims and it was here they would get their first glimpse of the Cathedral. To the east of Canterbury the village of **Wingham** is home to the Four Seasons restaurant which opens at night only and has superb food in a wonderful setting.

Another village to the south east of Canterbury is **Bridge,** a place of beauty and tranquillity. Many of the buildings are listed and Skippers of Bridge in the High Street is one of them. Built about 200 years ago it has a sense of permanence about it; a place that will continue to delight long after we have gone. It has been described as somewhere one goes as if to a dinner party rather than going out for a meal. Skippers is famous for its Bread and Butter Pudding - something not to be missed.

Supposing one were to decide on a longish tour that took one around the coast of Kent which is possible from Canterbury, then within fifteen minutes to the north you would come to **Whitstable** long renowned for its oysters but it has more than that to offer. There is good fishing, bathing from a shingle beach and good yachting facilities. A spit of land, known as 'The Street' juts about a mile and a half into the sea and provides a pleasant promenade at low tide. The Castle dates mainly from the 19th century but has a 15th century brick tower originally used as a look out post. Its parkland is open to the public. Whitstable has railway connections. Stevenson's Invicta (now preserved at Canterbury) pulled a train on the Whitstable-Canterbury line - the first passenger line to be opened in 1830. The tunnel through Tyler Hill was the first railway tunnel to be built in Britain and the line was finally closed in 1953. **The Oyster Fishing Exhibition** at Whitstable Harbour gave me a totally different outlook on this industry. Quite fascinating.

To the east the seaside resorts of **Westgate on Sea** and **Margate** have been popular for generations. The former is less boisterous than the latter but both have their adherents who would not go anywhere else. I cannot say that it is a holiday that would appeal to me but the countryside and the sea are both beautiful and you see a lot of happy, smiling faces so who am I to judge!

Broadstairs just round the North Foreland is a different kettle of fish. Here is a Regency resort which has not changed much since the society of those times put their stamp on it. It has miles of sheltered and sandy bays and to the north stand the chalk cliffs and lighthouses of the North Foreland, with wide views over the Thames Estuary. Bleak House is now a Dickens Museum containing early editions of his books, pictures, photographs and some personal items. Nearby Dickens House which also contains a museum was immortalised as the home of Betsy Trotwood in 'David Coppereld', written while Dickens was living in Broadstairs. In June every year a Dickens Festival is held, when the local people throng the streets in costumes of the period.

Down past **Ramsgate**, Sandwich and **Deal,** one comes to the beautiful St Margaret's Bay, part of the South Foreland Heritage Coast. Here at **West Cliff** is the stunning Wallets Court Hotel with the tiny church of St Peters opposite. It is a fascinating hotel in its own right but add that to the history of the building which first gets its mention in the Domesday Book and you cannot help being enthralled.

The garden at Wallet's is open to the rolling fields and the bracing sea air with its regularly swirling mists. It now contains a rather unusual treehouse, an all weather tennis court and a recently restored granary on Kentish straddle stones. During your wanderings from here you might visit the tiny church of St Peter where the Gibbon family who restored the house in the early 17th century, are all buried, or take a stroll up Pond Lane to a local vantage point. If you are feeling more energetic strike out for the White Cliffs and St Margaret's Bay. These have provided great inspiration for many writers, poets and artists over the years. The quintessential Englishman Noel Coward and also the man who created James Bond, Ian Fleming, both lived in the Bay at one time. The spectacular cliff tops just over a mile away from Wallet's are famous for their rare wild flowers and birds. One can lie there in the long grass for hours listening to the skylarks and watching the traffic on the Channel. On a clear day you can even see the French coastline which lies just over twenty miles away.

Dover at the end of the North Downs is famous for its White Cliffs but it is also of great historical importance. Apart from being an ancient port linking Britain with the Continent, it was once the walled Roman town of Dubris, and the start of the Roman road, Watling Street. Later it became the chief of the Cinque ports, which as I have written about in the Sussex chapter, were expected to supply ships for the Royal fleet. It is the largely Norman castle which dominates the town although the enormous activity of the port with its merchant shipping and busy ferry services keeps traffic flowing through the town almost twenty four hours a day. One of the best vantage points from which to view Dover is from Langdon Cliffs belonging to the National Trust, where you will have a birds eye view of the bustling Eastern Docks and miles of way marked footpaths across the flower rich cliff tops. Nowhere either will give you such a panoramic view over the straits of Dover.

The next part of my travels takes me to 'The Garden Coast' encompassing **Folke-stone, Hythe** & **Romney Marsh** which offers me endless pleasure both in the beautiful countryside, the sea and the history of the area together with the monasticism of the Romney Marshes.

Instead of returning to Canterbury directly, the M20 will take me to the busy town of **Ashford** and to the small medieval village of **Woodchurch** dating from about the 11th century. Here is another Wolsey Lodge, this time Prospect House. The house overlooks the large village green where cricket and football are played in season. There are two houses nearby which are both over 400 years old. It dates from 1789 but could be older as it has some very old beams in places. An old redbrick wall surrounds the house on two sides and the other sides are hedges. On warm summer days guests frequently have breakfast outside or sit in the shade under a large apple tree for tea. A wonderful house to stay in made even better by the owners Fiona Adams-Cairns and her South African husband. They are a fascinating couple who are widely travelled. Look at their visitors book and you will find comments such as ' Every night is a dinner party'. Le Shuttle is 25 minutes away. An hours drive will take you to Glyndebourne, Canterbury, of course, Dover Castle, the moated Leeds Castle, Churchill's home Chartwell and some wonderful gardens including Sissinghurst. Great place to stay. Just a little further south is **Appledore** where The Railway Inn offers hospitality to all weary travellers, and is an excellent spot for visiting the many surrounding attractions.

Royal Tunbridge Wells is beyond Sissinghurst to the west from Ashford. This is a town that must delight the eye. A distinguished spa at one time especially among persons of fashion in the 18th century, though the waters can still be drunk. Samuel Pepys and John Evelyn both visited and Beau Nash left Bath to become the master of Tunbridge Wells ceremonies in 1735. However it was Lord North who had made the waters popular a hundred years earlier. Charles I's wife Henrietta Maria came here after the birth of their son, the future Charles II in 1630. This was when the building of the town began. The Pantiles, the spa's oldest street was started in 1700. How beautiful this elegant arcade is enhanced by lime trees; its Italianate pillars supporting diverse frontages and a music balcony. The tiles were laid because Princess Anne - later to become Queen - threatened not to return after her son slipped on the original walk. Today flagstones have replaced almost all the tiles.

Royal Tunbridge Wells is blessed with many parks and gardens and a fine common with outcrops of weathered sandstone rocks. Such rocks are typical of the area, the source of its mineral waters, and an attraction for climbers: the nearby High Rocks, the Toad Rocks on Rushall Common; Bowles Rocks, Eridge, Harrison's Rocks, Groombridge and the Happy Valley. Lying at the heart of one of the most scenic stretches of countryside in England and surrounded by the unspoilt beauty of the Weald, Royal Tunbridge Wells is the perfect place for a short break or for a leisurely tour of the Kentish countryside.

You are spoilt for choice in the number of places you can visit. What about a leisurely cruise around **Bewl Water,** Southern water's beautiful reservoir at Lamberhurst? This is the largest area of inland water in south east England and set in the most attractive countryside. Also at Lamberhurst is **Scotney Castle Garden**, one of England's most romantic gardens surrounding the ruins of a 14th century moated castle. Rhododendrons, azaleas, waterlilies and wisteria flower in profusion.

Groombridge Place Gardens and **Enchanted Forest** provide another stunning day out. Surrounded by breathtaking parkland this mystical medieval site includes the famous Grade I Listed 17th century walled gardens set against the backdrop of the classical moated mansion and Enchanted Forest, which have inspired writers, artists and connoisseurs of beauty for hundreds of years.

To the north of Tunbridge Wells is **Tonbridge** a prosperous market town at the navigable extremity of the River Medway, where it diverges into formidable streams. A settlement that has been strategically important since Anglo Saxon and probably Roman times. The River Walk along the Medway, through willow-lined meadows gives a fine view of **Tonbridge Castle**. Its Norman to 13th century ruins, on a site defended since 1088, are substantial: the shell of the keep, curtain walls, round-towered gatehouse. Some of Tonbridge's 18th century houses are built of castle stone. It is an exciting place to visit and you are invited to travel back over 700 years to join the Lords of Tonbridge Castle and experience a vivid recreation of the sights, sounds and excitement of 13th century castle life.

Penshurst Place and **Gardens** near Tonbridge must be visited. The beautiful medieval stately home of Viscount de L'Isle, with its magnificent Barons Hall dates from 1341. The splendid gardens were first laid out in the 16th century. Travelling further north takes us to **Maidstone** where the beautiful **Langley Oast** is one of my favourite places to stay.

Two of the loveliest castles in Kent and some say in the world, are **Leeds Castle** 4 miles east of Maidstone and **Hever Castle** near Edenbridge, the childhood home of Anne Boleyn. Both will provide you with hours of delight and will remain in your memory for years to come.

The Medway towns must not be forgotten. They have always been places of great interest. Made up of **Strood, Gillingham, Chatham** and **Rochester**, they are steeped in history and none more so than the ancient cathedral city of Rochester on the lower reaches of the River Medway. It is a major port and an industrial centre and such a busy place but Rochester's older buildings are clustered around the Cathedral and in the High Street where they were confined by the medieval walls. The city is closely associated with the novelist Charles Dickens, and features more often in his books than any other place, apart from London, although Portsmouth, where he was born, has The Charles Dickens Birthplace Museum. Many great cities have been built around a river. Rochester is no exception.

Rochester's Norman legacy cannot be missed. The great square keep of The Castle towers above the River Medway, a daunting reminder of the history of the city. It was on this site that the Romans originally built the first fort to guard the bridge which connected the Imperial Route of Watling Street, leading from London to Dover. The Cathedral is the second oldest in England and is a regular place of pilgrimage for historians and worshippers alike. It has many visitors from all over the world who delight in the majesty even though it is much altered and reconstructed, with a spire dating only from the early years of this century.

Chatham has had a long and distinguished history and until recent years been inextricably involved in the life of Her Majesty's Navy. Those days are gone but a visit to **The Historic Dockyard** will give you at least five hours of absorbing interest. There are no less than 47 Scheduled Ancient Monuments, forming the most completely preserved Georgian dockyard in the world, dry docks and covered slips, timber mast houses and seasoning sheds, huge storehouses and the quarter mile long working ropery stand beside the elegant Commissioner's house and garden, officers' terrace and dockyard church. Now a living working museum this tells of the lives of the dockyard craftsmen whose skills - from carpentry and caulking to rigging and forging - made the British fleet the finest in the world. No one can fail to be fascinated by what they see. With seven main attractions plus skills and crafts in action, it is not surprising visitors stay an average of 5 hours.

Kent has so much beauty to offer in every direction. Its name 'The Garden of England' is fully justified. I constantly promise myself that the next time I come here I will spend more time - it is never long enough.

I lived in Suffolk for a while on the Shotley Peninsula looking over the River Stour to **Harwich.** This allowed me to become happily familiar with the corner of Essex that includes the old Roman town of **Colchester**, and the glorious Dedham Vale as well as many of the smaller villages including **Wix** between Harwich and Colchester, bypassed by the A120 which is a direct route to London. It is a place surrounded by local beauty spots like **Mistley** where one of Great Britain's largest population of mute swans live and the twin 'Mistley Towers' stand the only remains of Robert Adams ecclesiastical work in England.

Colchester is Britain's oldest recorded town and has 2000 years of fascinating history and heritage to discover. It is a history involving the Romans, the Saxons and the Normans which has been interpreted and displayed using the most exciting and up-to-date methods in the town's museums.

When the Emperor Claudius received the surrender of the British Kings here in AD 43, Colchester had been inhabited for something like a thousand years. It was at that period named Camulodunum, and was the capital of Cunobelin (Shakespeare's Cymbeline), ruler of south-east England and the most powerful man in pre-Roman Britain.

This was the first city the Roman's founded and it was later sacked by Boadecia and the Iceni, but after her defeat it was rebuilt as a walled city and became one of the most important centres of Roman administration. Parts of the walls may still be seen, and the arch of the Balkerns gate remains, which marked the entrance of the Roman road from London. The many Roman remains are the nucleus of the museum contained in the massive keep of the Norman castle, built in 1085 on the vaults of the Roman Temple of Claudius. In the medieval period, Colchester was a centre of the cloth industry and many Flemish refugees settled here in the 17th and 18th centuries in the area around West Stockwell Street known as the Dutch Quarter. This has been restored.

Colchester oysters were famous in Roman days and are still so today, but as a fishing and trading port, the town is no longer significant. The town however is significant for the 1000 acres of public gardens and parks. You should not fail to walk in the glorious park surrounding the Castle which was built by William the Conqueror in 1076 and a visit to its museum is strongly recommended.

A stroll away from the castle and close to the heart of the town is The Globe Hotel, in North Station Road. Here they offer a truly comprehensive service aiming to cater for the entire family as well as the unaccompanied traveller. The Salisbury Hotel at 112 Butt Road, is a Freehouse which offers good food, comfortable en suite rooms and great hospitality. If you would rather stay outside the town, The Cross Inn and Motel, at Burnt Heath Ardleigh Road, Great Bromley between Colchester and Harwich is the answer. This small and unpretentious country pub has only one sign of modernity and that is in its two en suite motel units. Its simplicity is charming; within the pub there is a welcoming, low ceilinged bar, soft lights, comfortable seats and in winter a roaring open fire. Food is all important and whilst no one would ever describe what is on offer as haute cuisine, it is genuinely home-cooked and you will never leave the table hungry.

The **Vale of Dedham** is something very special and immortalised by John Constable. This north-east corner of Essex is where the River Stour forms the boundary with Suffolk and is an area of outstanding scenic beauty. It is still possible to stroll through the meadows and along the river banks with their abundance of flora and fauna, or explore the delightful villages with their impressive medieval churches and old pubs. It is constantly changing scenery. From **Bures** to **Harwich** the river loses its quiet willow-lined banks enclosing the gently flowing water, home to colourful ducks, elegant swans, and moorhens and becomes tidal flats beyond Manningtree and the dominant east coast. From here it is easy to reach the enchanting wool towns and villages like **Lavenham, Hadleigh, Kersey** and **East Bergholt,** just over the Suffolk border and of course Dedham itself.

Finally away down the river where the Stour and the Orwell estuaries form Harwich Harbour, The Pier at Harwich Restaurant and Hotel is excellent. It has two restaurants - the à la carte Pier restaurant specialising in the finest seafood or, alternately, the Ha'penny Pier offering more modestly priced fish dishes, ideal for the family. The hotel has six bedrooms with ensuite bathrooms and splendid views over the busy harbour.

Further south many places have been encroached by the ever stretching tentacles of London, but there are still places to visit and stay that will delight and enthral you. One of these charming towns is **Burnham-on-Crouch**, where **The Copper Kettle** is a popular haunt for visitors and locals. First class food, a range of teas and coffees, smiling, friendly service. Owners Mr and Mrs Howard Watling have built an excellent reputation. Seats 30 people comfortably is open all year. No Credit Cards. Well behaved pets and Children welcome. Free Tourism Information. It can be found at 159 Station Road. Tel No 01621 782203.

Southend-on-Sea is very much a beach type holiday resort and caters very well for the family. Nearby at **Thorpe Bay** you can stay at the **Roslin Hotel** which boasts one of the finest views of the Thames Estuary. This top class hotel offers superb accommodation and exquisite English cuisine.

THE RAILWAY HOTEL,
Station Road,
Appledore,
Kent TN26 2DF
Tel: 01233 758253/758668 Fax: 01233 758705

Family-run hotels invariably offer guests hospitality that is friendly, informal and above all welcoming. This is certainly true of The Railway Hotel which has been there, in various guises, since the railway came to Appledore in 1851. The first hotel completed in 1853 was named 'Man of Kent Railway Tavern' and from that day on it has been a favourite port of call for locals as well as station staff and linesmen employed by the railway. The tavern flourished until 1893 when the landlord noticed that huge cracks had appeared in the cellar. When they looked into it further it was discovered that the whole building was gradually slipping into the nearby dyke. The building was condemned and finally demolished in 1894. A new and much larger tavern arose from the rubble and was named 'The Railway Hotel'. Since that day it has become more and more popular and has been part of fascinating bits of history. Imagine the scene in 1914, the beginning of World War I, when the Railway Hotel and the station yard would have been the scene of many tearful farewells. The Hotel has seen many changes since it was first built but the aim has always been to give out generous warmth and hospitality, and so it does today in the hands of Monty and Virginia Lowry.

The Railway Hotel has 12 en suite bedrooms, all furnished in a modern fashion and of a good standard. Each room has television, direct dial telephone and an abundant hospitality tray. The bars are cheerful places and the food is excellent. One can dine in the comfortable restaurant or the bar. The menu is largely traditional English with a good choice and every day there are tasty and tempting Daily Specials. You would have to have an enormous appetite to tackle the magnificent Railway Hotel Porterhouse Steak! Above all The Railway Hotel offers value for money.

One of the facilities the Hotel offers is conference accommodation and can cater for receptions for up to 100 people. Efficiently planned and run, these occasions highlight the expertise that the Lowrys have.

Appledore is surrounded by places of interest to visit including Canterbury, Eastbourne, Hastings, Rye and New Romney with its smallest Railway. Cycles are available for use by guests and for the sporting minded there are plenty of activities locally including Golf, Bowls and Dancing.

USEFUL INFORMATION

OPEN; *All year*
CHILDREN; *Yes*
CREDIT CARDS; *All major cards*
LICENSED; *Full On*
ACCOMMODATION; *12 en suite rooms*
PETS; *Yes* **GARDEN;** *Yes*

RESTAURANT; *Traditional English delicious and value for money*
BAR FOOD; *Good choice*
VEGETARIAN; *Always a choice*
DISABLED ACCESS; *Yes*

THE DUKE OF YORK

Southend Road,
South Green,
Billericay, Essex CM12PR

Tel: 01277 651403 Fax:: 01277 632621

This is a fascinating hostelry with a great history albeit only going back as far as the beginning of the 19th century. There has been a Duke of York on this site since before 1837, converted from two cottages built around 1801 by Thomas Smith, a millwright. From about 1856 it reverted to a private house and then after several changes it was leased as a beerhouse to Gray & Sons who finally bought it on the 31st December 1896. Over the years it has acquired great character and many features remain from the early days including the old beams in the bar and a ghost called Swanee who shows his disapproval of change by moving things about and causing pictures to fall! If you would like to learn more about the Duke of York, Mrs White, the present landlord will show you a hand-written account by two brothers whose grandparents, Mr and Mrs Swann, became the tenants in 1896. Everything you see or read about the Duke of York confirms what an interesting place it is to be. What has also happened over the years is the gradual building of a tremendous atmosphere of well being. Mrs White ensures this continues. She and her staff are friendly and welcoming and know how to look after customers.

The Duke of York has become synonymous with good food and good wine. The latter is international in its range and one of the most comprehensive wine lists you will find in any hostelry. It has been chosen with care to ensure both the quality and price is acceptable to wine lovers. The attractive restaurant which was added in 1975, seats 55 comfortably and is a popular place with people from miles around. The set menu has several choices of starters and at least four main courses which may well include Halibut steak with mussel sauce, strips of veal in a marsala sauce or a tender Minute steak with dijon mustard sauce. There are always delectable sweets from the trolley or cheese and biscuits. On the à la carte menu you will find at least 13 starters excluding soups. Lobster soup or the Chef's soup of the day are both delicious. Grills , Fish, Entrees together with a wide range of fresh seasonal vegetables makes it difficult to choose a main course. Whatever you choose it will be delicious, beautifully presented and the whole meal will be memorable.

Billericay has much to offer in its own right and is surrounded by such places as Ingatestone Hall, Hyde Garden, the Cater Museum and at Chelmsford, the old Cathedral.

USEFUL INFORMATION

OPEN; *All year*
CHILDREN; *Yes, if well behaved*
CREDIT CARDS; *All major cards*
LICENSED; *Yes*
ACCOMMODATION; *None*

RESTAURANT; *Wide range, good food.*
Table d'hôte & à la Carte
BAR FOOD; *Good choice*
VEGETARIAN; *Always a choice*
DISABLED ACCESS; *Yes*

BEAU'S RESTAURANT

8 Charlotte Street,
Broadstairs,
Kent CT10 1LR

Tel: 01843 862771

From Breakfast to Brunch, Luncheon and Afternoon Teas to the elegant, mouth-watering dinners served Bistro style on Fridays and Saturdays, Beau's Restaurant provides probably the best food in Broadstairs. It is an attractive, welcoming environment right in the heart of the town. Built about 100 years ago it has had time to acquire a pleasant ambience which is enhanced by the owner, Richard Tebbutt-Ford and his friendly and efficient staff. With 36 covers it is small enough to be intimate but spacious enough to provide comfort for everyone. In the summer months the outside is adorned with colourful hanging baskets which entice one to step inside and discover what is on offer. Brunch served between 10am and 11.30am offers a tempting choice from a delicious full English Breakfast to Poached or Scrambled Eggs on Muffins, Welsh Rarebit and Buck Rarebit. Luncheon, available between 12 and 3pm has a wide choice of dishes. Fish is very popular and includes Roast Fillet of Plaice with a spring onion, pepper and cream sauce, Classic Fish and Chips in a crispy Kentish ale batter or maybe a Breaded Seafood Platter. Meat Dishes include a delicious traditional Steak and Kidney Pie cooked in Guinness, a Bookmakers Sandwich - Steak served on French bread, Sausages and Mash with Onion Gravy and lots of other favourite dishes. Vegetarians have a choice of seven dishes and for those who enjoy Salads, the Mixed Leaf Salad drizzled with balsamic vinegar and olive oil dressing is accompanied by your choice of Tuna, Roast Beef, Roast Chicken, Pate, Sausage, Cottage Cheese or Avocado. All the dishes are freshly prepared and the vegetables are bought fresh from local farms and are cooked 'al dente' to preserve their flavour and vitamins. Sunday Roast Lunches are always very popular with several choices and all the trimmings.

Beau's Restaurant takes Afternoon Tea seriously and between 3pm and 4.45pm you will find a simple choice if you require it but most people are intrigued by the Prince Regent - a selection of Finger Sandwiches, Cakes, Scones, Jam & Devon Clotted Cream, Beau Brummell - Scone, Jam and Devon Clotted Cream, Fruit Cake served or Sir Percy Blakeney - Scones, Jam & Devon Clotted Cream served. On Friday and Saturday evenings the menu is exciting with dishes from around the world. For example a Caesar salad from Italy, Hot Chilli Con Carne from South America, Thai Fish Cakes from Thailand or Ostrich Steak from Africa among many others. The meal starts with a choice of six starters including Moules Marinière and Red Onion Soup with cheesy croutons. Finally the Desserts are delectable and definitely different. How about Grown-ups Banana and Custard (baked banana with an almond and brandy custard). Beau's is certainly the place to go in Broadstairs.

USEFUL INFORMATION

OPEN; *10am-5pm. 7.30-10.30pm*
CHILDREN; *Welcome*
CREDIT CARDS; *All major cards*
LICENSED; *Yes*

RESTAURANT; *Delicious and varied food to suit all tastes*
VEGETARIAN; *Yes*
DISABLED ACCESS; *Yes*

CAFE ROUGE

53 St Peters Street,
Canterbury, Kent
CT1 2BE
Tel: 01227 763833   Fax:01227 763830

When you come to the Cafe Rouge today you are entering into one of Canterbury's most
famous buildings, the 12th century Cogan House. It has a fascinating history which you can
explore when you visit the restaurant. As one would expect the restaurant is full of character
and furnished attractively with smart darkwood tables and matching chairs, lots of
nick-nacks everywhere creating a comfortable and pleasant atmosphere. The French menu
is wide ranging, prepared by chefs who create and prepare food with passion. The delicious
starters - 7 to choose from, the main courses including fish, meat and poultry, are cooked to
perfection. One can choose simple salads, freshly made, exciting sandwiches or perhaps the
'Menu Rapide' Three Courses for ten pounds. Excellent value, charming service and food
that is memorable.

USEFUL INFORMATION

OPEN; *All year*
CHILDREN; *Welcome*
CREDIT CARDS; *Yes*
LICENSED; *Yes*
PETS; *No*

RESTAURANT; *Delicious French cuisine*
Main meals, salads and snacks
VEGETARIAN; *No*
DISABLED ACCESS; *Yes*

THE CLARENDON HOTEL
Beach Street
Deal,
Kent CT 14 6HY

Tel:01304 374748

The Clarendon Hotel which is the focus of much of the social life of the town was built in the mid-18th century for the 4th Earl of Clarendon who was Foreign Secretary in the Earl of Aberdeen's Cabinet. It is a three storey, listed building with a mansard roof and for the lovers of architecture it is of great interest, especially for its delicately shaped dormer windows. The Clarendon stands a few hundred yards from the spot where Julius Caesar landed in 55 BC. Nearby is Deal castle, the rose-shaped fortress which was erected by Henry VIII as part of Britain's coastal defences.

Modern day visitors coming to Deal either for business or pleasure find that the atmosphere of the past has been soaked into 20th century activity and the hotel is a wonderful mix of the simple and the exotic. Nothing could be simpler, or more panoramic than the view from the hotel's windows where one can see, not only shipping, but on clear days, the rocky coastline of Cap Gris Nez. Inside, the Gaiety Bar bubbles with life. It has a serving area draped with gilt-trimmed pink curtains, like the proscenium arch of a stage, and among the pictures on the red damask walls are several portraits of great actors and famous Edwardian beauties. A great place for a drink, The Clarendon is regarded as the Premier night-spot in the town with live entertainment. The three bars have discos on Thursday, Friday and Saturdays and on Sunday lunchtime there is live music with jazz in the evening. More live bands play on Wednesday evenings.

The hotel has 17 comfortable bedrooms of which ten are en suite. Each has television and a hostess tray. Breakfast is a super meal with several choices and one which will set you up for the day whether you have to work or you are going to explore the area. The restaurant has a well chosen menu both at lunch and dinner. Brenda Lewis, who with her husband Jim, runs the hotel, is renowned for her cooking in which she specialises in traditional English fare. Sunday Lunch is a great favourite.

USEFUL INFORMATION

OPEN; *l0am-2am*
CHILDREN; *Welcome*
CREDIT CARDS; *Visa/Master*
LICENSED; *Full On*
DISABLED ACCESS; *No*
ACCOMMODATION; *17 rooms 10 en suite*

RESTAURANT; *Good, home-cooked English Fare*
BAR FOOD; *Wide range*
VEGETARIAN; *Catered for*
PETS; *Yes*

THE NEW INN
High Street,
Deal.
Kent CT14 6HE

Tel: 01304 369115

This is one of those inns one is always hoping to find in the centre of a town and seldom does. It is right in the heart of Deal. Built in 1605 it has had four centuries of caring for travellers, each century producing more and more atmosphere and mainly without losing the original charm. Today in the hands of Mr and Mrs Burgess it has never been better. If one were to say it is immaculate it would be nothing short of the truth but that almost detracts from the fact that the ambience is warm, welcoming and relaxing without a trace of formality except in manners. This is not a place for the badly behaved. It is an inn to which one can bring ones friends, of whatever age, for a drink in a peaceful environment. Those who eat here regularly will tell you that the food is second to none and the prices are very reasonable. At lunchtime it is busy with local people coming away from their places of work to enjoy the splendid sandwiches on offer or to select a tasty 'special' from the blackboard which may well include a seafood dish for which The new Inn is renowned. In the evenings people dine here in intimate surroundings and great comfort. The menu has all sorts of delights but probably the favourites are the Sizzle Platters with 8oz steaks cooked to perfection and served with chips, mushrooms, peppers, onions and tomato. Home-made Tagliatelli is another favourite and if you enjoy Mussels, the Green Lipped variety are cooked in garlic butter and served with salad and French Bread. Many people enjoy taking their drinks outside to the front patio where they watch the world go by.

On Sundays the traditional Roast Lunch is served with a choice of meat or poultry, seafood or a Vegetarian dish. There is always a choice of freshly cooked vegetables and to follow there are home-made fruit pies served with cream, ice-cream or custard and with pastry that melts in the mouth.

If you come to Deal as a visitor you will find there is a lot to see and do including visiting the old Castle. You can play Badminton, swim, fish, walk or play golf. All of which will ensure you have a good appetite when you visit the New Inn.

USEFUL INFORMATION

OPEN; *10.30am-11pm*   **RESTAURANT;** *Good food at sensible prices*
CHILDREN; *Welcome*   **BAR FOOD;** *Always a good choice*
CREDIT CARDS; *None taken*   **VEGETARIAN;** *Catered for*
LICENSED; *Full On*   **DISABLED ACCESS;** *Yes*
PETS; *No* **GARDEN;** *Front* Patio

ST BRELADES GUEST HOUSE

80/82 Buckland Avenue,
Dover,
Kent CT16 2NW

Tel: 01304 206126
E MAIL;STBRELADE@COMPUSERVE:com
Fax: 01304 211486
WEB PAGE:HTTP://WWW.SMOOTHHOUND.CO.UK./HOTELS/STBRELAD.HTML

*St Brelades Guest House deserves its 3 Crowns Commended status. It is a friendly,
beautifully run house in which the needs of the guests are paramount and the owner Gaye
Govier goes out of her way to ensure that everyone who enters the house feels welcome and
at home. Whether you are planning a holiday in Kent, a short break or an overnight stay on
your way to or from the Continent, this is the place for you. The 6 en suite rooms are
attractively appointed, very comfortable and complete with television, a hostess tray and
central heating. Breakfast is a delicious, freshly cooked meal and in the evenings St Brelades
has a name for its super food, including particularly good Indian curries. The house is
licensed and some good wines accompany the meal. In the cosy bar many a happy evening
is spent by residents enjoying entertaining conversation and a drink. Well lit, off street parking
is available with longer term parking if required. St Brelades is situated in Dover's town
centre, minutes away from the port and its new cruise terminal and 15 minutes easy drive to
the Channel Tunnel. You are within moments of Dover's famous Castle and many other
sights and only 25 minutes from Canterbury. Help is available with car and bicycle hire,
ferry tickets, taxis, pick-up from the bus and train station and much more. Your holiday
really does start from the moment you check in.*

USEFUL INFORMATION

OPEN; *All year*
CHILDREN; *No*
CREDIT CARDS; *All major cards except*
Amex/Switch/Diners
LICENSED; *Yes*
ACCOMMODATION; *6 en suite rooms*

DINING ROOM; *Excellent breakfast and
evening meals. Indian curries a speciality*
VEGETARIAN; *Catered for*
DISABLED ACCESS; *No*
PETS; *No*

WALLETT'S COURT HOTEL & RESTAURANT

West Cliff, St Margarets-at-Cliffe,
Dover,
Kent CT15 6EW
Tel: 01304 852424 Fax: 01304 853430

Wallet's Court is an old manor house set in lovely open countryside within easy reach of spectacular cliff scenery, the Channel ports, championship golf courses and the Cathedral City of Canterbury. Steeped in history the house has a very special atmosphere. 20 years ago it was a ruin and then in the loving and understanding hands of the Oakley family it has emerged as one of the most beautiful and delightful hotels in the country. Although the frontage of the house seems quite stark and uninspiring, once you are inside it is plain to see why prestigious historical figures were attracted to Wallet's Court. In the 13th century the manor came into the ownership of Eleanor of Castile and between the years of 1804 and 1806 William Pitt the Younger rented Wallet's Court. Now listed Grade II and awarded ' Historic Building of Kent' status, the building contains some fine and unusual features, which reflect its history. There are moulded plaster fireplaces, 17th century wall-paintings, an original wooden porch, an ancient carved oak staircase and even a priesthole in the roof.

When you come back to Wallet's Court after a days exertion, you will feel sufficiently at home to sink into the soft leather sofa by the roaring fire with a book, or just put your feet up and listen to the tick of the old grandfather clock, perhaps taking a glance at the menu in anticipation of the evening ahead. The table d'hôte menu is chosen to reflect the historic background of the house and changes each month in order to facilitate the use of fresh local ingredients. Whatever you choose will be delicious. Chris Oakley, who owns Wallet's Court with his wife Lea, is an inspired cook. The accommodation at Wallett's is fairly varied in style with a price range to match. The three rooms in the main house are large and full of character. Queen Eleanor's Room has a chunky oak-panelled four poster bed. Other rooms, with charming decor are situated in converted farm buildings. All rooms are en suite and equipped with everything you could wish for. Each is given a name rather than a number, so you might well end up in the Prince's Room, the Stable, Winnie's or Gunner Gregory's. Breakfast is a feast and if need be can be served for those catching an early ferry (quarter to seven for the eight o'clock) with prior notice, or a continental tray is supplied for those travelling at more unearthly hours. The Oakley family are totally sincere in wanting you to enjoy your stay in what is not only their home but also a hotel. You will be hard to please if you do not. No pets permitted.

USEFUL INFORMATION

OPEN; *All year except Christmas*
CHILDREN; *Yes. Cots. Baby listening*
CREDIT CARDS; *Master/Visa/Amex*
VEGETARIAN; *Always suitable dishes*
LICENSED; *Residential & Supper*
ACCOMMODATION; *10 en suite rooms*

RESTAURANT; *French/English.*
Seasonal with robust Jacobean flavours
to reflect the house
BAR FOOD; *Not applicable*
DISABLED ACCESS; *Not specially suited*
GARDEN; *Large with tennis court,*
tree-house tables and chairs etc

LEAVERS MANOR HOTEL
Goose Green, Hadlow,
Tonbridge,
Kent TN11 OJH
Tel; 01732 851442 Fax: 01732 851875

What is so nice about the 18th century listed Georgian Leavers Manor Hotel is the sympathetic and skilful manner in which extensions have been added without in any way taking away the elegant features of the house. You will find Leavers Manor in the heart of the Kent countryside, ideally situated for those wanting to explore this historic part of Kent which has so much to offer including Hever, Leeds and Lamberhurst Castles. In addition the hotel is adjacent to the motorway making many places easily accessible as well as the Continent. For those who enjoy outdoor activities there are six good golf courses within easy distance.

Standing in its own beautiful grounds, the hotel has thirty magnificently appointed bedrooms, all en suite of course, and each with colour television, direct dial telephone, hairdryer, trouser press, alarm clock/radio and a hostess tray. The furnishing throughout the hotel is designed for comfort but is stylish and has fine pieces in keeping with the age of the original part of the house. Ten of the bedrooms are in the Manor and another twenty are in the Walled Garden Suite.

For those who enjoy a drink before a meal the comfortable friendly bar has a welcoming log fire in winter and is just the place to unwind and relax with a quiet drink. The bar is well-stocked with a range of wines, beers and spirits and you can also have bar snacks here. The pretty restaurant which is open to non-residents, has a delicious à la carte menu with lamp cooking and for Residents there is an excellent table d'hôte menu.

One of the great advantages of the additions to the house is the availability of an entire suite which can be reserved for one party booking which can cater for up to 200 guests. A full range of menu choices are available ranging from a Finger Buffet to silver service hot or cold Dinner. You will find the Banqueting Suite is fully self contained and has been specially designed for a variety of uses. It is great for a Dinner Dance or a Wedding Reception and for business people it is a well appointed venue for a Conference.

The hotel is a very friendly place, owned and run with great professionalism by Leslie and Ulla Cserjen aided by their efficient and welcoming staff.

USEFUL INFORMATION

OPEN; *All year*
CHILDREN; *Welcome*
CREDIT CARDS; *All major cards*
LICENSED; *Yes*
ACCOMMODATION; *30 en suite rooms*
PETS; *Yes*

RESTAURANT; *English & French cuisine Specialising in fish dishes*
BAR FOOD; *Wide range of bar snacks*
VEGETARIAN; *Catered for*
DISABLED ACCESS; *Yes. Facilities*
GARDEN; *Yes Car parking facilities in courtyard*

LANGLEY OAST

Langley,
Maidstone
Kent ME17 3NQ.

Tel/ Fax : 01622 863523

    Langley Oast is remarkable in many ways but probably in the first instance it is because it is so unusual and quite dramatic in its appearance. It was built in 1873 as part of Langley Park Farm, which was owned at the time by 'Fremlins' the local Brewery. It remained a 'working' farm until 1985 when the farm buildings were sold for conversion to homes. Langley Park, as it is now known ,forms a secluded hamlet of twelve homes, a quarter of a mile away from the main road, the A274, about two miles from the centre of Maidstone and two miles from Leeds Castle. The setting of The Oast is idyllic in the heart of Kentish countryside. It has an air of well-being and tranquillity about it that wraps itself around everyone who stays here. You are totally unaware of the noise and bustle of the hectic life we lead today. You can see fields as far as the eye can see and at the bottom of the nearest field there is a lake. An ideal walk at anytime and somehow there is a therapeutic quality when one gazes at a lake, or any other form of water. Staying here is one of life's pleasures. The Oast has been lovingly and skilfully converted by Peter and Margaret Clifford. That they love and have pride in their home is there for anyone to see. You are greeted in the friendliest manner, without fuss but in such a relaxed way that you feel immediately at ease. The bedrooms are exquisitely furnished with beautiful colour co-ordinated drapes and bedcovers. Each of the rooms is full of character. Maybe you will sleep in the large Roundel rooms, one of which has a Jacuzzi, or in twin rooms with Half Tester Canopies. Whichever you choose you will find the beds the epitome of comfort and the additional touches of television and a hospitality tray, very welcome. One of the rooms is en suite. The whole charm of the Oast is the unexpected with a Spiral staircase leading to the rooms, lots of lovely antique furniture and pictures. Breakfast is delicious and freshly prepared to your order. There are no evening meals but the Clifford's will be happy to point you in the right direction for the many good eateries in and around Maidstone.

    One of the great benefits of staying in The Oast is its convenient situation. It makes an ideal touring base, one can reach London easily and Kent itself is full of tourist attractions. It is also ideal for those wanting a 'Stopover' to or from the Continent with Folkestone and Dover just 35 minutes away.

USEFUL INFORMATION

OPEN; *All year except Christmas & New Year*
CHILDREN; *Welcome*
CREDIT CARDS; *No*
LICENSED; *No*
ACCOMMODATION; *3 rooms 1 en suite*

DINING ROOM; *Excellent breakfast*
VEGETARIAN; *Yes*
DISABLED ACCESS; *Not suitable*
GARDEN; *Yes*
PETS; *No*

VALE HOUSE,
Old Loose Hill, Loose,
Maidstone,
Kent ME15 0BH

Tel:44 (0) 1622 743339 Fax: 44 (0) 1622 743103

What strikes one first about Vale House, is its warmth and charm from the outside. The mellow red brick has an abundance of creepers flourishing in the sun , the manicured lawns and the backdrop of evergreen trees present almost a picture postcard aspect. It is no less delightful when you step inside to be welcomed by your hosts Vanse and Tony Gethin. The house, rebuilt in 1720 on the site of a Tudor farmhouse is the Gethin's home and one in which much loving care and an eye for colour and harmony has been given to its furnishing and decor. Vanse is an interior decorator and her considerable skills have never been better displayed than in her own home. Everywhere there are attractive fabrics and period and original furnishings. Vale House is an ideal place to stay for anyone touring the local area. There are five beautifully appointed guest bedrooms, all with television, direct dial telephones and a generously supplied hostess tray. None are en suite but that is of no importance when the bathrooms are spacious, have lots of fluffy towels and toiletries and never short of hot water. Breakfast served in the elegant dining room is a memorable meal and one that will stand you in good stead for the rest of the day. There are no evening meals but the Gethins will point you in the right direction of local hostelries including The Chequers at the bottom of their drive, and the many good eateries in Maidstone.

Loose is a picturesque village and at one point there were many fulling and dying mills on the Loose stream which under Hugenot influence then were converted to papermills, the evidence of which can be seen on a walk through this charming valley. This is very interesting countryside and cries out to be explored. Maidstone itself is steeped in history and everywhere around has some fascinating story to tell. Vale House is easy to find. Just south of Maidstone, opposite the Chequers pub in the village. The house is set back from the road down a drive. It is an ideal place in which to stay whether you come for a well earned break, a longer stay or because you have business in the area. It would be hard to find a house in which you will be better cared for.

USEFUL INFORMATION

OPEN; *All year(Except Xmas/New Year)*   **DINING ROOM;** *Delicious, traditional breakfast*
CHILDREN; *Yes*   *No evening meals*
CREDIT CARDS; *None taken*   **VEGETARIAN;** *Upon request*
LICENSED; *No*   **DISABLED ACCESS;** *No*
ACCOMMODATION; *5 guest rooms*   **GARDEN;** *Beautiful, well maintained*
PETS; *No*

CHIGBOROUGH LODGE RESTAURANT

Chigborough Road, Heybridge,
Nr Maldon,
Essex CM9 4RE

Tel: 01621 853590

Set close to the banks of the River Blackwater Chigborough Lodge Restaurant could not have a more idyllic, rural spot and it is no wonder that so many local people make their way out from Maldon , Heybridge and other nearby places to enjoy the hospitality, the excellent food and appreciate the reasonable prices. Stephen and Ilse Chamberlain are the proprietors and they, together with their friendly staff, ensure that everyone is made to feel welcome and important; something that is lacking so often these days in restaurants. Closed at lunchtime on Saturdays but for the rest of the year the opening times Wednesday to Sunday 12-2pm and 7.30pm until late from Wednesday to Saturday inclusive. Sunday lunch time is a particular favourite and makes it advisable to book. Stephen Chamberlain is the chef and he never fails to use quality ingredients in the careful preparation, cooking and serving of dishes. He has an instinctive flair for achieving just the right textures and flavours. The fresh vegetables are cooked perfectly and a selection is left on your table for you to help yourself. The menu changes daily with an emphasis on traditional but imaginative English fare. Lobsters and fresh Crabs play a large part on the menu when they are available.

You might well choose to start your meal with Parma Ham, Rocket and fresh figs with a lemon and olive oil dressing, followed by Grilled Fillet of Sea Bass with Beurre Blanc and finish with a delectable Strawberry, Rhubarb and Mascarpone Gratin. A delicious and beautifully balanced meal. There are many more choices, of course, including Veal, Lamb, Salmon and many other tempting dishes. Whatever you choose it will be perfectly presented and as much a visual treat as a gourmet one.

This is a restaurant where children are welcome and if the day is nice they can enjoy the vine covered patio area rather than be cooped up indoors. You will find the visitors book is full of complimentary comments from 'This is a haven of good food' to 'Excellent food, very friendly atmosphere, discreet service and reasonable prices. What more could you ask for?' The latter quote sums up Chigborough Lodge perfectly.

USEFUL INFORMATION

OPEN; *Wed-Sun 12-2pm*
Dinner from 7.30pm Wed-Sat
Closed for Lunch Saturdays
CHILDREN; *Welcome*
CREDIT CARDS; *All major cards except Amex*
LICENSED; *Yes*

RESTAURANT; *Perfect food in an idyllic setting*
VEGETARIAN; *Always a choice*
DISABLED ACCESS; *Yes*
GARDEN; *Vine covered patio*

ROSLIN HOTEL,
Thorpe Esplanade,
Thorpe Bay,
Essex SSI 3BG

Tel: 01702 586375

Situated on the Sea Front at Thorpe Bay, the Roslin Hotel boasts one of the finest views of the Thames, something which the many contented visitors to this friendly, comfortable hotel , look forward to enjoying from the Continental style terrace where they can sip a drink in the sun. The terrace is one of the many attractive features of the Roslin which is owned and run by Keith and Janet Oliver aided by their son and daughter-in-law, Matthew and Hayley. Inside the hotel you will find it relaxing, informal and friendly. The Olivers recognise the need that their guests have to relax and unwind when they come away for a holiday, a short break or perhaps just a weekend. There are many pleasant walks for those who feel in need of exercise or for the more energetic, there is free membership of the local sports and leisure club, also tennis courts and golf courses are nearby. If you prefer to do absolutely nothing you may well use the comfortable lounge bar which also overlooks the Estuary, and here you can have not only a drink but a scrumptious afternoon tea or a bar snack from a varied menu. Many of the pretty bedrooms overlook the sea, but whichever room you have you will find it very comfortably appointed with full facilities, direct dial telephones, Sky television, tea/coffee makers and hair dryers. Food is all important at anytime but perhaps especially so when you are on holiday and have time to enjoy it without any sense of urgency. The Mulberry Restaurant which is open to non-residents offers a delicious à la carte or table d'hôte menu. There is also a healthy low-fat menu for those who need to watch their diet. At lunch and dinner the table d'hôte menu has a choice of six starters, six main courses, sweets plus a choice of vegetarian dishes. This menu changes regularly and the large à la carte menu two or three times a year. The talented chef ensures that all food is prepared freshly on the premises. The hotel caters for weddings and other celebrations and has Conference facilities for up to 34 delegates.

USEFUL INFORMATION

OPEN; *All year*
CHILDREN; *Very welcome*
CREDIT CARDS; *All major cards*
LICENSED; *Yes*
ACCOMMODATION; *39 en suite rooms*
GARDEN; *No but super front terrace*
PETS; *Yes.*

RESTAURANT; *À la Carte & Table d'hôte*
Excellent traditional English breakfast
BAR FOOD; *Afternoon tea & Bar snacks*
VEGETARIAN; *Always a choice*
DISABLED ACCESS; *Yes but check first*
PARKING; *Yes*

Chapter 10

LANCASHIRE, CUMBRIA & NORTHUMBRIA

INCLUDES

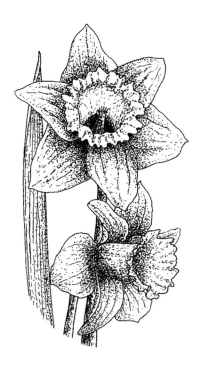

Chapter 10

LANCASHIRE, CUMBRIA AND NORTHUMBRIA

It is not my intention to lead you astray by including Lancashire in this chapter and then only introducing you to two places which in no way paints the picture of this diverse county. Lancashire holds the most famous playground of all **Blackpool**, and the wonderful county town of **Lancaster** which went down in the Domesday Book as a hamlet of the great manor of Halton, but Halton is now a tiny place near the Crook of Lune, while Lancaster has given its name to a famous castle, a great county, a historic duchy, and a proud line of kings, and maintains its title as capital of Lancashire.

My visits were in a way equally diverse. I wanted to see the **Blackburn Cathedral**. Most people are almost unaware that this busy place even has a cathedral. I found it to be fascinating, an example of what a town can produce from its own efforts if it so wishes. You cannot compare it to its venerable superiors like Winchester and Salisbury or even closeby Manchester, but nonetheless it is worth taking a look at. From Blackburn I made my way eastwards across the county to **Southport**, somewhere I had never been before but I had heard much about it. In my young days my Mother who was a keen bridge player used to take off from Plymouth to play in Bridge Congresses which were held in the town. Ever since then I have always wanted to come here and I was right to do so.

Southport has always been an all year round resort as exciting in the winter as in the summer. Over the years it has gained a reputation as being the floral capital of England's North West. Every year the **Southport Flower Show** which is held in Victoria Park in August is the premier English summer flower show, featuring exhibitors both professional and amateur from all over the world. There are many beautifully designed Victorian formal parks and gardens in Southport, including Hesketh Park and Botanic Gardens in Churchtown which features a fernery and a magnificent boating lake. You can relax with a morning coffee or an afternoon tea and scones in the Botanic Gardens cafe and then take a stroll around the fascinating museum which features displays of Southport's history, going right back to medieval times. There is also a gallery of Victoriana and a magnificent display of childrens' dolls. Brass bands, a feature of Northern England life, are another great attraction for both young and old.

The Southport Theatre and Floral Complex on the promenade is the main live entertainment centre with all the year round shows, concerts and performances to suit everyone. With modern variety shows, talent nights, old time dancing, music hall, wrestling and Lancashire nights - what more could you ask for? For the shopping addicts Southport has justifiably earned a reputation as one of the UK's most popular shopping centres. The Southport Air Show and Southport Pier festival are two of the many very important occasions every year.

Serious golfers will already know that Southport has the famous Royal Birkdale Course but it also fortunate enough to have several more famous course including Hillside, Southport and Ainsdale and Hesketh, all of which are championship status and qualifying courses for the 'Open' which comes to Southport again in 1998. Aintree Race-course, home of the Grand National is only 15 miles away and Haydock Racecourse features the Southport handicap race. You can swim in the large heated indoor pool on the esplanade or you could even treat yourself to a refreshing Turkish bath! Maybe Croquet or Crown Green and Flat Bowling would suit you better - it is all available in Southport. Lancashire Cricket Club regularly play at the Southport and Birkdale cricket ground.

One thing Southport has more than most is sand! There are over seven miles of firm golden sand with unspoilt natural dunes. It is possible to walk the full length of the coastline from Southport to **Formby** - nearly seven miles away - and then return by train.

On the other side of Southport to the north, stretch the extensive marshes of the Ribble estuary which are very important feeding grounds for migrating birds and further inland can be found the internationally acclaimed **Martin Mere Wildfowl Trust** which is an impressive natural habitat for hundreds of different species of migrating birds that can be studied from special 'hides' and walkways.

Gourmets will never go hungry in this town. In fact there are over 180 places to eat of every conceivable kind from the very top restaurants to the humble fish and chips. For me there was only one place to stay and that is **Stutelea Hotel** in Alexandra Road. Set in its own peaceful grounds with picturesque gardens it is so tranquil. It has every amenity including a splendid Leisure Club complete with an indoor swimming pool and much more. Wonderful food, super bedrooms some with balcony views and sumptuous four-poster beds, and a lift to all floors which is a Godsend for some of us.

Enjoy Stutelea Hotel and all that Southport has to offer. I wish I had come here years ago.

My travels in Cumbria this time have spread themselves about a bit from **Grange-over-Sands** to **Carlisle**. Once again I have picked on places I have enjoyed and I hope you will as well.

Taking the M6 to junction 36 I turned east very briefly on the A65 to **Lupton**, on the Kendal to Skipton road. I had been recommended to **The Plough Hotel** standing at the foot of the picturesque Farleton Knott, and only minutes away from the delightful town of **Kirby Lonsdale**. The hotel is everything anyone could wish for and if its comfort was not enough, it straddles the distinctive landscape of the Yorkshire Dales and the majestic scenic splendour of the Lake District. It is a welcoming informal establishment run with a degree of professionalism that is enviable. It was only the knowledge that I had a lot of ground to cover that made me move on.

Next stop **The Hare and Hounds Country Inn** at **Bowland Bridge**, Grange-Over-Sands. Here another change of scenery. The Inn which dates from the 17th century is situated in the beautiful Winster Valley in the hamlet of Bowland Bridge. Stay here and you will have the best of both worlds; the excitement of Lake Windermere yet far enough away to avoid the thronging crowds. Owned and run by ex-international soccer player Peter Thompson and his wife Debbie, The Hare and Hounds has a tremendous reputation for good food. I visualised spending a traditional Christmas here. It would be wonderful, warm, cosy, great wines, superb food, convivial company and thoroughly relaxing.

Grange-over-Sands is not the place for safe bathing but that loss is more than compensated for by the extensive gardens and promenade along the sea front. The climate is unusually mild and helps subtropical plants and alpines to flourish. It became fashionable by the coming of the Furness Railway linking it with Lancaster. There are some lovely walks and none more rewarding than a path which leads to Hampsfell Summit and The Hospice, a small stone tower from which there is an unforgettable views of Morecambe Bay and the craggy peaks of the Lake District. The 'Cistercian Way' starts at Grange. This 37 mile footpath goes through Fumes to Barrow linking many sites of Cistercian history.

Coniston Water and Lake Windermere flank the Grizedale Forest Park in Furness Fells. Wondrous countryside making it difficult to decide which stretch of water is lovelier. I decided on **Coniston** first. Leaving the West bound A590 from Grange to Ulverston, I headed north on the A5084 which runs alongside Coniston Water and eventually brought me to Coniston itself. Made famous by the late Donald Campbell during his record speed attempts on Coniston water, somehow it has managed to stay an unspoilt village in the heart of the mountains. It is a working village where tourism has not enveloped traditional local industries like the slate Quarries and the hill farms. The area is a haven for walkers and climbers, with something to suit everyone from quiet walks through woodland to Long Ridge and the 'classic' rock climbing routes in Dow Crags.

Anthony and Elizabeth Robinson who own **Coniston Lodge** where Donald Campbell used to stay with the family, are both experienced fell walkers. A delightful couple, they are only too willing to give their guests advice and guidance. Coniston Lodge is wonderful for a relaxed holiday. It only has six de luxe en suite rooms which means you have personal attention at all times as well as wonderful food. The hotel has a first class reputation for serving traditional home-cooked English and Lakeland dishes.

Leaving here you could make for the head of Windermere where at **Ambleside**, **The Crow How Hotel** reflects the character of Cumbria, built in local slate with many architectural features including the traditional round chimney stacks. It is only half a mile from busy Ambleside and nestles in peaceful seclusion within the Rydal Valley. It is a fell walkers paradise with inspiring fells on the doorsteps of the hotel. Crow How has footpath access from the garden to the Rydal stepping stones and thence to the lakes of Rydal Water and Grasmere.

Windermere is always beautiful, even in the depth of winter. In fact, I am not at all sure that I do not like it late in the year when it is quieter. It is ten miles long and the biggest lake in England. Here is all the charm of blue water, mountain peaks, fells and islands. Probably the best place to see it is from Orrest head. From here you can see the Langdales in all their severity, the gentle Grasmere mountains, the great peak of Ill Bell and the fascinating curves of Coniston fells. After a fall of snow, Windermere is spellbinding, only equalled by the sight on a summer's eveing when the lake and hills are wrapped in a golden mist.

Wordsworth is everywhere; he lived at Dove cottage, a very small house tucked away in the trees near the old Ambleside road. From here his genius blossomed, although when you see how small the house is you cannot help wondering how on earth he wrote anything at all. Not only did he bring his Mary Hutchinson there, but his sister Dorothy, Mary's sister, De Quincey and Coleridge as well. Visit the house and you will see the house and its furnishings almost as they were when he moved out and De Quincey became the tenant.
From the spectacular North Pennines, through the rolling fields and sandstone

villages of the lush river valleys below, to the staggering beauty of the northern lakes, **Eden** waits to be discovered by those who seek country pursuits and tranquillity.

This is an area surrounded by awe-inspiring uplands - the Lakeland Mountains and, to the south, the Howgill fells and Mallerstang, an isolated corner of old Westmorland where the River Eden has its source. Along the wooded river valley are numerous picturesque villages and the stations of the famous Settle Carlisle Railway, renowned throughout the British Isles for its spectacular views.

Eden's charm lies in its illusion of remoteness. Although it is easily accessible from the M6 motorway and major rail routes, half a million acres of some of the most breathtaking landscapes in England lie in this little known stretch of Cumbria, undiscovered by all but a discerning few. My first stop in this enchanted land was **Alston**, a delightful town of stone houses and steep cobbled streets a thousand feet above sea level; the highest market town in England. Surrounded by the magnificent scenery of the North Pennines - the backbone of England -Alston and nearby villages like **Nenthead** and **Garrigill** grew prosperous in the past as important centres for lead mining.

There is a delightful country house hotel close to Alston, **Nent Hall**. It is situated in a beautiful valley, with 17 en suite bedrooms it is a quiet peaceful retreat, and has real open fires to relax in front of after dinner. Totally charming, Nent Hall is the stuff that dreams are made of.

Penrith is a pleasant market town of red sandstone and a popular shopping destination in Eden, known for its sophisticated arcades and traditional markets. Linked to the M6 motorway and the London-Glasgow Intercity line, Penrith has been the focus for travellers since Roman times and is still the main northern gateway to the Lake District and the North Pennines. The town is dominated by Beacon Hill, which dates back to the Border Wars and there are a wealth of interesting and historic buildings to explore.

Just north of Penrith is **Kirkoswald**, one of the most charming little towns in Cumbria, it is nearly all built of red sandstone and delightfully embowered in trees. Hereabouts many things are found left behind by the Romans and the Saxons, and the town has a grim memory of the Scots who raided and burned it after Bannockburn. The church is very odd, it has a 19th century tower 200 yards away, small, low and square. You cannot even see it until you walk a little way up the churchyard, and then it comes into view perched on a hilltop. What has been described as 'the best little hotel in the world' is here. Prospect Hill Hotel, just outside the town. A creatively restored 18th century farmhouse and out-buildings have become an original country hotel that offers exceptional value for money. Then in the little village of **Staffield** is Nunnery House Hotel situated in the Eden Valley between the villages of Kirkoswald and Armathwaite just 15 minutes drive from the M6 at Penrith or Carlisle. Charming in its own right it has, within its own grounds, the spectacular Nunnery walks, an example of the savage or wild garden, using the natural woodland and the stream described as 'the most beautiful landform in the Eden Valley'. The romantic Wordsworth came here as a boy, and was so impressed by the tumbling Croglin Beck with its dramatic waterfall and gorge that he wrote a poem about it in later life.

The Northern lakes are dominated by Haweswater and Ullswater, thought by many to be the most beautiful lakes of all. The whole area is one of unrivalled scenery and a host of beautiful villages. **Martindale**, on Ullswater's eastern shore is home to the last herd of wild red deer in England. Steamers cruise for nine miles from Pooley Bridge to Glenridding, passing mountains which are mirrored in the Lake, against the backdrop of the mighty Helvellyn.

Once the county town of Westmorland, **Appleby** is one of the finest market towns in the North and this ancient borough is justly proud of its Royal Charters dating from 1174. Situated astride the River Eden, Appleby is also within easy reach of the magnificent scenery of the Pennines.

Life in the historic market town of **Kirkby Stephen** still centres on the market square, which bustles with activity for the traditional Monday market. There are a number of interesting shops and the town is particularly interesting for antique lovers. In the very centre of things in Market Street, is The Kings Arms. It is a 17th century former Posting Inn and offers comfortable accommodation with that added bonus of personal service from the resident Proprietors.

The Settle Carlisle railway reaches its highest point below Wild Boar Fell at the head of the dramatic dale of Mallerstang. The nearby villages of **Brough** with a castle built by the Normans, and **Ravenstonedale** should certainly be visited. Ravenstonedale especially because it is within hail of Yorkshire and sees all the glory of the Pennines. Hidden among mountains it has Gallows Hill in Lord's Park, a curious cattle refuge cut in the rocks below Ash Fell, and traces of Ancient Britons.

Two more good places to stay, eat or drink are here. At **Crossbank**, Ravestonedale, **The Fat Lamb Country Inn** was originally a 17th century farmhouse, and its solid stone walls and open fires still create a warm and welcoming atmosphere. **The Black Swan** is a comfortable hotel built of Lakeland stone at the turn of the century. All the 16 bedrooms are en suite and there are three ground floor rooms suitable for the disabled. The hotel has an excellent reputation for food.

Everywhere within Eden, the great outdoors is there to tempt you. It is wonderful walking country, whether for a gentle stroll or the challenge of the Pennine Way's highest point at Cross Fell. You can join a guided walk or minibus tour led by local experts or find your own way around this wonderful area. Cyclists can follow the Cumbria Cycleway, a way marked circular County route, or take to the byways which also provide excellent horse-riding and pony trekking. You can try your hand at sailing, windsurfing or canoeing on **Ullswater** or relax with the gentler pursuits of fishing or birdwatching. There is something for everyone.

Once you have discovered the North West Lake District with its more dramatic scenery than its southern sisters, and realised how much quieter it is - you will not find encroaching coaches on minor roads and it is so easy to get away from people - you will wonder why you have not always made this a first choice for a holiday or perhaps a restful short break. Having made this discovery, there can be few better places to stay than Tom and Gail Ryan's charming, family run **Appletbwaite Country House Hotel** situated one and a half miles from Keswick.

On now to **Carlisle**. I have to admit that I find the town slightly forbidding but it does have an excellent shopping centre.

Finally in Cumbria I went to **Talkin Village**, 9 miles east of Carlisle and 6 miles east of the M6 and only one and a half miles from Brampton. The village is charming, Talkin Tarn is half a mile distant and the surrounding area is particularly delightful. There is an excellent Golf Course at Brampton and The Blacksmiths Arms is right in the heart of all sorts of country pursuits; walking, golfing, fishing, pony trekking. The Border, Hadrian's Wall and the Lake District as well as many other places of interest are all within easy reach.

Northumberland I love, for its isolation, its rugged grandeur and its majestic coast line complete with romantic castles. Time limited my visits and eventually I had to settle for a drive along the Carlisle-Newcastle-upon-Tyne road and turning off onto the A6079 to **Wall Village** where The Hadrian Hotel has to be one of the best places to stay for miles around. Privately owned, it is beautifully run and perfect for anyone wanting to take a look at Hadrian's Wall.

From there I went much further east and just had time to call in to see an old favourite, Embleton Hall Hotel, at **Longframlington** just north of **Morpeth** on the A697. This small country house hotel, built in 1730 sits in its own grounds of five acres which are composed of landscaped gardens, a ha-ha, a grass tennis court and deciduous woodland. From here one can reach all sorts of exciting places in this staggeringly beautiful part of England. Finally and before I bade a reluctant farewell, if only temporarily, to Northumbria, I went to the Waren House Hotel at **Belford**. Just off the A1 west of **Bamburgh** with its forbidding castle, it is the most comfortable, warm and welcoming hotel and an ideal place to stay if you want to take a look, not only at Bamburgh, but **Alnwick**, **Lindisfarne**, and **Berwick-on-Tweed**, all exciting and very rewarding.

THE WHITE LION HOTEL

High Cross Street,
Brampton,
Cumbria CA8 1RP
3 Crowns Commended

Tel: 016977 2338 Fax: 016977 41618

The village of Brampton was the headquarters of Bonnie Prince Charlie in his siege of Carlisle in 1745 and the house he stayed in is just opposite the 17th century coaching inn, The White Lion Hotel, an atmospheric hostelry that is warm and welcoming and an ideal centre from which to explore this area rich in history. Brampton itself is historically fascinating. After the suppression by the Duke of Cumberland of the Jacobite rebellion six local supporters were hanged from a tree in the town, the tree survived until the last century and in its place now stands a monument to commemorate this fact. Hadrian's Wall and Birdoswald Fort are only four miles away, with Lanercost Priory, founded by Robert de Vaux, Lord of Gilsland, in 1169, even closer. For the energetic there is Coarse and Fly fishing - you will find the Brampton Angling Association very active and very helpful. It is some of the finest fly fishing in the North of England. There is Talkin Tarn Country Park, a beautiful stretch of water surrounded by woodlands. There are boats for hire and windsurfing is also permitted. Brampton Golf Course, one of the most demanding and picturesque you'll ever encounter, Brampton Bowling Green, horse riding and many other activities will keep you occupied. The border town of Carlisle with excellent shopping facilities is only 12 miles away.

Steven and his team carry on the tradition of hospitality that will have started three centuries ago and will never have been better than today. The hotel buzzes with activity and the bars are filled with locals enjoying the chatter and the well kept ale. Every day the menu has the addition of Daily Specials. The food is traditional English with a touch of Continental and an excellent home-made Indian curry. Vegetarians have a large menu so there are always exciting dishes for non-meat eaters. Children have their own 'Lion Cub' menu.

The nine bedrooms, some of them beamed are all attractively furnished and six are en suite. Every room has television, direct dial telephone, hair dryer, shoe polishing equipment and a hospitality tray complete with tea, coffee and drinking chocolate. An iron is available on request. A first class Cumbrian breakfast is served every morning - a great start to the day whether you are working in the district or on holiday and if you just want to sit and read a book, there is a Residents Lounge..

USEFUL INFORMATION

OPEN; 10am-11pm
CHILDREN; Welcome
CREDIT CARDS; All major cards
LICENSED; Full On
ACCOMMODATION; 9 rooms, 6 en suite
PETS; By special arrangement

DINING ROOM; Good, wholesome
English/Continental Cuisine
BAR FOOD; Wide range
VEGETARIAN; Ever changing choice
DISABLED ACCESS; None

THE SUN INN,
Main Street,
Hawkshead,
Cumbria LA22 0NT
Tel:015394 36236 Fax: 015394 36352
www.insites.co.uk/guide/cumbria/accom/sun-inn

Those who visit Cumbria and the Lake District with any regularity have found its special magic already but it never fails to enchant them and never fails to offer them the opportunity to discover even more about its history. Hawkshead is a delightful unspoilt village, steeped in its own history which includes the Grammar School where William Wordsworth perhaps learnt something about the use of words. Then there is Anne Tysons 17th century cottage and the ever popular Beatrix Potter Museum. It is a village proud of its beauty, its beautiful church and grounds and the magnificent views of Esthwaite water and the surrounding fells. It is a lively place with a busy square, quaint coffee houses and small shops full of gifts and other tempting products. In the centre of the village and very much the focal point, is the 17th century Sun Inn, one of the most atmospheric and charming inns in Cumbria.

One can imagine travellers coming into the warmth and comfort of The Sun Inn after they had braved the discomfort of travelling by coach and horses. They would have been made immediately welcome, offered excellent ale and good food. Nothing has really changed, the interior is still enchanting with its low ceilings and nooks and crannies. Here you do feel as if you have taken a step back in time and shut out the hustle and bustle of modern day life. The food is superb, both the proprietors, Stefan and Kay Forsgardh are skilled chefs and have trained and worked in some notable hotels in Switzerland, Sweden and Britain. Their combined talent makes every menu exciting and every dish delicious. It is no wonder that The Sun Inn is renowned for its food and attracts people from miles around.

Stay here in one of the eight individually furnished bedrooms, all of which have   private facilities, tea and coffee making facilities and colour television, and you will enjoy not only a good nights sleep but be amused to notice that one of the treasures of a building of this age is that the walls may not be perfectly square and the floors not quite even. It is a happy place to stay, great for tourists and especially welcoming to business people who prefer this sort of atmosphere rather than a conventional hotel.

USEFUL INFORMATION

OPEN; *All year*
CHILDREN; *Welcome*
CREDIT CARDS; *All major cards*
LICENSED; *Full On*
ACCOMMODATION; *8 en suite rooms*
AA QQQQ Commended

RESTAURANT; *The best of traditional English fare with many choices*
BAR FOOD; *A wide selection*
VEGETARIAN; *Yes*
DISABLED ACCESS; *No*
PETS; *No*

THE UNION TAVERN,
159, Stricklandgate,
Kendal,
Cumbria LA9 4RF

Tel: 01539 724004

Apart from running a very, happy successful Inn, Tom and Maureen O'Shea take a keen interest in the well-being of guests who stay with them. For example they organise golf parties, provide plenty of information and directions about the splendid walks in the area and for those who enjoy fishing this can also be arranged. Nothing ever appears to be too much trouble for this friendly, hospitable couple and this creates a great atmosphere throughout the Inn which was built in the 1800's. With a name like O'Shea it is no wonder that The Union Tavern has an Irish flavour with live Irish and Country Music twice weekly.

The Union Tavern is the first and the last watering hole in Kendal as you enter or leave the town on the main route to and from Windermere. Try to take a look down from the Fell-side in the evening when the tavern is lit. It glows invitingly, proclaiming its warmth, companionship and comfort. It is a glorious building, attractively and comfortably furnished in a modern fashion with wonderful colour co-ordinated drapes and decor. Recently refurbished it is just right for anyone wanting a quiet drink, a good meal or to stay awhile while discovering the glories of Kendal and the Lake District. In the bars you will find locals chattering over a pint at the bar. They are a friendly crowd and no visitor ever feels isolated. The food is good traditional fare in context with the occasional surprises such as the speciality Irish Meals. Everything is freshly cooked and the O'Sheas insist on using as much local produce as possible. Daily Specials are eagerly looked forward to on the Blackboard and if you haven't time for a full meal you will find the range of sandwiches, Ploughmans and other snacks both satisfying and at sensible prices. Dining in O'Shea's Restaurant is a pleasureable and relaxing experience. No one ever hurries you although the service is fast and efficient. On Sundays there is a Sunday Roast served between 12noon and 3pm which is always popular. It offers for under £6 a three course meal with choices of Roast meats, fresh vegetables and crispy roast potatoes. The Union Tavern would make an excellent base for anyone wanting to explore the area. There are ten ensuite bedrooms each well appointed and complete with television, direct-dial telephones and a hostess tray. You are free to come and go as you please and as a good start for every day, the breakfast is delicious and very generous in its portions.

USEFUL INFORMATION

OPEN; *All year*
CHILDREN; *Welcome*
CREDIT CARDS; *All major cards*
LICENSED; *Full On*
ACCOMMODATION; *10 en suite rooms*

RESTAURANT; *Delicious food*
with Speciality Irish Meals
BAR FOOD; *Wide choice*
DISABLED ACCESS; *No*
PETS; *Yes*

LAIRBECK HOTEL,
Vicarage Hill,
Keswick,
Cumbria CA12 5QB

Tel: 017687 73373 Fax: 017687 73144
Email: rogerc@lairbeck.demon.co.uk

Every holiday or break is enriched by the place in which you stay no matter how beautiful the area. Lairbeck Hotel is delightful and ideal from the visitor's point of view. Traditionally built in Lakeland stone, Lairbeck is a fine Victorian country house standing in its own secluded gardens, in walking distance of the town and within easy reach of the Keswick bypass. The owners, Roger and Irene Coy, run the house with the emphasis on peace and comfort for their guests. They are a friendly couple who enjoy people and this shows very much in their approach to hotel keeping.

The house retains much of its original character with large spacious rooms, each attractively furnished and very well maintained with an excellent standard of housekeeping. Certain modernisation has taken place to add to the creature comforts required by today's traveller but at no time has the period feel of the house been lost. The fourteen bedrooms come in a variety of sizes and each is named after the original use when the house was a private residence. You may well find yourself sleeping in the Housekeeper's Room, the Maid's Room, the School Room or perhaps the impressive Drawing Room. There are 9 en-suite Bathrooms, 5 en-suite Shower Rooms, all rooms have Direct-Dial Telephones, Colour TVs and a hostess tray. The pretty dining room with its relaxing views of the hotel gardens, is the perfect place in which to enjoy your hosts' excellent food and wine. Breakfast is a sumptuous meal and the five course evening meal, home-cooked and using freshly prepared local produce, is s omething to look forward to. There is a cosy resident's bar with a magnificent marble fireplace and while the dining room and bedrooms are strictly non-smoking, you are welcome to enjoy a cigarette in the bar.

Keswick is a friendly market town surrounded by magnificent hills and mountains with the River Greta flowing picturesquely through it. Meandering, narrow streets and interesting buildings lead you to the stunning shores of Derwentwater. It is no wonder that Keswick has been such a popular holiday centre since Victorian times and where better to stay than Lairbeck Hotel.

USEFUL INFORMATION

OPEN; *1st March-31st Nov plus Christmas week*
CHILDREN; *Over 5 years*
CREDIT CARDS; *Yes. Not Diners/Amex*
LICENSED; *Yes*
ACCOMMODATION; *14 en suite rooms*
PARKING; *20 cars*

DINING ROOM; *Delicious home-cooked fare*
VEGETARIAN; *Always a choice*
DISABLED ACCESS; *Partial*
GARDENS; *Yes*
PETS; *No*

THORNBANK PRIVATE HOTEL,
Thornbarrow Road, Windemere,
Cumbria LA23 2E

Tel/Fax: 015394 43724

A more beautiful part of the country would be difficult to imagine, and Thornbank is situated in just the right spot for visiting the lake and the wonderful surrounding countryside. It is a family run hotel in a quiet, residential area of Windemere which is owned by Roger and Carole Vernon, and offers a warm hospitality and homely atmosphere to guests.

There are seven en suite bedrooms, all charmingly furnished, and with colour TV as well as Sky, Clock Radio, and a tea and coffee tray. There are thoughtful additions of personal toiletries such as hand and body lotions, shower gels and shampoos. Each bedroom has a front door key which enables you to come and go as you please, and have access to your room at all times.

Breakfast and an evening meal are available, and all the food is good, home-cooked English fayre. Choose from a menu which includes pork loin steaks in a wild mushroom sauce, or chicken fillets in white wine, mushroom, red and green pepper sauce. There is a comprehensive wine list to compliment your evening meal. Breakfast is either full English served in the attractive dining room, or continental served in your room. Vegetarian and special diets are cheerfully catered for upon request. For those wishing to spend the day out and about, you can order a packed lunch the evening before. Thornbank provides you with lovely accommodation and with a great deal of thought included in the service for guests. You are advised to book early to avoid disappointment. There is excellent parking to the rear of the hotel.

This is a beautiful area with plenty of sporting facilities, watersports, boating, pony trekking, fishing, golf and walking available. You can also use the facilities at Parkland Country Club nearby, which is an all weather environment with swimming pool, spa bath, badminton, squash courts and much more. There is a lovely club lounge and bar, and all are designed and equipped to the highest standards. There is something for all in this part of the country, and the stunning scenery and enchanting view, along with charming hosts and good accommodation which will ensure a holiday to remember!

USEFUL INFORMATION

OPEN; *All year except Xmas & New Year*
CHILDREN; *Welcome*
PETS; *No*
CREDIT CARDS; *Visa & Master*
ACCOMMODATION; *7 en suite bedrooms*

DINING ROOM; *Good English fayre*
VEGETARIANS; *Catered for*
SPECIAL DIETS; *Catered for*
DISABLED ACCESS; *No*

LONDON

Chapter 11

LONDON

INCLUDES

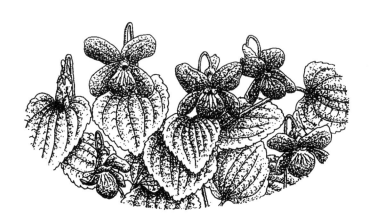

Chapter 11

LONDON

How can anyone possibly cover the majesty, the excitement and the spirit of **London** in a single chapter. I am not even going to try because suffice it to say there is so much literature available to the visitor, and totally up to date data, that any in put of mine would be trivial. I know that the years I spent living in London were probably the most exciting of my life. I lived just behind Oxford Street in Montagu Square and so I was in the heart of the West End. Theatreland was only a short distance, and I think I saw every play, musical, opera and ballet that was performed. It was a mental and visual experience that is unrepeatable and for which I will always be grateful that I had sufficient money to do it. The London stage attracts the very best in the world.

Strangely enough when I lived in the great metropolis I seldom visited any of the tourist attractions like the Tower of London unless I had visitors staying with me. It was American friends from Texas who really made me take a look at things and places I took for granted. I will always be grateful to them and would urge you to see as much as you can whether it is from the river or on foot or maybe using one of the many sightseeing buses. It is frequently the unexpected vista that enchants or the sun glistening on the water of the River Thames throwing odd lights onto familiar buildings. The Houses of Parliament, Lambeth Palace, the great Savoy Hotel all seen from the river look totally different. You can take boat trips the length of the River and it is more than rewarding. It will leave you with indelible memories.

London probably has the most varied and best restaurants in the world - the French would not agree with me! It would be invidious to choose any one place in which to eat but because I knew **The Portobello Hotel** and discovered that **Julie's Restaurant** was under the same management it therefore gave me a sound reason for going. If the standard was anything like that of The Portobello I would not be disappointed - and I was not. What an astonishing place. A labyrinthine fantasy warren made up of five rooms decorated in different styles, housed in three terraced houses and an ex builder's yard. The five rooms are Gothic: with chairs salvaged from nearby St Paul's church; Forge, decorated in pink with an original forge as a set-piece; Back, with a pulpit and huge oval table that required a wall to be ' demolished to fit it in (this is the stag party room where the Prince of Wales, Mark Phillips, Mark Knopfler and Sting bade farewell to bachelorhood; the Garden, which has a removable canvas roof, and the Conservatory.

Each room can be reserved for parties. The theatrical look evokes the novels of Jules Verne, but makes a congenial atmosphere for stars who want to let their hair down. It is a calm, romantic place and uncrowded. Somewhere to enjoy dinner by downlighters and candles. At lunch, most customers are on business, usually from the local fashion and record industries. In the evenings, locals and stars alike enjoy the intimate atmosphere and well-known absence of paparazzi. You may see anyone from Joanna Lumley eating vegetarian to Princess Margaret, Sean Connery, Roger Moore, Kenneth Branagh, Madonna - a never ending list. When booking regulars specify rooms not tables. George Michael, for example likes Table F6 in the Forge, somewhere to see and be seen! Sunday Brunch goes on from 12.30-7.30pm, there is a Morning Coffee Menu and delicious, imaginative food throughout. You will find Julie's at 135 Portland Road, W11. Tel: 0171 229 8331 and Julie's Bar at 137 Portland Road, W11. Tel: 0171 727 7985.

Where to stay? Well, the list is endless but I have chosen a small selection of places that I can personally recommend having either stayed there or had friends who have. Firstly **The Goring Hotel**, a distinguished, dignified hotel, privately owned and run immaculately. It is delightful, has beautiful gardens which provide the view for many of the bedrooms, some balconied. The service, like its sister hotel, **The Spa** in **Tunbridge Wells**, is faultless.

Next the old family hotel in George Street, **Durrants**. It has been owned by the Miller family for over 70 years and provides a service that meets the needs of today's travellers in an atmosphere of yesteryear. This quintessentially English hotel has been awarded the 'Which Hotel Guide' Best London Hotel for Value, on two consecutive years. Situated off Manchester Square it is close to Theatreland, Harley Street and Mayfair, with the Wallace Collection directly opposite and West End shopping within walking distance. Ideally situated for both business and pleasure. The whole of the hotel is elegant and beautifully appointed. Every room has character. Reached off narrow sloping corridors with creaking floorboards, each bedroom is individually furnished with every modern comfort. Pine panelled walls, brass labelled post box, an impressive staircase and a frock-coated concierge make one believe that one has stepped back in time. Hard to believe that Durrants was once a country inn.

To find a tranquil haven in the heart of London is a godsend. **Number Sixteen**, **Sumner Place** in South Kensington is that place. This elegant 'Town House Hotel' comprises of 4 Victorian houses side by side in a quiet thoroughfare. The premises just ooze warmth and a sense of being in your own private dwelling cared for by an efficient and friendly staff. The hotel serves breakfast only. Guests are invited to pour themselves drinks from the 'Honour Bar' in the relaxed surroundings of the lounge, a perfect setting in which to meet friends or business associates. My American friends told me that in addition to the pleasure they get from staying in such an elegant environment, they think the sumptuous English breakfast is memorable.

Another such place is **11 Cadogan Gardens, Sloane Square** which was the first exclusive Town House Hotel ever. It is set in a tree-lined square in the heart of Chelsea, just a few minutes walk from Sloane Square, close to Harrods and the shopping delights of Knightsbridge and the Kings Road. The hotel was established by an eccentric Swiss gentleman in the summer of 1949 for his friends and 'such ladies and gentlemen as can furnish me with acceptable introductions'. It has been the London home to discerning visitors throughout the intervening years.

The spirit of the 1970's lives on in the well kept and efficiently run **Portobello** at 22 Stanley Gardens. It gets its name from the thriving Notting Hill Portobello Market although Stanley Gardens is a quiet street. You will recognise the hotel quite easily in this porticoed terrace by its bay trees guarding the entrance. Inside it is gorgeous, if a trifle Bohemian. A hotel to be enjoyed and very well situated.

Tea Dances are synonymous with the Palm Court Lounge at **The Waldorf Hotel** in the Aldwych. Taking tea and dancing the afternoon away in the magical terraced **Palm Court** is a truly unique experience, popular with Londoners and visitors alike. Held every Saturday and Sunday, the tea dance has also become a favourite pre-theatre venue - The Waldorf's location on the Aldwych, in the heart of theatreland, makes most theatres within easy walking distance. The Waldorf which is the flagship hotel in the Forte Grand Collection of 29 international luxury hotels, has recently undergone a 12.5 million pound programme to restore and enhance the original character of the hotel. The Palm Court Lounge was totally decorated in the refurbishment with great care taken to maintain and enhance the room's cherished character and tradition. I love it. A visit to London without tea a tea dance at the Waldorf would be incomplete. Afternoon tea at **The Ritz** is another thrilling experience, quite different but equally memorable. Wonderful service, exquisitely thin sandwiches, delicious cakes and pastries and the lush greenery of St James Park outside the tall, elegant windows. Both The Waldorf and The Ritz takes one back in time.

DURRANTS HOTEL
George Street,
London W 1 H 6BJ
Tel: 0171 935 8131 Fax: 0171 487 3510

Durrants Hotel has been owned by the Miller family for over 70 years and provides a service that meets the needs of today's travellers in an atmosphere of yesteryear. This quintessentially English hotel has been awarded the 'Which Hotel Guide' Best London Hotel for Value on two consecutive years and offers quality, individual style, and fine service in the heart of London Durrants is situated off Manchester Square and is close to theatreland, Harley Street and Mayfair. With the Wallace Collection directly opposite and West End shopping within walking distance, it is ideally situated for both business and pleasure. The whole of the hotel is elegant and beautifully appointed. Every room has character. Reached off narrow sloping corridors with creaking floorboards, each bedroom is individually furnished with its own private bathroom or shower, and every modern comfort. Pine-panelled walls, brass-labelled post box, an impressive staircase and a frock-coated concierge make one believe that one has stepped back in time. The rooms used for private parties, conferences and meetings are almost all panelled and look stunning when the tables are laid. With such a good reputation it is almost an impertinence to talk about the food. Suffice it to say that the kitchen is run by masters of their craft who produce delicious and superbly presented dishes from around the world but with the main emphasis on traditional and modern English cuisine. The service comes from a staff, including the head waiter, who have been at Durrants for years. It is caring, efficient and unobtrusive. Hard to believe that Durrants was once a country inn, but one is reminded by the faithful recreation in the cosy hunting themed bar, with its brass tables and cast-iron coal burning fireplace, and in the intimate surrounding of the restaurant. There are conference facilities for up to 100 non-residents.

USEFUL INFORMATION

OPEN; *All year. 24 hours*
CHILDREN; *Welcome, family rooms*
CREDIT CARDS; *Mastercard/Amex/Visa*
LICENSED; *Full on*
ACCOMMODATION; *19 sgl, 40 twn, 30 dbl, 3 family, 3 suites*
GARDEN; *No. Dogs not permitted*

RESTAURANT; *Intimate, mainly traditional English*
BAR FOOD; *Available*
VEGETARIAN; *Always dishes on menu*
DISABLED ACCESS; *Wheelchair access 3 steps. 7 ground floor bedrooms*

ELEVEN CADOGAN GARDENS
Sloane Square, Chelsea,
London SW3 2RJ
Tel: 0171 730 3426 Fax: 0171 730 5217

Eleven Cadogan Gardens was the first of the exclusive private Town House hotels in London. It is set in a tree-lined square in the heart of Chelsea, just a few minutes walk from Sloan Square, close to Harrods and the shopping delights of Knightsbridge and Kings Road, a seven minute taxi ride to the Roman Catholic Westminster Cathedral at Victoria and 25 minutes to St Paul's Cathedral or Westminster Abbey.

The hotel was established by an eccentric Swiss gentleman in the summer of 1949 for his friends and 'such ladies and gentlemen as can furnish me with acceptable introductions'. It has been the London home to discerning visitors throughout the intervening years. With its own health and beauty spa at No 1 Synergy, just a few doors away it provides a haven of peace and tranquillity amid the hustle and bustle of the city. Guests have free use of the facilities. There are 60 beautifully appointed rooms including 5 suites. Each has its en suite bathroom and every modern comfort. There is a boardroom large enough to take 12 people and a Chauffeur driven limousine service.

Not surprisingly the service is impeccable, discreet and efficient. From the moment of arrival when the butler meets you at the door it is the epitome of Victorian hospitality. Room service is around the clock and can provide light meals and refreshments in a moment. The chauffeur driven limousine service is fantastic for those wanting to take in some sightseeing or a little shopping.

USEFUL INFORMATION

OPEN; 24 hours
CHILDREN; Yes. No special facilities
CREDIT CARDS; Amex/Visa/Diners/ Mastercard
LICENSED; Liquor licence
ACCOMMODATION; 60 en suite rooms including 5 suites

RESTAURANT; Room service only
BAR FOOD; No Bar
VEGETARIAN; Always a vegetarian dish of the day
DISABLED ACCESS; None
GARDEN' Deck chairs can be arranged in the communal gardens opposite

NUMBER SIXTEEN

16 Sumner Place,
London SW7 3EG
Tel: 0171 589 5232 Fax: 0171 584 8615

To find a quiet, tranquil haven in the heart of London, close to the shops, restaurants and theatres, is a godsend and almost unheard of. Number Sixteen Sumner Place in South Kensington is that place. The elegant 'Town House Hotel' comprises of 4 Victorian houses side by side in a quiet thoroughfare. The premises just ooze warmth and a sense of being in your own private dwelling cared for by an efficient and friendly staff. The whole of Number Sixteen is decorated and furnished with exquisite good taste. Guests are invited to pour themselves a drink from the 'Honour Bar' in the relaxed surroundings of the lounge, a perfect setting in which to meet friends or business associates. The comfortable informality of the drawing room will encourage you to curl up in front of the blazing fire with a book or magazines thoughtfully provided. The conservatory opens onto a secluded garden which has been tended with green fingers and loving care. It is no wonder that Number Sixteen is an award-winner. In 1991 it won the prestigious 'Spencer Trophy' and the 'London in Bloom' award. Both are well deserved, and only serve to confirm that there are few better places to stay in the metropolis than in the embracing comfort of this excellent hotel. Our American friends will tell you that in addition to the pleasure they get from staying in such an elegant environment, they think the sumptuous English breakfast is memorable.

USEFUL INFORMATION

OPEN: *All year*
CHILDREN: *Over 12 years*
CREDIT CARDS: *All major cards*
LICENSED: *Residential Licence*
ACCOMMODATION: *Elegant, spacious en suite rooms*

RESTAURANT: *Hotel and Breakfast only*
BAR FOOD: *Not applicable*
VEGETARIAN: *Not applicable*
DISABLED ACCESS: *No. Willing to assist*
GARDEN: *Secluded. Award-winning*

THE GORING HOTEL
Beeston Place, Grosvenor Gardens,
London SW 1 W OJW
Tel: 0171 396 9000 Fax: 0171 834 4393 Telex 919166

For three generations the Goring family have harmonised traditional standards of hotel keeping with progressive management. They are proud to operate two of the very best privately-owned hotels in England, The Goring Hotel in London and The Spa Hotel in Tunbridge Wells. A warm and dignified atmosphere, excellent service and outstanding facilities in either of the hotels make them a wise choice. Here in London, The Goring is to be found in a quiet haven ideally located, adjacent to Buckingham Palace and within walking distance of the Royal Parks, London's principal shopping areas and the heart of the West End and theatreland. The Houses of Parliament and Westminster Abbey are close by.

Within the hotel there are seventy eight bedrooms, individually designed and decorated. They are luxuriously appointed and some have enchanting balconies; the ideal place to have breakfast overlooking the lawns and flower beds. Room service is available twenty four hours a day, with valeting and evening maid service. The traditional elegance of the lovely restaurant makes it popular for both lunch and dinner. Guests may enjoy excellent food accompanied by some of the best wines in London which are chosen by George Goring and William Coupe. The Private Dining Rooms will accommodate between four and one hundred guests for Breakfast, Luncheons, Dinners, Cocktail Parties and Wedding Receptions. These rooms are ideal for small private parties, board meetings or formal luncheons. The Garden Bar is an excellent venue for friends or business associates to meet and enjoy a glass of champagne overlooking the beautiful Goring garden. The charming Garden Lounge is the place to relax over a pot of coffee, or enjoy the delights of warm scones and fresh cream with a Traditional English afternoon tea. Since the 2nd March 1910 when O.R. Goring opened the hotel; the first in the world with private bathroom and central heating in every bedroom, each guest has contributed something to the character, warmth and homeliness of this fine hotel which the Goring family run with the long standing General Manager, William Cowpe. They genuinely enjoy making their guests feel at home and now have the pleasure of being able to welcome the children and grandchildren of families they have known for generations.

USEFUL INFORMATION

OPEN: All year. 24 hours
CHILDREN: Welcome
CREDIT CARDS: All major cards
LICENSED: Full. Fine wines
ACCOMMODATION: 78 en suite rooms

RESTAURANT: Traditional, elegant, superb food
BAR FOOD: Yes. 24 hr Room service
VEGETARIAN: Selection of dishes daily
DISABLED ACCESS: Yes
GARDEN: Yes, lawns and flowerbeds

THE PORTOBELLO

22 Stanley Gardens,
London W 11 2NG
Tel: 0171 727 2777 Fax: 0171 792 9641

This exciting hotel is not quite the run of the mill. Originally two whitewashed town houses in a quiet street, within easy reach of the heart of London's West End and Theatres, it gets its name from Notting Hill's lively Portobello Market. You cannot fail to see it amidst the pretty porticoed terrace; luscious green bay trees stand guard at the entrance. Inside the furnishings, mainly antique, are set off with the help of elegant arched windows, wrought iron, ceiling mouldings and trompe l'oeil wall-beading. The atmosphere is wonderful and although it may appear totally laid back, this is an exceptionally well-kept and efficiently run hotel. The bedrooms all have a lot of character although if you are happy to spend a little more money, one of the special rooms - Room 16 for example, is an indulgent choice with its round bed, oriental gold and flower wallpaper and Victorian shower bath on legs. Every room is well equipped and there is 24 hour room service. There is no access to the communal gardens behind but from the lounge it is very restful to look out at the floral displays and the well kept grass. This is a room that is nothing short of splendid with its Victorian antiques, abundant greenery and deep seated chairs. Downstairs from reception is a conservatory style bar and restaurant room which looks out to a pretty seashell wall-mosaic and a little fountain. The menu is not vast but it does have some interesting dishes - monkfish and wild mushroom pie for example. The nicest thing about The Portobello is its warmth. You feel welcome and important - very good for the ego.

USEFUL INFORMATION

OPEN: All year except 23 Dec-2 Jan
CHILDREN: Welcome
CREDIT CARDS: Mastercard/Amex/
Diners/Visa
ACCOMMODATION: 7 suites, 5 dbl,
3 twn, 9 sgl
GARDEN: Not applicable

RESTAURANT: Small but interesting menu
LICENSED: Yes
BAR FOOD: Not applicable
VEGETARIAN: Always a choice
DISABLED ACCESS: Wheelchair. 2
ground floor rooms

UPTOWN RESERVATIONS
50 Christchurch Street,
Chelsea, London SW3 4AR
Tel: 0171 351 3445 Fax: 0171351 9383

This unique reservation service is reserved for those who prefer to stay in the comfort of a very nice home rather than the more impersonal hotel. Upton Reservations has a carefully chosen number of clients from all walks of life, from peers of the realm to actors and actresses who welcome guests on a bed and breakfast basis to their homes which are all in the heart of London; Mayfair, Knightsbridge, Chelsea and so on. Every house has been inspected by the agency and everyone is delightful. You have the freedom to come and go as you please, enjoy the beauty of the house you are staying in and know that you will be both extremely comfortable and provided with a first class breakfast. This leaves you with the opportunity to explore London's wide variety of restaurants at lunchtime and for dinner. You will find that none of the establishments on Uptown Reservations list is ever advertised publicly, in other words you will not be provided with a brochure from which to select a venue. When you ring to book accommodation, various houses will be offered to you to suit your requirements and you will never be disappointed. The reason is a simple one - security. The houses are all so beautifully furnished, frequently with valuable antique furniture and paintings, that the risk would be too great. You will be agreeably surprised at the cost of staying in these elegant properties and having once decided to use this service you will no doubt be eager to book again.

USEFUL INFORMATION

OPEN; All year
CHILDREN; No
CREDIT CARDS; Yes with agency
ACCOMMODATION; Rooms en suite

DINING ROOM; Breakfast only
DISABLED ACCESS; Not suitable
PETS; No

Chapter 12

LEICESTERSHIRE, NOTTINGHAMSHIRE, DERBYSHIRE, LINCOLNSHIRE, RUTLAND

INCLUDES

Chapter 12

LEICESTERSHIRE, NOTTINGHAMSHIRE, DERBYSHIRE, LINCOLNSHIRE, RUTLAND

Rutland, the smallest of all counties, is a gem and once again exists in its own right not as an appendage of Leicestershire. Anyone who lives here will tell you without equivocation that they live in Rutland and not in Leicestershire. It would take 300 Rutlands to make up England and 40 to cover Yorkshire but that does not phase this little brother of the Shires.

The earliest mention of Rutland as a county was seven centuries ago, in the days of King John. The north part of the county is a fertile plateau of grassland; it has the Leicestershire Wolds to the west and the Lincolnshire lowlands to the east, the River Welland separates it from Northants on the south. It perhaps lacks some of the grandest of English scenery but from its high places there are some wonderful views. It has gentle wooded hills, fertile valleys and serene villages with thatched cottages. Industry takes very much a back seat. Its unique qualities are summed up in its motto 'multum in parvo' - much in little.

I started my journey in **Uppingham**, a small town which is home to one of England's finest schools, known throughout the world. The great school with its splendid halls and courtyards appears to stand sentinel over the quiet town with its attractive bow fronted shops, peaceful streets and sombre ironstone houses.

From April to September you can visit **The Bede House** at **Lyddington** just a couple of miles to the south of Uppingham. It was built by Bishop Russell as an Episcopal residence late in the 15th century and has not changed much since. The home of bishops for over a century it was refashioned by Thomas Cecil, the son of Elizabeth I's Lord Burleigh. He converted it into an almshouse for a warden, 12 men and two women, adding to it, for the comfort of pensioners, the stone-roofed veranda running along the north side. The old house is domestic Gothic at its best.

I would like you to take a look at Glaston, a neat little place which has a good pub, The Monkton Arms and a very unusual church with its central towers described as being 'crowned with a Peter Pan of spires that seem never to have grown up high enough to give the church true dignity'. A perfect description.

Just up the road is **Wing** which has one of the oddest survivals of any English village. The ancient turf maze is forty feet across and still preserved, a wonderful example of the mazes that once were commonplace in England. Here the maze is made up of little turf banks about a foot high, winding round and round. If you ever wondered for what purpose mazes were built, tradition has it that they were devised by the Church as a means of penance, the wrongdoer was put in and left to find his own way out! The old church still watches over this one but modern man is too smart not to find his way out.

316

Tinwell is a small village complete with a green and an excellent hostelry, **The Crown**. Just a few yards from the A6121 between Stamford and Ketton, it is very close to the magnificent Burghley House, home of the Cecil family. It is no surprise therefore to know that the pub is actually owned by the Burghley Estate. The village church has a massive tower and a saddleback roof, the only one in Rutland. The nave arcade and the chancel arch are 13th century; the chancel and the clerestory 15th century. In the chancel lies Elizabeth Cecil, sister of Lord Burleigh, Elizabeth I's counsellor and founder of the House of Cecil.

There are many places I want to revisit in England and one of them is definitely Burghley House. It is one of the finest examples of late Elizabethan design in England. Entering it is like walking into an Aladdin's cave, full with every imaginable treasure. There is one of the finest private collections of Italian Art unique examples of Chinese and Japanese porcelain and superb items of 18th century-furniture. The remodelling work of the 17th century meant that examples of the work of the principal artists and craftsmen are to be found here; amongst others Antonio Verrio, Grinling Gibbons and Louis Laguerre made major contributions to the beautiful interiors.

If the interior beauty was not sufficient, you have the additional thrill of walking in a 300 acre Deer Park landscaped by the inimitable Capability Brown under the direction of the 9th Earl. Capability Brown created a lake and delightful avenues of mature trees. The park is open all the year round and the house from Good Friday to October 1st every day from 11am-5pm.

From Tinwell you are only moments away from the man made masterpiece, **Rutland Water**. Spanning 3,100 acres, it is the largest man-made lake in Western Europe. Built in the 1970's to satisfy the rising demand for water from the developing towns of Northampton, Peterborough, Corby, Milton Keynes, Daventry and Wellingborough, the reservoir's storage capacity of 124,000 million litres provides not only water for domestic and industrial consumption but also gives recreational facilities and enormous pleasure to everyone who visits it.

What do you look at first? I am not sure so I will just try and tell you some of the pleasurable things you can see and do. For example visit **The Barnsdale Drought Garden** which is completely innovative. Created by Anglian Water its purpose is to demonstrate the wide variety of attractive plants and shrubs which can be grown successfully in the British climate and which require no extra watering.

The name Barnsdale conjures up something else that is quite special and that is **The Barnsdale Lodge** in Exton Avenue, Rutland Water. It is a thoroughly revamped farmhouse with extensive converted barns and an Edwardian theme.

A good place to stay and you will find it attracts a lively crowd, sometimes people there for conferences and frequently fishermen revelling in the sport to be had on Rutland Water. You can have elevenses, snack lunches or afternoon tea in the Buttery.

From the car park at **Whitwell** you can board the Rutland Belle giving yourselves a chance to cruise around the reservoir taking in the views that are usually only enjoyed by fishermen and sailors. A regular service runs each day during the season except Mondays, but including Bank Holidays. The trip takes about 45 minutes.

Rutland is especially noted for its fine churches covering the whole range of architectural styles. One of these you will find at the medieval village of **Empingham**, and for me it is the most beautiful. Set amongst fine trees with the river Gwash running drowsily by, its 14th century tower has a spire ornamented with arcading that rises grace-fully towards the sky. Inside, peeps of old wall paintings and old glass strengthen the impression of past glory. Empingham also has one of the most unusual and magnificent of dovecotes. Built of stone, it is circular and has over 700 nests.

As you turn the corner at the head of the Dam you will see the **Normanton Park Hotel**, once part of Normanton Hall, owned by the Earl of Ancaster. In 1927 the main hall was demolished but the Georgian coach house and stable block survived and in 1980 was converted into this fine hotel. It is a Grade II Listed Building in which the working clock chimes throughout the day at the appropriate times. For the comfort of guests the chimes are silenced between midnight and 8am. The hotel has commanding views across Rutland Water and is a joy to stay in.

You may wonder how the village of **Edith Weston** got its name. Edward the Confessor was responsible, for he gave his Queen Edith this western part of Rutland. What a lovely village it is, lapping the edge of Rutland Water, with its thatched cottages and stately trees. The tower and spire of St Mary the Virgin are well over 500 years old and well justify the rhyme inscribed in the church below:

> *'Crown of all the neighbouring land.*
> *High and lifted up it stands.'*

The church is open daily during daylight hours. **Old Hall Coach House** in Edith Weston is a member of the Wolsey Lodge Consortium and a truly delightful place in which to stay. Just half a mile along the bank you can see St Matthews Church appearing mysteriously above the water's surface, raised before the meadow where it stood, was metamorphosed into a lake.

My journey round Rutland Water finished at the capital of this small county, **Oakham**. It is the very heart of Rutland and quite lovely. The wide streets have delightful houses and flower filled gardens. Glimpses of green hills and wooded lanes can be seen even from the ancient cobbled market square. All that is good has been preserved including the ancient stocks and buttercross. It is all quaint and it would not evoke much surprise if one saw a prisoner in the five hole stocks.

Oakham is famous for its magnificent church, its old school and what is left of its castle. If you look upwards you will see high above All Saints, Cock Peter, a weather vane which must be the oldest in England. It is said to have shown the way of the wind to men who went to the Battle of Agincourt.

Oakham Castle is part of a late 12th-century manor house of which the timber buildings and most of the fortifications perished long ago. What we see today is an aisled hall with curious carvings on its doors. It is beautiful and is enhanced by a unique collection of horseshoes dating from the 11th century when William I's farrier lived here. Through many centuries it has been the custom to take a horseshoe from every peer passing through the town, and on the walls is one said to have been given by Elizabeth I.

You should take a look at the 14th century merchant's dwelling known as

Flore's House. It has an early 14th century doorway between two faces, and a stone washing bowl with a head carved among foliage. It may once have been the home of a group of priests in the 13th century but it certainly was the home of Roger Flore, who put the top on the church spire. Titus Oates was born in Oakham in 1649 and in Jeffrey Hudson's Cottage an interesting thatched building on the Melton Road, was born a little man of that name in 1619. Nine years later he gained fame by hopping out of a pie in the presence of Charles I. He was only eighteen inches high!

One of the pleasures of writing a guide book is that your attention is constantly drawn to places and areas that are entirely new to you; even though the names may have been familiar since childhood. As far as I am concerned the County of Nottinghamshire is a prime example of this and I think the reason has as much to do with the shire's legendary hero, Robin Hood, as with its geographical position close to the Heart of England. Bounded to the West by the country's first motorway, the M1, and with its predecessor, the A1, running up through from the East, there is a natural tendency to take this fascinating county for granted as we travel north or south; we feel we know the area because of the exploits of the 'Merrie Men' on page and screen, and we are reluctant to stop because we are on the way to somewhere else. We could not be more wrong.

Nottinghamshire is a delight, redolent in history, landscape and culture, yet intensely alive; taking advantage of its very centrality to attract business and visitors from all over the world. It borders with Yorkshire to the north, Lincolnshire to the East, Leicestershire to the south, and Derbyshire to the west, and the land is fairly flat with the highest country being in the western region - perhaps the only off putting fact about the county is that its name is derived from the Saxon for 'the followers of Snot'!

For this visit I had three centres in mind. The first, the county town **Nottingham** which has a history stretching back to pre-Roman times and being a romantic at heart, I thought it appropriate to start at **The Castle** since it is both synonymous with the history of the city and is also situated high on an impressive rocky outcrop giving panoramic views of the city. Demolished after the Civil War, it was gutted by fire some 150 years later during a riot. The wealthy and far-seeing Corporation then restored and converted it to its present day role. Making my way down from the sandstone bluff to town, I was struck by the sheer concentration of antiquity that is to be found around, on top of, and even inside this unusual physical feature. Remains of earlier fortifications are to be found around the present 'castle', whilst grouped around the foot are many other attractions including the excellent museum, **Brewhouse Yard**, which is a beautifully presented display of daily life over the last three hundred years of Nottingham's history, housed within a group of restored 17th century cottages. There is also that celebrated inn, **'The Trip to Jerusalem'**, reputedly the oldest in the country and where, it is said, Crusaders once stopped to slake their thirsts before setting off for drier climes. Finally, there are the tunnels and the caves that honeycomb the rock - and for that matter, most of Nottingham.

Nottingham has everything from theatre to concert hall, Trent Bridge catering for cricket fans at county and Test level, whilst soccer enthusiasts can choose between the oldest football league club in the world, Notts County, or Nottingham Forest. Particularly impressive is the **National Watersports Centre at Holme Pierrepoint**, a 250 acre country park complete with 2,000 metre Olympic rowing course and white water slalom canoeing course - all this just four miles from the city centre.

CHAPTER TWELVE

My recommendation for somewhere to stay, or dine, is **Walton's** at 2, North Road, The Park. Within walking distance of the City Centre it is an early 19th century hunting-lodge, once an exquisite and extensive residence which for the past number of years has been a distinctive hotel and restaurant. It occupies a unique rural location, yet within easy walking distance of the city and the castle, theatres and other centres of entertainment. Beautifully restored and refurbished and lovingly decorated with English, French and Oriental antiques, it has a spacious patio looking out over the well stocked garden. The food is excellent and the service top class. I enjoyed it thoroughly.

Somewhere incredibly special in which to stay is **Langar Hall** in the small hamlet of the same name. You approach it via Bingham on the A52 which is halfway between Nottingham and Grantham. You will find it sign posted and the house adjoining the church is slightly hidden behind it. Craig Brown of the Sunday Times wrote of it 'Once in a blue moon it is still possible to come across a country house that makes one want to jump for joy'. Langar Hall is such a place. An unforgettable experience of graciousness, elegance, superb food and comfort and totally relaxed. A must for anyone who wants pampering and does not mind paying for it.

The second **Newstead Abbey**, the ancestral home of one of England's greatest poets, Lord Byron. Strictly speaking it was a priory and never an abbey. It is an appropriately romantic house with a dramatic past set in extensive parklands. It owes its origins to the guilt that Henry II felt over the murder of Beckett, for it was on this spot that he founded a monastery in memory of the dead Archbishop. After the Dissolution the estate was bought by one Sir John Byron of Colwick who turned the priory into a home for himself and his descendants. Two and a half centuries later, one of these descendants, the lame and impoverished Lord George Gordon Byron, first set eyes on Newstead and later recorded his impressions.

> *'Through thy battlements, Newstead the hollow winds whistle*
> *Thou, the hall of my fathers are gone to decay*
> *In thy once smiling garden the hemlock and thistle*
> *have choked up the rose which late bloomed in the way.'*

The reason for this somewhat gloomy description was that his great uncle, whom Byron succeeded, had let the place fall into disrepair after having been ostracised by society, as a result of killing his cousin in a duel, and was convicted of manslaughter. The poet who was greatly attached to Newstead, but, deeply in debt, was eventually forced to sell. The buyer, an old friend, spent over a quarter of a million pounds on remodelling the house into its present style incorporating the ruins of the priory. It is a site worthy of a romantic such as Byron, and the surrounding parkland with its lakes and waterfalls and gardens provide the appropriate backdrop. Thanks to another two great benefactors the house and land were presented to the City of Nottingham, whilst a third bequeathed a unique collection of Byronic relics.

A wonderful place to visit but where to stay? The answer is simple, at my third choice, **Papplewick Hall**, a superb Grade I Listed Georgian house set in 12 acres of glorious rolling grounds on the edge of Sherwood Forest. You reach it from the MI exit 27, taking the A608 and A611 in the direction of Hucknall, turning left after 3 miles on the A6011 to Linby and Papplewick village. It is a wonderful place to stay at anytime between April and October and in such easy reach of not only

Newstead Abbey but Thoresby, Chatsworth, Hardwick, Haddon, Calke Abbey, Kedleston, Belton, Sudbury and Belvoir Castles, Southwell and Lincoln Cathedrals. The owners, Dr Richard and Jane Godwin-Austen ensure a delightfully relaxed atmosphere for their guests.

Newark, my next place of exploration, is almost a guide book cliche - an ancient market town with a strong sense of its own importance in the history of our country. Situated where the ancient Fosse Way crossed the Great North road and by the banks of the River Trent, where wool was once shipped to Calais via the Lincolnshire port of Boston, it was an important geo-political centre from earliest times and it was considered the Key to the North in the turbulent days of the first King of All England. The town's buildings reflect its importance in historical terms, particularly around the large cobbled market square with an enchanting blend of architecture, predominantly medieval and Georgian inlet with narrow streets and alleys. The tall and well proportioned spire of the parish church of St Mary Magdalene rises to well over 200ft from behind the square and the building is mainly 14th century although there has been a church here since Saxon times. The beauty and elegance of the construction is ounterbalanced by a strong human element in its decoration; for both internally and externally, the church bears witness to the skills of the carver in both stone and wood with innumerable gargoyles, figures, scenes and shields to be found where one looks. However, to my mind, the town's greatest glory is to be found in the forbidding and noble ruins of **Newark Castle**, which stands guard over the entrance to the old town from the north. It is a wonderfully impressive structure and I think, best viewed from one of the cruise boats that sail past the ancient walls.

The Castle, constructed over 700 years ago, played host to many of our Kings and Queens; John died here in 1216 and in 1487 Henry VII prepared his army here prior to the last great battle of the Wars of the Roses at nearby Stoke Field. The last and most glorious chapter of the castle's active life came during the Civil War when it and the inhabitants resisted three determined sieges by the Parliamentarians, surrendering only at the King's command. The castle was then ordered to be demolished, but thankfully the job was never completed - probably due to a lack of enthusiasm on the part of the local populace combined with the massive strength of its structure.

There is an enormous amount to see and do, in and around this enchanting town. Certainly enough to warrant staying a while and for that purpose I have two   charming places for you. Lying in the village of **Langford** just north of Newark is **The Old Vicarage**, a Victorian house in secluded grounds next to one of the oldest and prettiest churches in Nottinghamshire. Here Jeremy and Jillie Steel offer you a very warm welcome to their elegant home. They enjoy people, are excellent hosts and Jillie has an enormous enthusiasm for cooking which ensures wonderful meals.

From here in addition to Newark itself, there is much to see and do. The National Water Sports Centre and Robin Hood country are nearby and the Peak District is easily accessible.

Before leaving Nottinghamshire I went, once again, to what has been described as 'England's least known Cathedral', the beautiful Mother Church of Nottinghamshire, Southwell Minster. If you admired the carvings in St Mary Magdalene, Newark, then you will be staggered by the work to be found in the 12th century Minster with its octagonal chapter-house and twin spires.

Southwell itself is an attractive small town and was once described by the late Sir John Betjeman as 'unspoilt', a description I would agree with. The heavily beamed **Saracens Head**

Hotel, an old coaching inn, was where Charles I spent his last night of freedom whilst **Burgage Manor** was the residence of Lord Byron prior to his taking up residence at Newstead Abbey, and it was friends in the town who first encouraged him to publish his poems.

I have always had an affinity with Derbyshire and this time I concentrated on **Eyam** as an example of one of the villages of the Peak. Each has its own charm and history and none more so than Eyam, known as the 'Queen of the Peak'. Here the old stone houses line the long, wide, old world street looking up to Eyam Edge towering 400ft above the village and reaching down to the gorge of **Middleton Dale** with its own delightful Cucklet Delf and Eyam Dale shut in by rocky heights. It looks at peace with itself but that is on the surface for no one living here has ever forgotten the terrible days of the plague.

It was in September 1665 that a box of tailor's cloth and some old clothes came from London to the cottage by the church, and with it a time that turned the village into a place of death, for it brought the plague that had raged in London for months. First the journeyman died within four days, five more by the end of the month and in October more than twenty. It continued its terrible path for the whole year only abating in the winter. The warmer weather set it off again and by March, 56 had perished.

All through this the villagers had been courageous and stoical people, who in the face of death, resigned themselves to their fate. Names that will live on forever are those of William Mompesson, the rector, his wife Catherine, and Thomas Stanley who had been ejected from the church for nonconformity, but had remained among his people. They set about isolating the village for the sake of other villages. They arranged for food to be brought from outside and left at certain places on the boundaries, the money left for payment being placed in vinegar to act as a disinfectant. One of these places has become known as Mompesson's Well and is covered with a block of stone, half a mile north of the village.

Deaths became so frequent that the passing bell ceased to be tolled. The Grave-yard could no longer take the dead. Graves were dug in gardens and fields often by the families of those who had died. One woman watched helplessly whilst her husband and six children died within eight days. Their graves can still be seen, a pathetic circle of six headstones and a tomb. Eventually the rector closed the church and took his ever decreasing flock to Cucklet Delf where Mompesson, whose wife Catherine was dead by this time, found comfort for himself and his followers in preaching from a picturesque rock with natural arches. By October the plague had run its course. Out of 350 villagers, 259 had died as well as 58 children. Mompesson and Thomas Stanley saw it through to the bitter end. Mompesson left the village afterwards and eventually became a Prebendary of York. Thomas Stanley, who remained at Eyam until he died, was not given such recognition. In fact had it not been for the Earl of Devonshire he would have still been turned out of the village for nonconformity.

It is a horrendous but moving story in its bravery. Eyam people are strong and welcoming, as can be witnessed if you visit the great church of St Lawrence. Be sure to see the 17th century wall paintings of emblems of the 12 tribes of Israel, the magnificent 8th-century cross, carved with bold vine scrolls and angels, and the 18th century sundial. It is open from 9am until dusk daily.

In Water Lane is **The Miners Arms** a 17th century inn with a great story to tell. It was used in lead mining times as the meeting place of the Great Barncote Court, which upheld the ancient and unique lead mining laws. The lead miners depended entirely on this Court to settle any disputes. Ghosts frequent The Miners, and they could well be disgruntled lead miners who found the Court's decisions had gone against them. The pub is fun and the hospitality excellent. The Miners also has excellent accommodation.

Next I would encourage you to visit **Baslow**, a pretty Derbyshire village situated on the edge of the magnificent Chatsworth Estate, four miles from the famous market town of **Bakewell** and within easy reach of all the Peak attractions. The towns of Manchester, Chesterfield and Sheffield are also only a short drive away. Pretty as the village may be, this was not my main reason for including it in this book. I want to introduce you to **Fischer's Baslow Hall** in Calver Road. This entrancing hilltop property built of local stone in 1907, stands on the village outskirts and is approached up a steep, snaking, tree-lined drive. You are invited to take drinks and canapés in the former hall which is dominated by a carved stone open fireplace and furnished in an attractive, comfortable country house style. The charming dining room seats 45 and here amidst candlelight you will enjoy a superb meal cooked by a culinary genius, Max Fischer. Simpler, but equally good meals are served everyday except Sunday in the 30-seater Café Max, a former living room off the entrance hall and at four tables on the terrace in summer. Open from 10am-10pm you can have everything from breakfast to afternoon tea. There are six bedrooms for those wanting to have the best of both worlds, a super place to stay and an ideal base for exploring.

Finally in Derbyshire I went to the little, historic village of **Repton**, just 9 miles away from the busy city of Derby. My reason was simply to see and experience the charms of **Bower Lodge**, a beautiful Victorian house at the end of the village. Here Peter and Liz Plant have built a reputation for being the most delightful and welcoming hosts. They are members of the Wolsey Lodge Consortium and make every one so welcome. It is also an excellent base for exploring so many wonderful places, Chatsworth House, Kedleston Hall, Calke Abbey to name just a few.

I have left Lincolnshire almost to the end of this chapter but in many ways you would be better taking a look at it after you visited Tinwell in Rutland because my first stop and my first love in Lincolnshire is the wonderful town of Stamford, just a few miles away. It took me a while to get to know this fascinating county. Until I did I had always thought of it as nothing else but fens and tulips with the occasional sausage and pork pie thrown in for good measure. It is no such thing, it burst forth upon me with a matchless beauty of its own. I suppose today I should refer to it as the County of Lincolnshire and South Humberside which is its official title.

You find yourself suddenly across the border from Norfolk or Rutland into an area of fenland that resembles a chequerboard with a skyline that is nothing short of phenomenal. It has a richness and a tranquillity, a sense of going backwards in time and a disbelief when you see the comparatively small amount of traffic on the roads.

This time I was determined to spend more time in and around Stamford. What an elegant town it is, probably the finest in the county, standing at its southern gateway, where Lincolnshire, Northamptonshire and Rutland meet and where the bustling River Welland makes a last dash down from hilly country to enter the Fenland plan. It was one of the five towns, Lincoln, Stamford, Leicester, Derby and Nottingham from which the Danes ruled Lincolnshire and the Midlands. For nearly a thousand years it has been a market town. Its beautiful buildings range mostly from medieval times to the Georgian era, and despite the centuries that separate them, the harmony is superb. No intrusion from either the 19th century, the age of the Industrial Revolution, or of our own 20th century have been allowed to spoil Stamford. It is full of surprises and charms which the centuries have bestowed. There are stone-slated roofs, steep gables, little bow windows, Tudor windows, Queen Anne houses, and Georgian mansions. Even inside these delightful houses, beautiful fireplaces, magnificent staircases and panelling still survive.

This time I stayed in Lady Anne's Hotel in **St Martin's Without** which takes its name from one of the earlier inhabitants of one of the houses that make up the present day hotel. Lady Anne Cecil was born on June 6th 1734 and was the much loved youngest sister of Brownlow, 9th Earl of Exeter. She would have spent her childhood at nearby **Burghley House** and later in her life moved to what was to become 38 High Street, St Martins Lady Anne's House the 5 bay building that now includes the main staircase of the hotel as well as the Old Sitting Room. Many local dignitaries lived in Lady Anne's House and a complete history of the building is available in the hotel.

Lady Anne's House is certainly delightful to stay in, has every comfort and the additional advantage of Hard and Lawn Tennis Courts available free of charge.

This is not the only interesting hotel in Stamford. **Candlesticks Hotel and Restaurant** at No 1 Church Lane has much to offer in a different sort of way. It has been recommended in many of the Food guides for the excellence of its cuisine and recently eight bedrooms have been upgraded making it a very comfortable place to stay.

You will have much to explore when you stay here including perhaps a visit to **The Steam Brewery Museum** in All Saints Street, where you can watch the brewing process from start to finish. In All Saints place is a church of that name, one of five medieval churches in the town. I visited three of them and found All Saints the most beautiful, with an exterior distinguished by the 13th century blank arcading and its fine Perpendicular steeple. It is a church that makes a statement about the wealth of the rich merchants who endowed the church and to whom there are splendid brasses.

A little to the east of Stamford, along the A16 is **Market Deeping** where the market is still a busy place and the rest of its name (with the other Deepings) reminds us that once its deep meadows were flooded every year by the River Welland from time immemorial. There are records that will tell you that the land was so fertile, gardens of great beauty were made out of its pits and bogs. The lands are still fertile, the flooding gone and the little town is a busy place. The old Market Place is where the A15 and A16 converge as well as several minor roads. Standing solidly on one side of the square is **The Deeping Stage Hotel**. It looks as though it has been there forever and I could imagine it being a welcome sight to the many weary travellers whose coaches would stop here to rest or change the horses, and give the occupants a chance to refresh themselves. Frequently it would have been an overnight stay and then, as today, the welcome into the warmth of the contented atmosphere of the hotel would have been a Godsend. The Deeping Stage provides not only comfort but good food, wines and beers.

The history of the Deepings is fascinating and centres round the great Wake family to whom Hereward the Wake belonged; he who resisted the Conqueror, and Hugh Wake, who looked after the affairs of the Forest of Kesteven for Henry III. Over a period of three hundred years the family grew in power and gained great possessions scattered all over England and into Scotland. Joan, the Fair Maid of Kent, was the heiress of the Wake family and daughter of Edmund Woodstock, Earl of Kent. Joan owned The Deepings among her 26 manors, most of them in Lincolnshire. She married her cousin the Black Prince as her second husband, and one of their two sons became Richard II.

In addition to Market Deeping, there is **Deeping Gate** and **Deeping St James** which today are really suburbs of Market Deeping. Deeping St James stretches alongside the Welland, a place of wide streets and many lovely old houses, stone-walled and stone-roofed with a particularly beautiful rectory beside the 15th century church.

It would be a pity not to take a look at **Woodhall Spa** which you will find on the B192 off the A153 between **Sleaford** and **Horncastle**. No longer operative as a spa town, the unique spa town atmosphere is still very much in evidence. It has excellent quality accommodation including the **Eagle Lodge Hotel** in The Broadway. Purpose built in 1891 it reigned supreme when Woodhall Spa was as well known to the high society of London as it is now to the golfing fraternity of the world. A super hotel, beautifully run.

By **The Golf Hotel** situated next door to the famous Woodhall Spa Championship Golf Course, there is a little **Cottage Museum** which will tell you how the town started and became a spa. You will then understand the enterprising John Parkinson who set out with three aims in the early 19th century; 1. Build a town. 2. Plant a forest. 3. Sink a coal mine. The town sadly was not built in Woodhall, but a fine street of town houses lies in the nearby village of **New Bolingbroke**. The forest was planted near Woodhall. As for the coalmine, John Parkinson chose a spot in Woodhall. When the shaft reached a depth of 540 feet, there was an inrush of clear salty water. So the Spa began. The Museum is open daily from Easter to October.

Throughout the year the woodlands in and around Woodhall Spa provide a cavalcade of colour. There are picturesque walks. The Viking Way, a long distance footpath from the Humber to Rutland Water, goes through the village. In the woods are two popular attractions, the **Kinema** and the **Teahouse**. The Kinema was an old cricket pavilion before becoming a cinema, and was christened 'the Flicks in the Sticks' during World War II by the armed forces billeted in the town. It still has a theatre organ rising up in the intermission to entertain the audience. The 'teahouse' was originally built in 1907 by the Misses Williams and has been providing refreshment ever since.

Going further towards the east coast, I made for **South Thoresby** at the foot of the Lincolnshire Wolds. You will find it one mile off the A16 and nine miles south of Louth. Ideal place for anyone to stay who wants to take a look at the coast. **The Vine Inn** is the place to visit. It has been there for about 300 years and replaced an earlier inn which goes back 500 years. I was made very welcome and cosseted in the small, intimate, dining room. The food was delicious and home-cooked and I was particularly pleased to find that smoking was not allowed! Good wine induced refreshing sleep and I was more than ready to wander round the villages and small towns of this lovely part of Lincolnshire.

An invitation to a race meeting at **Market Rasen** took me up the A16 to Louth and then on the A631 to the bustling town. Here is a delightful course, just east of the town and is acknowledged as one of the finest small tracks in the country. The recently built stand in the course enclosure is excellent, and for those who want to bring children there is a picnic area and a children's playground. The course sees seventeen days of National Hunt racing annually with a mix of exciting steeplechases and hurdle races. Particularly popular are the four evening meetings during May, June and August. A telephone call to 01673 843434 will give you the dates of the fixtures.

Market Rasen is a pleasant and prosperous small market town. The setting is lovely with woodlands all around, and the high Wolds sheltering it on the east. From the Wolds, at Bully Hill, the dancing little River Rase flows contentedly into the town. There is nothing spectacular about its architecture, the big church by the square has been considerably rebuilt but the richly moulded Norman doorway within the porch is superb. A good place to stay is Limes Country House Hotel in Gainsborough Road. Friendly, welcoming and comfortable it is very conveniently situated. A thoroughly nice hotel with the addition of Tea-rooms which stay open all year. The Limes will always stay in my mind for two reasons, firstly the sheer pleasure of sitting on the lawn on a warm summer's day enjoying a wickedly fattening Cream Tea and secondly, the unbelievable beauty of the sunset when seen through the unusual curved glass of the Furlong Bar.

With the intention of looking at **Brigg** and **Broughton**, to the north of **Caistor**, I was told that I could not do better than seek out **Arties Mill Lodge** in Wressle Road, Castlethorpe, Brigg. The information was good. The Mill is a charming old windmill, sadly without its sails built around 1790. The adjoining grain sheds and mill interior have been converted into bars, restaurant and function rooms. It is a friendly place and still retains many of the features of its Mill history. To get to it you drive out of Brigg for one mile on the A18. It is only five miles from Scunthorpe, 18 miles from Hull and Grimsby, with Lincoln just 22 miles distant. You will find that the 17 bedrooms are in **The Lodge** which is totally separate from the main bars and the restaurant. I found the food good, the owners and staff very friendly and helpful.

It is hard to believe that Brigg was once just a fishing hamlet. It is now busy with its markets and fairs and a riverside, where the trees meet with the water. The bridges span the old river and its straight new cut. Between the town and the Humber, this straight new River Ancholme has the Weir Dyke running beside it.

There have been some extraordinary finds here in the last hundred years or so. For example in 1886, when excavations were being made to provide for a gas-works, an ancient boat was unearthed. Shaped out of an enormous oak tree, it was between four and five feet wide, three to four feet deep, and nearly fifty feet long. It could carry fifty men. A few years earlier, a bed of clay in the brickyard disgorged a causeway fashioned of huge oak logs set on a layer of oak, hazel, and yew boughs. Another find was an oak raft, some 40ft long and almost 6ft wide. Both of these are thought to have belonged to the Early Iron Age.

THE JINGLERS INN
THE FOX AND HOUNDS,
Belper Road, A517 Bradley,
Ashbourne,
Derbyshire DE6 3EN

Tel/Fax: 01335 370855

You may wonder why this splendid old coaching inn has two names! If you approach it from Ashbourne, the Inn says, 'The Jinglers'. From Belper side it is called the more traditional 'Fox and Hounds'. The reason is that it was given the nickname of The Jinglers by the locals in the time when the road outside was a gated toll road. The old road then ran north-south past the pub then down Jinglers Lane, what is now a bridle path to the north and Jinglers Lane to the south. When the Mail Passenger Coach approached the pub, the bells on the horses' harnesses could be heard jingling in the distance, and Locals said 'Here it comes Jingling on in'.

It really is a delightful place to visit. Very much a family pub with old beams everywhere adding to the great atmosphere. All the walls and ledges are decorated with brass, silver and mugs, Horse leathers, Farm utensils, foreign notes and all manner of other bric-a-brac. Furnished exactly as a pub should be, it is warm and cosy, and above all things friendly to the visitor entering its doors for the first time. Much of this friendliness stems from the genuine welcome that the owner, Paula Catlin extends to everyone and this is something that is carried on by her staff. If you stay here you will find the guest bedrooms are attractively appointed and either en suite or with private bathrooms. Each room is self-contained and has its own entrance and kitchenette and has television. You cook your own breakfast from the plentiful ingredients supplied by your host. It does not detract from the enjoyment of the pub but it gives you total freedom - a great idea.

The food at Jinglers is delicious. Home-cooked bar meals are served at lunchtime and in the evening. The menu ranges from filled cobs to pizzas, chicken, steaks and salads and many other dishes. Jinglers run its own clay pigeon shoot on alternate weekends. Sporting, Skeet and Down the Line. Guns and tuition are available for beginners. Jinglers is an ideal base for visiting the many nearby attractions. A certified caravan location takes 34 caravans with hard standings for 27. Ashbourne is known as the Gateway to Dovedale - a truly beautiful place to explore. Just 2 miles away is Carrsinton water which provides excellent sailing, windsurfing and a walk around it of 9-10 miles.

USEFUL INFORMATION

OPEN; *All year*
CHILDREN; *Welcome*
CREDIT CARDS; *None taken*
LICENSED; *Full On*
ACCOMMODATION; *6 en suite*
bedrooms, self-contained with kitchenette

RESTAURANT; *Bar Meals*
BAR MEALS; *Wide range, good value*
VEGETARIAN; *Always a choice*
DISABLED ACCESS; *By arrangement*
GARDEN; *18 acres*
PETS; *Yes*

CALLADINE HOUSE,
17, Charnwood Street,
Derby, Derbyshire DE1 2FU
Tel: 01332 349106

Built at the turn of the century, it would best describe Calladine House as one of the most informal and friendly, unpretentious guest houses in which one could ever stay. Situated in the heart of Derby, it is convenient for people on business, indeed the main number of guests comes from this sector. They find it a home-from-home which is exactly what Andrea Costello tries hard to provide and succeeds admirably. This is also why the stranger to Derby finds it a happy house to be in. From here you can set out to explore the magnificent scenery that the surrounding provides, visit all sorts of fascinating places including Eyam, the plague village, which also has a wonderful church. Derby Cathedral does not rank as one of the foremost in the country but it has many superb facets including the glorious stained glass windows. It is a place for quiet contemplation, far more so than some of its more famous counterparts. Chatsworth House, the home of the Duke and Duchess of Devonshire, is within easy reach and will provide you with a wonderful day out, in a house that is full of old masters, fine furniture, magnificent architecture and perfectly maintained gardens and parkland. Alton Towers, Uttoxeter Race Course, the American Adventure and Matlock famous for its spa, are all nearby.

When you return to Calladine House at the end of a day out, it will be to the pleasant smell of an evening meal being cooked - everything is home-made. Breakfast is equally good and substantial making sure you never leave the table hungry. Andrea is happy to provide vegetarian dishes, or any other diet for that matter, providing she is given prior notice. At this present moment Calladine House is not licensed but expects to be soon. In the meantime you are more than welcome to bring your own wine.

USEFUL INFORMATION

OPEN; *All year*

CHILDREN; *Welcome*

CREDIT CARDS; *No*

LICENSED; *Shortly. BYO*

ACCOMMODATION; *7 rooms 1 en suite*

DINING ROOM; *Home cooked-fare*

VEGETARIAN; *& other diets by arrangement*

DISABLED ACCESS; *No*

GARDEN; *Yes + Patio*

PETS; *No .*

THE BELL INN,

Main Street, East Langtan,
Market Harborough,
Leicestershire LEl6 7TW
Tel:01858 545278 Fax: 01858 545 '748

Built in mid 1600 The Bell Inn is the epitome of what one expects an English traditional inn to be. The ceilings are low, the beams exposed and open fires send out a welcoming warmth from every room. The furnishings are in keeping with the age of the inn, deep sofas and armchairs are in abundance, old pine is everywhere and above all there is that indefinable something in the air which comes from a contented atmosphere acquired over the centuries. Whilst The Bell does not boast any ghosts you can feel the presence of the past. The hospitality that will have been in existence here for well nigh four hundred years is better today than it has ever been in the hands of the genial landlord, Alastair Chapman and his friendly, efficient staff. Apart from the excellence of the ale and other drinks in the well-stocked bar, The Bell is renowned for its food which is served every day of the week both at lunchtime and in the evenings with a full Carvery Lunch as well as Snacks available on Sundays. The range of food is tempting and exciting although the menu does not exclude some of the time-honoured favourites. There are Starters and Light Bites,. Mains and Middlers, an excellent and very tasty selection of Daily Specials on the Blackboard and for those who have a sweet tooth, The Bell's famous home-made sweets are irresistible. The menu is regularly changed and each time produces delicious food. Everything is cooked to order so please be patient - it is well worth waiting for. For those who would like to stay in this comfortable inn, there are two en suite bedrooms, beautifully appointed and each with television, a tea and coffee tray, biscuit barrel and trouser press. Breakfast like every other meal, is a feast.

USEFUL INFORMATION

OPEN; *11.30-2.30pm & 7-11pm*
CHILDREN; *Yes at Lunch and early evening*
CREDIT CARDS; *All major cards*
LICENSED; *Yes. Excellent Wine List*
ACCOMMODATION; *2 en suite rooms*
GARDEN; *Yes with rustic furniture*

RESTAURANT; *High class English fare*
BAR FOOD; *Excellent Daily Specials.*
VEGETARIAN; *Always a choice*
DISABLED ACCESS; *Yes*
PETS; *Yes, if well behaved*

THE BULL I'TH'THORN

Ashbourne Road,
Hurdlow, Nr Buxton,
Derbyshire SK17 9QQ
Tel: 01298 83348

The unusual name is enough to tempt you to discover The Bull I' th' Thorn and when you arrive you will be delighted with what you find beneath its ancient walls. This is an inn which is 1600 in part and goes back even further to 1472. It is full of atmosphere and full of antiques and artifacts which have been gathered over the years. All of it is authentic from the Cromwellian Armour to Swords, Gin Traps to Cross Band Winches and Powder Horns. Its earliest date 1472 is recorded and engraved on a plinth over the original fireplace. Farmhouse settles abound with Hibbert chairs and a very special William Cavendish Chair which used to be at Chatsworth House. Apart from the excellence of the food, drink and accommodation, it is simply a delightful, fascinating and memorable place to be.

In the Restaurant which is intimate and relaxed in spite of seating 50 people comfortably, the menu offers more than thirty choices mostly traditional English with the emphasis on Fish, Meat and Fowl with Game in Season. Annette Maltby-Baker is mine host and her partner, Graham is the talented chef. He is innovative and takes great pride and pleasure in producing and serving beautifully cooked and presented dishes. If you only wish to eat in the Bar there is always a choice from freshly cut, well filled sandwiches to the dish of the day. There is a good, well chosen wine list to complement the food. In the summer months the Beer Garden is popular with both adults and children; the latter have their own play area.

For those wanting to stay in this wonderful inn, there are four en suite guest rooms, newly refurbished and interestingly furnished in a 1930's style. One room has a splendid four poster and all the rooms have colour television and a hostess tray.

Breakfast, like every other meal at the Bull I' th' Thorn, is a delicious meal; very definitely something to look forward to at the start of the day whether you are at the inn for business or pleasure. Hurdlow is an excellent base for anyone wanting to explore the glories of Derbyshire including a feast of Stately homes, interesting villages, Well Dressings and all manner of other rituals that are part of the life of the county. Sheffield, Chesterfield and Derby are within easy distance and nearby Buxton is one of the finest towns in Derbyshire.

USEFUL INFORMATION

OPEN; *All year*
CHILDREN; *Welcome*
CREDIT CARDS; *Yes*
LICENSED; *Full On*
ACCOMMODATION; *4 en suite rooms one with four-poster*

RESTAURANT; *Delicious, traditional fare*
BAR FOOD; *Wide selection*
VEGETARIAN; *Daily choice*
DISABLED ACCESS; *No*
GARDEN; *Yes. Play area*
PETS; *Yes*

THE FALCON HOTEL

Castle Ashby,
Northampton NN7 1LF

Tel: 01604 696200 Fax: 01604 696673
E Mail: Falcon @ Castle Ashby.co.uk.

Just six miles south east of Northampton, this traditional 16th century country cottage hotel is made for relaxation. Privately owned and managed by the resident proprietors Jo and Neville Watson, it epitomises the best of England's cottage hotels. The Watsons have an eye for beauty which is apparent throughout the hotel. The overall atmosphere is cosy, warm and comfortable and enhanced in the winter with a blazing log fire. One of the nicest things is the presence of fresh flowers everywhere, lovingly arranged. Special weekend breaks are very popular and for those who have been fortunate enough to have a private party, wedding reception or small conference here, they will tell you with one voice that nothing seems to be too much trouble and the end result is perfect.

All 16 bedrooms have private bathroom or shower en suite, colour television, direct dial telephone, tea and coffee making facilities, hairdryer, bath robes and electric trouser press. Friendly faces greet you on arrival; French, Spanish and German is spoken. People come from far and wide for the restaurant alone. The food is outstanding but it is more than that. In summer the pretty restaurant seating 60, and pavilion marquee overlooks a luscious green lawn, surrounded by willow and walnut and in winter, you can sit by the roaring fire, enjoying a drink whilst you peruse the exciting menu. Local asparagus in May and June is a speciality. As part of an extensive wine list, which includes well tried traditional varieties, Neville has introduced a good selection of interesting half bottles. For less formal meals the friendly Cellar Bar with its wealth of exposed beams and fine selection of real ales, has an excellent menu. The hotel is a member of the Best Western Consortium and a Relais du Silence.

Situated,minutes from Castle Ashby House, The Falcon is within easy walking distance of the magnificent grounds. The 10,000 acre estate has been owned by the Marquess of Northampton's family for over four centuries. There are many fun things to do close by including golf, riding, fishing, clay pigeon shooting and water sports and a little further afield Silverstone, Stratford, Bedford, Woburn and Althorp.

USEFUL INFORMATION

OPEN; *All year Bar 12-3pm & 6.30-11pm*
CHILDREN; *Welcome*
CREDIT CARDS; *Visa/Master/Amex/JCB*
LICENSED; *Yes. Good wine list*
ACCOMMODATION; *16 en suite rooms*
GARDEN; *Yes, very pretty*

RESTAURANT; *Renowned for its food*
In summer outside dining
BAR FOOD; *Wide choice*
VEGETARIAN; *Always a choice*
DISABLED ACCESS; *One room equipped*

WASHINGBOROUGH HALL COUNTRY HOUSE HOTEL

Church Hill,
Washingborough,
Lincoln LN4 1BE
Tel: 01522 790340 Fax: 01522 792936

The Cathedral city of Lincoln is just two miles away from Washingborough Hall which is a Grade II Listed Georgian Manor House set in extensive and secluded grounds. It makes a superb base for anyone wanting an informal and relaxing holiday or a short break, or for those people on business who value the welcome they get from this privately owned and personally run hotel. Mary and Brian Shillaker are the joint proprietors and the emphasis throughout the Hotel is on high standards, good service and comfort. Every room is charmingly furnished with some antique pieces and other furniture that fits in beautifully. The 12 bedrooms, 6 doubles and 6 twin-bedded are all en suite and some have four-poster beds or Spa Baths. Every room has colour television, hair dryers, trouser presses, complimentary toiletries and a generously supplied beverage tray as well as direct dial telephones.

Washingborough Hall is renowned for its food and in the elegant Wedgwood Dining Room, overlooking the gardens, you will be offered a choice of dishes from a traditional menu which delights the eye as much as it does the palate. A comprehensive and well chosen wine list offers something to suit everyone's taste and pocket. After your meal you are invited to help yourself to coffee and relax in the hall where there is a log fire burning in the colder months. The comfortable bar, serving real ale, is an ideal place to have a quiet drink and order your meal.

The grounds are secluded and contain many mature trees and there is a large lawned area where you may play croquet during the Summer months. The Hall is well known for its flower display. These are all grown from seeds or cuttings by Mary Shillaker who specialises in fushias. A heated, outdoor swimming pool is available for your use in the Summer months. There is so much to do in this area of Lincolnshire. Apart from the magnificent Cathedral and Castle in Lincoln, the county is famous for the Battle of Britain flight at Coningsby and several other aviation museums. The Lincolnshire Wolds offer miles and miles of traffic free roads across beautiful countryside. There are many unspoilt villages, market towns and historic houses. Once across the Wolds enjoy the Fens, the windmills, and the long east coast with its nature reserves and golden sands.

USEFUL INFORMATION

OPEN; *All year. 8am-11pm*
CHILDREN; *Welcome*
CREDIT CARDS; *All major cards*
LICENSED; *Yes. Fine wines + Real Ale*
ACCOMMODATION; *12 en suite rooms*
PETS; *Well behaved pets welcome*
AA + RAC 3 STAR RATING

DINING ROOM; *Delicious food, superbly presented. Open to non-residents*
VEGETARIAN; *Upon request*
DISABLED ACCESS; *No.*
(Only to Dining Room)
GARDEN; *Beautiful & secluded*
With heated outdoor pool

THE KINGS ARMS COUNTRY INN & RESTAURANT

Top Street, Wing,
Oakham,
Rutland LE15 8SE
Tel: 01572 737634   Fax: 01572 737255

No one comes to the Kings Arms without being enchanted by it and happy to enjoy all that it has to offer. Built in 1643 it is full of an atmosphere which has been created over the centuries. Low ceilings, beams, inglenooks and all sorts of nooks and crannies add to the environment and this is enhanced by the friendly, hospitable owners Neil and Karen Hornsby, who, together with their staff, make sure everyone feels relaxed and welcome once they enter the door. Wing is a small Rutland village with a character of its own and has the oldest Maze in the world. Rutland Water is only 2 miles away which offers many activities including, fishing, sailing, great walks and cycle routes. Alternately just sit on the water's edge and watch life on the water! The Kings Arms also has a special arrangement with a local golf club. Leicester and Peterborough are both within easy distance and so is the fine old Lincolnshire town of Stamford. Burleigh House is just one of the Stately homes one can visit.

The Kings Arms has an excellent chef and is renowned for the high standard of its food. From the 6 Starters one can have Half Shell Mussels filled with Crabmeat topped with Melted Cheese or Smoked Haddock and Leek Soup finished with Chives and Cream. The Main Dishes are equally delicious with Lamb Steak marinaded in Rosemary and Garlic, chargrilled and served with a Port and Redcurrant Sauce, a firm favourite on the menu. There is always a choice for Vegetarians and a good selection of Bar Meals. You will find specialty dishes and bar snacks featured daily on the two chalkboards. A well chosen wine list is there to complement the meal.

The 8 bedrooms are all en suite. Four of them can be either double or family. There is one splendid Four-poster room and a Special Occasion Suite included. Attractively furnished in a traditional country style, every bedroom has television, direct dial telephone, a hospitality tray, trouser press and hairdryer. The recent conversion of the old village Bakehouse has provided four of these very comfortable bedrooms. There are no special provisions for disabled people but there are rooms on the ground floor. The garden is always popular in fine weather and it has a good play area for children.

If you cannot find the time to stay here, do make the effort to discover how good the Kings Arms Country Inn and Restaurant is - you will not be disappointed.

USEFUL INFORMATION

OPEN; *12-3pm. 6pm-midnight*
CHILDREN; *Welcome*
CREDIT CARDS; *All except Amex/Diners*
LICENSED; *Full On*
ACCOMMODATION; *8 en suite rooms*
Four-poster. Special Occasion Suite

RESTAURANT; *Super, imaginative food*
BAR FOOD; *Wide range*
VEGETARIAN; *Yes*
DISABLED ACCESS; *No*
GARDEN; *Yes. Play area*
PETS; *No*

GUY WELLS,
Eastgate,
Whaplode, Spalding,
Lincolnshire, PE12 6TZ.

Tel : 01406 422239

This beautiful 18th century Queen Anne Farmhouse gets it's name from the wells in the land which surround the house. Situated deep in the Fenland countryside, this charming listed building is home to Richard and Anne Thompson, who create an atmosphere of conviviality and hospitality that ensures the relaxation and enjoyment of all their guests. The house is set in old fashioned country gardens, surrounded by trees, creating a haven of peace and tranquillity that will delight and soothe you. Inside is delightful, with those little touches that make this a comfortable home from home. Each bedroom is attractively furnished and decorated, with good facilities such as full central heating, clock radio, and a hospitality tray of tea and coffee. Downstairs is a comfortable lounge with low ceilings and old beams, where you can relax in one of the raspberry tub chairs in front of the wood burning stove, and perhaps watch a bit of TV, or chat about your day's activities. Anne's superb style of cooking is wholefood, and their own vegetables and free range eggs are used where possible. An evening meal or a light supper can be arranged, as can vegetarian dishes, upon request. This is a working farm growing arable crops and flowers like daffodils, tulips, lilies and chrysanthemums.

This is a great base from which to explore much of Lincolnshire and of Cambridgeshire. Spalding itself is home to Springfield Gardens; 25 acres of lawns, flowerbeds and woodlands with wonderful displays of tulips in April and May. Boston has the 14th century Church of St Botolph with it's fine carvings and painted roof. There are many great churches in this area, and also many stately homes. The great Sandringham is within visiting distance, and others include the medieval Grantham House, Belton and Burghley. Peterborough is a great day out with it's excellent shopping centre, river trips and magnificent cathedral. There is something for everyone in this charming part of the country, and to end the day in the warm atmosphere of Guy Wells can only be described as one of life's memories to be treasured.

USEFUL INFORMATION

OPEN; *All year*
CHILDREN; *Well behaved welcome*
PETS; *Not indoors*
CREDIT CARDS; *None taken*
ACCOMMODATION; *3 rooms : 2 en suite.*

DINING ROOM; *Excellent English fayre*
VEGETARIANS; *By request*
DISABLED ACCESS; *Not really*
GARDEN; *1 acre beautifully managed*

Chapter 13

**EAST ANGLIA including
NORFOLK & SUFFOLK**

INCLUDES

Chapter 13

EAST ANGLIA including
NORFOLK & SUFFOLK

For this chapter of the book I have changed the format slightly and in so doing I will endeavour to give you a glimpse, alphabetically, of as many places as I can. East Anglia is so full of charm from its county town of Norwich, to its country villages, its busy coastal resorts and the timeless beauty of The Norfolk Broads, that it becomes impossible to include everything. Explore it for yourselves and use my input as the basis for a memorable tour.

Everything seems to have an exception to the rule and so going away from my scheme I am writing separately about Norwich; my excuse, well it is the county town - and I love it.

Perhaps **Norwich** gets its European air from the fact that it is almost as quick to get to Amsterdam as it is to London. In the past this has certainly been a facet of its trading habits. Whatever the reason this is one of the most exciting cities in the country. It is full of history but that has never prevented the City fathers from seeing into the future and continuing to do so even today. It is a city with two sides to its face. The first in this day and age has to be its commercial face which shines with success, the second and the one in which I am primarily concerned is its past and its leisure.

The very special atmosphere of the city might first of all be savoured in the market place where stalls are covered by brightly coloured 'tilts' - awnings to those of us who do not know the local terminology. It is a bustling place and it is with some difficulty that you will pass down the narrow lanes between the stalls. One of the landmarks of the city is **St Peter Mancroft** church in Market Place which is dramatically floodlit at night, as are many of the city's wonderful buildings. There is no other word for it but stunning. The building which dominates the market place is City Hall. It is the most popular building with the people of Norwich but Pesvner described it as 'likely to go down in history as the foremost English public building of between the wars'. For me it is the Guildhall, a contemporary almost of St Peter Mancroft, which delights the eye with its striking pattern of stone and flint. It was begun in 1407 and constructed by forced labour.

Norwich is somewhere you should explore on foot. For example at the Back of Inns is the **Royal Arcade**, which has a tessellated pavement, laid by imported Italian workmen, and over the delightful Victorian/Edwardian shops, the walls and glass roof can only be described as Art Nouveau. In Theatre Street is **The Assembly House** set back behind wrought iron gates and well manicured lawns. It is the venue for thousands of people every year who flock here to enjoy concerts, exhibitions and meetings. Norwich has more pre-Reformation churches than London, York and Bristol put together. One of them is St Stephens in Theatre Street. It was the last of the great series of Norwich churches to be built. It is eye catching. the tower is superbly decorative in contrasting flint and stone in roundels, diamonds and window outlines. The 16 clerestory windows have some notable glass and the sun shining through them throws immense light on the glorious hammerbeam roof. **Chapelfields** once was the place where archery was practised in Elizabeth I's reign. This was not for fun but was enforced; a sort of conscription.

Bacon's House in Colegate on the corner with St George Street is one building that has been tenderly restored. It was the 16th century residence of a prosperous worsted merchant who was Lord Mayor of the city. It is a fine timber-framed house.

Regency houses line Quayside and will lead you to Fye Bridge built in medieval style. The bridge stands at the beginning of Magdalene Street which was rescued from decay by the Civic Trust in the 1950's. The houses glow with colour and every now and then one will surprise you with its charming medieval courtyard.

Using Fye Bridge and Wensum Street as your guide, the first turning to the right is **Elm Hill**, surely the showpiece of the city. It has everything. Narrow winding streets are covered in cobblestones. The quaint houses, partly dating from the 15th century, are painted almost all the colours of the rainbow. There is the 16th century half timbered Pettus House, the 17th-century Flint House and the 15th-century church of St Simon and St Jude, now a centre for the Norwich Boy Scouts. As in almost every part of central Norwich there are more alleys to explore. Wrights Court just up from the church, was rescued from decay and takes its name from Wright & Son who, in the last century, had a factory in Elm Hill employing something like fifteen hundred hand-loom weavers. Within its courtyard, on the first floor facing the street, is a long weaver's window which was the only way, at that time, Wrights would have been able to give maximum light to their workroom. In spite of Elm Hill looking almost like a film setting, it is a busy place full of shops carrying on trades that harmonise with the surroundings, yet creating business in its own right.

A visit to **The Castle** and **The Cathedral** are musts. The battlements of the castle provide a fine vantage point to look down on many of the sights and streets you have already seen. It really does dominate the city and all the streets go round it. Built by Roger Bigod in the 12th century its purpose was to block the way to the city. Its peaceful role today is that of a museum which has the reputation of being the finest provincial museum in the kingdom.

Unlike many cities, the cathedral does not dominate the skyline. It is quite low lying and surrounded by buildings which make its spire - one of the tallest in the country - hide its beauty for privileged eyes. What a wondrous place it is. Before you enter you will find yourself embraced by the arms of the Cathedral Close. Its effect is immediately to make you feel withdrawn from the modern world. You can choose to enter this enchanted world through the Bishop's Gate in Palace Street, the Erpingham Gate or St Ethelbert's Gate in Tombland. Any of them reveal the stunning beauty of Upper Close and Lower Close as well as Green Yard and Almery Green. The grander houses are in upper Close with delightful cottages in Hook's Walk. At every corner there is another vista upon which to feast your eyes. Lovingly tended gardens are an offering to the Lord, and when the sun shimmers on the mullioned windows you know you are in a magical land.

The Cathedral was begun in 1096 by Bishop Herbert de Losinga on the orders of the Pope, as a penance for the sin of simony. The penance could not have been performed better. I have my own special favourite spots in the cathedral, one of which is going in through the south transept door, passing through the transept and then turning left into the nave south aisle until I reach the end of the nave. From here I have a view of the full length of the building which takes my breath away every time.

It is almost a relief to leave so much beauty and if your departure happens to be at eventide when The Close is at its best, I suggest you walk slowly through to Pull's Ferry from which you can turn back and see the cathedral from the river, remembering all its glory.

You could spend a long time in Norwich and never see all its treasures. This makes it all the more reason to come back.

What I have not told you about, are my favourite places to stay, drink and eat.

In Earlham Road, just ten minutes stroll from the centre of Norwich is **The Beeches Hotel and Victorian Gardens**. Two listed and sympathetically restored Victorian houses together with a new annexe make up this enchanting hotel which stands in 3 acres of tranquil wooded grounds. Over the years the garden became neglected as the house passed through the hands of various owners but in 1980 the house and its 'secret garden' were rediscovered. Today it is restored to much of its former glory and guests are free to wander through the delights of this important reminder of our Victorian heritage, with its ornate Gothic fountain and Italianate terrace. **The Garden House Hotel** at Salhouse Road, Rackheath has a reputation far and wide for the superb quality of its food. The hotel is totally charming and run by Jill and John Smart whose high standards are reflected throughout the hotel. They have certainly achieved a winning formula.

I always liked the greeting we had from **The Georgian House Hotel** in Unthank Road; 'Comfortable we may be, expensive we are not'! This is entirely true and accounts for the frequently returning guests enjoying the hotels ever popular Weekend or Mid-Week Breaks. Literally 5 minutes walk from the historic heart of Norwich.

Brasteds Restaurant on St Andrews Hill, just off Elm Hill, is a gastronomic experience. The menu offers classic European cuisine and regular customers will tell you that part of the pleasure in going there is to experience the peculiarly welcoming and friendly atmosphere that emits from the ghost who has haunted 8-10 St Andrews Hill since the 17th century!

St Benedicts Restaurant at No.9 St Benedicts Street is a City centre restaurant in a bustling street full of atmosphere. The cooking is top quality with a well chosen wine list and it is all at affordable prices.

Now for the places I have visited on this tour of Norfolk.

Banham on the B113 from Forcett St Mary is a lovely village, just 5 miles north-west of Diss and has a wealth of historic houses. It surrounds a rectangular green. The beautiful 13th century church has a churchyard from which, at the eastern end, you can see the Priory, a fine Georgian house with Dutch gables and, beyond Norfolk House with an original 19th century pedimented top window. To the left is the timber-framed Guildhall with a jettied upper floor. If you wonder where the brick came from to build all these fine houses, there used to be kilns at Hunts Corner, half a mile to the west of the village. They supplied much of south Norfolk with brick and tile.

When you have feasted your eyes sufficiently on the delights of the village may I suggest you turn your thoughts to delighting the inner man and repair to the splendid 17th century **Red Lion**, an establishment that caters for locals of all ages and welcomes visitors.

Billingford just west of Diss, has a handsome five storied windmill. It has been lovingly tended by the Norfolk Windmills Trust and is open to the public at weekends in summer. The village is dominated by a fine lofty church, with some remains of the 13th and 15th centuries. The tower is octagonal and embattled. Two fine arcades with clustered pillars divide the nave and aisles and over them are the quatrefoil windows of the clerestory. The bench ends are carved with 15th century tracery and old poppyheads but it is the lectern which is most interesting. Some 450 years old, it is vast with four lions at the foot. It is said to have come from the same foundry as its mighty counterpart in Peterborough Cathedral. Of little importance today is that the village once was the home of Sir Simon Burley, a favourite of Richard II who despatched him to Bohemia to bring Anne to England to be his queen. His fame and fortune did not serve him well; he died not in peaceful Billingford but by losing his head on Tower Hill.

Blickling one mile north of Aylsham has **Blickling Hall** owned by the National Trust, undoubtedly Norfolk's most wonderful Jacobean house. You approach it along a drive between clipped hedges of yew and rows of limes, and then over an   ornamental bridge astride the dry moat. At the end of the drive the Tudor splendour of the house bewitches you with its gables, turrets and oriel windows. It is built round two open courts, and the garden front looks on a garden of roses, box hedges and flowering borders a mile round.

In the great park of some 600 acres, a lake glistens in the sunlight and every now and again you come across a little statue and at one point, a summer house, which is a copy of a Greek temple. The fountains which toss their floating streams of water in the air, come from Oxnead. What appears to be a pyramid is the tomb of the second Earl of Buckinghamshire and his family. He was our Ambassador to Russia and sufficiently respected by the court of the Tsars to be presented by Catherine the Great, with a tapestry of Peter the Great at the battle of Poltowa. This is now in the house with portraits by Gainsborough and Zucchero amongst others. The massive library has a remarkable plaster ceiling with rows of symbolical figures representing Learning and the Five Senses in the centre. There is a priceless collection of manuscripts including a copy of the Maintz Bible - the first one printed - a Miles Coverdale Bible and two books printed by Caxton.

Brancaster Staithe, just three miles from Burnham is renowned for its salt marshes and is said to be the least polluted in Europe. It certainly produces the finest quality mussels and other seafood delicacies which you can enjoy when you visit **The Lobster Pot**. The pub provides a great atmosphere and the restaurant looks out over the harbour to Scuit Head Island, one of the best views on the North Norfolk coastline.

Bressingham just outside Diss, off the A1066 has an interesting **Steam Museum** in which there are hundreds of steam driven things plus Victorian fairground gallopers and the **Dell Garden** next door. There is a busy summer and autumn   programme of rallies and events. For details ring 01379 88382. It is open from mid-April to mid-October from 10-5.30pm

Buckenham is a little village which once had a ferry. Those days have gone but there are still some delightful cottages and a village green whilst nearby there is a Steam Museum for your entertainment.

Burnham Market - When you see the signposts for Burnham just off the A149 Sheringham to Hunstanton coast road, you might be confused because in all there are seven pretty villages in this group. Three of them Westgate, Sutton and Ulph have joined together and become the small town of **Burnham Market**. All the villages seem to be in sight of the sea and you reach them through a network of high hedged narrow lanes. It is somewhere you want to linger. The village green is surrounded by pretty 18th century buildings with red-tiled roofs. In amongst them is **Fishes**, a simple but not unsophisticated restaurant run by Gillian Cape, an ex-school teacher who will tell you she came into the business by accident. That may be so but she is totally professional and it is a pleasure to eat there. **The Lord Nelson** is the appropriately named village inn -Admiral Lord Nelson was born in the rectory at **Burnham Thorpe**. Valerie Jordan who runs the pub with her husband Peter, is a local artist and they hold Art Exhibitions in their stable. There are no lack of subjects for artists in this lovely part of Norfolk. Migrating birds are to be seen in the marshes, seascapes vary all the time and the lush green countryside with delightful cottages and houses attracts many artists. **Burnham Overy** has a fine group of 18th-century mill buildings, Burnham Norton is an unspoilt hamlet and **Burnham Deepdale's** church contains one of the finest fonts in East Anglia.

Beulagh lies one mile off the B1354 south of Coltishall. Worth making the effort if only to stand on the high bank in the churchyard of St Peters. There is nothing below but the River Bure and you get an extraordinary sense of tranquillity, as though you had left the outside world momentarily.

Burgh-Next-Aylsham on the Blickling Road is **Aylsham Old Hall** surrounded by Dutch-gabled farm buildings. It is a perfect example of a late 17th century house. Millgate Street will take you to the River Bure and give you a chance to look in wonder at the 18th century mill.

Colkirk is almost into Fakenham and is a pretty little village standing on high ground. It gets on with its own life, quietly enjoying the luxury of being surrounded by lovely countryside and having a village pub, **The Crown** which is the focal point of its being.

Coltishall is a village you must find time for. It is at the head of navigation on the River Bure and a favourite place for boating people. It has pleasant, mellow brick Georgian houses with many of the gardens running down to the river bank. People have lived here throughout history. Roman urns have been unearthed and Roman tiles frame two of the Saxon windows in the hilltop church. There is still Saxon masonry in the walls although most of the church is of the 13th and 14th centuries. The Norman font is lovely and so too is the little 17th century gallery beneath the tower. I stopped for a drink and a sandwich in the lively **Kings Head** which has plentiful moorings. I was told I should have tried the superb Pacific prawns in garlic butter which are one of the specialities of the informal restaurant. You may stay here for bed and breakfast if you wish at very reasonable prices.

Cromer is a fishing village that was developed into a seaside resort by the coming of the railways at the end of the 19th century and has been bustling ever since. It has great charm especially round the centre which highlights the old flint buildings of the fishing village it once was. Here stands the church of St Peter and St Paul, at 160 feet the tallest of any parish in Norfolk. The sea has always been important to Cromer and even today the Crab boats work daily except in the stormiest of conditions. If you like crab you will find there is little to rival a freshly boiled Cromer crab which is almost always on the menu of the many inns and restaurants. With the sea so much part of the life of the community it is not surprising that the town's lifeboat has one of the most decorated histories of any in Britain. There is a lifeboat museum in The Gangway which will tell you much more of the bravery of these men.

Dickleburgh. I would stay here in **The King's Head**. The 600 years old pub dates back to the reign of Richard II. It is steeped in history, friendly, feeds you well and has comfortable accommodation at incredibly reasonable prices. The village is only 3 miles from Diss and has an Otter Trust nearby as well as Wild Life Parks, and is also within easy reach of the coast.

Edingthorpe two miles to the north of North Walsham has All Saints Church which keeps watch as it stands on a little hill alone in a field. It has a delightful thatched nave and is worth the trek. Wellies might not be a bad idea though! A little 14th century church, still lit by oil lamps at **Crostwight** also called All Saints stands bravely facing the elements in another field. One that looks out on the sea in splendid isolation is the Saxon church of St Margarets at **Witton**.

Erpington near Cromer on the Norwich Road has **Alby Crafts** where old and mellow flint and brick farm buildings have been converted into an attractive craft centre surrounded by gardens. The Lace Museum is exquisite with some of the delicate work over 300 years old. The deft, nimble fingers of the laceworkers always fascinates me - I cannot even sew a button on properly. When you have watched long enough and perhaps been inspired to have a go for yourselves, you may buy lacemakers requisites if you wish, as well as books on the subject, and finished pieces of handmade lace. In addition to the Lace Museum there is a Bottle Museum with all sorts, shapes and sizes and some extremely old and rare. The Furniture showroom is an eye-opener on craftsmanship. Exhibitions are held here throughout the year and you are quite likely to see sculptors or stained glass designers at work as well as glass engravers, silversmiths and potters. At the end of your visit the Buttery will provide you with a welcome cup of tea.

Fakenham is on my list because it is all that you would expect of a market town. Go there on a Thursday and you will find it transformed into an open air market full of bustling shoppers and friendly chatter. It is a splendid centre for antique auctions too. There is a racecourse with regular meetings and on the outskirts of the town is the village of **Thursford** which is the home of **The Thursford Collection**. I was there just before Christmas a few years ago when this exciting place was playing host to Songs of Praise. It was magical.

Forncett St Mary to the east of Attleborough is a tiny village which is the home of The Forncett Industrial Steam Museum. It houses an amazing collection of large, stationary steam engines, including one of the pumping engines which started its life as the force that went behind opening Tower Bridge in London. There are 28 different engines seven of which can be seen running on Steam Days; the 1st Sunday of every month from May to October and also the 3rd Sunday in July, August and September plus Spring and August Bank Holiday Sunday and Monday from May until the end of September 2-6pm. It is certainly an insight into what has driven industry of all kinds from the 19th century to the present.

Fritton is a straggling village scattered around a vast marshy common. Its glory is the church of St Catherine, reached up a grassy track. It is a thatched building with a little round tower. It has some fine paintings, the most striking is St George and the Dragon. The knight, in coloured armour, flourishes a sword above his head as his horse rears up. Nearby is **Fritton Lake Country Park** part of the Somerleyton estate, which offers hours of interest and activity to the visitor. The lake is two and a quarter miles long and probably one of the most beautiful expanses of water in East Anglia. You can fish, play pitch and putt, go boating, windsurfing, walk looking for wildfowl or just simply sit and do nothing. The adventure play area is paradise for children and they will probably plague you for pony rides, but who could resist these gentle animals.

A house filled with love is how I would describe **Somerleyton Hall**, the family home of Lord and Lady Somerleyton and their five children. It is a perfect   example of a house built to show off the wealth of new Victorian aristocracy. Sir Morton Peto made a vast fortune from the railways and promptly spent a large part of it taking what was a comparatively small 17th-century manor at Somerleyton and creating around it an extravagant concoction of red brick and white stone. Inside he made it nothing less than lavish. He went too far and subsequently went bankrupt, selling his beloved house to Sir Francis Crossley, whose great grandson is the present Lord Somerleyton.

The Somerleytons run it as a family home but always with the knowledge that in order to preserve it for their children, they must share it with the many visitors who come each year to enjoy the house and particularly the gardens. The Oak Room stands out with its carved oak panelling and Stuart atmosphere. Here, between the windows of the northern wall hangs an exquisite silver and gilt moulded mirror originally made for the private apartments of the Doge's Palace in Venice, and at one time owned by Queen Anne. The other rooms are richly Victorian full of fine antiques and some delightful silver Meissen. The Ballroom is stunning in its grandeur. You can almost hear the music playing and the soft swish of lovely evening gowns as the ladies waltz in the arms of their elegantly attired menfolk. It has sumptuous crimson and damask walls reflected in rows of long white and gilt mirrors. In the Dining Room there is a rare portrait of Rembrandt and his wife as Ferdinand and Isabella, as well as paintings by many other famous artists. Some of these were collected by Sir Morton Peto in his heyday, who not only purchased old masters but commissioned painters such as Landseer to do new work. The Library houses a fine collection of books and there will not be a visitor who is not charmed by the Victorian Dolls House.

The 12 acres of garden are justly renowned. The yew maze planted by Nesfield in 1846 is one of the few Victorian mazes in Britain. Somerleyton Hall is open to the public from Easter until the end of September, Wednesdays, Thursdays and Sundays from 2-5.30pm and Bank Holiday Mondays. The Gardens open on Monday and Friday as well from 2-5.30pm.

Gorleston-by-the-Sea just four miles from Gt Yarmouth is as different as chalk and cheese. It has two faces, one side of it is the dockland of the River Yare but then you come to the beach and the whole scene changes. This quiet, slightly old   fashioned place has a special fascination. The people who live here take life calmly, look in the churchyard and you will find at least eight gravestones of centenarians which proves it. The great church stands on a bank and it was quite likely that Felix, Bishop of Dunwich built a small wooden church on the site in the 7th century. The fine flint tower stands 90ft high and if you want to climb to the top you will need a lot of puff; there are 127 steps. The marine drive which goes along for about two miles is wonderful and not an amusement arcade in sight. Just the cliffs above and the sea ahead. If I were staying in the Yarmouth area this is where I would come. There are two good hotels with splendid views, **The Cliff Hotel** on Cliff Hill and **The Pier Hotel** at the Harbourmouth.

Great Ryburgh nestles in the verdant Wensum valley approximately 3 miles south east of Fakenham in North Norfolk. This is a delightful corner of rural England, teeming with wild life - there are over 20 nature reserves and bird sanctuaries in the county. In addition the area is full of charming villages, small towns, a varied coastline and a rich range of tourist attractions. At the end of the village opposite the round towered Saxon parish church lies **The Boar Inn**, just a few yards away from the peacefully flowing River Wensum. Staying here at anytime is pleasant but sitting on the sun-trapped patio of this delightful inn looking out on the garden, enjoying a good lunch on a summer's day, is one of life's great pleasures.

Great Snoring is a small rural village just 2 miles north east of Fakenham from the A148 King's Lynn-Cromer Road. It is quiet and peaceful and has The Old Rectory, a secluded haven that dates back to 1500 and promises the discerning traveller old fashioned charm with a homely warmth and friendliness.

Great Yarmouth is one of the busiest places, sometimes a bit too garish but nonetheless a town that delights many visitors year in and year out. It is long and narrow, hemmed in by the River Yare. Once its economy relied entirely on the herring fisheries but when the Victorians discovered its sandy beaches and started coming for holidays, the town changed its thinking away from the fish quays and concentrated on this new way of making a living. There is a happy balance between the two with some fine 18th century buildings on South Quay. The sea-front is totally different and has become engulfed in all the 20th century holiday attractions. The town has its share of museums - five to be precise which I have listed at the back of the book for you.

Happisburgh is a coastal village not far from North Walsham. It has wonderful views and none more so than from **The Hill House**, an old coaching inn which dates back to the 16th century. Here Sir Arthur Conan Doyle was a regular visitor. Hill House stands high on a hill and has wonderful views of the Norfolk countryside. It is full of character, offers good food and is a friendly and relaxed place to be. There is limited accommodation.

Herringfleet just a mile to the west of Somerleyton Hall, has an odd little round-towered church with an east window filled with foreign glass. A south window however makes up for it with two figures of the 14th century. One curious thing about this church is that its priest is never instituted.

Hevingham three miles south of Aylsham is beautifully wooded through the generosity of Robert Marsham, a member of a local family, who was a keen naturalist and squire of the next door village **Stratton Strawless**. This was in the late 18th century and many of the trees he planted then still line the A140. Hevingham has benefited too from H.P. Marsham, who in 1881, gave St Botolph's church a number of stained glass panels. These were originally made in Germany for a monastery but were looted at the end of the 18th century by French soldiers who sold them into willing English hands.

The name Marsham appears again in the friendly Freehouse and Hotel, **The Marsham Arms**. This story too concerns Robert Marsham because in 1832 on a dark and windy night on the Holt road some seven miles from Norwich, he was attacked and robbed. Thinking that his attackers were poor farm labourers on their way to Norwich Market, penniless and with nowhere to stay, he decided, with remarkable generosity under the circumstances, to build a hostel for such men as these. The Hostel was later licensed and is now known as the Marsham Arms. The wood beams and massive open fireplace in the entrance bar are original features from the hostel.

Horning is one of the best loved Broadland boating centres. Because of its position it is dedicated to the needs of those holidaying or visiting the Broads. For me it is the charm of the place that is more important. It has one long street with a happy mixture of inns, shops, cottages and boatyards. Many of the buildings have reed thatch and most of them are built with brick that has mellowed with age. The pretty half timbered houses have moorings and thatched boathouses alongside. The river winds in and out until it nears the old church, which hides its face behind trees but still manages to catch glimpses of the shining water and the gaily coloured sails of the boats.

The Petersfield House Hotel is an elegant and comfortable, family run 18 bedroomed hotel a riverside retreat set well back from the banks and surrounded by two acres of beautifully tended landscaped gardens. The hotel has access to its own moorings and fishing facilities. Its impressive restaurant overlooks the garden. The regular Saturday night Dinner Dance is a major attraction for both guests and non-residents throughout the year.

Some friends of mine had dinner in The Swan Hotel here not so long ago and loved it. The restaurant has an intimacy created no doubt by the wealth of oak beams, the sparkling china and glass and the gentle light that emanates from the oil lamps. A walk across the lawns brings you to the rivers edge

Ingworth has the little church of St Lawrence of which only the stump of the tower remains and that is thatched. Inside the church is simply furnished but it is the views down to the Mill House and the water meadows which makes it so pleasing. Mills abound around the waters of the River Bure. A humped back bridge over the river at **Oxnead** lets you see an old mill on the right and there is yet another clapboard water mill by the Bure as you reach **Burgh-Next-Aylsham**.

Kenningham is a beautiful conservation village next to Banham, and is the home of **The Particular Pottery** where you can watch fine pottery being made by traditional methods, or wonder round the superb gallery which houses the work of many of East Anglia's finest craft people. The distinctive building was once a Baptist Chapel and retains much of the original character. Framed prints and original paintings, turned wood and small items of furniture complete a display of unique, handmade arts and crafts. The Particular Pottery can be found at Church Street, and the telephone number for opening hours is 01953 888476.

Kings Lynn you will either love or hate and you will also learn to refer to it as 'Lynn'. There is so much that is beautiful here and so much that has been spoilt in careless development because of the need for new industry, which became obvious almost immediately after World War II. Saturday Market is probably the best place to start a tour of Lynn. St Margaret's Church here reflects the wealth resulting in the medieval port's export trade in wool and cloth. The two west towers begun in the 12th century are magnificent and between them is a beautiful and very wide window. Storms, which can be ferocious in this part of the world, blew down a lead spire in 1741 wrecking the nave, the transepts and central lantern necessitating rebuilding. Lynn's most famous building is **The Guildhall**. It is fabulous, with its handsome facade of chequered flint and stone. Built in 1421, it was originally the hall of the Trinity Guild, a wealthy   merchant guild, existing before King John gave the town its charter. Since it was first built it has had extensions built on either side at different times but you would be hard put to differentiate which is which. Inside the l5th century Hall leads to the Georgian Assembly Rooms and the Card Room. If you are outside at night when the light shines through the massive window, illuminating Saturday Market, you will think you are in fairyland.

Next to the Guildhall is **The Rococo Restaurant**, a 300 year old grade 2 Listed Building of great charm which serves high quality food and has a comfortable lounge in which you may have morning coffee, indulge in afternoon tea or pre-dinner drinks before enjoying an excellent dinner. Another of Lynn's treasures is **The Customs House**, built in the l7th century. You come to it down King Staithe's Lane to the Purfleet Dock and there alongside the Purfleet is this perfectly proportioned building. It was designed by Henry Bell. a rich merchant who was an architect and twice Mayor of Lynn.

King's Lynn has the perfect place in which to stay. **The Park View** Hotel in Blackfriars Street was once a stagecoach stop between Lincoln and London. It has been carefully and sympathetically modernised and if you read some of the letters from visitors you will see it described as 'The friendliest hotel in which we have ever stayed, from management to chambermaids. It is well run and unfussy. A good choice.'

Langley is one of Norfolk's prettiest villages. It has a fine 18th century mansion, Langley Park, which architecturally pinched its design from Holkham Hall. It is a school now and not open to the public but you can catch glimpses of the park with its spring carpet of snowdrops and daffodils. On the edge of the park is the church whose l3th century doorway leads into a l4th century church with a l5th century tower. It is very long and a bit barnlike with no arch between the nave and the chancel. The nave is filled with high-backed and horsebox pews, from one of which rises a three decker pulpit. The font is 600 years old.

Litcham has hooded doorways which remind one of days long gone. One house by the bridge that crosses the little River Yar was once a house of rest for pilgrims. The church is mainly l5th century with a font that has traceried shields and a pulpit adorned with 1500 traceried panels. Above all the glorious screen, which must be well over 500 years old, is a work of art with its tracery painted and gilded. In the village you will find a genuine old coaching house complete with arch and stables. **The Bull Inn** in Church Street no longer has stables but that does nothing to detract from the atmosphere nor from the hospitable welcome you will receive. It is worth noting that if you have someone with you who uses a wheelchair, the door near the dining room is suitable. The food will suit everybody with no less than 40 items on the menu.

Loddon is everything one could wish for in a busy little market town. It has many houses, shops and inns that are mainly l7th and 18th century. The buildings lining the square are mainly Georgian with the exception of the flamboyant Gothic school built in 1857. The impressive church which lies to the east suffered in the hands of careless restorers but it does have some good paintings. An effigy in white marble of Lady Williamson should be noticed. This was the lady who was the biggest single contributor to the rebuild-ing of St Paul's Cathedral after London's Great fire in 1666. **The Loddon Swan Inn**, one of my favourite pubs because of its caring and happy atmosphere, is on Church Plain, just a stones throw from the River Chet. The Chet is part of the Southern Norfolk Broads system and feeds into the Yare. Although Loddon is mainly agricultural it also has a thriving tourist trade based on its 7 Hire Fleet and Boat Repair yards.

If you enjoy the weather-boarded mills that are so much part of the landscape round here, **Loddon Staithe** has an attractive white one, and is also the site for a well laid out marina development complete with car park and the boat yards I have already mentioned. This is the navigable head of the River Chet which runs into the Yare about three miles away.

Lound you might possibly ignore because it has nothing remarkable about it except for the duck pond and, beyond, a friendly pub, **The Village Maid Marian**. What is different is the rather severe church with its round tower. Inside it has been beautifully restored by the 20th century genius, Sir Ninian Comper. His fee came not from the church but entirely from the pocket of the incumbent, the Reverend Lynes. Sir Ninian was known for his sense of humour and it did not fail him here. Take a look at the big St Christopher wall painting on the north wall into which Sir Ninian has added himself driving his Rolls Royce! Not to be outdone when more restoration work was carried out in 1963, the craftsmen added a Bristol Britannia aircraft flying in the sky above St Christopher's head.

Mundesley has one of the nicest sandy beaches on the Norfolk Coast. It is unspoilt, a place for families and for those who just enjoy a walk across an uncrowded beach watching for the 'lowies' at low tide. This is the odd name the locals use for small rock pools. You will see a number of fishermen casting their rods in the hope of catching cod, Dover sole, eel or skate.

Neatishead in the Broadland triangle of Wroxham, Stalham and Potter Heigham, is an attractive little village with Georgian houses, standing at the head of a wooded creek which runs westward from Barton Broad. On the Irestead Road you will find **The Barton Angler Country Inn**, adjacent to Gay's Staithe on Barton Broad, probably the least spoilt of the Norfolk Broads. It has seven letting rooms, two with four-posters, offers excellent food and is an informal and welcoming establishment.

North Elmham, like all the villages and small towns in this part of Norfolk you are surrounded by lovely countryside but in fact very close to Norwich. It has a long village street lined with high brick and flint walls which sadly hide some of the fine houses from public view. One you can visit however is Elham House with its extensive park, wild garden and vineyards which produce excellent wine. There is the fine parish church of St Mary the Virgin with an imposing Perpendicular tower attached to a church of Norman origin. Normally the church is open from 9am-dusk.

North Walsham's quaint Market Cross, built by the Bishop of Norwich in 1550 is still the focal point of this prosperous market town which caters for Mundesley, Bacton Happisburgh and the northern part of The Broads. It has a handsome cross with three tiers of bell-like roofs each lessening in size. It had to be rebuilt in 1602 when much of the town was destroyed by fire. The Paston Grammar School taught Horatio Nelson for three years before he went to sea. Not all the houses were destroyed by fire and it is a delight to wander down the numerous alleys that run off the market place and take a look. Pretty gardens and houses back up to the church in contentment because that is the sort of town North Walsham is. What better place to stay than Scarborough **Hill House Hotel** on the Old Yarmouth road. It stands in 8 acres and was named after Sir Charles

Scarborough, physician to Charles II. The long, wooded drive is a picture in spring time when it is flanked by masses of daffodils and bluebells. The Broads and sandy beaches are only 5 miles away. It is a cheerful, friendly hotel, beautifully run.

Northwold, near Thetford is situated in the centre of East Anglia and is very central for the Norfolk and Suffolk coast, four National Trust properties and the historic cities of Norwich, Cambridge, Bury St Edmunds and Kings Lynn. There are wonderful forest walks and superb activity for bird watchers. **The Grange**, a Regency rectory set in 5 acres of garden with a stream running through and complete with a swimming pool, is the ideal place to stay. It is small and friendly.

Oulton Broad is one of the finest inland yachting lakes in the country. The road crosses the lock connecting the eastern end of Oulton Broad with Lake Lothing and so to the sea. At the other end there is a dyke that links the River Waveney and the Broadland water system. It is here that is a noted spot for fishing. Oulton tends to put the emphasis on family fun but whatever age you are **Nicholas Everitt Park** is a great outing. Nature has already adorned it with a natural beauty but man has added to it successfully. There is boating and fishing as one would expect. A children's play area conforms with all the safety standards that are required and has equipment that will delight any child. You will see people picnicking on the grass and then suddenly everyone makes for the water where one of the weekly and spectacular power boat races will be taking place. In the Boulevard Centre there is a swimming pool, crazy golf and trampolines and a small Pets Corner. It is also a place to enjoy a cup of tea in the cafe.

On the waterfront there is a large and imposing Freehouse, **The Wherry Hotel** with numerous stern on moorings. There is no fee if you are only stopping a couple of hours. It is open all day in summer and you can get bar meals at lunchtime. The speciality is Yorkshire Pudding which I am told is famed throughout Norfolk. There is a good Sunday lunch as well.

Overstrand next to Trimingham is where Lutyens designed two quite lovely houses, the Pleasaunce and the Hall. **The Pleasaunce** originally had gardens laid out by Gertrude Jekyll but these have been considerably modified. Nonetheless it is a delightful place to visit and is open from the Spring Bank Holiday until the end of October, Monday, Wednesday and Thursday from 2-5pm and a cream tea is included in the price.

Reedham is an interesting small place. Once it was a North sea port and a battlefield for Romans, Danes and Saxons. The River Yare runs beside its streets. It is an area of marshes in which grow the reeds which gave it its name. The big church of St John the Baptist suffered badly from a fire in 1981 but it produced something unexpected when plaster was stripped from the walls after the fire. There was the Saxon nave wall constructed from alternate courses of herringbone and horizontal tiles.

The railway bridge is important to the village. It was built to pivot allowing tall-masted ships through. Close to it is the chain ferry, the only crossing for vehicles between Norwich, 15 miles to the west, and Great Yarmouth almost ten miles to the east. The ferry is controlled by **The Reedham Ferry Inn**, a delightful pub to visit, l6th century and full of character. Imagine the scene; it sits on the junction of the B1140 and the bank of the river surrounded by picturesque marshland, mills, cattle, sheep and of course the reeds. The ferry is the only working car ferry in East Anglia. It starts in the morning at 8am, with a continuous service until l0pm daily with the exception of Christmas, Boxing Day and New Years Day.

Rockland Staithe deserves a line or two because there is good fishing from **Rockland Broad**, about a quarter of a mile down the dyke. You can sit on the grass and look over the peaceful scene before setting off for the New Inn, beloved by local people who will make you welcome. There is no charge for mooring a boat here. The pub is only about 25 yards away from the water.

Salle pronounced Saul has the marvellous church of St Peter and St Paul which rises high above the land. Great local magnates built it on a grand scale befitting their wealth and rank. The foundations were laid in the 15th century and it was built to last, as it has done and been saved the fate of restoration by the sometimes over zealous Victorians. The noble families included the Boleyns, and there are many brasses to the family but none to the sad Anne, Henry VIII's second Queen. It has been said though that she is secretly buried here and not in the Tower of London. It is worth visiting the church if only to see the great coats of arms carved in the frieze all the way round the high tower, above a doorcase carved with obedient angels. The church must have been completed by 1420 because the Royal Arms of Henry V are there too. It is a church of uncluttered, simple magnificence. Your eyes are drawn upwards to the angel studded nave roof and bosses with biblical scenes on the boarded chancel roof. The stalls are covered in   carvings of faces and monsters, and then you espy the faces accompanied by flowers on the misericords. The Seven Sacraments font has one of Norfolk's finest canopies. It is complete with a pulley used to lift the cover. The church is open during daylight hours.

Sandringham - 'Dear old Sandringham, the place that I love better than anywhere in the world' wrote King George VI about the most private and beloved Royal home. Only Edward VIII hated it and spent just one night there. It is an escape for the Royals, somewhere they can relax and feel they are simply local squires. The Queen and the Queen Mother take an active interest in what goes on locally. Gone are the glittering days when Edward VII, its first royal occupant, made it a focal point for society during the 49 years he owned it. Tempered with time, so too has gone the sadness of the death in his sleep here of George VI. Anyone who watched the television documentary Elizabeth R will feel they were privileged to see the family at home at Sandringham. The present house was built in 1869-71, it has a front 150 yards long and stands in an estate of 20,000 acres taking in several villages. The grounds at Sandringham are open to the public from April-September, when the family are not in residence. You enter by an oak door set in the perimeter wall and it is suggested that you take the route following a gravel path which leads to the shrubbery's. The plants and shrubs have been meticulously labelled with the name and date of planting. Opposite the heather bed by the wall are an array of camellias amongst many other shrubs including hydrangeas. The smell of the lavender beds draw your attention next and then comes a woodland glade which is filled with rhododendrons and azaleas. When they are in bloom they are stunning. Of course there is colour all the time especially from the polyanthus which bloom all summer and   unusual polar bear rhododendrons which flower in July. The museum in the grounds is chock full of royal possessions. You can see Royal Vintage Motor cars and a wonderful collection of photographs.

Edward VII might have been a leader of society but he never neglected his attendance at the 16th-century church at the corner of the park where the family still worship today. Here too are reminders of the Royal Family with memorial brasses and two little headstones over graves in the churchyard are of little princes. One of the brasses to the Duke of Clarence, Edward VII's eldest son, says 'To my darling Eddy' from his mother, Queen Alexandra.

Sheringham on the North Coast is designated an area of outstanding natural beauty. This small, attractive town has one of the finest seaside golf links to be found anywhere. I would recommend you to stay at **Southlands Hotel**, a friendly, privately owned family hotel situated in quiet and pleasant surroundings within three minutes walk of the town, golf links and sea.

Stody close to Melton Constable, a village that came into being entirely as a railway town in 1881. The village is very pretty with a church standing quietly above a stream, with an early round tower and a 15th century nave, chancel and transepts. Its roof is truly beautiful and it is fitting that nearby **Stody Lodge** built by the first Lord Rothermere should have a very pretty water garden, glorious azaleas and one of the finest displays of rhododendrons you will ever see.

Surlingham's church has a round Norman tower which was given its octagonal belfry when the rest of the church was made new in the 14th century. Its most modern attribute is the beautifully carved lectern with a little owl nestling in the base. From here you will get pleasant views over the river and the marshes. You will discover that Surlingham has a ferry but not for vehicles. After a drink in the white painted **Ferry Inn** you might care to take a walk around the nearby Nature reserve. One of the loveliest Yare riverside places is **Bramerton Woods End** where the trees dip down to the water and the wide grassy banks invite you to get out of your car and sit awhile.

Swaffham is an elegant, small town with some lovely buildings situated around a triangular market place. One of them is the Assembly Room, built in 1817, which was the scene of many social events of the Norfolk gentry who would bring their daughters to be seen in society before they went to London for the traditional coming out season. The Butter Cross, which is not a cross at all, immediately demands attention. It is a circular pavilion built by Lord Oxford in 1738 and at its apex sits a life-sized figure of Ceres. East of the market place is the church of St Peter and St Paul in which the north aisle was built by a wealthy man, John Chapman, known as the peddler of Swaffham who discovered two pots of gold in his garden. According to legend, John Chapman, a poor peddler, dreamed that if he went to London he would hear on London Bridge something to his advantage. He obeyed his dream and on the bridge he met a stranger who told him to go to Swaffliam and there seek the garden of one John Chapman, the peddler. Under a tree he would find buried a crock of gold. John hastened home, dug furiously and not one but two pots of gold appeared. John Chapman's pew is still in the church and he is portrayed on the town sign, carved by a local man, Harry Carter. Signs such as these were conceived by Edward VII who wanted them on the villages of the Sandringham estate to encourage the inhabitants to take an interest in local history. Today they are to be found all over Norfolk and many of them are still being made at the Queen's Carving School at Sandringham.

Thorpe Market on the A149 just north of North Walsham and close to the coast at Trimingham, is a quiet place and has the attractive Elderton Lodge, a charming hotel where everyone is welcome.

Trimingham close to Mundesley is where the cliffs rise 300 feet and on a clear day you can see the spire of Norwich Cathedral 20 miles away.

Wells-Next-The-Sea has a name that enchants. It manages to combine a working port with tourism successfully. Wandering the narrow yards - lanes to us - is a delight. Staithe Street with its Edwardian and Victorian shop fronts is a place to browse. Then you will come to Butlands, once used for archery practice. The Green, overhung by lime trees, is surrounded by sedate and fairly grand Georgian and Victorian houses apart from the lively Globe Inn. Here you can stay as well as get good meals and well kept beer.

You should visit **The Wells and Walsingham Light Railway** just east of the town which starts at Wells and runs along the course of the old Great Eastern line. It ends at **Walsingham** famed for centuries as centre of pilgrimage.

West Runton is the home of **The Norfolk Shire Horse Centre and Country Collection** which is open daily from Easter until the end of October from 10-5pm. It is closed on Saturdays except at Bank Holidays. Shire horses are such majestic animals and it is a privilege to watch the Shire Suffolks and the other breeds of draught horses demonstrated. You can see this twice daily at 11.15am and 3pm with an indoor demonstration area for the wet weather. It is not only horses here, there are also mountain and moorland ponies, some with foals , and farm animals on display. You can watch a video film of working horses, see a photographic display of draught horses, past and present, and finally a super collection of horse-drawn machinery, wagons and carts. Children love the cart rides and for every adult it is a time of nostalgia.

Wolverton railway station is now a museum filled with royal memorabilia but once it played host to Kings, Tsars and other Royals from many countries who were on their way to Sandringham. Frequently they would be greeted on the station by their Royal hosts. The station may be small, not in use, yet it definitely has an air of grandeur.

Worstead is a village you might like to seek out to the south of North Walsham. In medieval times this was a busy place renowned for its worsted cloth. Today it is quietly prosperous and has a square flanked by Georgian and Queen Anne houses. Sometime between 1379 and 1450 the wealthy merchants of Worstead built the beautiful church of St Mary with its fine hammerbeam roof and Box pews with intricate carvings and a traceried font.

Worthing a tiny hamlet lying a mile to the south east of North Elmham in the Wensum valley has a delightful mill and pond and a tiny Saxon church with a round tower. It looks almost abandoned, standing as it does alone by the river. I am assured though that it is still used.

Wroxham which considers itself to be the unofficial capital of the Broads is linked with **Hoveton** by a hump backed bridge over the River Bure. The banks of the river are alive with boatyards, and the waterway is so busy that traffic lights would not come amiss! The marina is the place to go if you would like to take a boat trip by paddleboat or motor launch through the adjacent broads.

I think it is a wonderful way of taking in this amazing area. It has everything, the colourful activity of the boats and then the peace of the less used areas where wildlife abounds and you get a chance to see the enormous amount of work carried out by the Broads Authority which was set up in 1978 to stop the degeneration of Broadland. It has to walk a very tight rope when you consider that it must please so many people. You have got a cross section of nature lovers, sailors, holidaymakers, farmers, water authorities and one must never forget the most important of all, the people who actually live here. Wroxham has the very nice **Broads Hotel** where visitors are treated like locals and locals as friends!

SUFFOLK

Going back to once happy stomping grounds can produce feelings of dismay because what was once treasured had disappeared to be replaced by foreign objects or completely erased to make way for a new road. My return to Suffolk in the 1990's has given me nothing but pleasure. Of course things have changed, but in most cases it has been for the good. I start my journey in **Ipswich**, a city close to where I once lived. It is England's oldest heritage town and as Suffolk's county town is a major commercial and shopping centre. After this I will list each place I visited in alphabetical order which I hope makes it simpler for the reader.

Ipswich offers a choice of many things to see and do. For a start there are no less than 12 medieval churches. The loveliest of these is St Margarets, flanking the north side of St Margaret's Plain. It is almost as beautiful as Norwich's St Peter's Mancroft with a spectacular 15th century roof, painted in the time of William III. Five of these churches are floodlit at night and most are open in daylight hours. Each of them has something to offer and will provide you with much of interest. If you want a place to eat which is totally different and totally memorable go to The Singing Chef at 200 St Helens Street. Here you will enjoy French Regional cooking at its best with a larger than life chef who literally does sing. It is wonderful.

The Claydon Country House Hotel at 16-18 Ipswich Road, Claydon, will allow you to stay in a true country house with first class cuisine and a superb wine list. It is small enough to ensure that every guest receives individual attention, yet spacious enough to allow for your complete comfort and relaxation. You will find it a few minutes drive from Ipswich on the A45, connecting Felixstowe, Bury St Edmunds and Cambridge.

The Tudor **Christchurch Mansion**, which was built in 1548 is furnished as a country house and contains the finest collection of Constable and Gainsborough paintings outside London. Set in superb parkland it is only 5 minutes from the town centre. **The Wolsey Art Gallery** is another must on a visitor's list remembering that Cardinal Wolsey was one of Ipswich's most famous sons. My favourite building is The Ancient House in the Butterwalk. Once a hiding place of Charles II, it is the finest example of pargetting in the country, used now as a bookshop.

One must not forget that Ipswich is still a busy port and there is much activity on the waterfront. There is **The Old Custom House** on Wet Dock. Much of the marine activity today is for leisure. Many yachts, large and small, berth here.

Whichever way you decide to drive deeper into Suffolk from Ipswich, it will be a delightful experience.

Aldeburgh has always been a gentle backwater and only came to prominence with the advent of the composer Benjamin Britten who, together with his friend Peter Pears, the opera singer, lived here for many years. **The Moot Hall** is one of Aldeburgh's treasures. Its beauty delights everyone and especially photographers. It is a herringbone brickwork building of the 15th-century and is still used as the Town Hall. Do not expect to find a great deal to do in Aldeburgh except to enjoy its tranquillity which is only shaken by the force of the winter storms sending waves pounding up the beach. **The Mill Inn** is the place to visit, just across from the Moot Hall. It has stood for centuries although at one time it was much further away from the sea, which has crept relentlessly nearer and nearer over the years. This haunt of smugglers in the past is now a welcoming hostelry offering good food. Looking for somewhere to stay, **New Austins Hotel**, is small, comfortable and well run. It is a popular venue for birdwatchers, ramblers and for those who come for a day out in Aldeburgh and are looking for somewhere to have an enjoyable meal.

Battisford just outside Stowmarket is a place you might pass by without realising it was the home of Sir Thomas Gresham, the founder of the Royal Exchange in London. This was an immensely rich and powerful man whose position was unique. He became King's Agent to Henry VIII and retained the position with hardly a break through the reigns of Edward and Mary, and in the early years of Elizabeth I. He was the unwilling custodian of Mary, a sister of Lady Jane Grey. He played host to many Protestant refugees and entertained Queen Elizabeth I in extraordinary style. Four centuries before his birth the village had famous builders in the Knights Hospitallers who raised one of their hospitals here. So when you are drinking an excellent pint of ale, or sipping a Gin and Tonic in the bar of **The Punch Bowl**, you are amongst great history.

Beccles is a Suffolk town, very much part of the life of The Broads but one that could easily put you off because so much has been eaten up by Industrial estates, especially on the eastern perimeter. You would be foolish though not to delve a little deeper. I know of no more tranquil place on which to stand than the old bridge at the end of Northgate Street. The River Waveney bubbles and bustles along beneath the picturesque parapets whilst your eyes become accustomed to the beauty of the riverside views. The church of St Michaels dominates the town. Narrow lanes or what are known locally as 'scores' run from the river bank to the foot of the tower. In spite of being severely damaged by fire in the several fires that swept through the town in the 17th century, it has been lovingly restored and refurnished by the Victorians. Probably the most beautiful part is the south-west porch which was built around 1455 and survived the devastation,

When you stand before the altar of St Michaels church you can tell yourself that it is here that one of the most thrilling chapters of English history began. In 1749 the curate of Beccles was married to Catherine Suckling; he was Edmund Nelson. Their son, of course, was Horatio Nelson. **The Waveney House Hotel** Puddingmoor, is the place to stay. Built in 1592 with Georgian extensions about 1760, this rich merchant's house stands in a quiet location on the banks of the River Waveney. Run with great professionalism it caters for all kinds of people and all ages. On the outskirts of Beccles at Gillingham, **The Swan Motel**, set in picturesque countryside makes an ideal base for exploring the Norfolk Broads.

Bentley on the other side of Alton water from Holbrook has a Victorianized medieval church set in a churchyard which seems almost oppressed by conifers. I always believed it was in this churchyard that I would find this splendid epitaph - but I was wrong; it is in Suffolk somewhere:

Here lies the body of Margaret Chowder
Who died through drinking fizzy powder
Oh may her spirit in heaven be blessed
Why she should have waited until it effervesced

Delightful isn't it? There are many such as this throughout the churchyards of Suffolk. Maybe a visit to **The Case is Altered**, a welcoming pub, will tell you where you will find this poetic treasure. If you wonder at the name then there are many versions of how it was acquired. The most likely one tells of a landlady who was over generous to her customers and did not fuss too much about how the money came in. When she died the new landlord had other ideas and so the case was altered!

Bildeston, halfway between Sudbury and Needham Market, is another charming spot. It has houses of rich cream plasterwork and dark oak half timbering of the kind especially concentrated in the late medieval clothing towns. The cottages that are linked in a row off the Square are my favourites. The church of St Mary Magdalene stands on a hill half a mile from the village. It is 15th century and well worth climbing the hill to see its splendid portal. Ironically its Perpendicular tower collapsed on Ascension Day in 1975 and has never been restored. Inside there is a little priest's chamber above the south porch. The beautiful nave arcades and fine roof of alternating hammerbeams and tie beams are outstanding. In the High Street, **The Crown Hotel** is reputed to be the most haunted pub in the country. I found it delightful and certainly would not be put off by a ghost or two!

Blaxhall has a pretty, 17th century pub, **The Ship** famous for its traditional Suffolk Folk Music and for the number of times it has been filmed by the BBC for different productions.

Bramford close to Ipswich is a village of picturesque houses and a beautiful church St Mary the Virgin. It has a handsome 14th century tower with an 18th century lead spire. Look closely and you will see panelled stone parapets and carved figures, including a monkey wearing a monk's cowl and hurling stones. The extraordinary presence of boulders round about is thought to indicate a pagan sacred site. Suffolk Water Park is here in the Gipping Valley providing ideal conditions for windsurfing, canoeing, spectating and picnics. For those who are brave enough to tackle a 17 mile walk, you can take off from Stoke Bridge, Ipswich and follow the former towpath of the river Gipping. It is never dull with plenty of natural history and industrial archaeology to interest you.

Brandeston not far from **Kettleburgh** is where, in the 17th century, they hung their octogenarian vicar for witchcraft. Also in the village is the cottage of Margaret Catchpole whose misdeeds caused her to be transported to Australia. This infamous lady is supposedly related to the landlord of **The Chequers** at Kettleburgh, through his great-grandmother. Apart from that this is a delightful village and has a good pub **The Queens Head**.

Bury St Edmunds is one of the most delightful and splendid of Suffolk towns. It is full of treasures and has managed to remain almost untouched by large scale modern developments. The way it was laid out in the 11th century has much to do with its charm because the rectangular grid of streets offers long vistas of varied architecture. Almost 1,000 buildings have preservation orders on them. Wander into Churchgate Street and you will see the impressive group of buildings erected by Abbot Anselm. The massive Norman Gate was begun about 1121 as a belfry. It was Abbot Anselm who gave Bury its two great churches. St Mary's in Crown Street is wonderful and lit by myriad tall windows. The 12th century St James's became the cathedral of the diocese of St Edmundsbury and Ipswich in

1914. The broad square, oddly named Angel Hill, has fine Georgian and Regency houses on the north and west sides amongst which is Number 8, an elegant Queen Anne house housing one of the finest collections of time measuring instruments in the country. Charles Dickens gave two of his celebrated public readings in The Athenaeum in the square and also made the nearby Angel Hotel forever famous, using it as the setting for one of Mr Pickwick's adventures. There is the beautiful Theatre Royal and Abbeygate, surely one of the loveliest shopping streets in the country. I found there at Number 34, **Grills and Gills**, an eating place with a difference, as unique in name as it is in its food and Mediterranean style interior. According to historians the rear of the building is 15th century and approximately 100 years later at the front section. The establishment has a sister restaurant 'Somewhere Else' at 1 Langton Place, Hatter Street, which was described in The Sunday Times as being 'without pomp or whimsy.'

Buxhall, just 3 miles south west of Stowmarket was the birth place in 1512 of Sir William Coppinger. He, like Dick Whittington, became Lord Mayor of London. Half his estate he left to the poor and half to his relations, whose hospitality was such that it produced a local saying 'To live like a Coppinger'. It was one of those relatives, Walter Coppinger to whom Henry VIII gave permission to wear his hat in the royal presence. The document giving this permission and signed Henry R, is in the possession of the lofty church which is well over 600 years old.

Cavendish to the west of Long Melford is a name that takes us back in history to one of the most ancient struggles between Government and workers; Wat Tyler's Rebellion. Sir John Cavendish lived here and was Chief Justice of the King's Bench at the time. His son helped to kill Wat Tyler and the news of this angered the mob so greatly that they ransacked Sir John's house, dragged him away and beheaded him after a mock trial. The old home of the Cavendishes is here by the beautiful, well manicured green. It is yet another delightful Suffolk village with immaculate cottages, whose ornately ridged thatched roofs have a sculptured air. **Netherhall Manor**, north of the parish church of St Mary, is a well-restored 16th century farmhouse at the centre of the famous Cavendish vineyards. Both of these are open to the public daily.

St Mary's Church has a tower built in the 13th century with a stair turret in one corner. The tower's ringing chamber is furnished as a living room with window seats in the casement window, and a fireplace whose chimney strikes one as being more than slightly eccentric, perched as it is on the impressive tower.

Clare named after the long line of the Earls of Clare from William the Conqueror. Gilbert the 7th earl, was one of the most powerful men in the land during King John's reign and his son founded the famous Priory of Clare. Another Gilbert, the 9th earl, fathered Elizabeth who became the Lady of Clare, and it is through her that the name of this Suffolk town is so well known in Cambridge, for she endowed and founded the second oldest college in the University. The town is beautiful with handsome houses, several of which are pargetted - intricately patterned plasterwork. The Bell on Market Hill is a good watering hole. It is a 16th-century coaching inn with an attractive black and white timbered facade. A comfortable place to stay as well as eat, with most of its rooms en-suite.

Cotton, 5 miles north of Stowmarket has **The Mechanical Music Museum**. It is quite fascinating with all types of organs, polyphones, musical boxes and many more unusual items.

Dunwich just fell into the sea and was no more! Without actually going there you cannot envisage quite what happened and quite how important it once was. Roman cavalry once patrolled the coast and after them the Saxons. It is certain that from those early times onward until finally the sea carried away the church, churchyard, market places, busy streets and monasteries, Dunwich played a major part in the growth of Suffolk. The final death knell came in the 20th century. How did it happen? It really started in the 12th century when, instead of riches from its trading success, silt came from the Suffolk shore and clogged the harbour which gave the storms and high tides the opportunity to batter the sea walls. It was relentless, year after year the sea swallowed up parts of the town. In the 13th century 400 houses, shops and churches disappeared and in the 14th century, the churches of St Martin and St Nicholas crumbled. By 1677 the sea had reached the market place. Yet people still stayed. By the 18th century, the Town Hall and St Patrick's church were no more. By then at low tide, ghostly buildings could be seen above the shingle. Nothing survives now except for the ruins of a friary, founded on the spot where St Felix landed in the 7th century bringing Christianity back to East Anglia.

What you will see are local fishermen whose timber huts on the beach, house their nets, and from which they sell their catches. Standing well back from the still crumbling cliffs, is a small village and in one of the cottages there is a museum containing relics dug from the shore. What remains of Dunwich is wild and awesome. The nature reserve of **Dunwich Common**, which belongs to the National Trust, and Westleton Heath take you along sandy heathland which once would have been full of sheep grazing; animals that made Suffolk a wealthy county.

East Bergholt was the birthplace of Constable in 1776 and he wrote 'I even love every stile and stump, and lane in the village.' He painted innumerable pictures of the village. Twenty one of them are now in the Victoria and Albert Museum in London. **Flatford Water Mill** and **Willy Lott's Cottage** are owned by the National Trust and not open to the public but you can visit **Bridge Cottage**, which nestles under Flatford Bridge. This also belongs to the National Trust and has a pleasant tea garden and shop. For stronger refreshment and good food you will do no better than visit the very pleasant Red Lion.

Felixstowe gained popularity as a south facing Edwardian seaside resort, round a wide shingly bay with totally safe bathing. The beach is divided into many sections by groynes and breakwaters. It lost its Pier at the end of World War II but it is still a favourite place for Ipswich people to be at weekends. Much of the activity in the newer part of Felixstowe is connected with the docks, not the most attractive of places, but it is a port that has thrived where others have failed. The port handles well over a million containers annually. Some achievement when you consider that in 1951 this was a run down port almost going out of existence. A little way up the coast is Felixstowe ferry which crosses from one side of the River Deben to the other. Here by the landing is **The Ferryboat Inn**, steeped in history. It was about to be refurbished when I was there last and I do hope that none of its character has been lost.

Framlingham is a little town of great charm and dignity. Its streets are narrow and graced by many fine buildings. The hilltop castle keeps a watchful eye on all that goes on in the town but it cannot find much of which to disapprove. Vineyards seem to thrive in this part of Sussex. Shawsgate Vineyard is just a mile out of Framlingham and specialises in the growth of Muller Thurgau and Seyval Blanc grapes as well as Bacchus and Reichensteiner, all of which become delightful white wines. It is a level area and especially good for anyone confined to a wheelchair. Opening hours 10-5pm. North on the B1120 is

Bruisyard Vineyard with the largest ornamental herb gardens in East Anglia as well as the vineyard. Open daily Easter until the end of November from 10.30-5pm

Harkstead sign-posted on the other side of the road from Pin Mill, off the B1456 is a small hamlet with a super pub, **The Bakers Arms**, which has the ring of the sea about it from the moment you enter its doors. It is a haunt of mariners of all ages. Those who come back here because of their time at HMS Ganges at **Shotley** and those who come today to sail their boats and yachts from the Marinas. The food is good and the company better. It is a marvellous stopping point for those who want to walk. No one minds how muddy or dirty your shoes or wellies are.

Kedington was the home of Lord Barnadiston, one of Cromwell's generals and inside the medieval church, which has Norman stones in the tower. Roman bricks and mosaic paving in the flint walls of the nave, you will find stone figures of seventeen members of the Barnadiston family - almost as man as I suspect they get in the Sunday congregation today. If you ever wondered how the Round-heads got their name, you will find the answer in the Barnadiston family. The story is that Charles Stuart s Queen was looking out of a window when she noticed a short-haired youth, Samuel Barnidiston, among a rebellious crowd in the street and commented 'Look at that handsome roundhead below'. The name stuck although Samuel took no part in the Civil War, biding his time until he was able to welcome Charles back to the throne, and so well was his welcome received, he was knighted. One useless piece of information I discovered about Samuel was that he built a reservoir for water on top of his house at Brightwell, which not only served for all domestic purposes but was also stocked with fish for the larder!

Kersey is designated as the prettiest village in Suffolk. It has to be quite out of the ordinary to earn such a description in a county rich in lovely places. It is just two miles north west of **Hadleigh** and set in something like a natural letter V, with the church looking down from one hill and lovely timbered houses, creeping up the other. A brook ripples between the houses and everyone seems to have green fingers; the gardens are glorious.

It is several centuries since the clack of looms could be heard weaving the now famous Kersey cloth. But as you look at the weaver's cottages, with their diamond paned windows twinkling in the sun, you can almost conjure up the sound and the smell of the cloth. The ruins of a 13th century Augustinian priory crown the slope opposite the fine church of St Mary. Its 15th century tower, with a delightful flushwork parapet dominates the village. Two ghosts who have both been seen within the last year or so, haunt **The Bell Inn**, largely, I suspect, because they enjoy its hospitality. It is a pub that attracts Film and TV companies who use it inside and out for various productions.

Lavenham is somewhere that must be visited. Jane Taylor, who wrote the nursery rhyme 'Twinkle, twinkle little star' lived here and whilst the star she had in mind was in the sky, the twinkling beauty of this glorious village is what most visitors would recognise. This is one of those places where nothing has changed in well over 400 years. You walk along and are swept up by the past. Quaint streets will lead you into enchanting medieval prospects, including those of the Guildhall, the Old Wool Hall, Tudor shop and Woolstaplers in Prentice Street, a house that is 14th century at the back and 16th century at the front, belonging to the last wool merchant in Lavenham.

Set at the end of this miraculously intact timber-framed Tudor wool town is the incomparable church of St Peter and St Paul, built by rich clothiers to celebrate the end of the Wars of the Roses in 1485. The foremost of these was Thomas Spryng and the Earl of Oxford. They began it in the 15th century and finished it in the 16th giving it the finest tower in the county. It soars 140ft high with shields on the buttresses and bands of roses and stars. Inside, the screens of the early 16th century are fabulously carved and detailed. **The Swan** in the High Street is the place to visit for sustenance, always supposing you are not suffering from too much mental indigestion.

This building, which is fitting for Lavenham, is an amalgam of a splendidly preserved Elizabethan house, inn and woolhall. Not the cheapest place to stay but worth every penny because of its history and hospitality.

Leiston pronounced Lacet'n on the B1122, stands on farmland near a beautiful stretch of coast. It has the most extensive monastic remains in Suffolk and one of the most interesting museums. **The Long Shop**, tells the history of the Garrett family who in the 18th century started a forge to manufacture ploughs, threshes and cast iron work. The family were innovators and aware of the future. They rapidly went into the market to build steam powered units in factories, mills and farms. One son, Richard Garrett was despatched to the United States to take a look at mass production methods and came back to report that Garrett's must design and build their own assembly hall on American lines. They endured the mockery of the locals who considered the new factory a folly and nicknamed it, irreverently, 'the cathedral'. It was not long before they realised that Garretts was successful and to be respected. Its official name was the Long Shop and the budding business constructed road rollers, steam engines and steam tractors. World War II was its finest hour and sadly now it is no longer operational, but what an exciting place to visit. **The White Horse Hotel** is the focal point of this ancient community which goes back before the Norman Conquest. It was purpose built in 1770 by the Gildersleeves, a well known inn-keeping family who supplemented their regular income by a heavy involvement in smuggling along the East Coast. For many years Garretts supplied their staff with tokens that could only be spent in the White Horse. Leiston is also close to **Minsmore Bird Reserve** and to the reserves of **North Warren** and **Havergate Island**.

Long Melford approached from the south might disappoint you, but be patient you will come to a mile-long High Street which is unusually wide and lined with timber-framed and Georgian houses which delight the eye. And then there is more because as the High Street narrows again to cross the Chad Brook, it reaches a wide green which is quite superb, bounded by the walls of **Melford Hall**, on one side and the beautiful church of the Holy Trinity.

Melford Hall is one of the best moated houses left from Tudor days. The house is owned by the National Trust and is open in the spring and summer. Beatrix Potter was a relation of the Parker family who have lived here since the 18th century. Quite a number of her pictures are on display.

Long Melford is unfairly blessed with two beautiful houses in the village. The second, **Kentwell Hall** lies to the north. This is a mellow, red-brick Tudor manor house which stands at the end of a mile-long drive, guarded by lime trees. It is moated and work was begun on it in the mid 16th century. The house is open in summer when you can see not only the house but the handsome brickwork maze in the form of a Tudor rose, that fills a courtyard. In order to raise money for all the restoration work that goes on constantly, the owners have what they describe as 'historical recreations' using actors and musicians. They are thoroughly enjoyable events.

The church is best of all and one of the great spectacles of England. It stands across the green with the Tudor almshouses in front of it. Its tower was burnt down but rebuilt superbly by Bodley at the end of the 19th century with dainty buttresses and stately pinnacles. The rest of it has not changed in 550 years. It is 260ft long and must have at least a hundred windows. You can see its great walls and proud tower for miles. The names of the clothiers who helped to build it are inscribed like a great chorus of petitions, below the battlement.

Moulton to the east of Newmarket has one of the loveliest packhorse bridges in Suffolk, sitting astride the River Kennet.

Nayland on the western end of Dedham Vale is a delightful old village and just on the outskirts is **Gladwins Farm**, no longer a working farm but somewhere to stay. The house faces south over the valley and the 500 year old Suffolk barn together with the stable block are centred in the 22 acres of wooded grounds which the owners are restoring and through which guests are welcome to wander. Bed and breakfast accommodation is offered in the farmhouse and self-catering is available in the six cottages in the barn and stable block.

Newmarket is where horse racing started 2,000 years ago when Boadecia set up camp at **Exning**, 2 miles down the road. Where thoroughbred horse come before everything today, she was probably more interested in chariot races. The Jockey Club controls the regulations of racing from their headquarters in Newmarket. The history of racing is told in **The National Horseracing Museum**. If you come to Newmarket for the racing you will find that in summer it takes place across the Heath where the crowds are free to mingle with the horses whilst they wait to be led into the paddock to take aboard their jockeys. Racing on the Rowley Mile which takes place in the spring and autumn is different. The Newmarket Classic Races are run here.

Orford always conjures up visions of the past. It was once a seaport but the greed of the giant gravel bank, **Orford Ness**, has gobbled up the entrance. It was on this exposed but secret shingle spit that scientists made their first experiments in radar; the year was 1935. Orford has the remains of a great 12th century royal castle, and if you climb the hummocky ramparts to the top of the formidable polyganal keep, you get a wonderful view over lush countryside and the coast.

Otley is a quiet village north of Ipswich and just five miles west of Woodbridge. A rural retreat and totally restful. Here you can stay in **Otley House Country House Hotel** in Helmingham Road. The standards are very high. There are four luxuriously furnished bedrooms, all en-suite. Wonderful food and hospitality and to be recommended.

Pin Mill Take the B1456 out of Ispwich and you are following the river down to the sea at **Shotley** opposite **Harwich**. This is a wonderful area for anyone who loves birds and marine life. Pin Mill has one the finest pubs in Suffolk -**The Butt and Oyster** - I am probably biased because I have known it for years and one time it was my local. Many a game of darts have I enjoyed as well as the more unusual Shut the Box and Pass le Temps. Right by the river it is home to Thames Barges. Good food, good company is still its strength.

Saxmundham is an unsophisticated small town dating back to Norman times and before that to the Danish Conquest. The church has suffered from too much restoration but it is still of interest, particularly in the south chancel aisle which has nine panels of Flemish Glass in a nice Victorian setting. **The Bell Hotel** under the same owner-ship as The White Horse at Leiston, offers good food and accommodation.

Saxtead is a little village close to Framlingham which has **The Saxtead Green Windmill**. This gem is preserved in beautiful order. It is an l8th century post mill with a 3 storey roundhouse. There are four patent sails, two pairs of stone and a fantail. Open from end of March until end of December, Monday to Saturday from 10-6pm.

Snape is the home of the **Aldeburgh Festival**. Set right on the banks of the River Alde, it is the trustee of a wonderful collection of l9th century buildings which includes the **Snape Maltings Concert Hall** where, from Easter until the end of   Decem-ber, you can listen to music performed by musicans from all over the world. Guided tours will help you appreciate all that goes on here. Take an afternoon's cruise on the Lady Moyra which operates between April and October and wends its peaceful way up the Alde estuary allowing one time to take in the beauty of the surroundings and trying to name the abundant birdlife.

Southwold with Blythburgh and Walberswick, cradle the River Blyth in their beautiful arms. **Blythburgh** is just a tiny village today and it is difficult to imagine it when it was a bustling little port. What a fantastic sight is the wonderful tower of Holy Trinity church soaring out of the reed beds where the tidal waters reach out to lap its feet. The devil is supposed to have caused the spire to topple in 1577 and to have left his signature in scorch marks on the north floor. This cannot be true, the presence of God is far too strong inside this majestic but sparsely furnished building. One of Cromwell's officers, William Dowsing in 1644, tried to wreak his vengeance on the church as well. He and his men left hundreds of bullet marks in both the ancient traceried doors.

There is a path that leads from **The White Horse Inn**, following a disused railway track, round the edge of the estuary and over the heathland to **Walberswick**. This enchanting place is in a world of its own. It never feels as if it belongs to this century. Even its residents seem to live at a slower place. You can sit on the stony beach watching the birds congregate to discuss their own business. If your eyes stray they will probably alight on the little medieval church of St Andrew which once was as grand as those at Blythburgh and Southwold. One unexpected gem here is the small restaurant **Marys of Walberswick**, which produces not only wonderful dinners but a cream tea it would be hard to equal anywhere. **Southwold** too has a sense of tranquillity about it. It allows the river Blyth to reach the sea unimpeded. The Dutch and Flemish influence jostle for pride of place. It has several beautiful greens and several good inns. My choice this time is **The Red Lion**, on South Green, a friendly unpretentious establishment with good home-cooking.

The beach is famous for its coloured pebbles and the old Edwardian pastel-painted beach huts. You will not find fast food shops, arcades or souvenir shops. Adnams beer is brewed in the town and delivered by horse-drawn dray - a fine sight. The relentless sea has prevented a harbour being built inspite of strenuous efforts. The history of this is told in the little museum on Bartholomew Green. There is a small lighthouse, a collection of fine Georgian houses and contrastingly simple fishermen's cottages. St Edmunds church rises proud and tall, a monument to light and airiness. 'Southwold Jack' stands by the tower at the rear of the church. It is he who strikes the bidding bell to mark the beginning of services. He has been doing so since the Wars of the Roses.

Stoke-by-Nayland has a church standing on a hillside among trees which Constable put into his famous Rainbow picture. Its 120ft high tower is a proud Suffolk landmark and certainly one of the grandest, built of warm, almost peach-coloured brick, with pinnacles on its beautiful parapet and at each corner, a huge buttress carrying canopied niches up to the belfry. In the village, which is three miles west of East Bergholt, there are many fine 16th century timber-framed buildings. At the crossroads in the centre is **The Angel Inn**. Its ancient name reflects the early connection between religious establishments and travellers' hostels. In 1536 when Henry VIII commenced the dissolution of the monasteries, the accommodation of travellers fell to the responsibility of local land-owning gentry. Although the subject of extensive restoration work over the centuries, much of the building survives from this time. Certainly the same hospitality is offered. It is a place both for a meal and a drink and to stay in comfort.

Stowmarket does not have the architectural beauty of some other Suffolk towns although it is a lively market town under which many a relic of Roman and Saxon England has been found. It has a fine medieval church with a timbered 16th century vicarage where the poet Milton used to visit his tutor. There is a small 17th century brass inside the church which touches the heart. It is to Ann Tyrell who lies there wearing a small shroud. The inscription says:

'By reason and Religion She at Seven
Prepared herself and found her way to heaven'

During the 17th and 18th century the town was a noted centre of the woollen trade and the River Gipping was canalised between Stowmarket and Ipswich to carry the town's trade. A pretty walk can be taken along the towpath through the woods and meadows by the river.

Sudbury has never lacked the courage to change over the centuries but has managed to save much of its heritage for the present residents. It was the centre of wool-weaving and later of silk production which gave it wealth. There are many fine buildings and none more so than **The Black Boy Hotel**, an example of timber-framing, its neo-Tudor front hiding an older structure. Opposite are a row of decorative brick buildings housing the banks except for the Corn Exchange, designed by H.E. Kendall in 1841. This flamboyant, Italianate baroque building has been converted in recent years by the county architect, Jack Digby. It is now a library and information centre. The house in which Gainsborough was born in 1727 stands in the street named after him, at the bottom of market hill. It is now a museum used to display paintings by Gainsborough and many of his contemporaries. Wander further along the street until it becomes Stour Street. Here there are some delightful, if slightly ornate, timber-framed houses. There is Salters Hall, a merchant's house and the old Moot Hall. Both date back to the 15th century and have oriel windows and some splendid carving. St Gregorys church has stood much as we see it now, since the 15th century but has relics of an earlier age. Inside it is elegant and lofty. The treasure of the church is the ancient cover of its modern font, one of only three covers of its kind. Apart from its beauty, what is exceptional is that the lower part pushes up ingeniously telescopewise.

In a small medieval chapel is an enormous altar tomb with an inscription to Thomas Carter who died in 1706, saying that he was rich and gone to heaven but in such delightful words:

Travellers I will relate a wondrous thing. On the day
on which Thomas Carter breathed his last, a Sudbury camel
passed through the eye of a needle; if thou hast wealth
go and do likewise.
Farewell

Westleton, a prize winning village has a wonderful thatched church whose dignity remains unimpaired, even though the low steeple is the result of the village fathers trying to build something grander on the base of the ancient tower which could not take the weight, and collapsed in 1770. The village green is famous for its large duckpond, and should be equally famous for **The White Horse Inn**, a delightful 16th-century inn. Here you may stay if you wish. Westleton is such a pretty place and there is so much to do close-by.

Woodbridge does not have one ugly building to my mind. You can approach it by six roads, each delightful although probably the most beautiful way in is by British Rail from London when the track runs along the Finn Valley bringing you to the station right at the salt-water's edge of the River Deben. One of the main roads of the town leads from the station and the quay-side with its 16th century houses and inns, its tall, ancient weather-boarded tide-mill and sheds with their old tiled roofs. Once it was a busy commercial port but now it offers a haven for those who love to sail. St Mary's Church is a must for you to visit. The 15th century tower and North porch are magnificently decorated. The font is of a type only found in Suffolk and Norfolk, depicting the Seven Sacraments. The church is always open during daylight hours.

The Seckford Hall Hotel is the place to stay - once the family home of Thomas Seckford once lord of the manor from 1580, who influenced much that happened in Woodbridge. The there is **The Cherry Tree Inn** in Cumberland Street, a welcoming hostelry and **The Captain's Table** in Quay Street, which is justly renowned as a Seafood restaurant.

Yoxford is known as 'The Garden of Suffolk'. This once coaching town is a pretty place with some charming old houses set in landscaped parks, through which flows the little River Yox. It is a centre of arts and crafts galleries and good antique shops. the church of St Peter's is medieval with a 14th century tower with a lead spire guarded by gargoyles.

THE COACH AND HORSES
77 Manor Road,
Dersingham,
Kings Lynn, Norfolk
PE31 6LD
Tel: (01485) 540391/ 540353

If you want a pub near to Sandringham and only 10 minutes drive to several beaches then the Coach and Horses at Dersingham has to be the answer. So far its history has been traced back to 1608 although it is believed to be considerably older. It actually stands on the Sandringham Estate and has welcomed many interesting visitors in its time. Pete and Madge Ashley are the proprietors and it is their outgoing friendly approach to their customers that has made the pub so popular. After enjoying a drink and some good pub food you can go on many lovely walks through Sandringham and whichever one you choose you will find a wealth of wild life deer, pheasants and many migratory birds. You can also stay here if you wish and it is in one of these comfortable rooms you will find there is no ceiling but just very old beams.

There are two bars, a games room and a dining room. Outside the beer garden tempts many people in good weather. It overlooks the Coach and Horses own Bowling Green on which you are welcome to play during pub hours at a small charge per person. The menu includes a number of home made specialities including a mouth watering steak and kidney pie, beef in beer, or pork cooked in cider. Seafood platters are very popular and so are the Vegetarian dishes. Crab salad is one of the many salads on offer. If you just want a snack then take a look at the range of sandwiches and Ploughman's. The prices are reasonable, the portions generous.

USEFUL INFORMATION

OPEN; Lunch: 11-3.00pm	**RESTAURANT;** Full & varied
Eve: 6-11.00pm menu	**BAR FOOD;** Basket meals, Ploughman's etc
CHILDREN; Welcome	**VEGETARIAN;** 3 dishes daily
CREDIT CARDS; None taken	**DISABLED ACCESS;** One small step
LICENSED; Full on Licence	**GARDEN;** Beer Garden.

THE PUNCH BOWL
Bildeston Road,
Battisford, Stowmarket,
Suffolk
Tel: (01449) 612302

What a pretty village is Battisford: a mixture of aged thatched cottages which sit in harmony with those built more recently. The main road, known as Straight Road, is one of the highest points around from which to look down on the surrounding beautiful countryside.

At one time the Punch Bowl was three cottages and you can still see the oak beams and the open log fires which were there originally. Part of the charm of this pub is its hospitable and friendly ambience. The proprietor, David Bumstead, knows exactly how to make visitors welcome and is a popular figure amongst the locals who use the pub regularly. In and around the bar there is plenty of highly polished brass which combined with the slightly rustic furniture, creates a truly rural picture. The well kept garden has swings and a play area for children which keeps them safely occupied whilst their elders enjoy a peaceful drink. Children are allowed inside to eat. If you are a caravanner you may like to know that there is a registered Caravan Parking Area available nearby.

The Punch Bowl is open for food every day of the week both at lunchtime and in the evenings. The menu is simple and all home-cooked. Every day there are different specials and on Sundays there is a traditional roast meal with all the trimmings, including a good pudding. For those wanting a quick snack there are sandwiches which are freshly made and a good Ploughman's lunch which is always popular. The prices are extremely reasonable and definitely value for money.

USEFUL INFORMATION

OPEN; 11-3pm 7-11pm   *RESTAURANT;* Traditional & home-cooked
CHILDREN; Garden &Restaurant *BAR FOOD;* Specials, sandwiches, etc
CREDIT CARDS; None taken *VEGETARIAN;* 2 or 3 dishes
LICENSED; Full Licence   *DISABLED ACCESS;* Level entrance
GARDEN; Swings, playarea, tables & chairs

THE GLOBE INN
The Buttlands
Wells-Next-The-Sea,
Norfolk.
NR23 1EU
Tel: (01328) 710206

Wells-next-the-Sea has clung on to its village atmosphere but acquired town status, with the facilities that go with it. Situated in the centre is a very trim and well kept pub, The Globe Inn, which also offers bed and breakfast accommodation. It stands facing a very large green overhung by lime trees. It is most attractive and no wonder that in summer, it is frequently used as an overspill for the Globe

Michael and Patricia Dickerson run this busy pub with great professionalism and efficiency. Even in the height of the summer when the place is buzzing, they manage to keep their cool. There is a public bar and a lounge bar both of which are comfortably furnished. The 4 bedrooms have a shared T.V. lounge, and in addition there is also a separate flat which sleeps five. A dining room which is used during the day for pub customers, also serves as a breakfast room for anyone staying, and you can be assured of a very good breakfast.

In addition to the full bar menu which is available lunchtimes and evenings, there is also a good range of bar snacks. So many of the dishes on offer are tempting that it is difficult to choose, but one of the most popular is 'Steak Michael Angelo' with green peppercorns, port and cream. All the steaks are particularly good; the meat used is prime steak reared locally. For those who prefer poultry or fish you will not be disappointed nor will the vegetarians!

USEFUL INFORMATION

OPEN; *Summer: 10.30am-1.lpm*
CHILDREN; *Yes in pool room*
CREDIT CARDS; *None taken*
LICENSED; *Full Licence*
GARDEN; *Tables front & back of pub*

RESTAURANT; *Full bar menu*
BAR FOOD; *Wide range including snacks*
VEGETARIAN; *Several dishes*
DISABLED ACCESS; *Yes*

GRILLS AND GILLS

34 Abbeygate Street,
Bury St Edmunds, Suffolk IP33 ILW
Tel:01284 706004

Bury St Edmunds is an historical gem and in the heart of the busy main High Street with a pedestrianised frontage opposite the ancient 11th Century Abbey Gate Gardens and Ruins, you will find Grills and Gills, an establishment as unique in name as it is in its food and Mediterranean style interior. The latter was designed by the three working directors using three primary colours for their wall scheme and upholstered iron chairs. The centrepiece being the three fabric wallhangings in an Aztec design. It all changes on the first floor of this Grade II 15th century Listed building. Here the timber beams and studding have been sympathetically retained and further enhanced by the use of mahogany dining chairs. The Abbeygate Lounge is used for private dining, meetings and as an overflow for the main restaurant. According to historians the rear of the building is 15th century, approximately 100 years later at the front section, and together with the buildings on either side once formed one large house.

The food is exciting, beautifully cooked, whether meat or fish, and offers a daily changing Fish Special Board, which also features an extension to the Lunch Menu with Pies, Cromer Crab, Mussels, Liver and Bacon and a host of other dishes. Grills and Gills is a sister restaurant to 'Somewhere Else at 1 Langton Place, Hatter Street, Bury St Edmunds - equally good and described by Craig Brown in the Sunday Times as being 'without pomp or whimsy'. Two places in which to relax and enjoy eating.

USEFUL INFORMATION

OPEN; *Mon-Sat: 12-2.30pm & 6-10.30pm*
CHILDREN; *Welcome*
CREDIT CARDS; *Visa/Access.JMaster*
LICENSED; *Full On Licence*
GARDEN; *No*

RESTAURANT; *Chargrilled. Large selection of meat & fish cuts*
BAR FOOD; *Not applicable*
VEGETARIAN; *10 dishes*
DISABLED ACCESS; *Two small steps*

**CLAYDON COUNTRY
HOUSE HOTEL**
*16-18 Ipswich Road,
Claydon, Ipswich IP6 0AR
Tel: 01473 - 830382*

English Country House charm is the essence of this very nice hotel which combined with first class cuisine and superb wine list makes it a must for any visitor in the area whether on business or pleasure. It is small enough to ensure that every guest receives individual attention, yet spacious enough to allow for your complete comfort and relaxation. You will find it a few minutes drive from Ipswich and the A45, connecting Felixstowe, Bury St Edmunds and Cambridge. From the A45 there is easy access to the Midlands, Norwich via the A140, and Ely via the A10.

Each bedroom has its own private bath or shower room. Beautifully furnished each offers restorative comfort at the end of a busy day! Family rooms are available with cots and high chairs if they are required. Naturally every room has colour television with satellite, direct dial telephone, tea and coffee making facilities, trouser press and hair-dryer. Most rooms offer delightful views over the village or the large gardens, and the Bridal Suite is most attractive with an elegant four poster bed. Wonderful place for a Special Weekend Break. The spacious Dining Room, open to non-residents, provides the perfect setting for lunch or dinner, whether you require a table for two, or the entire room! Silver cutlery, starched table linen, fresh flowers and Regency style decor, add undoubted elegance to the occasion. The standard of cuisine is equally high with a chef who creates, cooks and uses great imagination in his kitchen. One of Claydon's particular features is its ability to cater for all manner of special functions from Wedding Receptions to Business Functions.Claydon is also an ideal venue for conferences and meetings.

USEFUL INFORMATION

OPEN; *All year.*
CHILDREN; *Yes. Cots. Baby listening*
CREDIT CARDS; *Visa/Access/Amex.*
LICENSED; *Restaurant & Residential*
ACCOMMODATION; *14 en-suite rooms*
GARDEN; *Large. Safe.*
Eat outside in summer.

RESTAURANT; *Traditional English & French.*
BAR FOOD; *Snacks available at anytime.*
VEGETARIAN; *Several dishes*
DISABLED ACCESS; *4 steps at front.*
Ground floor bedrooms.

RYEGATE HOUSE

Stoke-by-Nayland,
Suffolk C06 4RA.
East Anglia

Tel: 01206 263679

Lying to the North of Colchester the Dedham Vale, well known as Constable Country, encompasses the River Stour from Nayland to Flatford. This beautiful vale has inspired many an artist with its watermills, quiet serene streams edged with willows and gently rolling meadows and fields. As you explore this picturesque area you will discover the delights of the riverside villages of Nayland, Dedham, Stratford-St Mary and Flatford. On the Northern flank lies the charming village of Stoke-by-Nayland where you will find shops, restaurants, public houses, a post office, garage and St Mary's Church, whose majestic tower dominates the skyline and overlooks the entire area

Here too you will find Ryegate House, an English Tourist Board '2 Crown Highly Commended' Bed and Breakfast establishment, owned and efficiently run by Margaret and Albert Geater, a very accommodating couple, who extend a warm and friendly welcome to you. The house itself is delightful, reminiscent of a traditional Suffolk farmhouse, exceptionally well kept with emphasis placed on cleanliness and attention to detail. The building is surrounded by a well tended garden with ample private off road parking. The furnishings are comfortable and in total keeping with the house. The guests sitting room is very welcoming with comfortable relaxing chairs, colour television and countryside views. The bedrooms, two double and one twin, are very well appointed with central heating, colour co-ordinated soft furnishings, en suite facilities, colour television, radio alarm, shaver point and a complimentary tea and coffee tray. Breakfast is served in the dining room where the outlook is across the garden to an old orchard left to nature. Here you can enjoy a full English, Continental or vegetarian meal. Evening meals are not available in house, but an excellent dinner or supper can easily be obtained from one of the restaurants or public houses in the village.

The surrounding area has much to offer the visitor. The market towns of Sudbury and Hadleigh with their historical backgrounds and ancient buildings. Many picturesque Suffolk villages and Long Melford with its baronial halls and ptethora of antique shops. Lavenham, the jewel in the crown and only a short distance away, regarded as the finest medieval village in England. Colchester, Britain's oldest recorded town, steeped in history and worthy of more than one days exploration. The unspoilt Suffolk coast and the ports of Felixstowe and Harwich are within easy reach and with fishing, golf and plenty of walking nearby, it makes Ryegate House a delightful place to stay.

USEFUL INFORMATION

OPEN; *All year except Christmas*
CHILDREN; *Over l0 years*
CREDIT CARDS: *None taken*
ACCOMMODATION; *3 en suite rooms*

DINING ROOM; *Choice of breakfast*
Evening meal is not available
VEGETARIAN; *Catered for*
DISABLED ACCESS; *No*

THE FERRY BOAT INN
Felixstowe Ferry,
Felixstowe
IP11 NRZ
Tel: (01394) 284203

This old pub dates from about 1450. Over the centuries it has played many roles: it was once a 'Fish House', and then a 'Ferry House', and even rented once to the Customs and Excise as a 'Customs House'. It was approximately 1680 when it was granted a licence to sell spirits, and to the present day this has been its main function.

It is a comfortable place, full of history and with the acquired warmth that an establishment of this kind has when it has given much pleasure to many people over centuries. It is not the smartest of places but that does not matter one iota because you will find a true welcome there and rapidly will want to know about the days when ferries ran regularly. Today there is only a summer service. You will also learn about the time when donkeys were stabled in a building at the rear of the pub. They were one of the many groups that paraded along the sea front. More interestingly, in the 17th century it was quite usual to see gaggles of geese on the roads. There might have been as many as 2,000 and they would have had their feet coated with tar and feathers before they were driven the loing way to the London markets. The hospitality of the Ferry Boat is renowned and the food is good home-cooked fare with a blackboard menu that changes frequently. Simple snacks are available as well as main meals. You can get some of the freshest sandwiches too. It is definitely a value for money pub.

USEFUL INFORMATION

OPEN; 11-2.30pm. 6-11pm.
Food: 12-2pm 7-(L/O)8.30pm
No food Sun eve.
CHILDREN; Dining area only
CREDIT CARDS; Access/Visa
LICENSED; Real ales straight from barrel
GARDEN; Yes

RESTAURANT; Not applicable
BAR FOOD; Home-cooked bar
food with accent on fish
VEGETARIAN; As required
DISABLED ACCESS; With assistance

THE CLIFF HOTEL
Cliff Hill, Gorleston,
Gt Yarmouth, Norfolk NR31 6DH
Tel: 01493 662179 Fax: 01493 653617

This attractive AA and RAC 3 star hotel offers as much to the businessman as it does to those who visit Gorleston on holiday. Its position is superb overlooking the harbour on the quieter side of Gt Yarmouth which is only a five minute drive away. Family owned and run by Rqdney and Janet Scott it has everything that one considers important in a traditional hotel but at the same time it has all that is necessary for the modern day businessman and woman. There are 39 bedrooms all of which are well appointed and en suite. For those with a discerning palate the food will prove to be of a very high standard offering a range of traditional dishes with the occasional inspired innovation. The wine list is extensive and provides something for every taste and purse. The Scott family have their own brewery so it is not surprising to see such beers as Golden Best Bitter, Blues and Bloater Festival Bitter, William French Strong Celebration Ale and Scotty's Dark Oast Ale prominently displayed in the cheerful bar.

For the visitor the safe clean beaches are an attraction but equally there is much else to see with stately homes, Wildlife parks, the Sea Life Centre at Great Yarmouth and many other places of interest within easy reach. The Cliff Hotel provides a quiet and relaxing environment for the businessman either for a small one day seminar or a larger residential conference. There are two conference rooms equipped with everything from a Flip Chart to a Projection screen. There is a special all in rate for delegates. What better way to end a days work than a stroll along Gorleston's upper and lower seaside promenades which are pleasant all year round, before returning to the hotel for drinks and an excellent dinner.

USEFUL INFORMATION

OPEN; All year, all hours

CHILDREN; Free accommodation when sharing with adults

CREDIT CARDS; Diners/Amex/Visa/Access

LICENSED; Full On

ACCOMMODATION; 40 en suite rooms

RESTAURANT; Traditional English

BAR FOOD; Wide range, inexpensive

VEGETARIAN; Several dishes daily

DISABLED ACCESS; Yes, no special facilities

GARDEN; Yes with tables and chairs

THE HILL HOUSE
Happisburgh,
Norfolk NRl2 0PW
Tel: 01692 650004

The coastal village of Happisburgh has wonderful views and none more so than The Hill House, an old coaching inn which dates back to the 16th century and was a favourite retreat of Sir Arthur Conan Doyle who wrote the famous Sherlock Holmes stories. Hill House as illustrated by its name, stands high on the hill with wonderful views of the Norfolk countryside. It is full of character developed over the years. Oak beams and large fireplaces in the main bar and restaurant give the rooms a splendid olde worlde ambience. Here you can relish Real Ales at their best, good home-cooked meals which are substantial and reasonably priced. Whether you sit down to a meal in the restaurant from which you can see the sea or enjoy a meal in the bar you will be offered a wide range of dishes including some very tasty specialities of the house.

There is a large, well maintained garden which seats 30, complete with a 1900 Signal Box and has fnendly barbecues dunng the summer, a Play Room and a Function Room. The Signal Box has been skilfully converted to provide a delightful double en suite bedroom whilst in the pub itself there are two more letting rooms with a shared bathroom, one of which sleeps three and the other five - ideal for families. The Hill House is friendly and relaxed; a good place to be.

USEFUL INFORMATION

OPEN; *11-3pm & 7-llpm*
CHILDREN; *Welcome*
CREDIT CARDS; *Visa, Access, Amex*
LICENCED; *Full On*
ACCOMMODATION; *3 letting rooms*
1 en suite, 2 family

RESTAURANT; *Good home-made food reasonable.*
BAR FOOD; *Wide range, inexpensive*
VEGETARIAN; *Always 2*
DISABLED ACCESS; *Yes*
GARDEN; *Large, seats 30, BBQ*

THE BEECHES HOTEL
& VICTORIAN GARDENS

4-6 Earlham Road,
Norwich, Norfolk NR2 3DB
Tel: 01603 621167 Fax: 01603 620151

Two listed and sympathetically restored Victorian houses together with a new annexe make up this enchanting hotel which stands in 3 acres of tranquil wooded grounds less than ten minutes stroll from the centre of Norwich. No one could walk through the front door and not recognise the love and care which has been applied to give it a relaxed and informal ambience. Each of the 27 attractive en suite bedroom has received an individual design; some are reserved for non-smokers, some overlook the famous Plantation Garden, designed in the mid 1800's by Henry Trevor. Sadly over the years the garden became neglected as the house passed through the hands of various owners. In 1980 the house and its 'secret garden' were rediscovered. Today it is restored to much of its former glory and guests are free to wander through the delights of this important reminder of our Victorian heritage, with its ornate Gothic fountain and Italianate terrace.

The restaurant offers an interesting menu with an Italian bias but using mostly fresh local produce and cooked to order at modest prices. The restaurant is open to non-residents. A small conference room seats up to 30 people. Pets are not permitted in the hotel. The Beeches has earned its 3 Crown Commended Classification by the English Tourist Board and its 2 Star AA Award -'an oasis in the heart of historic Norwich.'

USEFUL INFORMATION

OPEN; *7am-10pm.Closed Xmas*
CHILDREN; *High chairs, cots*
CREDIT CARDS; *Visa, Master, Amex Diners,Switch*
LICENCED; *Hotel & Restaurant*
ACCOMMODATION; *27 en-suite*
GARDEN; *3 acres, beautiful English Heritage*

RESTAURANT; *Italian bias, fresh produce reasonable prices*
BAR FOOD; *Not applicable*
VEGETARIAN; *Two dishes daily*
DISABLED ACCESS; *Level entrance one special double room*

**THE GEORGIAN
HOUSE HOTEL**
*32-34 Unthank Road,
Norwich NR2 2RB
Tel:01603 615655 Fax: 01603 765689*

The Goodwins who own and run this particularly nice hotel will tell you 'comfortable we may be but expensive we are not? This is entirely true and accounts for the frequently returning guests enjoying the hotels ever popular Weekend or Mid-Week Breaks. Literally 5 minutes walk from the historic heart of Norwich the hotel is an ideal base for exploring the hidden charms both of the city and the county. Both the Georgian House and Norwich have, using current parlance, the 'feelgood' factor. There are no motorways to speed hordes of visitors in this direction. Life is quieter and a safer place. Shopping is a delight, plenty of department stores, market stalls by the score and not a shopping mall in sight. The hotel consists of two well furnished Victorian houses linked together and set in beautiful gardens. It is a friendly, welcoming establishment where your comfort and well being is far more important than formality. The 27 en suite bedrooms each with Colour TV, Radio, Direct Dial Telephone, Hospitality Tray and Hairdryer ensure a good nights rest whether for the visitor or the businessman. For the latter there is a Fax and 48 hour laundry service. Non-smoking bedrooms are available. The small, intimate well-stocked bar is a pleasant place in which to enjoy a drink before or after dinner whilst in the Restaurant the food lives up to its reputation offering a varied table d'hote and a la carte menu, all prepared from carefully selected local produce. The wine list is not vast but it has been chosen to provide a world wide range and at sensible prices. Dinner is to be enjoyed and the whole atmosphere of the Restaurant and indeed, the whole hotel, has this emphasis. The Georgian House is somewhere to enjoy and to remember with pleasure.

USEFUL INFORMATION

OPEN; *All Year*
CHILDREN; *Welcome*
CREDIT CARDS; *Amex/Diners.Visa/ Mastercard/Electron/Switch available Carte Bleu/J.C.B*
LICENSED; *Residential/Restaurant*
ACCOMMODATION; *27 en suite*

RESTAURANT; *High standard Table d'hôte and Á La Carte*
BAR FOOD; *Sandwiches & snacks always*
VEGETARIAN; *Yes both Table d'hôte & Á La Carte*
DISABLED ACCESS; *No*
GARDEN; *Very large. Car Parking*

THE REEDHAM FERRY INN
Reedham,
Norwich, Norfolk. Inn f~ Restaurant
NR13 3HA
Tel: (0493) 700429

This well maintained, late 16th-century, Ferry Inn is a renowned, distinctive landmark and a welcome site to both yachtsmen and weary travellers. It stands on the junction of the B 1140 and the bank of the River Yare, surrounded by picturesque marshland scenery and of course the Reeds whence Reedham village derives its name.

Alongside the Ferry Inn is the only working car ferry in East Anglia. In the summer, visitors spend many idyllic hours sitting on the attractive riverside patio, watching the world float by, and the ferry plying to and fro across the River Yare. The ferry provides the only crossing place between the city of Norwich and the busy port of Gt. Yarmouth, on the coast. Some forty years ago, when the Archer family first settled at the Ferry Inn, the 'Horse Ferry' was cranked by hand, before its conversion to diesel power. A few yards upstream, trailed boats may be launched from the slipway. A further facility offered is the 4 acre, landscaped camping and caravaning park with every modern facility.

As one enters the bar through the 'Family Sun Lounge', a feeling of warmth envelops one. Numerous artefacts from a bygone marshland era abound, under the oak beams. The Restaurant serves traditional English and Continental fayre, with some interesting and unusual dishes. David Archer selects only the best of various game in season, and dishes are prepared only using fresh produce; prime meats personally chosen fish and home grown herbs. Bar food is equally good and varied

USEFUL INFORMATION

OPEN: *Sum:ll-3pm 6.30-llpm*
Sun:12-3pm Win:ll-2.30pm 7-llpm
Sun:12-3pm 7-10.30pm
CHILDREN: *Sun Lounge.*
Res't until 9pm.
CREDIT CARDS: *Access/ Visa only*
LICENSED: *Full Licence*

RESTAURANT: *English & Continental*
BAR FOOD: *Fresh & varied*
VEGETARIAN: *3 dishes*
DISABLED ACCESS: *Wide Doorways*
GARDEN: *Roadside & waterside patio*

THE ANGEL INN
Stoke-By-Nayland,
Suffolk.IP84 DX3
Tel: (01206) 263245

The Angel Inn is at the crossroads in the centre of Stoke-by-Nayland, one of Constable's most favourite villages. The village stands on a bluff of land that rises above the water meadows and fields of the Dedham Vale, now a conservation area. The surrounding countryside with its many footpaths and country lanes is ideal for exploring on foot or cycling. The Angel has stood since 1536 and although much restoration work has been done over the centuries, much of the original building survives from this time.
Today the Angel continues its long tradition of hospitality to travellers. Comfortably furnished rooms, beamed bars with log fires in winter, good food, wine and local ales. There are 6 guest bedrooms, all with bathrooms en suite. A full English Breakfast is included in the tariff. The restaurant offers a wonderful a la carte menu for lunch and dinner Tuesday to Saturday evenings and on Sunday, a traditional roast lunch. Due to its local popularity it is advisable to reserve a table. Lunch and supper are also served in the bar every day from an extensive chalkboard menu which is revised twice daily. Here informality is the order. All the food is prepared on the premises from fresh ingredients using local produce wherever possible, particularly fresh fish and shellfish from east coast ports. The head chef, Mark Johnson's style strikes a balance between the adventurous and the traditional with the emphasis on flavour. The Angel is one of Suffolk's treasures.

USEFUL INFORMATION

OPEN; *Weekdays: 11-2.30pm 6-11lpm*
Sundays: 12-3pm 7-10.30pm
CHILDREN; *No*
CREDIT CARDS; *Access/Visa AmexlDiners*
ACCOMMODATION: *6 en suit rooms*

RESTAURANT; *All fresh, International cuisine*
BAR FOOD; *Wide selection, changes twice daily*
VEGETARIAN; *One per day*
DISABLED ACCESS; *Yes*
GARDEN; *Patio*
LICENSED; *Full on Licence*

THE FOX INN,

The Street, Newbourne,
Woodbridge,
Suffolk, IP12 4NY.

Tel : 01473 736307

The history of this charming inn dating from 1634 actually goes back a lot further. It is said that in the 13th century, the river flowed near to what is now The Fox, and that an upturned boat was used as a dwelling. Eventually, a permanent dwelling was built around this boat, even using some of it's wood. Since 1634, The Fox Inn has been known as a haven for travellers and locals, and the present owners, Joye and David Ponsford, continue to ensure that a warm and friendly welcome is afforded to all their customers.

The inn today also boasts a very fine restaurant, which has an excellent range of varied English foods. Vegetarians and special diets are cheerfully catered for, as are children, and fish dishes are one of their specialities. Freshly prepared food is offered daily, and home grown herbs and fresh local produce are used where possible. There is a variety of special daily dishes which are advertised on the blackboard menu, and this includes a home made vegetarian dish. For those who prefer more of a snack meal there is an excellent bar menu.

An exciting new venture which Joye and David have embarked on is the erection of marquees in a section of the garden, which can be booked for those special events such as family gatherings, or even an indulgent business event! (A great way to impress those foreign businessmen with a English garden party!) This is a great way of making those 'special occasions' really unique, and ensuring a memorable time!

Another service that Joye and David offer is the arrangement of booking bed & breakfast for visitors to the area. This is a great idea in that you can state your price range and needs, and have good local accommodation which is recommended. This is a very worthwhile service which can make your holiday or visit much easier to plan.

Local facilities are very good. You are only 5 miles from Ipswich and 2 miles from the coastline. Fishing, golf, and walking are just some of the local pursuits and Woodbridge is on the cycling route which takes you through the heaths and marshlands with their wild beauty and soothing landscapes. This is a delightful part of the country, and with good food, company and accommodation, you are sure to have a great time!

USEFUL INFORMATION

OPEN; *All year - 7 days a week*　　　**RESTAURANT;** *Excellent choices*
CHILDRE; *Welcome*　　　　　　　　**VEGETARIANS;** *Catered for*
PETS; *No*　　　　　　　　　　　　　**SPECIAL DIETS;** *Catered for*
CREDIT CARDS; *All major*　　　　　**DISABLED ACCESS;** *Yes*

YAXHAM MILL,
Freehouse & Restaurant
Norwich Road,
Yaxham, Dereham,
Norfolk
Tel: 01362 693144 Fax: 01362 858556

Standing on the historic site of a Norfolk tower windmill dating from 1860, the present complex is the result of careful, loving use of old buildings and melding them with the present time. Former mill cottages have become individually designed self catering accommodation, beautifully equipped, warm and comfortable. For example The Baker's shop, Stables, Blacksmith's and Forge Cottages were all part of the original hamlet.

You will find Yaxham Mill in open countryside approximately 2 miles from the market town of Dereham in the Heart of Norfolk. A wonderful area to visit, it is rich in history, superbly scenic and has a plethora of wonderful places to visit whether it is taking off for the Broads, going to the coast or exploring the villages and market towns and gazing with awe at the beauty of some of the National Trust properties and gardens.

The owner, Eileen Leveridge, is an established breeder of Norfolk ducklings but she nonetheless finds time to personally supervise the running of Yaxham Mill, in which she is ably assisted by a cheerful and very efficient staff. Her chef, Charles Newcombe, is a wizard with food with a preference for Italian cooking but he insists on there being a wide range of English and foreign dishes always available. This is a man who has created meals for   Princess Margaret and Lady Thatcher and many other celebrities. He considers catering for 900 people at a Coldstream Guards charity event to be the pinnacle of his career - so far! The menu is always exciting and you dine in the superb 44 seater restaurant at tables laid with pretty linen cloths, cutlery that gleams and glass that sparkles. Bar snacks are available in a separate bar. For those who possibly have a wedding or a corporate function in mind you will find Yaxham Mill ideal. The organisation is perfect, marquees can be set up in the ground and live entertainment is readily available.

USEFUL INFORMATION

OPEN; All year. 11-3pm & 6.30-11pm
Weekends: All day
CHILDREN; Welcome
CREDIT CARDS; Visa/Mastercard
LICENSED; Yes
ACCOMMODATION; Self catering cottages
Overnight & Overnight caravan park
Short Breaks

RESTAURANT; Excellent, interesting
fare Including Italian dishes. Booking
advisable Especially for Sunday Lunch
BAR SNACKS; Wide range
VEGETARIAN; Catered for
DISABLED ACCESS; Yes Ramp. Toilets
GARDEN; Beer Garden

Chapter 14

SOMERSET & AVON

INCLUDES

Chapter 14

SOMERSET AND AVON

I spent Christmas last year with my daughter and son-in-law, grandchildren; in fact a whole house-party, in a village just outside Sherborne, very close to the Somerset border and this gave me the opportunity to visit some of the delightful areas of Somerset in this book. The first was in the estate village of **Hinton St George**, a stone's throw from **Crewkerne**. Hinton St George until recently was entirely owned by the Earls Paulett and fortunately has been left almost untouched by subsequent owners. Today restoration and protection are the name of the game. The church is a gem, showing ham stone work at its very best. It was endowed with money in 1486 and a tower was built with a splendid crown and pinnacles. The body of the church belongs to the same period though the font is 13th century, recut to go with the building. There is a wealth of fascinating memorials most of them to members of the Paulett family.

The Priory in the village is the oldest house in Hinton, which includes a 14th century window in the chapel at its east end although the house itself dates from the 16th century. I went to the local pub, The Poulett Arms with my family and some of their friends together with a very old friend who lives in the village. She lives in a delightful tiny cottage next door to an amazing shop which sells everything and if there is no one there to serve you, it is suggested you help yourself and leave the money on the counter - wonderful to see in this day and age.

The Poulett Arms is a fascinating building full of a sense of the past and the comfort of the present. Rough stone walls, enormous inglenook fireplaces, original beams and a wealth of splendid old signs hanging below the original beams. One states 'Rooms 7/6d per night with attendant female staff'. Would that were the price today and I did wonder who might be described as attendant female staff? The pub was packed when we were there and there had just been a change of management so I cannot comment on the standard or type of food but the welcome was just as warm as ever and the atmosphere delightful.

A choice of small country roads will take you from here to **Ilminster,** which as the name implies, was once a Saxon missionary centre, the minster on the River Ile, and said to have been founded by King Ine in 726. That is what the monks of Mulcheney Abbey claimed anyway in a charter in their archives which subsequently was found to be forged but the facts true! Ilminster has a charming market place. Queen Victoria stayed here in the George Hotel just before she became Queen. The Georgian houses in Court Barton demonstrate the prosperity of the 18th century which for over a hundred years had been an important cloth-making and gloving centre.

The superb crossing tower of the minster is reminiscent of the central tower at Wells Cathedral, with battlements and pinnacles. It is truly splendid. behind the church in Court Barton is a 15th century chantry house, partly Georgianized and the former grammar school, founded by Humphrey Walrond in 1549, a successor to a school at least a century older.

Yeovil does not draw the visitor in the usual way but it should not be ignored. It has an excellent shopping centre, some good hostelries and is a good base from which to strike out into Dorset if one wishes - it is right on the boundary.

I have a great love of Somerset and its wondrous beauty whether it is in the Exmoor National Park, the Somerset Levels, Glastonbury, the tiny cathedral city of Wells, or the hundreds of pretty villages and small towns. The limited number of words devoted to the county in no way reflects my feelings - rather those of my publishers who cannot permit me the number of pages I would like to have!

Bridgwater, now an industrial centre, was a busy port until Bristol overshadowed it. The town grew up around what was the best crossing point of a river which could not be forded. At the Norman Conquest it was held by a Saxon, Merleswain who lost it to Walter de la Douai. At that time it was known as Brugie but became the Bridge of Walter, hence it's name today. By the 26th June 1200, King John granted a Royal Charter giving borough status and permission to build a castle to protect the flourishing port. The River Parrett has been used for commercial shipping since pre-Roman times and a relic of Phoenician ring money was found near the site of the old town bridge. In the 13th century the port was used as a victualling base for forays into Wales and Ireland, and by the 15th century had become a major port ranking 12th in the whole country. Woolen cloth was the principle export, the wool trade forming the basis of the West Country wealth, and the main import was french wine.

It became the main point of entry and outlet for much of central and western Somerset, Taunton, Langport, Illchester and even Yeovil sent, and received, goods through the estuary of the River Parrett and by the canal to Taunton and beyond.

Many commuters to **Bristol** live in the pleasant town of **Burnham-on-Sea.** It has a laid back feel about it and no one seems to be in a hurry. You can walk for miles along the beach, enjoy the shops and find one or two very good hostelries. The medieval church of St Andrew contains a 17th century marble reredos designed by Inigo Jones and carved by Grinling Gibbons; originally made for the chapel of Whitehall Palace, it passed to Hampton Court and Westminster Abbey before coming to rest here in the 19th century. The tower of the church tilts three feet from the vertical - the subsidence being due to its sandy foundations.

A little further north is the popular resort of **Weston-Super-Mare**. A perfect place this for families with young children, they can ride donkeys along the wide beach and watch artists creating huge models in the sands. Maybe they will watch a Punch and Judy show and then retire tired but happy to one of the many guest houses or hotels, all of which boast nothing less than the comforts of home.

Ignoring the magnificent city of **Bristol**, I have chosen to write about **Thornbury Castle** at **Thornbury** just to the north of the city and the exquisite Daneswood House Hotel at Shipham off the A38 coming south. Thornbury a thriving country town has managed to achieve a certain isolation. Yes, it does have traffic problems, but they are home grown ones. The A38 passes to the east of the town, and long before its existence, the old turnpike road avoided it as far back as 1769. It has become a splendid backwater, keeping its old streets and buildings. The main street layout, which forms the letter Y, by the junction of Castle Street, High Street and the Plane, has not changed since medieval times. In the High Street you will see two fine 18th-century inns, **The Swan** and the **White Lion**, both excellent places to visit, and at number 24, the **Coffee Lounge at Heritage Shops**, a place that is regarded by the local civic society as being of special architectural interest. The shop, selling fine china, crystal and gifts has retained and incorporated the original black oak beams and low ceilings into its fittings. Built partly from local stone, as an extension to the rear some 15 years ago, the coffee lounge allows superb views from two wide sets of sliding doors of the garden and beyond across the valley to the river and to Wales. There is a well-preserved old market house and a small Greek temple built in 1839 which was the old registry office.

In 1511 Edward Stafford, 3rd Duke of Buckingham, started to build his castle at Thornbury. Ten years later he was beheaded for treason and the castle appropriated by Henry VIII, who stayed here in 1535 with Anne Boleyn. Mary Tudor lived here for some years and when she became Queen she returned the castle to the descendants of the late Duke. Today, with its own vineyard and the oldest Tudor garden in England, Thornbury Castle is the only Tudor castle to be run as an hotel, and as you would suspect, it is superb. It is rated as one of the best 300 hotels in the world. Quite a reputation to uphold. The resident proprietor, the Baron of Portlethen has a fine appreciation of old buildings and cultural heritage. Since he bought it in 1968 it has thrived and been lovingly cared for. You will still find reminders of Buckingham everywhere. A stone carved doorway bears his emblem in relief, the Brecknock mantle, the Stafford Knot, among other devices. The Knot even appears on the mounting block in the courtyard. Fireplaces too, display the emblems. A wonderful place to stay and it would be insulting to suppose that the food, the wines and the service would be anything other than superb. It is unashamedly expensive and deserves to be.

Shipham in the heart of the Mendip Hills is a quiet place, undisturbed by the hurly burly of modern life. The drive from Shipham to Bristol is a mere 20 minutes, making it an ideal base for access to many towns, to Bristol's Ludgate airport, and easily accessible from the M4/M5. Not perhaps the most exciting of places but for me it has great importance as the home of Daneswood House Hotel standing in a leafy valley. From here on a clear day, the views stretch as far as Wales. It was built during the Edwardian era as a homeopathic health hydro, and it must rank as one of the finest hotels in the south west.

Staying at Daneswood House you wll find it is wonderful for the surrounding scenic walks in the Mendip Hills. The grounds of the hotel are included in the route of the famous 'Mendip Walkway'. It is an excellent area for horse riding and pony trekking. There are numerous golf courses within easy reach and fly fishing is available in the nearby rivers and the lakes of Blagdon and Chew Valley. For the more energetic, a dry ski slope and sports and leisure centre are both within 5 to 10 minutes drive.

The village of **Cheddar** is one of Somerset's many pretty villages, the original home of Cheddar Cheese and the awesome 40ft deep cleft in the rocks which covers two miles and is **Cheddar Gorge**. A few short miles to the east on the outskirts of Wells is the famed **Wookey Hole.** A real must for the tourist, Wookey Hole is divided into stunning underground caverns, a 19th century penny arcade, Madame Tussaud's waxworks and a traditional working paper mill.

And so to **Bath**. A frisson of excitement courses through me whenever I think about this wonderful city. I treat it like an old friend but always with decorum and an awareness that Beau Nash together with the Master of Ceremonies at the Assembly and

Pump Room insisted on the highest degree of civility and manners. It is always with a certain amount of impatience and eager anticipation that I seek out this incomparable city. I prefer to behave in the manner of an ostrich and bury my head in the sand when it comes to the outskirts or the 'new' Bath which arose because of indifferent planning. Thankfully, Georgian Bath still remains. It is not the individual buildings that make this city so wonderful but the whole architectural assembly. Take a walk down through Laura Place looking at the houses in which society used to dwell in its heyday when Bath was a fashionable watering hole, cross Argyle Street and so to Pulteney Bridge which spans the Avon. You could be forgiven for thinking you were in Florence as you cross this enchanting bridge which has small shops on either side of it not unlike the Ponte Vecchio. The Abbey must come high on your list of places to see. It is probably the most beautiful place in the city. There is more glass than stone in the walls which fill it with light. It is sometimes called the Lantern of the West.

It is the west front that is the greatest glory. It looks down on the square where all the visitors gather outside the Roman Baths. The west door itself is heavily carved with heraldic shields set in a triple arch, and on each side are wonderful stone canopies covering ancient figures of St Peter and St Paul. The Abbey will give you hours of pleasure and especially if you seek out the hidden treasures. I have been going there for years and see something new to me every time.

Bath owes its abbey to the energy of Oliver King, Bishop of Bath and Wells, who had a dream in which angels climbed up and down ladders to heaven and a voice exhorted a 'king to restore the church' which he did between 1495 and 1503. His dream is carved in stone in the abbey.

THE BATH TASBURGH HOTEL,
Warminster Road,
Bath BA2 6SH

Tel: 01225 425096 Fax: 01225 463842

Built in 1890 for a photographer to the Royal Family, The Bath Tasburgh Hotel is a grand Victorian mansion standing away from the main road, set in beautiful gardens with terraced lawns overlooking the River Avon and Kennet and Avon Canal, a beautiful leisureway. A Country House setting yet on the A36 and a few minutes from all the Tourist attractions in the centre of Bath. Lovely original stained glass windows on two spacious landings throw a rich light across the elegant interior. Magnificent fireplaces dominate the ground floor rooms and appear in some of the bedrooms as well. It is an hotel that has been taken to the top of the small hotels in Bath by the dedication and sheer professionalism of its owners, David and Susan Keeling. The fine decor reflects their interest in interior design which is apparent everywhere you go in this well appointed house. Each of the 12 en suite bedrooms is individually furnished to a very high standard including telephone, colour TV, tea and coffee making facilities, radio and clock alarm.

The smart decor of the beautiful dining room makes Breakfast a great pleasure. Every day there is a full 4 course English breakfast offering a choice. For those who like a lighter meal, fresh rolls, fruit and yoghurt are always available. A three course gourmet dinner is served at night from a menu that changes daily. Food is available all day including delicious afternoon teas served in the conservatory or on the lawn in fine weather. One can also relax and enjoy drinks either in the conservatory or on the peaceful lawns, whilst idly watching a game of croquet in progress. The Bath Tasburgh has acquired quite a reputation for the care and skill with which special occasions, weddings and small conferences for up to 20 persons are handled.

Guests come from all over the world to stay in the Bath Tasburgh, not surprisingly. Nor is it surprising to know that it has received many accolades including ETB Three Crown - Highly Commended, AA - Two Star Hotel, RAC - Two Star Hotel and has been written about in many guides including the English Johansens Recommended Private Country Houses. There are 2 ground floor rooms for the partially disabled but not for wheelchairs.

USEFUL INFORMATION

OPEN; all year
CHILDREN; Welcome Half price if
Sharing with parents
CREDIT CARDS; Master/Visa/Amex/Debit
LICENSED; Residential
ACCOMMODATION; 12 en suite rooms
DISABLED ACCESS; No

DINING ROOM; Excellent breakfast.
3 course Gourmet Dinner. Menu changed daily
Afternoon teas. Food available all day
VEGETARIAN; As requested
GARDEN; Large gardens overlooking the
Kennet and Avon Canal with it's
towpath-walk into Bath centre.

BROMPTON HOUSE,
St Johns Road,
Bath, Somerset BA26 PT

Tel: 01225 420972 Fax: 01225 420505
Email BROMPTON_ HOUSE @ compuserve.com

Many of the historic and architectural gems of Bath are within a 5 minutes level walk of Brompton House, in it's own right one of Bath's gems. Because of its excellent position it is the ideal place to stay for guests who want to explore the magic of Bath without the chore of having to find, and then paying expensively for, car parking. You will also find that Brompton House makes an excellent base from which to tour the Cotswolds, the Cathedral cities of Salisbury and Wells, Stonehenge and Glastonbury.

Its position is only one of the reasons why it is such a pleasure and a privilege to stay here. Brompton House richly deserved the Les Routiers Guest House of the year award in 1996 as you will soon discover. It is an elegant Grad II Listed Georgian residence which was originally the Old Rectory for St Mary's Church. Built on the foundations of a much earlier 16th century Manor Farm House it occupies a site that has experienced both Roman and Saxon settlements. The strictly non-smoking house is owned and run by the Selby family (Sue and David with their daughter Belinda and son Tim) who genuinely wish to ensure that every comfort and service is offered for their guests well being. You have only to look in the visitor's book to see they achieve this. You will find glowing comments such as 'Idyllic setting - great service- we enjoyed it all' and 'wonderful atmosphere, beautiful surroundings'. The whole house is tranquil and set in beautiful mature gardens surrounded by three acres of trees and churchyard, antique furniture everywhere, rich with the patina of age, pretty, colourful drapes and an abundance of fresh flowers completes the picture. The bedrooms are all en suite, charmingly decorated and furnished and equipped with colour TV, radio/alarm clocks, direct dial telephone, hair dryers and tea/coffee making facilities. One large bedroom with easy access on the ground floor is perfect for guests with limited mobility. Breakfast served in the elegant dining room is delicious and with so many choices that it becomes difficult to decide. Traditional full English, continental or wholefood meals are all available. To add the opportunity to enjoy a bottle of chilled wine in the enchanting garden in the summer or perhaps a bottle of champagne for a special occasion in the sitting room or bedrooms at any time of the year, just sums up the style and the delights of this wonderful house.

USEFUL INFORMATION

OPEN; *All Year except Christmas & New Year*
CREDIT CARDS; *All except Diners*
LICENSED; *Residential*
ACCOMMODATION; *19 en suite rooms*
GARDEN; *Beautiful, mature gardens*

DINING ROOM; *Breakfast only. One of the most delicious meals anywhere*
VEGETARIAN; *Catered for*
DISABLED ACCESS; *Limited mobility*
PETS; *No*

THE KINGS HEAD INN

12 High Street,
Cannington,
Bridgwater, Somerset TA5 2HE

Tel: 01278 652293

What impresses most people when they see The King's Head Inn on the main A39 North Devon road to the coast, at the foot of the Quantock Hills, is the gleaming white building with its black Tudor style shutters all highlighted by the profusion of flowers in hanging baskets and pots spaced out along the pavement. It is a stunning sight and once inside the doors you are by no means disappointed by the interior. It is warm and welcoming with low ceilings and beams befitting to a 17th century building. It has that sense of timelessness that makes one realise that the art of hospitality really has not changed down the centuries and in this inn, in the friendly, competent hands of Linda and Michael Andison, the tradition of the past continues. The chatter amongst the local in the bar is always friendly and they soon make you feel at home.

You have the happy choice of being able to stay here if you wish. There are 7 bedrooms, mainly en suite and all charmingly furnished in keeping with the pub. Each room has colour TV and a Teasmade. The King's Head is renowned for its food and the reason is apparent when you come down to breakfast and enjoy the splendid breakfast which will set you up for the day. At lunchtime the busy bars provide food at reasonable prices and the Carvery is extremely popular with a choice of meat or poultry and a selection of freshly cooked vegetables as well as crisp roast potatoes and light Yorkshire Puddings. In addition there are many other choices including the tasty Daily Specials and a selection of simple things like Jacket Potatoes with a variety of fillings or freshly cut sandwiches. Food is available 7 days a week both at lunch and in the evening. This is when the Á La Carte comes into its own with a menu that offers delicious grills, chicken dishes of all kinds, fish, vegetarian choices and a lot more. There is something for everyone beautifully cooked and definitely value for money.

USEFUL INFORMATION

OPEN; *All year, all day except 3-6pm*
CHILDREN; *Welcome*
CREDIT CARDS; *All major cards*
LICENSED; *Full On*
ACCOMMODATION; *7 rooms*
mainly en suite

RESTAURANT; *Excellent choice home-cooked*
BAR FOOD; *Wide range. Carvery. Good value*
VEGETARIAN; *Always a choice*
DISABLED ACCESS; *No special facility*
GARDEN; *Yes*
PETS; *No*

THE OLD PIER TAVERN,

*Pier Street, Burnham-on-Sea,
Somerset TA8 1BT.*

Tel : 01278 783161

Diane Sprague is the proprietor of this friendly establishment which offers traditional British hospitality within it's welcoming walls. Along with the pub is a restaurant which can seat up to 30 guests and offers an extremely good value meal from a varied menu. Diane caters for children with a special smaller menu, and also for vegetarians on request. The pub offers a good variety of 'ales', and for your entertainment there is a games room. It is renowned for live music on Friday and Saturday nights, and there is a nice dance floor for those more active revellers. This is a fun pub, with awards being won for 'bus pulling' for charity, and you are not likely to have a dull moment here! Everybody is welcome and you cannot help but become enthusiastic about this pub and it's friendly locals. It has been around for a few hundred years, as it is told that when nobility stayed at the Queen's Hotel, the servants stayed here at the Old Pier Tavern. Upstairs are three good bedrooms, nicely decorated, and with a welcoming tea ad coffee tray.

Somerset is a lovely county, and there are lots of wonderful walks and stunning scenery for you to enjoy. Close by is the historic town of Wells with it's 12th century cathedral, and lovely historic buildings. Bridgwater has the Admiral Blake Museum which is devoted to Robert Blake, Cromwell's most famous admiral. There is great history in this part of the world, but if this is not to your taste there is a wealth of other activities for you to enjoy. Weston-Super-Mare is just along the coast with it's water sports and family orientated attractions, and with beautiful sandy beaches for your pleasure. Enjoy this county, and especially the friendly atmosphere of this great pub where you will find a warm welcome awaits you at any time.

USEFUL INFORMATION

OPEN; *11am till 11pm*
CHILDREN; *Welcome*
CREDIT CARDS; *None taken*
ACCOMMODATION; *3 rooms 1dbl, 1 twin, 1 fml.*

RESTAURANT; *Good English fayre*
VEGETARIANS; *Catered for*
LICENSED; *Full*
DISABLED ACCESS; *Not really*

MARKET CROSS HOTEL,

Church Street,
Cheddar,
Somerset BS27 3RA

Tel: 01934 742264

Anne Fieldhouse is the friendly owner of the Market Cross Hotel which she runs in a professional manner yet managing to make it appear informal to all the guests who stay under her roof. The atmosphere is warm and welcoming The Hotel's bedrooms are furnished attractively in a modern style. Every room is centrally heated, most are en suite and they all have colour television and tea/coffee making facilities. The bar in the comfortable lounge is a great meeting place for guests and particularly in the winter when the roaring log fire acts as a magnet for guests coming in from the cold weather outside. The Market Cross Hotel serves an excellent breakfast, freshly cooked to order and in the evening the licensed restaurant, where the food is of a high standard, is open to residents and non-residents. Light refreshments are also available up to 10pm. Bargain breaks are available from October through May and provide an excellent opportunity for those who would rather explore Cheddar when there are not quite so many tourists about.

Going a little further afield, the beautiful cathedral city of Wells and the historic town of Glastonbury will provide a wonderful day out. Bath, with its famous Georgian buildings and Roman Baths is only 25 miles away and Bristol, with its large shopping centres, museums, theatres etc is just 18 miles from Cheddar. If you would rather spend a day on the beach, Weston-Super-Mare, complete with its donkeys, is only ten miles away. The Market Cross Hotel could not be better situated for anyone wanting to discover Somerset. Cheddar itself, famous for its wonderful caves, which are to be found in the mighty Cheddar Gorge, is also famous for its strawberries and its cheese. The Hotel is within walking distance of the shops, golf driving range, adventure caving, indoor children's play centre, riding stables, Cheddar Gorge itself and some wonderful walking prospects in the picturesque Mendip Hills from which there are truly magnificent views.

Anne Fieldhouse also has some excellent self-catering apartments in the adjacent 'Sungate' Georgian house.

USEFUL INFORMATION

OPEN; *All year*
CHILDREN; *Welcome*
CREDIT CARDS; *Visa/Mastercard*
LICENSED; *Yes*
ACCOMMODATION; *6 rooms mainly en suite*
PETS; *No*

RESTAURANT; *High standard cooking*
BAR FOOD; *Light refreshments available*
VEGETARIAN; *Catered for*
DISABLED ACCESS; *Not suitable*
GARDEN; *Yes*

STOCKLEIGH LODGE
Exford,
Somerset TA24 7PZ

Tel: 01643 831500
Fax: 01643 831595

What could be more beautiful than the heart of Exmoor, for the setting of this wonderful country lodge, run by the amiable Myra and Mike. Sitting in it's own wooded grounds, surrounded by the open moors, it is ideal for riding, walking, fishing and all outdoor sports. The stables in the grounds cater for all abilities of riding. Riding is a wonderful way to see the moor, and believe me, is not that painful! Myra and Mike are a mine of information regarding the local activities and are only too happy to share their knowledge.

The bedrooms are south facing and have a lovely sunny outlook, and are en suite or have their own private bathroom. All are comfortably furnished with complimentary tea and coffee, and are centrally heated for those winter breaks! Breakfast is an excellent meal; full English , and vegetarians are extremely well catered for. There is an optional three course evening meal, and both meals are served in the dining room overlooking the splendid well kept garden. A packed lunch can be provided for those wishing to spend the day exploring the majestic countryside.

The drawing room is large and elegant with a grand piano and an open fire. Just sitting there on a winter's evening after an eventful day. with the hauntingly romantic moor all around makes me shiver deliciously, warm and content in the knowledge that someone will replace my drink when the glass is empty! Does sound good, doesn't it? This is not just the place for those wishing to relax or enjoy the moor, it is also ideal for business weekends or just a party of friends enjoying the company. You will feel welcome here no matter the occasion, and Myra and Mike will ensure that you and your friends will return again and again!

USEFUL INFORMATION

OPEN; *All year*
CHILDREN; *Welcome*
CREDIT CARDS; *None taken*
LICENSED; *Residential*
PETS; *Welcome*
ACCOMMODATION; *9 rooms,*
7 dbl, 1 sgl, 1tw

DINING ROOM; *Optional evening meal*
BAR MEALS; *Not applicable*
VEGETARIAN; *Well catered for*
DISABLED ACCESS; *No but welcome*
GARDEN; *3 acres*

THE CENTURION HOTEL & COUNTRY CLUB

Charlton Lane,
Midsomer Norton,
Bath BA3 4BD

Tel: 01761 417711 (5 lines) Fax: 01761 418357

Just 15 minutes from Bath and 30 minutes from Bristol The Centurion Hotel at Midsomer Norton is ideally placed for exploring the natural beauty and fascinating towns, villages and cities of the west country. Who can resist the elegance of Georgian Bath or fail to be amazed by the beauty of Cheddar Gorge and the Mendip Hills. Perhaps one of the favourite places is the tiny, cathedral city of Wells where the cathedral is stunning and swans ring a bell outside its walls when they want feeding! Whatever reason you have for coming into this area whether it is holidaying or business you will find this modern, purpose built hotel has everything to offer you. It is a family run complex which includes the Fosseway Country Club giving access to a superb range of leisure and business facilities for guests. Hotel guests are able to use the family size indoor swimming pool. Squash is also very popular and there are two courts available at a modest cost. A new addition is a four rink indoor bowling green. The parkland golf course has nine holes and is a par 4 course and there is more. The Centurion with its 5 crown luxury has forty four en suite, beautifully furnished and decorated bedrooms and yet manages to give you the feel of a much smaller and more homely establishment. All the bedrooms have remote control TV, telephones, radios, hairdryers and tea/coffee making facilities. Some rooms are specially designed for family use whilst others are equipped to welcome wheelchaired guests.

The Centurion has gained a good reputation for the excellence of its food. The menu offers English and Continental dishes cooked and presented with imagination and flair. There is both an a la carte and a table d'hôte menu. The restaurant adjoins the resident's lounge bar, but if that does not appeal to you there are three other bars which also provide daily fresh bar meals.

This is a wonderful setting for wedding receptions, business meetings, seminars and all sorts of social events. The ballroom is large enough to seat 160 people. However it is the personal touch that comes from the management and the staff that makes it such a pleasure to be at The Centurion for whatever reason.

USEFUL INFORMATION

OPEN; *All year*

CHILDREN; *Welcome*

CREDIT CARDS; *All major cards*

LICENSED; *Yes*

ACCOMMODATION; *44 en suite rooms*
Conference, wedding, seminar facilities

GARDEN; *Yes*

RESTAURANT; *First class menu*

BAR FOOD; *Wide variety*

VEGETARIAN; *Good choice*

DISABLED ACCESS; *Yes. Purpose built*
Bedrooms

PETS; *Guide Dogs only*

THE MIDLAND HOTEL,
40 - 42 Knightstone Road,
Weston-Super-Mare,
N. Somerset, BS23 2BD.

Tel : 01934 621217
Fax : 01934 641497

Personally owned by the Aston family for over 35 years, this family run hotel welcomes it's guests with an atmosphere of warmth and congeniality that immediately makes one feel at home. Bryan and Mary are your hosts, and endeavour to provide a superb service for their guests, ensuring comfort and relaxation is their prime concern. The hotel has a total of 30 bedrooms which are all en suite and decorated to a high standard. All have facilities of colour TV, direct dial, and a hospitality tray of tea and coffee. There are lifts to all main floors and access for the disabled is good. There are both a residents lounge and bar, which are comfortably furnished with stunning views over the sea. During the summer season, evening entertainment is provided several nights a week. The Waverley   Restaurant is also open to non guests and provides an excellent English menu in very cordial   surroundings. The Slipway Bar is an attractive bar where resident and non resident guests can enjoy a drink and again admire the panoramic views.

This hotel is in an excellent spot as it is just across the road from the sea front, and (weather permitting) you can wander straight on to the sandy beach after breakfast! The beaches at Weston-Super-Mare are excellent, and many happy family holidays are spent here. This hotel offers good quality accommodation coupled with easy access to many of the facilities of the town. There are lots of activities to keep the children amused, and there is a host of sports for those who wish to partake of a more active holiday. For those who like a quiet stroll, then the Avon and Somerset countryside is ideal, and for the shorter distance try some of the promenade walks. There are many historic cities within easy reach such as Bath, with it's 15th century abbey, and wonderful antique shops, or Wells with it's lovely historic streets and 12th century cathedral. There is something for everyone in this area, and with the hospitality offered by Bryan and Mary, you are sure to have a wonderful stay in this finest of family hotels.

USEFUL INFORMATION

OPEN; *All year*
CHILDREN; *Welcome*
PETS; *No*
CREDIT CARDS; *All major*
ACCOMMODATION; *30 rooms en suite:*
8 dble, 12 twin, 6 sgl & 4 fmly.

RESTAURANT; *Good English fayre*
VEGETARIAN; *Catered for*
DISABLED *ACCESS; Yes*
LICENSED; *Full*

SEEBURG,
138 Sherborne Road,
Yeovil,
Somerset BA21 4HQ

Tel: 01935 72159

Unless you have stayed in this exceptionally friendly guest house you cannot possibly appreciate all that it has to offer. It is not that it is so different from other establishments which I am sure are equally well furnished, have equally comfortable beds and offer their guests just as good food. What is different to many places is that Chris and Val Abel are so flexible. If needs be they will shift rooms around to accommodate a family or some special circumstance. Whilst they naturally need to earn a living from running Seeburg, they have the good common sense to be open to negotiations on their prices. All of this does not detract from the genuine welcome you receive.

Built in 1883 in the Edwardian era, the house is sturdy and yet has an elegance which is applicable to this age. The rooms are spacious with large windows. Every room is light and airy and decorated individually. There are 6 bedrooms, none of which are ensuite but there are three bathrooms with both baths and showers so this in no way causes a problem. Every room has a hostess tray - always a welcome sight for any traveller. The attractive dining room is where you will be served a substantial breakfast with several choices, although if you prefer it you can have something lighter. Vegetarians are catered for by arrangement. For those who require an evening meal this can be arranged although Yeovil is not short of good eating places.

Yeovil is right on the border of Dorset and only five miles from the old town of Sherborne with its two castles and famous school. There are many National Trust properties within easy distance including Montacute. For the energetic there is fishing on the River Yeo, golf within 5 minutes walk, a dry ski slope, riding stables nearby and it is splendid walking countryside.

USEFUL INFORMATION

OPEN; *All year*
CHILDREN; *Welcome*
CREDIT CARDS; *None taken*
ACCOMMODATION; *6 rooms,*
3 bathrooms
PETS; *By arrangement*

DINING ROOM; *Good traditional breakfast*
Evening meals by arrangement
VEGETARIAN; *Upon request*
DISABLED ACCESS; *No*
GARDEN; *Yes*

SHROPSHIRE AND STAFFORDSHIRE

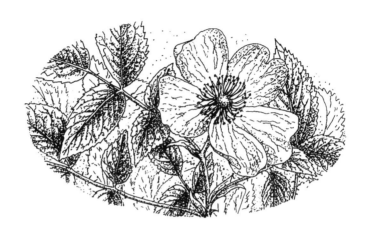

INCLUDES

Chapter 15

SHROPSHIRE AND STAFFORDSHIRE

Shropshire is such a wonderful mixture of countryside, architecture, agriculture and industry. It has wonderful places to visit, history which is fascinating and at times awe inspiring, stately homes, gardens, and all manner of other attractions. In this chapter I will try to cover as many places as I can but inevitably I will miss much that is worth seeing - a good excuse to come again very soon.

The temptation, when you come to South Shropshire, is to seek out immediately places like Ludlow, a place of historical romance and one of the most beautiful country towns in England. This is what I have always done in the past but this time I was invited to stay with friends in **Telford**, a new town that is light years ahead. My friends had moved there with reluctance when a new posting for the husband made it imperative. To their surprise they have found living in this new town a good experience. Some of their enthusiasm rubbed off on me and I, too, was agreeably surprised at the great effort that has been made to make it a 'green and pleasant land'. For example, over a million trees, plants and shrubs have been planted throughout the town. The park is a mixture of landscaped and natural scenery complete with a lake at the side of which is an amphitheatre and a sports arena. The town offers all sorts of facilities and seems to me to be full of young and enthusiastic people who enjoy what it has to offer.

One of the reasons that made my friends happy with Telford was the unique range of top class sporting facilities, with everything from golf and tennis to skiing provided in a range of superb modern sports centres. In addition to the National Sports Centre at nearby Lilleshall, Telford has six fully equipped sports and leisure centres of its own. The Telford Ice Rink is one of the finest in the Midlands, and it is the home of one of the country's top ice hockey teams.

A visit to Lilleshall allowed me to see the imposing ruin of the Abbey which makes an unforgettable picture as you approach it from the west. The view looks through the monumental gateway along the Abbey's full 228 ft length, with the leafy countryside beyond framed in the great east window. It is breathtaking. The abbey dates from the 12th century and there are extensive remains of its impressive masonry still standing. It is open to the public daily.

On the outskirts of Telford is **Priorslee** which has a charming pub, **The Lion Inn,** less than five minutes from Junction 4 or 5 off the M54. It has little to do with the 1990s, apart from modern amenities. It is a 16th century coaching inn, with oak beams, shining brass and a vast inglenook fireplace which houses a roaring log fire. I arrived there having spent a fascinating but tiring time at **Cosford Aerospace Museum** which is just 15 minutes away.

This is one of the world's most spectacular collections of civil and military aircraft, with more than 70 aircraft, missiles and engines on display. For me a feeling of nostalgia appeared when I saw the famous fighting machines of World War II - at least those that belonged to the Allied Forces. There was the legendary Spitfire, the Mosquito and the vast American Liberator bomber. You can see inside the interiors of the JUS2 and Field Marshal Montgomery's personal Dakota DC3. It is outstanding and for anyone with a feel for aircraft, Cosford has to be seen. Allow plenty of time, one afternoon is hardly sufficient.

The official address is Cosford, Shifnal and it is to **Shifnal** I will take you next. Dickens would not be pleased if he were to visit the town today. He mentioned the place in the Old Curiosity Shop; it was an important coaching-stop on the Holyhead Road and he thought of it as a pleasant village. This is no longer so, it has been industrialised but there are still delightful buildings including The Nell Gwynn, a restaurant in Park Street, which must be one of the most beautiful half timbered buildings in the whole of Shropshire. The moment you step inside its welcoming doors you are filled with a sense of history. People come from miles around to eat in this wonderful atmosphere. Next door is the equally interesting old pub, The Charles II which is part of the Nell Gwynn.

Market days are good fun and very lively, held on Wednesdays and apart from that you can just imagine you are walking with Dickens when you see some of the narrow streets, under timbered eaves and gables burdened with age. In a quiet corner of the town the 750 year old tower of the parish church rises in glory, unperturbed by the twentieth century activity below.

On the main Telford to Bridgnorth road (A442) is the pleasant rural village of **Norton**, home to a very special hostelry, The Hundred House Hotel. The original inn dates from medieval times although the present building is largely 18th century. It was totally refurbished in 1986 and is an hotel and inn of enchantment. It has so much to offer and it is, to quote from two of the many people who love The Hundred House, 'An excursion into the past with superb up-to-date food and service. Delightful beyond description.'

Newport is only eight miles to the north-east of Telford and is as different as chalk from cheese. Here I found a pleasant, unspoilt market town, centred around the broad, elegant High Street, a street just asking to be explored. At number 68 is The Pheasant Inn, a hostelry that has been dispensing hospitality for 250 years or more. You can stay in this welcoming place; the accommodation is unpretentious but comfortable and your hosts have a nice brand of humour and a great understanding of people's needs. I lunched on Fish Pie, one of the specialities of the house - and very good it was.

The town has a large and graceful church, **St Nicholas**, standing on an island site in the middle of the High Street. There is a font from the year of the restoration, a coffin lid carved quite wonderfully 700 years ago, and a list of rectors going back to the Normans.

The most famous son of Newport was the wise and extraordinary man, Sir Oliver Lodge, who experimented in wireless and sent wireless telegrams long before Marconi. He interested himself in all sorts of things from the mysterious problems of telepathy to the conquering of fog.

Just 3 miles north of Junction 3 on the M54 is **Weston Park** on the A5 at **Weston-under-Lizard**. This classic 17th century stately house is the historic home of the Earls of Bradford. The interior has been superbly restored and holds one of the country's finest collection of paintings, with originals by many of the great masters. There are fine tapestries from the famous 18th century makers Gobelin and Aubusson, and letters from Disraeli which provide a fascinating commentary on Victorian history. It is quite wonderful. It is used all the year round for Conferences, Banquets, Product Launches, Wedding Receptions and for very special gourmet 'Dine and Stay' evenings which are open to the public. These are truly wonderful occasions and will long stay in your memory.

From Weston Park it is only a short distance to **Boscobel House**, in which Charles Stuart sought refuge after his defeat at Worcester. As I drove along the quiet road I wondered if the King had wished he was just a simple Shropshire man, secure in his everyday life rather than a royal. The Giffords of Chillington owned Boscobel and as staunch Catholics they had honeycombed the house with hiding places for priests. If you see the house today many of them still exist. One will be pointed out to you as the kings, which is reached by a short flight of stairs leading to the cheese room.

William Penderel tenanted Boscobel and he was one of six brothers who were loyal supporters of the Stuart cause. However, it was not Boscobel which hid Charles Stuart but **Whiteladies**, where Humphrey Penderel lived. Here, he left all his retinue but Lord Richard Wilmot and became a countryman wearing a coarse shirt, darned stockings, a leather doublet with pewter buttons, a ragged coat and breeches, a battered old hat and rough boots. He darkened his face and his hands with soot and accompanied only by Richard, he crept out, avoiding troops that he knew to be in the neighbourhood. He was attempting to make his way over the Severn into Wales, stopping at Madeley, the home of Francis Woolf. The journey was fraught with danger and at one stage he and Richard were chased by a miller and a number of soldiers. The journey became so fraught that the only thing they could do was to return to Boscobel. The only way to do this was to swim across a river but Richard could not swim. Charles helped him over but by this time the King's feet were so blistered and torn and his boots so full of grit, that he felt he could not go on. It was Richard Penderel who kept him going and at last they reached the safety of Boscobel. Here Charles's feet were doctored, he was given a change of stockings and his boots were dried. Outside the house was a great oak and into this Charles climbed. He slept during the day but woke to the sound of Cromwell's men hunting in the wood searching for the King. There was a price of a thousand pounds on the King's head: something all the Penderels knew about but such was their loyalty that not one of them even thought of betraying him They would have died in his cause if need be. For two more days and nights Charles stayed at Boscobel, sleeping in the hole   beneath the trapdoor in the cheese room until finally it was thought safe enough for him to set out on the long journey which would eventually end in France.

You must visit **Tong**. It is only a small village but the magnificent 14th century church of St Bartholomew would not be out of place in a city. It is frequently referred to as 'the cathedral of the West Midlands'. Just north of the village, off the A41, you can see a peculiar pyramid-shaped building set back a few hundred yards from the road. It s called the **Egyptian Aviary**, and it is a bizarre hen-house designed by a celebrated local eccentric, George Durant in the early 19th century.

The whole of the **Ironbridge Gorge** is one big real-life museum that tells you every chapter of the fascinating story, on the spot, where it happened. There is no other place anywhere in the world like it. Make sure you allow yourself plenty of time to enjoy it.

The Severn flows through this deep gorge and the houses cling to the hillsides, looking as though a puff of wind would blow them into the swirling river, but they have been there for hundreds of years and are as much a part of this incredible place as the Museums. The chief distinction is, of course, the bridge, believed to be the first iron bridge ever built. It was built by Abraham Darby of Coalbrookdale in 1777. It is 196ft long with one span of 100feet and two smaller ones, the total weight of iron being about 380 tons. So much for the statistics, worth knowing but fading almost into insignificance alongside the many things one has to see. Over 250 years ago the Severn Gorge witnessed momentous events which culminated in the Industrial Revolution and it was the fortunate combination of coal, iron, water power and transport, all concentrated in this Shropshire Valley, which sparked off the series of events which affected all of us. Of the many places to visit perhaps **Rosehill House**, one of the elegant mansions where the Darby family lived in the 18th and 19th centuries, is probably my favourite. It is sheer pleasure to wander through the beautifully restored rooms with original period furniture. The house gives you an understanding of how a wealthy ironmaster would have lived.

In total contrast is **Carpenters' Row**, a terrace of workers' houses built by the company in the late 18th century. There is nothing grand about them. Four cottages have been restored and furnished to recreate a home from different periods between 1780 and 1930. Carpenters' Row is open to small groups by special appointment only. You will find many more places listed under 'Attractions' at the back of the book.

After the strenuous activity in Ironbridge it might be as well to take a look at **Broseley** across the Gorge. This was the great urban centre of the Coalbrookdale coalfield during the Industrial Revolution. The ironmaster, John Wilkinson, built his furnace here, and in its heyday it was a rival to Coalbrookdale itself as a centre of the iron industry. John Wilkinson was the man who had the idea of building iron barges. He persevered in spite of being laughed at and he had the last laugh when, on one summer's day in 1787, the first iron barge was launched on the Severn. From this the idea of an iron ship was born and Broseley was its birthplace. John Wilkinson was so dedicated to the use of iron that he asked to be buried in an iron coffin!

A visit to **The Forest Arms** in Avenue Road would not come amiss. It is on the edge of this small town and has nothing but fields and a small, colourful copse on one side of it. The oak trees have a beauty of their own particularly when they first come into leaf, and in the Autumn when their leaves take on a golden reddish hue. The pub is over 250 years old and its friendly landlords describe it as a country pub run by country people. An apt description.

Benthall Hall, a mile away to the north-west, belongs to the National Trust who have made sure that it remains as it would have been when it was built in the 16th century. It really is an excellent example of domestic architecture of that period. Built of local sandstone, the interior contains a magnificent oak staircase of 1618 wonderfully ornate plaster ceilings, and a charming white panelled drawing room. The Gardens are beautiful and to go there is sheer pleasure.

Much Wenlock cries out to be visited; it is a lovely old market town full of history. Arthur Mee described it as somewhere that 'sleeps in the hills, dreaming of all that has been, stirring with the memory of warrior kings and the ancient strife of the Border valleys, and inspired by the natural spectacle of Wenlock Edge.'

The ancient Tudor Guildhall is still in use as a court house and council chamber. There are charming timber-framed buildings in the Bull Ring. You will find picturesque half timbered cottages, a wealth of graceful Georgian houses and a 15th century house near St Owen's Well, which features an archway made from oak boughs.

I recommend to you **The Talbot Inn** which dates from 1360 and was originally known as the Abbot's Hall. It was once part of Wenlock Abbey and is thought to have been the Almoner's House. Tim and Meriel Lathe, mine hosts, aim to uphold the traditions of this ancient hostelry by providing good food and good company in congenial surroundings.

The steep wooded escarpment known as Wenlock Edge, runs for 16 miles and provides a series of spectacular viewpoints across to the Stretton Hills and the Long Mynd. It is essentially a geological phenomenon; the rock, Wenlock limestone, was formed more than 400 million years ago in a tropical sea. It developed as a barrier reef built up largely from the skeletons and shells of sea creatures.

Three miles north-east of Much Wenlock on the B4378 you will come to **Buildwas Abbey**. Standing in a beautiful situation on the banks of the River Severn quite close to Ironbridge Gorge, it is a worthwhile place to visit. It must be one of the country's finest ruined abbeys. Dating back over 800 years to Norman times it is surprising that so much is still standing today. The imposing walls of the abbey church with 14 wonderful Norman arches remain. It was probably completed in 1200 with the Norman and Early English architecture remaining virtually unaltered since the Dissolution in the 1530s.

When you are in Telford, Wellington, Ironbridge or Much Wenlock you should make the effort to reach the summit of **The Wrekin**. It is a curiosity and one of the most distinctive landmarks in the Shropshire Hills. The Wrekin is 1335 foot high, rising sharply from the flatness of the surrounding countryside. It is the site of an ancient Iron Age hill fort and it has been the focus of local legends and superstitions for hundreds of years My favourite is that the hill was formed by a giant who had quarrelled with the people of Shrewsbury. The giant was determined to punish the townsfolk and set off with a huge spadeful of earth to bury the whole town. On the way he met a cobbler by the roadside carrying a sack of shoes to be mended. the cobbler thought the giant was up to no good so he persuaded him that Shrewsbury was too far to walk, showing him the whole bag of shoes he had worn out walking the enormous distance from the town. The giant decided the cobbler was right: he ditched the spadeful of earth on the spot - and the Wrekin was formed.

Bridgnorth is two towns in one perched dramatically on a steep cliff above the River Severn. It is naturally beautiful and quite unlike anywhere else in England. This picturesque market town has High Town and Low Town linked by the famous Cliff Railway, which climbs up a hair raising incline. The only other I know like it, is the Cliff Railway which joins Lynton and Lynmouth in Devon.

Knowing I would find much to see and do here I stayed in the 17th century **Falcon Hotel**, in St John Street, Low Town. I could not have made a better choice. The 15 bedrooms are all en suite and it is the epitome of comfort and good service. Just 15 minutes from the M54, it is an ideal base for business trips in the West Midlands, for a family holiday or mini-break.

There is something reminiscent of old Italian towns as you climb the Stoneway Steps cut sheer through the rocks, or wander about the maze of old half timbered buildings and elegant 18th century houses. One of these is the curious 17th century Town Hall. This timber framed building is built on an arched sandstone base partly across the roadway in the middle of the High Street. At the east end of the street is The North Gate, the only remaining one of five gates in the town's fortifications. There is a Museum over the arches.

Bridgnorth Castle is famous for its leaning tower which is 17 degrees out of straight. The leaning Tower of Pisa is only 5 degrees! It has survived safely for 850 years. The castle grounds are now a public park where you can admire a splendid view over the river and Low Town. Take time out to discover this delightful town and its many interesting buildings which include the **Church of St Mary Magdalene, Bishop Percy's House** and the **Bridgnorth Costume** and **Childhood Museum.**

I would think that almost everyone would be enchanted by the long established **Midland Motor Museum**, the only one of its kind in Europe. Added to the collection of some of the world's fastest cars and motorcycles are the more laborious, but equally absorbing relics of the steam era. The exhibition covers a 25 acre site in the converted stable area of **Stanmore Hall**, an historic house on the outskirts of Bridgnorth.

To the east of Bridgnorth is **Claverley**, a pretty village with black and white houses and a fine Norman church. There is a nice story told about a friend of this village who left eight shillings a year for a man to drive dogs out of the church and wake up sleeping people. The man was given a long rod with a knob at one end and a fox's brush at the other. He would tap the heads of sleeping men with the knob and touch the faces of sleeping women with the tail.

Just down the A458 you will come to **Quatt**, a village which has become commuter housing land and lost much of its community spirit. What it does have is Dudmaston Hall, now in the care of the National Trust but still the home of Sir George and Lady Labouchere. Their rooms in the main house are small on the whole and filled with Sir George and Lady Labouchere's personal possessions, and it is this intimacy that makes the house so good to visit.

There are few better ways of seeing the Shropshire countryside with its wooded valleys and changeable moods than from the **Severn Valley Steam Railway** which runs from Shrewsbury to Hartlebury, north of Worcester. It is designed to capture the atmosphere of railway history to the last detail with captivating, evocative little stations like Highley, Hampton Loade and Arley, signal boxes and railway inns. Some two hundred thousand people, many of whom come from overseas, travel on the Railway each year, making it one of the most popular tourist attractions in the Midlands. It has become the home of the largest collection of working steam locomotives and restored railway coaches and wagons in Britain.

Ludlow beckoned and I happily answered the call, first having ensured that I could stay at one of my favourite places **The Charlton Arms Hotel** at **Ludford Bridge**, a fine and early medieval packhorse bridge just outside Ludlow alongside the River Teme. It is only ten minutes walk from Ludlow Castle. Apart from the hospitality it is such a pleasure to wake up in the morning and hear the sound of the river flowing almost beneath your bedroom window.

Here is a town that has few equals. Its river rings it like a moat and to walk about its castle and streets is quite thrilling. We are lucky to claim it as part of England because it is almost on the Welsh border. It became a fortress from which Wales's unruly and mutinous tribes were eventually knocked into submission.

The church of St Laurence soars upwards and vies with the castle for supremacy. It is an outstandingly beautiful Perpendicular church with an earlier foundation, twice restored in the 19th century. The church is open in summer from 9-5pm and in winter until 4pm.

The Wheatsheaf Inn in Lower Broad Street, first licensed in 1753, nestles under Ludlow's historic Broad Gate, the last of seven town gates, built in the 13th century. This family run inn offers an atmospheric, convenient and comfortable base from which to explore and enjoy the whole of the **Marches region**.

A break at **Dinham Hall** will give you the opportunity to combine the joy of exploring Ludlow with fine food and the elegant luxury of a Georgian house hotel. Built in 1792 Dinham Hall lies only forty metres from the castle, is beautifully furnished and offers its guests a wide range of leisure activities including a gymnasium and sauna.

There are some beautiful places to visit between Ludlow and Shrewsbury. One of my favourite haunts is **Stokesay Castle**. It stands just off the Ludlow-Shrewsbury Road half a mile south of Craven Arms. There is a car park up the signposted lane and past the church, only a few yards from this romantic ruin.

The marvellous state of preservation does give a very clear idea of the conditions in which well-to-do medieval families lived. It is one of the earliest fortified manor houses in England with the oldest parts dating from the 12th century and the Great Hall from the 13th. It is an extraordinary structure with massive stone towers topped with a timber-framed house.

The A49 going towards Shrewsbury will take you to **Little Stretton** which must be one of the most beautiful villages in Shropshire complete with a little thatched church and a village inn that is 250 years old. **The Green Dragon** is a real village inn with no juke boxes or gaming machines, just fine ale and freshly cooked food. The pub is a popular haunt of walkers on the **Long Mynd Hills** and **Ashers Hollow**.

Little Stretton's big neighbour, **Church Stretton** is somewhere else you should visit. Houses dot the valley and climb the slopes. To the west is the great moorland ridge of the Longmynd rising nearly 1700 ft, with the beautiful Cardingmill Valley below and the prehistoric Portway running along the top. To the east are the rugged Caradoc Hills with Watling Street at the foot, and the banks and trenches of Caer Caradoc's stronghold 1500ft up.

The strange cross-shaped church goes back 850 years and in the old church-yard is a stone of 1814 to Ann Cook which says:

On a Thursday she was born
On a Thursday made a bride
On a Thursday broke a leg
And on a Thursday died '

Thursday was not a lucky day for Ann Cook!

Bishops Castle to the west and surrounded by the beauty of the South Shropshire hills, was plundered by Royalists during the Civil War in 1645 but somehow they missed out the inn, **The Boars Head Hotel**, in which Roundheads were slaking their thirst. So today you are able to enjoy the exposed beams, the roaring log fire in winter, the hospitality, the fine ale and the beautifully cooked food as well as stay in one of the attractive en suite rooms.

Here you are on the edge of the Clun Forest, a delightful place and if you have ever read A.E. Housman's 'A Shropshire Lad' you will know his description of the Cluns. He thought it a quiet area:

> *Clunton and Clunbury*
> *Clungunford and Clun*
> *Are the quietest places*
> *Under the sun.'*

And so to Shrewsbury where once again A.E.Housman says it all.

> *'High the vanes of Shrewsbury gleam*
> *Islanded in Severn stream,*
> *The bridges from the steepled crest*
> *Cross the water east to West.' '*

It is almost an island with its castle standing in a narrow strait and more than half a-dozen bridges crossing to and fro. It has old black and white houses, half timbered of the Elizabethan era, fine brick buildings of the 17th century and wonderfully elegant Queen Anne and Georgian town houses, narrow streets and alleyways with strange names - Grope Lane, Shoplatch, Dogpole, Wyle Cop and Pride Hill. Everywhere oozes history and clamours for your attention.

You will want to visit **Rowley's House** in Barker Street which is set in a magnificent timber-framed building of the late 16th century. Housed here is the largest collection of material from the Roman city of Virconium at Wroxeter including the silver mirror unique to Roman Britain. On College Hill is **Clive House**, just five minutes from Rowley's House. Clive of India lived here in 1762 when he was Mayor of Shrewsbury and one or two momentoes of this great man remain. Several rooms have period settings and a magnificent collection of Shropshire ceramics. The gardens are open to visitors.

In **The Castle** you will find **The Shropshire Regimental Museum** with wonderful displays of all things military, even a lock of Napoleon's hair. The Castle dates back to 1083 but last saw service during the Civil War when Charles I is reputed to have stayed there for a short period. Thomas Telford later remodelled the interior as a private house in the late 18th century.

I stayed a night in **The Tudor House** in Fish Street, built in 1460. It is charming, warm and comfortable, and full of character. Not far outside Shrewsbury at **Weston-under-Redcastle** is **The Citadel**, a truly wonderful house with superb grounds. It is castellated and built in the early 19th century as a dower house for the famous Hill family who lived nearby at Hawkstone Hall. It stands in a spectacular position overlooking the North Shropshire countryside with views to the Welsh Hills. Anyone who appreciates the glory of the English countryside will soon fall in love with the house and the enchanting village.

CHAPTER FIFTEEN

In recent years people have travelled from far and wide to play golf at Hawkstone Park, made famous by Sandy Lyle. But now there is a new interest in the magical paths, caves, monuments, grottos and obelisk which have been hidden by nature for so many years. They are just a walk away from The Citadel.

From here you might well visit **Attingham Park** bequeathed by the 8th Lord Berwick to the National Trust in 1947. In the mansion, the splendid Regenry State Rooms are open to the public. They are full of silver, much of it collected by the 3rd Lord Berwick when he was Ambassador to Italy in 1807-1832. There is also a fine collection of French and Italian paintings and furniture, brought to England by the 2nd Lord Berwick and his brother, the 3rd Lord Berwick.

There are people who may tell you that North Shropshire is dull. That is absolutely untrue; it may be flatter than the south but within it you will discover it has miles of gentle green countryside, reed fringed meres, the excitement of the Shropshire Union and Llangollen Canals, red sandstone hills, a wealth of small villages and five historic market towns, Oswestry, Ellesmere, Whitchurch, Wem and Market Drayton.

It may well be out of your way to drive along the little lanes from the oddly named village of **Knockin**, where there was once a castle, to **Melverley**. You will be well rewarded if you do when you see **St Peter's Church** founded in 1406 and the oldest church in Shropshire. It is perched precariously on the banks of the River Vrynwy, a picturesque timber-framed building which has survived many floods. It is peaceful, serene and has a sense of belonging that is hard to compare. There is a quaint entry into the register which goes back to 1766 and tells of the marriage of Matthew Dodd and Elinor Foster. It must have been written by the Parish Clerk, one John Lewis:

This morning I have put a Tye
No man could put it faster
Tween, Matthew Dodd the man of God
And modest Nelly Foster.

Having looked at the church which is open during daylight hours, I stopped for a while and took a look at the fascinating Pastoral Crafts Centre which boasts a good tea room where I had a true country tea.

Powys Castle you will find south of **Welshpool** on the A483. Not in Shropshire of course, but as you are so near the Welsh border it would be a pity to miss it out. What an atmosphere it has, that has been steadily increasing since it was built around 1200AD by Welsh Princes. The Castle contained the finest country house collection in Wales. The 17th century terraced gardens are wonderful and both historically and horticulturally important. So much history has gone into the centuries since the Castle was built and it has many associations. It houses the **Clive of India Museum**.

One and a half miles from Welshpool on the A458 Dolgellau road is a charming hotel and restaurant standing on a hillside overlooking a delightful wooded valley through which runs the famous narrow guage, Welshpool and Llanfair Steam Light Railway. Originally **The Golfa Hall Hotel** was a substantial farmhouse on the Powys Castle estate and was converted into an hotel approximately 10 years ago. There is a very attractive restaurant open to non-residents.

Oswestry is back on the Shropshire side of the border but it does have very strong ties with Wales. Apart from being a delightful market town to explore it is equally splendid to wander the hilly, sparsely populated border country. This is a town that has so much to do and see that you could well stay here for a month and still not have seen everything.

Market days are full of life with one of the busiest street markets in the county. Over 120 traders set up their stalls with every imaginable kind of product and produce. The Market days are all the year round on Wednesdays with an additional market on Saturdays in the summer. There is ample car parking near the town centre.

One of the best ways to discover the secrets of this historic town is to use the Town Trail which wends its way through medieval streets, past ancient buildings like **The Fox Inn** in Church Street, an old timber building which once had a gable projecting over the street. It had to be removed after a passer by damaged his silk top hat on it. Church Street has many fine buildings of historic and architectural merit such as the impressive **Wynsstay Hotel**, with its grand entrance.

A super place for refreshment and in English Walls, is **The Grape Escape**, a Wine Bar and Bistro that offers something splendid from 10.30am until well after midnight. It is a popular meeting place for those who live in Oswestry and one, that a visitor having once tried, will want to go back.

Canals are very important to the way of life in this part of Shropshire and provide so much more than just water transport. Following the canal or 'the cut' is a wonderful way of exploring North Shropshire whether you have a boat or not. The towpath is a splendid, traffic free footpath on the level for miles albeit in some places it is distinctly rough going and very muddy. You are rewarded though by the wildlife that abounds on the water, in the bankside vegetation, and along the hedges. You can learn so much for the canal which tells its own story of our industrial and architectural heritage.

At **Whittington** you will meet with the **Llangollen Canal**, which wends its way across the country right up into Cheshire where it joins the main Shropshire Union Canal close to **Nantwich**. Whttington is a very large village in the centre of which is the remains of Whittington Castle. All that you can see today of this important border castle is the magnificent gatehouse and the moat. It is a delightful place to visit, with a children's play area, ducks to feed and a tea-room in which to relax. The village is reputed to have been the birthplace of Dick Whittington, the famous Lord Mayor of London and cat owner!

For nearly two centuries Bridge No 5 of the Canal was virtually on its own, only a small cottage with a large orchard kept it company. Now the cottage has grown and become a pub, **The Narrowboat Inn**, and instead of the clucking chickens in the orchard there are ducks swimming in the canal lay-by, dug out to accommodate the 24 hire boats known as **Maestermyn** (Hire Cruisers Ltd) which has a gift shop an off licence and chandlery. It is an exciting venture and in a marvellous spot. In spring the high grassy banks are full of cowslips and primroses and even in the very height of the season there is something peaceful and reassuring about this little piece of an English Canal.

From here I went north a little until I came to **Chirk** where it is the only way to cruise from England into Wales over the aqueduct on the Llangollen Canal, one of the seven wonders of Wales. This is quite a place with a lot of history, right on the border of Shropshire and Clwyd; it has withstood the slings and arrows of outrageous fortune. **Chirk Castle** which belongs to the National Trust, is a place you must visit and you should make sure you get to **Llanrhaedr Falls**, another of the seven wonders of Wales. They are   stunning.

The Shropshire Union Canal, a popular waterway for pleasure craft, has played a great part in the history of Ellesmere, and the Old Wharf with its warehouse and crane is a reminder of a prosperous period for the development of the town when it was a centre of plans for a link to the River Mersey (at what was to become Ellesmere port). This was nearly 200 years ago when some of Britain's leading industrialists first met to discuss the project, Thomas Telford included. Circumstances caused them to build instead a most attractive canal from Llangollen's Horseshoe Falls to Hurleston Junction near Nantwich.

If you can spare the time you will find the towpath a place of fascination. A short distance from the wharf is the old canal headquarters. Beech House stands opposite the spur to Ellesmere, while next door is the Ellesmere Works of British Waterways. Much of its equipment has been removed to museums but it is still an important maintenance depot. If you look closely at the east end of White Bridge you will see the outline of an old dry dock among the bushes.

The second place to join the canal is by the junction of the Whitchurch to Shrewsbury roads east of Ellesmere. The junction stands above one of the earliest tunnels to carry a towpath through it. To the east of this is Blakemere, a lake left by glaciers some 12,000 years ago. In Autumn the trees of the opposite bank attract innumerable artists trying to capture their elusive beauty.

Ellesmere is not blessed with any major historical buildings but it is known as the capital of Shropshire's Lake Country because it stands on the biggest of ten wonderful meres. The most important are **Blake Mere, Kettle Mere, Newton Mere, Cole Mere, White Mere, Crose Mere**, and the biggest of all called simply, **The Mere**. The very nature of the lakes makes them unique in Britain and indeed a rarity in global terms.

The word 'mere' is an old Anglo Saxon word for lake although unlike lakes they do not have streams flowing in or out. They receive their water from the slow drainage of the surrounding soils, and this nutrient rich water encourages the great variety of animal and plant life.

Naturalists have long been interested in these meres because of the phenomenon, which occurs occasionally after a period of warm, calm weather millions of tiny water plants, that we call algae, suddenly appear on the surface, so that the mere becomes like thick soup. This indicates the abundance and importance of this tiny plant life as the basis of food chains supporting the wildlife of the mere.

Fringed by trees and rushes, **The Mere** covers 116 acres. It is home to swans and abundant wildlife, a place of beauty and peace. It offers boating and fishing and is an ideal place for bird watching, most especially in the Winter Migration season when many rare birds are seen here. On the shores of the Mere are the **Cremorne Gardens**, given by Lord Brownlow for the use of the people of Ellesmere. This lovely waterside park is a place beloved by the people of the town. It is a sheer delight to walk amongst its well kept lawns and avenues of trees always with The Mere and its wildlife in sight.

Quite by chance I discovered **Ellesmere Restaurant Boat** on which you can enjoy the luxury of dining aboard as you glide along the Llangollen canal through the meres. It is something very different. The trips are available at the weekends for the general public but during the week the boat can be booked for private parties with a minimum of 20 people and a maximum of 52. For more information about this and the many other occasions catered for you need to ring 01691 75322 One outing is specially interesting. You meet and then set forth for **Welsh Frankton** where you are taken to visit Alf Strange who is both a Blacksmith and an Author. He demonstrates his craft and tells you tales of his life. It is quite riveting, as indeed are his books. From there you go to **The Narrowboat Inn** at bridge 5 - somewhere I wrote about earlier - and then to **Llangollen** over the Aqueduct. The whole trip is called 'A Step Back in Time' and I am quite sure you will enjoy every minute of it.

Hanmer is to the north east of Ellesmere and has its own Mere. Strictly speaking, this lovely, typically English village is in Clwyd, Wales but geographically it is considered to be part of the 'Shropshire Lake District'. It is one of the most peaceful places you could possibly find, indeed sometimes the only sound is the soft noise of the wind stirring the water as it laps the shore of the lake.

In the midst of the attractive cottages that are so much part of this village, is **The Hanmer Arms**, a very special place where tradition is paramount. It has not forgotten its role as the village pub, but discreetly and very comfortably, 20 en suite rooms have been added. A wonderful place for a break or for business people wanting a Seminar in quiet surroundings.

Wem is a town that still manages to preserve more of the old market town atmosphere than most others. It is delightful and dates back before the Conquest in 1066. In fact it is the only town mentioned in the Domesday Book which can trace descendants from before and after the Conquest. The fire of 1677 destroyed many of the ancient houses and it suffered for its staunch support of the Protestant Cause in the Civil War, being the first town to declare for Parliament and hence became a prime target for the Royalists of Whitchurch and Shrewsbury who laid siege to it for a long period without success. The church dates from the 14th century and has an uncommon doorway of that period, and a Perpendicular style upper tower.

Whitchurch is the most ancient of the market towns dating from AD6O when it was founded as a garrison for the Roman legions marching between Chester and Wroxeter. Many Roman artefacts and buildings have been found in the town centre notably in 1967 and 1977, and Pepper Street, High Street and Bluegates occupy the same situation as the Roman streets.

It is here that the composer Edward German was born, remembered by choirs today when they perform his every popular 'Merrie England'. He is not the only famous son of Whitchurch. John Talbot first Earl of Shrewsbury and virtually Shakespeare's hero of Henry VI Part one, is buried in the handsome Georgian church of St Alkmund.

Three and a half miles north of **Market Drayton** my final stop in this unexpectedly interesting and beautiful county, is **Bridgmere** and **Stapely Water Gardens**, not to be missed.

Market in name and market by nature, ideally you should come to Market Drayton on a Wednesday and join in the bustling bargain hunting tradition that has been going one for over 750 years. Since the Norman Conquest, this seemingly sleepy and isolated town has been the scene of revolt, riot, murder, adventure and trade; its links have extended worldwide. Clive of India was born here and he will never be forgotten for many reasons and not the least because of The Clive and Coffyne, a splendid inn made famous by its co-tenant, Paul Roberts who makes Clive pies from a recipe that Clive gave in 1768 to the French town of Pezanas. The recipe has been adapted and Clive's Petit Pates, have brought his home town much fame in recent years Paul won the Guiness Best Food Pub award with his Clive Pie. This fine timber-framed inn is to be found in Shropshire Street. If you are worried about the second part of the name, don't be - a coffyne is the local name for a pie crust.

You will find much to enjoy in Market Drayton, including the celebrated product of the local bakers' shops - Gingerbread Men, which come in a range of novelty shapes and packages, all faithful to recipes over 200 years old. A true taste of history.

You must find time to travel 6 miles down the A53 to **Hodnet** where the **Hodnet Hall Gardens** covering 60 acres are unrivalled for their beauty and natural valley setting. The magnificent trees, lawns and lakes provide a background to an ever changing seasonal colour and interest. Between April and July the rhododendrons are fantastic. The gardens are famous nationally and have been the subject of several TV and radio programmes. This was a visit to remember among the many very happy recollections I have of this county.

With limited time to spend in Staffordshire I decided to devote my time to a few places which interest me and in so doing hopefully stir in the reader a desire to see more of this most versatile and handsome county.

Thomas Telford's sixty-six mile canal was built to link the industrial city of Birmingham with the great port of Liverpool and was originally named the Birmingham and Liverpool Junction Canal. Looking at the peaceful waters running straight through the lovely countryside, it is difficult to see them as the 17th and 18th equivalent of our motorways - yet that is what they were. Quiet tree-fringed stretches where the tranquillity is only disturbed by the quacking of the mallard and the puttering of an occasional leisure boat, were once bustling highways where entire generations of families lived their lives afloat. Goods of every conceivable kind were carried by boat, together with passengers and even livestock, and a community such as Gnosall, situated beside both canal and major road, would have been important as a distribution centre. The popularity of the canals can be understood when one realises the appalling state of the majority of roads which were virtually impassable except by packhorse. Almost overnight the waterways enabled vast quantities of raw materials and finished goods to be moved quickly and economically - thus contributing enormously to the prosperity of the nation as a whole.

It is easy to forget the logistics involved in such a venture as our own century places an enormous reliance on powerful and sophisticated machinery to construct the roads and motorways - today's equivalent of the canal systems. Labour in enormous numbers had to be accommodated, fed and paid during the building of such projects; to drive the great waterways through the heart of our country relied chiefly upon the speed and expertise of men aided with little more than picks, shovels and wheelbarrows. The problems were not over once the canal was built, for there was the continual problem of maintenance - reinforcing banks, clearing weed, surfacing towpaths, breaking ice in winter and all the more skilled work involving locks their gates and associated machinery.   Failure in any of these departments could lead to blockage of the canal, or worse still, to loss of water, leaving boats and their cargoes stranded for days, even weeks. Gangs of men were allocated a length of canal to maintain, and many spent their lives working to keep the waterway running. Close to the aqueduct carrying the 'Shroppy' across the attractive country-side at **Shebdon**, is **The Wharf Inn**, once headquarters for a maintenance gang of 'lengthmen'. These gangs were noted for the prodigious amounts of food and drink they could consume - The Wharf obviously did a good job in these departments and carries on the tradition by catering to today's visitor with the same cheerful generosity.

Shebdon is close to the Shropshire border, a mile or so to the north of the A519 which runs through **Eccleshall**. The beauty of the surrounding undulating and wooded countryside, together with the architecture and charm of this small town make it one of the most attractive communities in Staffordshire. Pronounced 'Eccle-shawl', it has a long history dating back to a Roman settlement and over the centuries became an   important strategic, ecclesiastic and market centre. Soldiers, bishops and traders have all gone but their legacy remains in the buildings they left behind. **Eccleshall Castle** was the principal residence of the Bishops of Lichfield for 600 years. Bishop Muschamp was granted a licence to fortify his house in 1200 and this led to the construction of the castle. Interesting to note that bureaucracy ruled even then, and one wonders whether there is still a department deep in the bowels of Whitehall dealing with requests of this nature. The Church of Holy Trinity has been described as one of the finest 13th century churches in the country. Restored in 1868, it is a tall, light and lofty building of considerable grace and contains the tombs of five of the Bishops of Lichfield. The place to stay is The St George Hotel made famous in coaching times and still going strong. A most attractive interior and the charming George's Bistro ensure its continuing popularity.

Stone is a thriving and good-looking town. Two local stories account for the name; some say it comes from a cairn of stones that marked the graves of two Christian Mercian princes murdered by their pagan father, while others maintain it derives from a mineral-rich local stream that petrifies plant life. Whatever the truth, the area has been inhabited for a long time - as shown by the number of fine stone axe-heads found locally. A market town which did well out of the Canal Era (the River Trent and the Trent and Mersey Canal run parallel south of the town), Stone produced two notable figures; Admiral John Jervis, later Earl St Vincent (1735-1823) and the water colourist Peter de Wint (1784-1849). The neat 18th-century Gothic Church of St Michael, with its galleries and box pews contains a memorial to the Admiral who lies with other members of his family in a small Palladian-style Mausoleum.

South down the A34 is the county town of **Stafford**, the city constructed on the site of a hermitage built by St Pertelin some 1200 years ago. Commercial development has left the town surprisingly untouched - apart from the jutting intrusion of a few tower blocks. Stafford still wears the bubolic air of a country town even though it has been an important manufacturing centre for centuries; manufacturing internal combustion engines and electrical equipment since the beginning of the present century. Nevertheless its ancient heritage is on proud display for all to admire. Here you have **Stafford Castle** built in 1070, an impressive example of an early Norman fortress. The central building in Stafford is the late Georgian Shire Hall, a most handsome building that fits the part well, while not far away is a positive triumph of the timber house-builders art, **The**

High House. Built in 1595 for a wool merchant, John Dorrington, it is the largest timber-framed town house in the country. Nor must one forget **Chetwynd House**, a handsome Georgian building that is now the Post Office Here the ebullient playwright, theatre-manager and MP for Stafford, Richard Brinsley Sheridan, would stay on visits to his constituency.

Due west of Stafford, on the very tip of Cannock Chase, is **Shugborough Estate**, ancestral home of the camera-wielding Earl of Lichfield. A beautiful mansion, dating back to 1693, and set within a magnificent 900 acre estate, Shugborough contains fine collections of 18th century ceramics, silver, paintings and French furniture. **The Staffordshire County Museum** is housed in the old servants quarters and there are splendid recreations of life behind the 'green baize door'. Shugborough Park Farm is a working agricultural museum where rare breeds are kept, horse drawn machinery used and an old mill grinds corn.

Whether you arrive by canal or car, **Cannock Chase** remains the greatest attraction of the region. As its name implies it was once a Royal hunting-ground, but Richard I, in need of funds, sold it to the Bishops of Lichfield. In those times, it was a much larger area, extending from the River Penk in the west to the Trent in the east, with Stafford to the north and including Wolverhampton and Walsall to the south. Now it is around 26 square miles of forest and heath land that have been declared an 'area of outstanding natural beauty'. Medieval industrial activities meant the loss of much of the native oakwoods while the southern part was given over to coalpits, but these activities have long ceased and the deer and wildlife have returned to their natural habitat. The highest point is at Castle Ring with wonderful views over the countryside and the site of an Iron Age hill fort, dating from around 500BC.

Close to the eastern side of Cannock Chase lies the ancient city of **Lichfield** with its unique Cathedral of St Mary and St Chad, a magnificent red sandstone structure with three spires, known as 'the Ladies of the vale'. The Cathedral is considered the Mother-church of the Midlands and is the third building on the site since it was consecrated in AD 700 by St Chad. The present structure is a magnificent example of Early English and Decorated work, a triumph of medieval craftsmanship. The surrounds of the cathedral are equally beautiful with attractive houses of the 14th and 15th centuries surrounding the green lawns of **Vicar's Close**.

Uttoexeter is the mecca for Midlands racing fans. This cheerful little market town (every Wednesday since 1309) has three different ways of pronouncing its name - 'Uxeter', 'Utcheter' or 'U-tox-eter' - and its name has been spelt in seventy-seven different ways since first recorded in the Domesday Book as Wotochesede. The town evidently suffers no neuroses as a result of all this confusion, but sits four-square in the delightful countryside and goes about its quiet business, waking up for market days and race meetings.

There is a tendency to think of the **Peak district** as belonging exclusively to Derbyshire but natural physical features have a distressing habit of ignoring man-made boundaries, and there is more than a little truth in the local boast that 'the best parts of Derbyshire are in Staffordshire'. This is fascinating countryside, almost cosy in scale one minute, then possessed of a wild grandeur, the next.

North-east of **Oakmoor**, through the hills and dales, lies one of the most beautiful valleys in the region, **The Manifold Valley**. The village of **Ilam**, standing at the southern end, makes a good starting point for exploring the area, and the old mansion **Ilam Hall**, is now a Youth Hostel. The valley is relatively flat at this point but becomes increasingly deep and narrow as one journeys northwards. The River Manifold has a disconcerting habit of disappearing underground and at Ilam Hall, it re-emerges from its subterranean journey from **Darfur Crags**.

Obviously this beautiful area has long been a favourite with those who love what is described in the glossy-brochure trade as 'the great Outdoors' - even if writers of such hyperbole rarely get nearer to the fresh air than kicking the cat out last thing at night! Over three hundred years ago, two learned gentlemen, close friends and 'Brothers of the Angle' rambled the length and breadth of the glorious river valleys in pursuit of the shy brook trout. Izaak Walton and Charles Cotton could discuss the classical poetry of Homer or the merits of a fishing lure with equal facility and enthusiasm, and had a particular fondness for the river that runs down the border between Staffordshire and Derbyshire, the Dove. Cotton, who was to contribute a chapter on the art of fly fishing in Walton's 'Complete Angler' was a poet and author in his own right who lived at **Beresford Hall** near **Alstonfield**. The Hall was pulled down in the 1800's but the fishing lodge by the river still survives, and the village church still contains the Cotton family pew.

Fishing is still a matter for much learned - not to mention heated - debate, best undertaken in the comfortable surrounds of a friendly hostelry; Alstonfield provides the venue in the shape of **The George**, a local pub for over 250 years. Not only anglers, but walkers, climbers, naturalists and campers enjoy the atmosphere of this well-run and most welcoming pub.

Longnor is a tiny market town in the furthermost corner of north-eastern Staffordshire on the same road the intrepid Greyhound rattled its way across the rutted pot-holes over the moors. The road may have improved, but Longnor is little altered; good looking l8th-century facades and a square with a small Market Hall dated 1873. Stone lined streets and alleyways with determined little houses of the same material give a sense of dogged continuity, yet change - and welcome change at that - has taken place; tucked discreetly down narrow Chapel Street is Parrotts Bistro restaurant. Authentic French cuisine is now dispensed with flair and imagination from attractive premises that not long ago were the semi-derelict remains of a l7th century inn.

Wandering westwards one comes across the highest village in England, set close by the high road from Leek to Buxton. The oddly named Flash claims the title at 1,158 ft above sea-level. A Nepalese would doubtless fall off his mountain laughing, but it is a respectable height for our 'sceptr'd isle' and probably just as cold in winter as the Himalayas.

'The Metropolis of the Moorland' was how one writer described **Leek**, though Dr Johnson was not so charitable 'An old church but a poor town'. Nowadays it is a neat mill town standing in magnificent countryside. Like so many of its kind Leek has a cheerful and generous nature and welcomes visitors; particularly on Wednesdays when the old cobbled market square is thronged with stalls and the air filled with cheerful banter. There are a surprisingly large number of antique shops and many of the mills have their own shops.

The great canal-builder, Brindley, started his working life as a mill-wright and the **Brindley Mill** in Mill Street, tells the story of his life and graphically demonstrates the many facets of this once, important craft. One of his later works was the **Caldon Canal** which runs with the River Churnet in the valley alongside the hillside village of **Cheddleton**. **Cheddleton Flint Mill** ground up flints from Kent and Sussex for use in the pottery industry, and the waterwheels and grinding equipment are on display, together with other items associated with the trade, including a restored canal barge. Today's canal boats and their crews, along with many other visitors to the area, make use of the hospitable facilities offered by the **Red Lion**, an attractive 18th century establishment situated beside the canal on the Cheadle Road. The canal's successor, the railway, is also commemorated at the **Cheddleton Railway** Centre, with displays, mementoes, engines and other paraphernalia set in and around the attractive Victorian station.

The two different forms of transport were obviously of major importance to the development of the industries of the north-western sector of the county.**Newcastle-under-Lyme** and **Stoke-on-Trent** lie side by side, geographically close yet separate in terms of history and character.

Coming from the east, the first is Stoke-on-Trent, a combination of the six communities of **Tunstall, Burslem, Hanley, Longton**, Stoke and **Fenton** - known the world over as the **Potteries**. The companies based here, both large and small, have a world-wide market for their products and their heritage dates back many centuries. Wherever fine china-ware is used and appreciated, names such as Spode, Copeland, Minton, Coalport, Royal Doulton and Wedgwood are revered and respected.

'The Potteries have the flavour of a rural area; a feeling of continuity and a sense of tradition. The same family names crop up time and time again and, even in these difficult times, there is a pride in the past and has made enormous efforts to clean up the detritus of yesteryear and make Stoke an attractive place in which to work and live. **Trentham Gardens** cover 800 acres of parklands, gardens and lakes with numerous sporting facilities. **Festival Park**, is an amazing 23 acre complex which includes a sub-tropical aquatic playground with flumes, water slides and rapids.

The architecture is predominantly Victorian red-brick since the city was in a constant state of development, but there are exceptions; the Minton family brought over French artists to decorate their wares and built them ornate Italianate villas their sense of geography being obviously inferior to their business acumen. However both Italian and French influences of another kind can be sampled at **Il Mago**, a stylish and totally delightful restaurant in Cobridge Road, Hanley.

Newcastle-under-Lyme is the oldest of the two cities, dating back to its incorporation as a borough in 1180, at a time when the neighbouring Potteries were hamlets or villages. Although Stoke-on-Trent and Newcastle have grown into each other, they still retain their separate identities; the delicate craft of the potteries being is host to **Keele University**. Markets and a fair date from medieval times.

The surrounding countryside is immensely attractive with villages containing much good domestic architecture and a number of beautiful gardens (such as the **Dorothy Clive Gardens** at **Willoughbridge**) and country parks like **Bathpool Park, Kidsgrove**.

Staffordshire is a little-known county of remarkable contrast, interest and beauty that will repay the curious a thousandfold.

THE CROFT HOTEL,
St Marys Street,
Bridgnorth,
Shropshire WVl6 4DW
Tel:01746 762416

This charming, family run hotel is housed in listed buildings in the centre of historic Bridgnorth. The town dating from the 10th century is divided by the River Severn forming High Town and Low Town. You approach High Town by steep streets with architectural gems almost commonplace. The Croft Hotel is part of this scene. It is a picturesque location and only a short distance from all sorts of activities including walking, fishing and golf. The fabulous scenery of the Shropshire countryside is re-nowned especially Long Mynd, Stretton Hills, Wenlock Edge and Cleehills. In addition there is The Iron Bridge Gorge Museum, Europe's most important Heritage Museum, just seven miles away, and Shrewsbury, the county town of Shropshire, which seems surrounded by rivers, is 20 miles. The Severn Valley Railway runs from Bridgnorth to Kidderminster and has the largest collection of working locomotives. The Motor Museum on the outskirts of the town is another popular attraction.

In order to enjoy all that Bridgnorth has to offer you can do no better than stay with the Wilding family in The Croft Hotel. Built in the 1700's it is friendly, welcoming, centrally heated throughout and as one might expect in a listed building, many interesting features including an Inglenook fireplace. Every room is beautifully decorated and furnished with colour co-ordinated drapes. The whole atmosphere pervading the hotel is one of well-being. The Wildings are meticulous in the running of the hotel but nonetheless it has a relaxed informality about it that makes it a pleasure to stay in.

Jill Wilding has a fund of stories to tell about all sort of subjects, especially Bridgnorth. The family are multi-talented and each can cook delicious meals. This is evident when you see the excellent breakfast set before you and re-enforced by the evening meal with its choices and frequently innovative dishes. There is a Vegetarian menu and special diets can be arranged. Each bedroom is individually furnished and ten of the twelve rooms are en suite. Each has television, direct dial telephone and a hospitality tray.

USEFUL INFORMATION

OPEN; *All year*
CHILDREN; *Welcome*
CREDIT CARDS; *All major cards*
LICENSED; *Yes*
ACCOMMODATION; *12 rooms 10 en suite*

DINING ROOM; *Delicious, home-cooked fare*
VEGETARIAN; *Yes + special diets*
DISABLED ACCESS; *Not suitable*
PETS; *Yes*

THE CROWN INN

Market Place,
Abbots Bromley
Nr. Rugeley,
Staffordshire WS15 3BS
Tel: 01283 840227 Fax: 01283 840016

This old 17th century coaching house is situated in the centre of Abbots Bromley, famous for the Horn Dance which has been performed here since 1226. It is a charming and picturesque conservation village complete with Buttercross and a fine old church which is open every day until dusk and rewards everyone who enters its welcoming portals. The Crown Inn is ideally situated for anyone visiting Stafford, Shugborough Hall, the home of the Queen's cousin Lord Lichfield, the internationally famous photographer, Alton Towers, Uttoxeter Races, Lichfield, Burton-on-Trent, Staffordshire Way, Sudbury Hall, Tutbury Crystal and the Potteries. Once you enter the friendly inn you will find a warm welcome extended to everyone. It is a pub much beloved by locals who create a great atmosphere when they gather round the bar for a well kept pint and to enjoy lively conversation on all sorts of subjects in which visitors are readily welcome to take part. Frank Robertson is the jovial proprietor and he and his well trained staff go out of their way to ensure everyone enjoys coming to the Black and White fronted Crown Inn. Inside it is furnished in a comfortable, homely style, in keeping with a village inn The well stocked bar has a fine selection of ales which one might expect in a Free House. In addition there is a good selection of reasonably priced wines and as Frank is a member of the Scottish Malt Whisky Society, there are some 24 Malt Whiskies covering those distilled in the farthest north and in the south. Meals are served every day both in the Lounge and the bar and on Sundays there is a traditional Sunday Lunch served between 12 and 2.30pm. Booking for this popular occasion is advisable. All the food is good wholesome English fare, home-cooked and generous in portion. The Beer Garden is much used in fine weather. There are six comfortable letting rooms each with television, telephone and a hostess tray. A Function Room is available for private parties up to 50 persons without catering and Buffets, Lunches and Dinners for up to 40 persons are catered for. Outside bars can be arranged. If you want to entertain a group of up to 30 people, it is fun to hire the Long Alley Skittle room.

USEFUL INFORMATION

OPEN; *Mon-Thurs 12-3pm & 6-11pm*   **DINING AREA;** *Good, wholesome fayre*
Fri 12-3pm & 5.30-1 1p. Sat:12-1 1pm
CHILDREN; *Welcome. Childrens menu*   **BAR FOOD;** *Wide selection*
CREDIT CARDS; *Visa/Master/Delta/Switch*   **VEGETARIAN;** *On request*
LICENSED; *Full On*   **DISABLED ACCESS;** *with assistance*
ACCOMMODATION; *6 letting rooms*   **GARDEN;** *Beer garden*
Not en suite ETB 1 Crown AA QQ Recommended

THE BEAR HOTEL COUNTRY INN

Hodnet, Nr Market Drayton,
Shropshire TF9 3NH

Tel: 01630 685214 Fax: 01630 685787

Just three minutes from the famous Hodnet Hall Gardens, the Bear Hotel is a 16th century coaching inn with a character and substance that is hard to equal. The substance referred to is none other than Jasper, the friendly ghost who lives in the attractive illuminated cellar garden! Everything about the Bear has charm. The character of the bygone age has been carefully preserved with oak beams and open fires creating a warm and inviting atmosphere. At the same time everything has been done to provide the comforts of the Twentieth Century.

The comfortable bar is just the place to meet friends for a drink or to relax before a meal after a busy day either on business or pleasure. Just looking at it one would not quite realise how large the restaurant is, because it is full of nooks and crannies creating a great feeling of intimacy. The food is excellent whether you dine in the restaurant or have a snack at the bar. The á la carte menu is exciting and innovative whilst the wide ranging Bar menu provides something for every taste and pocket. The Bear is proud of its standards both of food and service which are highlighted by the excellent manner in which Conferences, Wedding Receptions and other occasions are dealt with in the atmospheric Baronial Hall style Function Room. This is also where The Bear holds its renowned Medieval Banquets throughout the year. They are nights of fun and revelry, frolics and professional entertainment, finishing with dancing until the early hours, for both small and large parties when guests are encouraged to come in period dress because it adds to the sense of occasion. However it is not compulsory and the dress can be smart casual.

For those who want to stay at The Bear and enjoy all it has to offer, there are six well appointed en suite guest rooms with colour television, direct dial telephones and hostess trays. It is certainly a great place to be and ideal for anyone wanting to enjoy the surrounding countryside with the opportunity to walk, ride, shoot, fish or play golf at Hawkestone Park Golf and Follies or the West Midlands Shooting Grounds which provides for the beginner as well as the expert.

USEFUL INFORMATION

OPEN; *All year*
CHILDREN; *Welcome*
CREDIT CARDS; *All major cards*
LICENSED; *Full On*
ACCOMMODATION; *6 rooms en suite*
PETS; *No*

RESTAURANT; *Good food, á la carte, in intimate surroundings. Value for money*
BAR FOOD; *Wide range*
VEGETARIAN; *Always a choice*
GARDEN; *Yes*
DISABLED ACCESS; *Partial. By arrangement*

THE LAURELS,
Star Bank,
Oakamoor,
North StaffordshiresT10 3BN
Tel: 01538 702629 Fax: 01538 702796
E.Mail 113235.1533@compuserve. com.

If ever you were looking for somewhere that would give you total value for money at very reasonable prices you should certainly stay at The Laurels. Situated within one and a half miles of Alton Towers with a short walk on country lanes direct from the house, and just four and a half miles from the market town of Cheadle, The Laurels at Star Bank, Oakamoor looks out over superb and spectacular countryside from which you can spend a day in romantic Dovedale, get your thrills at Alton Towers, or take a walk in the beautiful Churnet Valley. Wild and unspoilt moorland-deep limestone valleys, the antique shops of Leek or the world famous Potteries with such names as Wedgwood, Minton and Spode. All this can be yours if you stay here in a beautifully furnished and very comfortable house. Owned by Lyndon and Pam Hall it is one of the friendliest establishments anywhere. All the rooms are individually decorated there are six en suite bedrooms, 2 double, and 4 family each with television and a generously supplied hospitality tray. A comfortable lounge and a cosy, residential bar is there for guests use and provides a good meeting place at the end of the day.

As a great start to your day, Breakfast is a feast with a choice of a full, traditional English meal or a lighter Continental Breakfast. It is all freshly cooked and substantial. There is a good choice of eateries within easy distance to which Lyndon and Pam will point you in the right direction. There is something very special about this part of the world, especially with the Peak National Park 5 miles away. It offers a wonderful holiday or break to the visitor and this is enhanced for anyone staying at The Laurels.

USEFUL INFORMATION

OPEN; All year   *DINING ROOM;* Great breakfast
CHILDREN; Very welcome   *VEGETARIAN;* Catered for
CREDIT CARDS; Visa/Master/Switch   *DISABLED ACCESS;* No
LICENSED; Yes   *GARDEN;* Yes
ACCOMMODATION; 2dbl, 4fam all en suite   *PETS;* No pets

SANDFORD HOUSE HOTEL

St Julian's Friars,
Shrewsbury,
Shropshire SYl 1XL
Tel/Fax: 01743 343829

Sandford House Hotel is a Grade II Listed Georgian townhouse, close to the Severn with its fine riverside walks, yet within a few minutes walk of the town centre. Anyone who knows Shrewsbury loves it. To the first time visitor it seems almost cut off from the outside world apart from the bridges crossing the rivers that meet here. It is a town full of fine architecture included in which is Sandford House. People come to Shrewsbury for all sorts of reasons. Many visit simply to enjoy its wealth of half timbered Tudor buildings, its narrow winding streets, its castle, its famous abbey and several museums, as well as the quiet restaurants and pubs full of character. Some come here on business, some to explore the many exciting places within easy reach, but whatever their reason, those who have discovered Sandford House find it friendly and full of atmosphere. It is a small family hotel with a delightfully informal air. The aim is to provide a homely tasteful environment with high standards in food and cleanliness. This is clearly achieved and whilst it essentially caters for bed and breakfast, packed lunches can be provided.

Each bedroom has been individually furnished and decorated, half the rooms are en suite and every room has a washbasin. A tea and coffee tray is provided as well as colour television. An ironing board and iron and a very loud alarm clock are available! The comfortable guest lounge has television and both this room and the attractive dining room have a good deal of the original plasterwork still intact which provides a particularly pleasant atmosphere in which to relax or eat. The food is excellent, freshly cooked and generous in portion. Guests are very welcome to use the pretty garden which is sheltered and quiet and an ideal place to spend a sunny summer afternoon. There is parking at the front of the hotel and when these spaces are taken there is a reasonably priced car park about 50 yards away. Sandford House has a hotel licence which enables them to serve a range of wines.

USEFUL INFORMATION

OPEN; *All year*
CHILDREN; *Welcome*
CREDIT CARDS; *Master/Euro*
LICENSED; *Hotel licence*
ACCOMMODATION; *Good, comfortable rooms, some en suite*

DINING ROOM; *Great breakfast*
Optional evening meal. Packed lunches
VEGETARIAN;: *Catered for*
DISABLED ACCESS; *Not easy*
GARDEN; *Yes. Sheltered*
PETS; *By arrangement*

THE WOODBRIDGE INN

Coalport, Nr Telford,
Shropshire TF8 7JF

Tel:01952 882054

The 16th century Woodbridge Inn, situated right on the banks of the River Severn, is full of character and as one would expect a plethora of old beams, uneven floors, low ceilings and an atmosphere that has built up over the centuries. Paul and Judi Symington are the cheerful, friendly and extremely professional mine hosts who have a reputation in the area for the welcoming and hospitable manner in which they greet regulars and newcomers alike. No one ever remains a stranger here for very long. There is plenty to do if you stay here. You can fish on site, go canoeing on the river, play golf at a course a mile away and certainly enjoy either a gentle stroll or an invigorating walk in the immediate countryside. Indeed it is a very rural area but near enough the remarkable town of Telford to enable one to enjoy what it has to offer - in particular a wonderful park complete with all kind of leisure activities.

If you decide to stay here you will find there are five, recently beautifully refurbished, en suite guest rooms - one with a four-poster. They are well-appointed and have colour television as well as a generously supplied beverage tray. When you come down in the morning it will be to a really excellent breakfast with a choice of fruit juices, cereals, plenty of toast and preserves and a traditional cooked English breakfast of your choice. The chef is a Sicilian and is both talented and innovative. The meals that he prepares and presents, seven days a week, are delicious. Mainly traditional English but with a strong Continental influence. For Dinner you might choose Fillet of Cornish Sea Bass baked and served with home-made tagliatelle verdi with ratatouille sauce and essence of capisicum or a Pot-roast Fillet of Pork cooked with Chateau Bramley Apple served with fresh herb polenta and finished with a ginger wine liquor amongst many other equally tempting dishes. The starters and the desserts are equally tempting. Simple, home-cooked Bar food is also available every day.

In summer there is nothing nicer than to take a drink outside and sit on the patio right on the water's edge. There are also weekly barbecues which are fun and very well attended. In addition to all this you will find, that in the informal garden, the Symingtons have quite a menagerie; 2 Geese, 2 Goats, 2 Pot Belly Pigs, 1 Rabbit, lots of chickens and family dogs. They all add to the happy atmosphere that pervades the whole of The Woodbridge Inn.

USEFUL INFORMATION

OPEN; All year, all day
CHILDREN; Welcome
CREDIT CARDS; All major cards
LICENSED; Yes
ACCOMMODATION; 5 en suite rooms
GARDEN; Patio by waters edge. Barbecue

RESTAURANT; Delicious, innovative food
English with a Continental influence
BAR FOOD; Wide variety, home-cooked
VEGETARIAN; Catered for
DISABLED ACCESS; Difficult
PETS; Yes

Chapter 16

SUSSEX & SURREY

INCLUDES

Chapter 16

SUSSEX

West Sussex takes in an area bounded to the west by the Hampshire Border, to the north with that of Surrey with an imaginary eastern division running south from the new urban mass of Crawley down to meet the coast at Angmering-on-Sea. As an introduction to the whole it serves well; there are great estates and houses, high hills where sheep graze and skylarks sing, ancient villages and hamlets nestling in natural folds and large stands of mature woodland, the remnants of mighty tracts of forest which once covered much of the county. Balanced against this rustic idyll are modern developments, new roads and a population that has expanded rapidly over the last few decades. Better communications and an increase in personal wealth has meant an influx of commuters, together with a large amount of light industry attracted to the area since the Second World War; all this is to the good, even if the aesthetics occasionally offend. Employment and prosperity had done much to preserve the rural charm that so attracted the likes of Belloc, even though that charm can often seem synthetic. But consider; the thatched farm-labourer's cottage with roses climbing over the porch would be no more than a weed-ridden mound of rubble if left to purely local concern. Estates, councils and conservation bodies have but limited budgets and must spend accordingly; a tumble-down cottage of uncertain ancestry has no priority in their scheme of things, and few private landowners have sufficiency of cash to modernise such places to the standards that today's agricultural worker rightly expects. It is the outsider, the commuter, weekender or retiree who has the money and the determination to conserve. There are many students of the countryside and its vernacular architecture who grumble a great deal about the 'chocolate-box' or 'stockbroker-belt' image of many of these small rural communities, but to my mind it is better that it should be thus rather than down-at-heel and crumbling, or worse abandoned. One may raise an eyebrow at a satellite dish or an ill-advised conservatory - but doubtless our more affected ancestors reacted in like manner when confronted with innovations such as glazed windows or inside sanitation.

The newcomer rarely receives thanks and seldom praise for his efforts. However, those who have chosen Sussex in which to settle and 'improve' have made a wise choice, for the natives have long been known for their pragmatic and friendly attitude to the outsider, whether Roman, Saxon, Norman or modern city worker. It is a county with an almost magical ability to absorb, adapt and change almost seamlessly. Throughout its long history, it has been directly affected by great political and economic upheavals, yet, when the dust has settled and the shouting died away, the essential Sussex still remains; quietly welcoming the visitor to its tranquil beauty.

My own tour began in the cathedral city of **Chichester**, just a few miles to the east of the border with Hampshire. Other than the cathedral spire, little of the city's fine heritage can be glimpsed from the outskirts by the passing traveller who sees a flat countryside bounded to the north by the distant South Downs. This fertile land, used for growing a wide variety of crops, is also home to numerous light industrial estates that seem to fringe the northern edge of the by-pass. Chichester is no grand cathedral city. Its scale is domestic and it has the air of a prosperous market town; friendly, unpretentious with nothing to intimidate. Even the lovely Cathedral seems to stand at the pavement edge without benefit of grand close or walled surround. No great avenues or parades, merely a sensible cross-roads of four main streets running out in the direction of the cardinal points and the areas in between being filled with a happy warren of lanes, narrow alley-ways and delightful little squares. Modern development has inevitably led to the introduction of pedestrian precincts, car parks and shopping arcades but happily the process has not been over-intrusive and the human scale remains. The cruciform layout owes much to the Romans, who found the area of fertile plain much to their liking when they arrived in AD43.

The lovely interior of this Norman cathedral contains some startlingly modern decorative art. The most obvious is John Piper's huge representative tapestry hanging behind the high altar; there is also a window by Chagall, a painting by Graham Sutherland and numerous other contemporary works including a pulpit of concrete and steel. George Bell was bishop from 1929 to 1958 and it was he who introduced the concept of modern art into the cathedral. A bold move, but one that added new dimensions of colour and life that had been effectively missing since the Parliamentarians destroyed so much of the decorative work during the Civil War.

The city fell after a brief siege in 1643, after Sir William Waller's troops had breached a section of the wall to the south of the cathedral, sacking the Deanery that lay in the small Close behind it. This was handsomely rebuilt in the Classical style in 1725, but does not intrude into the cosy feeling of the close, which is not the open surround to be found in cities such as Exeter or Salisbury, but a delightful small area attached to the southside. There was no monastery here, and with the establishment of the Church of England, the deans and canons were permitted to marry and over the years the houses of the Close, were altered from celibate accommodation to comfortable family homes; there is very much a family atmosphere in the area to this day.

The Pallants is a charming area of principally Georgian redbrick and once under the exclusive jurisdiction of the Archbishop of Canterbury. Pallant House, built in 1713, is the finest of these buildings and has a link with the cathedral as it contains a fine collection of modern art, the bequest of the late Dean, Doctor Walter Hussey. There is also a wonderful collection of porcelain and a beautifully reconstructed small garden in keeping with the period of the house. It is both museum and gallery and succeeds in either sphere.

An old granary houses the excellent **Chichester Museum** while nearby stands **St Marys Hospital**, built in 1290 as an infirmary and converted in the 1600's into eight small dwellings for old people. It has been little altered since and is often held up as an example of excellent planning for the needs of the elderly. Further north of this area is **Priory park**, a large open space named after the Franciscan priors who established themselves here in the early 13th-century. The choir of their church survives as a museum and within the bounds of the Park is a grassy mound that once was the site of Chichester Castle, dismantled around the time of Henry III.

Chichester is representative of much of the county in that its prosperity comes from its ability to adapt without losing its essential character. As the visitor can see, ancient and modern co-exist happily and one of the principal examples of this is to be found in Oaklands Park, to the north of the old city walls. The **Chichester Festival Theatre** was constructed in the 1960's and now has an international reputation, attracting audiences from all over the world to see productions of the highest quality. The city also has a major Arts Festival, inaugurated some 20 years ago which takes place every July.

The stylish Georgian **Suffolk House Hotel** in No. 3 East Row, is the place to stay and eat. Once the Town House of the Dukes of Richmond, it is privately owned and run efficiently and comfortably by a small staff providing a tranquil atmosphere combined with everything that today's traveller expects. Cordon Bleu cuisine attracts non-residents who enjoy nothing better than dining in the beautiful restaurant on delectable dishes.

Outside the city one does not have to travel far in order to find something of interest. **Chilgrove** is the quintessential English hamlet, six miles north west of the town on the B2141. Here you will find **Forge Cottage Inn and Restaurant** set on rising ground on the edge of the village green, overlooking The White Horse, the village pub, and with the cricket pitch in the middle distance.

To the west is **Fishbourne** where **The Fishbourne Roman Palace and Museum** is one of the most important Roman relics in Britain and contains much of the remains of a magnificent 1st-century villa. For todays visitor apart from this gem there is an interesting if slightly eccentric pub, **The Woolpack Inn** where you will be well fed at sensible prices.

Just west of Fishbourne lies one of the jewels of the Sussex shore, the small Saxon village of **Bosham** (pronounced 'Bozzum'). Lying at the top of an arm of Chichester Harbour, this is a delightful little community jumbled around the waters of Bosham Creek. Canute had a palace here and it was on the foreshore that he was reputed to have commanded the tide to retreat. Anyone able to work such a miracle would undoubtedly be in much demand at the **Anchor Bleu**, a cosy pub by the creek, where the unwary motorist is frequently caught out by the rapidly rising tide which can cover the shore road. The Anchor is the sole survivor of several small pubs which once traded in the tiny and attractive High Street.

Northwards to the very border with Hampshire, I was off to visit **Stansted Park** near Rowlands Castle. Ancient woodland, once part of the Forest of Bere, sets off this most decorative Wren-style house, which is full of treasures. There is an extraordinary and highly-decorative chapel which owes its appearance to a previous owner of the house who spent most of his time trying to convert Jews to Christianity.

From here, head across the country to the B2147, a splendid Downland drive, where thick woodland alternates with pasture and plough and the road steadily climbs to the crest of the chalk hills. The Mardens, West, North, Up and East are all worth a diversion to visit the small churches and to admire the way in which the little communities seem to typify the essential South Down village. If you feel like stretching your legs, the **Stoughton Down Forest walk** can be found to the south of East Marden.

Uppark is a National Trust property which was partially destroyed by fire in 1989 and is now restored to its former glory. It has the most handsome facade, the gardens are by Humphrey Repton and the views are breath-taking. Uppark has had a number of owners since it was built at the end of the 17th century and the most colourful of these must have been the splendidly rakish Sir Henry Featherstonhaugh. He was in his early twenties when he inherited the house and in no time at all it housed his mistress, the beautiful Emma Hart. Before long she had left the rackety Sir Harry to marry the diplomat Sir William Hamilton and later achieved further notoriety by becoming Lord Nelson's mistress. Her former lover never forgot her though, and when she fell on hard times after Nelson's death in 1805, Sir Harry helped her out. His own life of debauchery and scandal continued until 1810 when he quarrelled with the Prince Regent and retired from London life to lead the life of a country squire. However, he was far from finished with the world of scandal and gossip, for at the age of seventy, he shocked the fashionable world by marrying his head dairymaid. He remained happily married until his death at the ripe old age of ninety-two.

The steep hill that runs down into **South Harting** is said to have deterred the Duke of Wellington when the house was offered to him after the Napoleonic Wars; the necessity for constant replenishment of horses was his excuse. The church here is unusual in that the short spire is clad in copper that has oxidised to a brilliant green; inside there are fine timbers in the roof and a sporting reminder of old Sir Harry from Uppark in the form of a grieving woman and a somewhat woebegone spaniel. In his time he would have undoubtedly patronised **The Ship Inn**, a suitably atmospheric establishment in the main street. You may think it odd that an inland pub should have a marine name. It was really because the pub was constructed of ship's timbers, a sort of 'quid pro quo' for the local timber being commandeered to build new ships for His Majesty's Navy. The Ship has been mentioned by Hilaire Belloc and also appears in one of Nevil Shute's novels when the hero takes tea in what was then the upstairs tea-rooms.

The country to the north of Chichester is both varied and well-endowed with numerous attractions, both natural and man-made. From West Stoke a delightful walk takes one up to the escarpment of **Kingley Vale**, now under the administration of the Nature Conservancy Council. The Vale is most notable for its ancient yew-woods, dark, dense and silent.

A cheerful and lively contrast to the mystical, perhaps Druidical, stillness of Kingley Vale can be found in the nearby village of **Lavant**, where the 17th century pub, **The Earl of March**, dispenses good food and hospitality. The pub's name is the honorary title given to the eldest sons of the Dukes of Richmond, owners of the famous estate of Goodwood. **Goodwood House**, set in lovely parkland, lies a couple of miles to the east. A handsome porticoed central section is flanked by two wings of flint construction with green-domed towers. As originally designed, this is only part of what would have been a truly palatial building and some idea of the projected scale can be gained by inspecting the enormous stable-block which was completed before money for the main house ran out. The house contains numerous treasures including Old Master portraits, tapestries, porcelain and furniture, but to me, the real attraction of Goodwood is the magnificent setting and the fact that the 12,000 acre estate is a diverse and working entity. Agriculture, forestry and recreation go hand in hand; the small airfield is surrounded by a once-famous motor racing track (now used for club events and testing) and there is a golf-course and a country park. The first Duke purchased the original Tudor house as a hunting lodge and, above all, it was the passion for all things equine that the Duke and his successors made the estate world famous. Today, international dressage competitions, horse trials and the principal attraction of 'Glorious Goodwood', Goodwood races, bring enthusiasts and competitors from all over the globe.

During the Second World War the skies over this region of sleepy Sussex reverberated to the sound of the supercharged aero-engines and cannon-fire. The Battle of Britain was fought principally from the airfields of Sussex and Kent: one of the most famous being just south of the A27 at **Tangmere**. headquarters of 11 Group, RAF Fighter Command. Tangmere played a key role in the Battle and its importance was reflected in the savage German air raids of 1940. Later in the conflict, units based there were instrumental in developing night-fighting techniques and also in the covert delivery and retrieval of Allied agents in France. The airfield was closed in 1970, but the small village of Saxon origin has never forgotten the tragedies and glories of those days; on the green, a simple stone monument commemorates the airfield and its squadrons. The graveyard of the little Early English Church of St Andrews contains the neat headstones of British, Allied and German airmen, lying amongst the older monuments to generations of Sussex folk who cold never have dreamt of war in the air. There is a small Military Aviation Museum close to the old runways with an excellent display of memorabilia and, fittingly the village pub is named after one of the most famous of all fighter pilots. **The Bader Arms**, open in 1981, is one of the nicest modern pubs I have visited and an apt way to remember 'The Few'.

The flat countryside was of course, ideal for the construction of an airfield, but for centuries its real worth has been agricultural and horticultural. The Selsey Peninsula has produced grain vegetables, fruit and flowers for generations, and its rich soil is keenly exploited. Nevertheless, it is an attractive area with small villages and reed-fringed rivulets, popular with holiday makers and yachtsmen. On the western side it is bounded by Chichester Harbour with the yachting centres of Dell Quay (once the original port of Chichester), Birdham, and Itchenor, neat and trim beside the water. On the westernmost tip, close to the popular sands of east Head, is the small resort of **West Wittering**. Sounding rather like the title of an old BBC radio comedy, the village is attractive with a most welcoming pub, The Lamb Inn and a church that is definitely organic, in that it is a happy mixture of period and styles. A walk along the seaward shore reveals some massive chunks of wave-smoothed rock; geological analysis shows they are probably originated in the Channel Islands, detritus from an Ice Age glacier.

At the beginning of the Chapter, I made mention of the fact that the great majority of country cottages owe their survival to the wealthy newcomer; at Singleton there is an exception to this at the **Weald and Downland Open Air Museum**. This is a collection of vernacular buildings from all over the county that have been painstakingly re-erected and restored to as near their original condition as possible. Cottages, mills and farm buildings are grouped attractively, and the site is brought alive by the presence of the rural crafts of the period - wheelwrights, potters, sawyers and charcoal burners. To inspect some of these 'idyllic' rural dwellings is to receive a salutary lesson; no sanitation or glazing and the 'central heating' being literally central - merely a fire in the middle of the earth floor!

Some five miles to the north 20th century comfort is to be found in 16th century surroundings. **The Crown** at **Midhurst** is everything a small country town inn should be warmly hospitable and full of character. The town is equally charming with a cheerful and prosperous air good brick and half timbered buildings from across the centuries line the streets around the centre. Its origins as a market town since the early 13th century are reflected in names such as Sheep Lane, Wool Lane, Duck Lane and Knockhundred Row. A curfew bell is still rung at eight o'clock every evening; a tradition that was begun when a lone traveller was lost in the mist one night and the tolling of the Midhurst bell led him to safety. In gratitude the man bequeathed a piece of land to enable the bell to be rung in perpetuity.

Cowdray is the name given to the large estate that virtually surrounds Midhurst and the great fire-blackened ruins of **Cowdray House** can be seen to the east of the town. It was begun in 1530, at the instigation of Shakespeare's patron, the Earl of Southampton and then passed to Viscount Montague, who had received Battle Abbey from Henry VIII. Legend has it that the last monk to leave the Abbey cursed Montague prophesying that his family would perish by fire and water. It was an effective, although somewhat slow-acting curse; the house was burnt down in 1793 and shortly afterwards, the then Viscount was drowned in Switzerland and his two sons at Bognor. The remains of the house have a tragic splendour and a look round gives an indication as to why it was once compared with Hampton Court as an example of courtly Tudor splendour. The estate, however, has prospered in the hands of the present owners, the Pearson family, and the great Park with its immense oaks, is internationally-known as a venue for polo. From Midhurst, a pleasant drive takes one north towards the gentler hills of the Surrey border, although to the east of the main road lies **Blackdown**, the highest point in Sussex at 919ft. It was a favourite beauty spot of Tennyson's, who described the view as 'green Sussex fading into the blue, with one grey glimpse of the sea'. The character of the countryside changes; it becomes more intimate with wood and copse interspersed by streams and small fields. The soil is healthy and acid with huge banks of rhododendrons hanging over some of the small lanes.

The third of Sussex's great estates is centred on **Petworth**, a lovely, if cramped little town, which has the reputation of being a centre of the antiques trade. It has a number of interesting 16th and 17th century buildings set around winding narrow streets and a small market-place with a simple arcaded **Town Hall** from the 18th century. The town's condensed effect comes from being huddled against the great east wall of Petworth House which, with its 700 acre deer park, dominates both town and surrounding countryside.

Although the House was built towards the end of the 17th century, Petworth has had a long association with great families and great houses. The Percys, Dukes of Northumberland, were here for 400 years until the direct male line died out in 1670; the chapel is the only surviving part of their medieval manor-house. The present Petworth House was begun as a result of the Percy fortunes being added to those of Charles Seymour, sixth Duke of Somerset, who married the heiress Elizabeth Percy. In 1688, he began the process of construction by demolishing that part of the old town that would have spoilt his prospective view to the south and erecting the boundary wall. Viewed from across the magnificent parkland, Petworth House is palatial yet restrained; without the enhancement of the later landscaping of Capability Brown, the house must have looked initially like a great London terrace, transplanted into the Sussex countryside. In 1750 another marriage meant that Petworth passed into the hands of a family who live there to this day, the Wyndhams, Earls of Egremont. Under their liberal and open-handed patronage, both town and house flourished; the third Earl in particular did much to turn Petworth into the great treasure-house that it is today. Petworth is now looked after by the National Trust.

To the east, the A283 runs close to the pretty village of **Fittleworth**, once the home of Sir Edward Elgar, and where the coach-horses were once changed at the 14th century **Swan Inn**. A little further along the main road, passing over the medieval bridge at **Stopham**, is the 'longest village in Sussex'. **Pulborough** settled since Neolithic times and lying beside a Flood plain of the river Arun, was once an important Roman encampment guarding Stane Street, which ran from Chichester to London.
In the hamlet of **Hardham**, a mile or so to the south, the little Norman church, contains a wonderful set of wall paintings, rendered around 1100; they rank amongst the most important treasures of their kind in England.

The South Down Way is some 80 miles of bridle and footpath that runs along the crest, affording riders and walkers views of some of the most lovely scenery in the country. South-west of Hardham, the Way runs close to **The Bignor Roman Villa**, site of an enormous farmstead and house, where the wonderful Roman mosaics, discovered in 1811, are displayed in a covered area.

The wealth and importance of Sussex in earlier times are also seen in three other major attractions that lie not far away to the east. **Amberley**, a truly lovely village seated at the foot of downland overlooking grazing marshes, was considered of such strategic importance in the 14th-century that the then Bishop of Chichester built a massive castle, the remains of which surround the ancient manor house. The name Amberley is reputed to mean 'fields yellow with buttercups', and the setting is truly exquisite.

The nearby **Amberley Chalk Pits Museum**, contains fascinating displays of bygone Sussex industries, crafts and skills. Further to the east is **Parham House**, one of the loveliest of Tudor mansions, set in a deer park with a church standing on the lawns, all that is left of a medieval village. Parham was built on the site of an earlier house that belonged to the Abbey of Westminster and was rebuilt around 1580 for Sir Thomas Palmer, a wealthy mercer, or textile merchant. Surrounded by beautiful gardens, the house contains some wonderful treasures, including needlework said to have been done by Mary, Queen of Scots, and her ladies-in-waiting, while imprisoned.

Returning to the south-west, the village of **Slindon** has a most attractive setting on the southern slope of the downs. In common with much of the area, flint and brick are the principal building materials and the National Trust looks after many of the cottages and the 3,500 acre Slindon Park Estate. Cricketing enthusiasts will know that Slindon was the birthplace, in 1718, of Richard Newland, considered by many to be the father of modern cricket. The 17th century **Spur Inn**, with its three acres of woodland gardens and excellent food and accommodation, makes a strong case for staying a while longer in this delightful part of the county.

Arundel is the home of the premier Duke and hereditary Earl Marshal of England, the Duke of Norfolk, and it undoubtedly looks the part. Narrow streets wind up from the fast-flowing River Arun towards the immense turreted mass of **Arundel Castle**, with a great grey cathedral thrusting alongside. Trees and hills provide a backdrop to a sight that has the air of a Gothic fairytale. The castle's owners have nearly always been Catholics and the fourth Duke of Norfolk's son, Philip Howard, was canonised in 1970; he kept faith, although persecuted and imprisoned during the reign of Elizabeth I. His remains are interred in the Cathedral of Our Lady and St Philip, which was designed in 1879 by A J. Hansom, of Hansom cab fame. It is a large but not particularly distinguished building, unlike the Parish Church of St Nicholas, a Perpendicular construction of the 14th century which is unique in containing the Catholic Fitzalan Chapel, divided from the Protestant main body by a screen. The town itself has a great deal of charm, with some handsome buildings of timber, flint and brick crowding the narrow steep streets.

The Arun flows into the sea at **Littlehampton**, a cheerful little portion of 'Sussex by the Sea', a popular family resort with all the usual attractions of an English sea-side town. Originally a small fishing settlement in Saxon times (mullet being the local delicacy, then as now), the arrival of the railway in 1863 helped develop the small port into resort status. However, medieval Littlehampton was a far cry from the cheerful and unpretentious town of today; stone from the vast quarries of Caen was landed here and some of Henry VIII's warships were constructed on the banks of the Arun.

Remains of a far more ancient industry are to be found in the downs to the east of **Findon**. A pick, made from an antler, has been carbon-dated to 4000BC, and was one of the tools used by Neolithic flint miners of **Cissbury Ring**. Artefacts from these mines have been found all over Western Europe and it is no exaggeration to describe the area as; 'the Sheffield of Flint', but Cissbury is better known for its enormous earthworks, built around 280BC during the Iron Age.

Findon today is renowned for its racehorse stables which have produced strings of winners including the famous Aldaniti and it is common to see champion jockey and Classic trainer Josh Gifford in the village. In the High Street **Findon Manor** standing in its own grounds is a charming hotel owned and run by Mike and Jan Parker-Hare whose welcoming presence adds to the pleasure of staying in this comfortable and friendly house. Excellent food, beautiful en suite bedrooms and ample parking are just additional reasons why one should bide a while.

Not far to the north lies an even better vantage point which must be the most famous landmark in Sussex. **Chanctonbury Ring** is a great clump of beeches planted around the remains of Neolithic earthworks. Although many of the beeches were blown down in the October 1987 storm, by a freak of nature it was principally the inner trees that suffered and not those on the perimeter. Although it is a stiffish walk, the views over the magnificent rolling hills are wonderful. The site has mystical significance; the Romans built a temple here and witches used to meet here on Midsummer's Eve.

Until the River Adur silted up in the l4th-century, Steyning was a busy port, but with the loss of navigable waterway, it turned its attention inland to become a busy market town and has retained much of the cheerful bustling atmosphere that goes with such activities. There are a number of good buildings including the splendid **Grammar School**, founded in 1614, and the handsome Queen Anne house facing the Green where W.B. Yeats wrote some of his later poems. The Norfolk Arms in Church Street, is a good example of the happy adaptability of so many Sussex buildings, since it began life as three cottages before being converted into the cheery pub of today.

Two very popular resorts lie along this coast. Just south of Chichester is **Bognor Regis**, beloved by King George V. Here the beaches are clean, the bathing safe and the people friendly. I discovered an interesting and very different place to stay just 2 miles outside the town on the A259 Bognor-Littlehampton Road. **The Camelot Hotel and Restaurant** built in 1931 and beautifully refurbished in 1991 has ten de-luxe bedrooms. Whether you are looking for an excellent restaurant or excellent hotel accommodation the hotel has a charm of its own. It has a reputation for good cuisine and a comprehensive selection of wines. Then on The Esplanade in Bognor is **The Royal Hotel**. Situated 30 yards from the sea, with glorious panoramic views of the Channel, it is only 3 minutes walk from the town centre and shopping precincts. It is superbly appointed with 24 hour service (Maximum security) and there is a lift to all floors to rooms which are all en suite and largely have sea views. The Royal has an acknowledged reputation for good food and for its service which is warm and friendly. The Coffee Shop which is open all day offers over 100 dishes!

Worthing is a quiet, dignified resort which is all the more surprising when one knows that the lively 'London by the Sea' Brighton is only a few miles along the coast. It has long been a place where people wanting a quiet, refreshing break, have found comfort and relaxation. There can be no better place to stay than **The Cavendish Hotel** on Marine Parade which is perfectly placed on the seafront, close to the town centre with its pedestrian precincts and within easy walking distance of the railway and bus stations. Worthing has theatres, cinemas and first class shops. There is a wide variety of indoor and outdoor sporting activity. The town's location on the south coast provides an ideal base for exploring the beautiful Sussex Downs and the villages.

When Steyning was a port, it was at the head of the Adur estuary and the task of guarding this strategic site fell to the lot of Bramber. Derived from the Saxon 'Brymmburh', meaning a fortified hill, there remains only a fragment of the grim Norman keep that kept watch atop the steep hill. The castle, which was torn down by the Parliamentary forces after the Civil War, guarded not only the approaches to Steyning but also a great stone bridge that crossed the Adur. The wardens of this bridge were monks and their home was the wonderful medieval **St Mary's House**, one of the finest timber-framed buildings in the county. Set in lovely gardens, the house contains finely panelled rooms including the Painted Room, said to have been decorated for a visit by Elizabeth I. The Virgin Queen was not the only Royal visitor for Charles II hid here on his way to France.

Bramber had a colourful history; pitched battles were fought in the street between tariff-collectors and ships' crews during the 11th and 12th centuries, the Knights Templars owned the Chapel House (now part of St Mary's) until they were ruthlessly suppressed for 'unlawful acts and gross immorality' in 1312, and the Benedictine Order which succeeded them was also accused of much the same charges in 1539. Finally in the era of the 'rotten boroughs' Bramber was described as the 'most rotten' - with eighteen voters returning two MPs! Things are distinctly quieter nowadays; the village has a unique little museum, **The House of Pipes**, devoted to what could best be   described as 'Smokiana' and an excellent hotel and restaurant, **The Old Tollgate**, which cleverly combines old and new in an attractive setting.

The vagaries of the sea which turned Steyning into a market town were to benefit **Shoreham**, a town that is a thriving port and with a history stretching back to Roman times. The modern part of Shoreham harbour is an enclosed dock, the largest between Southampton and Dover handling a tonnage nearly as great as the latter. Shoreham itself, a friendly and busy town, is on the western edge of the harbour by the mouth of the Adur, an area popular with small boats and sailing dinghies. Shoreham Harbour is a recent innovation; the old port was on the eastern side of the estuary and was of major importance from Saxon times until around the beginning of the 15th century. The little port saw great military expeditions setting out for the French wars whilst trade with that same country continued. From an historical point of view, this has been an almost continuous process; in 1347, soldiers left from here to capture Calais and throughout the centuries, the campaigns continued, culminating in the D-Day invasion in 1944. Hopefully, this process is now at an end although the trading aspect still continues and it is worth noting that one of the   principal imports in the 14th century was wine - a commodity still brought into Shoreham to this day.

Several places worth taking a look at are **Ashurst**, an unspoilt village surrounded by half timbered and tile hung farms. **Littleworth** has the restored **King's Mill**, which lies some three miles to the west. Once belonging to Hilaire Belloc, it was rebuilt in 1957 and now houses an exhibition of his life and work. Close by is the sporting and hospitable **Windmill Inn**, once three cottages built for the miller's assistants.

To the south lies another ruin, **Knepp Castle**, built by the Broase family from Bramber in the 11th century. A new, and private castle was built by John Nash in 1809. **West Grinstead** should not be confused with its larger, but far distant relation East Grinstead. They lie some 17 miles apart and whereas **East Grinstead** is a town, West Grinstead is little more than a hamlet. The great house of West Grinstead Park was demolished many years ago, but the battlemented stables, once headquarters of the   National Stud can still be seen. The real attraction of the village is the Church of St George, tucked away at the end of a lane overlooking the river. Once again the homely exterior belies the treasures inside. There are several brasses, one to a knight who fought at Agincourt, and a number of classical-style monuments. The pews have the names of local farms carved on them and there is a large scale parish map showing where these lie; the names are redolent of the Wealden countryside, Priors Bine, Thistleworth, Hobshorts, Sunt and Figland.

The monastery of St Hugh's Charterhouse at **Cowfold**, is a huge building, home to the white-robed Carthusians, who live a strict and contemplative life. The building can be glimpsed amongst the trees just south of the village. The parish church contains a noted brass to one Thomas Nelond, Prior of Lewes in the 1420's.

Lower Beeding is separated, like the Grinsteads, from **Upper Beeding**, by several miles of countryside. Also, for some unaccountable reason, Lower Beeding is well to the north and higher than Upper! However, the real reason to visit has nothing to do with the somewhat eccentric nomenclature, but to see the wonderful gardens at **Leonardslee**. The Loder family have lived here since 1889 and have created magnificent woodland gardens within a deep valley. Streams and ponds lead the visitor past magnificent trees and shrubs, including world famous displays of rhododendrons, azaleas and camellias. Although springtime is obviously the most spectacular, the gardens are a year-round attraction with deer, and, believe-it-or-believe-it-not, wallabies living semi-wild among the trees and grassy banks.

Leonardslee takes its name from the surrounding forest of St Leonard, where the saint, a French hermit is reputed to have slain a dragon. The blood from St Leonard's wound ripped on the ground, where lilies of the-valley immediately sprang up. Later, the hermit, who must have been more than a touch grouchy, hat they disturbed his meditations. Whatever the truth, it is a fact that lilies still grow there and the nightingale is never heard.

Horsham is not unlike Chichester, in that it has a sensible arrangement of streets in the centre based on the cardinal points. The market town stands on the western edge of St Leonards Forest, and although it has become a commuter town, modernisation has not spoilt the charm to be found around the Carfax, the old centre (the word means a cross-roads), and in particular the Causeway, a delightful tree-lined street of mainly 17th century houses. **Causeway House**, a lovely late Tudor building which houses the fascinating **Horsham Museum**. In the Middle Ages, the town was renowned for the manufacture of horseshoes, crossbows and quarrels, and in the early 19th century it had a bloody reputation as an Assize town. Those who escaped the gallows were sentenced to transportation and it is a sad reflection of the times that so many place names in Australia owe their origin to this harsh penalty.

Just south of the town is **Christ's Hospital School**, and the pupils can often be seen walking around in their distinctive uniform of dark blue coat, white neck-band and yellow stockings. The dress is based on the Tudor uniform worn by those who attended the original school established by Edward IV in 1553. The school moved from London to Horsham in 1902.

The iron works that once were found all over the Weald used water to drive the bellows and trip-hammers, and many of these mill, or hammer ponds still exist. There is one at **Warnham**, a well kept village just off the A24, which was once the home of the poet Shelley, and who was reputed to have sailed model boats on the pond. **The Warnham War Museum**, outside the village on the A24, contains an impressive collection of relics and memorabilia from the two World Wars.

Ignore the bland New Town of **Crawley** and neighbouring Gatwick Airport. Noisy and busy places. It is much pleasanter to take the network of minor roads that skirt around the north of Crawley towards the Surrey border. **Charlwood** is only ten minutes away from the busy airport yet retains a pleasant and calm rural air. The Norman church has a fine chancel screen, re-coloured and gilded in 1858 and a number of memorials to the Saunders family, including a good brass of 1553. In Rosemary Lane is the 18th century village prison, a small squat brick building. Of the same period but much nicer and more welcoming, is the attractive white-painted frontage which houses the excellent Limes Bistro.

South of Crawley, close to the small community of **Handcross**, are the lovely National Trust Gardens at **Nymans**. These are a whole series of quite different gardens set in 30 acres around the gaunt but romantic shell of a burnt-out house. The gardens are both formal and informal yet not in the least overpowering; Nymans has been described as a domestic garden on a grand scale rather than a grand garden on a domestic scale. Without a doubt, this is a truly Sussex garden.

Place names are often a delight; the Saxon word of 'Cucufelda', meaning a field full of cuckoos, is said to be the origination of **Cuckfield**, a friendly village on the western outskirts of **Haywards Heath**. The two communities have a common link in that their prosperity was based on transport; Cuckfield was a major coaching centre and in 1828, it was recorded that over 50 coaches were passing through every day, on the London to Brighton run. Naturally, this trade employed vast numbers of people such as grooms, wheelwrights, harness makers and smiths, to say nothing of the staff employed by coaching inns, such as **The Kings Head**, a favourite of George IV then Prince of Wales, and deservedly popular to this day. Although a coach service ran until as late as the first World War, the advent of the railway in the middle of the 19th century effectively killed off this lucrative and colourful trade almost overnight. However by refusing to accommodate this new fangled innovation, Cuckfield lost the financial rewards but retained its rural charm, while nearby the hamlet of Haywards Heath rapidly expanded into the commuting and shopping centre of today.

The other community to refuse the benefits of steam was **Lindfield**, on the opposite side of Haywards Heath. Although the financial penalties must have been severe at the time, the village's loss has been Sussex's gain; this is truly picturesque, situated on a gentle slope with the village pond at the bottom and the church with its tall spire, at the top. The houses are nearly all a delight, ranging from Tudor through to Georgian. There is a wonderful story concerning the Church house, which was once a pub called the Tiger Inn; apparently the ale it served to the bellringers in 1588, triumphantly signalling the defeat of the Spanish Armada, was so strong that it caused them to crack a bell and break all the ropes.

Hickstead, is internationally famous in the equestrian world as the home of the **All England Show Jumping Ground**; the arena with its grandstand and supporting facilities is set in an attractive area just to the west of the A23 and close to the pleasant little village of **Sayers Common**.

The rear escarpment of the South Downs, the last geographical obstacle before reaching the coast is breached by the **Devil's Dyke**, where the devil is said to have tried to dig a giant ditch through the downs in order to let the sea through. His intention was to flood the lower Weald and drown the churches, but he was foiled by a woman holding a candle. The Devil, who could only work in the dark, mistook the light for the rising sun and fled.

It's well worth a diversion to the east, to skirt the hills on their northern side and to visit **Newtimber Place**. Although the busy traffic rushes by within a few hundred yards, the moated house, built in 1681, is close to perfection with mellow brick and Flint facade. The steep woodlands of Newtimber Hill, together with the dewponds, are owned and maintained by the National Trust.

The up-and-down route to the east takes one through the village of **Pycombe**, best known as a centre of the crook-maker's craft; an ornately carved shepherd's crook was once both badge of office and indispensable tool of Downland shepherds. The road to Layton takes one past some odd chimney-like structures which are just that; ventilators for the steam trains that once ran through the chalk hills. The tunnel entrance near the village is an imposing Victorian Gothic affair with turrets and battlements, with a small house actually built over the entrance itself. One cannot help feeling inhabitants must be extremely fond of railways! Clayton's other claim to fame is in the simple little village church with its marvellous wall paintings that are thought to have been created as early as 1080. They portray scenes such as the Last Judgement and the Fall of Satan, with the centre-piece of Christ in Judgement over the pre-Norman chancel arch.

High above the village stand two well-loved landmarks, a pair of windmills christened Jack and Jill. A mile or so to the east, one of the highest vantage points of the South Downs gives some wonderful views. **Ditchling Beacon** stands at 813 feet above sea-level, towering over the village of **Ditchling** that lies on the lee of the Downs. Artists such as Sir Frank Brangwyn and Eric Gill lived here and the village has some lovely buildings; the best-known being **Wing's Place**, said to have been given by Henry VIII to Anne of Cleves.

South of the Downs is truly 'Sussex by the Sea', and **Brighton**, its capital the best known and loved town in the country - although there is really nothing of Sussex about the place since the influences that created it are distinctly metropolitan in tone. Invasion, Royal patronage, scandal, outrageous architecture, culture, sport and tragedy have combined in equal parts to create a town with a history both rackety and respectable. Like the favourite aunt of fiction, Brighton is settling into quiet and prosperous middle age although a fondness for eccentric dress and garish makeup hint at lowly beginnings and a picaresque past.

Brighton owes its fame - or notoriety - to its discovery by the Prince Regent, son of George III. An aficionado of the newly invented 'dirty weekend' (A Brighton speciality in the years to come), and obviously in need of Dr Russell's glandular treatment, he instigated the construction of the **Royal Pavilion**. In this extraordinary Indo-Chinese confection he secretly married his favourite mistress Maria Fitzherbert, a Catholic. Naturally, this was in direct contravention of the Act of Succession and the Royal Marriages Act and was thus doomed to end in politic divorce; nevertheless, His Royal Highness, later George IV, set the tone for the centuries ahead.

If the Royal Pavilion was, not to put too fine a point on it, outrageous, then much of the other contemporary development was in restrained, albeit fashionable form. Great crescents and squares, in classical Regency style, were built to house the cognoscenti and their households, and the town expanded into the neighbouring borough of Hove. The popularity of Brighton grew steadily and with the advent of the railway in the 1840's the town was brought within the reach of almost everybody. Hotels and boarding houses sprang up to cater for this new trade, and the three miles of sea-front were provided with elegant wide promenades, splendid piers, amusements and fairgrounds. That great British institution, the Seaside Holiday, was now firmly established, along with that redoubtable figure, the Seaside Landlady.

The visitor is spoilt for choice; where to go and what to see? Perhaps the best plan is to establish a basecamp, and Brighton is renowned for the quality and range of its accommodation. For those wanting just bed and breakfast in the most comfortable of surroundings **The Ambassador Hotel** and **The Athina Hotel** side by side at numbers 22 and 23 New Steine, Marine Parade cannot be bettered. Owned and run by Mr and Mrs Koullas, the rooms are gracious, the breakfast excellent and there is complete freedom to come and go as you please. Within minutes on foot from the town centre, you will find masses of places to eat and prices to suit every pocket. Another excellent bed and breakfast establishment is **New Steine Hotel** at 12a New Steine, Marine Parade, beautifully run and recently refurbished and upgraded to a very high standard. The breakfast menu is diverse, generous in portions and somewhere that Vegetarians will be very happy. In Regency

Square, **The Regency Hotel**, is a Town House built as a private dwelling and still has much of the original interior. English Heritage recognises the uniqueness by granting the house a Grade II listing and by starring its beautiful interior detailing and proportions. Here you will recapture for a few moments, pride and achievement in a house once owned by Jane, Dowager Duchess of Marlborough from 1870-1886. She was the third wife of the Duke of Marlborough and a great grandmother of Sir Winston Churchill. Sit in the drawing room where as a little boy he must have met this great lady, relax on the balcony and gaze across the lawned square and out to sea at a scene which has changed little since these early days.

If you prefer the quieter and possibly more dignified Hove then the friendly **Adastral Hotel** at 8 Westbourne Villas, is the place for those who might contemplate a longer stay than just a night or two. A very informal hotel and very friendly. **The Duke Hotel** at 3, Waterloo Street stands opposite the famous church of St Andrew, now sadly closed, but one that was designed by Charles Barry who was the architect for the Houses of Parliament. This is somewhere that is always lively, where you will be greeted as a friend rather than a stranger and you would be hard to please if you did not enjoy the well presented, well-cooked food. It is presided over by the landlord, Michael Baker and his partner, Chris Dolphin. The former is a great advocate of good beer as his somewhat robust figure will confirm!

Seaford was the principal port of this area until a series of events caused the mouth of the river Ouse to be diverted to Newhaven. Now a quiet and prosperous seaside town. From Seaford Head, where there was once a Roman cemetery, there is a fine view of the Seven Sisters, the dramatic vertical chalk cliffs that mark the end of the South Downs. At their far end stands the towering bulk of **Beachy Head**; on a clear day the seaward view extends to over 60 miles from the 536 ft cliff.

Between Seaford Head and the first of the Sisters, Haven Brow, lies **Cuckmere Haven** where the meandering River Cuckmere runs into the Channel. This was a favourite haunt of those Sussex gentlemen averse to paying import duty; in particular, of the Alfriston Gang, a notorious bunch of cut-throat smugglers who terrorised the area for years. Almost hidden by the tall cliffs and with the river winding its way inland through marsh and tall reed, the Haven and surrounding area attract a wide range of flora and fauna, and 700 acres of marsh and Downland to the east of the river have been turned into the **Seven Sisters Country Park**. This includes a unique mini zoo, **The Living World**, which displays marine creatures, reptiles and insects.

Close to the river, to the north of the secluded and idyllic village of **Westdean**, is the lovely **Charleston Manor**. The house dates in parts, back to Norman times and is reputed to have been built for William the Conqueror's cup-bearer. Later additions are Tudor and Georgian with medieval dovecote. This splendid mixture is handsomely set off by a remarkable garden, created by the artist Sir Oswald Birley (1880-1952). The rich alluvial soil has been planted in terraces divided by low yew hedges to give an effect that is a delightful combination of English and European.

Some three miles further up the river valley and set amidst lush water meadows is Alfriston, once the smuggler's headquarters. Stanton Collins, the leader of the gang lived in the Market Cross Inn, otherwise known as the Smugglers Inn. By a trick of fate, he was eventually caught and sentenced to transportation - but for sheep-stealing not smuggling!

The Star Inn dates from the 15th century, when it was probably built to house pilgrims on their way to visit the shrine of St Richard at Chichester. There are some splendid medieval carvings on the timbered facade, including one of a basilisk being slain by St Michael. There is also a small **Heritage Centre** and **Blacksmith's Museum**, housed in the Old Forge in Sloe Lane.

Drusillas Park, to the north of the village, has been a favourite with families for over 60 years; a winning combination of children's zoo, gardens, workshops, amusements and restaurants. Attached to this is the rather more grown up attraction of The English Wine Centre, which has its own vineyard and museum.

Wilmington's attraction is obvious; carved into the chalkface of the downs above the village is the outline of a giant, with a staff in either hand. No one knows the origin of **The Long Man of Wilmington**, first recorded as late as 1779; it has been variously suggested that he was a Bronze Age Chieftain, or the Saxon King Harold, or even an advertisement to guide pilgrims to **Wilmington Priory**. The Priory fell on hard times well before the Dissolution and became a farmhouse which now houses a museum specialising in bygone agricultural equipment. The little church next door is overshadowed by a huge and ancient yew, which probably dates back to when the priory was completed.

At **West Firle**, **Firle Place**, a Tudor mansion extensively remodelled in the 18th century has been the home of the Gage family for 500 years. Set amongst wooded parkland beneath the 700 ft Firle Beacon, the house contains a fine collection of paintings and furniture. The family include Henry VIII's Comptroller of Calais, a Governor of Massachusetts and the importer of the greengage, and the 13th century village church has a fine family chapel, containing amongst other memorials and brasses, an exquisitely-carved alabaster memorial to Sir John and Lady Phillipa Gage, and a window by John Piper, commemorating the sixth Viscount Gage. The village pub, **The Ram Inn** dating from 1540 is well worth a visit.

North of the main road lies another handsome house, **Glynde Place**, also a mix of Tudor and Georgian architecture. The house was built for William Morley whose descendant Colonel Herbert Morley was one of the Parliamentarian judges at the trial of Charles I, although he refused to sign the death-warrant. The house contains much of interest, including collections of Bronzes, needlework and a small aviary. The small parish church is in the Wren style, not unlike a miniature version of St Paul's Covent Garden.

Glyndebourne, which was also a Morley home is world-renowned for the quality of its opera. For over 50 years, opera lovers have flocked here to listen to the music and to enjoy picnicking in full evening dress, during the long interval. This year the new Opera House, purpose built has been opened and is thrilling audiences.

There is a solid, respectable charm about Lewes with the old houses clustered around the castle on the hill, and its steep narrow streets and alleyways. **Anne of Cleves House**, Southover, once belonged to Henry VIII's 'Flanders Mare' and is an excellent place to begin a tour of the town since it is also a museum containing items of local and country life and history.

That early 'Hooray Henry' the Prince Regent, often stayed at **Southover Grange** in Keere Street and doubtless this was where the coaching wager was laid. A wager in which the Prince Regent drove a coach and four down Keere Street, a street which is narrow and precipitous.

Simon de Montford spent the night before the Battle of Lewes in prayerful vigil at the church of St Mary and St Andrew, **Fletching**. The village's name probably originated with the medieval industry of arrow making; a Fletcher is the name given to such craftsmen.

Edward Gibbon (1737-94), the historian and author of 'The Decline and Fall of the Roman Empire' spent the last months of his life staying at **Sheffield Park**. The battlemented lodge and gateway lie just across the road from the church where Gibbon is buried. The Park, landscaped by both Capability Brown and Humphrey Repton and now administered by the National Trust, was at one time as renowned for its cricket as it is for its beauty; the Australians used to play their first tour game here before Arundel became the venue and the Lord Sheffield of the day was such an enthusiast that he played on the lakes in the park when they were frozen over, and once aboard his yacht off the coast of Spitzbergen! James Wyatt built the lovely Gothic Revival house in the 1770's and it is perfectly complemented by the superb landscape with rare trees and shrubs arranged around five lakes, set at different levels and linked by cascades.

One of the finest steam railways in the country is the **Bluebell Railway** which has its southern depot, headquarters and museum close to the park entrance. Named after the flowers which grow along the entire length of the line, this famous railway has operated steam locomotives to Horsted Keynes for over thirty years, and it is a sheer delight to chuff gently through the wooded Sussex countryside.

Uckfield grew with the advent of the railway although originally it was a small village at the intersection of the London to Brighton turnpike and the more ancient pilgrim's route from Winchester to Canterbury. Framfield has a church that is long and low and built in 1288. An attractive village square with a number of pretty tile-hung houses face the church, which seems to have been lucky to survive, having been severely damaged by Ire in 1509, while the tower collapsed in 1667, and was not replaced for two centuries. According to one authority, Framfield once fielded a cricket team of 15 men whose combined ages added up to 1,000 years -sadly they could find no suitably aged opponents!

Ashdown Forest is a mere shadow of what it once was when it was a mighty blanket of woodland that filled the valley between the North and South Downs. In the three heather thatched wooden barns of the **Ashdown Forest Centre** at **Wych Cross**, you can learn all about its history and see what is going on in conservation work alongside the natural process of regeneration.

In the old days the area was favoured by outlaws such as cut-throats, highwaymen and of course, smugglers. **West Hoathly**, high on the ridge at the westernmost end of the forest, and once a centre of the iron industry, was a great favourite of the unofficial import brigade.

Sensibly **The Cat Inn**, was their headquarters and the church tower, their look-out post. The 15th century **Priest's House**, with its roof of massive Horsham stone, is now a museum, and a fine Norman church and manor face each other across the street. With proper Sussex contempt for geographical exactitude, East Hoathly is some 15 miles to the south.....

Across the border with Surrey is the attractive Wealden village of **Lingfield** with its 15th century buildings and fine race-course. Eastwards the Sussex border runs with that of Kent, and at **Hammerwood Park** there are strong links with the capital of the United States. Benjamin Latrobe, who also designed the Capitol and the White House in Washington DC, built Hammerwood in 1792. As the name implies, Hammerwood was an iron-working community, as was the nearby village of **Cowden**. Today's visitor will find this hard to believe when gazing at the community of half timbered houses nestling amongst the hills. Nevertheless, to the west of the village are the 30 reed-fringed acres of Furnace Pond, which gives some indication of the size of the industry in times past. **The Cowden Crown**, in

Market Square, is an excellent institution; an hospitable inn and fine restaurant under the same cheerful roof.

Returning south towards the forest, the B2026 passes through the River Medway and enters the immaculate and substantial village of **Hartfield** with its weatherboarded stone, brick and tile-hung cottages. The church with a magnificent spire, acting as a landmark for miles around, has a most unusual lych-gate, half under the projecting upper floor of a fine little timber cottage.

There is something cosy and comforting about this part of Sussex, and that feeling is engendered, together with childhood memories, by the sight of a small wooden bridge over a stream; this is the bridge where Winnie-the-Pooh and Christopher Robin first dropped twigs into the water, thus inventing the immortal game of 'Pooh-sticks'. Somehow fiction becomes reality in this timeless part of the old Andredsweald.

The easternmost area of Sussex stretches along the coast from Eastbourne to Rye. It is lower lying than the country to the west, a pleasant, welcoming and varied landscape where small winding lanes take the visitor past farms, hamlets and villages which possess an almost timeless air. Deer browse in the shelter of thickets and wood, while fat fleecy sheep graze in gentle rolling pasture and ancient meadows. Well pruned orchards are laid out with military precision and, along the Kentish border, the coned towers of oast houses denote hop-growing. Although the vast majority of these buildings seem to have been converted into what an estate agent's love of abbreviation would describe as a 'des-res', the hop is still grown to flavour our ale.

If Brighton is 'London by the Sea' then **Eastbourne** is more akin to 'Bath by the Sea'; refined, elegant and restrained, it has a three mile seafront with its terraced parades and fountained gardens. In contrast to other South coast resorts, one is immediately struck by the absence on the front of shops and the more raucous form of entertainment and amusement emporiums. At night, with gardens and fountains floodlit, the effect can be breathtaking. After having seen the sweeping grandeur of the front, with the sea breaking gently on the shingle and sand beach it no longer seems unusual or incongruous that Claude Debussy should have written his greatest orchestral work, 'La Mer' while staying here in 1905. In keeping with the elegance of the town **The Lansdowne Hotel** on King Edwards Parade, offers 125 en suite rooms with every modern facility in an establishment which has been run by the same family since 1912. The hotel is a member of the Best Western Group, and meets the high standards the group require from all their members. Smaller, but nonetheless offering good old fashioned service, **Brownings Hotel** in Upperton Road has 10 en suite rooms and prides itself on the high standard of its cuisine which attracts a lot of local people. One of the most popular features of the hotel is the beautiful outdoor swimming pool.

Martello towers are to be seen from the shore road leading eastwards but at **Pevensey** there are traces of an older and greater fortification. The Saxon Shore Forts were built by the Romans and at Pevensey they constructed the fortress of Adnerida to repel the northern invaders. When the Romans departed, the Romano-British took the fortress over, but after a six month siege in AD 491, the Saxons took the castle and slaughtered every inhabitant. It is said that the Saxons never inhabited Anderida because of the savage deeds done that day and that the village was thus created. They took the name of the fortress and applied it to the vast hinterland of forest - Andreadswald, the Forest of Andred, later known as The Weald.

For such a small and seemingly insignificant community, Pevensey has had a long, important and violent history. Nearly six hundred years after the Saxon massacre, the long ships of William of Normandy loomed out of the Channel haze and grounded in the creeks and inlets of what was then a swampy natural harbour. This was the beginning of the Norman Conquest; Pevensey was where they landed and where they consolidated their position before moving on to capture Hastings and ultimately, to defeat Harold at Battle. **Pevensey Castle's** Roman curtain walls still stand, along with the 11th and 13th century gatehouse and keep.

The Pevensey Levels is the name given to the low lying area of marsh   inland from the town, once a region of shallow dykes and creeks until silting and storms filled the watery shallows. At the head of this area stands the striking shape of **Herstmonceaux Castle**, built of Flemish brick in 1440. By the time it was finished, the introduction of the cannon had made that form of medieval fortress redundant; nevertheless, it is a satisfyingly solid structure that could grace any romance involving knights in armour and damsels in distress. When it was finished it had a window for every day of the year and a chimney for every week; it was restored after decades of decay in 1913 and occupied by the Royal Observatory until recently.

Turning southwards towards the shore, **Bexhill** is the next coastal town to the east. Its history is not dissimilar to that of Eastbourne; a small village developed by the major landowner as a resort. The landowner was Lord De La Warr, who in 1885 began by building on his land that lay between the original village and the sea. Perhaps it was because it was a latecomer to the resort scene, Bexhill never achieved the size and status of its fellows and still retains something of a village atmosphere. However the town has led the way on many occasions. It had the first mixed bathing in the country in 1901 and followed this piece of daring by holding the first Motor Races in 1902. The De La Warr Pavilion is the town's best known building; a grade one listed architectural masterpiece, designed in 1933 by the German Erich Mendelsohn. Overlooking the sea, it houses an 1100 seat theatre, restaurants, bars and function rooms. In delightful contrast to the sweeping modern design are the neighbouring Edwardian designs of Marine Arcade and Marina Court Avenue, with their passing resemblance to Brighton's Royal Pavilion.

Hastings in common with other towns on this once-troubled shore, has had an epic history; a past that is not easy to divine at first sight of this cheerful and easy-going seaside resort. The town was one of the Cinque Ports, a confederation that supplied the medieval monarchs with ships and men in time of war in exchange for certain privileges, such as the right to hold their own courts and to keep the revenue from fines. The other ports were Sandwich, Dover, Romney and Hythe, all in Kent. Until the 12th century, Hastings was a rich and powerful town, but then events both natural and political conspired to drastically reduce its importance. The first was the loss of Normandy in 1204, which led to a considerable reduction in trade and the partial dismantling of the castle by King John, who feared that it might be seized by the French. Great storms during the 13th century led to the loss and silting-up of the harbour. In addition during the Hundred Years War (1338-1453), the French attacked and razed the town four times. Although Henry III restored the castle, erosion by the sea and subsequent collapse of the cliff face led to its collapse and abandonment. West Hill Cliff Railway takes the modern visitor to the top of the hill where the ruins lie. There is an audio-visual presentation called 'The 1066 Story' while nearby St Clements Caves, which honeycomb the hill, contain an entertainment entitled 'The Smuggler's Adventure'.

From the 14th century onwards smuggling, fishing and boat building appear to have been the principal occupation of the inhabitants, who managed these occupations from the unprotected shingle beach. Immediately below the East Cliff is an area known as the Stade, from the Saxon word meaning a landing place. To this day, boats are still drawn up the shingle by winch to lie alongside the extraordinary tall net-sheds. These structures date from Tudor times and were built in this odd manner for two remarkably good reasons. The small base area meant paying less ground rent, and the tall height meant that the fishermen could work out of doorways on the mast and rigging as well as the hull. The nearby fishmarket is also of historic interest; by local custom the auctioneer starts with a high price and works down, leaving the bidder just one chance to buy. Along the quaintly named Rock-a-Nore road there is also a Fisherman's Museum, Shipwreck Heritage Centre and an aquarium, the Sea-Life Centre.

To complete the story of Hastings it is important to head north-west to **Battle**, where Harold met William at what is known as the Battle of Hastings, although it actually took place some six miles from the town at Senlac Hill on October l4th 1066. After Harold's defeat, William vowed to build an abbey with the high altar on the spot where Harold fell. The abbey, dedicated to St Martin, was consecrated in 1094 and the town grew up around its walls.

The town is delightful, with a mainly Georgian High street running up from the Abbey with a number of arched entrances between buildings acting as a reminder of the days when coaches needed to pull into yards of inns.

Returning to the coast east of Hastings, the A259 takes one past the oldest windmill in Sussex, dating from 1670, at Icklesham, and on to Winchelsea, sometimes described as 'the smallest town in England'. It is really no more than a small village, although it still boasts a mayor and corporation. Peaceful and utterly charming in the late 20th century, its past is every bit as bloodthirsty and tragic as any of the ancient towns of the Sussex Shore, having been destroyed by storm, razed by French raids and de-populated by plague.

The original town, part of the Cinque Ports confederation, was set below Igham Hill on a shingle spit, and was the principal cross-Channel port. The violent storms of 1250 destroyed much of the town, and, under the direction of Edward I, a new community was built on the hill, 'where only coneys did dwell', the rabbits quickly lost possession of the area, for another storm in 1287 washed away the remainder of the old town, and construction of the new, neatly laid out in grid pattern, continued apace. However, further disasters were to strike; the French attacked Winchelsea seven times in the 14th and 15th centuries, while over the same period, the harbour was gradually silting up to the extent that the coastline today lies nearly two miles to the south of the town.

Roses and wisteria cling to the attractive remains of England's first planned town since Roman times. Although the town was never completed, the existing buildings are a delight. The Church of St Thomas the Martyr was largely destroyed in one of the French raids but what remains is wonderful; the original building was of cathedral-like proportions although all that is left is the chancel and a ruined transept.

Looking eastwards across the flats where the River Brede wanders is arguably one of the most beautiful small towns in Britain, **Rye**. Like its neighbour, it also suffered at the hands of the sea and the French but survived through a combination of good fortune and the tenaciousness of its citizens. Julius Caesar noted that they were 'fierce and hostile' and the citizens of the little town had no compunction about turning to piracy and smuggling when times were hard.

The town stands on a hill-top, now two miles from its harbour mouth. Its narrow cobbled streets probably have a greater concentration of old houses and more of the atmosphere of a l6th century town than anywhere else in the country. The waters of three rivers, the Tillingham, the Brede and the Rother combine to scour a channel through the marshy flats to the sea, and small craft can still make their way up on the tide to lie alongside the ancient wharves under the town.

Although the town is a major tourist attraction, it is still very much a working community and there is no feeling of being 'preserved in the Aspic of Time'. Rye is a market town and still retains a fishing fleet. There are boat yards, chandlers and marine engineers alongside the more obvious attractions of the antique shops and craft galleries. **The Old Borough Arms Hotel** on The Strand is situated at the foot of the famous 'Mermaid Street' where the cobbled streets of Rye begin to wind up to the Church of St Mary. A flower decked patio overlooks the bustling 'Strand' full of interesting antique centres. The River Tilling passes nearby with riverside walks to the fishing quarter, where the local catch can be bought. The hotel is a 300 year old former sailor's inn, incorporating the Rye Town wall built in the 14th century. The Borough Arms that were above the Strand Gate are now set into the hotel wall. Anyone staying in this friendly, small hotel will take away happy memories.

Rye Harbour lies some two miles south, the road going over bleak and flat countryside. Some measure of the shore's vagaries can be seen by the fact that **Camber Castle**, built in the 1530's to protect the Harbour entrance, is now stranded well inland. Rye Harbour consists of a few houses, a pub and a stark Victorian church with a tragic memorial to the crew of the lifeboat, all drowned in full view of their families earlier this century.

North of the town is **Rye Foreign**. There are two theories as to the origin of this odd name and both equally convincing since they are based on fact. The first is that the Manor of Rye was given by King Canute to the Abbey of Fecamp in Normandy. This was fine until King John lost Normandy in 1204; a legal and political wrangle then began which was not resolved until Henry III negotiated the town's return to crown governance. However, one small area was not returned - hence Rye Foreign. The other theory is that most of the French Protestant refugees, the Hugenots, who settled in Rye during the 17th century, chose to live in their own community on the edge of the town - hence Rye Foreign. Take your pick!

Just north of Rye Foreign is the pretty village of **Peasmarsh** and within it is the **Flackley Ash Hotel and Restaurant** with its 5 acres of beautiful grounds. It is just the place for a restful break. The staff will cosset you with good food and wines and send you home relaxed and refreshed.

There are many pretty villages around to discover and several interesting historical buildings including **Bateman's** at **Burwash**, an attractive village of little more than one street. Bateman's is best known for being the home of Rudyard Kipling from 1902 until his death in 1936. It contains many of his manuscripts and personal possessions. At the bottom of the lovely garden, a restored watermill grinds flour alongside a water turbine that once provided electricity for the house.

Robertsbridge is a small town on the River Rother with a large number of Wealden Hall houses, built as a result of prosperity in the 14th and early 15th century. In 1794 Horace Walpole when visiting the area, found that one of the inns was full of smugglers and another full of excise-men, and a pitched battle at nearby Silverbill resulted in victory for the smugglers and the death of a captain of dragoons.

A splendid eccentric, 'Mad Jack' Fuller, is buried in the pyramidal mausoleum in **Brightling** churchyard; he declined to be buried conventionally as he had a fear of being eaten by his relatives - 'the worms would eat me, the ducks would eat the worms and my relatives would eat the ducks.' Legend has it that he was buried sitting in an armchair, holding a bottle of claret. Far from mad he was an MP and a great benefactor, a patron of

Turner, and a builder of numerous follies, such as to alleviate unemployment. An exception is the conical Sugar Loaf at **Dallington**. The story goes that Fuller, over a good dinner, bet a substantial sum of money that he could see the distinctive spire of Dallington church from his home at Brightling. On returning home from the meal, he found to his consternation that he was wrong; he immediately summoned help and had the folly built overnight in a field, so that, from a distance it resembled the tip of a spire!

Finally to **Hailsham** where the cattle market once attracted drovers from as far away as Wales, and is still one of the most important in Sussex. A couple of miles to the west, **Michelham Priory** stands in beautiful grounds surrounded by a moat. Founded in 1229, the Augustinian Priory had a fairly uneventful history until it was dissolved in 1536. Two thirds of the buildings, including the church, were destroyed and the remainder, together with the estate, became a large working farm belonging to the Pelham and Sackville families. Now the buildings belong to the Sussex Archaeological Society and are run as a fascinating and lively museum with numerous events being held in and around the Priory and its grounds. There are displays of crafts and separate museums related to skills such as that of the wheelwright, locksmith and rope-maker. The last named is an industry still continued in Hailsham, which also made the special ropes used for executions.

Perhaps one of these gruesome products dispatched the evil Lord Dacre who murdered a gamekeeper at Hellingly in 1541. He was hung at Tyburn after Henry VIII refused his pleas for clemency. The evil deed occurred close to the magnificent **Horselunges Manor**, a moated timber-framed manor house built in the late 15th century. The unusual name is thought to be a corruption of two of the original owners, Herst and Lyngyver.

The pretty little village has a Saxon churchyard, probably dating from the 8th century, although the church was built much later, around 1190. Appropriately for a village whose appearance and history represents much that is best about Sussex, the village inn bears the name of the county's heraldic bird, **The Golden Martlet**.

WHITE BARN

Crede Lane, Bosham,
West Sussex PO18 8NX
Tel: 01243 573113 Fax: 01243 573113

The village of Bosham, to the local people is pronounced 'Bozzum', is very attractive with lovely cottages topped with thatch, little lanes to stroll along and all surrounded by creeks belonging to the harbour of Chichester. Sailors will be in their element as sailing and boating are the main pastimes. In the Saxon church of Holy Trinity there is a copy of the panel of The Bayeux tapestry featuring the church, and King Harold is said to have prayed here before going into the Battle of Hastings in 1066. In this idyllic setting is White Barn owned and very well run by Sue and Tony Trotman. White Barn is not actually a barn but an architecturally designed single storey house, standing in the peace, tranquillity and privacy of a former orchard, at the end of a private road. The house is very impressive with much open plan, making it light, airy and spacious. The furnishings are original in design, with lots of pine. The bedrooms have been well thought out, especially the family complex with adjoining rooms, one having twin beds the other has children's bunk beds and resembles a ships cabin. The `Honeysuckle' is a twin bedded room, and a beamed studio in the garden is another double. All these rooms are en suite with shaver points, tea and coffee making facilities, colour television and overlook the garden. The house is very warm and comfortable with a welcoming atmosphere, making it very easy to relax here. Sue and Tony are very good at making you feel at home. The sitting room has a colour television and a crackling log fire on chilly evenings, there are also leaflets and local guides to peruse so you can plan your day trips. The dining area overlooks the landscaped garden and a small patio. It is in this room you are served a sumptuous breakfast, a full English meal with all the trimmings cooked superbly on the Aga. Sue is an excellent cook and takes great care in the preparation and presentation of food, she always combines the finest ingredients creating irresistible dishes with her own individual flair. To compliment Sue's wonderful food you are more than welcome to bring you own wine. White Barn is ideally situated for visiting the surrounding area, being just 3 miles from the historic city of Chichester in one direction and to the Royal Naval port of Portsmouth, with all it has to offer in the other, with plenty to see in between; Goodwood, Arundel and of course the lovely countryside of Hampshire and West Sussex. You are assured of a wonderful warm and happy stay with super food. You couldn't ask for more.

USEFUL INFORMATION

OPEN; *All year*
CHILDREN; *Welcome, over 10 years*
CREDIT CARDS; *Mastercard/Visa*
ACCOMMODATION; *3 en suite rooms*
1 double, 1 family, 1 twin
PETS; *No*

DINING ROOM; *Excellent home-cooked fare using fresh local produce*
VEGETARIAN; *Catered for*
DISABLED ACCESS; *No*
GARDEN; *Yes*

ST ANDREW S LODGE

Chichester Road, Selsey,
Chichester, West Sussex P020 OLX
Tel: 01243 606899 Fax: 01243 607826

This family run hotel situated on the Manhood Peninsula lies 7 miles south of the ancient city of Chichester close to the sea and beaches and a short distance from the scenic South Downs. An abundance of attractions are situated within the area guaranteed to gratify visitors whatever their interests, making St Andrews Lodge the perfect base in which to establish oneself. Here you can rest assured that your every need is catered for by a friendly and caring hostess, whose aim is to provide her guests with comfort and a home from home ambience. The neat and tidy garden laid mostly to lawn is favoured with a patio area with sun lounges and garden furniture. Overlooking the garden is the very large and very restful lounge, with colour television and for those wishing to read or chat, a quiet area has been set aside. There is a cosy log fire for the winter evenings. Residents can enjoy the facilities of the small licensed bar where you may smoke, however smoking is not permitted in the bedrooms. All en suite bedrooms are well appointed with their own individual style and pretty colour co-ordinated quality soft fabrics, offering a tea and coffee tray, colour television, radio and hair dryer. There are ground floor bedrooms with wheelchair accessibility and for guests unable to manipulate the stairs. The property benefits from full central heating. There is plenty of secure car parking space. The cuisine is worthy of a special mention, dishes are creative and prepared using fresh produce. The hotel is renowned for their excellent Farmhouse Breakfasts. Prior arrangement is requested for evening meals which come highly recommended and vegetarian diets are catered for. Mrs Valma Kennedy has been awarded a 'Grade 1 Excellent Wheelchair Access' by the English Tourist Board, and '3 Crown Commended' and '4Q Selected' and one can understand why. St Andrews Lodge is well situated being close to the coast with water sports, including boating, surfing, swimming and fishing and a choice of three beaches. Golf and horse riding can also be arranged locally. Along the coast from Selsey is a 1000 acre reserve at Pagham, which is home to many species of birds, butterflies and moths. Bognor Regis still retains some of the sedate charms of years gone by and benefits from a long stretch of beach and safe bathing. Chichester is renowned for its historical interest and the Festival Theatre which presents a yearly summer season of thespian delights. Museums, country houses, fascinating villages, parks and gardens are all within easy driving distance.

USEFUL INFORMATION

OPEN; *All year*
CHILDREN; *Welcome*
CREDIT CARDS; *All except Switch*
LICENSED; *Yes*
ACCOMMODATION; *10 guest rooms*
All en suite
PETS; *Yes by arrangement*

DINING ROOM; *Delicious home-cooking.*
Evening meal by prior arrangement
Highly recommended
VEGETARIAN; *Catered for*
DISABLED ACCESS; *Excellent facilities.*
Awarded 'Grade 1 Excellent Wheelchair
Access' ETB

THE LANSDOWNE HOTEL

King Edwards Parade,
Eastbourne, East Sussex BN21 4EE
Tel: 01323 725174 Fax: 01323 739721
RAC & AA ***. AA Courtesy & Care Award 1992
RAC Merit Awards for Hospitality & Comfort 1995/96/97

Sheltered by the rolling South Downs and the towering white cliffs of Beachy Head, Eastbourne has gained an enviable reputation for its remarkably mild climate during the winter months and for the brilliance of colour in the Spring and Summer. From the foot of the lovely South Downs the uncommercialised promenades stretch for three miles towards the eastern boundaries of the resort. Eastbourne offers so much. There is an abundance of facilities for the sporting enthusiast including the Leisure Pool complex, 3 interesting 18 hole golf courses, tennis, squash and badminton courts. For those who enjoy walking the South Downs and Beachy Head (part of the Heritage Coast and an area of outstanding natural beauty). For the family, the Sovereign Centre is Eastbourne's beach palace with a wave pool, children's waterslide and squirter fountain. Bubble Pool for tiny tots and full size swimming pool. Eastbourne has an elegant pier with an amusement centre and recently the Sovereign Harbour has opened for yachting enthusiasts.

On the sea front, in a prime position, stands The Lansdowne, a traditional and privately owned hotel run by the same family since 1912. It has 122 en suite bedrooms with every modern facility including satellite TV. Here you can stay in complete comfort. All the public rooms are elegant and spacious; one lounge is entirely for non-smokers. There are 2 lifts to all floors, 2 Snooker Rooms, Games/Card rooms and 23 lock up garages as well as unrestricted parking in front and at the side of the hotel. A small charge is made for the use of a lock up garage. 24 hour Porterage. The attractive Regency Bar is a popular meeting place especially in the evening before dining in the Devonshire Restaurant which is also open for traditional Sunday Lunch. The food is delicious and the service faultless. A comprehensive Bar and Lounge Menu is available 7 days a week. Afternoon Tea is served daily in the restful Lounges and Foyer. Ideal for a holiday at any time, The Lansdowne offers Bargain Breaks from November until May including very popular Duplicate/Rubber Bridge weekends. Golfing Holidays are available all year. Dogs are allowed in the hotel but not in the Public Rooms. The hotel, a member of the Best Western consortium of independent hotels is RAC and AA recommended and was the recipient of the AA's prestigious 'Courtesy and Care' award in 1992.

USEFUL INFORMATION

OPEN; *All year except New Year &*
the first 2 weeks in January
CHILDREN; *Under 15 sharing parents*
room accommodation free
CREDIT CARDS; *All major cards*
LICENSED; *Full On Licence*
Extensive wine list from around the world
ACCOMMODATION; *122 en suite bedrooms*

RESTAURANT; *High standard*
Delicious. Open to non-residents
BAR FOOD; *Excellent Bar & Lounge menu*
VEGETARIAN; *Dish of the day*
DISABLED ACCESS; *Yes. 2 Lifts to all floors*
GARDEN; *No*

STREET FARM

Lower Street,
Fittleworth,
West Sussex RH2O lEN

Tel: 01798 865885 Fax: 01798 865870

All the family welcome you to Street Farm including 'Galahad' the family retriever who is not averse to accompanying you on walks in what is some of the best walking countryside in Sussex. Street Farm was originally the barn and outbuildings of an 18th century working dairy farm and was converted in 1988/89 to a very high standard using locally quarried stone. It is a delightful establishment and since 1995 has been the family home of Martin and Joanne Sturgis. They are ably assisted by Joanne's mother Lesley who has recently returned from Port Isaac, North Cornwall, where she helped to establish another great place to stay, the 'Old School' Hotel in conjunction with Mike Warner who commutes between the two establishments. There are only three guest rooms, all of which are en suite, attractively furnished and have colour televisions as well as beverage trays. It is hard to believe that these rooms used to be the old 'Pig Sty', and the Dining Room where you will be served a delicious full English breakfast, is where the milk was once stored. The Sturgis's will hastily assure you that the pigs are long gone and the milk is safely stored in a fridge! This is a very easy going household and you can virtually have breakfast when you like providing you have arranged it the night before. Normally the meal is served between 8.30 and 9.00am. There are no evening meals but this does not present a problem, there is a wide selection of excellent pubs and restaurants both in the village and the surrounding area. If you would like to take a picnic with you when you set off for the day simply discuss it with Joanne or Lesley the day before. If you want any help in planning your outings, they will gladly help you and even arrange a tour to your own requirements. There are plenty of maps and information available to help you make the most of this part of Sussex with its wealth of places to visit.

USEFUL INFORMATION

OPEN; *All year*
CHILDREN; *Welcome*
CREDIT CARDS; *None taken*
LICENSED; *No*
ACCOMMODATION; *2dbl 1tw all en suite*
PETS; *No*

DINING ROOM; *Full English breakfast*
No evening meals
VEGETARIAN; *Yes & special diets*
DISABLED ACCESS; *Not suitable*
GARDEN; *Yes*

THE CROWN
Edinburgh Square,
Midhurst,
West Sussex GU29 9NL

Tel: 01730 813462

Daria Stevens, who with her husband Paul are the landlords of this unusual and very beautiful 16th century hostelry, will tell you that she regards the bar to be an extension of her front room, where she entertains people. This warm and welcoming atmosphere pervades the whole of The Crown Inn at Midhurst. In the summer the outside of the inn is ablaze with colourful hanging baskets and inside it is charming with low ceilings, sloping floors and two bars, one at the back and one at the front. It is definitely a true pub where local and other people from further afield gather to enjoy the ambiance, the Real Ales for which it is renowned and of course the excellent food, traditional English in content and great value for money.

The Crown has a popular monthly event - a spit roast. On the first Sunday of the month a cult following enjoys either the spit roast lamb or 'a chunk in a bap'. It was started about eight years ago for a bit of fun after the fireplace had been rebuilt but it became so popular that it has remained ever since. Imagine the delicious smell that emanates from the spit as the motor turns the lamb making sure it is perfectly cooked. The slight hiss of fat hitting the smouldering fire and the crackle of the crisping skin makes ones mouth water. The biggest and most popular spit roast of the year is lunch time on New Year's day when the scene is enhanced by a local team of Morris Dancers.

Staying at The Crown is another delightful experience. It is a bit like staying in an old cottage, the three beautifully decorated and appointed rooms are in the oldest part of the inn dating from 1580. Don't expect them to be en suite - it would totally destroy the character. On Friday and Saturday nights it is a hive of activity and has a great, robust atmosphere. The Crown is a must on anyone's visiting list when in Sussex and Midhurst itself is a fascinating place with some fine old buildings and ideally situated for anyone wanting to explore the glories of the county.

USEFUL INFORMATION

OPEN; *All year*　　　　　　　**RESTAURANT;** *Not as such, eat anywhere*
CHILDREN; *By arrangement*　　**BAR FOOD;** *Popular dishes, value for money*
CREDIT CARDS; *None taken*　　**VEGETARIAN;** *Good choice*
LICENSED; *Full On*　　　　　　**DISABLED ACCESS;** *No*
ACCOMMODATION; *3 rooms*　　**PETS;** *Yes*

THE BEAR

237 Pagham Road,
Nyetimber,
Pagham,
West Sussex PO21 3QB

Tel: 01243 262157

If for no other reason you must visit The Bear at Nyetimber to take a look at the hundreds and hundreds of artefacts of all kinds that adorn every spare inch of space. It is a fascinating experience from the 1/6 scale Tiger Moth plane powered by a lawn mower engine which hangs from the Dining Room ceiling, to 2 other planes, flags, cannons, swords, model sailing ships, musical instruments and almost life size Disney etchings carved in wood and authentically painted. There is a superb print of a Roy Miller painting entitled 'Evergreen Champions' which depicts a horse racing scene and from the mass of green foliage in the trees in the background one catches sight of the faces of famous jockeys, Lester Piggot, Willie Carson, John Francombe and so on. There are too many things to mention but you can spend a long time simply enjoying them and especially enjoying the lively and extrovert landlord Bob Tomlinson and his wife Val who are all that good innkeepers should be. The atmosphere is superb, warm, relaxed and welcoming, the ale is well kept and the food delicious. In fact it is one of the nicest, true pubs in Sussex.

Val is responsible for the food and her menus are traditional English but with a definite hint of the Continent. There are always five interesting starters, succulent steaks with or without sauces, Gammon Steaks, Rosemary Lamb Cutlets, Pork Musdell and for the very hungry, Val's Challenge Grill which includes a 4oz rump steak, 3oz lamb cutlet, sausage, liver, pork escalop, burger, gammon, mushrooms, onion rings, grilled tomato and topped with fried egg, served with chips, peas and a salad garnish. There is always a choice of fish and some delicious salads as well as vegetarian meals. The Blackboard Menu has Chef's Daily Specials as well as several other interesting dishes. Whatever you choose will be beautifully presented and excellent value for money including the selection of wines.

For those wanting to stay in this great pub there are 5 guest rooms, comfortably furnished and complete with television and a generously supplied hostess tray. In the summer the Beer Garden is always popular. Nyetimber is a great base for people visiting this part of Sussex especially for those interested in nature and bird-watching. Pagham Natural Reserve is within short walking distance.

USEFUL INFORMATION

OPEN; *All year*
CHILDREN; *Welcome*
CREDIT CARDS; *All major cards*
LICENSED; *Full On*
ACCOMMODATION; *5 rooms not en suite*

RESTAURANT; *Good food, good value*
BAR FOOD; *Daily specials*
VEGETARIAN; *Always a choice*
DISABLED ACCESS; *No*
GARDEN; *Beer Garden*

THE FORGE

Splaynes Green, Fletching,
Uckfield,
East Sussex TN22 3TL

Tel: 01825 712960 Fax: 01825 713422

This is a most unusual and totally delightful house to which the owners, Stewart and Joy Partridge welcome guests into their home. They are friendly people with a charming   informality which has the virtue of making everyone immediately relaxed and at home. You will find The Forge situated on the edge of the old village of Fletching, a quiet place which encourages one to unwind and take in the splendid countryside and the invigorating fresh air that is so much a part of the Sussex scene. The garden of the house is attractively laid out and guests are welcome to enjoy its serenity.

Within its welcoming doors the rooms are elegantly and tastefully furnished with pretty drapes and a lot of pine wood. The sitting room has an attractive bay window and a full length window looks onto the garden. In the colder weather a cheering log fire burns in the grate throwing out a welcoming heat when you come in from a less than clement day. One of the great pleasures of Sussex is the ever changing scene throughout the year, making a stay at The Forge as good in summer as it is off season. The three comfortable bedrooms are all en suite and each has television and a hospitality tray. No smoking is the rule throughout the house. Breakfast is a delicious meal, freshly prepared and with several choices. No evening meals are served but there are many good eating places within easy reach. Stewart and Joy will be happy to point you in the right direction whatever your choice might be.

This part of Sussex is full of historical interest and there are several Stately Homes and Gardens within striking distance. There are castles and museums, small villages and a number of quaint old country inns which are worth visiting. The countryside pleases walkers and for golfers and others who like sporting activities, there are many sports one can enjoy.

USEFUL INFORMATION

OPEN; *All year*
CHILDREN; *Welcome*
CREDIT CARDS; *None taken*
LICENSED; *No*
ACCOMMODATION; *3 en suite*
PRIVATE PARKING

DINING ROOM; *Excellent breakfast*
VEGETARIAN; *By arrangement*
DISABLED ACCESS; *No*
GARDEN; *Yes*
PETS; *No*

450

Chapter 17

WARWICKSHIRE

INCLUDES

Chapter 17

WARWICKSHIRE
This other Eden, demi- paradise,
This fortress built by Nature for herself. . '

Those lines from Richard II conjure up images of a rural idyll and doubtless the beautiful countryside around Stratford-upon-Avon did much to inspire Warwick shire's most famous son. More than two centuries later Shakespeare's affection for his native county was to be echoed in the words of the eminent novelist, Henry James, who described Warwickshire as 'The core and centre of the English world; midmost England, unmitigated England... the genius of pastoral Britain'. James was an   American and his words have done much to encourage his fellow countrymen and women to visit this quintessentially English region. Although the late twentieth century has left its mark with evidence of industrialisation, the construction of motorways and some of the less appealing manifestations of the intensive tourist industry, there is still much of the gentle grace and beauty beloved by both men; turn off the coach-laden main roads and one can enjoy pastoral scenery little changed since the Bard's day or, turning away from a modern shopping precinct, one can delight in architectural gems that would have been equally familiar to the great playwright and his contemporaries.

Many facets of the history and culture of our 'sceptr'd isle' are inextricably bound with that of Warwickshire; great houses and estates bear witness to political power and wealth whilst enterprise and ingenuity are reflected in the industrial bases that were created within the old county boundaries in towns such as Birmingham and Coven-try. At the height of the British Empire it can be fairly said that this area at the heart of England exerted an influence out of all proportion to its size. The Empire has gone and the boundaries have been re-drawn to exclude the largest of the commercial conurbation's (now part of the newly created West Midlands) but dramatic change is not new to this gently undulating countryside which rose to greatness through war and peace yet whose humble beginnings are reflected in its earliest recorded name of Waeinewiscsr meaning 'the dairy farm by a river dam'.

If Warwickshire can be described as the heartland of England then the Avon must be its principal artery in that its waters have provided the means of irrigation, transport and power. Stratford-Upon-Avon is without doubt the central tourist attraction of the county - perhaps of the entire country. Shakespeare may be   syn-onymous with Stratford, but the town was of importance long before his birth   (reput-edly on St George's Day, 23rd April 1564) and had its beginnings as a Roman camp, and a Saxon monastic settlement. The name Stratford simply means 'a ford where the street crosses the river' and a market was first recorded in 1196. King John granted the right to hold a three-day fair in 1214 and in 1553 the town was incorporated as a borough and, regardless of Shakespeareama, Stratford is still an attractive and prosperous market town.

The central part of the town which contains its chief attractions is arranged along the north bank of the Avon with three streets running parallel to the river and three at right angles, the names being unchanged since before Shakespeare's time. The predominant style of architecture is Tudor/Jacobean half timbering, much of it genuine but with more than the occasional false facade; nevertheless the overall effect is pleasing and the town is an attraction in its own right.

Holy Trinity Church, lying beside the banks of the Avon, is an excellent place to start exploring the town for it is a dignified and graceful building that reflects both the early importance and history of the town as well as being the last resting place of England s greatest dramatist. The proportions and spaciousness are almost cathedral-like and the church was granted collegiate status by Henry V in the year of Agincourt (1415) and remained as an important theological centre until the Reformation in the l6th century. Throughout the building there are numerous memorials to many local worthies and associations and the former Lady Chapel is almost entirely given over to the Cloptons who contributed much to the growth and development of Warwickshire and to Stratford-Upon-Avon in particular. They, like many of their medieval neighbours, made their fortune from the wool-trade and Sir Hugh Clopton is doubly remembered for having built the multi-arched bridge upstream from Holy Trinity and for being a Lord Mayor of London in 1492.

William Shakespeare died at the age of fifty-two on St George's Day, April 23rd 1616 and is buried, along with his wife Anne and other members of his family, in the chancel, and every year, on the anniversary of his death, the whole area around the tomb is covered with floral tributes from all over the world. We sometimes forget how great a man he was and just how much his works are appreciated throughout the world; he would not be forgotten even if he had been buried in an unmarked grave and perhaps this is best summed up by the epitaph written by his friend and contemporary, Ben Jonson;

'Thou art a monument without a tomb,
And art alive still, while thy book doth live
And we have wits to read and praise to give'

At the age of eighteen Shakespeare married Anne Hathaway and it is believed he earned his living at this time as a schoolmaster although a year or so later after his marriage he left for London. However he was to return to Stratford at regular intervals and, with the prospering of his fortunes, he purchased **New Place** in 1597 and twelve years later settled there permanently with his family. That the house no longer exists is ascribed to the fact that a later owner, the Reverend Francis Gaskell, irritated by rating assessments and constant pestering by Shakesperean enthusiasts was moved to pull down the entire house! That there is nothing new about the pressures that can be caused by tourism is evidenced by the fact that the demolition took place in 1759. The foundations have been preserved together with a beautifully re-created Elizabethan garden. The entrance is by way of **Nash's house**, once the home of Thomas Nash who married Shakespeare's grand-daughter, and now containing what is effectively the town museum.

Quite rightly, Stratford-upon-Avon is home to the **Royal Shakespeare Theatre**. Originally known as the memorial theatre, it was designed by Miss Elizabeth Scott, a niece of the great Victorian architect Sir Gilbert Scott, and was opened by Edward, Prince of Wales in 1932. Considered controversial and innovative when first built, it stands massively beside the river and is a wonderful place to spend an evening being entertained by one of the greatest companies in the world. In the **Bancroft Gardens**, adjacent to the theatre is the impressive Shakespeare Monument, cast from sixty-five tons of bronze which shows the dramatist seated on a plinth surrounded by four of his principal characters (Hamlet, Lady Macbeth, Falstaff and Prince Hal). Also in close proximity to the Theatre are the **Other Place**, a small intimate theatre which presents a wide range of drama, and the **Black Swan Inn**, a favourite theatrical haunt that is better known as the Dirty Duck.

The town and surrounding area is naturally well-provided with pubs, hotels, restaurants and guest houses, ranging from the cheap-and-cheerful to the plush and expensive. My recommendation is **The Falcon Hotel** in Chapel Street, part of the Queens Moat House group, it is truly splendid. The friendly olde worlde charm of this 16th century Inn has been lovingly maintained, whilst having a skilfully blended extension at the rear, enabling the hotel to provide all the facilities that we 20th century visitors expect. This together with a beautiful walled garden and large private car park - almost unknown in Stratford - make the Falcon perfect for families, business people or those just wanting to get away from the pace of the city.

On the whole the town copes well with its immense number of visitors and has developed an infrastructure that operates extremely efficiently but it should be appreciated that Stratford-upon-Avon is perhaps the country's premier tourist attraction. A little planning will pay dividends in enabling you to enjoy your visit and the **Tourist Information Centre** at **Bridgefoot**, Stratford-upon-Avon (Tel: 01789 293127) can provide considerable help and advice including details of guided tours.

West Warwickshire is often referred to as Shakespeare country, providing numerous literary and historical connections, some true and some apocryphal, but one does not have to travel far from the centre of Stratford to find one of the most famous sites associated with the Bard of Avon. His wife, Anne, came from the picturesque little village of **Shottery**, now part of the modern borough of Stratford, and her family home, once called Hewland's Farm and now known as **Anne Hathaway's Cottage**, still exists. With its thatched roof, tall brick chimneys, latticed windows and half timbered construction, it stands in a most attractive old-fashioned garden complete with a mass of traditional flowers including foxgloves, hollyhocks, violets, primroses and traditional roses. The cottage (really a sizeable house) belonged to the Hathaways until 1892.

Shakespeare's mother came from a well-to-do farming family who lived at **Wilmcote**, three miles north-west of Stratford, and, to my mind, **Mary Arden's House** is the most fascinating of the properties managed by the Birthplace Trust. The farmhouse and its outbuildings contain much of interest including a fascinating collection of agricultural and rural implements.

It is only natural that stories and legends should abound with a man of Shakespeare's stature, and one of the best-known concerns the stately home of the Lucy family since 1118, **Charlecote Park**. Now in the hands of the National Trust, it was in the grounds surrounding the magnificent house that Shakespeare was reputedly caught poaching deer. The story tells that in consequence of this disgrace he was obliged to leave the neighbourhood and make his way to London, and thus to fortune. There is no evidence to support this tale although some cite the following lines from Titus Andronicus for proof of the Bard's youthful misdemeanours:

'What has thou not full often struck a doe,
And borne her cleanly by the keeper's nose?'

In 1769, the grounds were landscaped by Capability Brown and are still home to herds of red and fallow deer who peacefully graze amongst the oaks and chestnuts. Close by lies the village of **Hampton Lucy** with its handsome Gothic Revival church and cast-iron bridge over the River Avon.

If the connection of Shakespeare with Charlecote is doubtful, then it is ertain with **Snitterfield**, some three miles to the north of Stratford. Richard Shakespeare and Henry Shakespeare, grandfather and uncle, both farmed here and worshipped at the 13th century church of St James the Great. The vicar from 1751-1784 was another literary figure, the poet Richard Jago, and there is a slab to , his memory in the vestry.

Kenilworth will always haunt me because of the extraordinary and impressive sight of tall windows rising beside a massive fireplace in the ruins of the 14th century Great Hall of Kenilworth Castle. Looking at it my imagination runs riot and I see the arrival of Queen Elizabeth I and her entourage to attend a lavish banquet in her honour. The whole castle would have been alive and busy. No doubt Her Majesty and her followers would have to be housed and their individual staffs cared for. On one occasion she stayed fifteen days. Quite wonderful. You will see the red-sandstone castle keep standing foursquare on a grassy slope, aloof from the bustling market town below, serene in its own world. Though its towers are crumbling and its windows as blank as sightless eyes, it still retains the imposing strength and grandeur that made it one of England's chief strongholds in Norman times.

Approach it on foot across the causeway that leads from the car park on the south side and you will see that much of the castle's outer wall still stands. Beyond it is the Norman keep standing dignified and alone, separated from the ravages of war, time and weather from the buildings added to it in later centuries. Only the walls remain of the great banqueting hall built by John of Gaunt in the 14th century and little more of the buildings added by Robert Dudley, Earl of Leicester in the 16th century.

The castle has not been lived in since the Restoration and the best preserved parts are Dudley's gatehouse, which was designed to impress distinguished visitors and still impresses with its tall corner towers and battlemented parapets. Then there are the stables built of dressed stone with a timbered upper storey. The Roundheads held the castle during the Civil War and destroyed the keep's north wall after the war.

Below the castle in the Old High Street is the **Clarendon House Hotel** in the centre of the Kenilworth Conservation Area. Full of nooks and crannies, staircases leading from one part to the other, the hotel is full of history. The original timber framed 'Castle Tavern' is incorporated in the hotel and dates back to 1430. To this day it is still supported by the old oak tree around which it was built. For those guests who enjoy going out for an hour or so after dinner, Clarendon House is ideally situated in the centre of the old part of Kenilworth with the Castle and Abbey Fields only a short walk away. Run by very friendly people it is a fun place to stay.

Shipston-on-Stour dates from Saxon times has the flavour of other days about it. The streets are lined with houses and inns of the Georgian period built when the woollen industry made Shipston a more prosperous place than now. It is charming with weathered roofs of Cotswold tiles, quaint little dormers and handsome doorways with old brass knockers. I came here to visit the George Hotel which dates back to the 15th century and a fireplace in the Front lobby dates to 1508 - just one of the fascinating features of this well loved and cared for hotel with its welcoming bars, restaurant and rooms. Queen Victoria stayed here before she became Queen and in more recent times it has been the haunt of famous racing people actors and writers including George Bernard Shaw. Very conveniently situated, The George is 10 miles south of Stratford and 30 miles north of Oxford on the A3400, 25 miles from Cheltenham and 15 miles through Banbury from the M40. A super place to stay surrounded by picturesque villages, some within walking distance. It is only 6 miles from Chipping Camden and so convenient to the Cotswolds from Broadway to Stow, Burford up to Cirencester.

The Grand Union Canal and the River Avon make their way through Royal **Leamington Spa**, whose tree-lined avenues, river-side walks and wealth of handsomely proportioned architecture are laid out in a grid pattern. Named after the River Leam, a tributary of the Avon Leamington (or Leamington Priors as it was then known) was little more than a hamlet until the beginning of the 19th century when the fame of the curative powers of the local spring-water became more widely known. Speculators and developers created the town we see today at the most astonishing speed; some idea of the rapid development that took place may be gained from the fact that in 1801 there were 315 inhabitants and yet by 1841 there were 13,000! As the town rapidly expanded, the rich and fashionable flocked in to see and be seen, to promenade, to take the waters and indulge in entertainment's. One writer declared the town to be the 'King of Spas' and Queen Victoria, shortly after coming to the throne in 1837, granted the prefix 'Royal'. The locals must have been somewhat bemused since the original use for the salty waters was for seasoning meat and curing rabid dogs! Although the town has expanded further since the 19th century, much of the architectural interest has been retained around the centre and the original source of prosperity, the spring water can still be sampled at the **Royal Pump Room and Baths**. This elegant building designed in the classical style with a colonnade, was first opened in 1814; the waters are described as being a mild aperient (a polite word for laxative) and 'particularly recommended in cases of gout, chronic and muscular rheumatism, lumbago, sciatica, inactivity of the liver and the digestive system, anaemia, chlorosis and certain skin disorders'.

The town is blessed with many parks and gardens, perhaps the best known being the **Jephson Gardens** whose entrance lodge faces the Pump Room. Originally planned as an arboretum, these spacious gardens contain mature specimens of many unusual trees together with magnificent floral displays, a lake, and two fountains modelled on those at Hampton Court. The gardens were named after Dr Henry Jephson who did much to promote the curative effects of the waters as well as much charitable work. His consulting rooms were in the main thoroughfare, the Parade, and in the adjacent Regency Arcade, his name, together with his sensible emphasis on the importance of good dietary principles, are further remembered in the excellent and deservedly popular Jephson's Restaurant, which is open throughout the day. The Arcade is one of a number of modern shopping developments to attract visitors to Leamington. For somewhere to stay **Buckland Lodge Hotel** is the answer. This welcoming hotel has all the air of professionalism about it but at the same time radiates a totally relaxed and informal atmosphere. Two star ETB and a member of Warwick District Tourist Association and Heart of England Tourist Board, it is owned by the Chandler family who make every effort to ensure your stay is a happy one. Certainly they have a high percentage of visitors who return regularly. Not expensive and very good value for money.

I have shared just a few thoughts and places in Warwickshire with you. It is a wonderful county - enjoy it.

THE CHAMBERLAIN HOTEL
Alcester Street,
Birmingham B12 0PJ
Tel: 0121 606 9000 Fax: 0121 606 9001
E-Mail:info@chamberlain.co.uk
http://www.chamberlain.co.uk

The Chamberlain Hotel claims to be the finest value hotel in Birmingham with superb Conference and Banqueting facilities and their claim is justified. With a position in the heart of the city and 250 beautifully appointed ensuite bedrooms complete with colour television, direct dial telephone and a beverage tray and sensible charges for rooms at forty pounds a double room and thirty five for a single which includes breakfast and VAT, it is unparalleled. The Princess Helena Restaurant is elegant, the service is immaculate and the food as good as any you will get in Birmingham. All this adds up to a very special hotel but there is more - much more.

The Chamberlain's Banqueting and Conference Centre is a major part of the hotel. There are 8 Conference rooms, a multifunctional Banqueting Suite and 4 Syndicate rooms. Conveniently situated on the ground floor with natural light, the Conference Rooms are well equipped and all rates include free use of equipment from Flip-Charts to OHP & Slide Projectors, AM/PM refreshments and Vat. For example a day rate per delegate is £20.00 including VAT and a Day Conference with evening meal and overnight accommodation from £50.00 including VAT. Unbeatable prices in a superb setting. The Chamberlain Hotel also creates the perfect ambience for special occasions. Luxurious suites can accommodate from 5 to 500, ranging from formal dinners for up to 350, to an exciting choice of buffet menus tailored to your individual needs. The Chamberlain can also provide a whole package, even the ceremony, for weddings. The hotel's wedding co-ordinator will help plan the ceremony and reception, advise on photographers, cars and flowers, organise entertainment and overnight accommodation for the wedding party and their guests.

By August 1998 there will be a second Chamberlain Hotel in the city centre on the site of the former BT Regional Headquarters in Broad Street. In addition to 445 rooms, there will be 230 car parking spaces, more than any other city-based hotel and facilities including a reception area, restaurants, bar, bistro, leisure facilities and high quality meeting space. There is no doubt that it will be every bit as good as the first Chamberlain Hotel.

USEFUL INFORMATION

OPEN; *All year round*
CHILDREN; *Welcome*
CREDIT CARDS; *All major cards*
LICENSED; *Yes. Wines from*
The New World
ACCOMMODATION; *250 en suite rooms*
Conference and Banqueting Centre

PRINCESS HELENA RESTAURANT; *Superb food*
BAR FOOD; *Wide range at sensible prices*
VEGETARIAN; *Several choices*
DISABLED ACCESS; *Yes*
PETS; *Yes*

THE GRAPEVINE HOTEL

Bed and Breakfast
28 Lower Holyhead Road,
Coventry,
Warwickshire CV1 3AU

Tel: 01203 555654

THE
Grapevine
Hotel
28 Lower Holyhead Road,
off Spon Street,Coventry,
CV1 3AU,
Tel:01203 555654

The Grapevine Hotel is just a quarter of a mile from Coventry's superb, if sometimes controversial cathedral, rebuilt since it was devastated by German Bombers in World War II. It has risen in all its glories to become a tribute to the people of Coventry. Thousands of people come here year by year to take a look at it and many have found their way to The Grapevine Hotel in Lower Holyhead Road which runs off Spon Street, the medieval part of the city. The hotel stands in a quiet cul de sac offering a peaceful retreat yet not distance from all the tourist attractions.

Built in Victorian times, The Grapevine managed to survive the bombing and has all the natural elegance with which the Victorians embellished their buildings. The rooms are all spacious with high ceilings. Sensibly, the furnishing of The Grapevine has been carried out in a manner which has an understanding of Victorian times. There are flowers, plants, comfortable chairs, warm rooms and beds which ensure one has a restful night's sleep.

There are 8 bedrooms, with one twin and one double en suite. Each room is welcoming and relaxing in which you are guaranteed a good night's sleep before waking in the morning to a new and exciting day. Breakfast is a first class meal and no one will ever leave the table hungry! The staff are all welcoming and more than willing to help visitors find their way about and get the best out of any visit. There is so much to see and do in Coventry and visiting the striking cathedral is a must on anyone's itinerary.

USEFUL INFORMATION

OPEN; *All year*
CHILDREN; *Welcome*
CREDIT CARDS; *Master/Visa*
ACCOMMODATION; *8 guest rooms*
1 twin and 1 double en suite

DINING ROOM; *First class breakfast*
BAR FOOD; *Not applicable*
DISABLED ACCESS; *No*
GARDEN; *Patio for BBQ's*
PETS; *No*

CLARENDON HOUSE
Old High Street,
Kenilworth
Warwickshire CV8 1LZ
Tel: 01926 57668 Fax: 01926 50669
Freephone Reservation 0800 616883

The Old High Street in which the Clarendon House Hotel is situated is part of the Conservation Area of Kenilworth. The 4 Crown ETB hotel is five minutes walk from Kenilworth Castle and ten minutes from the town. On entering its welcoming portals it is quite an eye opener to discover how big it is and how full of history. The rich mahogany colour of wood panelling aligned with warm red carpeting gives the interior a welcoming feeling. The Restaurant and Bar dating back to 1430, are still supported by the old oak tree around which it was built. The original tavern was reputedly used as a billet and housed some of Cromwells Troops during the siege of the Castle. The Clarendon is full of atmosphere. The 30 en-suite rooms include four poster rooms and several singles. The friendly welcome of the Royalist Retreat Bar makes it a popular meeting place for locals and for visitors. In Cromwells Bistro Restaurant with its beams and low ceilings you can dine on well cooked and imaginative dishes. The menu includes many Daily Specials which are also available in the bar from 12-2pm. There are always several choices for Vegetarians. A wide ranging wine list gives one an excellent choice at reasonable prices. The Clarendon House is the perfect venue for business and leisure in the Heart of England. For those who come here to work it is useful to know that the Fieldgate Suite has conference facilities for up to 120 delegates whilst the Latimer Suite is ideal for private board meetings for up to 18 people. There is frequently live entertainment especially Jazz every Thursday evening.

USEFUL INFORMATION

OPEN; *All Year.*
CREDIT CARDS; *Visa/Master/Switch*
CHILDREN; *Allowed. No special facilities*
LICENSED; *Full On License. Good wine list*
ACCOMMODATION; *30 en-suite*
Fourposters.Singles

RESTAURANT; *Extensive menu*
BAR FOOD; *Good selection.*
Daily Specials 12-2pm
VEGETARIAN; *5 dishes daily*
DISABLED ACCESS; *No*
GARDEN; *Small Patio at rear*

BUCKLAND LODGE HOTEL

35 Avenue Road,
Leamington Spa,
Warwickshire CV31 3PG
Tel/Fax: 01926 423843/423815

Close to Leamington Spa Town Centre with its beautiful parks and gardens, elegant architecture and charming shopping malls, Buckland Lodge is ideal for those who want to enjoy this pretty town and at the same time be within easy reach of the glorious Warwickshire countryside, Stratford-upon-Avon and many other fascinating places. Buckland Lodge Hotel is situated on a wide tree lined avenue, less than 3 miles from the M40.

This welcoming hotel has all the air of professionalism about it but at the same time radiates a totally relaxed and informal atmosphere. It is sufficiently small to make sure every guest receives personal attention. Built in 1846 it is a tastefully converted detached, Victorian Villa, established in 1977 as an hotel by the Chandler family. Every bedroom has been carefully furnished, many of the rooms are en-suite and all are equipped with Colour TV, direct dial telephone and hot beverage making facilities - such a welcoming feature after a day out or late at night. Avenue Road is a quiet area and so after a peaceful nights sleep in comfortable beds you come downstairs to the attractive dining room ready to enjoy a first class full English breakfast with several choices. Evening meals are available on request. If you decide to eat in you will find the meal is home~cooked using as much fresh local produce as possible. If you are a Vegetarian you will be well catered for.

Two star ETB and a member of Warwick District Tourist Association and Heart of England Tourist Board, the Chandler family make every effort to ensure your stay is a happy one. Certainly they have a high percentage of visitors who return regularly. Not expensive and very good value for money

USEFUL INFORMATION

OPEN; *All year*
CHILDREN; *Welcome*
CREDIT CARDS; *Access/Visa/Amex Diners/JCB*
LICENSED; *Yes*
ACCOMMODATION; *Most rooms en suite*

DINING ROOM; *Full English breakfast Evening meal by arrangement*
BAR FOOD; *Not applicable*
VEGETARIAN; *Yes, welcome*
DISABLED ACCESS; *Yes, with assistance*
GARDEN; *Yes*

MELITA HOTEL,
37 Shipston Road,
Stratford-upon-Avon,
Warwickshire CV37 7LN
Tel: 01789 292432 Fax: 01789 204867

Regarded as one of the premier private hotels in Stratford-upon-Avon, Melita Hotel has everything that the visitor to this beautiful, medieval market town could wish for. Built in Victorian times as a family home, it has retained all the magnificence of the architecture of this period both inside and out and yet has sympathetically added what the travellers of today demand. It is a charming and friendly establishment which opened its doors to theatregoers and visitors from all over the world, some sixty years ago. It is elegant, efficiently and professionally run but manages to remain a family home into which the owners, Patricia and Russell Andrews welcome their guests. Their philosophy on hotel keeping is that the creatur comforts of their guests comes first whether it is in the luxury of the beautifully appointed ensuite bedrooms - (two have private facilities)or in the public rooms. Each bedroom has a generously supplied hostess tray, direct dial telephone as well as colour television. The comfortable and cosy Lounge with its 'Honesty Bar' is a great place in which to relax or in the summer months most guests are tempted to explore the award winning gardens which came out top in the 'Stratford in Bloom' competition in 1997. Breakfast is a sumptuous meal with a wide choice providing for all tastes. There are no evening meals but Stratford is blessed with any number of excellent restaurants, inns, etc which cater for everyone.

You will find Melita Hotel standing off the A3400 and very easy to find. It is a mere 200 yards from the famous medieval Clopton Bridge, spanning the River Avon and only a short stroll from the Royal Shakespeare theatres and town centre. It also has ample car parking - a rarity in Stratford. From Melita Hotel you can set out to visit exciting places like Warwick Castle, Blenheim Palace, Coventry Cathedral and the delightful tucked away villages in the Cotswolds. It is a great place to stay and the welcome is genuine.

USEFUL INFORMATION

OPEN; *All year, except 10 days at Xmas*
CHILDREN; *Welcome*
CREDIT CARDS; *All except Diners*
LICENSED; *Yes*
ACCOMMODATION; *10 en suite rooms + 2 with private facilities*

AMPLE ON SITE PARKING

DINING ROOM; *Excellent breakfast*
VEGETARIAN; *Yes*
DISABLED ACCESS; *Not really*
PETS; *By arrangement*
GARDEN; *Award winning*

Chapter 18

YORKSHIRE, COUNTY DURHAM, CLEVELAND & NEWCASTLE

INCLUDES

Chapter 18

YORKSHIRE, COUNTY DURHAM, CLEVELAND & NEWCASTLE

Whatever you want from a holiday, you will find it in Yorkshire, a region with a unique mixture of history, beautiful countryside and coastline, lively cities and a host of different activities.

For glorious countryside, the scenery of the Yorkshire Dales is difficult to beat. Miles upon miles of National Park with a stunning landscape which includes high peaks and sleepy valleys, pretty villages and bustling market towns, as well as great castles like Middleham and Castle Bolton. More unspoilt beauty can be found in the forests, hills and vales of the North York Moors National Park, with heather covered moorland stretching from the Vale of York to the sea.

The region has 120 miles of stunning coastline to discover. Full of character and individuality, it has a very special charm of its own. Cliffs, coves and sandy beaches overlook quiet fishing villages like Robin Hood's Bay and tiny Staithes, and each of the main towns of Scarborough, Whitby, Filey, Cleethorpes, and Bridlington has its own atmosphere.

The towns and cities of South and West Yorkshire make interesting destinations, their powerful industrial heritage combines with a new spirit of renovation and renewal. **Bradford** is a testimony to this, with the National Museum of Photography, Film and Television. Nearby is the Bronte village of **Haworth**, high on the Pennine Moors.

In Yorkshire you will never be bored, whichever time of the year you visit. There are many historic houses and abbeys to explore, like Harewood House near Leeds, and Fountains Abbey near Ripon, and more than 100 museums and art galleries, ranging from small folk museums to the award winning Jorvik Viking Centre in York.

Yorkshire is easy to reach from any part of the world, and once here the region offers such a wide range of things to do and see, and you can be sure of a warm welcome wherever you venture. This is only a taste of what's on offer in Yorkshire. I have chosen little pockets of this stunning county, in order to whet your appetite further but if you want more then do send for one of the very competent and instructive brochures issued by the Yorkshire and Humberside Tourist Board at 312 Tadcaster Road, York Y02 2HF. Tel: 01904 707070.

Naturally I have chosen to start with **York**. I lived here for a while on the outskirts and loved the sheer beauty of the city dominated by the majestic and magnificent York Minster. This glorious building has three times been brought to its knees by fire. The first in 1829 was started by a fanatic, Jonathon Martin, who believed he was acting on divine instructions; the second in 1840 was started simply by a careless workman who left a candle burning and the third in 1984 was witnessed around the world. The South transept roof was destroyed and the precious Rose Window badly damaged. The task of restoration was put in the hands of master craftsmen once more and now, thankfully is complete. In a delightful gesture, children were invited to suggest designs for some of the new wooden roof bosses, and a competition was run by the Blue Peter programme. The winning entries are in place and the children of the 20th century have made their contribution to the Minster's history.

There is a well documented walk around the walls of York, but it isn't unreasonable to suggest it may have once been a well documented stagger! In 1870 Walmgate for example contained 28 pubs and every other house was a brothel. There is now only one pub and that is The Spread Eagle. Needless to say, but for the sensibilities of the residents the other 'business' establishments have gone too!

There is no better way to appreciate the marvels of York than by viewing it from the medieval walls. The distance of this walk is about two and a half miles, but you would be advised to allow an afternoon to stroll at your leisure there are too many points of interest to rush. The walls are now well maintained but during the l9th century they were falling into a neglected state of disrepair. Fortunately they were saved by the endeavour of local citizens led by the York painter, William Etty. York attracts millions of visitors and perhaps for that reason it is best explored out of season when you can take the time to stand and stare without being hustled by the crowds.

From York I went to renew my acquaintance with the glorious Abbey at **Selby**. It is truly stunning - even after the majesty of York Minster. Just down the A63 from there is the tiny hamlet of **Hemingbrough**. It is very rural and has a fine l2th century church.

Harrogate has always been the Eastbourne of the north to me but in reality this busy, dignified town has a much more demanding role. It has retained its gorgeous flower beds, its discreet ambience but it has opened its doors to become one of the leading Conference venues in the whole of the country. The Spa town is known as a 'floral resort' and is beautiful.

You will obviously want to visit **The Royal Pump Room Museum**, the site of the original sulphur well. Here you can sample the spa waters as the earliest visitors did - although in much more comfortable surroundings. It also houses the History Museum. There are 200 acres of land given to the people of Harrogate under an award of 1778 known as the Stray. It was here that Tewit Well was discovered in 1571. **The Valley Gardens** are utterly lovely. Acres of floral displays lead into beautiful pinewoods with rhododendron bushes. There is a boating lake, a paddling pool, playground, tennis courts, pitch and run and a mini golf course. On Sunday afternoon in summer the band strikes up and you can sit and listen to a concert which will cost you nothing.

It would be invidious to even try to give you advice as to where to stay in Harrogate. The information is available from the well organised town and all encompassing. However I must recommend The Ruskin Hotel and Restaurant. Built in Victorian times about 1870, this most charming private hotel, set in lovely grounds in a quiet conservation area but only a few minutes walk from the centre of town and close to the famous Valley Gardens.

Knaresborough was well established centuries before its neighbour Harrogate even came into existence. Stand in the grounds of the ruined Norman and Plantagenet Castle and you will be rewarded with the most dramatic views of this fascinating town. On one side trees clothe the steep bank to enhance the prospect from the north-east slope where Knaresborough's red-roofed houses climb one above the other in a manner that reminded me of the fishing villages of Devon and Cornwall. There are attractive Georgian buildings to be seen everywhere. Their dignified doorways and elegant windows enhance every street. The cobbled market square is a visitor's paradise and has the 'Oldest Chemyst Shoppe' in England dating from 1720. You will not find a day long enough to discover all that this enchanting town has to offer.

Beside Knaresborough Castle, which you must see, is **Mother Shipton's Cave** and **The Petrifying Well,** probably England's oldest tourist attraction. Mother Shipton is England's most famous Prophetess. She lived some 500 years ago in the times of King Henry VIII and Queen Elizabeth I. She was born in a cave beside Knaresborough's mysterious Petrifying Well, delivered as lightning crackled and burned in a violent storm!

The Cave and the Well lie at the heart of the Mother Shipton estate - a relic of the Ancient Forest of Knaresborough. The beautiful riverside walks and carriage drive were classically landscaped with beech trees in the 18th century. Sir Henry Slingsby's Long Walk leads you to the Cave and Well. There is an excellent children's adventure playground, picnic area and plenty of car parking. In Mother Shipton's Kitchen you will find delicious Yorkshire dishes all day long.

Sitting on the banks of the River Nidd opposite Mother Shipton's Cave and within walking distance of Knaresborough, The Yorkshire Lass is a super hostelry both for food and for somewhere to stay. Perhaps one of the nicest features of this delightful pub is the magnificent array of flowers outside with which Derek and Bridget Speirs, the landlords, win. the 'Britain in Bloom', for the area every year. The display is stunning.

I also like the 17th century, Grade II Listed, former coaching inn, Newton House Hotel in York Place which is reputed to be built from the old stones of Knaresborough Castle and to have housed prisoners en route to York. The hotel is just ten minutes from Harrogate, 20 minutes from York and 30 minutes from the Dales and five minutes from the A1 so it serves as a base for those on business and those wanting to enjoy the sights and scenery of this wonderful part of North Yorkshire.

You might take a drive along the little B6165 frequently in sight of the River Nidd, until you come to **Pateley Bridge**. This popular Nidderdale centre for walkers and bird watchers is an attractive small town with plenty going on.

The Nidderdale Museum in Pately Bridge houses a fascinating collection in what was the Victorian Workhouse. It leaves you under no illusion how difficult life was for the dales folk. **Stump Cross Caverns** on **Greenhow Hill** is an experience not to be missed. 500,000 years ago the Stump Cross area was a wilderness over which bison, reindeer, fox, wolf and wolverine roamed, preying on one another, Sealed off in the last Ice Age, the caves were not discovered until the mid 19th century. From then on exploration has yielded a richness of animal remains, the untold wonders of stalactite and stalagmite, and fossils between 30,000 and 200,000 years old. The cave is skilfully lit to enhance the underground wonders and easily reached via steps and gravel paths.

I was also impressed by what is known as 'Yorkshire's Little Switzerland' Correctly it should be called **How Stean Gorge** where the caves are just waiting to be explored.To allow children to work off some surplus energy there is a children's play area.

Within easy reach of Harrogate I visited three places. The first is **Otley** whose most famous son is Thomas Chippendale. Joseph Mallord William Turner, although born in London became a son of Otley, by adoption. Ruskin the art critic said, 'Of all his drawings, those of Yorkshire have the most heart in them, the most unwearied, serious, finishing truth'. One wonders who gained most, Yorkshire or Turner. Both, I suspect. Farnley Hall today contains probably the largest private collection of Turner paintings in the world.

Otley does not need to hang on the coat tails of the famous. It is an attraction in its own right. Standing near the southern end of the beautiful Washburn Valley and on the River Wharfe, it is full of interesting buildings and an old Victorian Maypole at Cross Green, or more correctly one should say a replacement for the Victorian Maypole which was struck by lightning and replaced in 1962. None the less it carries on a tradition that is probably as old as the town itself. Otley shelters below The Chevin, an 841ft escarpment with a viewpoint at the summit. For keen 'Soap' addicts it is the 'Hotton' of Emmerdale Farm. The Chevin is much more than a backdrop for this historic market town. It is worthy of a Turner landscape and provides a wonderful area in which to wander. The rambler will find it a mini paradise, the kite flyer somewhere in which there is total freedom to enjoy this ever increasing sport. Horse riding, climbing, walking the dog, all is possible. **The White House** is the visitor centre from which you can find out all sorts of information. It has a Victorian farmhouse kitchen, a natural history display and a small shop as well for refreshments. If you are fit, a well signed path leads from the town centre to The Chevin. It is far too steep for me and I found it easier to take my car around the back and park close to what is known as 'Surprise View' from where the outlook is stunning. You look right out over Wharfedale beyond the valley to Almscliffe crag and the thickly wooded Norwood Edge.

The medieval street patterns make exploring Otley a pleasure. The town has held a market since Saxon times but the recorded history dates are Fridays and Saturdays with the addition of Tuesdays during the summer. In December Otley holds its annual Victorian Fayre when traders dress up in Victorian costumes and you can hear the sounds of a massive Victorian steam organ and children's choirs singing traditional carols. It is a wonderful occasion.

Kirkgate is the main street of Otley and here you will find The Red Lion Hotel where warm hospitality is the order of the day. It was built in the 17th century and still maintains the air of the coaching inn it once was. In Yorkgate is The Chevin Lodge Country Park Hotel. It is outstanding and very different. From the moment you arrive you will know you are in an extraordinary hotel, the combination of the woodland surroundings and the warmth of the solid log construction immediately tells you that you are in the right place. Unique in Britain the lakeside restaurant forms the centrepiece of what is the largest log building in Britain.

From Otley and Bolton Bridge there is a road on either side of the river. It is one on the east bank that I made for because it is so pretty. Much narrower than the other side but equally much quieter. I had been told by someone in The Red Lion that I should turn beyond the bridge into Weston Lane and a mile on I would see the gates of **Weston Hall**. They in themselves were impressively ornamental but it was the footpath I wanted, in order to be able to cut across a corner of the park and so get an excellent view of the Hall with its Tudor wings. The middle is 18th century - fire having destroyed the building earlier. What I was looking for was a sight of the unique glass turret which surmounts the 18th century Banqueting Hall. It certainly is extraordinary and was worth the detour.

To people not in the know one always thinks about **Ilkley** and its famous song 'On Ilkley Moor Bartat' and this does not conjure up at all what one does see in this superbly set town. There it lies in the arms of a narrow section of the valley between great curves of heather moorland, gritstone outcrop and thickly wooded hillside. It is somewhere that has attracted visitors since before the Iron Age. A quiet, pleasant place to live, it was happy to be in the backwater and leave the hustle and bustle to its sister towns of Otley and Skipton, until in the 18th century someone discovered a healing moorland spring in White Wells. The local squire, who lived across the river, saw the benefit of exploiting it and built a small bath-house to which were brought elderly patients who benefited from total immersion in the stone bath, built for that purpose. The development from this simple beginning was amazing hotels and boarding houses sprang up, and by early Victorian times, the previously quiet Ilkley was a fully fledged spa town.

The advent of the railway changed the scene once more. It became fashionable for the wool manufacturers and their senior management to live in what would now be called a commuter town. They built fine residences which can still be seen today. The incoming wealth brought other advantages. A splendid Town Hall was built and so was the Library, the Winter Gardens and Kings Hall. The Grove became the place to be seen and even today there is a sense of elegance with good dress shops, antiques and the famous coffee shop, Betty's. Behind the Grove are pedestrian areas around the small market square, beyond which is a well preserved Victorian Arcade complete with potted palms.

Ilkley is a place in which you want to abandon your car and just walk. the riverside parkland is charming. From Grove Road you can stroll gently to Heber's Ghyll, a natural wooded ravine with a stream which tumbles down from the moors, and man has built a series of footbridges. It is enchanting. Nearby Heber's Ghyll is the site of the Swastika Stone, a unique carved relic believed to have been instrumental in ritual fire worship.

Pickering almost older than time itself has records that show it was firmly established by 270BC. Today it is a lively market town with steep narrow streets climbing the hillside. Standing watch over the town above the market place is the parish church, the walls of its nave decorated with a series of remarkably vivid wall paintings, depicting the legends of the saints. It is believed to date from the 15th century.

Pickering Castle stands high above the town but it is in ruins. It has a fine motte-and-bailey with shell keep founded by William the Conqueror. The remains include later curtain walls with three towers, a keep and two halls. There is a delightful country hotel tucked away one and a half miles up a single track road at the foot of Cropton Forest and the North Yorkshire Moors. South facing, Cottage Leas Country Cottage Hotel stands in 2 acres of garden with splendid views over the Vale of Pickering. Certainly somewhere that needs to be visited to appreciate all that it offers.

A little way out of Pickering and on the edge of the North York Moors is the small village of **Sinnington** complete with a fine arched bridge and an old Rover's stone bridge as well as an ancient church and a plethora of lovely stone houses. It is somewhere that demonstrates what an English village should be. In the Main Street and totally in keeping is the Fox and Hounds Country Hotel with its friendly bars and welcoming en suite bedrooms. It is another Grade II Listed Building and in the 18th century was a thriving coaching inn on the main east Coast route to Thirsk. The date 1792 is clearly visible scratched on one of the window panes and a stone mounting block still awaits horsemen outside.

I loved **Lastingham Grange** in the village of **Lastingham**. Owned and loved by the Wood family it embodies all that is best in the way of traditional English values - good food, comfort and courteous service.

Next door in the pretty village of **Hutton-Le Hole** is the delightful **Hammer & Hand Country House.** This building, dating from 1784 was originally the village Beer House, but it would be difficult to guess its original purpose today. It is a warm, comfortable place to stay with olde world charm and superb accommodation.

Scarborough has been a holiday destination for the British tourist from as early as 1735! Today it offers a wealth of attractions for young and old making it a platform for all types of holidays from golfing to windsurfing, with beautiful gardens and excellent walking, and a variety of night-life to suit all. Midsummer finds the attraction of Scarborough Fair when you will find a multitude of entertainment and a gay time is on every street corner. One thing of note is the beautifully restored steam railway which winds its way to York from this pleasing town. There is a fascinating assortment of architecture down by the harbour where chapels, cafes and curio shops sit side by side with stands selling whelks, cockles and all types of sea life. It is an interesting place and one which should definitely be experienced.

Whitby is the stuff that fairy tales are made of. The quaint character of the town is a result of its long maritime tradition. The people built their homes as close to the harbour as possible, covering the steep valley sides on both banks of the River Esk at its mouth. The lofty ruins of **Whitby Abbey** stand guard over the narrow streets, compact houses and red rooftops nestling below. Visitors love this fascinating little town with a setting that has inspired many writers. At the bottom of the 199 steps in a very dramatic, picturesque harbour-side position, with a small sandy beach in front and an old Abbey on the cliff top immediately above, The Duke of York is a splendid pub. This is where Bram Stoker spent a great deal of time when he was writing 'Dracula' indeed he featured the sandy beach in his story. To get to the pub you have to walk the length of a narrow, cobbled street in old Whitby and you can just imagine the surreptitious way in which smugglers would have crept along with their ill-gotten gains. Whitby was the centre of much smuggling activity in times past and most of the small town seems to have had some involvement with the trade; certainly fooling and outwitting the Excise Men was one of the great pastimes. The Whitby Piers date from the time of Henry VIII, who owned much of the town. He ordered that they should be maintained at Royal expense with timber from the Royal Forests. Later in 1632 they were reconstructed in stone. It was not until 1906 that the harbour management was taken over by the town who immediately commenced adding on to their length. It was a huge task and was completed in 1914. Fortunately the German bombardment of the town by two cruisers on 16th December 1914 did them no harm although the Abbey was damaged. I was intrigued to discover that one of the features of the piers is that they line up with the North Pole. This is a result of the town, although on the east coast, facing north. It is an astonishing sight to stand on the cliffs in the middle of summer and see the sun rise and set into the sea.

The famous 199 steps accompanied by the adjacent, narrow cobbled 'donkey' road lead to the eastern cliff top and to St Mary's church which dates from 1110. It has been added to throughout its history especially to help its protection against the easterly gales. The church itself is of unusual design with its 17th century roof having been made by ships' carpenters and displaying the style of their trade. Dracula is reputed to be buried in the churchyard!

You should go to **Egton Bridge** close to Whitby in the North Yorkshire Moors. Here the pretty, creeper covered Postgate Inn, named after Father Postgate who was hung, drawn and quartered for practising Catholicism in the village. The Inn is popular with television companies, one of whom uses it for the popular 'Heartbeat' series. The first Tuesday in August is very special to the village when the famous 'Gooseberry Show' is held here.

Goathland was my next stop. The name was familiar to me because my first husband was serving in H.M.S. Goathland when I first met him back in the 1940's. The memories were happy ones and so I looked forward to my visit and intended stay there. **The Mallyan Spout Hotel** answered everything I had hoped for. Charming en suite bedrooms, friendly bars and a pleasant dining room, but above all a hospitable and friendly welcome. If you wonder at the name of the hotel; it comes from the cascading waterfall which is immediately behind it. Moorland streams cascade over rocks in several spectacular waterfalls, the best known is the 70ft high Mallyan Spout.

Sturdy grey stone houses surround the large sheep-grazed greens of the scattered village which is a popular starting point for walks on the North York Moors. More recently Goathland is yet another place that has acquired fame because, in this case, it is the village at the heart of the 'Heartbeat' television series, which is one of my favourites.

There is a little village tucked away, close to Danby on the River Esk which I like. **Ainthorpe** is friendly and attractive, deep in the North Yorkshire Moors and has a most welcoming pub, **The Fox and Hounds Inn**.

Way across to the East at the edge of the Yorkshire Dales I went to see **Leyburn** and **Middleham**. Taking the latter first I found myself in the smallest town in the country and one of the most beautiful, which clings to the rocky hillside with true Yorkshire determination. The river runs beneath, and above it all lies **Middleham Castle**, the childhood home of Richard III. A magnificent fortress, it lies on the edge of the enchanting scenery of the Dales with a sort of brooding acceptance of the beauty it   perceives. If you climb to the top of the massive keep you will enjoy marvellous views over Coverdale and Wensleydale. Middleham Castle is one of the largest ever built in England, The great tower contained all the main living rooms, while crowded around are later buildings - a chapel, gatehouse and chambers, built to supplement it.

The presence of the castle made Middleham one of the great seats of power in the 15th century and as you search out all the nooks and crannies of the town, you will inevitably pick up a sense of its past history and imagine what life in the castle must have been like in its heyday. With its back nestling into the original boundary wall to Middleham Castle, is the appropriately named hotel, The Richard III. It is a nice establishment and certainly relished by its resident ghost who is attached to one of the four-poster bedrooms.

The drive from Bedale along the A684 will reward you with superb scenery and a good stopping place is **Leyburn**. Five main roads meet here and it lies on a shelf on the northern side of the valley some distance from the river. Visiting Leyburn on a Friday is good fun. It is market day, full of bustle, and very colourful. It takes place in the Broad Market which received its Charter from Charles II. What it does lack is the old market cross, the bull ring and the stocks which were removed many moons ago.

For unrivalled views you will do no better than go to **The Shawl**, along a natural terrace running parallel with the valley. Somewhere along here at a place known as 'Queen's Gap', history tells us that Mary Queen of Scots was recaptured after an abortive attempt to escape from imprisonment in Bolton Castle. It is thought that The Shawl had much to do with the Ancient Britons, and implements used by pre-historic man have been discovered here.

Bolton Castle is just off the A684, four miles west of Leyburn. Seen from the valley below it looks almost intact. Its massive square towers, though crumbling away at the top, stand over 100 ft high. Many of the rooms remain roofed and you can catch glimpses of the windows glittering in the sunlight. It was built in the late 14th century as the fortress home of Richard le Scrope, Chancellor of England during the reign of Richard II.

I found it saddened me when I looked at a room in the south west tower which is known as Mary's room, and is supposed to be where this tragic Queen of Scots was imprisoned. In reality she would have been given the State Apartments in the north-west tower and certainly with a far greater degree of comfort than the prisoners in the dungeon of the north turret - a grim chamber with only one entry - a square trap through which the victims were dropped! The five storeys of this tower are now without floors and roofless.

Further west on the same road, you would come to a sign post that said **Askrigg-in-Wensleydale,** a charming village which will be familiar to anyone who watched the television series of James Herriot's 'All Creatures Great and Small'. Askrigg is the Darowby of the story and the village pub, the splendid and atmospheric Kings Arms Hotel was 'The Drovers'. Excellent food and a tremendously friendly welcome.

I came south to **Doncaster** for the sole reason of attending the races. Horse racing is a great love of mine and there are few more exciting courses than Doncaster especially for the St Ledger. Just south of the town I found the Duke William at Haxey on the A161. This pub is one of the villages favourites and offers a great deal to those wanting to stay or to eat and drink. It dates back approximately to 1730 and has been refurbished recently to provide a host of facilities in a warm and friendly atmosphere. Duke William has 6 en suite motel rooms, family owned and excellent value for money. Indeed I have to say that Yorkshire is synonymous with good value.

Another place that epitomises this is the charming **Merrils** in the nearby town of **Rotherham.** This delightful cafe and restaurant is well worth a visit to sample the delicious cooking of the proprietors. Something of a gamble for a couple who had no background in the industry, the Merrils has become a great success with its varied and innovative menu, and friendly hospitality.

Before we investigate the fascinating place that is **County Durham**, let me explain something of its history. It is unique. Separated from the rest of the country, its autonomy springs from a very troubled past. The story of the Prince Bishops of Durham starts approximately 900 years ago in Norman England. The border region of Northumberland came under constant conflict from the invading Scots and as a result was extremely difficult to administer, becoming something of a thorn in the flesh for the king. The area was too far removed from his domain in Southern England to allow sufficient control. He needed reliable representatives of this valuable land, if it were to be of any benefit. In an unprecedented move he decided to give regal power to the Bishop of Durham, thereby removing the threat of competition from the immensely powerful, hereditary Lords of the North.

With one move the Bishop of Durham became a Prince Bishop. From the role of churchman, he had to be a combined politician, funded administrator and soldier. It was this unusually homogenous role of Civil and Religious leader that he was to endure for the next eight centuries, shaping the county and founding all aspects of its rural and urban life.

The territories governed by the Prince Bishops were extensive and known as the Palatinate, consisting of lands in Northumberland including the lonely Holy Island. They stretched into North Yorkshire and of course, the central hub of Durham county. This kingdom within a kingdom, as it became known, had the authority to raise their own armies, appoint their own chancellor and Court, mint their own coins of the realm, and consequently levy taxes. They could create barons and grant charters for markets and fairs, and probably, most crucially, determine their own negotiations with the troublesome Scots.

Palatinate power reached its zenith in the 13th and 14th centuries when Bishop Anthony Bek presided over a court which mirrored that of the Monarch. With flourishing, romantic style, the Keeper of the Isle of Man and Patriarch of Jerusalem, Bek, the grand military leader and man of God, marched at the head of the army against the Scots. This is summed up by Sir Walter Scott when he wrote:

'Grey towers of Durham yetwell I love thy mixed and massive piles,
Half Church of God, half Castle against the Scots'.

The decline in the power did not begin until the 18th century, however the rights and privileges were not restored to the Crown until 1836. Even then the Palatinate courts survived until 1971 when they were finally abolished, leaving behind the wealth of unique heritage that we see today. Anyone complaining of boredom in Durham County must have had their imagination surgically removed! So diverse is this county that, in the limited room I have to write about it, I have had to select just a few places which I hope you enjoy.

The majestic sight of **Durham Cathedral** seen from a train is something never forgotten. That short glimpse fills me with delight and is for me the beginning of a love affair with the Cathedral and the City.

From the Dunholme of the Saxons and the Dureme of the Normans comes the ancient City of **Durham**. In 687, Cuthbert, Bishop of Lindisfarne and a most reverend man, died and was buried on his Holy Island. Two hundred years later the island came under the threat of Danish invasion, and the monks exhumed the miraculously preserved body of Cuthbert and fled. For a hundred years they roamed the north of England.

Eventually they came upon the naturally defensive peninsula of Durham. Their original church was replaced by the 'white church', which in turn made way for the new cathedral and shrine to St Cuthbert. The foundation stone for the new Cathedral was laid on the 11th August 1093 by William Carileph in the presence of King Malcolm of Scotland. The massive and gloriously ornate cathedral was complete in a mere forty years. In 1993 Durham celebrated the 900th anniversary of its Cathedral with visiting Archbishops, Choirs and Exhibitions in a fitting tribute to a symbol of consistency and strength. Sir Walter Scott's 'half church of God, half Castle against the Scots' rises from the banks of the River Wear and has been called the greatest and grandest Norman Church in England. From the moment you enter the North West Door with its replica of the original 12th century knocker, you will be captivated by the magic of the design. From the great piers, some plain, some ornately carved, and rib vault ceiling, the earliest in England, to the delicate beauty of James Wyatts' rose window, the delights are slowly revealed. At the west end of the nave stands Bishop Cosins marble font with its richly decorated towering canopy. After the drama of this elaborate interior it comes as quite a surprise to see the restrained simplicity of St Cuthbert's tomb. It stands on the raised feretory, surrounded by an oak screen, just a simple stone slab on the site of the medieval shrine which was destroyed at the Reformation.

There is no room for a West Door, the cathedral being on the very edge of the river. Instead huge windows allow a view over the river and flood the cathedral with light. Close to the altar is the tomb of the Venerable Bede, author, if that is not too understated a title for the great 'Ecclesiastical history'.

The cloisters are to the South of the building and are Norman and medieval in origin. They were rebuilt in the 18th century and the windows display lovely Gothic tracery. The museum can be found in what was the monks dormitory and contains many treasures including St Cuthberts's pectoral cross, removed from his coffin in 1827.

Fortunately a great many of Durham's monastic buildings have survived. The last Prince Bishop, Van Mildert, realised that after his death the Palatinate Empire would be abolished. This would result in all the powers and endowments thus far enjoyed by the Bishops and the City, would be passed to the crown. Van Mildert persuaded the Dean and Chapter to establish the University which was to receive a percentage of the Ecclesiastical funds. He also contributed £2000 per annum from his own income on the project. The Castle, home to the Prince Bishops for nearly 800 years dates from the Norman Conquest. It was to become the new home for Durham University College. Today both the Castle and Cathedral have been designated World Heritage sites.

A super way to enjoy the Cathedral is from the River Wear, there are pleasure cruisers available for hire, or if you feel energetic you can take out rowing boats. Downhill from the Castle, the narrow medieval streets merge gradually with the modern shopping developments, blending old and new successfully. Even the glass roofed ultra modern Milburngate Shopping Centre is not incongruous. Eating out in Durham is not a problem whatever your taste. There are plenty of traditional teashops selling delicious home-made cakes and a wide range of pubs and bars.

Nowhere represents the romance and the power of the Prince Bishops better than **Bishop Auckland**. Their symbols, the sword of state crossed by the Bishop's Crook and the Coronetted Mitre are to be found throughout the Bishopric and especially in their palaces at Durham and Bishop Auckland. Auckland was held in great esteem by the Bishops and was considered their favourite residence long before the gift of Durham Castle to the newly founded University in 1832, required them to make Auckland their main seat.

Standing commandingly above the River Wear, **Auckland Castle** has been a residence of the Bishops of Durham for over 800 years and is their only residence. The Gothic gatehouse was constructed for Bishop Trevor about 1750 by the amateur architect, Sir Thomas Robinson, Squire of Rokeby. The Gatehouse with its ornate pinnacles and battlements and square clock tower mounted with a large weather vane, is a fitting introduction to the castle. The broad driveway sweeps on to the park and the River Gaunless as it passes on its way to join up with the River Wear. The final stage of the drive leads through the triple arched gateway of John Wyatt's open Gothic Screen. The buildings are an astonishing mixture of seemingly disparate styles of architecture, but the size of the structure can best be felt on entering St Peter's Chapel. From the vast array of Cosins woodwork to the elaborate figured and panelled ceiling, one would assume this to be a great church, not a private chapel. At the West end of the South aisle is an imposing monument to Bishop Trevor who did more for Auckland than any other Bishop. King George II nicknamed him the beauty of holiness' and Horace Walpole 'St Durham'. He was, in his own right, Squire of Glynde in Sussex, and he had the distinction of having been enthroned by proxy in his Northern Cathedral.

Beyond the Castle stretches a rolling 800 acre deer park, with an unusual 'deer shelter' built in 1760. The public are admitted to the castle from mid-May until Mid-September on Sundays and Wednesdays in the afternoon. The chapel is also open on Thursday morning. The Park is open daily throughout the year.

Seven miles south-west of Bishop Auckland is **Raby Castle**. Herds of red and fallow deer graze in Raby's zoo acres of rolling parkland, which provides a peaceful foreground to this impressive castle's massive battlemented walls and towers. The Nevill family are responsible for building the present castle towards the end of the 14th century, and the hands of the restorers seem to have been kept away until the 18th century, by which time it had come into the possession of the Vane family who were ancestors of the present owner. It is a superb place to visit and is open to the public Easter, May and Spring Bank Holiday weekend, Saturday-Wednesday in the afternoons. May and June, Wednesday and Sunday afternoons, July September every afternoon except Saturdays, but open the Saturday of the Bank Holiday weekend.

9 miles due west of Bishop Auckland, the Forestry Commission's **Hamsterley Forest** is wonderful. The rolling moorland rises to more than 1500 feet. It is open to the public. There is a 4 mile Forest Drive or way-marked walks.

My next port of call was **Barnard Castle**. This solemn faced and imposing dinosaur of a Norman stronghold has grown from a rocky cliff above the River Tees. It is still, despite its ruined state, an awesome spectacle. The size of the building immediately tells us two things. Firstly how vital it was to be protected from the barrage of terrifying invasions and secondly the astonishing wealth which blessed the Baliol family. The Baliols built the castle in the 12th century. The foundations were laid by Bernard de Baliol, the fearless son of a Norman baron who fought alongside William the Conqueror at the Battle of Hastings. Over the following 200 years, Bernard's descendants enlarged and fortified it until it covered 7 acres and had facilities for some 800 troops. The Baliols were an important family whose influence spread far from this northern seat. Students of Baliol College, Oxford, can be grateful to the 13th century ancestors who founded their seat of education. Over the generations it was inevitable that some of the strength and power would abandon the family and the two members who became kings of Scotland did little to distinguish their careers. John de Baliol was king for only four years before abdicating after a disastrous defeat by the English in 1296. Consequently the family estates around Barnard Castle were seized by Edward I. No doubt there were mitigating circumstances but unfortunately it was John's son Edward who was to concede most of Southern Scotland to Edward III. The castle was returned to the hands of Richard III and remained in Royal possession until the Civil War of the mid 17th century. In 1569, the north of England was thrown into turmoil, and a great storm tore apart the peace of Elizabethan England. The great Catholic families resented being ruled by the Protestant Elizabeth I and in the Baronial Hall of Raby Castle began to plot her downfall, to replace her with their favoured Catholic Queen Mary of Scotland. The Steward of Barnard Castle, Sir George Bowes of Streatham held out against the rebellious Earls for eleven days. He could not however rely on the townsfolk for support and feared that the castle staff might be swayed to join the mob. In the face of possible treachery, he was forced to surrender. History records the defeat of the Earls of Northumberland and Westmorland, and the seizure of their estates by the crown. Barnard Castle was not to recover and by 1630 had become a ruin.

I imagine much of the castle's stonework has been artfully remodelled into the buildings of the town. Still today the town radiates out from the original market place established by the Baliols. At the centre stands the market cross. This impressive eight-sided stone pavilion was built in 1747. It is a two storey building with the cool, dark, lower floor used to sell butter and other dairy produce, while on the top floor was housed the local courtroom. The weather vane on the roof is punctured by two bullet holes. These are the result of a challenge match between a volunteer soldier and a gamekeeper in 1804. We are not told exactly what sparked it off, but the fact that they were standing outside The Turks Head when they drew their pistols, could lead those of a suspicious nature to conclude that alcohol may have been partly responsible. Anyway it was an amicable contest and when both men took aim and managed to hit the vane, the match was declared a draw. I expect they then withdrew to the public bar for a post mortem!

Also in Market Square is **Blagrave House**. Originally a private dwelling, it became an inn and is now a restaurant. Cromwell rode into the town on October 24th 1648 and according to a diarist of the time, may well have been taken to the Blagrave. The writer states 'the people of the town rode out to greet him and escort him to his lodgings, where he was served with mulled wine and shortcake'.

You will be glad to learn that Barnard Castle can offer more varied meals than Cromwells. Pubs, cafes and restaurants abound. I found the Raby Arms an excellent hostelry in which to stay. This elegant building was once the town house of Lord Barnard and is well over 300 years old. A Grade II Listed building, it has only been an inn for 100 years. It has a strong and enthusiastic local following.

The area has inspired at least two famous authors. It was the view from the ruined castle that moved Sir Walter Scott to compose his narrative poem 'Rokeby'. The much travelled Charles Dickens stayed at the Kings Head Hotel in the Market Place, while he researched Nicholas Nickleby. The hotel even has a recommendation in the novel.

A drive up the B6277 was suggested to me, and my first stop was at **Cotherstone** where the dramatic scenery that surrounds this pleasant village was reason enough to halt awhile. Cotherstone stands at the point where Balder Beck meets the River Tees. Near the watersmeet are the slight remains of a Norman castle.

The village of **Romaldkirk** lies five miles north west of Barnard Castle. It is a pretty place centred round its series of village greens, on which stand stocks and pumps, one bearing the date 1866. There is a marvellous legend surrounding the name of the village. Saint Romald, to whom the fine 12th century cruciform parish church is dedicated was the son of a Northumbrian Prince. In AD800, while heavily pregnant, his mother was forced to flee South to escape a fierce war. Legend tells us that at the moment of his birth the tiny infant cried out 'I am a Christian' and proceeded to preach a most enlightening sermon!

Romaldkirk sits on a terrace with the wild moorland behind it and the River Tees flowing through a gentle valley before it. There was once a working corn mill in the grounds of Collingwood House which is beside the 17th century Egglestone Bridge crossing the Tees. The prosperity of the town, founded on its wool and cloth trades is reflected in the splendour of the church. Within it is the tomb of Hugh FitzHenry, Lord of Bedale, Ravensworth and Cotherstone, a Knight of Edward I gravely wounded in the Kings War against Scotland in the 14th century. There are only two pubs remaining of the five which once served the village, but either will be a welcome stop before exploring the rest of this intriguing countryside.

Further up the Teesdale Valley is **Middleton in Teesdale**. The village grew in the 19th century with the expansion of the lead industry. The Headquarters of the London Lead Company were here in Middleton House, and the Bainbridge Memorial Fountain beneath its delightful cast iron canopy, is a tribute to the manager. To the west, two miles upstream the Winch Bridge was the first suspension bridge to be built in Europe.

Strong Quaker influence is evident in the no-frills orderliness of this stern little town. This is because the local lead mines, the mainstay of Middleton's economy until they were closed at the start of this century, were run by members of that denomination. The local church dates from the 19th century and shares its churchyard with various remains of a predecessor. In the Market Square, The Teesdale Hotel, is a family run, old coaching inn which has been carefully and lovingly modernised still with its fine stone-built exterior and archway which displays much olde worlde charm. Warm and friendly with super food and 10 en suite bedrooms as well as self catering cottages, you can set out from the front doorstep to walk part of the **Pennine Way** which passes through **Middleton**. There is also the new **Teesdale Way**, a long distance footpath which ends in this beautiful village. Some of Durham's most charming scenery lies within the broad Teesdale vale and none more fantastic than **High Force**, where one of England's loveliest waterfalls plunges 70ft over the menacing black cliff of the great Whin Sill, to be caught in a deep pool surrounded by shrubs and rocks. Cauldron Snout will not allow you to ignore it. This is a fantastic sight. More of a tiered cascade than a proper waterfall, it tumbles 200 ft down a natural staircase of hard dolerite rock.

The Morritt Arms Hotel at **Greta Bridge**, just outside Barnard Castle going south, is an excellent hotel. An ideal place to stay, not only to enjoy the local, spectacular scenery but also as a stopping point en route to the Lake District and the west coast of Scotland. It is an Olde 17th Century Coaching Inn, full of romanticism, unspoilt character and charm, with coal and log fires creating a traditional atmosphere which takes one back in time. Charles Dickens stayed here whilst researching 'Nicholas Nickleby'.

Perhaps you might not consider visiting **Darlington.** That would be a mistake. The extensive Roman Port at Piercebridge was built to defend Dere Street, the main eastern route for Roman soldiers as they travelled from York to Hadrian's Wall. In the fabric of this diverse town, Darlington shows its evolution. During the day there is plenty to see and there is no room for boredom in the evening either. The carefully restored Civic Theatre is acclaimed as one of the best provincial theatres in the country, and the Arts Centre offers an intoxicating programme of films, theatre, music and exhibitions. Do not let these modern attractions prevent you from appreciating the wonder of historic Darlington. Originally the Saxons established the town 900 years ago, wisely choosing a site on the banks of the River Skerne. Having survived, just about, the ravages of the Norman Conquest, the town was graced by the building of a Bishop's Palace and a new church of St Cuthbert. A huge market place was set out, in fact one of the largest in England, and this became the centrepiece for a Chartered Borough administered by the Bishop Pudsey's Bailiff.

The Market Hall and Open markets provide the focus for Darlington's shopping. Surrounding them small boutiques in characteristic 'Wynds' and modern arcades, offer a contrast to the traditional market atmosphere.

In the Covered market there are 73 stalls selling anything from a range of exotic fruits to fresh meat, fish and dairy supplies. You can find home produce, fresh herbs, or extensive delicatessens. Plus a large selection of varied goods for the home, all offered in an atmosphere of warm Northern friendliness. The Open markets have 200 stalls which open on Saturday and Monday from 9am-4pm, and a small fish market which opens on Mondays, Fridays, and Saturdays. The open markets are fascinating with something for all ages and interests. The competitive prices tempt the discerning shopper as well as the bargain hunter. From music and crafts to household goods and gardening, you are sure to find something to make you let the moths out of your purse.

There is an interesting town trail which meanders around the centre, starting in the market place, passing the old Town Hall with its famous Clock Tower designed by Alfred Waterhouse in 1864. It leads on to St Cuthbert's Church and the site of Bishop Pudsey's Palace and beyond that to the Royal Free Grammar School of Queen Elizabeth which was refounded by Charter in 1563. The school still exists today albeit on a new site, as the Queen Elizabeth Sixth Form College.

The trail ends at a footbridge over the River Skerne, which used to hold quantities of trout, pike, salmon and eel, which no doubt appeared on the menu at many feasts. The footbridge leads to Pease's Low Mill, from here it is possible to see the Clock Tower of the main line Railway Station at Bank Top which dates from 1887.

Railway enthusiasts are responsible for the **Darlington Railway Centre and Museum**. It is just one mile north of the town centre, off the A167. At a first glance you might be forgiven for thinking that the sash windows, the cream painted walls, and the elegant colonnade of Darlington's North Road Station looked more like a small country mansion than one of the world's first railway stations. Dating from 1842 when it was a place of great importance and activity, it degenerated into an unstaffed halt by the 1960's and became virtually derelict. In the nick of time it was saved by the campaigning of a group of railway enthusiasts, restored and turned into a museum commemorating the birth of the railway.

The date for the opening was 27th September 1975, 150 years to the day after the historic opening of the Stockton and Darlington railway. The railway was built to take coal from the South Durham coalfields near Shildon down to the River Tees at Stockton, via Darlington. But the railway Company soon realised that the future lay with passengers, as well as goods, and in 1833 they introduced regular steamhauled passenger trains.

The collection is built around two of the world's pioneer locomotives - the little Locomotion, built by Robert Stephenson and Company which hauled the first ever steam-train on a public railway in 1825, and the Derwent of 1845, designed by Timothy Hackworth, George Stephenson's successor as engineer to the Stockton and Darlington Railway. The so called - affectionately I may add -'Coffee Pot' which looks like a pot upended on a platform, was an efficient locomotive which hauled coal for almost a century. There are railway paintings everywhere accompanied by a wealth of photographs, posters and nameboards which hang around the walls. There are a number of detailed scale models, some built by the Darlington Rail Workshop staff in their spare time. You will learn from this museum that train speeds may have increased from the 12 miles per hour achieved by the Locomotion, but the continuity has never been broken from George Stephenson to Inter-City. It is a fascinating place and you will come away much better versed in every aspect of the railway of yesteryear, the present and a glimpse into the future. The Darlington Railway Centre and Museum is open daily throughout the year.

From Darlington it might be an idea to take a look at **The Beamish Open Air Museum** - a faithful recreation of Victorian life in the North East, amongst the many other places of interest and the spectacular countryside round and about.

Just three miles slightly north west of Darlington on the A68 is an unusual hotel, the 12th century **Walworth Castle** standing in 18 acres of lawns and wood. It is quite unique and has a long and illustrious history. Full of interesting rooms, each different, it has everything. It goes without saying that the food is wonderful and served in a superb dining room. The Farmers Bar is full of character and includes a Carvery. Walworth Castle successfully runs Conferences, takes excellent care of Weddings - the beautiful ballroom is frequently used for this and other functions. There are Murder Mystery Evenings, a full programme of special dinner parties with celebrity speakers. Hospitality has been the hallmark of Walworth Castle through the centuries and this tradition continues.

Having been born by the sea I always yearn to see it which is why I made my way from Darlington eastwards, past Middlesborough, to **Saltburn-by-the-Sea.** Victorian charm probably describes this slightly unfashionable little town. We owe its presence to Henry Pease, a Quaker and director of the Stockton and Darlington Railway. He perched himself on the 140 foot cliffs overlooking old Saltburn, a smuggling and fishing village, and contemplated how he might bring financial success to the people. He conceived the brilliant notion of building a brand new holiday resort around a railhead. His new Saltburn dates from 1861 and has served the town enormously well. I read somewhere that one miserable creature tried to deter Henry Pease by saying 'Saltburn is a very bad speculation. I live in the neighbourhood, and it is a nasty, bleak place, and the sand is horrid'. The man was so wrong. Yes, it does have bleak days like any other place, but it is captivating when the weather is fine and interesting enough to enjoy when it is not. The old railway station and the former Zetland Hotel with its yellow bricks, its terrace and its curious round central tower, are examples of the buildings that were completed under Henry Pease's grand plan. The Italian gardens are still a fine sight and would be easily recognisable to any Victorian. A little miniature railway from the seafront takes you there, and of course there is the cliff tramway and pier.

With so much Victorian heritage, it is hardly surprising to discover that Saltburn celebrates its past with a week-long summer festival every August when over 700 townsfolk dress the part and bring the Victorian era to life. You will find there are more than 60 events, culminating in a spectacular fireworks display.

In 1924 Saltburn was thrown into near financial chaos, not by its own economy but because the schooner Ovenburg, on passage from Fowey to Leith with a cargo of china clay got into difficulties and anchored in the bay. The gusting north-west wind blew up, the schooner ran aground, broke her back and demolished a section of the pier. Fortunately the people of Saltburn were not responsible for the repairs because the pier was the property of the Middlesborough Estate Company. The company decided they did not like the idea of spending £3,000 to effect the repairs and instead offered the pier and the cliff tramway together with the Italian garden to the local urban council for £15,000 - a massive sum in those days. The money was raised and Saltburn has been the proud owner of these jewels in its crown ever since. The pier, as we know, was rebuilt and has remained one of Saltburn's attractions ever since. The Cliff tramway is the oldest of its kind and just has to be visited - it links the town to one of the few remaining pleasure piers on Britain's East Coast.

You may wonder why I have chosen the unlikely named **Burnopfield** for the last place to visit whilst I am in this part of England. The answer is that it has a good pub, **The Plough Inn**, which stands 800ft above sea level from which I can see the glory of the **Cheviot Hills** on a clear day and enjoy a restful traditional pub lunch. I discovered it first when I was staying in Newcastle and had ventured into the countryside away from the hurly burly that is busy Newcastle.

THE FLANEBURG HOTEL

North Marine Road,
Flamborough, Bridlington,
East Yorkshire YO15 1LF
Tel: 01262 850284   0500 657846

The Flaneburg Hotel takes its name from the ancient name for Flamborough and whilst it was built in the first quarter of this century it stands proudly in its own grounds within the rural surroundings on the historic Flamborough headland. The hotel gleams with its white paint on the outside highlighted quite dramatically by the black shutters at each window. This Heritage Coast is superb and offers the visitor endless hours of pleasure. The Flaneburg gives you the freedom from the bustle of the nearby resorts but is still close enough for easy access to all the amenities. It is just 5 miles from Bridlington and close to uncrowded beaches and many golf courses. Right on the doorstep of the Flaneburg is North Landing with its massive white cliffs providing a natural sheltered sun trap, a sandy beach with plenty of caves at low water. Fishing trips can be arranged from the hotel. There is a Cliff top footpath from North Landing round the Headland which provides probably one of the finest walks in England. Big and Little Thornwick Bays are a geologists delight, where a natural amphitheatre has been eroded out of the white cliffs. Danes Dyke has a nature trail to an excellent beach. From the Lighthouse there are stunning views of the headland and North Sea shipping lanes and the old church of St Oswald demands to be explored.

Within the hotel you will find a warm, contented atmosphere redolent of the memories of holidays of the many people who have stayed here over the years. The public rooms are comfortably furnished and the cocktail bar and restaurant attract not only residents but local people as well. There are fourteen attractive bedrooms most of which are en suite. Each has colour TV and tea/coffee making facilities. Hair dryers and irons are available on request. The Flaneburg is well known for the high quality of its food and you will find   breakfast is a sumptuous meal which sets you up for a days exploration. At night you will return to a delicious dinner prepared by a chef who not only knows his job but loves doing it. The menu will include fresh seafood when it is available as well as other exciting dishes. Vegetarians are catered for. Non-residents will find the restaurant and bar very friendly places where you will be accorded the same welcome as the guests staying in the hotel - not always the case. The Wine List is not vast but it is very well selected with a choice of wines from France and around the world and all at sensible prices.

USEFUL INFORMATION

OPEN; *All year*
CHILDREN; *Welcome*
CREDIT CARDS; *Yes*
LICENSED; *Yes*
ACCOMMODATION;
14 mainly en-suite rooms

RESTAURANT; *Interesting menu.*
Open to Non-residents
VEGETARIAN; *Catered for*
DISABLED ACCESS; *Restaurant & bar only*
GARDEN; *Yes*
PETS; *No*

HAMMER AND HAND COUNTRY GUEST HOUSE,
Hutton-le-Hole,
North Yorkshire YO6 6UA

Tel: 01751 417300 Fax: 01751 417711

'By Hammer and Hand All Arts Do Stand' is the motto of this delightful house with its door knocker designed as a hammer and a hand wrapped around it. To stay here is a privilege. The house and its owner Ann Willis are welcoming. No one could fail to enjoy the 1784 building with its mellow York Stone and few would guess that its original role was as the village Beer House. It stands in a sheltered spot on the east side of the pretty village of Hutton-le-Hole, facing the green and beck within the North York Moors National Park. It is such a beautiful area and there is so much to do. Glorious walks and touring routes abound - Castle Howard, North York's Steam Railway, Dalby Forest Drive, to name but a few. Hutton is the home of the Ryedale Folk Museum. York and the famous coastal resorts of Scarborough and Whitby are within striking distance. All sorts of sporting activities can be arranged for you.

The interior of the house lives up to ones expectations. It contains many original features; old stone fireplaces, cruck beams, panelled doors, antique and reproduction furniture providing character accommodation and a wonderful olde worlde atmosphere. There is a comfortable sitting room with beamed ceiling and superb Georgian fireplace with an open log fire. The house makes one feel relaxed and be happy to absorb all it has to offer. The delightfully named bedrooms, The Fitzherbert, The Snug and The Hutton are all individually furnished with beautiful fittings and luxury en-suite bathrooms. Fitzherbert has an ornate King-size bed and The Hutton a double canopied bed whilst The Snug is the prettiest of country bedrooms with double sized oak bedstead. Each room has TV, Tea/coffee making facilities and hairdryers with a lot of other nice touches. Breakfast is a delicious meal of five courses served in the oak panelled Old Tap Room and Dinner is memorable with every evening becoming a great occasion.

USEFUL INFORMATION

OPEN; *All year*

CHILDREN; *By arrangement*

CREDIT CARDS; *None taken*

LICENSED; *Yes*

ACCOMMODATION; *3 en suite rooms*

DINING ROOM; *Memorable food*

VEGETARIAN; *Yes + diets by arrangement*

DISABLED ACCESS; *No*

GARDEN; *Yes with seats front & back*

PETS; *Yes*

LASTINGHAM GRANGE COUNTRY HOUSE HOTEL

Lastingham, Nr Kirkbymoorside,
York Y06 6TH
Tel: 01751 417345 or 417402 Fax: 01751 417358

To find this delightfully situated country house, leave the A170 at Kirkbymoorside and make for Hutton-le-Hole. Lastingham is a lovely old village, a peaceful backwater in the heart of the National Park and has a recorded history stretching back over 1,300years. Lastingham Grange is stone-walled and built round a courtyard. It would be hard to find a more restful place in which to spend a holiday or a short break. The gardens, like the house, are beautiful and perfectly maintained. There are ten acres with terraces, pergolas, rose beds, lawns and some magnificent specimen trees; wonderful to stroll in at anytime of the year. The road peters out at Lastingham and becomes a bridle path across the moors to Rosedale and farther afield, giving visitors perfect access to the wonderful scenery and countryside. From Lastingham Grange you can fish, play golf, walk, set off for some of the National Trust properties within easy reach, including Castle Howard. Lastingham Grange became a hotel in 1946 having been transformed in the nineteen twenties from a seventeenth century farmhouse into the gracious country house it is today. Since the nineteen fifties it has been in the hands of the Wood family whose love affair with the house has made it what it now is, a superb place to stay in which you will be cosseted, pampered and wonderfully cared for in the most unobtrusive manner. The low, welcoming entrance hall leads to a beautifully furnished long lounge with carefully chosen antiques and to an elegant dining room, both of which look onto the terrace and the rose garden beyond. The twelve bedrooms, all with private bathrooms are individually styled, luxuriously furnished and all have colour television, a hostess tray and direct dial telephones. You wake in the morning to find the only sound is the sound of the morning birdsong. The hotel is renowned for its food and whether it is breakfast or dinner, the choice is delicious and prepared using as much local produce as possible. The immaculately chosen wine list complements the food perfectly. Open to non-residents.

USEFUL INFORMATION

OPEN; *March-November inc.*
CHILDREN; *Welcome*
CREDIT CARDS; *None taken*
LICENSED; *Yes*
ACCOMMODATION; *12 en suite rooms*

DINING ROOM; *Superb menu*
VEGETARIAN; *Catered for*
DISABLED ACCESS; *Not really*
GARDEN; *10 beautiful acres*
PETS; *Yes but not in public rooms*

MERRILLS

16, Church Street,
Rotherham, South Yorkshire S60 1PD

Tel: 01709 364077

Merrills was once a Council cafe. That era has gone and now Keith and Rita Merrill have achieved a delightful Restaurant and Coffee Shop within its walls which additionally has one of the most attractive shop fronts in Rotherham. Furnished in a pleasing modern style, it is a relaxed pleasant place in which to eat whether it is for a full meal or for a quick snack. Reading the menu does not do justice to the excellence of the food. The Merrills believe strongly in traditional home-made cooking and the results are mouth-watering. Succulent hams fall from the bone, quiches burst with crisp fresh vegetables, home-made soups warm the cockles of your heart and no one can resist the high-rise cream cakes. Every day there are tasty 'Specials' at lunchtime. English fare at its very best. The reputation of Merrills has grown steadily over the years and it is sought out, not only by local people but some who come from miles around. The restaurant is licensed and is open every day from Monday to Saturday.

What makes Merrills out of the ordinary is that when Keith and Rita bought the premises in 1990, they were tackling something they had never done before. They had neither of them any catering experience but it was something they both wanted to do. Rita gave up nursing and Keith abandoned his engineering business and gave their full commitment to making Merrills succeed. Their philosophy basically was that the restaurant should be slightly upmarket and the food had to be what they would enjoy eating themselves and at sensible prices. This they have achieved superbly. All sorts of touches exist that make it a good place to eat. Simple things like sugar bowls rather than those horrid little packets, are on the tables.

The success of their party catering service is another story. They will cook and bake to order anything from Quiches to exotic desserts and deliver them to the clients door. Something that has become very popular. Together with the exciting and varied salads, two or three different quiches followed by a Strawberry Roulade, oozing with strawberries and cream, a Pavlova with fresh fruit and perhaps a Charlotte Russe, and you have a meal that will delight any guest and without you having to do any cooking at all. Wonderful way to entertain.

USEFUL INFORMATION

OPEN; *Monday-Saturday*
CHILDREN; *Welcome. Special portions*
CREDIT CARDS; *Yes*
LICENSED; *Yes*

RESTAURANT; *Excellent home-made fare*
COFFEE SHOP; *Good food, sensible prices*
VEGETARIAN; *Always a choice*
DISABLED ACCESS; *Yes*

ESPLANADE HOTEL,

Belmont Road,
Scarborough,
North Yorkshire, YO11 2AA.
Tel : 01723 360382
Fax : 01723 376137

This beautiful hotel, in its unique position on the South Cliff, commands wonderful views over Scarborough Bay and the surrounding area. Whether you are here on business or just enjoying a well deserved break, the Esplanade Hotel will cater for your every need. Concentrating on good old fashioned values and service, you will be delighted by this charming hotel and its friendly welcoming staff. Accolades include AA/RAC three star and ETB four crowns (commended), but the best must be those visitors who return again and again to stay in this peaceful haven in a charming harbour town.

There are 72 en suite rooms all attractively decorated and furnished, with full facilities of colour TV, direct dial telephones, radio alarms and hospitality trays. Each is very individual, and all are designed to aid a pleasant nights rest. A lift is available to all floors and there is a laundry service on offer. The Parlour Bar with its traditional and cosy furnishings, is the perfect place to relax and unwind after a days activities, enjoying a drink from the bar or even just a coffee. It is also open for morning coffee, bar meals and delicious cream teas. In the summer, the adjoining Roof Terrace grants an additional area where you can enjoy the breathtaking views over the harbour and bay. The Landau Restaurant is rather special with its magnificent oriel bay window where views of Scarborough, the harbour and castle compliment the fine food on offer. The intimate charm and warm ambience of this restaurant is enhanced by the friendly service and unobtrusive staff which cater to your requirements. Food is good fresh produce where possible, and vegetarians have a varied selection on offer. The restaurant is non smoking as is one of the lounges.

The Esplanade has many special breaks during the winter months, and a phone call will inform you of the offers available. It has excellent facilities for conferences, meetings and exhibitions, and hotel staff are always happy to discuss the requirements of any individual function. The professionalism and helpfulness of these experienced staff will confirm that your business or holiday requirements are in the best of hands.

Scarborough itself is the perfect place for a holiday or a short break. In addition, you are at the heart of a very unique part of the country. The Yorkshire Dales with their haunting beauty, the Heritage coast and Seascape with its bountiful walks and stunning views, Herriot country, Castle Howard (home of Brideshead Revisited), all ensure that your days can be filled with many activities, while your evenings can be spent relaxing in the splendour and warmth of a first class hotel, where the ambience and charm will delight and soothe.

USEFUL INFORMATION

OPEN; *All year*
CHILDREN; *Welcome*
PETS; *By arrangement*
LICENSED; *Full*
CREDIT CARDS; *All major*
ACCOMMODATION; *72 en suite rooms;*
21 dbl, 26 twin, 18 sgl, 7 fml.

RESTAURANT; *Quality English*
VEGETARIANS; *Catered for*
DISABLED ACCESS; *Not really*
BAR SNACKS; *Yes*
GARDEN; *Yes*

LARPOOL HALL
Whitby,

For Reservations
HF Holidays Ltd
Imperial House
Edgware Road
London
NW9 5AL
Tel. 0181 905 9558
Fax. 0181 205 0506

This exquisite Georgian Manor stands in its own grounds overlooking the beautiful Esk Valley. Once owned by Sir John Turton, physician to king George III, the present building was built by Lady Jonathan Lacey in 1796 but there has been a building on this site since the twelfth century. It has served many purposes such as an orphanage, service quarters in the Second World War, an outdoor pursuits centre, more lately returned to its delightful former glory. Today, it is a wonderful 'escape', and offers a range of walking and special interest breaks. Everything is of the utmost quality, and you will find the character and ambience of this Country House hotel enchanting.

The bedrooms are large, airy rooms with full central heating. All are en suite and offer that ever essential tea/coffee tray. They are charmingly furnished in period pine. The public rooms include Chomley Lounge, a restful, pleasing room with views over the Esk Valley, where you can relax in one of the cosy chairs enjoying a pre dinner drink, chatting and planning your next day's activities. Dales Restaurant is a beautiful setting for any meal with its 17th century fireplace and bay window. There is a good variety of vegetarian dishes on offer and special diets are easily catered for by prior arrangement.

With the recent addition of the beautiful self contained Lady Jonathan Lacey Suite, the hotel can cater for almost any occasion from that important conference to a family wedding reception or private party.

Whitby itself offers the visitor many attractions, and is a very pleasant town to wander round. Nearby is the North York Moors Railway where you can enjoy a 'steam' trip from Grosmont to Pickering, and there are lots of walks for all abilities in this area of great beauty. The magnificent York is within a car journey and Castle Howard (the setting for Brideshead Revisited) is an excellent choice for a day's excursion.

USEFUL INFORMATION

OPEN; *All year*
CHILDREN; *Welcome*
CREDIT CARDS; *All major*
ACCOMMODATION;
20 rooms en suite: 11 dbl,
5 twin, 3 sgl, 1 fml

VEGETARIANS; *Good choice*
SPECIAL DIETS; *Catered for*
PETS; *No*
LICENSED; *Full*

THE MALLYAN SPOUT HOTEL,
Goathland,
Nr. Whitby,
North Yorkshire YO22 5AN

Tel: 01947 86486 Fax: 01947 896327

Goathland is an attractive village and in an unique position on the village green is the Mallyan Spout Hotel built in 1892 to accommodate shooting parties and visitors to Goathland who came by train - Stephenson's first railway ran through Goathland and still runs today on the North York Moors Railway. For people who love outdoor pursuits and enjoy walking there can hardly be a lovelier place in Britain. The least explored North York Moors are superb all the year round but probably at their most beautiful in August and September when the richness of the purple heather adds a regal touch.

You may think the name of the hotel is unusual; it comes from the cascading waterfall immediately behind it and just a quarter of an hours walk from the hotel. Inside you will find 24 en suite bedrooms with every facility, two of which are luxury suites and look over the valley and moors. There are friendly bars, a pleasant dining room and above all an hospitable and friendly welcome from Judith and Peter Heslop and their friendly and efficient staff. Whether you stay here or merely come in for a drink and a meal you will receive excellent service.

Open to non-residents, in the dining room there is a set price for either a three or four course meal which includes a whole range of delicious dishes prepared by two loyal and long serving chefs, David Flecther and Martin Shelton, as well as á la carte dishes. In the bars there is food also of a very high standard and served daily from 12-2.30pm & 6.30-9pm. If you enjoy fish you will find that it comes fresh every day from Whitby, 10 miles away, an attractive place to visit and spend time on the beach.

USEFUL INFORMATION

OPEN; *All day, 8am-midnight*
CHILDREN; *Yes.*
Lounge only. Not under 6 years in dining room
CREDIT CARDS; *Diners/Visa/Master*
Amex/Switch
LICENSED; *Full Licence*
ACCOMMODATION; *24 en-suite rooms*

RESTAURANT; *Good, wholesome English fare*
BAR FOOD; *Freshly cooked. Wide range*
High teas
VEGETARIAN; *Yes, several dishes*
DISABLED ACCESS; *Ground floor only*
GARDEN; *Very large with patio at back*
overlooking valley and moors

SAXONVILLE HOTEL

Ladysmith Avenue,
Whitby,
North Yorkshire YO21 3HX

Freephone: 0500 334454 Fax: 01947 820523

Whitby must be one of the most fascinating and historic towns in North Yorkshire. Its winding streets and alleyways, the sea, the fishing fleet and the beaches make it an ideal place for a holiday. Situated on Whitby's West Cliff, the Saxonville Hotel has been owned and run by three generations of the Newton family since 1946 and like all well run family hotels it has a contented air about it which brings visitors back again and again. It has a two star rating with both the AA and RAC (the AA at 70% being the highest in Whitby) and is 4 Crown Commended by the English Tourist Board. The hotel has been developed from 4 town houses built about 100 years ago. It is very a comfortable place, furnished with excellent taste. First impressions are all important and when you walk in you will find the spacious Reception area has an abundance of fresh flowers and a splendid Grandfather clock which provide a welcoming atmosphere which is enhanced by the friendly, efficient staff whose sole aim is to ensure you have a happy and carefree stay.

There are 24 en suite bedrooms, comprising singles, doubles, twins and large family rooms. Decorated individually and with pretty drapes, every room has colour television, tea and coffee making facilities, radio and direct dial telephones. When you come down to breakfast in the spacious and attractive Fairfield Restaurant you will be given a breakfast that is wide in choice and delicious and certainly enough to set you up for the day. At night, the restaurant which is open to non-residents, is well known for its traditional English fare from the Table d'hôte menu and for the wide ranging À la Carte menu. Choose either and you will find both are complemented by an irresistible sweet trolley. Before and after dinner guests get into the habit of meeting in the cosy bar to enjoy a drink and a chat about the days explorations and the plans for the next day.

Whitby, as well as its own history - Captain James Cook sailed from here to change the history of the world- is surrounded by an area full of interest. There is the Captain Cook Heritage Trail, the quaint and picturesque fishing villages of Staithes and Runswick Bay. Scarborough is not far off and within an easy drive are the cities of Durham, Ripon and York and, to the North, Hardrian's Wall and the Border Country.

USEFUL INFORMATION

OPEN; *Easter to November*
CHILDREN; *Welcome*
CREDIT CARDS; *Yes. Not Diners/Amex*
LICENSED; *Yes*
ACCOMMODATION; *24 en suite rooms*

RESTAURANT; *Open to non-residents*
Renowned for its good food
VEGETARIAN; *Catered for*
DISABLED ACCESS; *No facilities*
PETS; *No*

PRUDOM HOUSE,

Goathland, Whitby,
North Yorkshire, Y022 SAN.
Tel & Fax : 01947 8%368

Situated in the charming village of Goathland, with access to some of the country's most beautiful scenery, is the lovely property of Prudom House. The original site dates back to the twelfth century, whilst the present building has been there since 1750. This old farmhouse has been renovated so that none of its character and charm has been lost, whilst also providing modern conveniences in a delightful house that exudes warmth and hospitality. The name Prudom probably derives from the French 'Prudhomme', who was one of the first settlers in Goathland, and is believed to have been hung for sheep stealing! Lew and Veronica Lewis are your hosts, and are anxious that your stay is a relaxing and happy one, and offers a level of service that ensures just that! The comfortable accommodation is furnished in a traditional English style and the six bedrooms are all en suite with hair dryers and tea/coffee facilities. The lounges are cosy and informal with open fires that invite you to sit round and chat after a day's activities, and Prudom House enjoys a residential license if you wish to partake of a little refreshment in the evenings. Breakfast is a full English meal, while the optional evening meal consists of good traditional food. For three or more nights stay, a 10% reduction is offered on the cost o£ your stay, and you are sure to want to take advantage of this offer.

Prudom House also incorporates a country style Tea Room which is open daily serving cream teas, home-made cakes and other delicacies. In addition there is a craft shop producing and selling locally made items.

Goathland is an ideal location offering great opportunities for walking and rambling on the moors and coastline. All are within easy distance, and the scenic beauty of the Moors will have you reaching for your camera to capture forever this stunning landscape. The North Yorkshire Moors Steam Railway runs right through the village and is great for enthusiasts, and those who enjoy the sights and sounds of these old trains. The picturesque fishing port of Whitby with its varied historical connections is well worth a visit, and the fine city of York is less than an hour away providing ample opportunity for those who wish to explore this medieval city.

USEFUL INFORMATION

OPEN; *March to Nov.*
TEA ROOMS & CRAFT SHOP; *10.00 - 6pm*
CHILDREN; *welcome*
PETS; *No*
CREDIT CARDS; *None taken*
ACCOMMODATION; *6 rooms en suite: 4 dbl, 1 fml, 1sgl.*

EVENING MEAL; *Traditional fayre*
VEGETARIANS; *By arrangement*
DISABLED ACCESS; *No*
GARDEN; *Large*
LICENSED; *Residential*

HOLMWOOD HOUSE

114 Holgate Road,
York,
Yorkshire YO2 4BB
Tel: + 44 01904 626183
Fax: +44 01904 670899
e-mail:holmwood.house@dial.pipex.com

By popular demand Holmwood House is strictly non-smoking. It is a friendly, relaxed establishment maintained quite beautifully and the sort of place in which having arrived, one sinks into one of the comfortable chairs in the sitting room on the ground floor, simply glad to be there and quite sure it is going to be enjoyable. Built as two houses in the middle of the 19th century, and backing on to one of the prettiest squares in York, the two listed buildings have been lovingly restored to retain this atmosphere of a private home. When you arrive you will be struck by the pretty, colourful hanging baskets adorning the walls outside and the tubs of flowers on the flagged approach. Having rung the doorbell you will be warmly greeted, politely asked to sign in, handed your bedroom and front door key. After that you are quite genuinely asked to treat the house as your home.

One of the features that makes this house so attractive is that all the rooms are different, both in decoration and size. They are charmingly appointed with pretty drapes and the beds are particularly comfortable. All the bedrooms have their own bathroom or shower-room and there are many extra touches in addition to the usual colour television, coffee and tea-making facilities, radio-alarm clock, hair dryer and direct-dial telephone.

Breakfast is superb. You are offered a choice of fruit juices; grapefruit segments and prunes; cereals, including Holmwood Houses special muesli (full of fruit and nuts); followed by a truly wide selection which includes the usual full English breakfast, kippers, fruit platter, vegetarian breakfast, hot croissants and toast, and to help the digestion, gentle classical music plays in the background. No evening meals but the range of restaurants in York is wide and covers almost all ethnic variations. For special occasions Holmwood House offers Gourmet Breaks in conjunction with one of York's top restaurants. There is a large private car park to the rear of the hotel. Leave your car here whilst you explore the city! The city walls are only 5 minutes walk away, with the National Railway Museum, the Minster, Jorvik Centre, The Shambles and many other attractions within easy walking distance. The night life offers a variety: the two fine theatres, good restaurants and country pubs. From the hotel you can set off to explore James Herriot's Dales, Castle Howard, Fountains Abbey, Rievaulx, Harewood House and Hutton-le-Hole. York has a famous racecourse and there are several golf courses.

USEFUL INFORMATION

OPEN; *All year*
CHILDREN; *Welcome*
CREDIT CARDS; *All major cards except Diners*
LICENSED; *No*
ACCOMMODATION; *11 en suite rooms*

DINING ROOM; *Superb breakfast*
No evening meal
VEGETARIAN; *Yes*
DISABLED ACCESS; *Not suitable*
PETS; *No*

Chapter 19

THE MILLENNIUM

East Anglia

East Midlands

Greater London

North

North West

South East

South West

West Midlands

Yorkshire and Humberside

Chapter 19

THE MILLENNIUM

T he era of a new age is always a momentous one, and to live through such a time is bound to be exciting and thrilling. All over the world there will be celebrations, parties, and coming together of peoples from all nations and societies. Sidney in Australia is tipped to be popular, and rumour has it that America will be producing the largest world fair ever seen, but our own fair isle is celebrating 'big time!' A great deal of money has been generated for a variety of projects and areas, and all over the country you will see the product of some wonderful ideas and schemes that will last well into the next century. Not only are we 'celebrating' but we are undertaking ventures that will generate employment, uplift areas, and encourage our tourist industry. The latter is what primarily concerns this chapter, and having mused upon this I have decided that the best way is to give you a listing of some of the events and happenings that should be in place by the year 2000, or shortly afterwards. This is by no means a full listing as we would probably have to dedicate a complete book, but I have chosen some which may be of interest.

EAST ANGLIA:

Clearwater 2000 is a really exciting project which will restore clear water and wildlife to the Barton Broads which is the second largest shallow lake in the Norfolk and Suffolk Broads. This has been ongoing since 1995 and public access is one of the many aims. There will be a Ecology Centre, Information Centre and Pleasure Island where the general public will be able to enjoy the rich wildlife and wonderful views. There will be regular boat trips and educational walks, as well as canoes and cycles for hire. Norwich itself will have a new Visitor Centre which will include a Heritage Attraction detailing the history of the city , a Multi-media Auditorium for a wide variety of events and entertainment, The Forum which will be the main entrance to the Centre, and many cafes and restaurants to meet the needs of visitors.

Peterborough Green Wheel is designed to provide a network of cycleways, footpaths and bridleways around the city. This will link tourist attractions, nature reserves, wildlife areas, picnic sites and parks and feature three heritage centres which will show the history, culture and environment of the area. It has been designed to encompass some of the most attractive and interesting parts of the countryside, and will also have access for the disabled.

EAST MIDLANDS

National Space Science Centre will provide an exciting education and leisure facility in the city of Leicester. This will have four main elements; the Exhibition Centre, the Millennium Dome, the Challenger Learning Centre, and the Research Centre. There will also be a tower which will house real rockets. Definitely one for the children whether young or old!

GREATER LONDON

Tate Gallery of Modern Art which will be sited at Bankside Power Station which is a powerful and architecturally distinguished building. It will provide a stunning setting for fine art displays, and occasional exhibitions of architecture, photography, design, film, and the decorative arts. One of the main aims is to educate and increase access to the general public, and to encourage regular visits from local and national schools and colleges at many levels. It will also bolster regeneration in the surrounding area of Southwark, and new transport links will make it easily accessible.

The British Museum The year 2000 will see the inner courtyard of the British Museum transformed into a spectacular covered square. This will open up the inner court for the first time in 150 years creating a new dramatic space where people will be able to meet and enjoy being close to one of the world's greatest cultural resources.

Croydon Skyline This is the largest, single urban lighting project ever conceived and will transform the central area of Croydon. Large images displaying public art and information will be projected onto buildings after dark using new lighting technology. Special performances will also feature and the project will demonstrate new lighting design and will include handling light pollution.

NORTH

International Centre for Life This complex on a 10 acre site in the heart of Newcastle upon Tyne is a science based venture which celebrates the greatest scientific discovery of all time. It is a genetics institute for human genetic research, combined with a bio science centre. The heart of the centre is an inter-active visitor attraction featuring six exciting zones including a Gene Dome which explores the influences of genes on life, and Health Quest, a huge exhibition which encourages healthy living. Timeline explores evolution to date, spanning over 3 billion years beginning with the 'soup' from which simple molecules developed. Sporting Heroes allows you to learn about the fitness and health regimes of your favourite sports personalities such as Alan Shearer and Sally Gunnell, or you can even score a goal against the virtual reality Pavel Srnicek!

Suzy The project is to create a an Eco Structure powered by natural energy sources which will house a futuristic Hydroponicum used for cultivating a wide variety of plants all year round. Practical demonstrations and interactive exhibition areas will feature environmental innovations to enhance living, leisure and working environments.

Turning the Tide This is a very worthwhile project by Durham County Council to restore England's only stretch of magnesium limestone cliffs. Coal waste and derelict structures will be removed, beaches restored and new cycle paths and walkways created. It will be a fantastic sight to see Durham's coast restored to it's former beauty.

Gateway City Project, Carlisle The aim is to reunite Carlisle castle with the historic city centre by creating and developing a Millennium Gallery, Castle and city walkways, a reconstruction of the city's original medieval Irish Gate, and new bridges.

NORTH WEST

The Lowry Centre This is a waterfront complex in Salford Quays which will include a theatre, a gallery to present works by the artist L S Lowry, a children's Hands On Gallery and a National Industrial centre for Virtual Reality. This project will bring life to the quays which have stood derelict for nearly ninety years and will be enjoyed by many people both young and old.

The Ribble Link   A new five mile canal at Preston, linking two stretches of inland waterways for the first time. The new link will link, enhance and preserve green spaces in Preston and assist in the regeneration of Preston Docks which are being developed as a tourist attraction.

National Wildflower Centre A focus for creative conservation in a suburban area which will offer research, education, leisure and commercial opportunities in the Merseyside region.

SOUTH EAST

The Millennium Seed Bank This aims to secure a safe future for approximately 25,000 species of flowering plants world-wide, as well as all the plants native to the UK. This will be at the already wonderful Royal Botanic Gardens at Kew where already they have been working for the last twenty years to save some of the species from extinction. Despite being the world's largest establishment dedicated to the collection of wild species, it contains less than 2% of the Earth's flora. In addition the project will provide a world class building of high architectural quality, access for the public to view the scientific process and the opportunity to train new scientists.

Weather Watch Discovery Centre An interactive Discovery/Science centre which will describe in an entertaining and educational way the forces shaping weather and climate, and a 'Weather Tower' which will reflect the weather.

Island 2000   A project to create two interpretation and visitor centres on the Isle of Wight. At Sandown there will be a dinosaur museum in the shape of a pterodactyl, which will display the island's palaeontological collection. At Ventor Botanical Gardens a new visitor centre will provide educational and community facilities for the island.

SOUTH WEST

Bristol 2000 A landmark project with major attractions. Science World and Wildscreens will be surrounded by squares and city spaces, and will regenerate a derelict site in Bristol.

The Eden Project This will demonstrate and explore the relationship between plants and humans. In a worked out china clay pit near St Austell, Cornwall, up to 60 metre high biomes will be built, capable of exhibiting plants from four climates; the rainforest, desert, mediterranean and temperate. For the first time scientific research of plants as a whole population rather than individual species will be made possible. The visitor centre will explore the wonders of the plant kingdom and the role of human communities within. It will make the world of plants accessible to a wide audience and provide education which is both relevant and stimulating. There will also be many restaurants celebrating food from around the world.

WEST MIDLANDS

Millennium Point Birmingham   This will be a world class centre of technology and learning.   The Discovery centre will integrate new multi-media technologies with historic and modern artefacts, the Technology Innovation Centre will become a centre of excellence for technology and innovation, the University of the First Age will provide a new learning experience for up to 90,000 young people in the West Midlands, and the Hub will link the component parts and contain numerous facilities including themed shops, an IMAX cinema using the latest 2D/3D technology and many cafes and restaurants.

Ceramica   A new major educational and visitor attraction at Stoke-on-Trent which aims to celebrate Staffordshire's world famous pottery industry.   There will be a children's area to explore the world of the potter, a multi-media room for the study of the industry, and the Arnold Bennet gallery which will illustrate the author's life and works through some of his personal possessions and the words of an actor.   There will be exciting displays of different aspects of the industry and samples of the various manufacturers wares.   The surrounding Wedgewood place will be remodelled and landscaped into an attractive public space.

YORKSHIRE AND HUMBERSIDE

Huddersfield Narrow Canal   This project will restore 32 miles of the Huddersfield Narrow Canal to navigastional standard.   The 5.5km long Standedge Tunnel which is the longest, deepest and highest canal tunnel in the UK will be reopened.   A new visitor attraction called 'The Standedge Experience' will include an canal museum and trips into the tunnel.

Trans Penine Way   This will create a linked route for walkers and cyclists extending 714kms across the country from Merseyside to Humberside.   Generally the trail will follow disused railways, canal towpaths, riverside parks and existing rights-of-way. There will be plenty of facilities including refreshments stops, cycle hire, stabling, and overnight accommodation.

500

M

N

A-Z INDEX

Y